UTSA LIBRARY

WITHDRAWN
UTSA LIBRARIES

A CITY OF ONE'S OWN

A City of One's Own
Blurring the Boundaries Between Private and Public

Edited by

SOPHIE BODY-GENDROT
Université Paris IV – Sorbonne, France

JACQUES CARRÉ
Université Paris IV – Sorbonne, France

ROMAIN GARBAYE
Université Paris IV – Sorbonne, France

ASHGATE

© Sophie Body-Gendrot, Jacques Carré and Romain Garbaye 2008

All rights reserved. No part of this publication may be reproduced, stored in a retrieval system, or transmitted in any form or by any means, electronic, mechanical, photocopying, recording or otherwise without the prior permission of the publisher.

Sophie Body-Gendrot, Jacques Carré and Romain Garbaye have asserted their right under the Copyright, Designs and Patents Act, 1988, to be identified as the editors of this work.

Published by
Ashgate Publishing Limited
Gower House
Croft Road
Aldershot
Hampshire GU11 3HR
England

Ashgate Publishing Company
Suite 420
101 Cherry Street
Burlington, VT 05401-4405
USA

www.ashgate.com

British Library Cataloguing in Publication Data
A city of one's own : blurring the boundaries between
  private and public
1. Sociology, Urban
I. Body-Gendrot, Sophie II. Carré, Jacques III. Garbaye,
  Romain
307.7'6

Library of Congress Cataloging-in-Publication Data
Body-Gendrot, Sophie.
 A city of one's own : blurring the boundaries between private and public / by Sophie Body-Gendrot, Jacques Carré and Romain Garbaye.
    p. cm.
  Includes index.
  ISBN 978-0-7546-7502-0
 1. Citizens' associations--United States. 2. Citizens' associations--Great Britain. 3. Neighborhood government--United States. 4. Neighborhood government--Great Britain. 5. Community organization--United States. 6. Community organization--Great Britain. 7. Public-private sector cooperation--United States. 8. Public-private sector cooperation--Great Britain. 9. Community power--United States. 10. Community power--Great Britain. 11. Political participation--United States. 12. Political participation--Great Britain. I. Carré, Jacques. II. Garbaye, Romain. III. Title.

JS303.5.B63 2008
320.8'50941--dc22

2008028141

ISBN 978-0-7546-7502-0

Library
University of Texas
at San Antonio

Printed and bound in Great Britain by
MPG Books Ltd, Bodmin, Cornwall.

Contents

List of Figures and Table	vii
Notes on Contributors	ix

Introduction   1
Sophie Body-Gendrot, Jacques Carré and Romain Garbaye

PART 1: PLANNING

1   'Private' and 'Public' in the Extension of Georgian London's West End   13
Jacques Carré

2   Making an Inclusive Urbanism: New York City's World Trade Memorial   25
Robert A. Beauregard

PART 2: HOUSING

3   The Privatization of Council-Housing in Britain: The Strange Death of Public Sector Housing?   41
David Fée

4   The Governance of New Communities in Britain, France and North America, 1815–2004: The Quest for the Public Interest?   57
Stéphane Sadoux, Frédéric Cantaroglou and Audrey Gloor

PART 3: SECURITY

5   Gated Communities: Generic Patterns in Suburban Landscapes?   77
Renaud Le Goix

6   From Self-Defence to Citizenry Involvement Participation in Law-and-Order Enforcement in the United States: Private Spheres and Public Space   103
Didier Combeau

7   The Future of Prison Privatization in the United States   115
Franck Vindevogel

PART 4: HEALTH

8   AIDS Prevention by Non-Governmental Organizations: Inside the
    American and French Responses   133
    *Laura Hobson Faure, Carla Dillard Smith, Gloria Lockett and
    Benjamin P. Bowser*

PART 5: EDUCATION

9   Education Management Organizations and For-Profit Education –
    An Overview and a Case-Study: Philadelphia   149
    Malie Montagutelli

10 'We Pay the Rates!' Catholic Voluntary Schools and Scottish School
    Boards (1872–1918)   163
    Geraldine Vaughan

PART 6: CITIZENSHIP

11 'To Serve and to Elect': The Women's Local Government Society,
    Britain 1888–1918   181
    Myriam Boussahba-Bravard

12 The 'Third Way' and the Governance of the Social in Britain   201
    Jérôme Tournadre-Plancq

Conclusion: Jane Jacobs Revisited?   213
Sophie Body-Gendrot, Jacques Carré and Romain Garbaye

Index   *217*

List of Figures and Table

Figures

4.1	Ebenezer Howard's Garden City diagram (1902)	69
4.2	Ebenezer Howard's 'Three Magnets' diagram (1902), showing 'Freedom' and 'Cooperation' as the rationale underpinning the Garden Cities project	70
5.1	Gated communities in the US – chronology and filiations (suburban housing developments, homeowners' associations, safety and exclusivity)	85
5.2	Location of some gated streets and residential enclaves in the Ile-de-France	93
5.3	Location of gated communities in the region of Los Angeles	97

Table

11.1	Women Guardians' Society members 1889 compared with Women's Local Government Society members 1903	186

Notes on Contributors

Robert A. Beauregard is Professor of Urban Planning in the Graduate School of Architecture, Planning, and Preservation, Columbia University (USA). His most recent book is *When America Became Suburban* (University of Minnesota Press, 2006). He writes extensively on urban theory, urban redevelopment and urban planning.

Sophie Body-Gendrot is Professor of Political Science and of American Studies and Co-Director of CEUMA (Center of Urban Studies) at the Sorbonne (Université Paris IV). She is an expert for the 'Urban Age' programme at the London School of Economics on safety and public space. Among her most recent books in English, she authored *The Social Control of Cities? A Comparative Perspective* (Blackwell 2000) and co-edited *Violence in Europe* (Springer 2007) and *Social Capital and Social Citizenship* (Lexington Books 2003).

Myriam Boussahba-Bravard is Senior Lecturer in British Political History in the British and American Studies Department, University of Rouen (France). Her research focuses on suffrage history and periodicals in the Edwardian period. She has edited *Suffrage Outside Suffragism, Women's Vote, Britain 1880–1914* (Palgrave, 2007) and is currently writing a book length biography of the feminist journalist Teresa Billington-Greig (1877–1964).

Benjamin P. Bowser is Professor and Chair of Sociology and Social Services at the California State University East Bay. His research over the past twenty years has focused on HIV/AID and drug abuse prevention among African Americans. He has a number of journal publications and he is lead editor of *Preventing AIDS: Community Science Collaborations* (Haworth Press, 2004) and *When Communities Assess their AIDS Epidemics: Results of Rapid Assessment of HIV/AIDS in Eleven US Cities* (Lexington Books, 2007).

Frédéric Cantaroglou holds degrees in political science and planning. He is currently Director of Information and Communication Technologies at Université Pierre Mendès France, Grenoble (France). He is also a part-time lecturer at Institut d'Urbanisme de Grenoble. His PhD thesis (Institut d'urbanisme de Grenoble, 2000) is entitled 'Le rôle de l'industrie dans la mise en œuvre de la planification urbaine et de la planification territoriale en France de 1850 à 1946'.

Jacques Carré is Professor of British Cultural History at the Sorbonne (Université Paris IV) and Co-Director of CEUMA. He works on architecture, space and society in eighteenth- and nineteenth-century Britain. He has recently co-edited *The Invisible Woman: Women's Work in Eighteenth-century Britain* (Ashgate,

2005). His latest book (in French) is entitled *Londres 1700–1900: naissance d'une capitale culturelle* (Presses de Paris-Sorbonne, 2008).

Didier Combeau is a researcher at CEUMA at the Sorbonne (Université Paris IV) and teaches American civilization at Université Paris III-Sorbonne Nouvelle. He has recently published a detailed study of the debate on gun control in the United States, entitled *Des Américains et des armes à feu: démocratie et violence aux Etats-Unis* (Editions Belin, 2007) as well as numerous articles.

Carla Dillard Smith has been Cal-Pep's Research Director since 1992. Under her guidance Cal-Pep has partnered academic and health organizations in several large-scale research projects targeting the African American community in Northern California. She has co-written a number of Cal-Pep reports and publications. She is a former member of Alameda County's HIV Prevention Planning Council and currently serves on the Alameda County African American State of Emergency Task Force.

David Fée is a Senior lecturer in the English Studies department of the Université Paris III-Sorbonne Nouvelle. He is the author of several articles on housing policies in England as well as co-editor of two books on urban renaissance and the housing crisis in England (to be published in 2008).

Romain Garbaye is Maître de Conférences in anglophone studies at the Sorbonne (Université Paris IV). He was previously a Jean Monnet post-doctoral fellow at the Robert Schuman Centre for Advanced Studies of the European University Institute in Florence and he obtained his DPhil in politics at Oxford University. He is the author of *Getting into Local Power, the Politics of Ethnic Minorities in British and French Cities* (Blackwell, 2005), and has published several articles and book chapters on subjects such as multiculturalism or the politics of Islam in urban settings in Britain and France.

Audrey Gloor is a geographer and a planner. She is currently advisor to the Chief executive of Etablissement public d'aménagement (EPA), St Etienne (France). She was previously researcher and part time lecturer at Institut d'Urbanisme de Grenoble. Her doctoral thesis (Institut d'Urbanisme de Grenoble, 2006) is entitled 'Los Angeles: un outil de compréhension de la ville post-moderne'.

Laura Hobson Faure worked with Cal-Pep as a grant writer from 2002–2003. Her research focuses on how minorities have responded to the crises affecting them. She has conducted research on the AIDS movement in France and the United States and is currently completing a doctorate at the Ecole des Hautes Etudes en Sciences Sociales, Paris, on the mobilization of American Jewish organizations in France after the Holocaust. She has taught at the Universities of Paris IV, VI, and VII, as well as at the École Polytechnique.

Renaud le Goix teaches human and urban geography as an Assistant Professor at the Université Paris 1-Panthéon-Sorbonne. He has been a member of the UMR Géographie-cités CNRS research team since 1999. He holds a PhD in geography (Université Paris I, 2003) and his urban geography researches about gated communities and private residential governance in the US aimed at addressing the impact of gated communities on segregation patterns. He was awarded in 2000 a Tocqueville Fellowship and in 2002 a Fulbright Research Fellowship at the University of California, Los Angeles and at the City University of New York. He leads an ANR junior research programme (2007–2010) on public-private interactions in the production of suburban patterns.

Gloria Lockett is co-founder of Cal-Pep and has been Cal-Pep's Executive Director since 1984. A former sex worker, she has worked to create and fund HIV/STD and substance abuse services for the African American community in Northern California. She is past Chairperson of the Alameda County Ryan White Planning Council. Sheis also a former member of the National Cities Advocating for Emergency Relief (CAER) Coalition on HIV/AIDS, and a member of COYOTE 'Call of Your Old Tired Ethics,' a prostitutes' rights organization.

Malie Montagutelli is Professor of American studies at the Université Paris III-Sorbonne Nouvelle. Her field of research is the history of American education. For the last five years, she has concentrated on the present situation of schools, with a special interest in the encroachment of private enterprise in the public system. She is the author of *Histoire de l'Enseignement aux Etats-Unis* (Belin, 2000) and *L'Education des Filles aux Etats-Unis* (Ophrys-Ploton, 2003).

Stéphane Sadoux holds planning degrees from the Universities of Newcastle (UK) and Grenoble (France). He is currently a lecturer and researcher in urban planning and social sciences at Ecole Nationale Supérieure d'Architecture de Grenoble. He also teaches at Geneva University and the Institut d'Urbanisme de Grenoble. Prior to that, he was a project development officer at the Town and Country Planning Association, London. He has published numerous articles on town planning in Britain.

Jérôme Tournadre-Plancq teaches political science at the Université Paris II-Panthéon-Assas). He is the author of *Au-delà de la gauche et de la droite, une troisième voie britannique?* (Dalloz, 2006).

Geraldine Vaughan completed a doctorate in 2007 at the Sorbonne (Paris I) on Irish immigrants in the West of Scotland (1851–1918) and their impact on religion, politics and identity in modern Scottish society. She is currently exploring the theme of Irish immigration in Scotland in the post-World War I era and is an Assistant Lecturer at the University of Rouen (France).

Franck Vindevogel is Senior Lecturer in American studies at the Université du Littoral–Côte d'Opale, Boulogne (France). He is a former Fulbright Researcher at John Jay College of Criminal Justice and holds a doctorate in American studies. He has published a number of articles and a book chapter on crime control and incarceration in the United States and was awarded the Marie-France Toinet Prize for the best doctoral thesis in American Studies in 2003.

Introduction

Sophie Body-Gendrot, Jacques Carré and Romain Garbaye

Students of local governance have frequently emphasized the growing influence of business interests in cities. In so doing, they have been led to question the notion of a clear distinction between public policy and private interest, and to redefine the contours of the public sphere in cities. At the same time, the concept of local governance makes it possible to conceptualize a possible renewal or transformation of community participation and citizenship. It provides an analytical framework to understand the conditions that may allow the emergence of new forms of citizenship in the context of evolving modes of government.

The authors of this volume take up these two issues and attempt to deal with them by focusing on governance's taken for granted premise – that current trends are new. The twelve chapters written by French, British and American scholars from four disciplines and two continents defend the idea that private initiative (and chaos) was always mainstream. It was municipal 'socialism' which was the 'orderly' exception. The volume sets out to examine current trends towards the privatization of cities in three countries, particularly in relation to their historical roots. Modern urban theory, often obsessed by quest of the new, tends indeed to ignore the agents of change in the past.

The contributions point to a long and rich history of partnership in British, American and French cities, showing that both private interests and community groups have long been involved in local policies. The British case is a clear case in point, with public-private partnerships a feature of nineteenth-century local politics. In fact, religious organizations preceded local authorities in some policy sectors, such as education.

More generally, private individuals and bodies rather than vestries or even corporations were the driving forces of urban change before the twentieth century. These private agents were often impelled to contribute to urban governance by religious or moral motives, although the pursuit of private interests was also, inevitably, a powerful factor. One well-identified feature of the history of cities in the English-speaking world is indeed that the two motivations were often combined (Weber 1930). Even utopian writers on the city, often suspected of being idealistic, were economy conscious. Victorian social prophets such as Robert Owen and Ebenezer Howard provided elaborate administrative and financial arrangements in order to demonstrate the feasibility of their projects (Owen 1821, Howard 1902). In general, the early private initiatives in urban governance concerned areas untouched by indifferent or inefficient local authorities. In the nineteenth century, with the advent of the industrial city and its growing pains, private interventions tended to be reactive, and to provide tentative solutions to some of the most unbearable living conditions imposed on the poorer urban residents (Carré and Révauger 1995). The numerous philanthropic networks established then are a good example of such contributions to urban governance (Owen 1960).

Organized, well-funded and interventionist local authorities only developed in the late nineteenth and early twentieth centuries, then had their heyday between 1945 and 1975. The 1970s, however, saw a major turning point, with the combination of ideological criticism of the welfare state and the economic difficulties which made it less sustainable than before. Private actors of city life, who in earlier centuries had complained about the near absence of local government and had compensated for its inertia, now complained about the failures of public urban policies, and proclaimed the benefits of voluntary action and the third sector (Brittan 1983). Local authorities then started to share the stage again with an array of organizations (see the review by Stoker 1997: 59–63). The 1945–1975 era of strong local government may thus be labeled a 'parenthesis' in a history otherwise dominated by private and third-sector intervention.

The exploration of historical precedents must by no means be limited to the last two centuries. The contrast between the under-regulated city of the eighteenth and early and mid-nineteenth centuries, on one side, and the overregulated city of the twentieth, on the other, should not obscure the fact that in liberal English-speaking societies since 1688 the freedom of initiative of private individuals and bodies has always been a major feature of the polity. Indeed the imprecision of the frontiers between the proper territories of private and public actors has long been a major dilemma of liberal governments. Then as now they have always hesitated about the proper boundaries of state action, and even about the definition of the public interest (Moroni 2004). It seems legitimate, then, to the authors of this book to identify the sources of the privatization of the city in the long historical perspective.

Urban sociologists and political scientists working in a European context in the last decade have emphasized a shift from 'government' to 'governance'. The concept of governance, derived from American studies of local politics, has taken two interlinked meanings in European contexts. First, it is based on a criticism of the traditional object of local government studies, focused on elected local councils and their administrative apparatus. Instead it emphasizes a set of 'new' actors such as private corporations, third sector organizations and non-elected administrative bodies. Second, it operates a shift from the conceptualization of power as monolithic, and based on constraint, to a more organizational and relational conception of power. In the new governance studies that are developed in this book, what is studied is networks, modes of negotiation, patterns of coalition-making between business interests and the local state that make it possible to continue to govern increasingly complex societies.

The originality of the authors' approach is to develop comparative case studies from the US, UK and France regarding six themes: planning, housing, security, health, education and citizenship. Each heading mixes historical and contemporary perspectives in order to evaluate the importance of private and public initiatives, according to long national traditions or time-periods. For instance, the culture of urban planning which marks the early twentieth century onward does not go much further than the 1970s. The rise of third-sector and for-profit actors in local affairs since then, appears as a return of earlier modes of social and political organization. We share Jane Jacobs' view according to which students of cities should work inductively, starting from empirical observations to gain an understanding of the logics of social, economic and political interactions that take place on complex urban territories and form the fabric of cities.

The book is organized as follows. The first chapter by Jacques Carré deals with the emergence of urban planning as a result of private initiative. Planning is traditionally perceived as the paradigmatic product of twentieth-century welfarist urban government, as a technique of land use that was supposed to wrench cities from the clutches of speculators and develop them, hopefully, in the public interest (Unwin 1909, Abercrombie 1933). It is useful to look at the historical example of planning in London's West End in the seventeenth and eighteenth centuries in light of the following chapter relative to the World Trade Center's planning after 9/11. The laying-out of Restoration and Georgian London's West End did not emanate from public authorities, but from individuals or associations. It was the result of a series of private developments by aristocratic ground landlords taking advantage of the building booms in that period. It is traditionally analysed as market orientated, its environmental attractiveness and architectural elegance being seen as features capable of attracting affluent residents to the area (Summerson 1945). Yet, as Carré demonstrates, the new estates were actually designed so as to integrate certain essential functions of cities: squares, markets, churches, workhouses, burying grounds were not only tolerated, but actually provided for by the ground landlords. The various needs of the local residents (social elites as well as their servants and tradesmen) seem to have conditioned the use of space. The geometrical grids of the West End, far from being a formal pattern arbitrarily imposed on faceless people, seem on the contrary to be a reflection of the needs of a society considering itself as both orderly and enlightened.

The contrast with the World Trade Center in the second chapter is not as stunning as might be expected. Analyzing theoretical links relative to private and public approaches to urbanism in Europe and in the US, Robert Beauregard highlights two sets of concerns regarding privatization: one has to do with the lack of social justice and the reinforcement of inequalities, a European concern and the other – the focus of his study – the neglect of serendipity and of different needs addressed to space. For some utopians, the function of space is to link all kinds of city users and of heterogeneous spaces. But is this is not what high modernist urbanism does when it creates spaces for a 'universal resident' and for a white, educated middle-class life-style? What rights do non-conformist people then have in commodified city spaces? Can public culture bloom in such places? Beauregard opposes an idealized version of European urbanism as elaborated by Lefebvre (2003) and redefined by Jane Jacobs (1961) (see conclusion) that is, public space focussing on people and allowing diverse uses, random encounters on sidewalks, street-level particularities and American standardized, controlled, predictable, 'sterile' urbanism. One is unintentional and indigenous and the other is produced by state and capitalist interventions. As an illustration, redesigning the World Trade Center space after 9/11 which is publicly owned has been left to a public authority, a non-profit corporation and a real estate developer whose visions are 'private' and dominated by commercial and financial interests. By contrast, Battery Park, an example of postmodern urbanism has attempted to replicate a more or less typical New York City neighbourhood, with its apartment buildings, small retail stores, streets and open spaces (Fainstein 2001). Here, as in eighteenth-century London West End, the care for local residents prevails on an abstract vision of visitors, users of office towers, patrons of art, etc. The human factor, the different scales and uses are put forward in an inclusive and heterogeneous conception of urbanism.

The third chapter is devoted to British housing as a thematic follow-up of considerations on urban planning, private/public initiatives. Fée takes the example of housing policy in historical perspective and points at the privatizing trend of the 1970s–1980s. At that time, the tide gradually turned indeed against the enduring supremacy of public power. The intervention of private interests in city governance became much more massive and acrimonious (Imrie and Thomas 1993). The Thatcherian mantra of 'rolling back the frontiers of the state' was of course the signal of this change. The systematic attack against public-sector housing by the Iron Lady is often described as the arch-example of her general encouragement of privatization of many previously state-controlled services and industries. And yet, as Fée brilliantly demonstrates, the apparent triumph of council housing in the mid-twentieth century was more fragile than it seemed. He points out that the so-called consensus on this question was limited to the short period 1939–1956, while it is possible to find a constant appeal to private sector housing in Conservative manifestoes of other periods. More radically, Fée suggests that the rapid demise of council housing under the Thatcher-Major-Blair governments, accompanied by an increasing recourse to the voluntary sector, merely echoes the Victorian approach to social housing (Burnett 1986). The model-housing companies and the philanthropic housing trusts, such as the Peabody Trust, were to some extent the forerunners of the present housing associations.

In the context of later, more conflictual ages, that of the nineteenth-century industrial city, and that of the postmodern late twentieth-century city, the planning of space by private initiatives can again be described less as technical solutions than as the expression of community needs and values. The fourth chapter by Sadoux, Cantaroglou and Gloor shows that the English Garden City movement and the current American New Urbanism movement, both independent from public authorities, were rather utopian in origin, but have led to a few interesting achievements, such as the post-World War II British New Towns (Schaffer 1972). What is most significant about them, as suggested, is that they address some fundamental problems of the societies they seem to challenge. They provide answers first to industrial and then to post-industrial urban problems in terms of way of life and socio-economic organization. They represent an alternative to urban chaos, not an expression of accepted order, as it was in the Georgian city. We find in the cases described here decisive attempts to submit urban space to the specific needs of people in given local contexts. They point to the ability of well-targeted associations to influence urban thinking (Duany 2003).

Concerning the American city, it is important to remember that Lewis Mumford himself as a member of the *Regional Planning Association of America* had been influenced by the English Garden City. The success of his ideas can be explained by the importance given to the 'community', that is, the micro-space model of social organization based on trust, empowerment and cooperation within a green environment. Currently, the success of New Urbanism in the United States is also based on a people sensitive socio-spatial system. But the concept of community is deeply ambiguous and it may refer to the 'Not In my Backyard' phenomenon as much as to progressive grass-roots actions (Body-Gendrot 2000).

Chapters 5, 6 and 7 deal with a new theme, security, in order to pursue the demonstration according to which private initiatives have always been mainstream. Case studies from France and the US examine the links between security, gated communities and law and order. An extreme example of spatial control to the benefit of a restricted number of people is offered by the development of gated communities all over the world. It is currently observed in Latin American, Asian, South African megapolises and it is common in Eastern Europe. Yet as pointed out by Le Goix in the fifth chapter, the United States, and California specifically, led the way, in continuity with the American philosophy linking the right of the people to control their space with their right to security as a dimension of freedom and a good per se. Security is not just a political aspiration, it is considered as a right by the 'haves' concerned both by property value and by the defence of their norms. Another interest of the chapter is to point out at a neglected aspect: French intellectuals so eager to criticize contemptuously American gated communities as an 'urban pathology', a 'social paranoia' and a 'segregationist ideology' have forgotten that in the nineteenth century, when the faubourgs of Paris were developing fast, municipal incorporations of private residential parks occurred, just as is the case currently in Los Angeles. With the examples of Montretout and Montmorency in point, Le Goix demonstrates that former concerns with value property and walls around parks are currently evolving into legitimate claims for safety.

By contrast with Le Goix's approach, Didier Combeau reintroduces the role of the regalian state in drawing boundaries regarding citizens' initiatives in his comparison of space and safety in France and in the US. The contrast between the two countries is again striking, both in the fields of political philosophy and in the involvement of private citizens in the enforcement of law and order. Whereas in a twisted interpretation of the Constitution, some American states have granted city residents an unrestricted right to bear arms, to conduct neighbourhood watches and to self-defend – including the use of deadly force to defend oneself and one's property – such is not the case in France: the use of force by individual citizens has never been considered, at least in the public debate, as an appropriate response to burglary (the UK stands closer to the US than to European laws which ban deadly force to defend property). These differences are obviously related to diversified modes of nation-building, to monarchy and to the state progressively moulding French society on the one hand, and on the other, to self-help being a necessity in the colonies and later, in an entrepreneurial American society. Maxwell Brown, who examined the history of the US, showed that when perceiving 'a grave menace to social stability in the conditions of frontier life and racial, ethnic, urban, and industrial unrest, solid citizens rallied to the cause of community order. [...] Violence was tinctured with social conservatism'. Violence was also on the side of the forces of law and order when confronted to the criminal and the disorderly. Many historical episodes in which nonconformists have been harshly punished by 'solid citizens' seem to give support to the idea of an American exceptionalism (Brown 1979: 31).

It is hardly surprising then due to the instrumentalization of fear against 'Dangerous Others' in a number of states that Florida would legitimize self-defence not only in the home but also in public places perceived both as part of the community and as a sum of private interests (Body-Gendrot, 2002). Another interesting distinction pointed at by Combeau relates to the concepts of person and property. A person is seen as a social entity in the US, and property is a natural right. Consequently, the boundary between self-help and law enforcement is very thin. In France, property is not part of the sphere of the person.

Such differences have obviously an impact on punishment and law enforcement. Criminologist Frank Zimring supports the idea of 'a deeply held American belief in violent social justice'. He points at the Southern communities in the nineteenth century, where a culture of lynching and of vigilantism expressed a mistrust of institutions. He emphasizes the populism of spontaneous and ephemeral mobs, taking the law in their hands and the legitimacy of self-help and of violence against those perceived as a threat to the community. Zimring draws a link between the past and today, explaining that the states which had high rates of (illegal) lynching in the 1890s are those with high rates of (legal) execution behaviours in the 1990s (Zimring 2005) but this last assumption has been contested. In *Harsh Justice*, another criminologist, James Whitman also emphasizes the comparative roughness of American punishment forged in the eighteenth century and reproduced ever since. He blames the absence of aristocratic codes of behaviour which, in Europe, gradually granted offenders the treatment previously reserved for elite offenders and which is largely absent in the US. 'Humiliation and degradation in punishment, he says, are not considered as inegalitarian practices in the US' (Whitman 2003). The legal implication of this trend of thought points at a tight relationship between American culture and punishment. But a timeless cultural explanation for American harshness cannot be sustained in light of cultural changes which occurred over time and space and over specific historical and political events. It would be unfair to compare the worst of American practices, especially in the South, with the best of European ideals and to downplay the importance of contexts and of time periods (Garland 2005). Yet mass incarceration in the late-twentieth century American society provides a feature of US exceptionalism in terms of 'fortress mentality'. Three per cent of the adult population is managed by the criminal justice system subcontracting a number of its prisons to private entrepreneurs. Exclusion strategies link the phenomenon of gated communities ('locking oneself in') to that of prisons ('locking others out') in what J. Simon calls a 'model of exile and exclusion' (Simon 2007: 278–9).

For Franck Vindevogel (Chapter 7) the phenomenon of prison privatization in the US is not a minor phenomenon. The US contains 83 per cent of all existing private prison facilities in the world. These facilities are found mostly in the states which were not part of the first colonies, that is, in the south and the west of the country. Until the end of the nineteenth century, states used to lease contract convict labour to private companies and some of them had transferred the whole correctional function to the private sector. These prisons were supposed to turn a profit for the states. Vindevogel has found that currently five states of the West have a quarter of their inmate population in private facilities. But whereas private policing is hardly a matter of debate (there are three private security guards for one policeman in Los Angeles) profit-seeking prisons have generated controversies: they involve constitutional rights (those of inmates) and the safety issue (that of surrounding communities). The impetus for private prisons is a follow up of the taxpayer resistance to government spending which first emerged in California with proposition 13 and then spread throughout the country, a philosophy boosted by the Reagan Administration. As currently observed in numerous megacities of the South (Johannesburg, Sao Paulo, Mexico City, Lagos), the state has been complacent and taken advantage of huge private companies' appetite for profit. However, disorders caused by inmates' overcrowding and poor standards of treatment as shown vividly in Sao Paulo public prisons, make privatization a necessity when justice systems are unwilling to replace incarceration with alternative sentencing for non-violent offenders. Another linked consideration concerns the inability of Republican states to exert quality requirements on private prison providers: the latter contribute heavily to the Republican party's campaigns. Scandals and negative evaluations have periodically tarnished private prisons' image in the states. But the Federal government's instrumentalization of fear, especially after 9/11, makes massive de-incarceration unlikely. Due to the carceral system cost, Zimring anticipates a 25 per cent decrease in the 25 years to come, but not much more (2005; Simon, 2007).

Chapter 8 introduces a new issue, health, with the cases of California and France, again to understand how much the private sector is comparatively involved vs the public one in the current trends. The case study on AIDS illustrates this differential approach of health in the US and in France. With the example of the California Prostitution Educational Program (Cal-Pep) in the Bay area, Laura Hobson Faure, Carla Dillard Smith, Gloria Lockett and Benjamin P. Bowser provide a brief history of non-governmental response against AIDS in the United States. Due to government inefficiency and mistrust by minority groups, to the reluctance of traditional Black churches to get involved with the AIDS problem and the class bias of some of the civil rights activists, Cal-Pep has worked to change culture and norms among marginalized HIV high risk groups. African-American homosexuals are indeed frequently rejected by their community. With multiple sex partners or as drug users, they are perceived as a risk for community norms and behaviours. In France, the over-representation of heterosexual immigrants in the AIDS epidemic has been ignored for lack of statistics regarding ethnicity, then hidden for politically correct reasons. When the problem was finally acknowledged, it posed challenges to public health officials who turned to organizations to outreach these populations. The comparison brings two striking differences: one related to the construction of race and ethnicity reveals the influence of this dimension on the public and private modes of intervention against AIDS. The second has to do with the relationship of NGOs and public officials in both counties. According to the authors, in the American case, the officials' reluctance to let Cal-Pep exert its leverage in the way it wished to operate forced the latter to work on its political connections instead of simply do its 'front-line' work. Moreover, perceived as 'private contractor', the staff is evaluated and accountable for its efficiency. In France, despite the centralization of the state, the NGOs have to turn to multiple sources of public and private funding. Yet they only act as junior partners and are cautious not to substitute themselves to the state for service delivery. A major problem is due to the lack of empirical data on the outcomes of funded programmes and of budgetary transparency in the annual activity reports. A third issue is related to the reluctance French officials have at identifying immigrant populations with specific needs, once they are French.

The next chapters focus both on education. While to the public, private schools may appear as new phenomena linked to the 1980s, historically, US schools have been run by private organizations. In Chapter 9 M. Montagutelli remarks that, historically, private companies have been involved in activities related to education and the running of American public schools. In recent years, however, Education Management Organizations (EMOs) have emerged and due to the dysfunctions of public education – and in the case of Philadelphia, the extreme distress in which some of the public schools are – have appeared as a successful option: they brought greater access to computers, the hiring teaching of assistants with college degrees, and the enhancement of the maintenance and repair of buildings. As in the case of private prisons, there are different degrees of involvement and of participation in the public system for these private companies, but due to their very presence, the overlapping of the public and the private sectors has reinforced. The controversy lies around the values of performance standards, efficiency, customer-requirements, etc., which import a market discipline in the urban schools. They may in the long-run alter the nature and long-term objectives of education. On the one hand, the improvement brought by privatization is not conclusive and opponents – some of them launching class-action in the courts – have not relented. It should be fair to say that the nature of the social problems plaguing the schools in very poor areas have their roots outside the schools. Is it then possible to improve the students' scores and moreover, to draw profits from school districts that are already underfunded and in trouble?

The historical example provided by Vaughan in Chapter 10 about the confrontation of certain minorities and underprivileged members of society with established institutions in the late Victorian and Edwardian age emphasizes similar questions. Vaughan studies the unexpected participation of Roman Catholics in the School Boards of Scotland in an age when Catholic schools voluntarily remained outside what they considered to be a Protestant system of education. By a strange process, the Catholic members of School Boards, who saw themselves as unfairly treated by the law, in fact acted as overzealous citizens, serving schools which their children did not attend. In reality this participation allowed them to make their grievances more public, and certainly contributed to the final equality of treatment of all achieved in 1918.

In the last chapters, which are focused on citizenship – women in government and 'third way' initiatives – the two authors have selected case-studies in the British context. Boussahba-Bravard's analysis of the Women's Local Government Society in Chapter 11 shows how an underprivileged group, that of women, skillfully tried to extend women's participation in local government. The self-confident middle-class ladies of the Local Government Society used existing loopholes in the law, strengthened their position by asking for expert legal advice, and generally demonstrated their contested abilities. Yet they were far from adopting a militantly feminist stance: they concentrated on areas of local government traditionally considered as suited to the female 'character', such as poor relief and education. Furthermore, the members of the Women's Local Government Society remained ostensibly a non-party organization. Thus we find in these chapters how through perfectly legal, and indeed, almost uncontroversial action, underprivileged citizens have made their influence felt on the urban scene.

Finally, Jérôme Tournadre-Plancq's essay traces the origins of the British 'Third Way' approach promoted by Labour Party modernizers to the culture of mutualism and friendly societies that permeated the British working-class until the early twentieth century. For instance, the fascination of authors associated with New Labour for 'social entrepreneurs', suggests, again, that the era of extensive delivery of welfare services by the State may be viewed as a parenthesis, and that it should give way to a greater emphasis on a reliance on local 'leadership' and 'social capital'. In the last resort, the doctrine of the Third Way redefines the state as a social regulator, focused on the management of private and voluntary programmes, and perhaps compensating for the privatization of policies with a renewed ability to set agendas and impose values on its 'partners'.

References

Abercrombie, P. (1933), *Town and Country Planning* (London: Oxford University Press).

Body-Gendrot, S. (2000), *The Social Control of the Cities? Comparative Perspectives* (Oxford: Blackwell).

Body-Gendrot, S. (2002), 'The Dangerous Others: Changing Views on Urban Risks and Violence in France and the US' in Eade, J. and Mele, C. (eds), *Understanding the City* (Oxford: Blackwell), 82–106.

Brittan, S. (1983), *The Role and Limits of Government: Essays in Political Economy* (London: Temple Smith).

Brown Maxwell, R. (1969), 'Historical Patterns of American Violence' in Graham, H.D. and Gurr, T.R. (eds), *The History of Violence in America* (New York: Bantam), 19–48.

Burnett, J. (1986), *A Social History of Housing, 1815–1985* (London: Methuen).

Carré, J. and Révauger, J.-P. (eds) (1995), *Ecrire la pauvreté: les enquêtes sociales britanniques aux XIXe et XXe siècles* (Paris: L'Harmattan).

Colls, R. and Rodger R. (eds) (2004), *Cities of Ideas: Civil Society and Urban Governance in Britain, 1800–2000, Essays in Honour of David Reeder* (Aldershot: Ashgate).

Duany, A. (2003), *New Civic Art : Elements of Town-Planning* (New York: Rizzoli).

Fainstein, S. (2001), *The City Builders* (Lawrence, KS: University Press of Kansas).

Garland, D. (2005), 'Beyond the Culture of Control' in Matravers M. (ed.), *Managing Modernity: Politics and the Culture of Control* (London: Routledge).

Howard, E. (1902), *Garden Cities of To-Morrow* (London: S. Sonnenschein and Co.).

Imrie, R. and Thomas, H. (eds) (1993), *British Urban Policy and the Urban Development Corporations* (London: Paul Chapman Publishing).

Jacobs, J. (1961), *The Death and Life of Great American Cities* (New York: Vintage, 1961).

Lefebvre, H. (2003), *The Urban Revolution* (translated from the French) (Minneapolis, MN: University of Minnesota Press).

Moroni, S. (2004), 'Towards a Reconstruction of the Public Interest Criterion', *Planning Theory* 3:2, 151–71.

Owen, D. (1964), *English Philanthropy, 1660–1960* (London: Oxford University Press).

Owen, R. (1821), *Report to the County of Lanark* (Glasgow: Glasgow University Press).

Schaffer, F. (1972), *The New Town Story* (London: Paladin).

Simon, J. (2007), *Governing Through Crime* (New York: Oxford University Press).

Stoker, G. (1997), 'The Privatization of Urban Services in the United Kingdom', in Lorrain, D. and Stoker, G. (eds), *The Privatization of Urban Services in Europe* (London: Pinter): 58–78.

Summerson, J. (1945), *Georgian London* (London: Pleiades Books).

Tournadre-Plancq, J. (2006), *Au delà de la gauche et de la droite, une troisième voie britannique?* (Paris : Dalloz).

Unwin, R. (1911), *Town Planning in Practice: An Introduction to the Art of Designing Cities and Suburbs* (London: T. Fisher Unwin).

Weber, M. (1930), *The Protestant Ethic and the Spirit of Capitalism* (New York: Scribner's).

Whitman, J. (2003), *Harsh Justice: Criminal Punishment and the Widening Divide between America and Europe* (New York: Oxford University Press).

Zimring, F. (2005), 'Capital Punishment, Mass Imprisonment – American Exceptionalism', paper presented at the XIVth World Congress of Criminology, University of Philadelphia (August 2005.)

PART 1
Planning

Chapter 1

'Private' and 'Public' in the Extension of Georgian London's West End

Jacques Carré

In his classic book on *Georgian London* John Summerson emphasized the fundamentally mercantile nature of London's physical growth in the long eighteenth century and beyond (Summerson 1945: 25–6). Building, and singularly housing, he argued, was mostly considered a profitable activity, just like any other form of business, well into the nineteenth century. For this reason, the capital grew piecemeal and somewhat haphazardly, following the decisions of those private ground landlords who decided to launch housing developments. Summerson particularly emphasized the triumph of private interest over any attempt at government intervention:

> Beside other eighteenth-century capitals, London is remarkable for the freedom with which it developed. It is the city raised by private, not public, wealth; the least authoritarian city in Europe. Whenever attempts have been made to overrule the individual in the public interest, they have failed (Summerson 1945, 25).

Compared to continental capitals, seventeenth- and eighteenth-century London did remain remarkably free from government interference. Neither the plan nor the appearance of the growing metropolis were altered or even controlled by government, even when opportunities such as the Great Fire of 1666 might have tempted Crown or State to impress their stamp on the capital.

However, such freedom was not universally approved. As early as the mid-eighteenth century there were dissentient voices, that saw licence rather than freedom, disorder rather harmony, in this triumph of private interest. We may note, for example, the journalist James Ralph's strictures on the development of West End squares, when he wrote in his *Critical Review* about the newly laid-out Grosvenor Square:

> It was meant to be very fine, but has miscarried very unfortunately in the execution: there is no harmony or agreement in the parts which compose it, neither is there one of those parts which can make us any thing like amends for the irregularity of the whole. (Ralph 1734: 108)

Some thirty years later, the architect John Gwynn, one of the first English promoters of public urban planning, was even more critical of the effects of private enterprise on the extension of the West End in his *London and Westminster Improved*:

> In the present state of building, the finest part of the town (where only real improvement can be hoped,) is left to the mercy of capricious, ignorant persons, and the vast number of buildings, now carrying on, are only so many convincing proofs of the necessity of adopting the following, or some better hints, in order to convince the world that blundering is not the only characteristic of English builders. (Gwynn 1766: ix–x)

The targets of the two writers were of course not only builders, but also the ground landlords who decided to develop their property by offering building leases. They stood implicitly accused of failing to develop London in the public interest, and of treating urban space only as private property, without any concern for its status as a capital city.

For both Ralph and Gwynn, and indeed for other writers, the meaning of the new districts far exceeded their capacity to provide residential accommodation. The rapidly extending West End of eighteenth-century London was part of a metropolis whose visual appearance had a social, economic and political significance that was of national interest. In the 1720s Defoe had already underlined the drawbacks of the shapelessness of London:

> It is the disaster of London, as to the beauty of its figure, that it is thus stretched out in buildings, just at the pleasure of every builder, or undertaker of buildings, and as the convenience of the people directs, whether for trade, or otherwise; and this has spread the face of it in a most straggling, confused manner, out of all shape, uncompact, and unequal; neither long or broad, round or square. (Defoe 1971: 286–7)

We cannot suspect Defoe, a proto-liberal, of deploring freedom of enterprise, yet he clearly sensed the symbolic import of planning and monumentality in a capital, deploring for example that the rebuilt St Paul's Cathedral was hemmed in by neighbouring buildings.

The new West End of London, on the other hand, was built on empty sites and did allow some street planning, as foreign visitors were quick to notice. The new squares were even compared sometimes to French *places royales*. Such comparisons may sound absurd, considering their radically different aims. Yet they raise the question of the relationship between the fundamentally private development of London's West End and the treatment of what was after all public space. Mandeville, in the same period, had famously explained in *The Fable of Bees* how the pursuit of private interest (and even of vice) could in fact bring public benefits. In the case of the development of the West End, it seems possible to say that private initiative was in fact deliberately concerned in certain ways with the public character and significance of the new streets and squares.

On the basis of the well-charted history of a number of residential estates I will suggest in this chapter that the ground landlords made decisive choices that concerned not just housing, but practically all aspects of urban life, and were therefore involved in what we would now call the governance of London. To what extent the pursuit of private interest is compatible with, and favourable to, the public interest is of course one of the recurrent problems of liberal societies. In the context of London, the weakness of local government left much scope for private enterprise, and consequently for the control of the organization of the new residential districts. At the same time, a consciousness of having public obligations was part of the image the ruling élites had of themselves, and may explain how they managed to combine private interest with a degree of public virtue. In order to identify this involvement of landlords and builders in what we may call the governance of London, I will look at such problems as their responsibility for the lay-out and architecture of the new districts, for the creation and decoration of public space, for the provision of shops and markets, for the building of churches and other parish institutions.

It would be simplistic, of course, to suggest that there were perfectly identical attitudes in the organization of all the new residential areas over a long period. As Elizabeth McKellar has shown, it is rewarding to take stock of local situations and developers (McKellar 1999). This is why I will concentrate on three different estates developed between the Restoration and the 1740s, in order to refine the analysis of different forms of urban governance through estate development: the development around St James's Square planned by Henry Jermyn, first earl of St Albans (1605–1684) soon after the Restoration; the Grosvenor estate, developed by the three brothers Richard, Thomas and Robert Grosvenor from the 1720s; and the Ten-Acre Close, gradually built up under the aegis of Richard Boyle, third earl of Burlington (1694–1753).

*

Eighteenth-century visitors to London were struck by the modern, regular lay-out of the new West End developments, that formed an obvious contrast with the narrow, crooked lanes of the old City. On this side of London, wide, straight, airy streets, close to Hyde Park, offered an obviously healthier environment (Sheppard 1960, 1963, 1977–1980). The location and the lay-out of the new developments were in fact ideally suited for the needs of their affluent residents, who were often members of the ruling élites, together with professional people whose incomes largely depended from their services to the former. All these people found it convenient to reside near the Court of St James, the Houses of Parliament and other government buildings in Westminster. In the early seventeenth century, before these estates were developed, aristocratic families in fact already resided in the central and western parts of the built-up metropolitan area. But, as Lawrence Stone has suggested, after the Restoration they increasingly preferred smaller accommodation to the large family houses which used to line the Strand (Stone 1980). The development of the St James's Square area, initiated in the early 1660s, was clearly situated in a most favourable position for the members of the political élites and the professional people. Charles II was explicitly favourable to this development, which would bring the nobility to its doorstep, and he gave concrete evidence of his approval by eventually granting the Earl of St Albans in 1665 the freehold of much of the land in the area.

Yet a notable feature of the layout of the new residential estates of the West End from the Restoration to the 1750s was their public image as isolated, semi-private areas. In many cases, the new estates were referred to by the names of their owners (for example the Bedford, Cavendish, Grosvenor, Berkeley estates), almost as if they were country estates or colonial plantations in the heart of the metropolis. Contemporaries sometimes referred to them as distinct towns. John Evelyn referred to the Earl of Southampton's Bloomsbury development as 'a little town' (Summerson 1945: 41). In 1724 Defoe compared the Cavendish estate (north of what is now Oxford Street) to 'a new city', and even asserted it was larger than the cities of Bristol, Exeter and York (Defoe 1971: 300). We also have to remember that the squares which formed the nucleus of each development were often bordered on one side by the grand town house of the ground landlord. This was the case, for example, of the Earl of Southampton in Bloomsbury Square. The space of such squares, at least initially, might then be construed as a kind of courtyard common to a number of private residences. This was clearly the intention of the Earl of St Albans, who in 1662 wished to have only a very few grand town-houses around St James's Square. The eventual failure of this plan, and the fact that a larger number of private residences were built around the square of course slightly transformed the meaning of the square. Still, there was a clearly semi-private character to the new estates, which, furthermore, was reinforced by the organization of the street pattern.

The lay-out of the new aristocratic estates can be described as inward-looking. An examination of the early maps of the West End suggests there was little concern for connecting the new districts with the existing thoroughfares around them. For example, the St James's area was well related only to Pall Mall, but on the other three sides, the outer streets of the estate (Bury Street, Jermyn Street and the former Market Lane) were only connected to the rest of London by a few narrow lanes and passageways, as is visible on Morgan's map of 1682 and even on Rocque's map of 1746. Another example of this inward-looking character is that of the Grosvenor estate, laid out in the 1720s. It was situated in the North West corner of Mayfair, and was originally in an almost rural situation:

> GROSVENOR-SQUARE Stands at the farthest Extent of the Town, upon a rising Ground, with the Fields on all Sides; which, with the fine Air it thereby enjoys, renders the Situation delightful. The Inside is surrounded with Rails in an Octagonal Form, different from all the Squares in *London*, and agreeably planted with Dwarf-Trees, intermixed with fine Walks. (Pote 1730: 122)

One must admit, however, that on the northwest side, Tyburn gallows (situated where Marble Arch now stands) was not a very attractive feature of this part of London. This may explain there was no direct access to this important crossroads from the estate. On the western side, the houses turned their backs on Hyde Park, while in the South, the few streets connecting with the Berkeley estate formed awkward angles, as is clearly visible on John Rocque's map of 1746. As for the Ten-Acre Close developed by Lord Burlington to the north of his own house in Piccadilly, it was also poorly related to neighbouring streets, being bordered on the South by the wall of the nobleman's garden, and having no street link with Conduit Street to the North.

This self-contained and inward-looking character of the new developments contributed to making of the new West End a kind of mosaic of districts without spatial cohesion. John Gwynn, a pioneering advocate of public control over new developments, wrote:

> Had authority interposed, we should very probably have had the pleasure of seeing buildings erected with more convenient room, and at the same time occupying less ground; we should have been utter strangers to the terminating of tolerably good streets with stables and dunghills; nor should we have seen the fronts of one pile of buildings opposed to the backs of another. (Gwynn 1766: 12)

Gwynn had clearly noted how awkwardly the lay-outs of the new estates were related to the neighbouring areas. But he failed to assess the more positive contributions of the developers and builders to the creation of the new West End.

The most visible advantage of the extended West End, for resident and visitor alike, was its modern, urbane appearance, resulting from a geometrical layout and the provision of attractive squares. Many members of the ruling élites had been abroad and had seen French *places* and Italian *piazzas*. The new squares gave the British capital a more sophisticated appearance than ever before, as we know from the testimonies of some foreign visitors. Louis-Sébastien Mercier, who was in London in 1780, favourably compared London to Paris for this reason:

> In London, the inconsiderable height of houses, the breadth of the streets, which are mostly long and straight, make it easy for the visitor to know where he stands; at regular intervals there are spacious squares, some with a statue in the middle, some with a bowling green, or a bason, or a shrubbery, remarkably well-kept and used by the residents as walking-space; these squares are huge and handsome; they can be found at regular intervals, and are innumerable. (Mercier 1982: 60)

Even if such a description may sound rather idealized, it is clear that the new districts contributed to changing the image of London from an antiquated and backward city to a modern capital. They had nothing in common with the older crowded parts of the metropolis, with their eternal congestion, stench, noise and bustle. Here traffic was easy and scarce, sewers were laid out under every street, hardly any shops were to be seen, and pedestrians could enjoy the pleasures of a quiet walk. Furthermore, the regular pattern of new streets organized according to a grid-pattern had a symbolic quality, as an emblem of rationality and modernity.

One of the more visible and public attractions of the new districts was the appearance of the new houses, particularly in the central square, expected to be a show-piece of modern architecture. However, few London squares of the seventeenth and early eighteenth centuries had uniform façades, and those that had failed to preserve them for more than a few decades. Inigo Jones's Covent Garden Piazza originally had uniform terraces, apparently inspired by Italian and French examples, but fires and neglect fairly rapidly occasioned irregular rebuilding. St James's Square is of course, a prime example of regularity in the early years of its existence. Here, the appearance of the terraced houses was clearly influenced by Parisian examples, as the Mansard roofs suggested. The earl of St Albans was a Francophile courtier that had spent the period of the Commonwealth in Paris, and was familiar with the Place Dauphine, finished in 1614, and the Place Royale (now Place des Vosges), finished around 1630, both with uniform houses. It is clear that he was influenced by these Parisian examples when he projected St James's Square. His own house in No. 9–11, St James's Square, was indistinguishable from neighbouring ones. Yet what is significant of the limitations of the ground landlords' influence is precisely the ephemeral nature of such uniformity. The pressure of the successive lessees wishing to follow specific designs was too strong to be resisted by the successive ground landlords. The stringent clauses of the early leases were simply abandoned in the interest of easier leasing.

It is clear, however, that the model of the uniformly-fronted square was still of great appeal during the whole of the eighteenth century in British towns, as the splendid examples in Bath and other spas suggest. In the 1720s, when Grosvenor Square was begun, there were hopes, especially among the Palladian architects, that uniformity of street front might be possible. Colen Campbell and Edward Shepherd unsuccessfully proposed palatial designs for one entire side of Grosvenor Square. The east side, designed by John Simmons, was symmetrical, with a more emphatic central building, but never equalled the monumentality found in Bath's Queen Square. The Palladian architects and critics expressed disappointment over the failure of the London squares of the 1720s and 1730s to rival John Wood's achievement. Robert Morris wrote specifically about the east side of Grosvenor Square in 1734:

> The Middle House breaks forwards, is of another Species than those adjoining, then consequently is independent of any Proportions belonging to them: It is a Design of itself, and not suppos'd to represent the range as one House, only to preserve a Regularity in the Disposition of the several Buildings which compose the Line. (Morris 1734: preface)

And the whole of Grosvenor Square was also fiercely criticized by James Ralph for its poor architectural quality:

> It was meant to be very fine, but has miscarried very unfortunately in the execution: there is no harmony or agreement in the parts which compose it, neither is there one of those parts which can make us any thing like amends for the irregularity of the whole. The triple house, of the north side, is a wretched attempt at something extraordinary; but I hope not many people, beside the purchasers, are deceiv'd in their opinions of its merits. (Ralph 1734: 108)

As for Lord Burlington, the arbiter of Palladian taste, he also failed to demand uniformity of design from the building lessees in the Ten-Acre Close. He even provided different designs for two neighbouring houses erected in Burlington Street for General Wade (No. 29) and Lord Mountrath (No. 30). Colen Campbell provided a uniform street-front for a number of houses (No. 31–34) in the same street, but there was again no attempt at monumentality in these otherwise fairly narrow streets. However, the northern termination of the three parallel streets of the estate was carefully stage-managed by Burlington. We know for example that the proportions of Burlington School, a new building that was visible at the northern end of Burlington Street, were dictated by the nobleman (Carré 1993: 426–8).

Such tentative, fragmentary attempts at controlling the architectural appearance of the new residential estates of the West End are significant of the difficulties faced by the ground landlords whenever they tried to give the new West End some sort of monumentality. The conditions of the market did not allow them to practise authoritarian planning, much as they might have preferred it. It was only in the 1770s that the nature and appearance of the London square were described in terms of a public ideal to be followed:

The notion I form to myself of a perfect square, or public place in a city, is a large opening, free and unencumbered, where not only carriages have room to turn and pass, but even where the people are able to assemble occasionally without confusion. It should appear to open naturally out of the street, for which reason all the avenues should form radii to the centre of the place. The sides or circumferences should be built in a stile above the common and churches and other public edifices ought to be properly introduced. In the middle there ought to be some fountain, group, or statue, railed in within a small compass, or perhaps only a bason of water, still, by its utility in cases of fire, &c. makes ample amends. (Stewart 1771: 7)

Still, it is possible to say that the early eighteenth-century squares came close to this model, not though any process of public planning, but through the mediation of private developers.

When one examines the evolution of the treatment of squares, however, one is again faced with the ambiguous relationship between private and public interest. The streets of the new districts were generally accessible to all (except in a few exclusive gated *cul-de-sacs*), but there was a distinct tendency in favour of the privatization of the squares in the 1720s. As McKellar has noted, they were gradually transformed into gardens, which made them differ radically from the French *places* (McKellar 1999: 204–5). Much work remains to be done on the use and significance of the London squares, who are too often described as unchanging in their appearance and function, while in fact there is considerable ambiguity about their role in the city. Many of the earlier ones, like Covent Garden Piazza and St James's Square, changed appearance early in the eighteenth century. St James's Square was originally an empty space, technically belonging to the Crown, open to all, and in fact rather uncared for. Its immediate benefit was that it provided residents with light and air, advantages not always forthcoming in the older parts of the capital. In the early eighteenth century, trees and booths seem to have occupied part of it in a haphazard way. When rubbish began to accumulate in the square, the residents petitioned Parliament which in 1726 allowed them to appoint Trustees that would clean and embellish the square. Some £5,000 was levied from the residents, and Charles Bridgeman, the famous landscape gardener, designed a circular basin surrounded by an octagonal railing ornamented with obelisks and lamps. The rest of the square was finely paved. The erection of a statue of William III was contemplated. Such sophisticated visual treatment certainly enhanced the status of the square, which thus became emblematic of a new kind of public space designed for polite deambulation. This was indeed a novelty in a city where open spaces in general had a bad reputation as being generally neglected, uncontrolled, and generally disreputable (Carré 2000). The ornamented square of early eighteenth-century London, on the contrary, was a civilized and attractive public space, whose elegance was illustrated by many engraved views of the period.

Grosvenor Square was designed in 1725, and from the start was ornamented in a similarly elegant manner at the expense of the ground landlord himself, even before the houses were finished. The centre featured an oval enclosure planted with shrubs and ornamented with a gilt statue of George I. It was surrounded by a low wall and its access was reserved to residents. Such haste sounds very much like a marketing device, aimed at setting the tone of the new district, in a way that could rival St James's Square. The erection of a statue of the reigning king in the middle of the square at the expense of the ground landlord was also a private gesture. As Charlotte Chastel-Rousseau has remarked, there was no 'dialogue between the sculpture and architecture of the square', as in the French *places royales* (Chastel-Rousseau 2005: 46). The Grosvenors were old-fashioned Tories, suspected of Jacobite sympathies, who simply needed to assert their loyalty to the Hanoverian dynasty in order to attract the dominant Whig élites to the area. There is no doubt that the new London squares of the eighteenth century were show-pieces, but what they advertised was not national grandeur, but rather the dynamism of private entrepreneurs capable of transforming the capital into a visually attractive city. The fact that most of the new squares were given the name of the corresponding ground landlord also indicated the private nature of London's development at the time.

This remarkable association of private and public in the governance of eighteenth-century London is not easy to interpret in historical terms. Should we connect it with the rise of liberalism in Britain, and with the enterprising spirit evident in the manufacturing and transport sectors? Or should we connect it with the traditional civic humanism which was supposed to urge the élites to take an active part in the management of public affairs? An examination of the provision of services in the newly developed estates may perhaps help us to suggest an answer.

*

The idea of the new residential development as a kind of self-contained city implied the availability of a number of services. It is remarkable that the services provided for or contributed to by the ground landlords were for the poor as well as for the rich. The presence of poor inhabitants in reputedly affluent districts of the West End of London has rightly been emphasized recently by a number of social historians (Shoemaker 1991, Boulton 2000). And one can suggest that to some extent the aristocratic ground landlords behaved in London as if they were managing their own country estate, where the sense of their obligations towards the community was still strong. The Earl of St Albans, the Grosvenors, as well as Lord Burlington, all had their territorial bases in the counties, which did not fail to remind them of their social duties. However, we must admit it is often difficult to decide whether the provision of a given service in the capital answered commercial motives, or was related to a sense of public obligations.

In the St James's development, a church was provided, the still existing St James's, Piccadilly. This was designed by Sir Christopher Wren with particular care and begun in 1676. It is worth noting that the body of the church was largely financed by the Earl of St Albans, although the steeple and the decoration of the church were paid for later on by contributions of the local residents. The estate was also equipped with a covered market, begun in 1665, on Crown land leased by the Earl of St Albans's. It is probable that the cost of the market-house was paid for by the Earl himself.

On the Ten-Acre Close, Lord Burlington provided land free of charge in 1719 in Noel Street for a charity school for girls. He also asked Colen Campbell to provide a design for its street front, but we do not know the extent of his financial contribution to the building. This institution, named Burlington School, was opened in 1725. It aims were a characteristic combination of philanthropy and social control, as we can see from a contemporary account of workhouses:

> There is built a strong commodious Fabrick in *Burlington Gardens*, near *Hanover Square*, which has open'd at *Lady-day* 1725 for the Reception of the Girls School in the Parish, where they are lodg'd, boarded, and set to Work at Spinning Flax, &c. Knitting, Sewing, Washing, and such other Parts of Housewifery, as may prepare them to be good Servants. (Marryott 1725: 23)

In the Grosvenor estate, in the same decade, the ground landlord leased some land at a moderate price for the provision of a chapel. Yet Sir Richard did not pay for the construction, and to some extent this chapel was a commercial venture, as the cost of the construction by four contractors was to be repaid by the profits to be made from the renting of pews. As in the case of the square, the provision of this public building was offered as an incentive to attract inhabitants. This is made clear in the agreement between Grosvenor and the builders:

> As well for the Conveniency and Accommodation of the severall Tenants or Inhabitants of new Houses lately built ... lyeing in or about Grosvenor Square ... As also for the Encouraging and promoting of building in Generall upon such parts of the said Estate as yet remain unbuilt It hath been adjudged and though proper to erect a Chappell. (Sheppard 1980: 298)

Although the Grosvenors were very attentive to their own interest in general, they were also prepared to allow the provision of some costly services. As their estate was being developed, they paid (at least until 1733) for the laying of sewers under the major streets. Fresh water was provided from the reservoir of the Chelsea water company in Hyde Park.

Yet we can also note that some of the facilities offered in their Mayfair estate certainly did not enhance the attractiveness of the area for potential middle or upper-class inhabitants. First many taverns were allowed in the minor streets of the estate, though possibly for the use of the workmen during the building phase. Secondly the ground landlord consented to sell land at a very cheap price for the creation of a burying ground for the parish of St George's, Hanover square. Two small barracks for Guards were also allowed on the estate. Most surprisingly Sir Richard Grosvenor even consented to lease land for the erection of a workhouse to accommodate the paupers of the neighbouring parishes. This was built in 1725 in Mount Street, according to an innovative design by B. Timbrell and T. Phillips. The plan of this model workhouse was even printed and circulated by the Society for the Promotion of Christian Knowledge (Morrison 1999: 15). Surely the inclusion of a workhouse in an upper-class residential area cannot be explained otherwise than by a sense of social obligation. Moreover, for about a dozen years, in the 1750s and 1760s, a Lying-In Hospital (for married *and* unmarried mothers) was accommodated in Duke Street, at the expense of a number of charitable subscribers (Sheppard 1980: 86). An anonymous poem celebrating the occasion emphasized the happy combination of private and public interest in striking terms:

> See public Love triumphant here rejoice!
> Here private *Charity's* a public Triumph.
> What complicated Benefits flow hence!
> What rich, what national Utility! (*Charity* 1759: 9)

One may tentatively conclude that the major aims of the developers of the new West End were both to take advantage of a favourable location and of the current building boom in London, and to fulfil the classic public duties of wealthy land-owning families. The Earl of St Albans, the Grosvenor brothers and Lord Burlington can probably be ranged among those Defoe calls 'honest projectors':

> But the Honest Projector is he, who having by fair and plain principles of Sense, Honesty, and Ingenuity, brought any Contrivance to a suitable Perfection, makes out what he pretends to, picks no body's pocket, putd his Project in Execution, and contents himself with the real Produce, as the profit of his Invention. (Defoe 1720: 35)

We must emphasize that what was produced in the new West End was more than profits for the ground landlords and housing for affluent Londoners. What was created was also a new image of the metropolis as a healthy and pleasant environment that took into account the spiritual as well as material needs of Londoners. That such apparent concern for the public interest resulted mainly from an attempt to make the houses marketable does not preclude a sense of public obligations. The distinction between 'private' and 'public' interest thus appears to be blurred when one considers the impact of these developments on London's urban scene. What was often described later as urban speculation showed the way to a general modernization of London, and offered a new image of the capital that could compare favourably with continental cities.

*

It seems possible therefore to argue that the development of London's West End in the seventeenth and early eighteenth centuries was not driven purely by unbridled individualism. There existed at that time a peculiar imbrication of private and public interest that contributed to the development of the urban system. The development of the West End estates, as we have seen, was conducted to some extent in the same way as that of a private country estate, where the quest for profit was tempered by a sense of duty to the local community. The Earl of St Albans no doubt felt he was doing service to his fellow citizens when he organized the development of the estate he leased from the Crown. The Grosvenors themselves, sixty years later, were still thinking partly in terms of public obligations when they developed the residential district in Mayfair.

Such a spirit, however, was in the process of rapid decline in the second half of the eighteenth century, as commercial values and *laissez-faire* ideas were gaining ground. As early as 1758, the moralist John Brown complained bitterly about the demise of public spirit among the élites:

> Can it be imagined, that, amidst this general Defect of *Religion* and *Honour*, the great and comprehensive Principle of *public Spirit,* or *Love of our Country*, can gain a Place in our Breasts? That mighty Principle, so often feigned, so seldom possessed; which requires the united Force of upright *Manners*, generous *Religion*, and unfeigned *Honour*, to support it. What Strength of Thought or conscious Merit can there be in effeminate Minds, sufficient to elevate them to this Principle, whose Object is, 'the Happiness of a Kingdom?' (Brown 1758: 62)

From a less moralizing perspective this supposed decline of public spirit can of course be explained simply as a growth of economic individualism. Another era in urban development was beginning, in which the lessons of pre-industrial governance were forgotten. The growing industrial cities of the late eighteenth century did not enjoy their benefits, and were quickly seen as a prey to building speculators. It was now argued that many of their evils such as overcrowding, pollution, poor sanitation and slum-housing could be remedied by some degree of government intervention. The advent of municipal socialism in the late nineteenth century, followed by the gradual setting up of planning authorities in the twentieth century, were understood as means of solving such problems. This familiar story of gradual urban improvement thanks to public intervention soon formed the backbone of the grand Whig narrative of local government. The time has perhaps now come to revise it, not in order to sing the praises of the oligarchs, but in order to understand how urban governance could work in the past.

References

Boulton, J. (2000), 'The Poor among the Rich: Paupers and the Parish in the West End, 1660–1724' in Griffiths, P. and Jenner, M.S.R. (eds), *Londinopolis, Essays in the Cultural and Social History of Early Modern London* (Manchester: Manchester University Press).

Brown, J. (1758), *An Estimate of the Manners and Principles of the Times*, I (London).

Carré, J. (1993), *Lord Burlington (1694–1753), le connaisseur, le mécène, l'architecte* (Clermont-Ferrand: ADOSA).

Carré, J. (2000), 'Le jardin urbain au XVIIIe siècle', *Bulletin de la société d'études anglo-américaines des XVIIe et XVIIIe siècles* 51.

Charity: or, the Sanctuary. A Poem (London, 1725).

Chastel-Rousseau, C. (2005), '*Rus in Urbe*: les squares en Grande-Bretagne à l'époque géorgienne, 1720–1774' in Rabreau, D. and Pascalis S. (eds), *La Nature citadine au siècle des Lumières* (Bordeaux: William Blake & Co.).

Defoe, D. (1702), *Essays Upon Projects* (London).

Defoe, D. (1971), *A Tour through the Whole Island of Great Britain* (Harmondsworth: Penguin Books).

Gwynn, J. (1766), *London and Westminster Improved* (London).

Marryott, M. (1725), *An Account of Several Work-Houses for Employing and Maintaining the Poor, setting forth the Rules by which they are Governed, their great Usefulness to the Publick, and particularly to the Parishes where they are erected* (London).

McKellar, E. (1999), *The Birth of Modern London: The Development and Design of the City, 1660–1720* (Manchester: Manchester University Press).

Mercier, L.S. (1982), *Parallèle de Paris et de Londres* (Paris: Didier-Erudition).

Morris, R. (1734), *Lectures on Architecture*, I (London).

Morrison, K. (1999), *The Workhouse, A Study of Poor-Law Buildings in England* (Swindon: English Heritage).

Pote, J. (1730) *The Foreigner's Guide* (London).

Ralph, J. (1734), *A Critical Review of the Publick Buildings, Statues and Ornaments in, and about London and Westminster* (London).

Sheppard, F.H.W. (ed.) (1960), *Survey of London*, vol. 29, *St. James's, Westminster, part 1* (London: The Athlone Press).

Sheppard, F.H.W. (ed.) (1963), *Survey of London*, vol. 29, *St. James's, Westminster, part 2* (London: The Athlone Press).

Sheppard, F.H.W. (ed.) (1977-1980), *Survey of London*, vols 39 and 40, *The Grosvenor Estate in Mayfair* (London: The Athlone Press).

Shoemaker, R. (1991), *Prosecution and Punishment: Petty Crime and the Law in London and Rural Middlesex c.1660–1725* (Cambridge: Cambridge University Press).

Stewart J. (1771), *Critical Observations on the Buildings and Improvements of London* (London).

Stone, L. (1980), 'The Residential Development of the West End of London in the Seventeenth Century' in Malament, B.C. (ed.), *After the Reformation: Essays in Honour of J.H. Hexter* (Philadelphia: University of Pennsylvania Press).

Summerson, J. (1945), *Georgian London* (London: Pleiades Books).

Chapter 2

Making an Inclusive Urbanism: New York City's World Trade Memorial[1]

Robert A. Beauregard

Any resistance to privatization, any attempt to preserve and enhance what belongs to the public, benefits from an understanding of how the interplay of private and public spaces can make a city tolerant, just, and cosmopolitan. Limitations on access to a public park or the constriction of the right to assembly weaken the city as a place of inclusion and difference. The way that public and private activities intersect at a particular moment and in a particular place is essential for how we experience the city.

The purpose of this chapter is to frame the privatization debate in relation to urban form. Specifically, it is to provide a more expansive perspective on the spaces of the city (Lehrer 1998) and the extent to which the city's urbanity depends on their configuration. My central theme is one of urbanism, of the spatial form. Of central importance is how that form juxtaposes diverse activities, particularly its mix of private and public spaces.

Ultimately, my interest is in urban design. Consequently, I will illustrate my argument using the rebuilding of the World Trade Center site in New York City and, specifically, the design of the memorial for the victims of the 11 September 2001 (9/11) terrorist attack there. The proposed plans and designs embrace an exclusionary urbanism that ignores the diversity of spaces that sustain a city. With overtones of high modernism, the resultant urbanism is driven by state imperatives and the logic of the real estate industry. As a result, it is inhospitable to the city's public qualities. An opportunity for making the city more inclusive and more experientially coherent has been squandered. Rather than simply pose a critique, however, I also offer an alternative. Urbanism allows us to do both; that is, to negate and also affirm.

Privatization and the City

Interest in the privatization of cities divides thematically into a set of concerns focused on public and private services and another set centred on urban spaces.

---

1 An earlier draft of this chapter was presented at 'The Privatization of Cities in Historical Perspective', Conference, Université Paris-Sorbonne (Paris IV), 4 June 2004.

The first includes the privatization of such public services as education, health care, and prison management as well as the market segmentation of already private services such as telephone and bank accounts (Esman 2000, Goldsmith 1996, Graham and Marvin 2001). Both forms of privatization have drawn criticism from Left intellectuals. With public services shrinking under neoliberalism and private providers marginalizing those less able to pay, working class and poor people are deprived of quality services. Moreover, social inequalities are exacerbated. The implicit premise is that these services should be provided by the state or by a private sector compelled by state regulations to pool risks and accept limited profit margins.

The second set of thematic concerns centres on the spaces of the city (Beauregard 1999, Kohn 2004: 4–14, Sorkin 1992). Three of the most common topics are gated communities, shopping malls and the commodification of public spaces such as plazas and parks. The privatization that gated communities represent has two undesirable consequences: first, the withdrawal of the affluent middle class from support of state activities and, second, the cleaving off of one group of people from the larger society and the resultant amplification of disinterest towards those who are less privileged (Caldeira 1996, Marcuse 1997, McKensie 1994). Here, the two general concerns about the privatization of the city – services and space – meet. For example, the spatial withdrawal of the affluent middle class diminishes public services when these families send their children to private schools and no longer participate in debates about the quality of the local public schools.

Shopping malls pose a different set of issues having to do with rights of free speech and assembly and, more generally, political protest (Kohn 2004, 69–92; Mitchell 2003). In the common spaces of shopping malls people come together as consumers. Over the last few decades, malls have become ubiquitous, particularly in the United States, and even taken the place of the traditional 'downtown' where people mingle as citizens rather than consumers. In many suburbs, they are the only such 'public' settings. Consequently, a mall functions much like a public plaza or town commons even though privately owned. Of major concern is the rights people have in such commodified spaces.

The undesirable consequence of this commodification (as with gated communities) is discrimination by status. Critics fear the diminution of the potential for people from various social strata to mingle with each other (Mitchell 2003). The public sphere is diminished, for example, when city governments in the United States allow for-profit businesses (such as restaurants) to take public land, soft-drink companies to place vending machines in public schools and purchase the right to deny competitors from doing so (Franks 2000), or place commercial uses (e.g., hotels) and for-profit housing in public parks in order to generate the tax revenues ostensibly needed to build and maintain them (Ulam 2006).

Interest in the spaces of the city extends beyond the anxiety engendered by creeping commodification though. Of equal moment is the state's role in limiting movement and behaviour in public places through surveillance technologies and anti-terrorist barriers (Koskela 2000) and the role of youth gangs, the homeless, and criminal elements in making the spaces of the city feel more dangerous

(Body-Gendrot 2000). These activities constrict the places available to the general public and make the city seem less tolerant and, it is feared, less democratic. Public spaces, as Sharon Zukin (1995: 259) has written, 'are the primary sites of public culture' without which democracy is severely harmed. At the same time, critics also warn against the invasion of private spaces by the state. Examples include homophobic laws regulating consensual sexual relations and monitoring of telephone calls to identify terrorist cells. Privatization, commodification and surveillance are the enemies of a shared culture and of a politically engaged, free and informed public. The battle is fought in the physical spaces of the city.

Urbanism

In the United States, urbanism is typically associated with the way of life that occurs in cities. It is equated with what is popularly labelled lifestyle. By contrast, urbanism on the European side of the Atlantic Ocean tends to focus on the physical form of the city, what would be labelled urban design in the United States (Beauregard 2005, Krieger 2006). It involves the spatial juxtaposition and interconnection of buildings and spaces, landscape elements, and various structures from bridges to monuments. When these elements take on a collective identity – when they make sense together – an urbanism appears. Urbanism, then, is about the form of the city and the coherence that form achieves as it emerges from the social and spatial forces that shape society (Ellin 1996, Sennett 2004). (European scholars have also constituted urbanism as a social practice, see Lefebvre 2003: 6.) Consequently, urbanists talk about a high modernist urbanism with roots in the work of Le Corbusier and the International Congress of Modern Architecture (CIAM); a postmodern urbanism of historic preservation, pedestrian-oriented spaces, and a fine-scaled urban fabric; and, more recently, a neo-traditional urbanism which attempts to bring back the small towns and villages of the early twentieth century (Relph 1987).

To illustrate these differences, consider the early writings of Jane Jacobs that inspired both postmodern and neo-traditional urbanism. Jacobs wrote about an ideal urbanism of diverse uses and activities, random encounters, and street-level experiences (Jacobs 1961) Her 'sidewalk' urbanism is both a way of life and an urban formation that captures the city's richness and complexity. In opposition is a modernist planning intent on standardization, control, and predictability (Scott 1998). Jacobs' ideal city depends on people and economic activities being relatively unconstrained in their geographic location, jumbled together in a rich and fertile mix, and encountering each other in multiple places.

Interestingly, distinctive ways of life are often associated with specific urbanisms. A good example is the suburbanism that was produced in the United States after World War II (Beauregard 2006, Hayden 2003: 128–80, Jackson 1985). It was characterized by endless rows of single-family detached houses clustered together in large-scale developments. Its retail areas were (and still are) located along major highways, distant from residential areas and appearing in their purest form as regional shopping malls. This suburban urbanism supported and encouraged a family-centred, privatized, consumption-based, and automobile-centric culture and lifestyle. Currently, it is the target of a 'New Urbanism' that focuses on income-mixing, quality planning, and high-production design meant to foster pedestrian activity and a sense of community (Bray 1993; Beauregard 2002, Kohn 2004: 126–33, Schuyler 1997).

In any large city, what actually exists are multiple ways-of-life and layered urbanisms. Income, ethnic, cultural, status, and behavioural differences generate diverse consumption patterns and lifestyles. At the same time, because the city is itself an historical construct, overlapping and intersecting urbanisms, each representing different historical moments, exist simultaneously (Beauregard and Haila 2000). This layering includes both the intentional urbanisms produced by state interventions and capitalist practices and the unintentional or indigenous urbanisms of people adapting to and making their way in the city.

The benefits of using the notion of urbanism to think about privatization are twofold. First, urbanism directs our attention to the mix – the plurality – of spaces that comprise a city. It reminds us that a city embraces a variety of spaces from the most intimate to the most public, from those that are controlled by a single entity (such as a business corporation or the police) to wild spaces – an abandoned house – where all surveillance has disappeared.

Second, urbanism reminds us that the spaces of a city are connected; that is, that the city is an organic entity. Consequently, it is a mistake to think solely in terms of a single space. Places in the city are functional and meaningful only in relation to each other. And, although these connections vary in adjacency and intensity, they undermine any sense that planning and development of one part of the city can proceed without attending to places 'off-site' (Burns and Kahn 2005).

More specifically, the elements of urbanism are the buildings and structures that occupy land as well as the spaces – streets, backyards, rivers – between them. In effect, an urbanism is a mix of interior and exterior spaces arranged, purposively or not, in relationship to each other. And like the debate on privatization of the city, urbanisms are mainly concerned with exterior spaces, shopping malls being the major exception on the privatization side.

Exterior spaces can have various qualities. Most often discussed is whether they are private or public, a distinction meant to capture issues of accessibility and control. Highly privatized spaces are those that can be entered only by persons authorized to do so. Once there, the permitted activities are frequently limited. As an example, think of a health club or a workplace. At the other end of the continuum are public spaces where access is open to all and behaviour is lightly circumscribed; illegalities are the exceptions. The best example here is a city sidewalk.

In this formulation, 'private' does not mean commodified; that is, used for profit and thus under the control of a business. It is not a direct reference to an ownership-model of (private) property (Blomley 2004), although ownership is part of the formulation. One can have a privatized family space or a privatized neighbourhood space or even a privatized space under the auspices of the government (for example, a jail or the mayor's office). In a related sense, public does not mean 'state' or 'governmental'. A shopping mall is a good illustration of a privately-owned space that is public; that is, that admits people without discrimination. Nor does public have only one meaning. For example, a family compound has a public quality about it, but it is better described as communal. In short, the private-public distinction describes a continuum that unfolds on multiple dimensions of access, control, and ownership (Lofland 1998).

The city is the quintessential public space as captured in the famous German expression *Stadtluft macht frei* (Martindale and Neuwirth 1958: 94). It is filled with places where access and control have been relaxed. It has marketplaces, public squares, and sidewalks where people freely roam (Jukes 1990). More to the point, the city is where residents mingle with strangers. The presence of strangers and the tolerance and anonymity that flow from this makes the spaces of the city 'free' and thus public in a particular way (Kahn 1987). Consider the example of foreign tourists, the quintessential strangers, who, in the contemporary city, are highly valued for their contribution to its vibrancy and economy.

The city's spaces also vary in size and quality. A big city will have large urban parks, much smaller playgrounds, and very small squares where people can sit and talk. Or, consider highways, boulevards, streets and alleys as another illustration of how similar types of functional spaces differ in size. In effect, the city encompasses a mix of activities taking place at a variety of scales.

Aesthetics are another dimension on which the spaces of the city are distinct from each other (Sennett 2004). Some spaces are formal, purposively designed, and well-maintained. Examples include the grounds of a corporate headquarters, the park in front of city hall, and subway stations. Others are informal, indigenous, and barely maintained; for example, a path along a river or the impromptu football ground laid out by local youth in a city park.

An interesting variation on the theme of differentiation is derelict spaces (Jakle and Wilson 1992). These marginal places are considered by urban designers and city planners to fall outside the bounds of good urbanism. I am thinking here of homeless encampments under elevated highways, wooded areas that have become sites for dumping burnt-out automobiles, and streets lined by abandoned buildings that serve as promenades for drug sales.

Of course, all spaces have the quality of location. Large public spaces (such as plazas or boulevards) are often found in the more commercial areas of the city; more intimate and parochial spaces in residential areas. Still, many exceptions exist to this rule; for example, large public parks in US cities can be found in residential areas – Prospect Park in New York City or Forest Park in St Louis – and small public sitting areas in business districts.

Any urbanism, particularly if it is intentional, attempts to make sense of this plurality of spaces by managing their functional relations. One of the most common ways to do this is in terms of movement. Consider the international business person making her way from the airport to a first-class hotel, then to a business meeting at the corporate offices of a transnational firm, and, later, to dinner at an expensive restaurant (Martinotti 1999). Urban designers and city planners want these trips to be as effortless and as pleasurable as possible. Or, reflect on the daily life of a waiter in that upscale restaurant who makes his way to work from a neighbourhood some distance away – walking to a metro stop, exiting at his destination, and strolling along the river before taking a side street to begin serving the restaurant's customers. For this waiter, no less than the business person, the effort involved in the trip and its enjoyment (or lack thereof) are important. Or, as a last example, take the mother accompanying her children to school, stopping briefly in the playground with the baby, shopping for the evening's dinner, meeting a friend for coffee at a local cafe, and strolling through the park with the family in the evening.

These movements tie together the spaces of the city and direct our attention to how spaces are experienced (Lehtovuori 2005) and networked through their use. What becomes obvious is that certain spaces appear in the itineraries of dissimilar people, while a single individual is likely to move through many different spaces during the average day. This means that no single space is complete in itself; it neither satisfies all the daily, public needs of a user of the city nor has meaning in isolation. Spaces within the city make sense only in terms of the other spaces with which they are functionally, aesthetically, symbolically, and/or visually related (Bender 2001).

The goal of the urban designer is to rationalize these spaces in order to enhance their aesthetic quality, the sequential and visual experience of moving through them, and the efficiency of passage. In reality, the size, quality, location and juxtaposition of urban spaces is a product less of a single mind than a 'chaos of intentions' (Klinkenberg 2004). A city is a layered, interpenetration of intentional urbanisms and indigenous urbanisms that are always slightly out of kilter with the ever-changing users of the city. To the extent that cities are comprised of numerous publics, each with unique and ever-changing habits and lifestyles, the physical city and its social life are never in equilibrium. The goal of urbanism is – should be – to capture this diversity and respect its indeterminateness.

Yet, intentional urbanisms, much like the utopian proposals of city planners, are frequently less concerned with capturing the diversity of spaces and lifestyles than with creating a city for the middle class. Underlying such urbanisms from high modernism to neo-traditional planning is a normative order that, for the most part, emphasizes and legitimizes only a single way of life. Such urbanisms strive for narrative mastery (Klein 1995).

High modernist urbanism is the most egregious example of this bias (Holston 1989). The residents of the city are conflated into a 'universal' user without qualities of gender, ethnicity, nationality, religion, or cultural inclinations. This 'modern man' is middle-class, educated, employed, living in a stable family and comfortable in a high density world. Even more salient is that the resident shares his (or her) lifestyle with all the other residents. High modernist urbanism plans for a single public; multiple publics are simply not imagined.

This perspective proposes a sterile city where the preferred norm exists without the deviances that give it meaning. One can dine *al fresco* in a restaurant adjacent to a verdant riverbank but not fix one's automobile on the sidewalk. One can sit on a grassy knoll listening to musicians but not play football in the street. One can have household plants in one's flat but not appropriate a public green space for a garden of peppers and leeks. Moreover, it is not just high modernist urbanism that has a utopian vision of who is ideally suited for its cities. All intentional urbanisms rest on such an image. Most recently, New Urbanists have posited a world in which people sit on their front porches, chat with their neighbours, and take nightly strolls through the neighbourhood, but do not pile construction materials on their lawn or linger in country-and-western bars until late into the night.

Intentional urbanisms, then, tend to be inattentive to people living the real plurality of the city. Their goal is an 'ideal' way of life joined to its corresponding urban form. Multiplicity is not recognized. Yet, any city, whether it be culturally diverse like London or Johannesburg or relatively homogeneous like Reykjavik or Port-au-Prince, is saturated with distinctions that invoke a multiplicity of lifestyles and thus compel a variety of spaces (Bickford 1996: 55–93).

A vibrant and inclusive urbanism enables – even requires – an engagement with the city's plurality (Sandercock 1998, Sennett 1992). The normative ideal of city life, as Iris Marion Young (1990: 227) has argued, is 'an openness to unassimilated otherness'. In this ideal city, strangers intermingle not just under the banner of tolerance but in an environment of respect and mutual obligation. This allows the city's residents to become a public; that is, to act together. Consequently, a heterogeneous public has the potential to be a just public, one in which domination and oppression, institutional or otherwise, are resisted.

What enhances or erodes a just public are the spaces of the city (Sennett 2004). Inclusive and pluralized, they make justice more likely; exclusive and isolated, they diminish it. Solidarity and engagement rest on visibility and contact. That people share similar experiences in similar places, jointly recognize the symbolism of places, and move along common paths is essential to political engagement and to social justice. By 'providing a forum for dissenting views', public spaces enable the negotiation of differences (Kohn 2004: 201).

In sum, an inclusive urbanism recognizes how the spaces of the city contribute to its organic quality (Sternberg 2000). Designed to knit together various urban fragments, the resultant, over-lapping spatial networks encourage the city's many differentiated publics to interact. By doing so, an inclusive urbanism sets the conditions for both a robust democracy and social justice. The goal is not a simple coherence but rather a heterogeneous incompleteness, a city organically in flux and devoid of divisiveness.

The World Trade Center Memorial

Thinking about the public spaces of the city in this fashion is useful for reflecting on the design for the memorial to the 2001 terrorist attack in New York City. The memorial is part of the larger rebuilding of the former World Trade Center site in lower Manhattan (Beauregard 2004, Fainstein 2005, Filler 2005, Goldberger 2002a, Nobel 2005). There is much that can be said about this event in terms of the privatization of public spaces. From a European perspective – that is, the perspective of countries where states are strong rather than weak – one of the truly astounding decisions was the failure to treat the site as a 'public' space under the control of the federal government (Goldberger 2002b). This would have been a perfectly defensible position given the tragedy of event and its symbolic weight in the national imagination. Instead, the decision was to give the responsibility for rebuilding to a bi-state, non-profit development corporation (i.e., a public authority) and a single real estate developer. The result is a commercial, real estate project dominated by financial interests, drawing comparisons – absent the memorial – to the renewed Potsdamer Platz in Berlin (Eakin 2004).

My concern is with the urbanism that is being crafted through the site plan and the memorial design. Specifically, I want to assess the memorial design against the notion of an inclusive urbanism that links the site to the fabric of the city and that recognizes the plurality of activities and people that will flow through and around this space.

Destruction of the World Trade Center's twin towers and adjacent buildings on 11 September 2001 left an approximately 16-acre site on which government and business leaders vowed to rebuild. The rebuilding process was initially overseen by the non-profit Lower Manhattan Development Corporation (LMDC) set up by the New York State government. (The LMDC was disbanded in 2006.) The two main property owners are the Port Authority of New York and New Jersey (a bi-state governmental agency) and Larry Silverstein, a major real estate developer and owner of office buildings. Just months before the terrorist attack, Silverstein Properties had purchased from the Port Authority a 99-year lease on the twin towers and the land underneath. In return, it would pay the Port Authority approximately US$120 million a year in rent.

To date, the rebuilding process has produced, through competitions, a site plan by the firm of Studio Daniel Libeskind and a design for a memorial to the victims. The program initially called for the replacement of most of the approximately 10 million square feet of office space, the 500,000 square feet of retail space, the repair of the transit stations and tracks, two cultural facilities, and a memorial. The final site plan, titled 'Memory Foundations', developed by Studio Daniel Libeskind consisted of three, central open spaces surrounded by four office towers (with retail services) along with the a fifth office tower (Freedom Tower) to be topped off at 1,776 feet in height, the number a reference to the year in which the United States declared independence from England.

This redevelopment project can be viewed as a clash between two types of urbanism. On the one side is the high modernist urbanism of the original office development. This corporate-centred urbanism celebrated commerce and its twin 110-story towers were modernist icons. The towers sat on a large monolithic base physically and aesthetically distinct from the surrounding urban fabric, a form made possible by the amalgamation of smaller city blocks to create a super-block. The two, identical towers were surrounded by other office towers, all designed in the International Style and all reflecting the high modernist urbanism in which they were embedded. Underneath, the concourses were dedicated to moving commuters to their offices and providing eating and shopping opportunities.

This high modernist approach, with its commercial mentality, has been continued into the current rebuilding process through the emphasis on replacing the office and retail space and retaining a large plaza-like space – the memorial –

as a central focal point. The architecture has changed, though less substantively than superficially. One of the adjacent office buildings that was destroyed has been replaced by a typical office building design. The Freedom Tower, the first of the above-ground projects, breaks with the rectangular form of the International Style but still retains core design elements such as the uniform, glass curtain wall.

More importantly, the spaces of the proposed rebuilding are high modernist spaces. They are designated for visitors to the memorial, commuters to the office towers, and office workers on their lunch breaks. Purposive and segregated, these spaces elevate control over serendipity. Moreover, the rebuilt site is quite likely to mimic its earlier incarnation and create a night-time sterility, a place inhabited only during office hours. In addition, the rebuilding does not engage its surroundings; it simply fills the land made available as a result of the destruction. The site is sharply distinguished from its surroundings in form and use. Property rights, security concerns, and the narrow mix of uses combine to produce an exclusionary space.

On the other side is a postmodernism urbanism represented by Battery Park City to the west, a project of the 1980s designed to replicate a more or less typical New York City neighbourhood of apartment buildings, retail activities, commercial uses, and open space (Fainstein 2001, Gordon 1997, Kohn 2004: 141–56). For decades, lower Manhattan, once the city's main and sole commercial district, has been becoming more residential. Consequently, a constituency exists for a rebuilding that recognizes the demand for mixed-use redevelopment and that emphasizes the needs of local residents, specifically the retail (dry cleaners, food stores) and public services (elementary schools, playgrounds) that enable people to function in their daily lives (Beauregard 2005a, Goldberger 2005).

These two types of urbanism privilege different variations and configurations of public spaces. The high modernist approach that is dominating the rebuilding process favours a single large public space, spaces for pedestrian movement and transit activities, and the more privatized office and retail spaces. By contrast, the postmodern urbanism of the 24-hour city privileges playgrounds and small parks and retail areas oriented to residents of the area rather than to office workers and tourists. One unfolds at a commercial scale; the other at a more human scale.

As for configuration, the Libeskind site plan offers a 'center' dominated in plan by the memorial and in section by the Freedom Tower. Around these focal points the other buildings and spaces are arranged. All of the elements are in close proximity and subordinate to the core. Eroding this clarity is that the commercial intent of the rebuilding is in tension, functionally and symbolically, with the memorial to the victims of the terrorist attack.

Just as for the site plan, a competition was held for the memorial. The process began in August of 2002 when the LMDC hired a manager for the design of the memorial (Goldberger 2004: 204–34, Young 2005). In April of 2003, the design competition was announced and over 5,000 designs were submitted. The competitors were required to locate the memorial on the former WTC site – still owned by the Port Authority – and use no more than one-quarter of it. The mission statement required the designers to memorialize the 'innocent men, women, and children murdered by terrorists, show respect for the place of the tragedy, and reflect the endurance and courage of the survivors (Young 2005: 147). By November of that year, the jury had narrowed the total submissions to eight finalists. The winning design, 'Reflecting Absences' by Michael Arad, was announced in January of 2004. Soon thereafter, Peter Walker, a landscape architect, was added to the design team.

Arad's original design consisted of a field of trees surrounding two, recessed pools with water cascading into them from the plaza level. Visitors would access the pools from ramps. Below ground, they would find spaces for contemplation, exhibition areas, and rooms for storing the unidentified remains of those who died there. The pools occupied the two footprints of the former twin towers.

Once the design was selected and Walker added to the design team, the LMDC and the designers began modifying the proposal in light of various engineering, security, and access issues, symbolic concerns (e.g., how and where to list the names of victims), and the relationship between the memorial and the two cultural facilities and office buildings that had been planned for the site. Simultaneously, the World Trade Center Memorial Foundation was established to raise private and public funds to build and manage the memorial. The Foundation was not initially successful and by 2006 the president had resigned and the budget had doubled to close to US$1 billion, excluding the US$80 million visitors' centre which had originally been designed as a cultural facility. A design review was initiated to reduce the costs to a manageable US$500 million.

The footprints of the twin towers had become sacred places – burial sites – for the victims' families and politicians, despite the fact that victim remains had been found blocks beyond the original site. Arad's casting of the footprints as 'absences' captured this sense of loss while the trees stood for the resilience of life. In addition, the mission statement left the commercial intentions of the rebuilding intact. The memorial was subordinated to the office and retail functions both in the physical confinement of the memorial and in the positioning of the memorial design only after the commercial aspects of the site had been determined (Goldberger 2004: 213). In response, Arad produced a modernist design that repeated the stock elements of many memorials and even of typical commercial public spaces; its boundaries are clear and its form monolithic. As the architectural critic Paul Goldberger (2004: 226) commented as regards all of the finalists, the design had 'the bland earnestness of a well-designed plaza'.

Clearly, the memorial design was not considered an event in a larger, layered, inclusive, and heterogeneous urbanism. It ignores the increasingly residential character of lower Manhattan and the organic nature of the city. It posits a single site for a tragedy that affected lives well beyond these 16 acres. Consequently, it marginalizes the way the meanings of that day rippled across the city, its region, the nation, and the world.

An alternative design drawing from an inclusive urbanism would have configured this public space much differently and connected it to the surrounding city. Likely, it would have crossed the boundaries of the site rather than remaining confined to an artificial centre (Sennett 2004) and thus have been knitted into the surrounding urban fabric. In this way, such a design would have become a remembrance *and* an affirmation of the city. It would have served as a symbol not of terrorism as an act perpetrated on the people who worked in the towers and those who tried to rescue them, but of a world in which such hatreds mark all of us as complicit. Thinking of the site and the memorial in this more expansive fashion was not allowed however.

In fact, the modernist centrality of the WTC memorial has been resisted. Across the country, and even outside of it, local groups and governments have built memorials to the victims. And, immediately after the terrorist attack numerous informal memorials appeared around New York City where people posted pictures of the victims and left flowers and candles. At one point, a series of floodlights were positioned near the site as a temporary memorial, their twin beams directed skyward.

By November of 2006, nearly 200 formal memorials had been created in the United States with another twenty or so in countries like Israel, France, Ireland, and New Zealand (www.911memorials.org). The largest number were located in the states of New York and New Jersey, with many fewer in Washington, DC, and Connecticut. They range in style from simple plaques to sculptures and from pieces of the destroyed buildings to flower gardens. Many were living memorials; that is, small parks, community and school gardens, and tree groves (www.livingmemorialsproject.net). Jersey City, just across the Hudson River from New York City, planned to erect two stainless-steel walls, while Westchester County north of the city proposed a series of steel rods rising from the ground and welded together at their top (Applebaum 2004, Boxer 2004, Nobel 2004).

These memorials emerged out of a localized grief and a need to remember the event and neighbours who died there. The result is a series of architectural fragments that appear in different places with no attempt at a design connection. (The memorials that use remnants of the buildings are the informal exception.) Their disconnectedness in aesthetic and urbanistic terms enables the WTC memorial to maintain its dominance. The goal is not necessarily to coordinate these many memorials, but to devise a scheme for taking a geographically disconnected 'field' of places of different scales and uses and relating them. Each place, each event, would then remind the visitor of the tragedy in a way that would strengthen the sense of it as having national meaning and not just having occurred 'at' the World Trade Center site.

One could address the centrality of the WTC memorial design in another way. Consider a memorial space that integrates the site with its surroundings; that is, that extends outward, not abandoning the 'site' but extending its tentacles into other areas of lower Manhattan and the city. This memorial space could capture the pathways along which visitors proceed to 'ground zero' from off the site. It could accommodate through different uses (e.g., bus shelters, sitting areas, public toilet facilities) those who live or work near-by and pass through the space on a daily basis. And, it could recognize that people grieve and remember in quite diverse ways, and provide them the opportunity to do so. This design would draw on an inclusive urbanism and react to the movements and varied and incommensurate meanings that people attach to the city and to that event.

Of course, all that I have suggested remains schematic. Nonetheless, it suggests that the memorial could have been done differently, could have broken away from a an exclusive, high modernist urbanism. It did not. The resultant urbanism reflects the commercial and state-centric nature of the rebuilding process.

Conclusion

Any attempt to think about the privatization of the city must recognize the diversity of its spaces, the manifest ways in which privatization and publicness materialize, and the plurality of the city's residents. To have done so for the World Trade Center site – to have thought and designed in terms of an inclusive, heterogeneous, and organic urbanism – would have meant a different memorial and a different site plan, making both in and of the city.

Negating any such approach are a combination of property rights, organizational imperatives, and political symbolism that privileges the site over the city. The Port Authority's control of the site, Silverstein's ownership of the leases, and the varied ownership of surrounding sites into which a memorial might be inserted pose formidable barriers to alternative schemes. Consequently, the World Trade Center site has become privatized despite being publicly owned. In addition, the Port Authority, Silverstein Properties, and the LMDC have mandates and agendas that limit perspective. Their mission is to rebuild on the site, not to rebuild lower Manhattan or the city. Finally, the symbolism of the site is extremely powerful. Many of the families of the victims see it as sacred space; its presence in the consciousness of most New Yorkers and many Americans is not to be denied. The death and destruction occurred there, not someplace else.

An inclusive and heterogeneous urbanism is a utopian project. This does not mean, though, that utopian visions should be abandoned (Friedmann 2002), nor that critique has to be confined to negation. If the privatization of the city is seen as inevitable, it will spread and thrive. Suppressing an engaged public will enable privatization and commodification to flourish. Until we can imagine what a different city would be, until we can embrace a counter-urbanism, neither critique nor resistance will be successful.

References

Applebaum, A. (2004), 'First Interpretations', *Metropolis* 24:2, 126–7.
Beauregard, R. (1999), 'Julkinen kaupunki' ('The Public City'), *Janus* 7:3, 214–23, available in English from the author.
Beauregard, R. (2002), 'New Urbanism: Ambiguous Certainties', *Journal of Architectural and Planning Research* 19:3, 181–94.
Beauregard, R.(2004), 'Mistakes Were Made: Rebuilding the World Trade Center, Phase 1', *International Planning Studies* 9:2, 139–53.
Beauregard, R. (2005a), 'The Textures of Property Markets: Downtown Housing and Office Conversions in New York City', *Urban Studies* 42:13, 2431–45.
Beauregard, R. (2005b), 'Urbanism' in Caves, R. (ed.), *Encyclopedia of the City* (New York: Routledge), 501–502.

Beauregard, R. (2006), *When America Became Suburban* (Minneapolis, MN: University of Minnesota Press).
Beauregard, R. and Haila, A. (2000), 'The Unavoidable Continuities of the City' in Marcuse, P. and Kempen, R. van (eds), *Globalizing Cities* (Oxford: Blackwell Publishers), 22–36.
Bender, T. (2001), 'The New Metropolitanism and the Pluralized Public', *Harvard Design Review* 13, 70–77.
Bickford, S. (1996), *The Dissonance of Democracy* (Ithaca, NY: Cornell University Press).
Blomley, N. (2004), *Unsettling the City* (New York: Routledge).
Body-Gendrot, S. (2000), *The Social Control of Cities?* (Oxford: Blackwell).
Boxer, S. (2004), 'New Jersey Selects its Sept. 11 Memorial', *The New York Times*, 1 August: E3.
Bray, P. (1993), 'The New Urbanism: Celebrating the City', *Places* 8:4, 56–65.
Burns, C. and Kahn A. (eds) (2005), *Site Matters: Design Concepts, Histories, and Strategies* (New York: Routledge).
Caldeira, T. (1996), 'Fortified Enclaves: The New Urban Segregation', *Public Culture* 8, 303–28.
Eakin, H. (2004), 'The Other Ground Zero', *Metropolis* 23.8, 52 3.
Ellin, N. (1996), *Postmodern Urbanism* (Cambridge, MA: Blackwell Publishers).
Esman, M. (2000), *Government Works: Why Americans Need the Feds* (Ithaca, NY: Cornell University Press).
Fainstein, S. (2001), *The City Builders* (Lawrence, KS: University Press of Kansas).
Fainstein, S. (2005), 'Ground Zero's Landlord: The Role of the Port Authority of New York and New Jersey in the Reconstruction of the World Trade Center' in Mollenkopf, J. (ed.), *Contentious City* (New York: Russell Sage Foundation), 73–94.
Filler, M. (2005), 'Filling the Hole', *New York Review of Books* 52:3, 6–11.
Franks, T. (2000), *One Market Under God* (New York: Doubleday).
Friedmann, J. (2002), *The Prospect of Cities* (Minneapolis, MN: University of Minnesota Press).
Goldberger, P. (2002a), 'Groundwork: How the Future of Ground Zero is Being Resolved', *The New Yorker* 78:12, 86–95.
Goldberger, P. (2002b), 'Up From Zero', *The New Yorker* 78:21, 29–30.
Goldberger, P. (2004), *Up From Zero: Politics, Architecture, and the Rebuilding of New York* (New York: Random House).
Goldberger, P. (2005), 'A New Beginning', *The New Yorker* 81:15, 54–7.
Goldsmith, S. (1996), 'New Hope for the Cities', *Civic Bulletin* 5.
Gordon, D. (1997), *Battery Park City* (New York: Gordon and Breach).
Graham, S. and Marvin S. (2001), *Splintering Urbanism: Network Infrastructures, Technological Mobilities, and the Urban Condition* (London: Routledge).
Hayden, D. (2003), *Building Suburbia: Green Fields and Urban Growth* (New York: Pantheon).
Holston, J. (1989), *The Modernist City: An Anthropological Critique of Brasilia* (Chicago: University of Chicago Press).
Jackson, K. (1985), *Crabgrass Frontier: The Suburbanization of the United States* (New York: Oxford University Press).
Jacobs, J. (1961), *The Death and Life of Great American Cities* (New York: Vintage).
Jakle, J. and Wilson, D. (1992), *Derelict Landscapes* (Savage, MD: Rowman and Littlefield).
Jukes, P. (1990), *A Shout in the Streets* (Berkeley, CA: University of California Press).

Kahn, B. (1987), *Cosmopolitan Culture* (New York: Atheneum).
Klein, K. (1995), 'In Search of Narrative Mastery: Postmodernism and the People Without History', *History and Theory* 34:4, 275–98.
Klinkenberg, V. (2004), 'Without Walls', *The New York Times Magazine* (16 May), 15.
Kohn, M. (2004), *Brave New Neighborhoods: The Privatization of Public Spaces* (New York: Routledge).
Koskela, H. (2000), '"The Gaze Without Eyes": Video Surveillance and the Changing Nature of Urban Space', *Progress in Human Geography* 24:2, 243–65.
Krieger, A. (2006), 'Where and How Does Urban Design Happen?', *Harvard Design Magazine* 24, 64–71.
Lefebvre, H. (2003), *The Urban Revolution* (Minneapolis, MN: University of Minnesota Press).
Lehrer, U. (1998), 'Is There Still Room for Public Space?' in INURA (ed.), *Possible Urban Worlds* (Basel: Birkhaeuser), 200–207.
Lehtovuori, P. (2005), *Experience and Conflict: The Dialectics of the Production of Public Urban Space in the Light of New Event Venues in Helsinki, 1993–2003* (Helsinki: Centre for Urban and Regional Studies, Helsinki University of Technology).
Lofland, L. (1998), *The Public Realm* (Hawthorne, NY: Aldine de Gruyter).
Marcuse, P. (1997), 'The Enclave, the Citadel, and the Ghetto: What Has Changed in the Post-Fordist US City', *Urban Affairs Review* 33:2, 228–64.
Martindale, D. and Neuwirth, G. (eds) (1958), *The City* (Glencoe, IL: The Free Press).
Martinotti, G. (1999), 'A City for Whom? Transients and Public Life in the Second-Generation Metropolis' in Beauregard, R. and Body-Gendrot, S. (eds), *The Urban Moment: Cosmopolitan Essays on the Late Twentieth-Century City* (Thousand Oaks, CA: Sage Publications), 155–84.
McKensie, E. (1994), *Privatopia: Homeowners Associations and the Rise of Residential Private Communities* (New Haven, CT: Yale University Press).
Mitchell, D. (2003), *The Right to the City* (New York: Guilford Press).
Nobel, P. (2005), *Sixteen Acres: Architecture and the Outrageous Struggle for the Future of Ground Zero* (New York: Henry Holt).
Nobel, P. (2004), 'Soaring Modesty', *Metropolis* 24:1, 62, 66.
Relph, E. (1987), *The Modern Urban Landscape* (Baltimore, MD: The Johns Hopkins University Press).
Sandercock, L. (1998), *Towards Cosmopolis* (Chichester, UK: John Wiley and Sons).
Schuyler, D. (1997), 'The New Urbanism and the Modern Metropolis', *Urban History* 24:3, 344–58.
Scott, J. (1998), *Seeing Like a State* (New Haven, CT: Yale University Press).
Sennett, R. (2004), 'The City as an Open System', paper presented at Conference on 'The Resurgent City', London School of Economics, London, 20 April.
Sennett, R. (1992) (orig. 1974), *The Fall of Public Man* (New York: W.W. Norton & Company).
Sorkin, M. (ed.) (1992), *Variations on a Theme Park* (New York: Noonday Press).
Sternberg, E. (2000), 'An Integrated Theory of Urban Design', *Journal of the American Planning Association* 66:3, 265–78.
Ulam, A. (2006), 'A Bridge Too Far?', *The Architect's Newsletter* 13, 27.
Young, J. (2005), 'The Memorial Process: A Juror's Report from Ground Zero' in Mollenkopf, J. (ed.), *Contentious City* (New York: Russell Sage Foundation), 140–62.
Young, I. (1990), *Justice and the Politics of Difference* (Princeton, NJ: Princeton University Press).
Zukin, S. (1995), *The Cultures of Cities* (Cambridge, MA: Blackwell).

PART 2
Housing

Chapter 3

The Privatization of Council Housing in Britain: The Strange Death of Public Sector Housing?

David Fée

The election of Margaret Thatcher as British Prime Minister in 1979, and the eighteen years of Conservative rule which followed, have given birth to a vast literature devoted to the analysis of Thatcherite policies. Writers have often argued that 1979 represents a turning point and have sought to demonstrate how successive Conservative governments put an end to some thirty years of political consensus (Kavanagh 1987: 1). They have been encouraged in their analysis by statements made by Margaret Thatcher herself expressing her determination to break with what she regarded as the stalemate of the British model. The post-war years, they say, were characterized by a high level of political agreement on the nature of public policies, as well as on the strategy favoured to implement these policies (mainly through negotiation and compromise) (ibid.: 6). This agreement included 'the acceptance of the legitimacy of the central role of the State in Welfare' (Deakin 1994: 54). Consequently, the social policies at the heart of the Welfare State, designed to promote the well-being of the individual and to guarantee social security, are often said to have developed within a climate of high level of agreement across political parties. This climate of opinion, illustrated by Harold Macmillan's decision to accept his chancellor's resignation rather than reduce public spending, was itself based on the belief that the Welfare State enjoyed widespread popular support and that no government withdrawing support from it would be re-elected. These writers often treat housing as one of the five main public services having been encouraged in their belief by Beveridge's inclusion of housing in his five Giants. As a consequence, they argue that housing illustrates most clearly the retreat from Welfare State principles and the deliberate break with post-war policies (Forrest and Murie 1988: 4, Kleinman 1996: 18–57, Balchin 1995: 8) that marked the post-1979 years. The sector is said to be somewhat of an exception in that, alone among other public services, it was targeted for change and has undergone a complete transformation and increasingly been relegated to the edge of the Welfare State. Recently some writers have challenged this idea (Malpass 2004: 209–27) and argued that housing reform, far from driving the sector away from other public services, has only anticipated the reform of the wider Welfare State. In fact, continuity and convergence are said to prevail over the long term.

The following chapter will seek to buttress this theory and qualify the general view that 1979 constitutes a turning point in housing policies.[1] It will attempt to demonstrate that post-1979 Conservative housing policies of privatization have not so much broken with the post-war consensus as followed lines sketched by late nineteenth- and early twentieth-century Conservatives.

The Conflictual Growth of Public Housing

When Margaret Thatcher was elected in 1979 the public housing sector was a force to be reckoned with. From the end of World War II until the election of the Conservative government in 1979 some 5 million houses or flats were built in British cities and new towns through state subsidies. Whereas council housing (that is housing subsidised by the central state, but built and managed by local authorities) represented less than 2 per cent of Great Britain's housing stock in 1913 and still only 13 per cent in 1947, by 1979 its share of the British housing stock had risen to 32 per cent (Balchin 1995: 120). By 1979 local authorities had become the largest landlord in the country. Contrary to popular belief, this spectacular expansion was not achieved on the basis of the post-war political consensus but in spite of a political disagreement about the role of the state in housing. A brief reminder of the history of conflicts surrounding the growth of the sector will help to put in perspective the post-1979 reform of council housing and qualify the radical nature of the conservative policies.

The strength of the public housing sector in 1979 was the result of the slow and gradual intervention of the state into the field of housing from the second half of the nineteenth century onwards. Although municipal housing was born in 1890 when a piece of legislation (Housing of the Working Classes Act) made it possible for local authorities to build for the working class to house them and no longer to re-house them, the state refused for a long time to shoulder the financial burden and left building to the discretion of local authorities. Only a few pioneers, such as the London County Council, Sheffield or Liverpool councils, took advantage of these new powers. The foundations of the central-local partnership that was to dominate housing policies until the early 1980s were only laid down in 1919. That year, a piece of legislation was passed by the government of Lloyd George, fearing social revolution in case millions of demobilized men were sent back to their insalubrious homes. The 1919 Housing and Town Planning Act made it compulsory for local authorities to assess their housing needs and submit plans to the ministry. It provided, for the first time, yearly state subsidies to local authorities to have houses built for the working classes.

Contrary to popular belief, far from growing smoothly between 1919 and 1979, public housing expanded fitfully, moving on by leaps and bounds, its history reflecting the priorities of the party in power. A change of government resulted

---

1   The chapter is based on the author's unpublished PhD thesis, 'Le logement public en Angleterre de 1885 à 1990: des politiques consensuelles?' (Université Paris 3–Sorbonne Nouvelle, 1998).

in change of tactics and emphasis (Lowe 1993: 245). Apart from a short period (1939–1956) when an artificial consensus was reached, the two main political parties never managed to agree beyond a minimum framework. This framework was to dominate housing policies until the 1970s economic recession forced a revision of it on governments. This 'enabling framework', as it has been defined by Peter Malpass, rested on five principles, state subsidies to local authorities, local control of capital expenditure programmes, rents set at reasonable levels, rent rebates schemes also subject to local determination and the principle that the housing revenue account was subject to a no profit rule (Malpass 1992: 13). That the political consensus over housing was a short and minimal one can be explained by an on-going and profound disagreement over two key related issues: the extent of state intervention and the question of universality. The inability of the two main parties to agree on these issues explains why, as an increasing number of scholars have pointed out (Malpass 2004: 211) housing stands apart from other public services and always enjoyed an ambiguous status within the Welfare State.

Seen in retrospect, the inter-war years heralded the ideological divide that was to become clear after World War II. For the Conservatives housing was synonymous with private enterprise and state intervention was to be time-limited and kept to a minimum. Clearly, with the benefit of hindsight, the Conservatives never conceived the post-1918 housing programmes as a more than a temporary expedient made necessary by exceptional circumstances. Their preference always lay with owner-occupation and the private sector. Although the Conservative Party committed itself in 1918, just like its political opponents, to a comprehensive national housing programme, their return to power heralded a withdrawal of the state. With a view to making savings, the Conservative-dominated government of Lloyd George had the 1921 Housing Act voted thus putting an end to the 1919 programme and to state subsidies paid to local authorities to build working class housing. After 1922, when the Conservatives found themselves finally alone in power until 1929, state subsidies to local authorities were increasingly reduced on several occasions (1923, 1926 and 1928). Meanwhile, private enterprise was favoured and home ownership given financial help (1923 Housing Act). These measures were dictated by the notion of 'filtering-up', the belief that the increase of the private housing stock would in the end benefit the poor as they would move into the homes left vacant by upwardly mobile middle-class people (Hansard 1924). They were also motivated by the idea that providing working-class housing was beyond the power of local authorities and that subsidising local authorities was unfair competition to the private sector (Hansard 1923, NUCUA 1933: 18). The Conservatives' belief that the state should play a minimum role in the field of housing and their trust in the market were further underlined in 1933. That year, the Housing Act put an end to state subsidies to local authorities for any building activity not related to slum clearance. Clearly, state intervention was to be limited to those working class people too poor to be provided for by the private sector and whose living conditions posed a threat to the rest of the population (National Housing Committee 1934: §1). These policies helped owner-occupation increase in the inter-war years from 10 per cent of the stock in 1914 to 32 per cent in 1938. In contrast, the Labour Party always supported the need for the state to intervene in order to build for the general needs of the whole of the working classes. It stressed the responsibility of the nation in housing working class people properly and so in going some way towards reducing poverty (Hansard 1924). When shortly in power in 1924, the party passed a housing act which officially established local authorities as part of the machinery set up to provide working class housing (Bowley 1945: 38). In opposition after 1931, it ceaselessly campaigned for the inclusion of housing into the emerging social policies (The Labour Party 1935).

Likewise, a study of the policy aims expressed between 1945 and 1979 by the two main parties in the housing field serves to dispel any myth of a consensus. Despite the acceptance by the party of planning and state intervention (as visible in *The Industrial Charter*) under the pressure of various Tory reform groups as well as the policy reforms introduced by R.A. Butler, housing remained at the heart of party conflict in the post-war years (Lowe 1993: 235). The acceptance of a mixed economy never meant to the Conservatives a far-reaching housing public service. More than any other public service, housing for the Conservatives was to be limited to a safety-net for the poorest. Unlike Labour governments, Conservative governments never saw their role as being a universal provider. The evolution of the parties' housing policies is aptly summed up by the metaphor of two trains running on parallel lines in opposite directions (Hennessy and Seldon 1987: 310–11). Because of the conclusions of the Committee on Reconstruction, the coalition government had agreed in the 1944 Housing Temporary Accommodation Act to a two-year housing programme which re-instated local authorities in the pivotal role they had lost in 1933. However, very quickly, what appeared to be a consensus turned out to be a mere compromise which did not survive the end of the coalition in May 1945. While in opposition the Conservatives criticized the restrictions imposed on private builders by the Labour Party and signalled their intention to restrict the intervention of the state to slum clearance and housing the poorest if re-elected (Conservative Research Department 1948–1949: 3). They denounced the principle of a universal housing public service enshrined in Labour's 1949 Housing Act which had removed the limitation placed on local authorities to build for the working classes only (see A. Eden, Hansard 1949). When they returned to government, however, they launched the housing crusade that the Conservative Party conference had committed itself to in 1950 for electoral reasons but they relied not just on local authorities but on private enterprise, too. However, they had to raise the amount of subsidies given to local authorities through the 1952 Housing Act in order to achieve their goal. This interventionist episode is probably what gave birth to the myth of a post-war consensus on housing. However, by 1954 there were signs that the party was moving back to its previous inter-war position. The 1954 Housing Repairs and Rent Act signalled a return to slum clearance after a parenthesis of 15 years. This step was officially justified by the need to cut public expenditure but also, tellingly, by the need to foster independence (MHLG 1953: 3). The war consensus came officially to an end on 17 November 1955, when the government announced its decision to cut back subsidies and to concentrate state help on 'special needs' housing, and passed the Housing Subsidies

Act one year later. The same year, in a striking example of policy differences, the Labour Party conference came down in favour of the municipalization of all private rentals. Whether it is 1954 (Malpass 2004: 210) or 1956, the mid-1950s, unquestionably marks a turning point. From then until 1979 the Conservative Party moved constantly further away from the Labour Party's ideal of a universal housing public service, 'retreating from the communal values that policymakers had initially tried to foster' (Lowe 1993: 259). In a climate of opinion which saw the publications of the party increasingly stressing the need for targeted selective social service (Joseph 1966: 5), they relentlessly pursued four aims, reinforcing the sanitary dimension of any housing programme, restricting access to council housing to people with special needs, encouraging home-ownership and widening housing provision to new participants. These priorities were at odds with Labour's policy aims of universality and state intervention, exemplified by it repeating its support for municipalization in 1954 (The Labour Party 1957: 95).

Contrary to the popular picture of a political consensus on the nature and aims of social policies, the study of the post-war years proves that the differences of opinion between Conservatives and Labour which had emerged in the inter-war years endured. Far from having accepted Labour's conception of housing as a universal public service on a par with other services, the Conservatives never ceased to strive to relegate housing to a safety-net dimension. This helps to qualify the popular idea of a complete break with post-war policies under Margaret Thatcher.

The New Right and Housing

Housing held a special place in the crusade to reform British society that the New Right in Britain launched after 1979. In the face of what they regarded as the failure of state intervention, the Conservatives embarked on an agenda designed to redraw the contours of the Welfare State so as to reduce state intervention in the social domain (Lowe 1993: 301–29) or as the former PM herself put it 'to roll back the existing activities of government' (Thatcher 1993: 599). They were determined to restore individual responsibility, consumer choice and put an end to the heavy burden of the Welfare State on the country. The Conservative manifestoes all devoted many pages to housing and stressed the determination of the party to widen home ownership and to privatize local authority housing, by giving tenants the right to buy the council home they were living in. They went as far as to compare it to the corner stone of the whole Thatcherite project (The Conservative Party 1987: 18).[2] In the words of Michael Heseltine, the Environment Minister from 1979 to 1983 and as such the minister responsible for housing, it was the only sector 'capable of generating the great revolution of our time' (Crick 1997: 199) and of making good the 'property-owning democracy' promised by Anthony Eden at the 1946 Tory party Conference. To Nicholas Ridley it was 'the

---

2 The expression used was 'The foundation stone of a capital owning democracy'.

area where Margaret Thatcher thought it was easiest to start to dismantle the dependency culture' (Ridley 1992: 87).

The decision to restructure council housing was not taken at random. Tellingly, of all the 90 think-tanks established by the Conservatives when in opposition, the housing committee was the only one to see its proposals included in the 1979 manifesto (Timmins 1996: 362–5). The fact is council housing was regarded as incompatible with several principles and objectives of the New Right. First, it ran against the Monetarist principle of the control of the money supply in order to curb inflation. For the Conservatives, the building and keeping up of council houses was seen as a strain on the state, a state living beyond its means as the 1977 IMF loan had clearly shown. The success of the monetarist venture depended on the reduction of public spending and so on controlling the budget of local authorities. Second, public housing was also at odds with the belief that the market is superior to state intervention in allocating goods and that the law of supply and demand was more efficient than administrative procedures (Kleinman 1996: 24). Third, council housing was considered to be the perfect illustration of what had gone wrong with the management of the Welfare State. Local authorities were regarded by the Conservative Party as being remote landlords and as having 'proved an insensitive, incompetent and corrupt landlord' (Thatcher 1993: 599). Their management was deemed to be bureaucratic, undemocratic and remote from their tenants. The solution lay in giving tenants the means of expressing their discontent by giving them an 'exit option', the possibility of exiting the system (Burns et al. 1994: 22). Finally, council housing was singled out for privatization for ideological reasons. Indeed, for the Conservatives it symbolized the culture of dependency which the Welfare State had created. By contrast, property was synonymous with self-dependency and decentralization. By reducing council housing the Conservatives were hoping to encourage responsibility, 'attitudes of independence and self-reliance that are the bedrock of a free society' (M. Heseltine, see Hansard 1980) and so to transform the nature of British society and mentalities.

For all these reasons the Conservatives mounted a triple attack on local authorities and their housing stock. The first stage was marked by the implementation of the programme of privatization announced in the 1979 manifesto (The Conservative Party 1979: 278), in the form of three housing acts in 1980, 1984 and 1986. The idea was to offer attractive discounts on the price of council homes, ranging from 30 per cent under the first act to 70 per cent for flat tenants in the last one. Success was instantaneous but varied according to the region, with London, the South East and the West Midlands experiencing the highest numbers of sales by 1999 (ONS 2000: Table 6.3). Nevertheless, as early as 1981, the number of council homes sold had outstripped that of new council buildings and by 1997 more than 1.7 million homes had been sold to their tenants (The Conservative Party 1997: 19). The financial fall-out was enormous, the receipts of the sales exceeding the budget devoted to housing as early as 1984/5 (Murie 1989: 7) and the total income dwarfed all other privatization schemes with the Treasury receiving £23 billion by mid-1992 (Balchin 1995: 179).

Up to 1986 the Conservatives mostly concentrated on widening owner-occupation but they went one step further in the privatization of council housing after the re-election of Margaret Thatcher in 1987. Complete local authority withdrawal from ownership was encouraged by the introduction of quasi market mechanisms, that is competition within a public service and consumer choice, so as to break up the quasi monopoly exercised by local authorities in the social housing sector. This was made possible by the 1988 Housing Act which sought to encourage privatization in three ways. First the act provided for the establishment, after a local ballot, of Housing Action Trusts which were to take over and to be in charge of the management and renovation of the worst housing estates and were to sell them off to new social or private landlords after rehabilitation, after a new ballot. Second the act encouraged local authorities to make use of the right given to them in the 1985 Housing Act and the 1986 Housing and Planning Act to transfer whole estates (Large Scale Voluntary Transfers) to housing associations or private landlords on a voluntary basis if a majority of tenants agreed. Third, the act also gave the right to individual tenants to transfer to another landlord. The result was a mixed one, with some 250,000 dwellings transferred from local authorities to new housing associations in the decade to 1997, but this further weakened the control of local authorities over housing.

This onset on municipal landlordism was accompanied by a fundamental redefinition of the role and functions of local authorities regarding housing. This was announced in the 1987 White Paper which ushered in a new era. In it the government drew a fundamental distinction between providers and enablers in the housing field, and between strategic and executive functions. The future role of local authorities was henceforth defined solely as 'a strategic one identifying housing needs and demands, encouraging innovative methods of provision by other bodies to meet such needs, maximizing the use of private finance and encouraging the new interest in the revival of the independent rented sector ...' (DOE 1987: 14). Clearly the government's intention was therefore to compel local authorities to abandon the building and management role they had been given in 1919, including for special needs tenants. They were meant to withdraw from all direct activity in the field of housing to the benefit of the voluntary or private sector and to concentrate on their planning and resource management role. The Conservative government first adopted a permissive approach. The 1988 Housing Act supported the setting up of Tenants Management Organizations (TMOs) and sought to revive the right given to tenants in the 1986 Housing and Planning Act to force local authorities to examine seriously any tenant-based proposal to form cooperatives to manage their estate. The disempowerment of local authorities became statutory with the 1992 Local Government Act which extended Compulsory Competitive Tendering to housing management, as the government had pledged in the 1991 White Paper, in order to create competition in this council service (Cabinet Office 1991: 16). Finally in 1994 the introduction of the Right to Manage gave all tenants groups covering twenty-five or more properties the right to take on a range of housing management responsibilities. There were more than 200 TMOs by 2005.

Thus, by 1997 housing had been relegated to the periphery of the Welfare State and the local/central partnership which had delivered millions of dwellings was a thing of the past. Local authorities had been almost entirely stripped of the housing responsibilities which they were given in 1919 and they had managed to retain until 1979 despite political disagreement over the extent of these responsibilities. Public building had almost ceased because of changes to the funding mechanisms with local authorities building 2,135 dwellings in 1995 in Britain compared to 86,027 in 1980 (ODPM 2005: Table 243).

A Long-Term Continuity

As it was argued above, the post-1979 Conservative policies of privatization and transfer of council housing do not seem to be such a fundamental break with a mythical post war consensus. Seen in a historical perspective, they can be construed as an attempt to restore continuity and the logical outcome of previous policies, too. What some writers considered to be a break with the post-war era philosophy of a strong public housing sector is in fact in keeping with the Conservative housing philosophy over the long term and as it was formulated very early on.

As we saw, apart from a brief three year-period after World War I and a ten-year period after World War II when the party agreed that only the state could make good the housing shortage, the Conservatives never really accepted the intervention of the state in the housing field. To them public housing was to be at most a temporary safety net for the poor. Opposition to state intervention on the basis that it was fostering dependency and destroying morals, an idea that was to echo down the decades, was formulated very early on. An article written by Lord Shaftesbury in 1883 thus reads:

> If the State is to be summoned not only to provide houses for the labouring classes, but also to supply such dwellings at nominal rents, it will, while doing something on behalf of their physical condition, utterly destroy their moral energies. It will be in fact an official proclamation that without any efforts of their own certain portions of the people shall enter into enjoyment of many good things, altogether at the expense of others. (Shaftesbury 1883: 934–5)

As Conservative records show, despite their opposition, they were forced to agree to limited state intervention by political forces, namely the extension of the franchise to working men, their repeated defeat in general elections between 1906 and 1910, and popular pressure after the two world wars. Their acceptance of public housing in the early twentieth century was purely pragmatic (Fforde 1990: 55–60), and fits the party's early conception of limited social reform as an antidote to socialism and a sop to the masses (Salisbury 1892: 6c). Gradual concession in the housing field was acceptable to the party if it made it possible to safeguard the wider Conservative edifice and benefited the whole of society. But it always remained a reluctant last resort measure. Instead of state intervention, they favoured three tenets, home ownership, private enterprise and voluntary action, which mirror post-1979 priorities.

The main lines of the Conservative housing philosophy began to emerge at the end of the nineteenth century. Very early on encouraging home ownership became a priority for the party. As early as 1885 the party had looked into the possibility of giving local authorities the right to make loan to would-be home-owners and to grant them tax relief (Churchill 1952: 15). The minutes of party conferences show that its leaders considered home-ownership as the surest means of upholding Conservatism and fostering responsibility. Just like their twentieth-century successors, many were of the opinion that home-ownership made better citizens, in so far as those owners felt they had 'a larger stake in the country' (see J. Chamberlain, Hansard 1899) and were more likely to look after their homes. To this argument was often added a political objective that was expressed at the 1892 conference in these terms: 'when working men became men of substance they naturally became conservative' (NUCUA 1892: 8). These beliefs explain why, from the end of the nineteenth century to the 1980s, the party, when in power, always sought to limit state intervention in housing and to help workers become home-owners. This was to be achieved by giving financial help to would-be home owners as early as 1899 in the Small Dwellings Acquisition Act and as we saw earlier in 1923 (Housing Act: §5). This was also to be achieved by selling council homes, which became an official party policy after 1979 as seen previously. As early as 1925 an ambiguous clause can be found in the Housing Act. This laid down that 'it shall not be obligatory upon a local authority to sell and dispose of any lands or houses acquired or constructed by them' and so implied that conversely local authorities could do so if they wished. This privatization policy, as it came to be known later, was made more explicit in 1936 when paragraph 79 (3) in the Housing Act passed by the Conservatives allowed local authorities to sell their stock 'on the only condition that they should obtain the best possible price'. Interestingly, the 1935 act (§25) also made it possible to transfer the management of the councils' stocks to a newly appointed Housing Management Commission, a forerunner of TMOs.

The post-war years illustrate the permanence of home-ownership as a Conservative objective. Indeed, as soon as World War II was over, despite the housing crisis, every Conservative Party annual conference between 1945 and 1951, save in 1948 and 1951, repeated the party's determination to promote home ownership on the basis that home-ownership fostered sound citizenship and was a natural trait of human nature. The policy of privatization resurfaced at the 1947 conference during which a motion was passed 'to give the fullest encouragement to the sale of council houses to existing tenants' (NUCUA 1947: 97). After 1950, home-ownership was justified by the wider ambition to create a 'property-owning democracy' as the 1950 manifesto, *This is the Road*, put it and became a key component of it. A 1951 circular reminded local authorities of their power to lend money to would-be home-owners and the 1959 House Purchase and Housing Act made £100 million available to building societies to encourage home-ownership. From 1952 on, when a circular was issued, the party, when in power, pursued a discreet policy of privatization (MHLG 1952). The 1957

Housing Act (§104) set in stone that right and another circular (MHLG 1960) followed in 1960 because the party felt local authorities were slow to respond. This drive to widen home-ownership cannot be dissociated from the increasing unease expressed after the mid 1950s by the Conservatives at what they perceived as the levelling and corrupting influence of the Welfare State. As a consequence the Conservatives embarked on a theoretical exercise which led them to formulate an alternative to the Welfare State. This alternative, named Opportunity-State, would both rest on basic Conservative values (choice, freedom and responsibility) and would guarantee a safety net for the most vulnerable citizens (Macmillan 1958: 9). It became all the more natural to encourage home-ownership. After their electoral victory in 1970 privatization took on a more systematic form and was justified by the need to provide increased financial resources to local authorities to concentrate on special needs (The Conservative Party 1970: 17).

A new circular lifted the ban introduced by Labour three years earlier on the sale of council housing and the white paper of 1973 asked local authorities to step up their sales and even to build houses for sale (DOE 1973: §20). A forerunning sign of what was to come five years later, the 1974 Conservative manifesto pledged to withdraw from local authorities their right to refuse to sell. Therefore, from a historical point of view, the policy of privatization led from 1979 to 1990 appears to be the logical outcome of the Conservative housing philosophy. It can be construed as a return to the core tenets of the housing policies that the party had sketched as early as the turn of the twentieth century and clearly formulated in the inter-war years.

Third Sector Revival

The withdrawal of local government from housing and the privatization of the council stock (carried on by the Labour governments of Tony Blair, but this is beyond the scope of this article) have led to a revival of the third sector. This has been achieved through the encouragement of the voluntary sector and the policy of transfer of local authority housing stock to housing associations. The outcome of these policies, namely the growth of non-municipal social housing, appears once again not so much as a break with post-war policies but as a return to a situation that predates the emergence of council housing in 1919.

The encouragement of the voluntary sector under the Conservatives stemmed from their dislike of council housing which they regarded as too costly, politicized and badly managed. Building by associations was seen on the contrary as less costly than council housing and so made it possible to achieve the New Right's aim of containing and cutting public expenditure. Second, housing associations unlike councils were thought to be outside the political arena and so less likely to foster socialism than local authorities; third, associations were considered as better managers than local authorities. The turning point for housing associations came in 1987 with the publication of a housing white paper (DOE 1987) and subsequently of the 1988 Housing Act. Their revival, as seen above, was made possible by the 1988 Housing Act which redefined the role of local authorities and gave tenants the right to change landlords. It was also encouraged by a reform of the financial regime of housing associations designed to give them officially greater control over their affairs. The 1988 Housing Act defined housing associations as non-public bodies, which freed them from public sector borrowing constraints. This gave them privilege access to private finance to raise money to renovate the housing stock and to borrow private cash to build. The idea was 'to increase the amount of rented housing built for a given volume of public expenditure' (Malpass 2000: 201). The transfer policy initiated under the Conservatives has also played a major part in the growth of the voluntary sector. The threat of tenant choice transfers had an unexpected consequence on the development of the voluntary housing sector. As a reaction to these perceived threats to the stock of social rented housing, some local authorities began to transfer their stock often to local housing companies especially set up for the purpose. Other reasons included the wish to get round Compulsory Competitive Tendering introduced in 1992 for housing management (Pawson and Fancy 2003: 5–6). As a consequence, by 1994 thirty-two local authorities had transferred the whole of their stock-some 149,478 dwellings-and some 250 were considering transfer (Balchin 1995: 185). The transfer process has gathered momentum since then, so much so that by 2003 it was estimated that 111 local authorities had transferred all their stock to housing associations (some 870,000 homes) (Pawson and Fancy 2003: vii).

As a result of Conservative policies, as well as of the Labour government's decision to speed up the transfer of housing out of local authority control after 1997, the landscape of social housing today, if we leave aside the issue of state funding to Housing Associations through the Housing Corporation, is increasingly similar to what it was in the nineteenth century. Indeed, the sector is today dominated by housing associations which have become the main providers of new rented social housing since 1990 (Langstaff 1992: 29). In 2003/04, the voluntary sector was responsible for completing 18,370 units in the UK while local authorities' share collapsed to 207 (ODPM 2005: Table 201). Not-for-profit housing associations manage almost half of all social dwellings in the UK (some 2.001 million in 2004), a threefold increase since 1991 while the size of the council stock is constantly dwindling and has fallen to 2.983 million (ODPM 2004: Table 101). This sea change in social housing policies since 1979, if it goes on, will gradually restore to the voluntary sector the place it held in social housing up to 1919. It has by any means already reversed the rise-and-fall history of the sector during most of the nineteenth century and twentieth century.

Indeed, prior to 1890 and the vote of the Housing of the Working Classes Act which empowered local authorities to build for the working classes regardless of slum clearance issues, social housing (if we can use the term in the nineteenth-century context) relied almost exclusively on the voluntary housing sector. Following the collection of data on the living conditions of the poor and the publication of books, such as *The Condition of the Working Class in England* by Frederick Engels in 1845, and official reports like the Chadwick Report in 1842, philanthropic housing associations developed in parallel with the public health movement after the 1840s. Unlike their modern successors these associations were not united in a coherent movement and did not benefit from state aid. They tried to demonstrate that it was possible to reconcile building model dwellings for the working class while ensuring some dividend to their shareholders, hence the nickname of '5 per cent philanthropy' given to the movement. But like their modern successors they aimed to raise minimum standards of accommodation while keeping rents below market level. Together, the two main types of voluntary housing organizations, the model dwellings companies and the charitable trusts (like the Peabody Trust or the Guinness Trusts) were housing more than 72,000 people by 1890 (Malpass 2000: 37), most of them in London and none of them among the poorest households. Despite the passing of the 1890 Housing Act, housing associations remain the main providers of social housing by far, building some 50,000 new homes between 1890 and 1914, far more than the 24,000 (ibid.: 50) built by forward-looking local authorities.

The dominance of the voluntary housing sector came to an end with World War I. From 1919 until 1988 the history of housing associations is a history of decline. The scale of the 'homes fit for heroes' programme launched by the coalition government in 1919 made local authorities the natural providers of working class housing with the financial help of the state. Although loans were offered to voluntary housing societies, the few houses they built in the inter-war years convinced political officials that they were unable to cope with demand in an emergency context and to help make good the housing shortage. The result was that the voluntary housing movement lost credibility over the long term. And although the debate went on about who should be relied on to build more houses, the idea of supporting the revival of the voluntary movement was repeatedly rejected (Ministry of Health 1933: §31). The 1935 Housing Act excluded them from urban governance in as much as the act left it to the discretion of local authorities to seek the cooperation of housing associations to deal with slum clearance and the rebuilding of their area. For most of the post-war years housing associations were overlooked by governments, determined to increase the public housing stock in the case of Labour, or to support home ownership in the case of the Conservatives. Despite receiving discretionary public financial support they were relegated to the margins of the Welfare State and expected to supplement the work of local authorities by building for special needs sections of the population (elderly people, ethnic minorities, disabled people) and help with slum clearance. Their image was 'tarnished by Victorian authoritarianism' and they were seen as 'undemocratic and unaccountable' (Malpass 2000: 132). Despite renewed government interest after 1961, as showed by the creation of the Housing Corporation in 1964 and Housing Associations Grants, and the significant growth in the number of associations, their contribution to the housing stock remained insignificant compared to private and public output. While local authorities in England and Wales built some 5 million homes between 1945 and 1979, housing associations only managed to build some 378,000 units. Although the 1974 Housing Act and circular 14/75 drew them one step further into urban governance as they made it clear that the government expected local authorities to cooperate with housing associations they were to remain secondary agents of housing policies until the late 1980s.

The policies implemented by the Conservative governments in the 1980s and early 1990s have profoundly altered the nature and role of public sector housing. As a consequence of these, council housing has changed beyond recognition as local authorities have been gradually stripped of most of their housing responsibilities. From a dominant and quasi-exclusive status in social housing provision, council housing has been moved to the periphery. This is the result of a deliberate policy to privatize the stock of local authorities, concentrate subsidies on the voluntary sector, prevent local authorities from building, and encourage the transfer of their stock to the third sector. Because of the 1980s and early 1990s Conservative agenda, social housing needs are met today by a variety of agencies working together, while up to 1979 the local government through the local authorities was almost the sole player in the housing field (Leach and Percy-Smith 2001: 1). The voluntary sector has become by far the main provider of new social dwellings. The policies introduced, or rather stepped up in some cases, have led to a return to a fragmented housing system dominated by non-elected providers quite similar to the pre-1890 situation, the main difference being the existence of a system of grants paid by the state to housing associations. The intervention of the state in social housing has been profoundly altered. These developments, although dramatic, have had another spectacular consequence, namely the residualization of council housing, that is the shrinking of the council sector to a residual tenure providing a safety net only for the more vulnerable people. While council housing used to be a privileged tenure compared to private renting after the war, today a strong stigma is attached to the sector. It is increasingly becoming synonymous with second-best housing and poverty housing as it has become dominated by retired and inactive tenants (Bramley and Munro 2004: 37).

Seen from a historical and political perspective, local authority housing appears then more like a parenthesis in the long tradition of private house-building and in the more recent one of social housing. It is possible to argue that the post-1979 Conservatives have simply followed lines sketched by the pre-war Conservative governments and implemented a radical version of policies outlined as early as 1930s. One can only talk of a Conservative revolution in the housing field for the post-1988 policies, when the party attempted to question the very existence of council housing. But even then the policies implemented were only a return to a conception of housing prevailing in the party before 1919. Council housing may truly become a thing of the past in Britain over the next decades if we are to judge by New Labour's housing policy. Far from reversing the policies of its predecessors the Labour governments of Tony Blair seemed indeed intent on stepping up the transfer of housing out of local authority control so as to improve management standards, reduce public spending and reach its decent homes target (ODPM 2000: §7.19). If this was to be followed through then local authorities would be left only with strategic housing responsibilities. Despite statements and publications (CLG 2007) implying that Gordon Brown was not as hostile as his predecessor to the idea of local authorities' house building programmes, so far there is little evidence to suggest that we are about to witness a halt in the decline of municipal ownership that has characterized the last thirty years.

References

Balchin, P. (1995), *Housing Policy* (London: Routledge).
Birchall, J. (ed.) (1992), *Housing Policy in the 1990s* (London: Routledge).
Bowley, M. (1945), *Housing and the State, 1919–1944* (London: Allen and Unwin).
Bramley, G. and Munro, M. (2004), *Key Issues in Housing Policies and Markets in Twenty-forst Century Britain* (London: Palgrave-Macmillan).
Burns, D., Hambleton, R. and Hoggett, P. (1994), *The Politics of Decentralisation, Revitalising Local Democracy* (London: Macmillan).
Cabinet Office (1991), *The Citizen's Charter: Raising the Standard*, White Paper, Cm. 1599 (London: HMSO).
Churchill, W. (1952), *Lord Randolph Churchill* (London: Odhams Press).
Communities and Local Government (2007), *Homes for the Future: More Affordable, More Sustainable* (London: HMSO).
Conservative Party (The) (1970), *A Better Tomorrow* (London: CCO).
Conservative Party (The) (1979), *The Conservative Party General Election Manifesto* (London: CCO).
Conservative Party (The) (1987), *The Next Move Forward* (London: CCO).
Conservative Party (The) (1997), *You Can Only Be Sure With the Conservatives* (London: CCO).
Conservative Research Department (1948–1949), *Amended Draft Statement on Housing Policy*, 2/24/6.
Crick, M. (1997), *Michael Heseltine: A Biography* (London : Hamish Hamilton).
Deakin, N. (1994), *The Politics of Welfare: Continuities and Change* (London: Harvester-Wheatsheaf).
Department of Environment (1973), *Widening the Choice, The Next Step in Housing*, Cmnd 5280 (London: HMSO).
Department of Environment (1987), *Housing: The Government's Proposals*, Cm 214 (London: HMSO).
Fforde, M. (1990), *Conservatism and Collectivism, 1886–1914* (Edinburgh: Edinburgh University Press).
Forrest, R. and Murie, A. (1988), *Selling the Welfare State: The Privatisation of Public Housing* (London: Routledge).
Hansard (1899), House of Commons, vol. 68, col. 786, 14/03/1899.
Hansard (1923), vol. 165, col. 1540, 20/06/1923.
Hansard (1924), vol. 174, col. 1294, 04/06/1924.
Hansard (1924), vol. 174, col. 1325, 04/06/1924.
Hansard (1949), vol. 468, col. 1365, 26/10/1949.
Hansard (1980), vol. 976, col.1444-5, 15/01/1980.
Henessy, P. and Seldon, A. (1987), *Ruling Performance* (Oxford: Blackwell).
Joseph, K. (1966), *The New Priorities* (London: CPC).
Kavanagh, D. (1987), *The End of Consensus, Thatcherism and British Politics* (Oxford: Oxford University Press).
Kleinman, M. (1996), *Housing, Welfare and the State in Europe, A comparative Analysis of Britain, France and Germany* (London: Edward Elgar).
Labour Party (The) (1935), *The Labour Manifesto: The Labour Party's Call to Power* (London: The Labour Party).
Labour Party (The) (1957), *Report of the 56th Annual Conference* (London: The Labour Party).
Langstaff, M. (1992), 'Housing Associations: A Move to the Centre' in Birchall (ed.).

Leach, R. and Percy-Smith, J. (2001), *Local Governance in Britain* (London: Palgrave).
Lowe, R. (1993), *The Welfare State in Britain since 1945* (London: Macmillan).
Malpass, P. (2004), 'Fifty Years of British Housing Policy. Leaving or Leading the Welfare State?', *European Journal of Housing Policy* 4:2, 209–27.
Malpass, P. (1992), 'Housing Policy and the Disabling of Local Authorities' in Birchall (ed.).
Malpass, P. (2000), *Housing Associations and Housing Policy* (London: Macmillan).
Macmillan, H. (1958), *The Middle Way, 20 Years After* (London: CPC).
Ministry of Health (1933), *Report of the Departmental Committee on Housing*, Cmd 4397 (London: HMSO).
Ministry of Housing and Local Government (1952), *Sales of Council Homes*, Circular 64/52 (London: MHLG).
Ministry of Housing and Local Government (1953), *The Next Step*, Cmd. 8996 (London: HMSO).
Ministry of Housing and Local Government (1960), *Housing Acts: Sales and Leasing of Houses*, Circular 5/60 (London: MHLG).
Murie, A. (1989), *Lost Opportunities: Council House Sales and Housing Policy in Britain, 1979–1989* (Bristol: SAUS).
National Housing Committee (1934), *A National Housing Policy* (London: P.S. King and Son Ltd).
National Union of Conservative and Unionist Associations (1892), *Verbatim report of the Conservative Conference* (London: NUCUA).
National Union of Conservative and Unionist Associations (1933), *Verbatim Report of the Conservative Conference,* (London: NUCUA).
National Union of Conservative and Unionist Associations (1947), *Verbatim report of the Conservative Conference* (London: NUCUA).
Office of National Statistics (2000), *Regional Trends 35* (London: The Stationery Office).
Office of Deputy Prime Minister (2000), *Quality and Choice: A decent Homes for All*, The Housing Green Paper (London: The Stationery Office).
Office of Deputy Prime Minister (2005), *Housebuilding: Permanent Dwellings Completed by Tenure* (London: HMSO).
Office of Deputy Prime Minister (2004), *Dwelling Stock by Tenure* (London: HMSO).
Pawson, H. and Fancy, C. (2003), *Maturing Assets. The Evolution of the Stock Transfer Housing Associations* (London: The Policy Press).
Ridley, N. (1992), *My Style of Government: The Thatcher Years* (London: Fontana).
Salisbury (Lord) (3 February 1892), 'Lord Salisbury at Exeter', *The Times*, 6c.
Shaftesbury (Earl of) (1883), 'The Mischief of State Aid', *The Nineteenth Century* 14, 934–9.
Thatcher, M. (1993), *The Downing Street Years* (London: HarperCollins).
Timmins, N. (1996), *The Five Giants, A Biography of the Welfare State* (London: Fontana Press).

Chapter 4

The Governance of New Communities in Britain, France and North America, 1815–2004: The Quest for the Public Interest?

Stéphane Sadoux, Frédéric Cantaroglou and Audrey Gloor

Since their appearance, new communities[1] have been an almost constant source of debate amongst practising planners and academics, in the countries we use here as case studies. But while a vast amount of literature has been produced about their architectural, environmental and historical planning techniques, little attention has been given to what we refer to here as their 'decentralized governance'. We propose to examine this here, from a comparative and historical perspective.

Setting the Scene: The Victorian City as a *Décor of Crisis*

To say that the Victorian city had become a health hazard by the early 1900s would be an understatement. John Snow's famous cholera maps produced in 1855 had already thrown light on emerging hygiene issues which only got worse as decades went by. The prevailing political faith in *laissez faire* during most of the nineteenth century had in fact allowed market forces to take control of most aspects of economic and social life. As a result, drainage and sanitary provision were generally poor, levels of control over building were practically non-existent and the housing stock was poorly built (Ward 2004, Cherry 1988).This rather bleak picture of British industrial cities was further tarnished by a number of influential publications. Perhaps most importantly, Engels (in his *Condition of the Working Class in England*) highlighted as early as 1845 that 'every working man, even the best, is therefore constantly exposed to loss of work and food, that is, to death and starvation, and many perish in this way'. Charles Booth's groundbreaking surveys of living conditions in London, published in the early 1900s, added to a growing amount of critical and utopian literature, and gave the unmanaged Victorian city its final blow, questioning its adequacy as a socio-spatial system. The same was to occur in France and North America.

---

1   By New Communities, we refer to 'planned' communities.

Framing the Picture: Philanthropy, Utopianism, Popular Reaction and Urban Governance

In the *Life and Labour of the People of London*, Booth (1902) mapped poverty levels throughout London and linked them to socio-cultural criteria, based on extensive surveys of the capital city. According to Peter Hall, 'Booth and his collaborators [...] had pioneered modern techniques of mass social observation in London in the 1880s, and had produced a still unequalled masterpiece of empirical urban sociology' (Hall 1988: 366).

Booth's contribution was however not limited to methodological issues. Drawing on Bales' views (1999), we argue that Booth was the first social investigator to provoke a *popular reaction*, following the publication of his alarming findings that a third of Londoners lived in poverty, in the 1880s. This led him to being the first social scientist to become a *household name*. In the following decades, the widespread publicizing of similar studies and reformist pamphlets gave the larger philanthropic, utopian and reformist movement a certain degree of credibility upon which they were later to act. This often-underestimated phenomenon played a major role in the development of new communities as intellectual, philosophical, political and physical alternatives to traditional living patterns and, most importantly, to urban governance frameworks found in Victorian cities. Since its foundation in 1899, Ebenezer Howard's Garden Cities Association, for instance, featured regularly in the written press – a credibility no doubt owed to the succession of leading British planners in the Chair. Later, still known as the Town and Country Planning Association, the think-tank campaigned for the reform of the British planning system, arguing that more weight should be given to the social dimension of urban planning as a means of achieving sustainable communities. In a sense, this paved the way for the current levels of influence of the New Urbanism movement in the United States, a movement which also relies on figureheads as a communication tool. Whether referred to as a popular reaction or as publicity, this notion should be kept in mind when examining the reasons underpinning the successes or failures of particular types of urban planning. Following Howard's theories, Lewis Mumford's success as a member of the *Regional Planning Association of America* clearly pointed to the levels of influence a movement can gain when it addresses issues which are identifiable by a large part of the population. The same is true for the success of New Urbanism, which is being increasingly copied, despite the fact that the movement is still young.

For the purpose of this study, we take the view that 'governance' simply refers to 'the action or manner of governing'[2] and is therefore not a new notion. The quasi-generalized rhetorical shift from '*government*' to '*governance*' has only recently invaded the political sphere. But a close examination of the development intricacies of new communities, within a historical perspective, brings to light the pioneering approach developed in this field in all three countries, in order to secure alternative ways of distributing power and wealth within an urban system.

---

2   *Oxford Online Dictionary*.

Van Kersbergen and Van Warden (2004) recently suggested that governance should be seen as a bridge between disciplines. Although the authors focused on recent shifts towards postmodernism, their writings could in a sense also be applied to the context of Victorian cities:

> In recent decades, traditional governance mechanisms have started to become destabilized and new governance arrangements have emerged. ... Changes have taken place in the forms and mechanisms of governance, the location of governance, governing capacities and styles of governance. These changes have been the subject of a variety of literatures and disciplines .... These literatures all give the term 'governance' different meanings. (Van Kersbergen and Van Warden 2004: 143)

The present paper can thus be considered as a cross-disciplinary attempt at revealing the diverse nature of urban governance in new communities over time, in contrast with traditional types of settlements and urban management, administration along with planning techniques.

Utopianism, Utopias and New Communities ... on Paper and in Practice

Carlos Nunes Silva (2003) recently reflected upon the two main utopian movements of the twentieth century: the Garden City movement, personified by Ebenezer Howard, and Le Corbusier's Modern Urbanism, represented by the Congrès internationaux d'architecture moderne (CIAM): 'Both discourses were responsible, directly or indirectly and for better or worse, for most of the urban design of the twentieth century' (Nunes Silva 2003: 327). Both sets of ideologies can be labelled as utopian, since they suggest an alternative way of life, most importantly in terms of their conception of *society* and *community*. This is perhaps where we should draw attention to one crucial aspect of the Garden Cities project which radically differs from the CIAM proposals. Howard's ideal city, the *sociable city*, is not solely concerned with the physical aspects of urban planning. Some have even suggested that these physical and design-related aspects of the Garden City project were far from being central to Howard's vision (March 2004). The Modernist movement, however, argued that only a radical shift in building design could save cities from chaos. Implicitly, this dangerously assumed that design itself was the one and only key to growing urban problems. Howard's proposal by contrast advocated the building of a town whose every aspect would favour the development of close links between members of the community. The Garden Cities Association's project, examined below, was fully exposed in Howard's unique set of proposals in *To-Morrow: A Peaceful Path to Real Reform*, later republished as *Garden Cities of To-Morrow* (Howard 1902). More recently, the Charter of the New Urbanism has followed this idea:

> *We recognize* that physical solutions by themselves will not solve social and economic problems, but neither can economic vitality, community stability, and environmental health be sustained without a coherent and supportive physical framework. (Congress for New Urbanism 2000)

Following Françoise Choay (1965), French approaches to planning theory have tended to contrast two kinds of utopias in urban planning: 'progressist' and 'culturalist'. Here, however, we suggest an alternative distinction. Firstly, we distinguish projects which were essentially of an architectural and technical nature, following the example of Claude-Nicolas Ledoux, among others. They developed in countries like Spain, with the works of Arturo Soria y Mata, or in Austria with projects by Camillo Sitte, and were also taken up in France by Eugène Hénard and Tony Garnier.

Our second distinction concerns projects which focus more on the social aspects of town planning, and draw heavily from the works of Robert Owen, most notably his *Book of the New Moral World*, published between 1834 and 1845. Other experiments following this social-oriented planning movement include Fourier and his development of the 'Phalanstère', Cabet's *Voyage en Icarie* (1840) or Ebenezer Howard's Garden City, which is used in this paper as the prime model of social cities. Having made this distinction, it is important to point out that although Howard's model does resemble Garnier's in terms of the importance of green spaces or low housing densities among other criteria, they differ radically. Howard justified the appropriateness of his model by the fact that it placed *people* at the centre of it. By contrast, Garnier's works can be seen as planning for *places*, not people, focusing essentially on architecture and design principles (Cantaroglou 2000).

Howard and his followers can thus be referred to as political utopians who sought to promote a transferable urban social model, aimed at founding a new type of social organization. But perhaps most importantly, Howard seemed convinced that the British industrial revolution was inevitable and, somehow, beneficial. Building upon the economic, social and political transformations inherited from the revolution, he proposed a new way of living, working and governing within the context of industrial Britain. Garnier, on the other hand, did not appear to have been convinced by the necessity of a French industrial revolution. This is perhaps one of the reasons for Howard's success: rather than assuming a community could exist as totally autonomous entity, thereby ignoring national contexts and legislation, he integrated his project in the wider context of Victorian Britain. Clearly the Garden City movement intended to implement its project on a national scale, thus pointing to the inadequacy of the current government's urban policy. The fact that F.J. Osborne once explained to Lewis Mumford that Howard had no belief in the state sums up this situation well (Hall and Ward 1999).

In France, the birth and development of social utopias did not however undermine the ongoing research to integrate factories better into expanding urban areas. Similarly, the relationship between urban and rural areas was also changing, as a result of urban sprawl. It soon became obvious, as it was to Ebenezer Howard, that the social dimension of industrial and urban development should be further explored. Robert Owen was the first to attempt this. From 1817 onwards, he created a series of cooperative villages built around manufactures, resulting in a new social system. Owenite communities would typically include agricultural land and farms, a park, an urban centre, cultural amenities both for adults and children and housing units containing vast apartments, all boasting central heating. Owen considered his social model to be universal and hence transferable. By raising living standards and establishing such a community life, the children of these villages would become a high quality workforce. Following Owen's theories, Charles Fourier put forward his conception of social reform built around the factory in 1829. This was to be of lasting influence amongst intellectuals and policymakers of that time, from Karl Marx to Jean Jaurès.

Fourier's theories stemmed from his assessment of the industrial city which he discovered was largely characterized by poverty and social inequality. He believed perfect harmony could exist, but only through the application of what he coined 'Le Plan de Dieu'. The 'Phalanstère' was born. Using his famous *phalanx* as a key element, his community was built for 810 men and 810 women. Profits were redistributed, and, symbolically, all members of the community would dine together. Although such community living could be compared to the Owenite communities, they did differ: unlike Owen's villages, that followed a leader who owned the land and buildings, the Phalanstère was more than a cooperative; it was effectively a *copropriété*. But most importantly, through his early use of zoning, Fourier had produced a prospective model for an ideal city.

In France, a number of experiments were implemented using the Fourierist model. The most famous of them all, the 'Familistère' at Guise (Aisne), was built around Jean-Baptiste Godin's foundry in 1846 and arguably remains the only successful scheme of this nature to date. But it was amongst French Socialists that Fourier's level of influence was greatest in his own country. From 1840 to 1856, they endorsed his claim that agriculture should be the cornerstone of any production system. In this respect, Godin adapted Fourier's model by putting industry rather than agriculture at the centre of the project. But most importantly, Godin was strongly opposed to the communitarian way of life to be found in Fourier's Phalanstère. Thus, even though Godin's Familistère is an autonomous socio-spatial system, encouraging social interaction between its members, its inhabitants benefit from individual housing units for each family. Interestingly however, Fourier's model was exported to North America, and received particular attention from Albert Brisbane who launched the North American Phalanx in the 1840s. At the same time, Victor Considérant and Fourier's disciples (*les orthodoxes*) largely contributed to the dissemination of Fourier's work. In 1854 for example, Considérant recruited 250 members in Texas for his *Société de Colonisation du Texas* experiment.

More recently, the American New Urbanist movement, deeply anchored in the Garden City tradition which we will analyse in further detail below, seems to have preferred a design-led approach in its quest for the ideal community, rather than combining this with the implementation of alternative patterns of power distribution. There is no apparent governance system associated with New Urbanism. Perhaps we should see this as a reiteration of the belief that urban planning and design, which encourages the building of community networks, brings about trust, empowerment and cooperation. This leads to efficient participative governance, rather than the reverse. In this sense, the New Urbanism could succeed where modernism clearly failed: the garden city as a people-sensitive, socio-spatial system is surely more inclined to generate the above-mentioned values than the modernist project which conceived housing units as living machines.

New Communities, Democracy and Governance: A Few Thoughts

Dallmayr recently commented that 'as it happens, democracy is easily one the most slippery words in political terminology, notwithstanding its long tradition'. (Dallmayr 1993: 101) In this chapter, we accept March's view that 'democracy is understood as being antinomic, embodying a series of internal contradictions or dilemmas in its core values' (March 2004: 409). This is a view which Etzioni-Halevy also endorses:

> The inherent contradiction or dilemma stems from the relationship between the principle of the acquisition of power on the basis of free elections by the entire population and the principle of freedom of organisation, both of which are part of the above definition of democracy. (Etzioni-Halevy 1988: 327)

How then, do new communities attempt to address these issues? Central to March's study of Garden Cities is the view that *democratic planning* can reconcile two of the main inherent contradictions of democracy, which he defines as an antinomy (March 2004). Firstly, by allowing the planning process to take place, each individual within a given community will benefit from the actions which would not have been possible without 'co-ordination beyond the individual and beyond the short term'. Secondly, the planning process seeks to reconcile the conflicts of government, 'the tension between the autonomy and interests of the individual, and restrictions upon individual autonomy being reconciled with the collective interest'.

New Communities and the Public Interest: Is This Relevant and If So, Who is the Public?

The notion of *collective interest*, otherwise known as the *public interest* has always more or less been taken for granted as part of the basics of professional ethics in the planning profession. For Mazza (1990), 'historically, the only standard common to different planning forms has been the public interest'.

Hague and McCourt (1974) once commented that the development of theory has been seen as an alternative to practice. Quoting Reade (1968), they remind us that 'planning, as a social reform movement and as a governmental activity has been concerned with *getting things done*'. As a result, the ideologies underpinning planning have tended to go unquestioned, a view also endorsed more recently by Ernest Alexander (1992). Hague and McCourt suggested that 'one way which may improve planning practice, then, is to improve the theoretical base for action, and one way to attempt this is through a re-examination of the fundamental assumptions on which planning is based' (Hague and McCourt 1974: 145). This now appears to be underway, as the concept of public interest has been under severe attack in recent years (Moroni 2004).

Planners and policy makers have tended to use the public interest as a constant justification of any action to be taken. Incidentally, it is worth pointing out that the rise of the public interest as a 'conciliatory' notion only occurred when it became clear that the transition from pre-industrial to industrial, and later the modern and postmodern city could not cater for each and every inhabitant. It is hence worth questioning the extent to which the public interest criterion as a key feature of public policy has led planners to assume that their assessment and plans would, in a way, ensure 'happiness' for all, among an increasingly-fragmented population and wide-ranging interests. Perhaps this is a key to understanding the relationship between new communities and the public interest. Indeed, we could fairly claim that the notion of public interest is irrelevant in the case of New Communities following the Garden City ideal, since the project itself implicitly assumes that all actors involved work towards the same goal. There is in this case (presumably) no divergence between interests: whether the planner is a mediator or an advocate is irrelevant.

Looking back and re-reading Patrick Geddes, there is a also a lot to say about re-exploring the theories he and his disciples instigated, giving birth to the short lived 'British Sociology' movement. Cultural and social factors are central to this approach. Rather than a top-down planning and governance framework, which assumes that national policy following the public interest should be taken for granted, as we have mentioned, this school of thought advocated strong regionalism as a way of securing social and cultural identity to build region-specific agendas. Similarly, New Urbanism seeks to reconcile the social and the cultural, as well as existing construction, in an attempt at creating successful communities. Are we therefore talking not about 'regional interest' or 'the community's interest', rather than about the public interest?

Quoting Fishman (1977), March (2004) states that it is instructive to recall Howard's vision 'because he sought to discover the minimum of organization that could allow the benefits of planning, while affording individuals the greatest possible control over their own lives'. This idea was put forward by Hall and Ward's Sociable Cities: *anarchism and cooperation* underpin Howard's project. In terms of municipal services for instance, they explain how some would 'come from citizens, in a series ... of pro-municipal experiments – or self help. ... People would build their own homes with capital provided through building societies, friendly societies, co-operations or trade-unions' (Hall and Ward 1998: 29). This was to be achieved without large scale central government intervention, reminding us of Howard's admiration for Kropotkin.

Could it therefore be said that Howard's freedom and cooperation, apart from strengthening social relationships between members of a community, actually engender a different way of life from the bottom up, rather than try to implement it from the top down? If such were the case, new communities are clearly not merely a type of physical form; they are also a vehicle of a specific type of philosophy based on consent and commitment. Euchner and McGovern have claimed that 'in democracy, reform requires winning the consent of the people, and so there is no choice but to find new ways to win public support' (Euchner and McGovern 2003: 10). This involves (regional and local) consensus and commitment, rather than (national) *coercive hegemony* backed by the public interest as rationale.

'The Community', Communities and New Communities

Community means different things to different people. In a recent series of essays, Gerard Delanty (2003) has explained how this notion is perhaps more relevant than ever. It is in fact relatively safe to claim that, 'much of the reorientation of moral and social philosophy is the consequence of the impact of the rediscovery of community in historical and sociological thought' (Nisbet 1967: 53).

What then, is the state of community in the countries we are interested in? David Hamer (2000) has explained on several occasions that today's planners look back more and more to what we might call *historical best practice*. Although he writes that 'American thinking on urban design and its development has, until recently, paid little heed to the past', he also asserts that this is now changing. The degradation of American neighbourhoods in the 1960s and 1970s, caused by the climax of the automobile's influence upon planning resulted in the destruction of communities. Hence 'there has been a revived interest in applying models from the past to the conceptualization and design of districts'. New Urbanism, he suggests, like modernism, rejects part of the legacy of urban planning and certainly its recent past, adding that 'a very important aspect of the New Urbanism has been what is referred to as the 'rediscovery of old communities'.

Judging by recent studies and surveys, communities in North America are not in good shape, a phenomenon which explains the slow but constant progression of New Urbanism. Talen (2000) reminds us that Sennett announced a general decline in citizenship and civility as early as 1978, whilst Bellah et al. exposed a profound forfeiture of public life in American culture (Bellah 1985). More recently, in a major study based on 500,000 interviews covering twenty-five years, Robert Putnam (2000) documented a sharp decline in social capital. Ironically, Lewis Mumford had widely publicized this loss of community through unplanned urban growth in his time. As Spann notes:

> [Mumford's] utopia would not be one but many, a world of as many as fifteen million communities each rooted in its own special bit of nature and of history, each of whose inhabitants 'will have familiarity with their local environment and its resources, and a sense of historic continuity'. (Spann 1996: 51)

In their quest for the perfect society, utopian thinkers have always developed similar themes in their works. In the case of Victorian cities, the problems associated with urban and economic growth were numerous and wide-ranging. But one stands out: the poor's living conditions brought to light by Charles Booth's surveys were often associated with landlordism, in sharp contrast with an idealized rural past in which community had flourished (March 2004). Ebenezer Howard's Garden City was a direct response to this generalized nostalgia; so were some earlier American examples, most notably Edward Bellamy's work. Given this striking opposition between the rather bleak and coercive ideas associated with industrial (and later modern) cities and the well being believed to exist in rural areas, 'this search for the new suburban environment expressed what seems to have been an ever-present element in our increasingly-urban culture, the use of changing morphology of residence to create or enhance new ideas as to the desirable lifestyle' (Vance 1972). It is no coincidence that one year after Vance wrote these lines, Fischer pointed out that popular imagery, along with various social science theories have tended to argue that urban life generates a sense of despair or malaise (Fischer 1973). Clearly, then, new communities (following the Garden City ideal) have looked back in history as a means of safeguarding social links which are debatably absent in the industrial megalopolis. They also do so as a way of ensuring the community does not reproduce the concentration of power and wealth patterns to be found in the modern city.

Who Actually Governs? Power, Representation and Accountability

Does utopia really exist? According to Kumar (1990), the answer is clearly *no*. Here, however, we suggest that two similar, yet distinct movements should be distinguished. The first one, which we could label 'paternalistic', refers to those new communities set up *for* and *around* a factory. Kumar points out that Owen's attempts at fostering new communities was not so much one of creating the utopian ideal, but rather one of responding to 'managerial necessity'. Thompson (1963) has similarly claimed: 'We should see that the great experiments at New Lanark were instituted to meet the same difficulties of labour discipline ... Owen was in a sense the *nec plus ultra* of utilitarianism.'

The second category, including Howard's Garden Cities and New Urbanism, do not place industrial paternalism at the centre of the project. Nor do they imply leadership by a single paternalistic figurehead. As March points out, democracy, 'by definition, requires the decision of all in decision-making' (March 2004: 412). But he also comments that due to major time and financial constraints, decision-making cannot occur if the full requirements of democracy are preserved: this would undermine the democracy by lengthening the decision-making process. Overall, the utopian communities which followed the paternalistic path failed to 'reconcile the need for members to influence while maintaining collective control' (March 2004, 413) – an issue which Howard's proposal addresses to a great extent.

The precise role of municipal government in the type of new communities we are concerned with here is in fact quite awkward to assess. Howard considered that the roles and influences of this government would vary according to the situation. Broadly speaking, his ideal communities imply a balance between collective action and individual enterprise, as ways of fostering the ideal community. In a nutshell,

> The exclusivity of the garden city is twofold: on the one hand, it is Schumpetarian, allowing an ostensibly democratic community to develop itself, but is also anarchistic and relativistic in that it seeks to ignore outside government to a large extent, giving

little opportunity to judge the 'goodness' or otherwise of the community within, except by its own standards. (March, 2004: 414)

This statement can in fact also be applied to the larger suburban movement and indeed to suburban communities currently in existence in North America. As Baldassare points out:

> [Suburban surveys have found] there are widely-held, negative perceptions that regional governments are unnecessary, large bureaucracies, less effective structures than local governments and authorities, and ones that threaten the system of local political power. These stereotypes are consistent with the suburban values that emphasise distrust of large, urban government bureaucracies, a preference for decentralized public services, and a strong desire for local rule. (Baldassare, 1992: 484)

Clearly, large urban areas may generate a feeling of political inefficacy (Fischer 1975). In 1968, Moss Kanter explained that since all social orders are supported by people, one of the issues which collectivities face is finding adequate ways to involve the population whilst ensuring that the population remains obedient. She raises the crucial issue of *commitment* –a notion which has since resurfaced in modern urban policy, disguised as 'civility'. New communities built on the various models associated with garden cities assume a high degree of commitment from the population. By commitment, we take Moss Kanter's view this is best defined as 'the process through which individual interests become attached to the carrying out of socially organized patterns of behaviour, which are seen as fulfilling these interests, as expressing the nature and needs of the person' (Moss Kanter 1968: 500). But as we shall see, experience has shown that this is perhaps unobtainable.

Taking land assembly and management as an example of the methods pioneered by Howard in his own projects, Dennis Hardy (2000) explains that even though his Garden City, was, in purely spatial terms, an attractive plan, 'what distinguishes it from other model schemes is its unique treatment of land values and tenure arrangements':

> The land for the settlement as a whole would be purchased by a sponsoring trust at agricultural land values (then about £40 an acre), with a rate of return for trustees of not more than four percent. All occupants would pay a rent ..., and the income received in this way would be used for three purposes: to pay interest on the initial capital sum, to pay back the capital and to pay for the general running costs and welfare of the garden city. ... The secret, claimed Howard, was to retain the land in common ownership and to plan the whole project systematically from the outset. (Hardy 2000: 62)

David Hall, a past Director of the Town and Country Planning Association, explains this further:

> Howard noted that the payment of interest and repayment of capital constitute a large proportion of local authority expenditure. The borrowings which require these capital charges were largely for the acquisition of land and buildings. The meaning Howard

gave to this pattern was that municipal debt largely constitutes the payments made by local governments to landlords. Rents are paid directly to landlords, but rates, in Howard's characterisation, are mostly paid to landlords indirectly – via government. (Hall 1985)

Howard had planned there would be a Board of Management, as part of the Garden City administration. Hall and Ward (1998) however highlight what he had *not* envisaged: 'apparently quite separately, there would be the limited-dividend company, concerned with the return on investment capital. Howard did not seem seriously to have grasped that the two bodies might come into conflict'. Further, they comment:

> The fact was that in his book, he failed properly to address the problem of the relationship between the trustees and the community; ... when the First Garden City Company was created there was no mention in its Memorandum and Articles of Association of any legal obligation to transfer power progressively to the community. And, though Howard persisted in asserting that this view was the ultimate intention of the Board, the Company's solicitor advised against it, and the idea was quietly dropped. (Hall and Ward 1998: 34)

To a certain degree, the debates raised in this paper severely undermine the notions underpinning democracy as we know it. As early as 1960, Harbold wrote:

> Certainly a pertinent question is whether that [democracy] is an appropriate contrivance of human wisdom to provide for human wants in the present day. Many have asserted over the years that it is not, claiming generally that democracy is neither an effective device for asserting what human wants are, nor for discovering and implementing appropriate means for their provision. (Harbold 1960: 135)

According to Warren (1992), there are two distinct schools of thought regarding the principles and applications of democracy. The first one seeks to limit the 'spheres of society which are organized democratically'. The second group considers that it is these limits which cause most of the ills of a democratic society. Exploring the idea of self-transformation in democracy, Warren argues:

> Autonomy and self-development are increased by institutions that take into account the characteristics of each kind of interest as it relates to the self. Only by differentiating the social relations implied by these interests can we grasp the full potentials of democratic processes and commitments, potentials that are ultimately rooted in how democracy protects and facilitates persons.

All these questions no doubt contributed to the birth of theories of *democratic administration* in the 1950s and are particularly useful within the scope of this study. As we know, there is no city without administration, minimal as this may be. The city as a place of democracy, by definition, requires some administration to function. So does the new community. Contemplating the emerging democratic, administration theories, Waldo (1952) raises an interesting point. According to him, 'a considerable measure of conflict is perhaps not only necessary but also socially desirable, the fabric of any democratic society must be woven to allow for the play of conflict without damage to the fabric itself' (Waldo 1952: 103). Conflict was in fact a major part of the Garden Cities' history: some of the initial plans as put forth in *A Peaceful Path to Real Reform* in terms of governance, were not implemented –or, rather, could not be. According to Howard himself, his project was to enable social reform without revolution. Presumably, the revolution was to occur in terms of administration and management.

What is the role of government in such communities? We take Griffith's views that 'governmental institutions are of course stimulus as well as response; positive conditioning factors as well as a product of conditioning' (Griffith et al. 1956: 101). Most people remember the Three Magnets (Figure 4.1) as the symbol of Howard's work. But few will recall the motto 'Freedom Co-operation' which sheds light on the issue of new communities' governance (Figure 4.2). The influence of early American experiments on the father of British Garden cities is obvious. Of particular interest to Howard were the works and projects of Edward Bellamy, who 'was equally disturbed by the chaos of the day-to-day life, the failure of politicians to respond to local problems, the coming of class warfare and the failure to have a balanced urban-rural continuum' (Mullin 2003: 144). The answer, for Howard, was the Development Corporation:

> Howard's lack of faith in parliamentary method would have been reinforced by the fate of his ideas on municipal ownership in new towns .... Howard envisaged that the new town estate would be held in trust, *by gentlemen of undoubted probity and honour* on behalf of the elected council for the town who could pay to the council whatever surplus was available from rent after interest charges had been met. For Howard, in other words, the public body representing the community, which would benefit from the urban property values created, would be the local council. [...]. (Hall 1985)

Here, we suggest that the Garden Cities project, as well as the various movements stemming from this philosophy, assumed that cooperation between decision-making bodies and the wider population would occur naturally under appropriate circumstances. Moreover, it assumed the efficacy of autonomous local communities:

> [Howard] paid little heed to the difficulties associated with the potential tyranny of a majority within a particular Garden City or the conflicts that might occur between different garden city communities, particularly if they were forced into competition with each other. (March 2004: 417)

Concluding and Looking Ahead ...

Shouldn't trust be central to urban policy, in a world which is, let's face it, increasingly suspicious about policy-making? Shouldn't something be done about the ever-increasing politicization of urban planning frameworks in which private interest prevails? Do the reasons for Howard's successes, and indeed failures, lie in

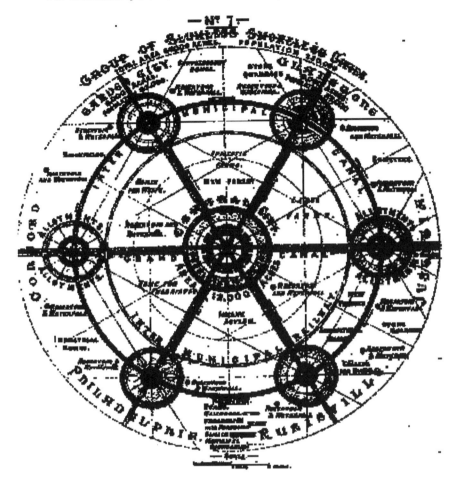

Figure 4.1 Ebenezer Howard's Garden City diagram (1902). © The Town and Country Planning Association

his non-acceptance of political issues which, according to him, would inevitably create conflict? Community politics, as defined by Liberal Democrats, were developed following this view as 'a dual approach to politics, acting both inside and outside the institutions of the political establishment ... to help organise people in their communities to take and use power ... to build a Liberal power-base in the major cities of this country ... to identify with the under-privileged in this country and the world ... to capture people's imagination as a credible political movement, with local roots and local successes'. But Meadowcroft (2001) has pointed out that although laudable, this objective has not really turned out to be convincing in practice:

> Councillors are under pressure, not least political pressure, to deliver the 'right' solutions to policy problems. Indeed, if Community Politics involves 'having views

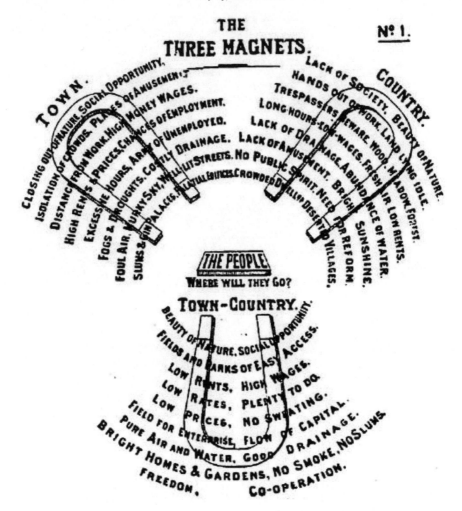

Figure 4.2 Ebenezer Howard's 'Three Magnets' diagram (1902), showing 'Freedom' and 'Cooperation' as the rationale underpinning the Garden Cities project. © The Town and Country Planning Association

on the wider and general good' then councillors may be justified in dismissing views which do not correspond to their perception of the common good or that they judge to be uninformed and undemocratic. (Meadowcroft 2001: 39)

It is therefore reasonable to assume that the perfect community (in economic, social, environmental and political terms) will always remain a utopia? Roland Warren (1970) explored the possibility of creating a non-utopian, normative model of community: 'four types of utopian investigation bear in one way or another on the questions of normative models in sociology for such entities as communities'. The first, including Plato's *Republic*, seeks to create imaginary societies, most often through the raising of philosophical issues such as the nature and roles of justice as in Plato's case. The second, the *intentional community*, goes beyond the imaginary stage and attempts at building those communities which would offer alternative sets of values. Warren then explains that New Towns are part of the third type of investigation: 'they do usually not present alternative value bases and social structures to those of contemporary society, but rather constitute presumably more efficient ways of attaining them.' The fourth and final category, the prescriptive models,

> attempt to urge the maximization of a particular set of community values, guides to action which swing back and forth between value statements, prescriptive admonitions and sociological findings, and attempts at a prescribed set of characteristics which strive for objectivity but nevertheless appears to conceal implicit value preferences. In this category probably belong as well as the various representatives of the 'community movement", that group of social scientists, philosophers, planners and others who admonish their colleagues that the community is dying, and seek to preserve and enhance the values which they purport to have found in the preindustrial, agricultural communities of another day. (Warren 1970: 219–20)

Where do Howard's new communities stand? Probably somewhere between the third and fourth categories. But surely, they are not purely utopian. As David Hall rightly points out:

> Howard's land reform and social city ideas would make it easy to label him as a kind of social ideologue. But Howard's ideology does not extent beyond opposition to large urban concentrations, which he also saw as concentrations of wealth and power. [...] If labels have to be found to describe his position they would be anarchist, consumerist, decentralist, ecologist, municipalist. Howard believed in private enterprise and voluntary activity as much as in public enterprise.

As the issues of accountability, representation, empowerment become increasingly important in today's fragmented policy-making apparatus, how can planners regain a certain degree of credibility and convince the population that they work in their interest? Along with the emergence of these questions in the current context of postmodernism, a new wave of urban utopian thinking has appeared. Leonie Sandercock, in her highly acclaimed *Towards Cosmopolis* (Sandercock 1998), has for example suggested a brighter future, founded on urban planning which respects cultural differences, civility and the environment. But to the best of our knowledge, no project or theory has surpassed Howard's in terms of identifying and attempting to resolve the full range of issues associated with urban development in the search for an ideal community, *the social city*. Although New Urbanism certainly addresses a number of decisive issues, these are, at best, environmentally and socially oriented. But the problem of attaining 'good governance' remains unaddressed, albeit extensively discussed and theorized, particularly in academic literature.

References

Alexander, E. (1992), 'The Public Interest in Planning: From Legitimation to Substantive Plan Evaluation', *Planning Theory* 1:3, 226–49.
Amin, A. and Graham, S. (1997), 'The Ordinary City', *Transactions of the Institute of British Geographers* 22:4, 411–29.
Baldassare, M. (1992), 'Suburban Communities', *Annual Review of Sociology* 18, 475–94.
Bales, K. (1999), 'Popular Reactions to Sociological Research: The Case of Charles Booth', *Sociology* 33:1, 153–8.
Bellah, R.N., Madsen, R., Sullivan, W., Swidler, A. and Tipton, S. (1985), *Habits of the Heart* (New York: Harper & Row).
Booth, C. (1902), *Life and Labour of the People of London* (London: Macmillan).
Cantaroglou, F. (2000), 'Le Rôle de l'industrie dans la mise en oeuvre de la planification urbaine et de la planification territoriale en France de 1850 à 1946', doctoral thesis, Institut d'Urbanisme de Grenoble, Université Pierre Mendès-France, Grenoble (France).
Cherry, G.E. (1988), *Cities and Plans: The Shaping of Urban Britain in the Nineteenth and Twentieth Centuries* (London: Edward Arnold).
Congress for New Urbanism (2000), *Charter of the New Urbanism* (New York: McGraw-Hill).
Dallmayr, F. (1993), 'Postmetaphysics and Democracy', *Political Theory* 21:1, 101–27.
Delanty, G. (2003), *Community* (London: Routledge).
Euchner, C.C. and McGovern, S. (2003), *Urban Policy Reconsidered: Dialogues on the Problems and Prospects of American Cities* (London: Routledge).
Fischer, C.S. (1975), 'The City and Political Psychology', *The American Political Science Review* 69:2, 559–71.
Fischer, C.S. (1973), 'Urban Malaise', *Social Forces* 52:2, 221–35.
Fishmann, R., (1977), *Urban Utopias in the Twentieth Century: Ebenezer Howard, Frank Lloyd Wright and Le Corbusier* (New York: Basic Books).
Gans, F.J. (1970), 'The Need for Planners to be Trained in Policy Formulation', in Erber, E. (ed.) *Urban Planning in Transition,* (New York: Grossman Publishers), 239–45.
Geddes, P. (1915), *Cities in Evolution* (London: Williams & Northgate).
Griffith, E.S., Plamenatz, J. and Pennock, J.R. (1956), 'Cultural Prerequisites to a Successfully Functioning Democracy: A Symposium', *The American Political Science Review* 50:1, 101–37.
Hague, C. and McCourt, A. (1974) 'Comprehensive Planning, Public Participation and the Public Interest', *Urban Studies* 11, 143–55.
Hall, P. (1985), 'Introduction' in Howard, E., *Garden-Cities of To-Morrow* (London: Faber).
Hall, P. (1988), *Cities of Tomorrow* (London: Blackwell).
Hall, P. and Ward, C. (1999), *Sociable Cities: The Legacy of Ebenezer Howard* (London: Wiley).
Hardy, D. (2000), *Utopian England: Community Experiments 1900–1945* (London, E. & F.N. Spon).
Kumar, K. (1990), 'Utopian Thought and Communal Practice: Robert Owen and the Owenite Communities', *Theory and Society* 19:1, 1–35.
March, A. (2004), 'Democratic Dilemmas, Planning and Ebenezer Howard's Garden City', *Planning Perspectives* 19, 409–33.
Mazza, L. (1990), 'Planning as a Moral Craft', *Planning Theory* 2:3, 47–50.

Meadowcroft, J. (2001), 'Community Politics, Representation and the Limits of Deliberative Democracy', *Local Government Studies* 27:3, 25–42.

Moroni, S. (2004), 'Towards a Reconstruction of the Public Interest Criterion', *Planning Theory* 3:2, 151–71.

Moss Kanter, R. (1968), 'Commitment and Social Organization: a Study of Commitment Mechanisms in Utopian Communities', *American Sociological Review* 33:4.

Mullin, J.R. (2003), 'Bellamy's Chicopee: A Laboratory for Utopia?' *Journal of Planning History* 29:2, 133–50.

Nisbet, R. (1967), *The Sociological Tradition* (London: Heinemann).

Nunes Silva, C. (2003), Review Essay: 'Urban Utopias in the Twentieth Century', *Journal of Urban History* 29:3, 327–32.

Reade, E. (1968), 'Some Notes Towards a Sociology of Planning: The Case for Self-Awareness', *Journal of the Town Planning Institute* 54:5, 214–18.

Sandercock, L. (1998), *Towards Cosmopolis* (London: Wiley).

Sennett, R. (1978), *The Fall of Public Man* (New York: Vintage).

Spann, E.K. (1996), *Designing Modern America: The Regional Planning Association of America and its Members* (Columbus: Ohio State University Press).

Storper, M. (1995), 'The Resurgence of Regional Economies, Ten Years Later', *European Urban and Regional Studies* 23, 191–221.

Talen, E. (2000), 'The Problem with Community Planning', *Journal of Planning Literature* 15:2, 171–83.

Thompson, E.P. (1963), *The Making of the English Working Class* (London: Gollancz).

Vance Jr, J.E. (1972), 'California and the Search for the Ideal', *Annals of the Association of American Geographers* 62:2, 185–210.

Van Kersbergen and Van Waarden, F. (2004), 'Governance as a Bridge between Disciplines: Cross-disciplinary Inspiration Regarding Shifts in Governance and Problems of Governability, Accountability and Legitimacy', *European Journal of Political Research* 43, 143–71.

Waldo, D. (1952), 'Development of a Theory of Democratic Administration', *The American Political Science Review* 46:1, 81–103.

Ward, S.V. (2004), *Planning and Urban Change,* 2nd edn (London: Sage Publications).

Warren, R.L. (1970), 'Towards a Non-Utopian Normative Model of the Community', *American Sociological Review* 35:2, 219–28.

PART 3
Security

Chapter 5

Gated Communities: Generic Patterns in Suburban Landscapes?[1]

Renaud Le Goix

Since the early 1990s a discourse has been steadily growing about a pattern of urban living that many thought to have been consigned to history: the so-called gated communities or privately governed urban territory. Their rise was initially fastest in the US and Latin America, where the media and academic commentators were quick to describe the phenomenon in terms of security-oriented privatized urbanism. A popular critique easily followed, warning of the social fragmentation of the city; out-of control urban segregation; secession; and the end of civic order as we know it. Gated communities became for some, both symbols and symptoms of a line that is being crossed from voice-based citizenship to exit-based citizenship; from politically-organized to market-organized civic society. While the discourse on gated urbanism seemed to spread from American sources, the phenomenon itself, had its own local history in every continent and country (Caldeira 2000, Carvalho et al. 1997, Thuillier 2005): in China (Giroir 2006, Webster et al. 2006), South-east Asia and Australia (Burke 2001), Europe (Glasze 2003, Billard et al. 2005), Eastern Europe (Lentz 2006), South Africa (Jürgens and Landman 2006) and the Arab world (Glasze 2000, Glasze and Alkhayyal 2002). Gating may thus be interpreted as a global trend. It is undoubtedly influenced in many ways by US models but it is developed according to local political, legal and architectural traditions (Glasze et al. 2002, Glasze 2005).

In the US for instance, the percentage of people living in gated communities is now estimated, according to the 2001 *American Housing Survey* up to 11.1 per cent in the west, 6.8 in the south, and less than 3 per cent in other regions (Sanchez et al. 2003). In the Los Angeles urban region,[2] this market represented a 12 per cent average of the new homes market in Southern California, but 21 per cent in

---

1   First draft of this chapter: July 2003. First revision: June 2004. This first version was presented at the International Conference: 'The Privatization of Cities in a Historical Perspective: US/British/French Comparisons', 3 and 4 June 2004. Université Paris-Sorbonne (Paris IV). Second revision: Le Goix (2006) 'Gated communities as generic patterns in suburban landscapes'. Presented at the Council for European Studies Conference, Chicago, 29 March–2 April, 2006. Final draft for publication: March 2008.

2   According to author's database. Because of the lack of a comprehensive survey of gated communities at a local or metropolitan scale (Blakely and Snyder 1997, Bjarnarsson 2000), the doctoral research is originally based on a database of gated communities built

Orange county, 31 per cent in San Fernando Valley and 50 per cent in the desert resort areas of Palm Springs.[3] As real-estate commodities, they are tailored to fit to specific prospective buyers. Gated communities are located within every kind of middle- and upper-class neighbourhoods, and are available for almost each market segment: half of them are located within the rich, upper-scale and mostly white neighbourhoods, and one third are located within the middle-class, average income and white suburban neighbourhoods. As a proof of the social diffusion of the phenomenon, 20 per cent of the gated communities surveyed are located within average and lower income Asian or Hispanic neighbourhoods, especially in the northern part of Orange County and in the North of San Fernando Valley (Le Goix, 2002; Le Goix, 2003).

In this chapter, I first propose a critical analysis of the discourse on gated communities, both as it is expressed in the American social science literature and in its French counterpart, motivated by the recent multiplication of private enclaves in France. Much of the French literature explains gating as an American model of a security-oriented urbanism, and I argue that this is only a partial explanation. In order to begin with a better understanding of the generic patterns of gating, I then propose a comparative study of the original forms of gating, which occurred in Paris *faubourgs* and early nineteenth-century suburbs and the originals forms of gating in the US. This historical comparison of spatial patterns diffusion provides a different perspective on the global emergence of gated residential estates. The demonstration develops two main sets of hypothesis. First, gated residential enclaves are indeed a profound expression of classical patterns in the production of suburban landscapes. Second, there is a resilience of gating in suburban areas: residential gates are erected where fences and gating were already present in land-use patterns.

Gated Communities as a Global Model

Because this urban phenomenon is perceived as deleterious for the social fabric, the media and fiction writing described them as seeds of a seceding elite in a not

---

with the same data as a prospective homebuyer would collect, and integrated within a Geographical Information System with 2000 Census data (Le Goix 2005, 2006).

3   The first gated developments were built in 1935 in Rolling Hills and in 1938 in Bradbury, and some well-known gated communities have been built early after World War II, like the upper-scale Hidden Hills (1950), and the original Leisure World at Seal Beach (1946) housing veterans and retired in Orange county. Less than 1700 housing units have been estimated to be gated in the Los Angeles area prior to 1960, with a major increase to 19,900 in 1970, because of the developments of major gated enclaves like Leisure World (1965) and Canyon Lake (1968). Although the growth rate decreased after 1970 because new developments were smaller than before, there were 31,000 gated units in 1980, 53,000 in 1990 and 80,000 in 2000. For the sample of gated communities for which the size is known, the number of dwelling units located behind gates in 2000 can be estimated to 80,000 (an estimate of 230,000 inhabitants), or 1.5 per cent of the housing stock, and increasing at a fast pace.

so distant future. Some sci-fi novels (Butler 1993, Stephenson 1992), inspired by themes connected to urban crime and secession, set the narration within a quasi-civil war between rich gated neighbourhoods and the rest of the city:

> Most Sundays, Dad holds church services in our front rooms. He's a Baptist minister, and even though not all of the people who live within our neighborhood walls are Baptists, those who feel the need to go to church are glad to come to us. That way they don't have to risk going outside where things are so dangerous and crazy. It's bad enough that some people – my father for one – have to go out to work at least once a week. None of us goes out to school any more. Adults get nervous about kids going outside. ... A lot of our ride was along one neighborhood wall after another; some a block long, some two blocks, some five. ... In fact we passed a couple of neighborhoods so poor that their walls were made up of unmortared rocks, chunks of concrete, and trash. Then there were the pitiful, unwalled residential areas. (Butler 1993, 7–9)

Stephenson's vision even encompasses the broader question of the production of Southern California urban space:

> Southern California doesn't know whether to bustle or just strangle itself on the spot. Not enough roads for the number of people. Fairlane, Inc. is laying new ones all the time. Have to bulldoze lots of neighborhoods to do it. But the seventies and eighties developments exist to be bulldozed, right? No sidewalks, no schools, no nothing. Don't have their own police force – no immigration control –, undesirables can walk right in without being frisked or even harassed. Now a burb' clave that's the place to live. A city-state with its own constitution, and borders, laws, cops, everything. (Stephenson 1992, 6).

Movies and TV drama have also been inspired by gates, thus developing the argument of a social paranoia due to the secured lifestyle. In 1998, *The Truman Show* (dir. Edward Harris), shot in Seaside, FL, used the secluded location of this private city as a set for this story of a young man tracked and observed by video camera ever since he was born. In this movie, as in the others, the enclosed location is pretext for a *huis-clos* and a plot based on the permanent control of a *Big Brother* on the neighbourhood and its inhabitants. Furthermore, an episode of the popular TV show *X-Files* (*Arcadia* 1999) and a TV movie (*The Sect* 1999), both plot the violent death of residents guilty of misconduct as regards the restrictive rules of the enclaves on the maintenance of the housing unit and the front yard in a gated community managed by some hegemonic guru. This short list, while incomplete, exemplifies the discourse developed about gated enclaves. If sci-fi is mostly inspired by contemporary events and usually develops a very accurate metaphor of the present society, it nevertheless conditions public conceptions about gated communities and is inspired by social science and media discourses.

Three major ideas emerge from the literature: gated communities belong to a recent trend of a security-oriented urbanism; gated communities are to be considered as an urban pathology leading to a secession of successful elites; although gated communities have been developed in other contexts and continents, the US represent the place where such developments are considered as the models and references all over the world, as a global, commodified real-estate good.

A Recent Trend of a Security-Oriented Urbanism

First, gated communities are described both as a recent, physical and obvious expression of the post-industrial society changes (fragmentation, individualism, rise of communities), and as a deep penetration of ideologies of fear and security developed by economic and political actors: municipalities, homebuilding industries and security businesses (Davis 1990, Flusty 1994, Marcuse 1997). This first argument elicits a noticeable consensus among authors describing security logics as a requirement in contemporary urbanism and architecture. The security features and guarded booths are another level of neighbourhood security, after the self-defence 'armed response' placards posted on lawns, the community programmes of 'neighbourhood watch' and community policing, and defensible space theories (Newman 1972). Because of this quest for residential security as well as the video surveillance devices in every parking and mall, Los Angeles has long been referred to as a carceral metropolis (Davis 1990, 1998). This discourse has been publicized in quite a dramatic way, as demonstrated by the following quotation from a French newspaper, *Le Monde Diplomatique*:

> Surveillance helicopters are humming above one's heads. Concrete walls dissimulate malls as gigantic as some cities may be. Paramilitary squadrons patrol in upper-scale neighborhoods. Buildings' roofs have been super-elevated in order to protect them from being targeted by a Molotov cocktail. Los Angeles is a city haunted by the fear of crime. ... Future architecture uses some gadgets that could refer to James Bond movies, because the people loudly claim for more and more order and security. (Lopez 1994)

Security claims are associated with a trend towards exclusion, as it is more related to a fear of others than to a desire for personal security (Davis 1990, Low 2003). In a city where fear of riots and violence boosts the security industry, security has become a commodity accessible only to who can afford to pay for it. Whites find in the suburbs a refuge from the impoverished city, as described in *Le Monde*:

> '72 per cent of district policemen, 50 per cent of the teachers and employees live outside the city. ... Blacks are leaving the district for the same reasons as Whites do; ... they try to escape the concentration of poverty', said Marguerite Turner. It is highly significant that gated communities, these highly guarded residential enclaves which were once a Californian specialty, tend to spread in and around Washington, housing a white, and black, bourgeoisie. (Zecchini 1997)

In this context stressing the fear of an American model of urbanism, gated communities are seen as a real-estate commodity, that is nevertheless detrimental to the social fabric and leads to a South-Africanization of American cities.

An Urban Pathology

As a consequence, a second set of arguments depicts gated communities as some obvious symptoms of urban pathologies, among which social exclusion is considered preeminent. The decline of public space in cities is addressed as detrimental to the poorest social classes: the voluntary gating is thus associated with an increase of social segregation (Blakely and Snyder 1997, Caldeira 2000, Glasze et al. 2002).

The most publicized occurrences of this discourse stress the effects of gated communities for an entire community, and especially its impact and spillover effects on the neighbouring areas. Citizen groups, such as documented in the 1994 *Citizens Against Gated Enclaves (CAGE) vs. Whitley Heights Civic Association* case, have sought to ban the gating of public streets (Kennedy 1995), arguing that gates would have forbidden the free access to a public property, even though the residential association proposed to pay for the cost of gating and street maintenance. Another group, the *Coalition for a Healthy Worcester* (Reville and Wilson 2000) was involved in fighting against gated communities in this Massachusetts community, promoting the following arguments:

- gates are a social threat by reducing 'the resident's civic involvement and disrupting the social contracts that cities and town are built on' (Reville and Wilson 2000);
- gating disrupts the American community ideals, as gated communities residents worry about crime for themselves, and don't address the issue as citizens of a community;
- the development of gated communities impacts the real-estate market, as they are more attractive, and may lead to a snow-ball effect;
- gated communities have a negative impact on the image of a city as a whole, leading prospective residents and businesses to think that crime is a significant problem in the city, even though it is not.

The idealized city with public spaces moving towards an urbanization built of private enclaves is thus argued to be a 'secession' from an elite opposed to the welfare redistribution system (Donzelot 1999, Reich 1991). Three words have been used to describe the spread of gated communities: '*secession*', used by Reich (1991) refers to the Civil War; '*balkanization*' used by Stewart (1996) refers to the political collapse of the Balkan region prior to 1914: both address the development of gated communities withdrawing from the public interest into a very homogeneous community driven by very local interests. '*Apartheid*' has also been used (Lopez 1996), thus comparing ethnic segregation in the US to the former separate citizenship status and residential assignments (townships) in South Africa. This stresses the argument of gated communities as being part of a social pathology and segregationist ideology.

All seem to agree with the explanation that gated communities are caused by a fear of crime, a rise of individualism, a decline of confidence upon public authorities, and a global move to private provision of public services. Nevertheless, the chain of causality leading to this situation is intricate. In an essay by the French journalist Zecchini (1999) he explains that public policies and private home-building industries have both led to the same growing exclusion. He describes the construction of a 'double enclosure' in the cities, and compares the French city crisis and US gated communities developments:

> With its suburban public housing developments where the police has no ambition other than containment, and closed correctional facilities for minors proposed by M. Chevènement [a former Interior Minister], this double closure stresses a ghetto phenomenon. This is rather clear in the US, where white populations are reluctant to live with racial minorities and worry about insecurity. ... Large cities in France have not yet been reached by American gated communities, those high security enclaves without racial diversity. But the rising ideological amalgam between Maghreb immigrants and security concerns threatens to lead to an auto-exclusionary drift. (Zecchini 1999)

This linking of gated communities with racial diversity is not isolated. Many arguments repeat over and over this fear of French cities of being haunted by 'wild urban gangs' and forecast the perspective of entire municipalities seceding with private police, following the model of a American gated communities (Lesnes 1999, Lopez 1994, 1996, Zecchini 1997). The same arguments have been integrated by French literature addressing the issues of a 'new urban question' (Donzelot et al. 1999). This issue is crucial at a moment old European cities are being transformed, from the classical center-periphery realm into an 'emergent city' realm built out of low-density suburban neighbourhoods and islands of affinity-based communities (such as gated enclaves) and isolated low-income ghettoes. This transformation of the former high-density, socially-mixed city landscape would ultimately lead to some secessions, thus threatening the capacity for a city to incorporate social diversity (Ascher 1995). In a context of deindustrialization and suburbanization, three explanations are discussed. First, social unrest and riots are connected with a contradiction between the location of employments and the residence of job applicants, leading to a failure of integration processes within the society, given the assumption that employment precisely founds this process. Donzelot, echoing spatial mismatch and skill mismatch hypothesis (Kain 1968, 1994), refers to the location of low-skill employments which does not match the place of residence of job applicants, whereas the highest skilled workers have to commute everyday to a 'Central Business District' located close to decayed neighbourhoods, thus maximizing the social contrasts.

Second, the social disintegration mechanisms and the processes leading to the enclosure is argued to be an effect of an 'urban disincorporation' (Ascher 1995), favoured by low-densities and loose urban landscapes made of freeways, undeveloped areas and a zoning emphasizing the separation of urban functions (basic production, services, commerce, residences, culture and leisure activities). A third explanation is related to class relationships, and gated enclaves are viewed as an ultimate quest for a neighbourhood based on individualistic desire of close knit sense of community and class-based exclusion strategies (Donzelot 1999, 106).

Within the exclusionary zoning in a distended metropolis, US gated communities are discussed as secessionist neighbourhoods getting their political autonomy. The recent city of Canyon Lake (9,500 inhabitants, incorporated[4] in 1991), and Leisure World-Laguna Woods (19,000 inhabitants, incorporated in 1999) were publicized in France by TV documentaries.[5] It is instructive to hear Jaillet (1999) arguing that French gated communities are too small and do not support the comparison with Americans enclaves. She also points out that municipal incorporation is impossible in an old nation like France:

> It seems difficult in a country that has been administered for a long time, where governments have organized the territory and set many inner boundaries, to imagine that territories could be still vacant of any control, without any status, and could possibly set up their own rules and make abstraction of the common rules. (Jaillet 1999, 145)

Writing this, the author seems to miss the point of the municipal incorporation in the US, which is in general a jurisdiction transfer from the county (unincorporated areas) to a city, empowered by the State under a Charter or a General Law (Elliot and Sheikh 1988). Nevertheless, the argument falls short of the historical facts. Between 1871 and 1875, when the suburban areas of Paris were developing fast and composed of upper-scale estates and private residential parks, municipal incorporations of private residential parks as municipality occurred the same way: Maison-Lafitte, an 1830 master-planned community, Le Vesinet development (Pinçon and Pinçon-Charlot 1994), Le Chesnais and Levallois-Perret in western Paris.

Furthermore, even though the sizes of the developments are not quite comparable, the historical processes seem to be quite comparable between the latest nineteenth century industrial city of Paris, and the earliest twenty-first century informational city of Los Angeles: a fast land development, increasing local interest and homeowners concerns willing to take control over local affairs in order to insure the slow-growth policy in a sprawling metropolis and to protect the property values against undesired land use (Marchand 1993, Miller 1981, Purcell 1997).

An American Commodity

Lastly, two sets of hypotheses sustain this discourse. The first set suggests the recent appearance of the phenomenon, and a second argues the diffusion of an American model of a real-estate commodity perceived as part of an all-American

---

4 Incorporation is the legal process by which unincorporated land (under county's jurisdiction) becomes a city, once approved by the state (in California, the LAFCO, Local Agency Formation Commissions are in charge of supervising the process) and by two-thirds of the voters. A new municipality can either be granted a charter by the State as large cities are, or be incorporated under the general law, which is the common case.

5 'Des Racines et des Ailes', March 1999, France 3 Public TV Network.

lifestyle, of which fast-food concessions and gated communities would be the ultimate archetypes (Schlosser 2001). When one argues that 'Large cities in France have not yet been reached by American gated communities' (Zecchini 1999), the assumption of the importation of a model is latent, as suggested by Donzelot:

> In Europe, the fashion for gated communities is very recent and their development still embryonic. But, if we look closely at the French case, they could have soon a rapid growth. (Donzelot 1999, 108)

Jaillet adds: 'It impossible, when one observes Old Europe's cities, to find an equivalent of gated communities .... Europe seems to be innocent of such attempts (Jaillet 1999, 145).

While these authors actually explore the capacity of dense and old European cities to prevent any secession, especially because of their vigorous municipal institutions, the north-American model nevertheless remains the recurring focus. Street-gating in South Africa and the post-apartheid evolution of townships has also been referred to as an Americanization of South African lifestyles and standards (Eidelberg 1996), which may seem contradictory with Davis referring to a 'South-Africanization' of Los Angeles, in a cross-referential metaphoric game.

In Lebanon, Glasze not only addresses the proximity between some *compounds* and American models, but he also describes the proximity between US models and Lebanese investors (Glasze 2000).

While acknowledging a global spread of a US model, some authors also notice the local specificity of gated communities development according to the national context, as stated about Latin America locations of gated communities. Many appeared in the 1970s as a middle- and upper-income exodus to suburban areas where lower-income had been settling since the 1940s (Caldeira 2000), and gates are justified to maintain a physical separation between classes, while physical distances between rich and poor are short (Carvalho et al. 1997).

In this context, such discourses understand gated communities as a recent and genuinely American form of residential developments. Nevertheless the word 'gated communities' itself, though recent and generically used by the press, the real-estate industry and also scholars, describes a phenomenon that is far more rooted in the history of cities than it appears at first sight.

Seeking the Origins of a Generic Model

Getting a better understanding of both the origins and the status of gates and walls requires retracing the processes which have inspired a generic model of gating during almost two centuries of evolution of the morphology of urbanization, of lifestyles and security concerns. Because gated communities are basically nothing else than residential developments, their characteristics are consistent with the ideological framework that has produced sprawling suburbs, as well as in the evolution of juridical basis of homeowners' associations.

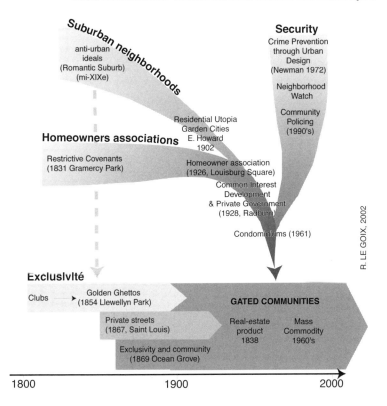

Figure 5.1   Gated communities in the US – chronology and filiations (suburban housing developments, homeowners' associations, safety and exclusivity). © Le Goix, 2002

The Romantic Suburb

A first source of inspiration for gated communities relates to the romantic suburban utopias and projects. Haskell's Llewellyn Park probably was the first gated community ever built in the US, continuously operating a gatehouse and a private police since 1854 (Jackson 1985). Jackson mentions that Davis, the architect, was inspired by romantic European architecture and introduced four main innovations, now standard features in suburban residential developments. First, a curvilinear street pattern emphasized a Jeffersonian pastoral ideal, while connecting the community to a natural setting located in the center of the neighbourhood. Olmsted later transposed this pattern to the master planned community of Riverside (Illinois) in 1868.

Secondly the concept of private governance of public spaces was introduced, as the central park was conserved as a natural landscape, and placed under the private jurisdiction of an association, the *Committee of Management*.

Third, a restrictive covenant prohibited any commercial or industrial activity within the residential park.

The fourth innovation was the enclosure and a sign post: 'Private Entrance. Do Not Enter'. The residential park thus provided its inhabitants with a protected environment, and introduced four basic elements of the contemporary suburb: the street patterns favouring low density and natural setting; the private governance realm; the restrictive covenants enforcing the stability and homogeneity of the neighbourhood; the exclusivity of the park. These elements derive from several philosophical sources (Romantic thought, Emerson's and Thoreau's transcendentalism), religious beliefs (the values of Protestantism) and early feminism (Ghorra-Gobin 1997, 2000, Jackson 1985) The very first master-planned community also was the first gated community in the US, thus linking both phenomena in a common family of urban projects.

It may seem a paradox to mention that the original conception of private cities and master-planned communities, as it was publicized in Howard's *Tomorrow: A Peaceful Path to Real Reform* (Howard 1898, 1902), was inspired by planned socialist communities such as Fourier's Phalanstère and 1804 Ledoux's industrial utopia at Arc-et-Senans (Schaer et al. 2000).[6] Garden-cities also became a source of inspiration both for an ideal master-planned community implemented in the US in 1924 in Radburn (Jackson 1985), and a quasi-private local governance that McKenzie describes as 'a democratically controlled corporate technocracy (McKenzie 1994, 5), paving the way for the rise of homeowners associations.

Common Interest Developments

A second thread links gated communities to the historical process that brought the Common Interest Development (CID) juridical structure from Europe to the US. McKenzie (1994) explores the long European history of restrictive covenants and residential associations. Common ownership of a structure started in the twelfth century with the *Stockwerkseigentum* (common property of a building) in German cities. The notion of shared property then appeared in France in 1804, in the early twentieth century in other countries in Europe before being transferred in 1928 to Latin America, to Porto-Rico en 1951 and finally to the US in 1961 under the concept of *Condominium*. Property-owners associations and restrictive covenants are distinct from the structure of ownership. It originated in Great Britain after the sixteenth-century enclosures and the abandon of collective use of communal lands, which raised the necessity for a body of law setting usage restrictions and rights of ways on private property. The first restrictive covenants for parks and leisure amenities appeared in the eighteenth century in Great Britain: since 1743, a fee has been levied on property owners around Leicester Square in London, and

---

6 Although incidental in regard to gated communities development, it can be mentioned here that utopia often refers to walls, gates and enclosures. Thomas More's 1516 Utopia was an island; the Phalanstère and Arc-et-Senans industrial utopias were enclosed. The 1734 idealistic master plan for a colony in Georgia projected the construction of a wall around the city of Savannah. See Schaer et al. 2000. Not to mention Howard quoting a William Blake poem referring to the fortified Celestial Jerusalem in an *incipit* to the 1902 second edition of *Garden-Cities of Tomorrow* (Howard 1902, 37).

they were granted an exclusive access to it (McKenzie 1994). McKenzie reports the same usage of restrictive covenants was later used the same way in Manhattan's Gramercy Park, managed by a trustee of homeowners. The first homeowners association *per se* was created in the US in 1844 in Boston's Louisburg Square, and Llewellyn Park and Roland Park (1891) were the first large privately owned and operated luxury subdivisions, exclusive neighbourhoods. They set the bases of private urban governance:

> To maintain the private parks, lakes and other amenities of the subdivisions, developers created provisions for common ownership of the land by all residents and private taxation of the owners. To ensure that the land would not be put to other uses by subsequent owners, developers attached 'restrictive covenants' to the deeds. (McKenzie 1994, 9).

In the first half of the twentieth century, this kind of subdivision became quite common (Mission Hills, Missouri in 1914, Kansas City Country Club District in 1930s, and Radburn in 1928). CIDs aim at protecting property values through various design policies and the application of Covenants, Conditions and Restrictions (CC&Rs). Throughout the first half of the twentieth century, the application of restrictive covenants to residential neighbourhoods has been an instrument of selection of the residents, especially on a race basis (Fox-Gotham 2000, McKenzie 1994), and both the developers and the government have backed such a discrimination (Massey and Denton 1993). Since the Supreme Court declared residential segregation illegal in 1948, restrictive covenants and POA membership have relied on age limitation (for retirement communities, the owner's age must be older than 55) and on required membership (i.e. cooperative housing or country-club), the membership being subject to the approval of the board of directors (Kennedy 1995, Webster 2002). Although no reference to race or color can be made during the membership application process, the issuance of the membership is discretionary, based on the principle that any club may regulate its membership (McKenzie 1994, 76), as far as the criteria for selecting prospective buyers remain reasonable. So far, sociability and congeniality have been considered reasonable criteria by courts (Brower 1992). Along with landscaping and architectural requirements, subjective criteria of social preference are common in many CIDs, thus helping to maintain a homogeneous social environment in the neighbourhood. Furthermore, CIDs are both public actors because of the nature of their provision of a public service to the residents and their right to collect a regular assessment. They act at the same time as private governments, based on a private contract (CC&Rs) enforced to protect the property values (Kennedy 1995, McKenzie 1994).

Exclusiveness

In order to be 'peaceful',[7] the use of a property should also be exclusive, and the protection of exclusivity is a third concept of importance in the design of gated

---

7   Term used in Canyon Lake CC&Rs.

communities. In fact, two main categories of exclusiveness must be discussed. First, the 'golden ghetto', also dubbed 'exclusive enclaves' (Blakely and Snyder 1997) where the gates protect the quietness of the rich and wealthy from the busy crowds and can be compared to a club estate and an approximation of private streets. Second, the quest for exclusiveness behind gates seeks to protect the sense of community. Both principles are present in today middle-class and lifestyle gated communities.

One preeminent reason for gating relates to the exclusive use of a private site and its amenities, in order to prevent any free-riding and unwanted visitor. Gated enclaves are operated like a club, the members paying for its private services. In Saint Louis (Missouri), forty-seven streets have been progressively closed between 1867 (Benton Place) and the early 1920s (University Hills, Portland Place, Westmoreland Place). Built in 1922, University Hills is a 187-unit subdivision with nine manually-operated gates, only one of them being opened each day according to a planning only released among the residents. While entrance was not completely prohibited, through traffic was diverted to other streets. The private streets were then extended to several early suburbs in Saint Louis. It was reported that residents chose to privatize the streets and gate them in order to locally control zoning and land use and to protect property values. Furthermore it appeared that the municipality of Saint Louis was unable to provide the residents with correct infrastructure, thus raising the need for local private arrangements (Lacour-Little and Malpezzi 2001; Newman et al. 1974.) It clearly appears that the exclusiveness was originally designed to protect an infrastructure paid in common by associated private property-owners. Defined as a club estate (Webster 2002), this association is neither a complete private realm (with complete exclusiveness of property rights) nor completely public (with collective consumption rights and free-riding). In a club, Webster explains that property rights over a local public facility (roads and infrastructure) are shared within a group, and denied to all external persons. Purchasing a house within a gated community, comes along with a required association membership that conditions the use of collective goods and shared amenities included in the development. Being part of the club is a first step toward being part of the community.

Although a quite blurred and complex notion involving political history, nostalgia, and religious connotations, the word 'community' can nevertheless be defined according to five components: a common territory bounded by identified limits (a neighbourhood, a village ...), shared values defining an identity (religion, ethnic identity ...), a shared public domain providing spaces for encounters and socialization, and a common destiny or a common interest (such as the protection of property values in POAs) (Blakely and Snyder 1997). This sense of community, rooted in local politics and attached to the notion of citizenship, also often sanctioned by religion, nevertheless needs to be protected against physical aggressions. In 1869, the community of Ocean Grove promoted an original way of avoiding detrimental effects against its sense of community by erecting a gate. Founded in 1869, Ocean Grove was a seaside resort where membership was based on faith and religion (Parnes 1978). New York businessmen, along with Methodist-Episcopal clergymen founded the community in order to build a leisure and religious vacation retreat. Residents and planners developed an urban idealism where faith defined regulations, landscape, and leisure activities. As in a congregation the rule of faith dominates the secular city as described in a 1881 *Annual Report*:

> *First* a religion [religious community] and *then* a town ... It is a town, but town and all its secularities are subsidized to the religious thought. (Parnes 1978, 34)

A local paper further explains in 1875:

> Religion and recreation should go hand in hand. Separate them, and religion grows morose, and recreation will soon be sinful. Blended both become more beautiful. (Parnes 1978, 34)

According to Parnes, observers described Ocean Grove as a medieval fortress governed by an autocrat (Bradley, founder of the community). Ocean Grove gate was the physical guarantee protecting this pious environment. Surrounded by two lakes and the Atlantic Ocean, the western gates and a bridge were the only accesses to the community, and were to remain closed on Sunday. A $10 fine was charged for trespassers and trains never stopped in Ocean Grove-Asbury Park on Sunday. Barnes reports that President Grant was once requested to walk into the community to attend a Sunday service, leaving his horse-car at the gate. The symbolic role of the gate might also be seen as a reference to the walls of the Celestial Jerusalem – an explicit reference as a model of the Holy City was exhibited in the community.

Then, gating and fencing a development reify a common territory encompassing shared values and identities. It also helps protecting a sense of community, as well as it probably helps creating this sense of community. In the 1930s, the mix of exclusiveness and lifestyle were already commercial arguments. In Rolling Hills gated development, commercial materials promoted in 1938 the lifestyle of a ranch estate near the already growing city of Los Angeles, advertising themes emphasizing the uniqueness of the architecture, the affordability of housing, and the exclusiveness of the neighbourhood:

> A slice of Old Virginia is being reborn in Rolling Hills ... the exclusive suburb of Long Beach and the Harbor District! ... Remember, only fourteen families can buy the homes which are priced no more than ordinary homes on ordinary communities. (Hanson 1978, 77)

Lifestyle was promoted at the same time: 'Own your own dude ranch in Rancho Palos Verdes ... not for profit but for pleasure' (Hanson 1978). In the 1930s Rolling Hills was already very close to the real-estate commodity generically known as gated communities: a community ideal based on lifestyle, an urban setting maintaining rural amenities and romantic references, a scenic location whose exclusiveness was guaranteed, and last but not least, the development was backed by powerful financial institutions, as the developer, the Palos Verdes

Corporation, belonged to Vanderlip, a New York banker (Hanson 1978). Rolling Hills is now a home for 2,076 inhabitants.

Exclusive lifestyle developments then became common by the turn of the 1960-70s, designed as mass-consumption real estate developments, financed by large corporations attracted by potential profits and backed by the Government through the Department of Housing and Urban Development (McKenzie, 1994). The Irvine Ranch private development is well documented (Baldassare 1986, Forsyth 2002, Kling et al. 1991), and is comparable in nature to the development of another Orange County area master-planned by the Laguna Niguel Corporation (1960–1970), the Moulton Daguerre Ranch. The initial project envisioned an utopian balanced community based on leisure and recreational facilities:

> A utopian community with recreational facilities – beach, lakes, parks, golf course and riding stables; industrial and research sites; custom homes with high quality design standards maintained by deed restrictions and architectural review; and schools, churches and shopping areas all conveniently located. (Decker and Decker 1990)

Not far from the retirement gated community of Leisure World, the first neighbourhood developed in this utopian project was Laguna Niguel, a 1,100 units gated community on the Pacific Ocean.

Security

The enclosure of an exclusive lifestyle is inherited from the club-realm and the exclusiveness of a site and its amenities, and shared community values. As an effect of contrast, the fourth and last lineage is far more recent and related to security concerns in residential areas. In Argentina and in Brazil (Caldeira 2000), in the US, in Europe (Querrien and Lassave 1999), in Mexico (Low 2001), gating is associated with a lack of confidence in the public security enforcement. In the US, the necessity of a well-regulated militia', the uninfringeable right of the people to bear arms, and to be secure in their houses, persons and belongings are guaranteed by the second and the fourth amendment of the Constitution. The first theorization of gated streets as a *defensible space* was developed by Newman (1972) and the *Institute for Community Design Analysis*. The results of these researches were then widely publicized and incorporated within public policies through urban design guidelines to prevent crime (Newman 1996). This is a set of theories and architecture practices called *Crime Prevention through Urban Design*, designed to increase safety in residential areas by acting over the perception of space, controlling the public circulation, and increasing the sense of property. In order to prevent urban decay, social control by the residents over the environment is improved especially by the mean of gating streets. An original research on the nineteenth-century gated streets of Saint Louis (Newman et al. 1974) helped to theorize the advantages of gating as it defines a private structure that the resident is willing to control and to improve. The diffusion of 'defensible space' guidelines gave a wide publicity to gated enclaves, as it promoted the implementation of 'mini-neighbourhoods'. The latter were experimented in Dayton (Ohio) to stop urban decay and instability in a neighbourhood named Five Oaks. Residents had to pay half the price of street gating.

The erection of street barriers in old residential neighbourhoods became a way to enforce public safety, to control gang activities, and was developed in several low-income and public housing development, such as Mar Vista Gardens and Imperial Courts in Los Angeles South Central , along with other community policing strategies (Leavitt and Loukaitou-Sideris 1994). Newman's set of guidelines was also exported abroad, and was used in France through various improvements of public space in decaying public housing (Lefrançois 2001).

As a consequence, gated communities belong to a global trend of community involvement to prevent crime in residential areas, and the public authorities back these programmes. Although the fear of urban crime is not specific to gated community residents, recent streets gating are clearly motivated by the fear of crime, among other factors, as demonstrated by several empirical researches (Low 2003, Wilkson-Doenges 2000).

The Resilient Enclosure

The intricate threads of filiation leading to gated communities clearly demonstrate that the development of gated enclaves is neither new, nor contradictory with the underlying logic producing suburban areas. It was in the nineteenth century that a class-based enclosure was experimented, hybridized with utopian ideals of the garden-cities, thus paving the path for the first gated communities as real-estate industry products in the 1930s.

It is well-known that gated communities and private urban governance are more likely to develop in fast growing cities, as this is a convenient way to transfer the cost of urban sprawl on private developers and homeowners (McKenzie 1994, Le Goix 2003, 2006). To sum up previously exposed arguments, gated enclaves are highly desirable in order to privately fund the development of infrastructure needed by the urban sprawl. Gated enclaves emerge from a partnership between local governments and private land developers. Both agree to charge the final consumer (i.e. the home buyer) with the overall cost of urban sprawl, since he will have to pay for the construction and the maintenance of urban infrastructures located within the gates. As compensation, the home buyer is granted a private and exclusive access to sites and former public spaces. Such a pattern was obvious in the way part of suburban properties (aristocratic domains, ranches, etc.) were dismantled and partially transformed into exclusive neighbourhoods. Because of the fiscal assets they produce, at almost no cost, gated communities are particularly desirable for local governments.

I wish to proceed further with an argument that has hardly been expressed in the existing literature. The diffusion of gated communities is not to be understood as a 'secession' from the public authority but as a public-private partnership, a local game where the gated community has a financial utility for the public authority, whilst the property owners' association is granted more autonomy in local governance. This ambiguous relation helps us to have a better understanding of the reasons leading to a sprawl of gated communities that cannot be simply explained by a rush for security.

As a consequence, I will discuss some examples of early gated developments in the fast growing nineteenth-century suburbs of Paris, which were not only aristocratic gated estates but also blue-collar gated developments. I first argue that a significant number of these enclaves were developed where gates and fences were already present in the landscape, producing a local resilience of the enclosure, the condition of appearance of gated communities being part of an heritage of land use patterns in fast growing suburban areas. Second, I proceed further with the argument that local conditions of urban sprawl favoured the development of private urban governance and gated communities.

Seeking the Origins of Nineteenth-Century Residential Gated Estates

Because of the industrial revolution and the early developments of railways in the 1840s, the development of the outskirts of Paris was rapid during the nineteenth century, and residential developments were a common pattern (Marchand 1993, Roncayolo 1980). Estates and private developments were mostly a concern of the rich and famous. The general picture is the same as in the US, as previously depicted, emphasizing the bucolic image of manors, villas, hunting-lodges and cottage residences. The builders had preferences for scenic locations, in the woods, or in the former park of a castle. Some of these developments were indeed gated already, part of an aristocratic fenced domain, that was divided, sold and ultimately developed.

On a scenic hill overlooking the Seine river, the Parc de Montretout in Saint-Cloud was a pioneer. The private estate was part of the royal domain of Saint-Cloud, and was used as residence for guards and officers. In 1832 the domain was partially dismantled and sold to a private developer, and a homeowners' association (*l'Assemblée syndicale des propriétaires*) was incorporated.[8] The first development was planned for thirty-seven properties, and there are today almost 50 distinct units housing about 400 persons. 1,855 covenants set several restrictions enforced to protect the property values. Housing units were to be built within the three years following the purchase of a lot, and businesses, cafés and ballrooms were prohibited in the development. In 1932, the regulations were amended in order to prevent any lot from being subdivided into less than a 1,000 square metre area, and to restrict the building of non-residential structures. The development has always been gated, but security was not a preeminent goal in the original concept: the restrictive covenants only mention a janitor's booth near the main gate.[9] There is no reference to the gate itself in the Covenants, and the walls and gate are physical remainders of the former park enclosure. The gate can

---

8 Association incorporated on 5 June 1832, according to the deeds, restrictive covenants and regulations recorded by M. Leroy, notary in Saint Cloud on 28 September 1855. Although substantially amended, these original covenants are still in use today.

9 Article III of 1855 Restrictive Covenants.

be considered as a resilience of former land-use: it used to be a gated residence for officers and royal guards.

According to a resident,[10] only one burglary has occurred in a five-year period, but many residents perceive safety concerns as an important issue and rely on the gate to provide more security. This concern seems to be relevant especially among the homeowners who recently moved in. Former residents consider the janitor and the monumental gate as effective enough to deter crime; but newer residents (such as the Front National's leader J.-M. Le Pen and some national and foreign industry CEO and top industry executives) requested the installation of electronic devices to control the gate. The implementation of a video-surveillance system at the gate was proposed but declined because illegal: it would have recorded public traffic on a public street for private purposes. Finally, the bucolic landscaping cautiously maintained by the association is regularly disturbed by journalists and TV reporters because of the political activities of the extremist leader in his headquarters.

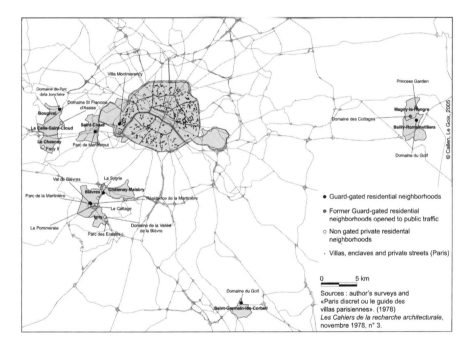

Figure 5.2   Location of some gated streets and residential enclaves in the Ile-de-France. © Le Goix, 2002

---

10   Anonymous interview in 2000, with the help of S. Degoutin.

'Villas' and Private Streets as a Classic Periurban Feature

Montretout was a very early example of a private gated development, yet is not an isolated case in Paris. Many apartment buildings and small individual houses are indeed located in a private street with a private square or in small streets where public traffic is banned. There were (according to a 1977 survey) 1,500 *villas* and private streets in Paris, operated by property owners associations. The *Villa Montmorency* in the upper-scale western side of the city (16th *arrondissement*) is one of the archetypal examples of gated residential villas in Paris and was built in 1853 with the completion of the Auteuil railway (restrictive covenants were set up in 1853; all lots were sold by 1857) (Pinçon and Pinçon-Charlot 2001). Although sources are unclear whether the Duchesse de Montmorency or the Comtesse de Boufflers[11] was the last owner, the land used to be a former gated aristocratic property. Publicized because of a murder investigation (Tourancheau 2003) (yet another proof that gates are not a protection against crime), the *Villa* is composed of 120 luxury units in large gardens, and used to be the home of writer André Gide and philosopher Henri Bergson. Security concerns are far stronger than in Montretout, and the gatekeeper strictly enforces the access restrictions.

Gates and private streets in the early nineteenth century are not restricted to the upper classes. Working-class villas and small private developments were also built, especially near the South-eastern industrial outskirts of Paris along the Seine River. In Athis (nowadays near Orly airport), the *Villa des Gravilliers* was built in 1897 for seventy-five inhabitants and was the property of a cooperative mutual society of factory workers in Paris. The mutual society built the private street and the fences, and a lottery was organized to designate the future occupants. The residents were given a seven-year lease with an option for purchasing the lot (Bastié 1964). It must be mentioned that this kind of mutual society stood then close to the utopian socialism, that later inspired Howard's Garden City. Usually, the villas are small developments built during the first half of the twentieth century, as the property ownership for the working class was favoured by a public policy allowing preferential loans (laws Ribot and Loucheur).

Gates in the Urban and Suburban Landscape: The Resilience of Enclosure

Some common patterns can be drawn from the examples in Paris, and from later examples in Los Angeles. These patterns can help us understand the context where and when gated residential areas might appear.

First, the enclosure is often inherited from a former fenced land use. Montretout and Montmorency used to be aristocratic domains which were fenced. It has also been documented that suburban development in the late nineteenth and early twentieth centuries in Paris partially occurred in former aristocratic forests, estates and hunting domains, some part of them being designed as fenced

---

11 Contradictory information is provided by the *Nomenclature des rues de Paris* (2002) and by the *Guide Bleu* (1995).

areas (Bastié 1964). Montmorency, the large developments of Maison-Lafitte, Le Chesnais near the Saint-Germain-en-Laye forest, as well as the smaller blue-collar villas on the south-eastern side of Paris, were all developed on such former domains. The street patterns of these neighbourhoods also recall the former hunting-trails ('*chasses royales*') (Pinçon and Pinçon-Charlot 1994, 2001). It is interesting at this point to mention the recent development of small upper and middle-class neighbourhoods, for example along the Bièvre valley, 20km south of Paris, in the municipality of Bièvres. Three gated developments were built there between 1985 and 1990, and are located within the walls of the former Parc de la Martinière. When the lots were developed after being sold by the municipality, the development maps were seen to fit the original limits of the park, and one of the neighbourhoods even preserved the original wall. This development's purpose was, in accordance with municipal authorities, to help finance the maintenance of the domain, the park and the estate. As a consequence, when purchasing the lots, the homeowners were charged a fee to fund the maintenance of the public park (Callen 2002, Le Goix 2007).

In the Los Angeles area as well, some enclaves are indeed the results of local resiliencies of former land uses, hybridized with residential development projects. Rolling Hills was first a ranch property of the Palos Verdes Corporation. Once developed, the owner (Vanderlip) and the developer (Hanson) agreed in 1935 to make improvements to the former ranch gate and to patrol the community (Hanson 1978). The gate thus remained at the same spot where it had always been, and its architecture still recalls the ranch-gate style. Hidden Hills' gates also fill the same purpose. Hidden Hills was first developed in the 1950s as a horse-oriented residential ranch, before it gradually transformed into an upper-scale development after 1970 (Ciotti 1992).

In Canyon Lake, a 9,500 inhabitants gated community, fencing also derives from a former land use. This large gated enclave used to be a summer trailer park nested around a lake (1968) with fences protecting the properties when owners were absent, before it became a full-time gated residence of homeowners.

Whatever the historical and cultural context, the enclosure is motivated by the sense of property (private streets of Saint Louis, Montretout, Villas and contemporary gated communities) and their effects on maintenance and tidiness in order to protect the property values. This well-known effect of gating (Brower 1992, Newman et al. 1974, Webster 2002) thus contributes to protecting and increasing property values (Lacour-Little and Malpezzi 2001, Le Goix 2002). Such common economic values among club-members are not exclusive of high-ends development and this sense of property among members has also motivated the gating of private streets in Parisian suburb based on a trade-union membership, as previously mentioned about the Villa des Gravilliers.

Urban Growth and the Diffusion of Enclosures

Second, the sprawl of private streets and private communities is connected with the pace of urban sprawl. In Los Angeles, the fastest increase in gated communities' population was recorded between 1960 and 1970 when the population living behind gates was multiplied by a factor of ten (Le Goix 2003). At the same time, the population of Orange county doubled (where most of these 1960s gated development are located). As a comparison, while Orange County's population was growing by 10.8 per cent in ten years in the 1990s (1990–2000), gated communities population increased an average of 30 per cent (still one of the fastest rate in the US). In Paris area, it seems reasonable to make a comparable statement. The fastest growing areas (Marne-la-Vallée for instance) are also targeted by developers for such gated developments. Many private enclaves near *Disneyland Resort* were developed by international developers (e.g. K&B Homes) in Magny-le-Hongre where population has increased by 2.5 between 1994 and 1999. Another recent example (La Résidence des Demeures du Golf, developed by Windsor, accommodating 400 residents) was built in the late 1980s near Corbeil-Essonne (south of Paris), when the rate of growth of Saint-Germain-lès-Corbeils topped at +38 per cent between 1982 and 1990 census and was still increasing between 1990 and 1999 (+15 per cent). Concurring evidences can be drawn from the late nineteenth-century development of private enclaves, as they occurred during the population boom on the outskirts of Paris, especially on the western edge of the city along with the development of suburban railroads. This development occurred in the yet rural sixteenth 'arrondissement', on the top of the hills of Saint-Cloud, and on other scenic locations along the Seine river (Le Vésinet, Le Chesnay). Between 1861 and 1891, inner-Paris population increased by 44 per cent while the suburban population was increasing by a factor of 2.7. Data about gated enclaves in Paris are still fragmentary and a comprehensive survey of gated enclaves is under way.[12]

Conclusion

First, gated enclaves are being developed in areas where gates and walls were already present, thus underlying a new way of using enclosures for residential purpose in a form of resilience of landscape patterns. Gated communities development usually depends on the willingness of public authorities to found urban sprawl by the means of transferring the cost of infrastructures (roads…) and amenities from the public authority to a private developer. The latter making the final owner to pay for these infrastructures, it indeed justifies gating and privatizing residential space. Finally, gated communities sprawl depends on public policies, and is more likely to appear in fast growing cities. Such logics were already at work in the Paris area in the nineteenth century, when land developers actively built the first residential estates near the railway stations. They are active now in

---

12 A comprehensive survey of enclaved neighbourhoods, both public and private, is conducted by the IAURIF and the UMR Geographie-cités 8504, sponsored by an ANR research programme on Public-Private Interactions and the Production of Periurban landscapes (2007–2010). Information and forthcoming publications on http://gated.parisgeo.cnrs.fr.

every metropolitan areas where the joint influences of individual transportation and land development favour the urban sprawl.

This chapter argues that gated enclaves should not be understood only as a radical and recent change in urban landscape, nor as a simplistic sign of the militarization of society. They are indeed a profound expression of classical patterns in the production of urban spaces and suburban landscapes. The diffusion of gated communities depends on a local path dependency towards gated patterns, either because enclosure have been traditional features, or because laws and regulations indeed favour this kind a residential scheme. In France and in the US, the legal framework of co-ownership and property owners associations and the planning practices have allowed the rise of private urban governance, in different parts of the cities and different historical contexts.

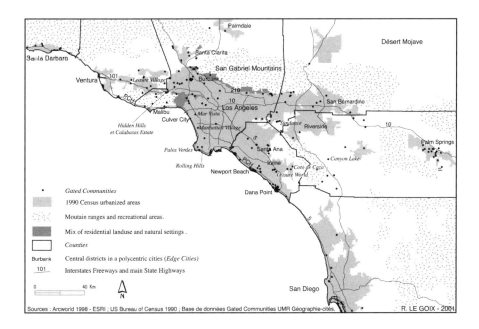

Figure 5.3   Location of gated communities in the region of Los Angeles. © Le Goix, 2002

References

Ascher, F. (1995), *Métapolis, ou l'avenir des villes* (Paris: Odile Jacob).
Baldassare, M. (1986), *Trouble in Paradise: the Suburban Transformation in America* (New York: Columbia University Press).
Bastié, J. (1964), *La croissance de la banlieue parisienne* (Paris: Presses Universitaires de France).

Billard, G., Chevalier, J. and Madore, F. (2005), *Ville fermée, ville surveillée: La sécurisation des espaces résidentiels en France et en Amérique du Nord* (Rennes: Presses Universitaires de Rennes).

Blakely, E.J. and Snyder, M.G. (1997), *Fortress America, Gated Communities in the United States* (Cambridge, MA: Brookings Institution Press and Washington DC: Lincoln Institute of Land Policy).

Body-Gendrot, S. (2001), *Les villes: la fin de la violence?* (Paris: Presses de Sciences Po).

Brower, T. (1992), 'Communities within the Community: Consent, Constitutionalism, and Other Failures of Legal Theory in Residential Associations'. *Land Use and Environmental Law Journal* 7:2, 203–73.

Burke, M. (2001), 'The Pedestrian Behaviour of Residents in Gated Communities', paper presented at the conference *Walking the 21st Century*, 20–22 February, Perth.

Butler, O.E. (1993), *Parable of the Sower* (New York: Four Walls Eight Windows).

Caldeira, T.P.R. (2000), *City of Walls: Crime, Segregation, and Citizenship in Sao Paulo* (Berkeley, CA: University of California Press).

Callen, D. and Le Goix, R. (2007), 'Fermeture et entre-soi dans les enclaves résidentielles' in Saint-Julien, T. and Le Goix, R. (eds) *La Métropole parisienne: Centralités, Inégalités, Proximités* (Paris: Belin), 209–32.

Carvalho, M., Varkki, G.R. and Anthony, K.H. (1997), 'Residential Satisfaction in *Condominios Exclusivos* (Gate Guarded Neighborhoods) in Brazil', *Environment and Behavior* 29:6, 734–68.

Ciotti, P. (1992), 'Forbidden City', *Los Angeles Times*, Los Angeles, B3.

Davis, M. (1990), *City of Quartz: Excavating the Future of Los Angeles* (London: Verso).

Davis, M. (1998), *Ecology of Fear: Los Angeles and the imagination of disaster* (New York: H. Holt).

Decker, D.M. and Decker, M.L. (1990), *Laguna Niguel: The Legacy and the Promise* (Laguna Niguel, CA: Royal Literary Publications).

Donzelot, J. (1999), 'La nouvelle question urbaine', *Esprit* 258, 87–114.

Donzelot, J. and Mevel, C. (2001), *La politique de la ville: une comparaison entre les USA et la France. Mixité sociale et développement communautaire* (Paris: Centre de Prospective et de Veille Scientifique, DRAST).

Eidelberg, P.G. (1996), 'Apartheid et ségrégation urbaine en Afrique du Sud', *L'Espace Géographique* 25:2, 97–112.

Elliot, J.M. and Sheikh, A.R. (1988), *The State and Local Government Political Dictionary* (Santa Barbara, CA: ABC-Clio/Jack C. Plano).

Flusty, S. (1994), *Building Paranoia: The Proliferation of Interdictory Space and the Erosion of Spatial Justice* (West Hollywood, CA: Los Angeles Forum for Architecture and Urban Design).

Foldvary, F. (1994), *Public Goods and Private Communities: the Market Provision of Social Services* (Aldershot: Edward Elgar).

Forsyth, A. (2002), 'Who Built Irvine? Private Planning and the Federal Government', *Urban Studies* 39:13, 2507–30.

Fox-Gotham, K. (2000), 'Urban Space, Restrictive Covenants and the Origins of Racial Segregation in a US City, 1900–50', *International Journal of Urban and Regional Research* 24:3, 616–33.

Ghorra-Gobin, C. (1997), *Los Angeles: le mythe américain inachevé* (Paris: CNRS Éditions).

Ghorra-Gobin, C. (2000), *Les États-Unis entre local et mondial* (Paris: Presses de Sciences Politiques).

Giroir, G. (2002), 'Les *Gated Communities* à Pékin, ou les nouvelles cités interdites', *Bulletin de l'Assocation des Géographes Français* 79:4, 423–36.

Giroir, G. (2006), 'The Purple Jade Vilas (Beijing): A Golden Ghetto in Red China' in Glasze et al. (eds), 142–52.

Glasze, G. (2000), 'Les complexes résidentiels fermés au Liban', *Observatoire de la Recherche sur Beyrouth* 13, 6–11.

Glasze, G. (2003), 'L'essor global des complexes résidentiels gardés atteint-il l'Europe?', *Etudes Foncières* 101, 8–13.

Glasze, G. (2005), 'Some Reflections on the Economic and Political Organisation of Private Neighbourhoods', *Housing Studies* 20:2, 221–33.

Glasze, G., and Alkhayyal, A. (2002), 'Gated Housing Estates in the Arab World: Case Studies in Lebanon and Riyadh, Saudi Arabia', *Environment and Planning B: Planning and Design* 29:3, 321–36.

Glasze, G., Frantz, K. and Webster, C.J. (1999), *Gated Communities as a Global Phenomenon*, available at <http://www.gated-communities.de>.

Glasze, G., Frantz, K. and Webster, C.J. (2002), 'The Global Spread of Gated Communities', *Environment and Planning B: Planning and Design* 29:3, 315–20.

Glasze, G., Frantz, K. and Webster, C.J. (eds) (2006), *Private Cities: Global and Local Perspectives* (London: Routledge, Taylor and Francis).

Guide Bleu (1995), *Paris* (Paris: Hachette).

Hanson, A.E. (1978), *Rolling Hills, The Early Years (February 1930 through December 7, 1941)* (Rolling Hills: City of Rolling Hills).

Howard, E. (1902), *Garden Cities of Tomorrow* (London: Sonnenschein).

Jackson, K.T. (1985), *Crabgrass Frontier: The Suburbanization of the United States* (Oxford: Oxford University Press).

Jaillet, M.-C. (1999), 'Peut-on parler de sécession urbaine à propos des villes européennes?', *Esprit* 11:258 (November), 145–67.

Jürgens, U. and Landman, K. (2006), 'Gated Communities in South Africa', in Glasze et al. (eds), 109–26.

Kain, J. (1968), 'Housing Segregation, Negro Employment, and Metropolitan Decentralization', *Quarterly Journal of Economics* 82, 175–87.

Kain, J. (1994), 'The Spatial Mismatch Hypothesis: Three Decades Later', *Housing Policy Debates* 3, 371–462.

Kennedy, D.J. (1995), 'Residential Associations as State Actors: Regulating the Impact of Gated Communities on Nonmembers', *Yale Law Journal* 105:3 (December).

Kling, R., Olin, S. and Poster, M. (1991), 'The Emergence of Postsuburbia: An Introduction' in Kling, R., Olin, S. and Poster, M. (eds), *Postsuburban California: the Transformation of Orange County since World War II* (Berkeley, CA: University of California Press) 1–30.

Lacour-Little, M. and Malpezzi, S. (2001), *Gated Communities and Property Values* (Madison, WI: Wells Fargo Home Mortgage and Department of Real Estate and Urban Land Economics, University of Wisconsin).

Le Goix, R. (2002), 'Les *gated communities* en Californie du Sud, un produit immobilier pas tout à fait comme les autres'. *L'Espace Géographique* 31:4, 328–44.

Le Goix, R. (2003), 'Les *gated communities* aux Etats-Unis. Morceaux de villes ou territoires à part entière?', doctoral thesis, Université Paris 1 Panthéon-Sorbonne. Available at <http://tel.ccsd.cnrs.fr/documents/archives0/00/00/41/41/index_fr.html>.

Le Goix, R. (2006), 'Gated Communities as Predators of Public Resources: The Outcomes of Fading Boundaries between Private Management and Public Authorities in Southern California' in Glasze et al. (eds), 76–91.

Leavitt, J. and Loukaitout-Sideri, A. (1994), 'Safe and Secure: Public Housing Residents in Los Angeles Define the Issues', *Future and Visions: Urban Public Housing* (November), 287–303.

Lefrançois, D. (2001), 'Vers l'émergence d'un modèle français d'espace défendable?', *Les Cahiers de la sécurité intérieure* 43, 63–80.

Lesnes, C. (1999), '21 questions au XXIe siècle. Des villes libres? Vers un monde urbain en expansion', *Le Monde*, Paris.

Lentz, S. (2006), 'More Gates, Less Community? Guarded Housing in Russia' in Glasze et al. (eds), 206–221.

Lopez, R. (1994), 'Les nouvelles armes du contrôle social: Délires d'autodéfense à Los Angeles', *Le Monde Diplomatique*.

Lopez, R. (1996), 'Un nouvel Apartheid social: hautes murailles pour villes de riches', *Le Monde Diplomatique*.

Low, S.M. (2001), 'The Edge and the Center: Gated Communities and the Discourse of Urban Fear'. *American Anthropologist* 103:1, 45.

Low, S.M. (2003), *Behind the Gates: Life, Security, and the Pursuit of Happiness in Fortress America* (New York: Routledge).

Marchand, B. (1993), *Paris, histoire d'une ville* (Paris: Seuil).

Marcuse,P. (1997), 'The Ghetto of Exclusion and the Fortified Enclave: New Patterns in the United States', *The American Behavioral Scientist* 41, 311–26.

Massey, D.S. and Denton, N.A. (1993), *American Apartheid: Segregation and the Making of the Underclass* (Cambridge, MA: Harvard University Press).

McKenzie, E. (1994), *Privatopia: Homeowner Associations and the Rise of Residential Private Government* (New Haven and London: Yale University Press).

Miller, G.J. (1981), *Cities by Contract* (Cambridge, MA: MIT Press).

Newman, O. (1972), *Defensible Space: Crime Prevention through Urban Design* (New York: MacMillan).

Newman, O. (1996), *Creating Defensible Space* (Washington, DC: US Department of Housing and Urban Development, Office of Policy Development and Research, Institute for Community Design Analysis, Center for Urban Policy Research, Rutgers University).

Newman, O., Grandin, D. and Wayno, F. (1974), *The Private Streets of St Louis* (New York: A National Science Foundation study, Institute for Community Design).

Paquot, T., Lussault, M. and Body-Gendrot, S. (eds) (2000), *La Ville et l'urbain: L'état des savoirs* (Paris: La Découverte).

Parnes, B. (1978), 'Ocean Grove: A Planned Leisure Environment' in Stellhorn, P.A. (ed.), *Planned and Utopian Experiments* (Trenton, NJ: New Jersey Historical Commission) 29–48.

Pinçon M. and Pinçon-Charlot, M. (1994), 'Propriété individuelle et gestion collective. Les lotissements chics', *Les Annales de la recherche urbaine* 65, 34–5.

Pinçon, M. and Pinçon-Charlot, M. (2001), *Paris Mosaïque* (Paris: Calmann-Lévy).

Prévôt-Schapira, M.-F. (1999), 'Amérique latine: la ville fragmentée', *Esprit* 258 (November), 128–44.

Purcell, M. (1997), 'Ruling Los Angeles: Neighborhood Movements, Urban Regimes, and the Production of Space in Southern California', *Urban Geography* 18:8, 684–704.

Querrien, A. and Lassave, P. (1999), 'Au risque des espaces publics', *Les Annales de la recherche urbaine* 83/84, 3.

Reich, R.B. (1991), 'Secession of the Successful', *New York Times Magazine*.

Reville, N. and Wilson, H. (2000), *Why We Oppose Gated Communities in Worcester*, Available at <http://www/nindy.com/chw>.

Roncayolo, M. (1980), 'Logiques urbaines' in Duby, G. (ed.), *Histoire de la France urbaine, XIXe siècle* (Paris: Seuil), 18–71.

Sanchez, T., Lang, R.E. and Davale, D. (2003), *Security versus Status? A First Look at the Census's Gated Communities Data* (Alexandria, VA: Metropolitan Institute, Virginia Tech).

Schaer, R., Claeys, G. and Sargent, L.T. (2000), *Utopia: the Search for the Ideal Society in the Western World* (New York: The New York Public Library and Oxford University Press).

Schlosser, E. (2001), *Fast Food Nation: The Dark Side of the All-American Meal* (Boston: Houghton Mifflin).

Stephenson, N. (1992), *Snow Crash* (New York: Bantam Books).

Stewart, J. (1996), 'The Next Eden: The New Social Order Behind Gated Communities', *California Lawyer*.

Tourancheau, P. (2003), 'Meurtres ordinaires au bout de la voie privée', *Libération*.

Thuillier, G., 2005, 'Gated Communities in the Metropolitan Area of Buenos Aires, Argentina: A Challenge for Town Planning', *Housing Studies* 20:2, 255–71.

Ville de Paris (2002), *Nomenclature officielle des rues de Paris*, Available at <http://www.paris.fr/fr/asp/carto/nomenclature.asp>.

Webster, C.J. (2002), 'Property Rights and the Public Realm: Gates, Green Belts, and Gemeinschaft', *Environment and Planning B: Planning and Design* 29:3, 397–412.

Webster, C.J., Wu, F. and Zhao, Y. (2006), 'China's Modern Walled Cities' in Glasze et al. (eds), 153–69.

Wilson-Doenges G. (2000), 'An Exploration of Sense of Community and Fear of Crime in Gated Communities', *Environment and Behavior* 32:5, 597–611.

Zecchini, L. (1997), 'Ségrégation ordinaire à Washington', *Le Monde*.

Zecchini, L. (1999, 'Insécurité urbaine: la déplorable spécificité française', *Le Monde*.

Chapter 6

From Self-Defence to Citizenry Involvement Participation in Law-and-Order Enforcement in the United States: Private Spheres and Public Space

Didier Combeau

Crime and violence are subjects of heated debate everywhere and the use of force, perhaps more than any other social issue, raises questions concerning that fine line that separates private spheres from public space. Among all areas worthy of scrutiny in the attempt to shed light on the tension that lies between public and private urban initiatives, one that ineluctably stands out is law and order. Still more illuminating in this area are the diverging cultural perceptions, revealed by even superficial transatlantic observation, of citizens from two given countries, say France and the United States, each having in common a national faith in the exemplarity of their political, economic and social organization. One of the most exotic concepts that a French mind might have to grasp, for example, is the American model of the so-called 'gated communities', where, in some cases, the citizens themselves take part in patrolling the streets.

In order to show how differently citizens from each side of the Atlantic apprehend and approach the domain of public safety, and to fully delineate the ontological roots of those diverging approaches, it is first primordial to trace the major differences between the French and the American notions of self-defence. This can but exemplify the reason why the idea of private involvement in the enforcement of law and order is much more present and deeply ingrained in the American, rather than French, psyche. Private involvement in the United States can take very extreme forms, unheard of in France, and an overview of the evolution of the statutes of several states, which most recently grant even more power to the individual to meet force with force in public places, shows how this may require a re-examination of the very notion of public space.

A Transatlantic Perspective on Self-Defence

Self-defence might appear as a transparent notion, yet using the same word in two different places may translate quite differently. Any transatlantic comparison of the legal implications of self-defence is, of course, made difficult by the sheer number of existing penal codes: one for each of the fifty American states and at least one for each of the European nations. But by placing the provisions of the penal codes of two large, but rather different states in terms of history and mentalities like New York and Texas, side by side with those of a European country – France – a solid enough base can be formed from which to widen our perspective and give ample grounds for interpretation.

In New York, as in Texas, there is an obligation, whenever possible, to avoid violent confrontation rather than using force, and especially deadly force – that is to say a degree of force likely to kill or seriously maim – encapsulated in the formula 'duty to retreat'. However, the New York Penal Code clearly states that there is no such 'duty to retreat' for anyone in his private home:

> A person in possession or control of [...] a dwelling or an occupied building, who reasonably believes that another person is committing or attempting to commit a burglary of such dwelling or building, may use deadly physical force upon such other person when he reasonably believes such to be necessary to prevent or terminate the commission or attempted commission of such burglary. (§ 35.20)

In everyday terms, this means that a New Yorker is allowed to kill a burglar when he or she is in his or her home if he or she believes that the circumstances are such that it is necessary to protect his or her property. This is popularly known as the 'castle doctrine': 'a man's house is his castle, and he is the king in his castle.' The Penal Code of Texas contains the same provision with only slight differences (sec. 9.42); a Texan is allowed to use deadly force to defend property only between sunset and sunrise. A Texan, however, is allowed to chase a burglar outside his or her home and use deadly force as long as he or she was able to maintain visual contact – which is not the case in New York State.

The use of force to protect property in France is governed by article L 122 – 5 of the French Penal Code:

> Shall not be held criminally liable a person who, to terminate a crime or a misdemeanour against property, accomplishes an act of self-defence, save from voluntary homicide, when such an act is strictly necessary to this end, provided that the means employed are proportional to the seriousness of the crime or misdemeanour.[1]

What is important to note here is the very clear stipulation that voluntary homicide is not an acceptable response when there is an attack on property. This means that while self-defence, as legal recourse, is also acceptable in France, it is certainly much more limited in scope than it is in either New York or in

---

1 My translation.

Texas. A homicide is justifiable according to French legislation, only to protect one's own physical integrity, not one's possessions. Interestingly, the distinction between two separate expressions in French for 'self-defence' becomes visible: one is *'légitime défense'*, which is most of the time understood as the defence of one's own person, and the other one is *'autodéfense'*, which is far less limitative and includes the defence of one's belongings. If *'légitime défense'* can go as far as voluntary homicide when one's own life is in jeopardy, *'autodéfense'* is a much more controversial concept.

This contrast automatically lessens when comparing the United States with the United Kingdom. Andrew Ashworth, in *Principles of Criminal Law*, writes that there is no duty in Britain to retreat in one's private home, and notes that 'in several cases in which a firearm, sword, or knife has been used against a burglar with fatal results, the householder has been either acquitted or not prosecuted' (146). But he also notes that the British common law, at least to this extent, is in violation of the European Convention on the Protection of Human Rights and Fundamental Freedoms, article 2, which includes language allowing the use of deadly force for the defence of one's person, but not of one's property:

1) Everyone's right to life shall be protected by law. No one shall be deprived of his life intentionally save in the execution of a sentence of a court following his conviction of a crime for which this penalty is provided by law.
2) Deprivation of life shall not be regarded as inflicted in contravention of this article when it results from the use of force which is no more than absolutely necessary:
    a) in defence of any person from unlawful violence;
    b) in order to effect a lawful arrest or to prevent the escape of a person lawfully detained;
    c) in action lawfully taken for the purpose of quelling a riot or insurrection.

The Citizen and the Enforcement of Law

It is easy to see how such a liberal definition of the legitimate use of deadly force has gone hand-in-hand with the participation of private citizens in the enforcement of law and order throughout American history, and well into recent times. The line that separates self-defence from law enforcement is thin, and personal armament has often been represented as an appropriate response in critical periods in the United States, as illustrated in this letter to the editor, published by the *New York Times* during the crime wave of the 1920s:

Let revolver and rifle shooting become a part of the required work of our public schools; teach the subject as it should be taught, and the recipient of such training will soon answer the question of how to suppress crime of this kind. (27 March 1927)

Seven decades later, just as the Y2K computer bug fear reached its apex, *Time Magazine* ran a cover story on the subject and published a picture of a family posing in front of a stock of canned food with the father holding a rifle, a perfect illustration of this inclination to arm when threatened (18 January 1999). A Time/

CNN poll published in the same issue revealed that 13 per cent of Americans had contemplated buying a rifle to be able to face the turmoil likely to be caused by the collapse of information systems. Again, after 9/11, and after airline pilot unions demanded the right for their members to carry guns on board to be able to defend their aircrafts and passengers from terrorist attacks, this new 'call to arms' was signed into law by President George W. Bush in 2002 (P.L. 107 – 296). The havoc wrought by Katrina brought descriptions of scenes taking place in New Orleans, as captured in the *New York Times* in an uncritical article entitled 'Owners Take Up Arms as Looters Press Their Advantage' (1 September 2005):

> Paul Cosma, 47, who owns a nearby auto shop, stood outside it along with a reporter and photographer he was taking around the neighborhood. He had pistols on both hips.
> Suddenly, he stepped forward toward a trio of young men and grabbed a pair of rusty bolt cutters out of the hands of one of them. The young man pulled back, glaring.
> Mr. Cosma, never claiming any official status, eventually jerked the bolt cutters away, saying 'You don't need these'.

Other evidence of the implication of American citizens in their own defence can be found in the success of numerous neighbourhood watch programmes or of television programmes like *America's Most Wanted* (Fox Television), which summons crime witnesses and broadcasts real-life scenes of citizens protecting themselves, their families and their neighbourhoods from criminals – sometimes at gun point. This kind of private involvement is not merely the defensive, knee-jerk reflex of a frightened individual. It has often been encouraged by public authorities. In 1922, New York police chief William Enright, facing criticism over the city's crime situation, announced on the front page of the *New York Times* that the police shooting range was opened to 'bank messengers and confidential men in the financial district whose employers wanted them to achieve greater proficiency in the use of the revolver' (7 April). He also declared that the number of gun permits delivered to New Yorkers since the beginning of that year was not 25,000, as had been said previously, but 35,000. A few years later, it was announced in the same newspaper that the Chicago authorities approved the decision of bankers to offer a $2,500 reward for each gangster killed (6 July 1925). Likewise, after 9/11, a sheriff from Portland, Oregon, suggested setting up units composed of volunteers equipped with their personal weapons to protect sensitive sites like power lines, pipe lines and nuclear plants from terrorist threats (*New York Times*, 3 November 2001). Further evidence of this kind of official inducement to 'get involved' can be found in the large diffusion of 'most-wanted' ads by the FBI, or in the programmes that associate civilians to police patrols in many American cities. It seems that even in extreme emergency situations, like the one that prevailed in New Orleans after Katrina, public authorities are hard pressed to claim any kind of monopoly on law and order enforcement:

> Mr. Compass, the police superintendent, said that after a week of near anarchy in the city, no civilians in New Orleans would be allowed to carry pistols, shotguns or other firearms of any kind. 'Only law enforcement are allowed to have weapons', he said.

That order apparently did not apply to the hundreds of security guards whom businesses and some wealthy individuals had hired to protect their property. The guards, who were civilians working for private security firms like Blackwater, were openly carrying M-16s and other assault rifles.

Mr Compass said that he was aware of the private guards but that the police had no plans to make them give up their weapons. (*New York Times*, 9 September 2005)

The participation of American citizens in fighting crime is not merely symbolic. Its reality can be found in numbers. According to the statistics published in the FBI Uniform Crime Reports, 4,749 of the 11,440 'felons killed during the commission of a felony' between 1987 and 2004 were killed by private citizens, and not by the police – that is to say four out of ten.

Voices clamouring for the rights of individuals to be armed when threatened, at the workplace or elsewhere, are often heard in the United States, from the already-mentioned, post-9/11 voices of airline pilots to those of Texan judges after courtroom attacks,[2] or from those of rampage victims such as Texas State representative Suzanna Gratia Hupp[3] following the deaths of her parents killed in Killeen in 1991 to the collective voice of the National Rifle Association advocating the arming of teachers to prevent school shootings.[4] This, again, stands in sharp contrast with France. Even if French society is usually considered as less violent, it has known, over the years, its share of tragedies. Tellingly, the use of force by individual citizens has never been considered, at least in the public debate, as an appropriate response. After the rape of a railroad employee in 2005, for example, the unions called not for the right to use more force, but for better security in their trains by increasing the workforce.[5] Similarly, doctors in down-ridden districts and confronted by racketeering, asked simply, passively, for police protection.[6] Even a decision by the government to mobilize retired policemen and military personnel to act as security guards after an attack on a court clerk in Rouen was sharply criticized by the magistrates' unions.[7] Maintaining security in courthouses, or elsewhere it seems, is seen, in France, as the task of the police. The country has experienced rampages just as tragic and as dramatic as any American state – in Tours, for instance, a madman killed four people in the street in 2001 while in Nanterre, another killed eight city council members during a meeting in 2002 – but there is not a single organization in the country, not even one single sportive shooting association, that supports the cause of victims being armed.[8] This extreme difference in sensibility is possibly best epitomized by the French-American controversy which broke out when American authorities required the

---

2   See for instance *Houston Chronicle*, 14 and 15 May 1996.
3   See for instance *Houston Chronicle*, 16 January 1993.
4   See for instance the NRA press release, 'NRA Calls for More Guns in Schools', 26 March 2005.
5   See for instance *Le Monde*, 26 January 2005.
6   See for instance *Le Parisien*, 25 March 2005.
7   See for instance *Agence France Presse*, 8 September 2005.
8   See for instance *Libération*, 29 March 2002.

presence of armed security agents on foreign carriers entering or leaving the United States, while French airline pilots were strongly opposed.[9]

The Ontological Roots of Diverging Attitudes towards Self-Defence

The tendency of the French to rely on the police and the judicial system rather than on self-defence for their security can of course be related to a political tradition of a strong central government that reaches back at least to Louis XIV, while the opposite readiness of Americans to take the law into their own hands, can probably be linked to the rustic conditions that prevailed during the colonial period and, later, during the frontier period. There is no doubt that the situation of the American colonist setting foot in new territories had not much in common with that of the French peasant leaving in the shadow of a *château fort*. However, the lingering, legendary view of the individual citizen obliged to join vigilante committees to make up for the lack of new-world institutions, may not be absolutely accurate, historically speaking. In fact, institutions seem to have arisen rather quickly in new communities according to historians specialized in the American West, such as W. Eugene Hollon, and this is best illustrated by the example of Guthrie, Oklahoma, built literally overnight when the Indian territories were opened to settlers in 1889:

> People from thirty-two states, three territories, and half a dozen foreign countries were represented at the first roll call in the late afternoon of April 22 in Guthrie. Hardly a man knew more than a dozen individuals present, outside his immediate family. Yet within thirty-six hours after everyone had arrived at the 'Magic City' on the Prairie, this heterogeneous mob had elected a mayor and a council of five members, adopted a city charter, and authorized the collection of a head tax. Within a week, Baptists, Methodists, and Presbyterians were holding church services in tents and planning the construction of permanent church buildings. The development of Oklahoma City, Edmond, Norman, and other towns that sprang up along the Santa Fe tracks on the same day paralleled that of Guthrie. (202–3)

American works of fiction run in the same vein, depicting citizen-involvement in law and order enforcement – whether that citizen be gunfighter, lone ranger or private eye – despite solidly existing institutions. There is no lack of judges, sheriffs, marshals and police officers in westerns, hardboiled detective stories, or gangster films and there is always some form of organized police and judicial system present in each of these seminal genres. But it turns out that they are either inefficient, or corrupted.

A shortcut from Louis XIV to the frontier and to the twenty-first century leaves as much in the shadow as it brings to light: why are the French ready to be so blindly confident in their police and in their judicial system, when the Americans look at theirs with so much distrust? It is difficult to know if American

---

9 See for instance the press release by the Syndicat National des Pilotes de Ligne, 5 January 2004.

police departments are more or less corrupted and more or less inefficient than the French national police or the *Gendarmerie*, but there is no doubt that the American judicial system is a lot harsher with criminals; the incarceration rate is much higher in the United States than it is in France. The comparison of crime rates from one country to another is always scientifically hazardous because the methodologies applied in gathering statistics are different, but the official rate of burglaries published by the FBI is very close to that published by the French Ministère de l'Intérieur. Yet as Maurice Cusson has underlined, it is in the domain of personal crime (murder, rape and aggravated assault) that the States breaks into the forefront, with rates that far exceed those exhibited in France. This can, in some ways, explain why Americans are more prone to self-defence; a response that can also be considered, at least in part, as a side-product of the ready availability of guns, itself justified by the necessity of being able to defend oneself.

Contingent factors, therefore, fall short in explaining why the French and the American representations of self-defence are so divergent. We must admit that there is something deeper and look to more philosophical arguments. After all, it may well be that the French are not as confident in their security institutions as might appear at first glance, and the temptation to take the law into one's own hands certainly exists at the individual level. But whereas the Americans tend to consider self-defence as a basic responsibility of each citizen, the French, at least in the public debate, see it as a mark of supreme egoism and of indifference towards the notion of public interest. This is but a specific declination of two trends: whereas the French tend to oppose private interest to public good, the Americans tend to consider the latter as the sum total of the former.

This brings us back to the penal codes of France, of Texas and of New York State. Underlined above is the fact that the use of deadly force is allowed to prevent property crime in the US, but that in France it is not. The French penal code does, however, permit resorting to deadly force in life-threatening situations. In setting these dissimilar legal provisions side by side, it seems that the distinction between personal crime and property crime is not as clear cut in the United States as it is in France. Yet turned the other way round and positioned under a different light, this may be exactly why private initiative in law and order enforcement is more prominent in the United States than in France.

Seen in this new light, one might consider that the justification for the use of deadly force is basically the same on both sides of the Atlantic, namely for the defence of one's person, but that it is the very definition of what a person is that differs. Whereas the French penal code conceives a person as a physiological entity limited to his or her own body, the penal codes of New York State and Texas consider a person as a social entity. In a tradition that can very well be traced back to the thought of John Locke, a person is not only a biological organism, but also one encompassing the possessions that are the product of his or her own industry: property is not a mere social compact, it is a natural right.

This fresh perspective allows us to reconsider the relation between self-defence and law and order enforcement. I use 'self-defence' here in a restrictive meaning, close to what would be called '*légitime défense*' in French, that is to say defence of one's own physical integrity. By 'law-and-order enforcement', I mean defence of all that constitutes the framework of society, in particular of a social structure based on a set of economic rules that define the way private property can be accumulated. Defending one's own property, which is of course 'personal' in so far as it is the product of one's own industry, but which is also, in many ways, the product of that set of social rules, belongs more to law and order enforcement than to self-defence in a restrictive meaning. By giving so much power to the individual to defend his own property – power that goes as far as inflicting death – the New York State and Texas penal codes tend to erase the line between self-defence and law and order enforcement. When a homeowner kills a burglar, he does not merely defend his property, he also acts as a responsible citizen uprightly thwarting an act of burglary, that is to say an activity that breaks the rules.

The fact that private property is considered as an inseparable part of a person, and that the right to private property can be, and is here, equated with the right to live, makes it virtually impossible to draw a line between self-defence and law and order enforcement. It is not then surprising, as a consequence, that American citizens are so involved in the maintenance of law and order. Divergently, law and order enforcement in France is more readily considered as what is called in French a *'prérogative régalienne'* – which, literally translated, means a 'royal privilege' – a duty which should not, or at least should rarely be delegated to private initiative. This does not mean, of course, that private police forces do not exist in France, but it does explains why they are much less common than in America, resting on far less established moral grounds. Recourse to them can either be justified by a lack of confidence in the government to efficiently police the city, or be seen as a first response before calling the police, but it is difficult here to call ontological arguments into the debate. This also explains why private police are generally not allowed to carry guns, their role appropriated to the defence of property and to something that lies well outside of the sphere of the person; a realm that is less valuable than life itself and whose defence does not justify the use of deadly force.[10]

No More Duty to Retreat

A recently-passed law in Florida goes a large step further than the penal codes of New York State and of Texas. Before 1 October 2005, the courts in Florida considered that a person acting in self-defence had 'a duty to use every reasonable means to avoid the danger, including retreat, prior to using deadly force',[11] even though such a duty was not statutory. Similarly, the courts applied the 'castle doctrine' which was not found in the statutes either. A section added by an act that was approved by ninety-four votes to twenty in the Florida House and unanimously in the Senate (sec. 776.013) transcribes an immoderate interpretation

---

10 In France, gun permits are delivered by the government on a 'may-issue' basis.
11 Weiand v. State, 732 So. 2d 1044 (Fla. 1999); State v. James, 867 So. 2d 414,416 (Fla. 3d DCA 2003), quoted in House of Representative Staff Analysis, Bill # HB 249 CS.

of the 'castle doctrine' into the print of the Florida statutes: for a person to be presumed to have held 'a reasonable fear of imminent peril of death or great bodily harm', it is enough that the person against whom he or she has used deadly force had been in 'the process of unlawfully and forcefully entering, or had unlawfully and forcefully entered, a dwelling, residence, or occupied vehicle'.

This would make Florida's law but a radicalized version of that of New York and Texas, in so far as deadly force can be used even if the person entering the building is not committing a burglary. But subsection 3 also states that:

> A person who is not engaged in an unlawful activity and who is attacked in any other place [than a dwelling, residence or occupied vehicle] where he or she has a right to be has no duty to retreat and has the right to stand his or her ground and meet force with force, including deadly force if he or she reasonably believes it is necessary to do so to prevent death or great bodily harm to himself or herself or another or to prevent the commission of a forcible felony.

The notion of forcible felony includes, of course, murder, manslaughter and sexual battery, but also offences that can imply the use of non-deadly force like robbery, burglary, aggravated assault or arson. The means employed, it follows, do not have to be 'proportional to the seriousness of the crime or misdemeanour', so distinct from France (see above article 122-5 of the French penal code). But what really represents a departure from the ontological basis of the French penal codes, but also those of New York and Texas, is that the person attacked 'has no duty to retreat and has a right to stand his or her ground and meet force with force', not only in his or her home but also in public places. This signifies then, that no penal or civil action can be taken against a person who pulls a gun at and shoots an aggressor on the street, in a bar or at a football field, even though fleeing would have been possible and would have been sufficient in averting any harm. The logic behind this law was that citizen involvement in their own defence, and that of their property, would deter crime. Governor Jeb Bush, before signing the law, highlighted the link between self-defence and law enforcement:

> Our crime rate is dropping, and it's because of measures that allow people to protect themselves and their properties, as well as putting habitual offenders away for longer periods of time.[12]

If Florida now seems to stand as an extreme case by its extravagant positioning on self-defence, such an extension of the 'castle' rule even outside one's 'own castle' is in no way unique. Since 1989, the Tennessee statutes clearly state that 'There is no duty to retreat before a person threatens or uses force' (39-11-611 (a)), and a bill similar to Florida's law has been introduced in Michigan in 2005 (House Bill 5153); in Louisiana, duty to retreat is not mentioned in statutes, which allowed the courts to consider that 'there is no unqualified duty to retreat' (*State v. Brown*, 414 So.2d 726 (La. 1982)).

---

12   Quoted in *Orlando Sentinel*, 6 April 2005.

Gun control advocacy groups have been alarmed by the enactment of the new law in Florida – which unsurprisingly had the backing of the National Rifle Association. The Brady Campaign to Prevent Gun Violence launched a national campaign against what they nicknamed as the 'Shoot First Law', acridly warning all Sunshine State tourists to avoid unnecessary arguments with local people, to make sure to keep their hands in plain sight if they were involved in a car accident, and to avoid making gestures that could be interpreted as threatening or instigative. The Brady Campaign explained its reasoning in the following terms:

> Individuals who are unfamiliar with Florida's roads, traffic regulations and customs, or who speak foreign languages, or look different than Florida residents, may face a higher risk of danger – because they may be more likely to be perceived as threatening by Floridians, and because they are unaware of Florida's new law that says individuals who feel their safety is threatened or their possessions are at risk are legally authorized to use deadly force.[13]

It goes without saying that their aim was to show just how detrimental such a law could be to the tourism industry of Florida. Yet even if one puts aside the will to press where it hurts, understandable on the part of an advocacy group, there is no doubt that such a law, giving a ample freedom to the individual citizen to use force against whoever he deems threatening, fosters the kind of conformism where even looking 'different' becomes very risky. Above and beyond all, it re-qualifies the very notion of public space. If an individual can behave in a public place in the same way as he can in his private home, then the concept of public space dissolves, to be replaced by that of an aggregation of private spheres. In such space, common good does not transcend private interests; it amounts to no more than their arithmetic sum, and public initiative, therefore, no longer makes sense.

*

The point made here is that privatization is more than a mere matter of economic efficiency, or of financially-vested interest, at least as far as self-defence and law and order are concerned. More factors have to be taken into consideration, beyond what meets the eye, if the involvement of private citizens in law and order enforcement is to be understood – whether it be under the form of direct individual participation or through private security companies, which are the logical prolongation of that individual involvement. There is certainly the belief that private ventures are more efficient than public intervention, weighted down, as it is perceived, by bureaucracy and red tape, and that the free play of market forces will ultimately result in the best possible social organization. But it must be recognized that whatever perceptions a given society has of its citizens and their involvement in law and order, is also inextricably hinged on ontology, namely on a representation of human beings which does or does not include, within the

---

13 http://www.shootfirstlaw.org.

sphere of the person, his or her property. In the American mindset, each person is in part physiological and in part social; a philosophical justification for private involvement in defending, at gun point if necessary, not only the physiological part of one's being but also the social part, through the defence of the legal and economic order that presides over the accumulation of wealth. From personal right, this can even be elevated to the stature of moral duty, as exemplified in the following excerpt of a letter to the editor published by the *New York Times* on 1 February 1927:

> The moral, or psychological, effect of removing from the citizens themselves their personal responsibility to protect all persons dependant on them, and also the fruit of their personal thrift and labor, from criminal aggression is another point to be considered. A citizenry which depends entirely on paid defenders for all protection soon becomes weak and helpless.

Such a view is now, and would have been at the time, largely foreign to most French citizens. That public security has largely been considered in France, at least until the present time, as a *'prérogative régalienne'*, a 'royal privilege' that can hardly be delegated, has to be linked with a much more limitative representation of human-beings, where even within his or her own castle, let alone in public places, a man or a woman is not an absolute king or queen. This may contribute to explaining why the sight of citizens patrolling and policing their own communities, visually undisturbing to some American landscapes, can appear so striking to French eyes.

References

Ashworth, A. (1999), *Principles of Criminal Law* (Oxford: Oxford University Press).
Brown, R.M. (1994), *No Duty to Retreat : Violence and Values in American History and Society* (Norman: University of Oklahoma Press).
Brown, R.M. (1975), *Strain of Violence: Historical Studies of American Violence and Vigilantism* (New York: Oxford University Press).
Combeau, D. (2007), *Des Américains et des armes à feu : démocratie et violence aux États-Unis* (Paris: Éditions Belin).
Cusson, M. (1999), 'Autodéfense et Homicides', *Revue internationale de Criminologie et de Police technique et scientifique*, 2 131-50.
Hollon, W.E. (1974), *Frontier Violence: Another Look*, (New York: Oxford University Press).
Kinkeade & McColloch, *Texas Penal Code Annotated* (1997) (Rochester: West Group).
Pelletier, H. and Perfetti J. (1999), *Code Pénal* (Paris: Éditions Litec).

Chapter 7

The Future of Prison Privatization in the United States

Franck Vindevogel

The involvement of private companies in the incarceration of prisoners has not only generated various studies but has also fuelled a debate among justice professionals, researchers, citizens and policymakers. The reason for this can be found both in the rapid growth of private prisons and in the fundamental questions raised by such a trend.

Burgeoning prison populations in various western countries with a neoliberal political agenda like Australia or the United Kingdom have led to a growing implication of the private sector in corrections. Nowhere, however, has the trend been so visible as in the United States where 83 per cent of all existing private prison facilities in the world were in operation in 2002 according to Corrections Corporation of America (CCA). As of December 2006, the latest available data, 113.791 US state and federal prisoners were incarcerated in privately operated correctional facilities in thirty two states primarily located in the South and West (Sabol Harrison and Couture 2007). Five states, all in the West, had at least a quarter of their inmate population in private facilities. Some twenty years ago, when the first contract was signed, nobody expected the privatization movement in corrections to gain such a momentum.

The development of for-profit incarceration has recently attracted wide public attention in the United States and frequent bewilderment overseas. This can easily be justified: in our contemporary societies, the incarceration of criminals has traditionally been viewed as one of the most symbolic government obligations to the public. Although much more common and widespread, the participation of the private sector in policing is not so much a topic of debate in the United States as it is in corrections. The reason for this partly lies in the fact that the implications for society are not the same: private involvement in policing, indeed, does not materialize in the takeover of police departments. The development of for-profit incarceration is particularly controversial because it raises some fundamental ethical, ideological, legal and political questions that pertain to the protection of prisoners' rights, the safety of surrounding communities, but also to their profit-seeking nature and the quality of services like food, health care, rehabilitation or education.

This chapter attempts to address a central question for the future of the US criminal justice system: on the basis of available information, will privately-operated prisons continue to replace publicly managed corrections in the coming years? In this objective and following a brief historical overview of the rebirth of private prisons in the United States, we will see if private prison operators have kept their promises and if the specific context that led government to turn to the private sector will continue to exist.

The Rebirth of Private Prisons

Private sector involvement in the provision of public infrastructures and services has a long history in the United States. For historical, cultural and ideological reasons, Americans have traditionally sought ways to reduce government involvement in the marketplace. In the eighteenth and nineteenth centuries, for example, private ventures played a major role in the construction of roads and railroads, in supplying water and electricity as well as in the development of urban mass transit systems.

Following decades of public sector growth initially encouraged by the effects of the Great Depression, taxpayer resistance to government spending recently led to a renewed interest in the virtues of the private sector. This trend has materialized in growing privatization and public/private partnerships. The phenomenon really gained visibility under Ronald Reagan's presidency, not excluding fields commonly viewed as the sole province of government. The criminal justice system is one of them.

Today, the most visible involvement of private ventures in the criminal justice system can be seen in the provision of security services contracted by economic interests, individuals, governments and residential or cultural communities. The pervasive problems of crime and fear of crime, the failure of government to provide adequate police protection and the development of mass private properties have created huge markets for private security companies. This booming industry has not only tapped the market of protection and crime prevention but also more recently that of punishment.

Contrary to popular belief, privatization in corrections and more generally in the US criminal justice system is an old story (McCrie 1992: 12–26). It actually dates as far back as the time when the British used to transport convicts to America and Australia, or when public service surveillance in cities was a responsibility shared by local government and the private sector. In fact, until the end of the nineteenth century, private prisons were the norm in the US. States used to lease contract convict labour to private companies and in some instances (e.g., Texas) the correctional function was entirely transferred to the private sector. These prisons were supposed to turn a profit for the state or, at least, pay for themselves and in return they promised to control delinquents at no cost to government. Private prisons, however, disappeared about one hundred years ago because of the combined opposition from labour and business interests, which complained that the use of convict labour was unfair competition, and from both the public and reformers, who felt outraged by the extensive corruption and frequent abuse (malnourishment, whippings, overwork, overcrowding) existing in private prisons. Private companies, however, never ceased to play a role in the history of corrections in America: constructing correctional facilities or providing medical, dental, education, maintenance or food services.

The 1980s marked the beginning of a new era in prison privatization. At this stage, the term requires some clarification: what is meant by private prisons exactly? Douglas McDonald has proposed a model that introduces a distinction between ownership and operating authority. Based on this model, three different types of private involvement in corrections can be identified, they include: (1) institutions both owned and operated by a private enterprise; (2) institutions owned by government but operated under contract by a private company; or (3) owned by a private company but operated by government on a lease or lease-purchase agreement (McDonald 1992: 365).

Depending on the jurisdiction, the local, state or federal government is then charged a per diem or monthly payment for each prisoner. Some states do not have privately operated prisons within their borders but contract with out-of-state private prisons to detain some of their inmates.

In 1984 and 1985, three different jurisdictions at the county, state and federal levels decided to contract with private firms for the management of correctional facilities. Corrections Corporation of America (CCA) and Hamilton County (Tennessee) signed the first county-level contract in 1984. Soon after this, the Immigration and Naturalization Service (INS) became the first federal agency to turn to private companies for the detention of illegal aliens. A year later, the state of Kentucky and Corrections Corporation of America signed the first state-level contract (Tabarrok 2003: 75). In 1985, CCA offered $200 million to take over the entire Tennessee state prison system. But following strong opposition from public employees and the reluctance of the state legislature, the initiative was eventually defeated (Cheung 2004). In the 1990s, private contractors gained new market shares. Encouraged by double digit annual growth rates and soaring stock prices, several CEOs began to build '*spec* prisons' (i.e. speculative): instead of responding to demand for beds, they actually attempted to create demand by building and staffing prisons and advertising the availability of beds nationwide. Over a nine-year period, the design capacity of US private prisons rose from 15,300 in 1990 to 119,000 in 1999 (Tabarrok 2003: 78). In 2006, 7.2 per cent of all US prisoners incarcerated in correctional facilities across the United States were managed by such firms as Corrections Corporation of America (CCA), the GEO Group,[1] Management and Training Corporation and others. Building on their early successes, some of these firms then sought to become global providers of correctional services and began signing contracts with correctional agencies in Australia, South Africa and the United Kingdom (Mattera et al. 2003).

---

1   The GEO Group was formerly known as Wackenhut.

Have Private Prisons Held their Promises?

Any discussion of the future of private prisons in the United States requires a prior understanding of the factors that led to their rebirth. What did government authorities expect from privatization? Has for-profit incarceration kept its promises?

As mentioned above, private prisons re-appeared recently, in the mid-1980s, when state and federal governments decided to transfer the management and/ or ownership of some corrections to private firms. How can such a turnaround be justified?

From the 1920s to the early 1970s, the US incarceration rate had remained relatively stable, around 110 per 100,000 residents. Since 1973, however, it has kept rising steadily and markedly above historical norms to reach a record rate of 751 in 2006 (Sabol et al. 2007: 4). Today some 2.26 million Americans are incarcerated in jail or prison (against half a million in 1980). For some observers, the United States has launched a wide scale experiment to test the assumption that crime can be dramatically reduced if a large number of offenders are sent behind bars (Clear 1994: 38, Austin 2001).

Such an increase, however, cannot be easily explained by a single cause but should rather be viewed as the result of the combination of five main factors. The adoption of 'law and order' political agendas at the local, state and federal levels was the driving force that led to a new war on drugs, an increased number of arrests and more likely imprisonment, the passing of tougher sentencing laws (mandatory minimum sentencing, truth-in-sentencing, three-strike laws, ...) by state and federal legislatures and finally to the massive construction of new prison cells. As we will see, the economic and social impacts of these political choices would reverberate nationwide in ways most elected officials and voters alike had not fully envisioned.

Starting in 1973, the sharp rise in the number of criminals sentenced to prison terms led to a shortage of prison space and rapidly deteriorating living conditions for inmates. In spite of massive prison construction programmes nationwide, overcrowding never ceased to be a serious concern for many state authorities during the 1980s and 1990s. In 1994, state prisons were operating at between 17 and 29 per cent above capacity, while the federal system was operating at 25 per cent over capacity (Gilliard and Beck 1995: 1). During the same year, 39 states plus the District of Columbia were under court order to reduce overcrowding or improve prison conditions (Donziger 1995, 45). Major urban jails have also been under consent decrees regarding medical, food, education and protection from harm issues.

Not surprisingly, the punitive approach to crime control has produced impressive and sometimes unexpected budgetary constraints at all levels of government. The combined cost of operating budgets and new prison construction programmes led more and more states to divert their tax dollars from other priorities like education or welfare. Between 1977 and 1999, corrections spending at the state level grew by 946 per cent but welfare programmes (except health care) 'only' by 510 per cent, health care by 411 per cent and education by 370 per cent

(Gifford 2002). American taxpayers have become increasingly puzzled by such a list of priorities and reluctant to pay more taxes to fund new prison cells.

As the US incarceration rate continued to swell during the 1980s, the corrections system increasingly lost its credibility with both public and policymakers. Several major prison disturbances (in California, Illinois, New Mexico, New York) led to growing public sentiment that government management was inefficient. This perception was reinforced by the occasional disclosure of corruption scandals involving prison staff. Between 1989 and 1994, for instance, 50 correctional officers employed by the District of Columbia were convicted of serious crime, 18 of them for smuggling drugs into prison (Donziger 1994: 45). With penal programmes failing to produce significant reduction in recidivism rates, the public also became further disillusioned about the capacity of the prison system to rehabilitate its inmates.

This whole context led some elected officials to look for alternative solutions; among them was the idea of turning to the private sector. The idea was particularly appealing in a culture that has traditionally been mistrustful of large bureaucracies and government authority but convinced of the superiority of free enterprise. In the 1980s, encouraged by Reagan's economic policy, private entrepreneurs claimed they could solve the most pressing problems of the American prison system. They contended their companies could not only build and manage prisons as effectively, safely and humanely as the government, but could also do it in a more cost-effective way to save taxpayers money. Prison privatization advocates first believed that the private sector would increase prison bed capacity rapidly, therefore reducing prison overcrowding and eliminating the heavy fines imposed by federal courts. Secondly, they were convinced of their capacity to operate facilities more effectively by targeting labour costs which traditionally account for about 65 to 70 per cent of all operating costs. Theoretically, labour costs could be cut by reducing the number of employees, staff salaries, fringe benefits and overtime. This is easier in the private sector where CEOs are accountable to their investors, where labour unions are much less powerful than in public facilities, and where political pressure from public opinion is much less problematic. There were also expectations that the private sector would improve the quality of service, confinement and public safety. By introducing competition into the correctional marketplace, corporations would logically have to improve quality to get their contracts renewed. Finally, contracting out was expected to give government more flexibility as private corrections can provide cells when needed and specialize in unique facility missions (Austin and Coventry 2001: 14–17). Understandably, all these claims became increasingly attractive to those government authorities confronted with mounting budgetary and political pressures.

Now it can reasonably be argued that if private entrepreneurs' promises have materialized, prison privatization is likely to become a permanent and rapidly growing feature of the US correctional system. There are now enough privately operated facilities and sufficient experience for researchers to measure their performance and for public officials to determine whether or not privatized prisons can serve the public interest. What do we know today?

Have private companies the capacity to reduce prison overcrowding? The answer is definitely yes: private corporations can increase prison bed capacity, they cannot only do it faster, in two or three years instead of five to six, but also more cheaply than public agencies. The main explanation is to be found in the absence of government rules which slow down the construction process: they simply do not apply to the private sector (Austin and Coventry 2001: 68).

Can private contractors reduce operational costs? This is definitely one of the most debated issues among researchers and professionals working on prison privatization. Studies abound, but few are scientifically reliable. Various reports suggest private companies can operate correctional facilities at 5 to 20 per cent less than state agencies, but they are frequently biased. The latest study conducted for the Bureau of Justice Assistance (BJA) in 2001 confirmed previous findings from a 1996 General Accounting Office review of various comparative studies. The researchers concluded that differences regarding costs were minimal or even nonexistent between public and private institutions and that the promise of a 20 per cent saving 'has simply not materialized' (Austin and Coventry 2001: 39). It may also be too early to determine if the initial cost saving, where it exists, can last over an extended period of time: indeed, a single major riot can greatly affect budgets (Austin and Coventry 2001: 29). In the absence of real and systematic evidence that contracting out can be cost effective, it is difficult to draw positive conclusions.

Has the private sector proved its capacity to improve the quality of services? Clearly, anecdotal evidence of disturbances abound. It is no secret that major scandals have plagued some private prison companies. Corrections Corporation of America, which has grown to become the leading corporation in this field with a prison bed capacity of 70,000, has received substantial negative national media attention (Mattera et al. 2003). The Clark Report focused on CCA's Northeast Ohio Correctional Center (a medium security 'spec' prison constructed in 1996 in Youngstown, Ohio). Within fifteen months of operations: two homicides were committed, seventeen inmates were stabbed and six inmates escaped. In addition, numerous assaults against staff and inmates were reported and homemade weapons discovered. The facility operated under partial or full lockdown for long periods of time to avoid further incidents (Clark 1998). One of various causes was the incarceration of some maximum-security inmates in violation of the contract and with the knowledge of both CCA and the District. The lawsuit that followed not only cost CCA $756,000 in legal fees (not including defence) but also generated much bad publicity for the whole industry. In recent years CCA, which currently manages 50 per cent of all beds under contract with private operators in the United States (Corrections Corporation of America), has been involved in lawsuits involving allegations of inadequate medical treatment, incapacity to control violence, criminal activity among employees, escapes. Other examples of mismanagement in private prisons were observed in Colorado, Louisiana, Oregon, Texas, and so on (Austin and Coventry 2001: 59). Serious trouble usually occurs in 'spec prisons' where contracting agencies (often out-of-state) usually have less control due to distance. CCA's joint ventures in the UK and Australia have also had their own scandals to the extent that the Australian government decided to buy one of CCA Australia's facilities after four years of ongoing problems (Mattera et al. 2003).

Academic studies that measure quality of service and recidivism rates are less common than studies measuring cost. Some researchers conclude that the private sector outperforms state and federal prisons while others argue that both public and private facilities operate at the same level. In truth, a thorough evaluative comparison of inmate services in public and private facilities remains to be made (McDonald and Patten 2003). Using existing data, however, a monograph by the Bureau of Justice Assistance (BJA) concluded that the assumption that privately operated prisons are safer than public facilities is not supported by available statistics. The BJA researchers found that the rate of major incidents (inmate-on-inmate and inmate-on-staff assaults) appeared to be higher at private facilities than at public facilities (Austin and Coventry 2001: 52). James Austin (George Washington University) found that the occurrence of inmate-on-staff assaults was 49 per cent higher in privately managed facilities while that of inmate-on-inmate was 65 per cent higher than in publicly run institutions (Greene 2001).

We believe that this conclusion is consistent with the problems induced by the profit-making nature of private prisons. This difference in the level of violence could possibly result from the objective of private prison operators: turning a profit by cutting costs. An inmate incarcerated for five years in private prisons noticed that many riots in private facilities were triggered by inadequate food (cold, poorly-prepared, small portions served on dirty trays). Frequent financial reward mechanisms encourage food service managers to squeeze spending therefore creating frustration and anger among the many inmates who cannot afford to buy food from the prison's commissary at inflated prices. Inspectors may not be able to actually witness this problem as it is easy for prison authorities to upgrade the menu after being informed of an upcoming inspection (Bowers 2004). Similar cost-cutting incentives have also been used to minimize health care spending. In an extreme case that resulted in a lawsuit, a Tennessee physician employed by CCA doubled his annual salary to $190,000 from $95,000 after he managed to substantially reduce the inmates' medical service expenditure (*Prison Legal News* 2001). Equally serious are the cuts on labour costs. Private facilities have had to deal with high employee turnover and their staffing level is 15 per cent below that of public institutions. These are two factors potentially aggravating security problems. The authors of the BJA study, however, suggested that the variation in the number of incidents could also possibly be explained by different reporting standards or management difficulties resulting from recent opening (Austin and Coventry 2001).

The hope that competition would force companies to enhance the quality of their services clashes with a simple reality: today, the number of providers from which government authorities can choose remains limited.

With such inconclusive findings, it is therefore difficult to form a clear opinion. Researchers are confronted with complex methodological problems, especially difficulties comparing facilities that are different (age) and that do not have the same inmate population (demography and classification level) (Austin and Coventry 2001). We also still lack those long-term studies necessary to draw definite conclusions. Finally, the problem with many existing reports is that they often reflect the ideological beliefs of their authors. Academic Charles Thomas, for example, argued that savings of 10 to 20 per cent could be expected from prison privatization. But the Florida Ethics Commission was alerted to the fact that the researcher had been paid $3 million in consultation fees by private prison corporations. Thomas was then penalized and had to shut down his research institute at the University of Florida (Greene 2001).

To this date, therefore, we have no real scientific evidence that private corrections can systematically keep their promises. Quite clearly, this uncertainty has not been favourable to prison privatization proponents and to the industry itself. Of course, it cannot be denied that publicly run prisons have not been spared by various scandals and mismanagement problems either, but the promise that private entrepreneurs would make a real difference and provide better services has clearly disappointed many. The various incidents and disturbances occurring in these privately operated prisons have been widely publicized and have affected the industry's business. North Carolina, for example, cancelled two contracts with CCA arguing that the prison was poorly managed and insufficiently staffed. The North Carolina legislature went further voting a law to prohibit the importing of out-of-state inmates. A year later, Arkansas took over control of two of its prisons from Wackenhut. The repercussions of such setbacks even hit the stock market: CCA's stock trading dropped as low as 18 cents in December 2000 from a high of $44 two years earlier (Cheung 2004).

Prison overcrowding has been the prime factor leading municipal, state and federal governments to support privatization. In a 1997 survey of 28 responding jurisdictions, 86 per cent cited the reduction of overcrowding as an objective; lowering cost of operations was of secondary importance (cited by 57 per cent of the respondents), as was improving the quality of services (cited by 43 per cent of the respondents.) (McDonald and Patten 2003).

The result of this survey raises a second major question: will overcrowding continue to be a problem in American corrections?

Will Private Corrections Still Be Needed?

In 2003, states faced their third consecutive year of budget crisis. Nationwide, the cumulative state budget shortfall amounted to $200 billion dollars. In this context, the annual price to pay for the nation's prisons and jails – $50 billion in 2000 against only $7 billion two decades earlier – is clearly fuelling a debate. In fiscal year 2007, an estimated one in every 15 state general fund dollar was spent on incarceration, making corrections the fifth-largest state budget category (The Pew Center on the States 2008: 14). Non-profit organizations and concerned citizens have increasingly been calling for smart on crime policies that can reduce cost and still be effective deterrents. With a cost approaching $30,000 per inmate per year (Beckett and Sasson 2005: 4), reform advocates argue taxpayers had better think twice before supporting laws that have the potential to send non-violent offenders behind bars for many years. Their lobbying activities have occasionally been successful, for example in Michigan where *Families Against Mandatory Minimums* (FAMM) obtained the repeal of the so-called '650 lifer law', one of the nation's harshest mandatory minimum sentences, in 2002. Budget cutters increasingly hear the message and choose corrections as their prime target arguing that they have been the fastest growing item in most state budgets (Butterfield 2002). Steadily declining crime statistics between 1993 and 2004 and diminished public anxiety about crime have also emboldened cash-strapped legislators to support shortening sentences and drug treatment programmes as an alternative to systematic incarceration. In the fiscal year 2000, 25 states reduced their corrections budgets either closing prisons, reducing staff or curtailing programmes. Only one government sector – higher education – was affected more often (29 states) (Wilhelm and Turner 2002).

Correctional professionals and researchers had long argued that sending offenders to prison massively was not an appropriate policy to solve the US crime problem. As early as 1973, the *National Advisory Commission on Criminal Justice Standards and Goals* stated that 'no new institutions for adults should be built and existing institutions for juveniles should be closed. ... The prison, the reformatory and the jail have achieved only a shocking level of failure' (National Advisory Commission on Criminal Justice Standards and Goals 1973). If experts' recommendations were most of the time ignored by 'law and order' politicians, we now have signs that the retributive mentality may be fading away. Recent scientific evidence shows that the huge investments made in prisons have not delivered a great result. On the basis of a study made for the Department of Justice, we know that among nearly 300,000 prisoners released in 15 states in 1994, 67.5 per cent were rearrested within three years, and 51.8 per cent went back to prison. A similar study published in 1983 had shown a lower recidivism rate: 62.5 per cent had been rearrested within a three-year period (Langan and Levin 2002). The mood is now even changing among conservative politicians: more now publicly admit it is time to stop the experiment of mass incarceration. An increasing number of Americans are also becoming aware that locking up and ignoring offenders has not been a cure-all for crime. Public support for harsher sentences fell from 42 per cent of respondents in 1994 to 32 per cent seven years later. In contrast, the proportion of respondents who favoured addressing the root causes of crime rose from 48 per cent in 1994 to 65 per cent in 2001 (Wilhelm and Turner 2002). This shift in public opinion, however, is neither universal nor radical. Support for reform seems to be strongest when it comes to low-level, non-violent crimes such as drug possession (Vindevogel 2007).

The combination of these two trends, the spiralling cost of incarceration and growing awareness that punitive policies have failed, has paved the way for a bi-partisan reform movement affecting a growing number of states, small and large. During the 2003 legislative sessions, more than 25 states reduced sentences and changed their sentencing and correctional policies (Wool and Stemen 2004). In an effort to reduce the inflow of new inmates, they have either: removed mandatory sentencing for certain non-violent offences (e.g., Michigan), sent drug offenders to treatment instead of jail (e.g., Kansas), limited application of three strike laws (e.g., Louisiana) or increased the number of inmates eligible for early release (Wilhelm and Turner 2002). By 2003, seventeen states had given up their mandatory minimum sentences and revised other tough penalties (Families Against Mandatory Minimums). Such laws had notoriously contributed to prison overcrowding. In 2007 alone, 18 states attempted to review the effectiveness of their criminal justice systems or pass reforms to cut recidivism and reduce sentence length (King 2008).

Although the US general prison population still continues to rise, the effect of these new trends is nonetheless already perceptible and does not bode very well for the business of private prison entrepreneurs. While the average annual growth in federal and state prison population had reached 7.8 per cent for the period between 1981 to 1998, it dropped to only 2.1 per cent for the years 1999 to 2003 (statistics computed from Gilliard and Beck 1995 and Harrison and Beck 2004).

The consequences on overcrowding are also becoming visible. As of 2003, state prisons were operating at full capacity to 116 per cent above capacity, which is nine percentage points below the 1995 figure (Harrison and Beck 2003). Although the full impact of this changing context remains to be measured, we can reasonably expect that if the reform movement gains momentum, prison overcrowding will continue to diminish, making it less pressing for elected officials to find alternative solutions to state prisons.

The impact of these recent developments on for-profit incarceration can already be measured at the state level. More states (Mississippi, Utah) have ended their contracts with private correctional firms or announced their intention to do so (Tabarrok 2003: 77, 96).

Despite this downturn, the number of inmates held in private facilities nationwide has continued to rise: from 90,542 in 2000 to 113.791 in 2006. This trend is partly due to the growing use of private prisons by the Federal Government. As of 2006, a quarter of all US inmates in private facilities were held for the Federal Government.

Originally, the Federal Bureau of Prisons (FBOP) had been reluctant to turn to privatization. It was only in 1997 that it awarded its first private prison contract to operate a low- and medium-security complex for federal prisoners in California. In the years that followed, the FBOP engaged in a much more ambitious privatization campaign throughout the country. This decision coincided with a fast-escalating federal prison population fuelled by the passing of harsh drug-sentencing laws. Between 1995 and 1999, the federal inmate population rose by 31 per cent, twice the nationwide rate over the same period (Greene 2001). Because federal prison facilities were then operating well above maximum capacity, members of Congress voted massive new construction programmes while also searching for additional cheap private prison cells. The drug war waged at the federal level is not the only factor generating profits for the private corrections industry. Another large proportion of Federal inmates sent to privately managed institutions happens to be non-citizen immigrants convicted of federal crimes. The number of people incarcerated by US immigration officials increased threefold between 1995 and 2005 to more than 21,000. In 1998, these immigrants – about half being Mexican citizens – made up 29 per cent of the Federal prison population. The

1996 Immigration Reform Act which greatly expanded the number of crimes for which 'criminal aliens' must be deported after serving their sentences along with the creation of the Department of Homeland Security following 9/11 have spurred a huge demand for additional prison beds and consequently created new opportunities for the private corrections industry.

Today, many of these detainees awaiting deportation are housed at facilities run either by CCA or the GEO Group (Crary 2005). According to the Bureau of Justice Statistics, one third of these non citizens were incarcerated for immigration violations but only 1.5 per cent for violent offences. Their specific profile therefore does not require high-security prisons and makes contracting with private prison operators a good choice for federal authorities (Greene 2001). These recent Federal contracts came just at the right time for CCA, when literally thousands of empty prison beds had placed the Nashville-based corporation at the brink of bankruptcy.

That federal corrections are currently operating well above capacity may not be the only reason why private prison bed providers are gaining new market shares with federal agencies. For an industry whose only customer is the public sector, it is no surprise that these companies have frequently tried to woo elected officials from state legislatures up to the federal government. Lobbying activities have taken various forms including campaign contributions to carefully selected politicians or the publication of favourable academic studies. But private prison corporations have also developed a more personal approach. Some of their senior managers appear to have particularly useful connections with the federal government. One of the most prominent examples is undoubtedly that of Michael J. Quinlan: just after serving as the Federal Bureau of Prisons (FBOP) director from 1987 to 1992 under President Bush, he was hired by CCA to hold various key positions in the company including that of President and Chief Operating Officer (Mattera et al. 2003: 22). As CCA's Senior Vice President, Quinlan still remained one of the firm's five top executives in 2002. The presence of Norman Carlson, a director of the FBOP under President Ronald Reagan, in Wackenhut's board of directors (Greene 2001) most likely served the same twofold objective of enhancing the company's credibility on the market and cultivating ties with federal authorities.

Of course we will never know for sure if the combined presence of two former FBOP directors among CCA's and Wackenhut's executive officers or board members and CCA's soft money contribution to the Republican party – about $100,000 between 1997 and 2003 (Mattera et al. 2003: 29) – can explain by themselves the awarding of the recent federal contracts. But we have good reasons to believe that it was a very important factor. The industry's connection with the political realm is an old story: CCA's co-founder, Tom Beasley, was the chairman of the Tennessee Republican party. Because private prison bed providers lobby for the protection and growth of their market shares, they are part of the 'prison industrial complex'. The phrase, first used in a 1994 article in the Wall Street Journal, refers to this iron triangle, existing between government bureaucracy, private industry and politicians, joining forces to promote incarceration for their own financial or political benefits. Much like the defence-industrial complex which took advantage of the Cold War in its time, the prison-industrial complex attempts to maximize the opportunities generated by the war on crime. The industry has repeatedly denied accusations of pushing tough-on-crime legislation and other policies favourable to its business interests.[2] But since 1994, researchers have gathered growing evidence about the connections formed between the political, business and administrative spheres to expand the criminal justice system.[3] One major example is the industry's contribution to the funding of the conservative *American Legislative Exchange Council* (ALEC), a public policy group that actively endorses tough sentencing policies while also promoting the benefits of privatization among state legislators. ALEC has successfully contributed to the implementation of 'three-strike' and 'truth-in-sentencing' laws in various states across the country. This implies that CCA and Wackenhut have therefore been in a position to directly influence sentencing legislation thanks their financial and political involvement in ALEC's *Criminal Justice Task Force* (Cheung 2004).

Equally troubling is evidence that citizens are losing some of their political power to the industry's advantage. The tax-exempt general-obligation bonds necessary for the construction of new state prisons or local jails typically require voter approval. One strategy that wary citizens have used against systematic use of incarceration as a punishment and costly continuous prison expansion has been to vote against additional prison construction in their jurisdiction. But the private prison industry which is not dependent on such favourable votes can still build new facilities 'on spec' from their own capital and then contract with government authorities. This amounts to charging taxpayers for new prison beds with or without their approval.

It has therefore become increasingly apparent that the industry's combined profit-making nature and political connections are not compatible with a sound public criminal justice policy.

But these ethical questions rarely bother the industry's CEOs and stockholders. In contrast, they have even shown relative confidence in the future. In an emblematic sign of optimism, the GEO group has recently bought its rival Correctional Services Corp. At first sight, it is true that prospects seem to be good for those private prison bed providers contracting with federal agencies: at year end 2005 indeed, the federal system was still operating at 34 per cent above capacity (Harrison and Beck 2006) and according to a Federal Bureau of Prison spokeswoman, the number of federal prisoners is expected to grow from 185,000 to 226,000 by 2010 (Crary 2005).

Nevertheless, we believe this confidence may be excessive. What is clearly happening is that the private corrections industry is becoming increasingly dependent on the Federal Government for its business. In 2002, Henry Coffey, a managing director and senior research analyst at Morgan Lewis, an investment banking firm, issued a stock analyst's report of the private prison industry in which he clearly identified slow or negative growth at the state level and a

---

2 A specific page on CCA's web site deal with the various myths existing on the industry. It can be accessed at <http://www.correctionscorp.com/myths.html>.

3 Examples include Donziger 1996 and Jacobson 2005.

concentrated dependence on the federal government for new prisoners as primary risk factors facing the industry (Coffey 2002). Clearly this process is underway. In 2003, the Federal Bureau of Prisons, the United States Marshals Service and the Immigration and Naturalization Service made up nearly one third of CCA's revenues (Mattera et al. 2003).

In addition, resistance to the industry is mounting and could possibly reduce the political influence of the 'prison-industrial complex'. Not surprisingly, public corrections unions have a vested interest in the defeat of the privatization movement and have been actively involved in the political debate. Opposition has also come from Congress where Ohio Representative Ted Strickland introduced twice a Public Safety Act in 2001 and 2005 in an attempt to prohibit the incarceration of inmates by private contractors. The bill received endorsement by members from both political parties. Additionally various groups have sprung up like *Not With Our Money*, a network of students and activists whose ambition is to hold entrepreneurs in the industry accountable for their actions. But opposition also comes from rural citizens. Private corrections corporations had traditionally relied on a convincing argument to encourage political leaders and rural communities to accept a prison. They laid emphasis on the creation of economic development opportunities such as job creation and new service contracts. But a group of researchers from the Sentencing Project, a Washington based criminal justice think tank, has recently cast doubt on the validity of such a claim. They studied conditions surrounding 32 rural prisons opened since 1982 in New York State and in 2003 they concluded that counties with prisons did not gain any significant jobs compared with those without prisons:

> Overall, over the course of 25 years, we find no significant difference or discernible pattern of economic trends between the seven rural counties in New York that hosted a prison and the seven rural counties that did not host a prison. (King et al. 2003: 2)

The explanation lies in the fact that local residents cannot really take advantage of employment opportunities because their career profile and qualifications are not necessarily compatible with the positions available in these prisons. Well-informed rural communities are no longer systematically lured by these so-called economic opportunities and now voice their opposition to the construction of new prisons. In 2004 for example, the '*Concerned Citizens*', a group of activists from Uniontown, Alabama, organized the community against the construction of a new private prison locally, arguing that it would keep better businesses away by stigmatizing their town: 'to get that little benefit, we're going to have from now on the stigma of a prison' (Crowder 2004).

The economic boom experienced by the private prison industry during most of the 1990s resulted from the combination of two main factors. The first one was the scarcity of available prison beds that resulted from a massive incarceration experiment. The second one was the absence of reliable scientific evidence about the performance of private prison providers when expectations were high that the private sector would provide a viable alternative to publicly-run institutions. About the first factor, evidence is now building up that this experiment has failed. The industry's use of sophisticated lobbying strategies will certainly help it maintain its market share and avoid massive contract termination, but in a context of changing attitudes towards incarceration, they will not be enough to allow massive business expansion. As regards the second factor, our analysis has shown that the industry's claims of better performance and lower costs have simply not proven true and that the only real advantage private corrections companies can offer is rapid construction of new facilities. Turning to private contractors is particularly appealing when prison overcrowding becomes unbearable and when state legislatures are reluctant to build new costly state facilities. Private prisons therefore only give public authorities management flexibility. Increased management flexibility is exactly what currently prompts state and federal agencies to turn to private companies. But is this really enough for the industry to ensure a vast increase of its market share in the long term? Probably not. We should not forget that this same flexibility also allows government authorities to make immediate and convenient reductions in prison contracts without the loss of public jobs and labour union protest. In fact, private prisons currently appear to be no more than a kind of buffer for cash-strapped and overcrowded departments of corrections. Bill Sessa, a spokesman with the California Department of Corrections and Rehabilitation, pertinently noted that turning to private prisons is 'not a policy of choice' but rather 'a policy of circumstances' (Lifsher 2007)

Quite clearly, we think that the future of prison privatization lies more in the diversification of services than in an extensive transfer of inmates from government facilities. Public authorities at all levels of government will certainly look favourably on the idea of contracting out some of their health and rehabilitation programmes. The rehabilitation function of prisons is being revived in many correctional systems. Lawmakers across the country now admit that with such high recidivism rates, it is time for reform. But to facilitate the re-entry of newly released inmates, unprepared prison systems nationwide will have to invest a lot in new programmes such as education and vocational training. At the same time, cash-strapped prison systems also have to deal with rapidly-mounting medical expenses. This other problem reflects a national trend: partly due to longer sentences, the US prison population is getting older and older. In years to come, record numbers of greying inmates suffering from chronic and geriatric illnesses will need expensive health care. The private prison corporations will probably want to tap these two huge market opportunities for the future development of their activities.

References

Austin, J. and Coventry, G. (2001), *Emerging Issues on Privatized Prisons* (Washington, DC: Bureau of Justice Assistance, US Department of Justice).
Beckett, K. and Sasson, T. (2005), *The Politics of Injustice: Crime and Punishment in America* (Thousand Oaks, CA: Sage).
Bowers, G.A. (2004), 'Dealing with the Devil: Colorado's Private Prison Experience', *Inside Justice* 4:5, <http://www.insidejustice.org/justice-0405.htm>

Bowman, G., Hakim, S. and Seidenstat, P. (eds) (2002), *Privatizing the United States Justice System* (Jefferson, NC: Mc Farland).
Bureau of Justice Statistics (2005), *Prison and jail inmates at Midyear 2004* (Washington, DC: Bureau of Justice, US Department of Justice).
Butterfield, F. (2002), 'Inmate Go Free to Help States Reduce Deficits', *New York Times*, 19 December.
Cheung, A. (2004), *Prison Privatization and the Use of Incarceration* (Washington, DC: The Sentencing Project).
Clark, J.L. (1998), *Report to the Attorney General: Inspection and Review of Northeast Ohio Correctional Center* (Washington, DC: Attorney General's Office).
Clear T.R. (1994), *Harm in American Penology* (Albany, NY: State University of New York Press).
Coffey, H.J. (2002), *Private Corrections Industry, Beds and Cons: Changing Dynamics, Areas of Potential Growth* (New York: Morgan Lewis Githens and Ahn, Inc.).
Corrections Corporation of America, <http://www.correctionscorp.com/aboutcca.html>, accessed September 2005.
Crary, D. (2005), 'Private Prisons Experience Business Surge', *ABC News*, 30 July.
Crowder, C. (2004), 'Resistance to private prison is strong', *The Birmingham News*, 28 October.
Darrell, G. and Beck, A. (1995), *Prisoners in 1994* (Washington, DC: Bureau of Justice Statistics, US Department of Justice, Office of Justice Programs).
Donziger, S.R. (1995), *The Real War on Crime* (New York: HarperPerennial).
Families Against Mandatory Minimums, <http://www.famm.org>, accessed September 2005.
Gifford S. (2002), *Justice Expenditure and Employment in the United States, 1999* (Washington, DC: Bureau of Justice Statistics, US Department of Justice, Office of Justice Programs).
Greene, J. (2001), 'Bailing out Private Jails', *The American Prospect*, 10 September.
Harrison, P. and Beck, A. (2003), *Prisoners in 2002* (Washington, DC: Bureau of Justice Statistics, US Department of Justice, Office of Justice Programs).
Harrison, P. and Beck, A. (2004), *Prisoners in 2003* (Washington, DC: Bureau of Justice Statistics, US Department of Justice, Office of Justice Programs).
Harrison, P. and Beck, A. (2006), *Prisoners in 2005* (Washington, DC: Bureau of Justice Statistics, US Department of Justice, Office of Justice Programs).
Irwin, J. and Austin, J. (2001), *It's About Time: America's Imprisonment Binge* (Belmon, CA: Wadsworth).
Jacobson, M. (2005), *Downsizing Prisons* (New York: New York University Press).
King, R.S. (2008), *The State of Sentencing 2007* (Washington, DC: The Sentencing Project).
King, R.S., Mauer, M. and Huling T. (2003), *Big Prisons, Small Towns: Prison Economics in Rural America* (Washington, DC: The Sentencing Project).
Langan, P. and Levin, D. (2002), *Recidivism of Prisoners Released in 1994* (Washington, DC: Bureau of Justice Statistics, US Department of Justice, Office of Justice Programs).
Lifsher, M. (2007), 'Increase in Inmates Opens Door to Private Prisons', *New York Times*, 24 August.
Mattera, P., Khan, M. and Nathan, S. (2003), *Corrections Corporation of America: A Critical Look at its First Twenty Years* (Charlotte, NC: Grassroots Leadership).
McCrie, R. (1992), 'Three Centuries of Criminal Justice privatization in the United States', in Bowman, Hakim and Seidenstat (eds).
McDonald, D. (1992), 'Private Penal Institutions', in Michael Tonry (ed.).

McDonald, D. and Patten, C. (2003), *Governments' Management of Private Prisons* (Cambridge, MA: Abt Associates).

National Advisory Commission on Criminal Justice Standards and Goals (1973), *A National Strategy to Reduce Crime: Final Report* (Washington DC: Government Printing Office).

Prison Legal News (2001), 'CCA Medical Cost-Saving Contract Unconstitutional', July.

Sabol, W., Harrison, P. and Couture, H. (2007), *Prisoners in 2006* (Washington, DC: Bureau of Justice Statistics, US Department of Justice, Office of Justice Programs).

Tabarrok, A. (2003), *Changing the Guard* (Oakland, CA: The Independent Institute).

The Pew Center on the States (2008), *One in 100: Behind Bars in America 2008* (Washington, DC: The Pew Charitable Trust).

Tonry, M. (ed.) (1992), *Crime and Justice: A Review of Research*, vol. 16 (Chicago: University of Chicago Press).

Vindevogel, F. (2007), 'La remise en question des politiques pénales ultra-répressives', *Revue Française d'Etudes Américaines*, 113.

Wilhelm, D.F. and Turner, N.R. (2002), *Is the Budget Crisis Changing the Way We Look at Sentencing and Incarceration?* (Washington, DC: Vera Institute of Justice).

Wool, J. and Stemen, D. (2004), *Changing Fortunes or Changng Attitude? Sentencing and Corrections Reforms in 2003* (Washington, DC: Vera Institute of Justice).

PART 4
Health

Chapter 8

AIDS Prevention by Non-Governmental Organizations: Inside the American and French Responses

Laura Hobson Faure, Carla Dillard Smith, Gloria Lockett and Benjamin P. Bowser

In both the United States and France, the AIDS epidemic began among gay and bisexual men. But it has now expanded to those who inject drugs with potentially contaminated needles – injection drug users (IDUs) – and those who engage in sex without condoms and with multiple partners – sexual high-risk behaviours (SRBs). In the United States, the most rapid increase in diagnosed AIDS cases is among IDUs and SRBs in African-American inner city and rural communities and in France among IDUs and heterosexuals, often of foreign descent, in central cities and their surrounding suburbs (CDC 2001, IVS 2004). Gay and bisexual men are a declining proportion of those infected by HIV as the proportion of HIV risk takers among African-Americans and immigrants increases (CDC 2003, Corbie-Smith et al. 2002, IVS 2004). Those at highest risk of contracting HIV in both the US and France are very difficult for public health authorities to reach and to get to change their behaviours. In the United States, the first difficulty is getting through their ethnic cultures and suspicion of authorities to reach high-risk takers and, secondly, they are hard to reach because their existence is often denied within their ethnic culture and communities, where they are stigmatized and hidden (Corbie-Smith et al. 2002). While these factors may also play a role in France, French public health authorities have been slow to recognize the specific prevention needs of immigrant populations and have only recently addressed the over-representation of foreigners in its AIDS epidemic (Fassin 1999). In order to respond to this alarming situation, public health authorities in both countries have come to depend on local and national non-governmental organizations (NGOs) in order to prevent HIV among hard-to-reach populations and help those who are infected with the virus.

This chapter will focus on the work of California Prevention Education Project (Cal-Pep), an American non-governmental organization that works with the African American population in the Bay Area of California, while comparing this organization to AIDS organizations in the Paris region of France.[1] The goal of this undertaking is to highlight the similarities and differences present in the non-governmental response to AIDS in both France and the United States. By focusing on minorities such as African-Americans in the United States and immigrants in France, we hope to shed light on how historical and sociological differences in the construction of race and ethnicity in these countries influence the fight against AIDS, while providing concrete examples of the relationship between non-governmental AIDS prevention organizations and government.

In the first section of this chapter, we will focus on Cal-Pep, and use public health behavioural research to demonstrate the need for non-governmental organizations to conduct AIDS prevention work among minority populations in the United States. We will then address non-governmental AIDS organizations in France to highlight the tensions specific to the French epidemic. In the second part of this chapter we will focus on the relationship between the NGO and the local and national governments of the United States and France. Without claiming to be comprehensive, we hope to inform the reader of the complexity of this relationship, and will concentrate on the funding strategies of AIDS prevention NGOs. We will conclude this chapter with a comparative analysis of the French and American cases.

AIDS Prevention in the United States

The California Prevention Education Project (Cal-Pep) based in Oakland, California demonstrates how to effectively reach and get behaviour change from IDUs and SRBs within the San Francisco-Oakland Bay Area African-American communities (Lockett et al. 2004). Cal-Pep's founder is an African American woman, Ms Gloria Lockett, who was once a prostitute who later worked in women's health issues prior to the AIDS epidemic. She was appalled at the lack of response to the AIDS epidemic in the poorest and most heavily impacted communities. She took direct action by starting Cal-Pep in 1984, whose primary intervention is street outreach, a technique in which community health outreach workers engage sex workers, IDUs and more recently, high risk adolescents on the streets at night where they congregate. Cal-Pep provides condoms and bleach kits to clean used needles, exchanges used needles for clean ones with IDUs, provides social service and health information and referrals, does prevention education, HIV testing, and health screenings from a mobile van. They have had a risk-reduction treatment programme for actively drug-using women, and currently have a case-management project for drug users who have recently been released for prison and a project for sexually-active drug using adolescents and young

---

1 This method will allow us to evoke specific French AIDS organizations when relevant. We recognize that our comparative method runs the risk of oversimplifying a rich and multilayered response to the HIV/AIDS epidemic in France. Observations on the French situation are based on research conducted by Laura Hobson Faure (2000, 2001, 2005) as well as secondary sources.

adults. Cal-Pep is right on the front-line of prevention services to socially and economically marginal African-Americans and others at risk of HIV infection in Oakland and San Francisco.

Why a Group Rather than Individual Focus?

Cal-Pep and other US agencies like it are reaching hidden, HIV high-risk groups in ethnic communities and demonstrating that they can reduce their HIV risks. These organizations work with individuals to impact groups. They do so because HIV is passed from person-to-person as a consequence of social relations and interactions that are not unique. HIV risk-taking behaviours are defined, learned, sustained and repeated thousands of times in multiple cultural contexts – first because risk-takers are members of ethnic communities and second because they are members of stigmatized groups within their ethnic communities. The most effective prevention requires getting these hidden and stigmatized groups to change their social norms to favour and reinforce HIV low-risk behaviours rather than HIV high-risk behaviours (Bowser 2002, CDC 2003). In doing so thousands of social relations are changed and many more individuals change their behaviour as a consequence of group change and pressure. Working to change group culture and norms is also more effective and efficient than trying to change one individual at a time (Emmons 2002). Both the pace of a rapidly moving AIDS epidemic and group pressure to continue engaging in HIV high-risk behaviours can easily overwhelm individual resolve to do otherwise.

Reaching hidden and stigmatized groups within ethnic sub-cultures is work that government cannot even begin to imagine doing. The first pre-condition for effective prevention within hidden groups is to educate them about HIV/AIDS and how to prevent infection (Ellickson 1995). But government-sponsored public service announcements are ineffective in reaching African-Americans and other minority IDUs and SRBs. This is not only because ethnic groups in the United States have distinct subcultures and communities. It is also because of past government abuse and neglect of social service and health needs among African-Americans in the South prior to 1965 and in urban ghettoes since then (McBride 1991; Byrd and Clayton 2002). In addition, generic public service messages do not address specific African-American beliefs about the drug and AIDS epidemics. Many African-Americans believe that heroin and crack cocaine have been brought to and sustained in black communities by the US government, that AIDS is primarily a white gay men's disease and that the AIDS virus was created by the US government to eliminate African peoples (Thomas and Quinn 1991, Corbie-Smith et al. 2002). For these reasons, many African-Americans view government sponsored public health efforts with deep suspicion.

Mistrust of government then compromises the second and third precondition for effective HIV prevention with groups: 1) those at risk must embrace the preventive prescription at an emotional or affective level; and 2) they must develop their own social norms that reinforce preventive practices such as using condoms and cleaning injection equipment (Bandura 1977). No government or external agency can get people to internalize the need for social and individual change, nor can outsiders define new and low HIV-risk behaviours for a cultural group. They have to do these things for themselves; outsiders can only support their efforts. Additional barriers to effective HIV prevention among African-Americans are the US government's refusal to provide adequate job training, health care and education in the inner cities as well as federal opposition to needle exchanges, inadequate funding of drug treatment on demand, and the lack of universal health care (Jaynes and Williams 1989, Normand et al. 1995). These are barriers because they further drive African-Americans and others at high-risk of HIV infection away from civil society and health services.

The Tradition of Non-Governmental Response in the United States

There is a long tradition in the United States for private citizens and associations addressing social needs especially where government has failed or is not trusted. This tradition is very well developed among African-Americans, as illustrated by Cal-Pep. AIDS prevention and advocacy organizations have emerged in African American communities because of the ineffective response of the federal government to the HIV/AIDS epidemic among African-Americans. They have also emerged because of the slow response to the epidemic by traditional black churches, which view HIV risk behaviours as immoral and HIV high risk-takers as outside their faith and congregations. Civil rights organizations have also been slow to respond because of their social class bias against lower class drug abusers and others who are not seen as deserving and respectable examples of the race. Non-governmental organizations (NGOs) such as Cal-Pep have been quick to mobilize, have developed ways to access and work closely with HIV risk-takers, have gained their trust, and have come to advocate for them and to know their issues and concerns.

The Fight Against AIDS in France: A Diverse Mobilization

The history of the non-governmental response against AIDS in France has been studied in numerous works (Pollak 1988, 1990, Hirsch 1991, Pollak 1993, Martel 2000, Pinell et al. 2002). In the Paris region, one observes that the first organizations, which resulted from the mobilization of HIV positive individuals and their loved ones, now co-exist alongside responses against AIDS from more traditional sectors of French civil society.[2] The Catholic Church has established its

---

2   When one speaks of AIDS organizations in France there is a tendency to focus on the organizations that have developed from a self-help experience, which was largely driven by a mobilization of male homosexuals (Pollak 1993: 282). Historical accounts and social science research in France have addressed organizations such as 'Vaincre le Sida' (established in 1983), AIDES (established in 1984), Arcat-Sida (established in 1985), and ACT-UP (established in 1989). One can attribute the 'coverage' of these organizations

own AIDS organizations; underfunded public hospitals have also used this legal structure as a means of accessing additional funding; and medical personnel has united to address their specific needs This latter group of organizations represents the flexibility of the 1901 French law, which legally recognized the structure of the NGO (*association* in French).[3]

In a similar pattern to the United States, the epidemic has changed in France, moving from homosexual to heterosexual transmission patterns, attacking new minority and socially disadvantaged populations. For example, among the AIDS cases that were declared between 1995 and 2001, 15 per cent were among foreign individuals. Yet foreigners made up only 5 per cent of the French population in 1999. In the year 2000, the percentage of foreigners among AIDS cases rose to 27 per cent (Delfraissy 2002). More recent data on HIV cases show that 57 per cent of the cases transmitted through heterosexual contact were among foreigners (IVS 2004).

The changing epidemic poses new challenges for existing NGOs. Many of these organizations were founded by a mobilization of homosexuals and based their responses on this specific experience with the illness; these organizations and others rely heavily on volunteer work (which requires individuals with time and resources), setting up a situation where the users of a NGO belong to a different social class than its volunteers. One volunteer from a Parisian AIDS agency explains this conflict:

> The majority of our organization is not gay anymore, there are a lot of third-world women. What can I offer to a Sub-Saharan African woman with HIV? I feel out of place, I cannot help her. But, it has to evolve ... The volunteers are all still gay and HIV– and the participants are not – [they are] Africans, drug users. Maybe there should be more of these people [volunteering and working], but where does that leave me? …. I'm not equipped to help these people. In the training they should say what it is, up-front, that only a few gay men ... who is better equipped to help the Africans? Other Africans, just like I have the understanding for a gay with HIV. You know how that person feels and it takes that from a volunteer. Or, you go to your doctor or your social worker and you get professional help. (Hobson 2000: 53)

to the fact that they were the first organizations to respond to HIV, yet it can also be attributed to the fact that a large number of intellectuals were founding members of these groups (Hirsch 1991: 38). These individuals facilitated and sometimes conducted their own research on their organizations. The important presence of members of the 'elite' also helps to explain the tremendous progress these organizations have made in gaining recognition from the French government, both for the HIV cause and their ability to provide services. For example, the organization AIDES speaks of an 'equal partnership' with the French government (Steffen 1992: 247).

3   On this specifically French structure, see Barthélemy (2000).

AIDS among Foreigners: the Need for Recognition and Prevention

The republican tradition of colour blindness in France casts a shadow over our ability to assess its AIDS epidemic as it relates to larger inequalities, such as institutionalized racism: it is currently illegal for the French government to collect statistical data based on race, religion and ethnicity (Gilloire 2000). In the meantime, Jean-Marie Le Pen's extreme right-wing National Front Party has referred to HIV positive individuals as '*sidaïques*' (a play on '*judaïque*', used frequently in the anti-Semitic language of Vichy France) and has suggested that these individuals be placed in '*sidatoriums*', an indirect reference to the crematoriums of Nazi-occupied Europe (Steffen 1992: 239). The public health establishment of France has been wary of releasing any statistics that could cast a negative light on the populations that are targeted by the discriminatory logic of the extreme right. As a result, there has been a late recognition of the over-representation of foreign individuals among reported AIDS cases. The first well-developed statistical analysis of the epidemic among foreigners was released in 1999 (Savignoni et al. 1999). The fear of associating AIDS with immigration has slowed the government response to adapting prevention campaigns and attributing specific funding.

The reluctance to recognize the growing AIDS epidemic among foreigners on the part of French public health authorities and in French culture in general has greatly affected prevention efforts towards minority populations in France (Fassin 1999). If late in coming (the first response was in 1996: the creation of a section on prevention for 'migrants' at the Centre régional d'information et de prévention du sida), there has been a mobilization of AIDS organizations in immigrant communities as well as outreach towards these communities in the first generation of AIDS organizations. A new at-risk group, 'migrants', has been identified. However, in the Paris region, organizations from within immigrant communities have been slow to gain the credibility needed for funding from public health authorities. Because the first generation of AIDS organizations have a certain standing with the government, it is common for them to advocate on behalf of 'migrants' and to make efforts to include them in their organizations. Some criticize these organizations for diverting funding from smaller, less established organizations that may have more access to and more appropriate services for 'migrants'.

Tension surrounding funding is also present in the United States, where AIDS organizations must compete with each other for limited sources of public and private monies. We will now explore the local and federal funding situation of Cal-Pep to highlight certain aspects of the relationship of the organization to government.

Local Funding: An American Example

Cal-Pep and community-based organizations like it all over the US are funded by a combination of local, state and federal funds. Cal-Pep does front-line prevention work at times and in places that the Alameda County Public Health Department (ACPHD), based in Oakland, cannot. For example, the ACPHD civil service contracts prevent them from hiring people without educational backgrounds but who are most knowledgeable of the high-risk groups and their cultures and who can best establish rapport with them. ACPHD staff cannot work late nights when HIV risk-takers are most accessible (Bowser and Hill 2007). Furthermore, this is not work that can be done through volunteers; services must be provided on a regular basis at a given time and place year-round regardless of weather. This can be very dangerous work and requires especially skilled and experienced staff. Non-governmental agencies such as Cal-Pep are subcontracted to do this prevention work. Given agencies like Cal-Pep's front-line role in the AIDS epidemic, one would think that their funding would be very stable, especially since independent evaluations have found them to be very effective.

The fact is funding for organizations such as Cal-Pep is constantly in question as a direct reflection of the ambivalence of the ACPHD for the populations at risk of AIDS and for those who serve and advocate for them. Street-identified, low-income African-Americans, most of whom have criminal records, are viewed by local authorities as taking scarce public health resources away from more 'worthy' and 'deserving' issues. Prenatal infant care, heart disease and stroke prevention, smoking and cancer reduction are less complex, can be done for less money and involve tax paying, 'deserving' citizens who appreciate and expect good public health services (Braithwaite and Taylor 1992).

In self-defence, NGOs such as Cal-Pep minimize local funder's control over them by having staff serve on county and state advisory committees. While non-profit governmentally funded organizations may not engage in political advocacy, individual staff may exercise their constitutional rights to do so. Being highly visible and active in one's community makes any negative ACPHD decision regarding one's programme highly visible and potentially embarrassing to public health authorities. Also one must cultivate political allies in local government who oversee the public health budgets and who hold county health officials accountable. The necessity to minimize local arbitrariness regarding funds puts constant pressure on NGOs to diversify their funding. They cannot just do their prevention work; they must also do political work and constantly seek new funding in order to simply do their 'front-line' work.

The State and National Puzzle

In the US the federal government is the primary funder of local HIV/AIDS prevention efforts. It does so through complex 'block grants' to State governments, which in turn fund county (local) governments. There are federal guidelines that specify that grants should be spent specifically for the purpose it was given, but these guidelines are poorly enforced. When it comes to AIDS prevention among people of colour, the federal government increasingly expects more and more primary funding to come from each state. The state's response is that it does not have the money and expects more from the federal government. Furthermore, whatever is the federal share of AIDS prevention funds, very little of it actually gets to the counties with the greatest need. There is a state policy for which county (local government) gets funding and how much. Counties with the highest proportion of white population get the highest per capita level of AIDS funding; counties with the highest proportion of black populations and highest HIV rates get the lowest per capita AIDS funding. So, rural white counties with few AIDS cases get higher per capita AIDS funding than do urban black counties with out-of-control AIDS epidemics. Ultimately, due to federal block grant formulas and politics very few prevention dollars make it to organizations like Cal-Pep to do street-based HIV/AIDS prevention work.

It was mentioned that Cal-Pep has had a treatment programme for actively using women and currently has a case management project for recently released ex-offenders and for sexually active adolescents and young adults. None of these advancements in prevention are funded by block grant monies. These are all directly funded by the federal Centers for Substance Abuse and Treatment (SAMHSA). The purpose of these grants is to develop effective and innovative prevention and treatment practices that are to then be continued by local and state funding. To our knowledge, not a single one of these projects in the Bay Area has been funded by state or local monies after federal funding ended. States do not have AIDS prevention as a primary agenda and therefore have very little money for it. As a result, instead of improving AIDS prevention work, these grants destabilize the organization because staff and office space must be rapidly increased to do the projects then let go when the project ends. The federal government has provided little leadership and funding to states, even under previous Democratic administrations. Since George W. Bush has become president, applicants for federal prevention monies have been warned to not propose projects that involve condom use, services to gay and bisexual men or sexual education to adolescents. In effect, national AIDS prevention is being moved away from public health to reflect the moral and ideological views of the current administration.

The fact is the US federal government is putting major resources into a biomedical solution to AIDS and has abandoned any hope of preventing the spread of AIDS at the local level among minorities. There is now more money in researching AIDS and monitoring the progress of the epidemic than in preventing it.[4] Ultimately, the large numbers of HIV-positive African-Americans in whom infections could be prevented will be very useful in the upcoming clinical trials for AIDS vaccines in development. Indeed, federal guidelines have been established to increase the participation of minorities, especially African Americans, in clinical trials in response to research showing significant racial disparities in such endeavours (King Jr 2002). Ironically, the new funds to which organizations like

---

4 The National Institute on Drug Abuse 2002 and 2004 budget reports list a number of clinical and biomedical research initiatives done through specific research centers and other research supports. Prevention is mentioned as 'on-going' and done through partnership with state governments. There is no center or other research budget line devoted specifically to prevention. We can infer that prevention is not a priority because its budget expenditure is one of the best-kept secrets in NIDA (NIDA 2002, NIDA 2004).

Cal-Pep have access are to develop protocol for the inclusion of HIV-positive African-Americans in large national clinical trials. Organizations like Cal-Pep have no way to pressure federal and state governments to prioritize prevention over research. This would require proactive leadership from national political and church leaders. With regard to AIDS, neither is forthcoming. So as African-Americans become an increasing proportion of those infected with AIDS in the United States, the national response is increasingly one of traditional benign neglect and racism.

While NGOs in the United States have less and less hope of finding the resources they need to serve their populations, the relationship between non-governmental AIDS prevention organizations and the French government appears to be better defined, in spite of recent budget cuts.

French Non-Governmental AIDS Organizations and the Government

Addressing the relationship between French AIDS organizations and local and national governments is not an easy task, because this relationship varies according to each organization. The issue of funding provides a means to better understanding this relationship.

France seems to represent a middle ground between the complex funding regimes in the United States (where organizations must 'diversify their portfolios' by seeking both public and private funding, from multiple foundations and government sources), and other countries of northern Europe, where the government may fund the majority of the budget of a few large organizations, leaving little room for new voices. For example, in the mid-1980s the German organization *Deutsche AIDS-HILFE* received 90 per cent of its budget from the German government, while the French organization, AIDES, received 39 per cent of its budget from public sources (Pollak 1993: 289).

French AIDS organizations may seek funding from both private foundations and public sources. Public sources reflect the centralized nature of the French State: the *Direction Générale de la Santé* (DGS), part of the Ministry of Health and Social Protection, determines the national priorities in the fight against AIDS. The DGS priorities are put into action by the National Institute of Health Prevention and Education (the INPES), which administrates grants to AIDS organizations throughout France. Certain specific problems and at-risk populations receive national priority and may seek what is called 'decentralized' funding, which comes through regional and departmental (similar to county) public health offices (the DRASS and the DDASS). Organizations may also seek funding from city officials, such as the mayor's office, but unlike the US, there are no city offices of public health. Other national governmental offices provide funding for specific populations, such as the Fonds d'Action Sociale, which provides financial aid to NGOs that help foreigners. While there are multiple sources of public funding, AIDS organizations are facing diminishing grants: the public budget dropped by 20 per cent between 2002 and 2003 (Sidaction 2003: 15). A third, private source of funding is Sidaction, formerly known as Ensemble Contre le Sida. This organization utilizes well-known public figures to operate a unified fundraising campaign that is used to support AIDS research and NGOs. In 2003, Sidaction supported 86 AIDS organizations throughout France (Sidaction 2003: 18).

In the context of diminishing funding, all French AIDS organizations are at risk of being considered superfluous by the government. How do they account for their activities and prove that they work? Empirical data on the outcomes of funded programmes, as well as budgetary transparency, while increasingly important to securing funding, are largely absent in the annual activity reports of French AIDS organizations. Evaluation techniques are not widespread, making it difficult to prove the efficiency of prevention efforts. Because the French world of HIV/AIDS is centralized and relatively small, certain government officials may play a protective role for some organizations. This informal, reputation-based construction of credibility makes it harder for new organizations to receive and keep funding.

Conclusion: Comparing France and the United States

Fundamental differences separate the fight against AIDS in France and the United States. These differences are often linked to the different constructions of race and ethnicity in these countries. In the United States it is largely accepted that HIV/AIDS is an illness that disproportionately affects people of colour due to institutionalized and direct forms of racism. The only way to begin such an analysis in France is to examine the cases of foreigners, who are often immigrants from former French colonies and people of colour. While we know where these individuals come from (and we can then extrapolate a link to France's colonial past), the current statistics cannot distinguish the French child of immigrants from the rest of the French HIV-positive population. When one considers the French AIDS epidemic through an American lens, we can imagine a situation similar to the US: an epidemic disproportionately affecting people of colour, linked to and exacerbated by past and current inequalities. While this is an accepted truth for American AIDS prevention organizations such as Cal-Pep and is fundamental to understanding its specific response to AIDS among African-Americans, this cannot be statistically proven in France and therefore this discourse remains somewhat taboo.

Whereas the United States embraces the 'particular' and has mobilized against AIDS according to group identities, (motivated by past-discrimination and the need to 'take care of one's own'), this is less true for France. For example, for the French organization AIDES, individuals mobilized in the name of the *malade*, the sick individual (Defert 1994). Social and ethnic diversity in the French AIDS epidemic creates a tension between the particular and the universal that one can observe throughout French society, especially in current debates on immigration and secularism. In this debate, the 'particular', represented by the group unit, threatens the traditional 'universal' French political model in which only the individual citizen is politically recognized by the state. Some fear that openly recognizing group identities within the French population would threaten this privileged relationship between the individual and the state (Schnapper 1991, Steffen 1992). This conflict is lived out in the fight against AIDS around the issue of creating special prevention tools and programmes for migrants.

Beyond these differences surrounding diversity, one notes a historical difference in volunteer work in the French and American mobilization. While NGOs in both countries rely heavily on this form of solidarity, sociologists have demonstrated the desire on the part of French AIDS organizations to break with past forms of assistance to the sick and needy. In France, where volunteerism (*le bénevolat*) was associated with bourgeois (and feminine) practices, the English term 'volunteer' was chosen to replace the French term '*bénévole*'. This can be contrasted with the American mobilization against AIDS, which utilized the momentum from the pre-existing gay rights movement, and also stressed historically American traditions such as volunteerism (Patton 1990: 21).

Other observations stem from the structural differences in the involvement of government in welfare (health, social services) and the consequent funding climate in the United States and France. American AIDS organizations have developed to fill perceived, and very real, gaps in state and federal social services and medical care. The beginning of the AIDS epidemic coincided with the Reagan Administration's dismantling of many social programmes. The later attack on welfare and its replacement with Temporary Aid for Needy Families (limiting an individual's access to aid to five years) has ended any belief in a social safety net. Under these conditions, AIDS organizations have stepped in to save as many lives as possible, essentially becoming the private contractors of an absent state. The role of the French AIDS NGO is entirely different: instead of being seen as replacing the state, the NGO has been seen as a complementary partner. Public Health authorities and NGOs seem to agree that AIDS organizations are necessary for reaching key populations, linking them to state services, and controlling the epidemic. However, NGOs remain vigilant because they do not want to replace public benefits, but improve access to them. It is also accepted that AIDS organizations have a role to play in a delicate 'checks and balances' system: they should challenge the state, propose new solutions, and work as laboratories for new programmes. This perception of the role of NGOs is exemplified in the following quote from the above-mentioned organization Sidaction: 'In 2003, Sidaction could only slightly compensate for the disengagement of the State. While it has been able to save some structures that were shamefully abandoned, this is not its role. Its job is to innovate' (Sidaction 2003: 15).[5]

Over time, some organizations have taken on new duties, such as managing state-sponsored apartments for HIV-positive individuals. Along with a decreasing state budget, this can be seen as a slow (and dangerous) shift towards a more American vision of AIDS organizations.

Fierce competition has forced American NGOs to prove why their services are cost-effective, better, with greater relevance to the targeted population. Programme

---

5 Our translation of the following: 'En 2003, Sidaction n'a pu que faiblement compenser ce désengagement des pouvoirs publics. Mais s'il lui est arrivé de sauver des structures honteusement lâchées, là n'est pas son rôle. Car sa vocation est d'innover.'

evaluators and grant writers are formal positions in almost all (funded) AIDS organizations in the United States. Statistics are taken systematically, and grant writing occupies a large portion of time and energy in organizational life. These activities are still not practised on a wide scale in France, although exceptions exist.[6]

In addition to these structural differences from French NGOs, vocabulary in American NGOs reflects their roles as 'private contractors' and has been borrowed from business management: 'clients', 'efficiency', and 'units of time'. (In France, one speaks of 'members' or 'users' of an organization, which sends a very different message.) Many American organizations have adapted the case management system as a cheaper alternative to social work, which relies on case managers, who do not need a Masters degree and can therefore be paid less than a social worker. In this system, 'clients' are linked to resources by their case manager, and units of time spent with the client are measured. This is for funding purposes, as each moment of the case manager's day must be accounted for. They also must evaluate their client's progress, so that one may say: 'with X units of time, we saw a reduction in high-HIV risk activity.'

In both France and the United States, it appears that funding opportunities depend on the social and cultural capital of the organization. This means that grass-roots organizations, such as Cal-Pep, which hire from the communities they serve in order to reinforce peer-based help, must develop the skill of presenting to two very different audiences: their funders and their clients. The ability of an AIDS organization to 'speak' to two (or more) audiences is largely determinant for its survival. The struggle for funding can take AIDS organizations away from their original goals, and de-legitimize the organization in the eyes of its clients or users. Caught between the needs of their users and the requirements of their funders, AIDS prevention organizations must continually reinvent themselves in order to survive. Yet at what point will larger structural constraints overtake the life-saving efforts of these organizations?

References

Bandura, A. (1977), *Social Learning Theory* (Englewood Cliffs, NJ: Prentice Hall).
Barthélemy, M. (2000), *Associations: Un nouvel âge de la participation?* (Paris: Presses de Sciences Po).
Berkman, L.F. and Kawachi, I. (eds) (2002), *Social Epidemiology* (New York: Oxford University Press).
Bowser, B. (2002), 'The social dimensions of the AIDS epidemic: a sociology of the AIDS epidemic', *International Journal of Sociology and Social Policy* 22:4–6, 1–20.
Bowser, B. and Hill, B. (2007), 'Rapid Assessment in Oakland: HIV, Race, Class and Bureaucracy', in Bowser et al. (eds).
Bowser, B., Mishra S., Reback, C. and Lemp, G. (eds) (2004), *Preventing Aids: Community-Science Collaborations* (New York: The Haworth Press).

---

6 The 2004 annual report of Ikambere shows a strong use of statistics (Ikambere 2004).

Bowser, B., Quimby, E. and Singer, M. (eds) (2007), *Communities Assessing Their Aids Epidemics: Results of the Rapid Assessment of HIV/Aids in US Cities* (Lanham, MD: Lexington Books).
Braithwaite, R. and Taylor, S. (eds) (1992), *Health Issues in the Black Community* (San Francisco: Jossey-Bass Publishers).
Byrd, W. M. and Clayton, L. (2002), *An American Health Dilemma: Race, Medicine, and Health Care in the United States 1900–2000. Volume II* (New York: Routledge).
CDC (2001), 'HIV/AIDS -United States, 1981–2000', *Morbidity and Mortality Weekly Report* 50:21, 430–433.
CDC (2003), 'Advancing HIV Prevention: New Strategies for a Changing Epidemic – United States, 2003', *Morbidity and Mortality Weekly Report* 52:15, 329–32.
Coombs, R. and Ziedonis, D. (eds) (1995) *Handbook on Drug Prevention* (Boston: Allyn and Bacon).
Corbie-Smith, G., Thomas, S.B. and St George, D.M. (2002), 'Distrust, race, and research', *Archives of Internal Medicine* 162:21, 2458–64.
Defert, D. (1994), 'Le malade du sida est un réformateur social', *Esprit* 203, 100–11.
Delfraissy, J.-F. (ed.) (2002), *Prise en charge des personnes infectées par le VIH: Recommandations du groupe d'experts, médicine-sciences* (Paris: Flammarion).
Ellickson, P. (1995), 'Schools', in Coombs and Ziedonis (eds).
Emmons, K. (2002), 'Health Behaviors in a Social Context', in Berkman and Kawachi (eds).
Fassin, D. (1999), 'L'indicible et l'impensé: la "question immigrée" dans les politiques du sida dans les politiques du sida', *Sciences Sociales et Santé* 17:4, 5–35.
Gilloire, A. (2000), 'Les catégories d'"origine" et de "nationalité" dans les statistiques du sida', *Hommes et migrations* 1225, 73–82.
Hirsch, E. (1991), *Aides Solidaires* (Paris: Editions du Cerf).
Hobson, L. (2000), 'Les associations Congreso De Latinos Unidos et Aides Ile-de-France: une comparaison internationale de deux réponses associatives dans la lutte contre le sida', Master's degree thesis, Université de Paris VIII.
Hobson, L. (2001), 'La construction de l'altérité dans sept associations de lutte contre le sida en région parisienne', Diploma of Higher Studies thesis, Université de Paris VII.
Hobson Faure, L. (2005), 'L'étranger séropostif: prise en charge et constructions de l'altérité en milieu associatif en France', *Face à Face, Regards sur la Santé* 7, 103–19.
Ikambere (2004), *Rapport d'activité de 2004* (St Denis: Ikambere).
IVS (2004), 'Premiers résultats du nouveau dispositif de surveillance de l'infection à VIH et situation du sida au 30 septembre 2003', *Bulletin Epidémiologique Hebdomadaire, Institut de Veille Sanitaire* 24–25, 102–8.
Jaynes, G. and Williams Jr, R. (1989), *A Common Destiny: Blacks and American Society,* (Washington, DC: National Academy Press).
King Jr, T.E., (2002), 'Racial Disparities in Clinical Trials', *New England Journal of Medicine* 346, 1400–402.
Kirp, D.L. and Bayer, R. (eds) (1992), *Aids in the Industrialized Democracies* (New Brunswick, NJ: Rutgers University Press).
Lockett, G., Dillard-Smith, C. and Bowser, B. (2004), 'Preventing AIDS among Injectors and Sex Workers. Preventing AIDS: Community-Science Collaborations', in Bowser et al. (eds).
Martel, F. (2000), *Le rose et le noir. Les homosexuels en France depuis 1968* (Paris: Editions du Seuil).
McBride, D. (1991), *From TB to Aids: Epidemics among Urban Blacks since 1900* (Albany, NY: State University of New York Press).

Normand, J., Vlahov, D. and Moses, L. (eds) (1995), *Preventing HIV Transmission: The Role of Sterile Needles and Bleach* (Washington, DC: National Academy Press).

NIDA (2002), Fiscal Year 2002 Budget Information, <www.nida.nih.gov/funding/budget02.html>, accessed 12 March 2008.

NIDA (2004), Fiscal Year 2004 Budget Information, <www.nida.nih.gov/funding/budget04.html>, accessed 12 March 2008.

Patton, C. (1990), *Inventing Aids* (New York: Routledge, Chapman and Hall, Inc.).

Pinell, P., Broqua, C., de Busscher, P.-O., Jauffret, M. and Thiaudière, C. (2002), *Une Epidémie politique: La lutte contre le sida en France. Science, histoire et société* (Paris: PUF).

Pollak, M. (1988), *Les Homosexuels et le sida: Sociologie d'une épidémie, leçons des choses* (Paris: Editions Métailié).

Pollak, M. (1990), 'Les associations de lutte contre le sida: éléments d'évaluation et de réflexion', *Mire Information* 19, 8–11.

Pollak, M. (1993), *Une identité blessée, Etudes de sociologie et d'histoire* (Paris: Editions de Métailié).

Savignoni, A., Lot, F., Pillonel, J. and Laporte, A. (1999), *Situation du sida dans la population étrangère domiciliée en France* (Saint-Maurice: Institut de Veille Sanitaire).

Schnapper, D. (1991), *La France de l'intégration. Sociologie de la nation en 1990* (Paris: Gallimard, 1991).

Sidaction (2003), *Rapport d'activité de 2003* (Paris: Sidaction).

Steffen, M. (1992), 'France: Social Solidarity and Scientific Expertise', in Kirp and Bayer (eds).

Thomas, S.B. and Quinn, S.C. (1991), 'The Tuskegee Syphilis Study, 1932 to 1972: Implications for HIV Education and AIDS Risk Education Programs in the Black Community', *American Journal of Public Health* 81:11, 1498–506.

PART 5
Education

Chapter 9

Education Management Organizations and For-Profit Education – An Overview and a Case-Study: Philadelphia

Malie Montagutelli

Private companies have been involved in activities related to education and the running of American public schools for a long time. In recent years, however, EMOs, Education Management Organizations (modelled after HMOs, Health Management Organizations), have emerged and expanded, moving surprisingly fast into areas that so far were traditionally placed under the exclusive control of – and operated by – public authorities. Today these new protagonists on the educational scene blur the line separating the public and private spheres. This chapter attempts to assess the impact, the efficiency, and the future of EMOs.

The presence of private companies in public educational establishments, as either partners of public institutions or full protagonists, is nothing new in America. Schools have long been contracting out some of the services that are peripheral to their educational mission, such as the transportation of students to and from school or the operation of cafeterias within the schools. Besides such services, ever since the nineteenth century, companies have commonly participated in the funding of certain school or educational projects, sometimes lavishly, whether by directly donating money or by creating foundations that channel funds to certain educational projects. More recently, some schools and whole districts have hired the services of counseling firms or efficiency experts to help streamline their bureaucracies or increase their efficiency in generally running the schools. Since the 1970s, more and more public establishments have devised various schemes of outright commercialism to bail themselves out of difficult financial situations; they have also called on private companies to provide certain teachings within their curricula, for instance maths courses, or reading methods, or some technological courses. In this last case, these firms may send out their own instructors to the schools or simply sell videos of their courses to be used in class by the school's own teachers.

However, the most recent development has been the intrusion of private companies directly into scholastic establishments, acting as managers and curriculum providers of public schools or owners/managers of private ones.

In this chapter we propose to look at how in some instances private companies have now completely taken over all of the activities involved in the process of providing education: devising curricula, teaching and hiring and training teachers. They have also managed to become an integral part of the public educational institution, albeit with special arrangements. Such expressions as for-profit education, education industry, education companies, edupreneurs, and EMOs have become household words.

There are different degrees of involvement and participation for these private companies, but in any case their presence has created a new, yet to be fully explored – as well as fully understood – environment caused by the interaction and overlapping of the public and the private sectors. In so doing, they are quickly affecting the philosophy underlying education and school policies by introducing new values and changing the way in which people look upon scholastic institutions, whether they be school administrators, parents, teachers – the latter however to a lesser degree, or the public at large. Concretely speaking, by placing schools and the act of teaching within the logic of the market, by integrating schools to the world of business, they introduce notions of competition, accountability, efficiency, new criteria, and new practices. This in turn is profoundly altering the very nature and long-term objectives of education.

Thus we will see what these new practices are and how they affect primary and secondary education, first by assessing what goes on nationally and then by looking more closely at the city of Philadelphia where the experiment being carried on today is the first of its kind in the United States in terms of its scale.

Let us first briefly state the direct origin of the fast development of these practices. They can essentially be traced back to the choices which have consistently been those of the federal government since the late 1980s. Even though the federal government cannot implement reforms to alter the states' institutions, in the field of education it has had a strong influence on school districts and their policies and, since the late 1980s, it has been constantly committed to such notions as choice (for parents), accountability (for schools and teachers) and adaptability (for schools) as the vectors of improvement of education and schools, of excellence in teaching and learning. These objectives have essentially given rise to two schemes, vouchers and charter schools, both of which have contributed to the blurring of the dividing line between public and private education, and have thus encouraged private companies to play a more direct and active role in the field.

In 1994, in his book entitled *Reinventing Education: Entrepreneurship in America's Public Schools*, Louis Gerstner, chairman and CEO of IBM and edupreneur himself, was presenting a new venture in education, that of RJR Nabisco Foundation, called The Next Century Schools. Here is what he had to say in favour of the introduction of such notions as innovation, competition, efficiency, productivity and performance in the schools:

> The lesson is clear: to succeed, public schools must be 'deregulated.' They must be free to meet their objectives. They must be held to high standards, but those standards must be of a special kind: performance standards. Schools must meet the test any high-performance organization must meet: results. And results are not achieved by

bureaucratic regulation. They are achieved by meeting customer requirement by rewards for success and penalties for failure. Market discipline is the key, the ultimate form of accountability. (Gerstner 1991: 22)

In *A Nation Still At Risk*,[1] the manifesto published in April 1998, a group of 37 reformers, who were calling for innovation in education, spoke of the need for more accountability, pluralism, competition, and choice:

> Every state needs a strong charter-school law, the kind that confers true freedom and flexibility on individual schools, that provides every charter school with adequate resources, and that holds it strictly accountable for its results.

At the time, Scott Hamilton, former Associate Commissioner of the Massachusetts Department of Education and one of the co-signers of the manifesto, declared in an interview:

> The charter school concept has the potential to utterly transform public education. Thanks to charter schools, the public is getting used to the idea that a school does not need to be operated directly by government in order to be public.

This has been the philosophy which the federal government has chosen to encourage, one that places public schools in a situation of competition amongst themselves. The latest Education Act signed into law in January 2002, 'No Child Left Behind', promotes the exact same policies. When he signed the bill, President Bush declared:

> We must confront the scandal of illiteracy in America, seen most clearly in high-poverty schools, where nearly 70 percent of 4th graders are unable to read at a basic level. We must address the low standing of America test scores amongst industrialized nations in math and science, the very subjects most likely to affect our future competitiveness. We must focus the spending of federal tax dollars on things that work. Too often we have spent without regard for results, without judging success or failure from year to year. In order for an accountability system to work, there has to be consequences. And I believe one of the most important consequences will be – after a period of time, giving the schools time to adjust and districts time to try different things – if they're failing, that parents ought to be given different options. If children are trapped in schools that will not teach and will not change, there has to be a different consequence.

Under this Act, if a public school does not show progress within a five-year span, it must be restructured or chartered out. Consequently across the nation, there are districts that are now confronted with takeovers of some of their public schools by just about anyone who can come up with a viable project: state authorities, local universities, any type of associations or organizations, foundations or the private companies that now form what is referred to as

---

[1] An allusion to the report entitled *A Nation At Risk* issued in 1983 by the National Commission on Excellence in Education.

the education industry. Thus charter schools provide the perfect vehicle for edupreneurs to enter the educational scene. They are the locus where public and private sectors join together in a somewhat unholy matrimony.

For-profit education in the United States is a relatively new phenomenon that first must be studied from a general standpoint.[2] Companies may provide a variety of educational products: early education and child care, K-12 education, post secondary education, corporate and government training, as well as various consumer products and services, such as on-line teaching for home schoolers or after-school study. In the area of K-12 education, for-profit companies may restructure or manage already existing establishments or create new ones, they may offer a range of services to existing schools, such as technologies, programmes to retrain teachers, and they may also facilitate education at home.[3]

According to a report published in April 1999, the dollar share of the general education market held by for-profit companies represented only about 10 per cent of the whole $ 740 billion education market (that is what the United States yearly spends on education altogether).[4] Approximately 75 per cent of that total amount was collected, controlled and spent by public, governmental institutions of all types,[5] government-run elementary and secondary schools taught, and still do, approximately 88 per cent of all students.[6] On a national scale, in the area of K-12 education, the for-profit industry receives only about 5 per cent of the total amount of dollars actually spent and for-profit schools serve a relatively small population, about 100,000 students in approximately 230 schools.[7] This K-12 sector is in fact the most difficult one within the education industry for companies to enter.

In view of these figures, private companies denounce the hold that public institutions have on the providing of education in the United States, a near-monopoly which they see as unfair competition in a sector of activity which they see as a competitive, potentially lucrative market. In a book published in 1992, former scientist Lewis Perelman (1992: 225) made the following critical commentary on this particular aspect of the situation:

---

2   A lot of the figures mentioned in the next paragraphs come from Carrie Lips (2000) at the Cato Institute. The Cato Institute is a non-profit public policy research foundation based in Washington, DC.

3   Since 1990, homeschooling has been expanding at a rate of 15 per cent per year. As of 1997–1998, there were approximately 1.5 million homeschoolers. See http://www.hslda.org/central/faqs/index.stm.

4   Lips, 2 (Moe et al. 1999: 9).

5   Lips, 4 (Moe et al. 1999: 23).

6   The Department of Education estimated that in 1999 4,724,4000 (approximately 88 per cent) of the 53,215,000 K-12 students were enrolled in public schools.

7   Estimates differ on the number of for-profit schools: Symonds et al. (2000: 66, Molnar et al. 2000: 1) placed that estimate at 200, while Mathews (2000: E1) thought there were 250 for-profit companies running US public schools.

In essence, the public school is America's collective farm. Innovation and productivity are lacking in American education for largely the same reasons they were scarce in Soviet agriculture: absence of competitive market forces.

Regarding charter schools, for-profit companies operate about 10 per cent of the total[8] and it is not very easy at present for them to start or to expand their operations. First of all, because opening a school, or taking over a failing one, requires a considerable initial investment. Besides the financial difficulties, teachers' unions often build up a strong opposition front and various local groups may express some hostility toward such endeavours. It may also be difficult for these companies to hire qualified teachers. Finally, because they depend on government funding, they may become casualties to political shifts in future elections. What appears today is that some existing for-profit schools have actually failed to turn a profit so far. For example, Edison Schools, which will be presented further on in this chapter, lost $49.4 million during fiscal year ending 30 June 1999 and Chancellor Beacon Academies, Inc., created by merger in 2002, has yet to show a profit (Chancellor Academies which existed since 1996 lost $2.7 million in fiscal year 2000 and nearly twice as much in fiscal year 2001).

In spite of the uncertainty of the general picture, even though the situation does not appear so flourishing at the moment, and even though the share of for-profit companies in this market is still small, these companies see huge potentialities in a relatively near future. Several factors may actually substantiate this optimism concerning for-profit education in general and more specifically for companies involved in K-12 education: a constant demand from business for a better trained workforce; a demand for retraining coming from consumers who need to keep pace with the evolving workplace; a demand coming from parents for alternatives to government-run schools (in fact, ever since 1991, the year when Minnesota opened the first charter school in the country, parents have increasingly supported school choice nationwide); an expanding educational market spurred by the policy reforms of the 1990s (growth of charter schools and private schools).[9] In 1999, as regards elementary and secondary education, there was a grand total of 116,000 public and private schools throughout the country receiving an estimated total of 53.5 million students at a cost of approximately $360 billion, and a non-negligible number of the public establishments were reported to be failing, a fact that edupreneurs were quick to see as their opportunity.[10] Analysts interpret these failures of public schools as one among a few positive factors creating more opportunities for private companies to enter the K-12 market in the future. Another one is the creation of more charter schools and more voucher plans, thus giving parents more choice. To this must be added more tax credit available as an incentive for parents to enter their children in private establishments. Thus Merrill Lynch estimates that the for-profit education market should be growing at

---

8   Lips, 5 (Moe et al. 1999: 74).
9   http://www.uscharterschools.org/gen_info/gi_main.htm.
10 *Digest of Education Statistics, 1999*, Table 2: 11/Table 5: 14.

a rate of 13 per cent per year and that within 10 years 10 per cent of all publicly funded K-12 schools will be privately managed.

In order to promote their own brand of K-12 education, the argument most often invoked by edupreneurs is the fact that the public school system hurts low-income students the most, precisely those it claims to be helping, because it is the low income students who attend the worst government-run schools and have the fewest alternatives to choose from. Edupreneurs also claim that free and open competition would bring costs and expenditures down. They also invoke the fact that funding should not be a problem for any family since, besides vouchers, which are still not available just anywhere, there are private charitable organizations, like the Children's Scholarship Fund for example, that specialize in funding the educational needs of low income children. In addition, there are private companies which can provide similar services.

Let us now look at how from an organizational standpoint for-profit companies operate within the public system. They can participate: either they only administer or manage a school, or they fully own it. The schools they are involved with can be charter schools or privatized schools. A charter school is a publicly funded school that operates without many of the traditional regulations found in other public schools. They are generally accountable to a state or local school board and their goals are basically to produce positive results and comply with the charter contract, as well as to turn a profit. This contract, which actually establishes the school, is a performance contract detailing the mission, programme, goals, students served, methods of assessment and ways to measure success. Most charters are granted for three to five years, renewable. They may be operated not only by for-profit companies, but also, as we saw earlier, by many other entities or groups as well.

Privatized schools are all operated by for-profit companies and administered by CEOs. In this case, the schools or school districts negotiate contracts with private firms, or EMOs, and pays them an amount that varies from district to district. Companies pay the schools' operating expenses and in some cases teacher salaries and they keep any capital remaining. They have the right to use their own curricula and create their own rules – while they still have to comply with state and local regulations and reporting requirements. Students must still take the same mandated standardized tests that all students in the state must take. In some cases, the companies behind these schools can hire and fire employees and do not have to answer to teacher unions. Finally, as with any business, contracts may be canceled if a district is dissatisfied with the company's product. In short, privatized schools are much more independent of control from state or district administrative scholastic authorities than charter schools.

Now we will take a brief look at the general operations of the two largest private companies in the United States. Both operate within the city of Philadelphia's school system: Edison Schools, Inc. and Chancellor Beacon Academies, Inc.

Edison Schools, Inc. was founded in 1992 by the now famous Christopher Whittle, who in 1989 launched Channel One, an advertiser-supported television programme for schools. Based in New York, Edison Schools opened its first four schools in 1995. Today it is the largest private operator of public schools throughout the United States. The company runs 150 schools for a combined enrollment of approximately 90,000 students in 24 states and Washington DC. Its curricula are based on the 'core curriculum' recommended by E.D. Hirsch Jr (1987, 1996), a retired teacher who wrote extensively on core knowledge and cultural literacy. Most of these schools feature a longer school year – approximately 198 days – as well as longer school days. They boast 'a technologically rich environment'. Edison went public in November 1999; it was the first public-traded EMO. Its stock went down from a high of $38 a share to a low of 14 cents (it managed to not go off the market). It operates under management contracts with local school districts and charter school boards.

Florida-based Chancellor Beacon Academies, Inc. is the second largest provider of both public charter and private day schools. It grew out of a merger in January 2002 between Chancellor Academies founded in 1996 and Beacon Educational Management founded in 1993. It serves approximately 19,000 students in charter-based schools, mostly elementary and middle schools. Its 81 schools are located in Arizona, Florida, Massachusetts, Michigan, Missouri, New York, Pennsylvania, Virginia and Washington DC. The company's on-line prospectus boasts of schools that 'feature technologically advanced instruction in small classes' and teach standard-based curricula.

This general information makes it easier to understand what has been happening in Pennsylvania, and more specifically in Philadelphia, in recent years. In view of the poor results students repeatedly scored all over the state of Pennsylvania in the standardized tests, the State Department of Education felt drastic measures were needed and in 1997 the Pennsylvania Charter School Law was passed. It allowed the opening of an unlimited number of charter schools, whether these were converted former public schools or new creations. The terms of the initial charters were to be up to five years renewable. These schools would benefit from automatic waiver from most state and district education laws, regulations, and policies; they were also to enjoy legal autonomy. Regarding their funding, they were to receive federal and school district funding but no state funding. In each establishment, at least 75 per cent of the faculty had to be certified. All charter schools had to come under the control of the Pennsylvania State Assessment System.

If we now turn more specifically to the city of Philadelphia, the general context has been one of great budgetary difficulties for a number of years now. Like many other school districts, the Philadelphia School District, which serves approximately 200,000 students, has been squeezed between the obligation of showing better student results because of the federally imposed higher standard requirements and sharp state budget reductions. Thus the structural reforms that were launched starting in 2001 grew out of the failure of a large number of public schools in the Philadelphia district, when measured in terms of results to the state standardized tests (the Pennsylvania State Assessment System). In an effort to find some solutions to its problems, the school district launched a broad school reform, the most extensive experiment in education ever seen in the recent history of American schools. In July 2001, it signed a $2.7 million contract with Edison Schools to evaluate the public schools of the city. Besides showing the failure of many local schools, Edison's report found that the school district was $215 million in the red. Following this assessment, in December 2001, the state took over control of the Philadelphia Public School District. This means that the mayor and the governor jointly dissolved the city school board and appointed a five-member School Reform Commission to replace it. The new commission then decided to turn over the running of 45 of the city's lowest-performing schools to entities outside of the school administration. Thirty-one companies competed for contracts.

The school reforms were made official by decision of the Philadelphia School Reform Commission which issued a statement on 31 July 2002 to be effective at the beginning of school year 2002–2003. The general goal of the Commission was to 'reprioritize spending and shift resources back to the classroom'. Five private companies, EMOs, and two universities were retained. The EMOs were Edison Schools, Inc., Chancellor Beacon Academies, Inc., Victory Schools, Inc., Foundations Academies, Inc., and Universal, Inc. They entered into partnerships with the state to assist in the redesigning and managing of these under-performing schools. Edison won the largest contract and was awarded 20 elementary and middle schools. Chancellor Beacon won five schools, three elementary and two middle schools. Victory Schools originally was assigned to run five schools as well, three elementary and two middle schools. In 2003, it was asked to take over another middle school and in addition to create two new small high schools in Northern Philadelphia. Foundations also won three elementary schools and two middle schools and Universal won an elementary school and a middle school. The University of Pennsylvania was mandated to run two elementary schools and one middle school and Temple University three primary schools and one K-8 school. Twenty-one other schools were restructured. In most of these establishments, new schedules extended the school day and allowed for after school programmes for underperforming students; curricula were redesigned with a 'back to basics' approach and special coaches were hired to counsel teachers.[11] The plans include after school and summer school programmes, a major reading initiative to ensure that all students are proficient in reading by the third grade, and a comprehensive plan to revitalize the high schools. In order to have the means to provide more support and training for their teachers, EMOs receive supplemental funding equal to the total difference between the district's average teacher salary and the actual teacher salaries for that school. In order to provide additional support and services to the students, they also receive a per-pupil equity supplement. They must ensure curriculum development, teacher and principal development and other technical assistance supports.

---

11 In addition, during the last few years, the city has authorized 46 charter schools. As examples of the diversity of the groups behind these schools, one of them is run by the Center for Economics and Law, another one by the Women's Christian Alliance, another one again by a local chapter of the Brotherhood of Electrical Workers, a union. There seems to be somewhat of a turnover among these charter schools, as some most recently did not get their charter renewed, while new ones are cropping up.

The Commission approved contracts with the EMOs and the two universities and defined their responsibilities. Under these contracts, school employees remained members in their unions and worked under collective bargaining agreements. It also approved a budget of $55 million in state funding to be divided among the EMOs, the two universities and the city's charter schools. The share of the EMOs totaled a little over $23 million. The contracts bound the providers to what the Commission called 'some of the strictest financial and academic accountability standards in the nation'. These contracts are all five years in length and 'can be terminated for cause or convenience', which gives the Commission more leverage.

This plan for for-profit companies to take over some of the city's public schools has met with hostility. Many were quick to point out the fact that this experiment was in direct violation of the city's regulations. In November 2002, this turned into an open conflict between state and city governments and the City Council filed a lawsuit asking the Pennsylvania Supreme Court to restore local control to the schools, contending that the governor had 'illegally taken over Philadelphia School District in order to privatize it'. The council asserted that the state takeover violated the city's Home Rule Charter, which calls for a nine-member Board of Education to be appointed by the mayor. The decision allowed EMOs to continue functioning.

The presence of for-profit education companies within the public school system raises questions of two types. The first one revolves around their efficiency and their ability to actually do better than the public system and improve a situation of failure which finds a lot of its causes outside of the school system. In the United States today, many people, among them decision makers and educators, are still unsure of the EMO's ability to raise the standards of achievement in the schools that they take over. Results are mixed, some EMOs have actually shown failing results. If we refer to the present situation in Philadelphia, as indicated earlier, reports show that EMOs are experiencing some operational difficulties: there are many teacher vacancies that are difficult to fill. In many instances, there was already a high teacher turnover in these schools before the takeover by an HMO, but certainly the new managers have not been able to correct this.

In view of such questioning on these new, non-traditional approaches to schooling, in 2002, Chaka Fattah, Congressman from Pennsylvania, requested that the General Accounting Office conduct a national review of privatized schools. The GAO had already reported on the private management of public schools back in 1996 (GAO/HEHS 1996). In that first report, the GAO surveyed the situation in the Baltimore City Public School District, Baltimore, Maryland; the Dade County Public School District, Dade County, Florida; the Hartford School District, Hartford, Connecticut; and the Minneapolis School District, Minneapolis, Minnesota. It concluded that many different experiments with varying degrees of authorities and responsibilities for the companies managing the schools showed very mixed results. Scores on mandated tests had not climbed substantially. The companies however had made some changes that benefited the students by improving attendance, by giving greater access to computers, by hiring teaching assistants with college degrees, and by enhancing the maintenance and the repair of buildings. In 2002, the new GAO report did not bring any new answers in the face of 'inconclusive results' because of, among other things, a lack of 'rigorous research' (GAO 2002).

In contrast, Edison Schools published its *Sixth Annual Report on School Performances* on 6 April 2004. The glowing self-congratulatory tone will not come as a surprise; the company toots its own horn just as it did in its previous reports. It asserts that there has been:

> A significant increase in the number of Edison school students who scored at or above proficiency levels. An average gain rate that is significantly higher than the gain rates of comparable schools. Specifically the data in the study show that between 2002 and 2003 Edison students posted an average gain of 6.7 percent points. This gain rate is more than 2 times the respective district and state gain rates where these Edison partnership schools are located. Last year's gains mark the largest overall average gains that we have experienced as a system.[12]

About parental satisfaction, the report adds: 'A majority of 51 percent gives their schools an A and 34 percent gives their schools a B, for a total of 85 percent of parents giving their Edison school an A or a B.'

More objectively, Alex Molnar, professor of Education Policy Studies and director of the Education Policy Studies Laboratory, EPSL,[13] at Arizona Sate University, Tempe, AR, has been doing research on what he calls 'schoolhouse commercialism'. For almost ten years now, Molnar has headed the Commercialism in Education Research Unit, CERU,[14] a unit of EPSL which has been studying and publishing reports on all forms of commercialism in the schoolhouse, naming rights (naming a school building or facility after a commercial company or business, national or local), sponsorship of programmes and activities, exclusive agreements (as do soda companies in schools to the exclusion of others), incentive programmes (such as rewarding students with commercial products), appropriation of space, sponsorship of educational materials (including the creation of curricula that promote corporations and commercial companies), electronic marketing, fund raising programmes and privatization. It would be difficult to question the integrity and the scientific quality of the research done by CERU, although its statement of purpose clearly indicates a position within the debate over commercialism in scholastic establishments that is not above the fray. Indeed, it unambiguously states that it 'is guided by the belief that mixing commercial activities with public education raises fundamental issues of public policy, curriculum content, the proper relationship of educators to the students entrusted to them, and the values that the schools embody'. This shows, as if it were still necessary, that the debate leaves no one indifferent. In spite of this, we

---

12 The Seventh Annual Report was released on 1 April 2005. It can be found on the official Edison Schools, www.edisonschools.com. It conveys exactly the same message as the previous report, practically unchanged in its wording.

13 http://edpolicylab.org.

14 CERU was formerly located at the University of Wisconsin, Milwaukee, under the name of Center for the Analysis of Commercialism in Education, CACE.

will review the results published under the auspices of the University of Arizona, as they are to this day the most extensive and reliable source of information on the subject.

In the scope of their research, Molnar and his team have been monitoring the performance of Edison schools and the overall conclusion is that 'their academic track record is not exemplary'. A 1992 CERU report published the results of a study which principally focused on Edison schools during 2001 and 2002 (Molnar 2002).[15] This report makes mention of the dissatisfaction that certain school districts voiced concerning this group, as there were various instances of dropping enrollment, high teacher turnover, and poor school results, and it also underlines the division among many local and state authorities over how to deal with the Edison schools. It details how the company became entangled with the United States Securities and Exchange Commission: in May 2002, the SEC started to investigate Edison's accounting proceedings and found that the corporation had inaccurately described some aspects of its business in SEC filings. It failed to reveal that an important portion of its reported revenues consisted of payments actually made by the school districts, in other words by Edison's very clients; something that Alex Molnar and his team uncovered. In fact, 'About one half of the company's fast-growing revenue consisted of money that its client school districts paid to others – teachers, bus companies and cafeteria vendors, for example – on Edison's behalf' (Molnar 2002: 22).

In a national perspective, the report concluded that, in 2002, there were indications that this young industry was in flux. As examples, it mentioned how Boston-based Advantage Schools had been acquired by Mosaica Education, Inc., Beacon Education Management, Inc. had been acquired by Chancelor Academies, and how Advantage Schools, Inc. was having fiscal problems. Besides, financiers were canceling some of their support of school privatization. In effect, the year 2002 seems to have been a turning point in the history of the development of EMOs between their first phase, prior to 2002, characterized by fast, vigorous growth and their new phase, after 2002, in which they had reached a plateau and were now looking for more modest and realistic growth targets. Even with this new maturity, the report was predicting a future that was uncertain:

> For-profit management of charter schools has been the principal vehicle for privatization in recent years, but their future, and therefore the future prospects of privatization, is not entirely clear. Although not directly related to commercialization, there were signs of second thoughts about charters generally in some school districts and some states - concerns that have implications for the future growth of private companies managing charter schools. ... In Ohio, legislators debated changes in state charter laws after only 18 per cent of 1,200 charter school fourth grade students passed a statewide reading test in March 2001, compared with 56 per cent of students in regular public schools. (Molnar 2002: 24)

---

15 Online: EPSL-0209-103-CERU at http://edpolicylab.org.

CERU has also been publishing an annual report entitled *Profiles of For-Profit Education Management Companies*. In the 2004 report, which covered school year 2003–2004, the authors concede that commercial involvement in education has now become a global phenomenon. Given that global framework, they also admit that the possibilities that have been offered EMOs look attractive:

> In the latter part of the 1990's, EMOs have taken the opportunity afforded by permissive charter school legislation and focused on the management of publicly funded charter schools. Charter schools, because they receive public funds but operate outside of the normal regulatory and accountability structures that govern the operation of traditional public schools, offer operators considerably more latitude in how money received from the state is spent. It appears that the combination of stable public funding and reduced accountability make charter schools attractive to EMO operators. (Molnar et al. 2004: 3)

But in that same report, they conclude that: 'Profitability and a positive return on investment (ROI) continue to be elusive goals for the EMO industry' (Molnar et al. 2004: 4).

This brings us to the second set of questions raised by EMOs, which have to do essentially with profitability as the obvious primary objective of any business company. In the logic of the market, it is normal for edupreneurs to run their operations in the perspective of reaping profits. The problem when they enter into partnerships with public school districts is that they intend to make their profits from school districts that are already under funded and in financial trouble. Not only is this a problem in itself but it creates a negative mood of resentment among the schools outside these partnerships. Another drawback is that it would also seem within that same business logic that they would feel more accountable to their investors than to school districts, parents and students and therefore that in the long run they would not really serve the educational needs of the students, something a public service can achieve in a more disinterested approach. As stressed in the *2004 Profile*:

> A major concern about for-profit schools is the tension between delivering a quality educational program to all students versus the pressure to achieve profits to the company stockholders. Critics point out that in business the company is primarily concerned with their own business interests and not the best interests of their customers. They fear that EMOs will make decisions based on their profit and loss statement rather than according to the best interests of their students. (Molnar 2002: 4)

In the end, what are the perspectives for EMOs? If we refer to the conclusions of the research team led by Alex Molnar, the situation for EMOs in America today is not as flourishing as might have been expected years back. The 2004 Profile already stated:

> The consensus view of investors, researchers, and others (was) that the evidence thus far (was) insufficient to demonstrate the quality of education (was) improved or that private management companies (could) profitably manage schools. (Molnar 2002: 4)

Many school officials realize that entering into partnership with EMOs is very costly, often beyond their means. They may find that EMOs do not perform up to accountability or expectations. Some critics also feel that EMOs were hired to remedy a situation of failure and that, whether they have succeeded or not, they should not remain in control of the schools indefinitely.

The 2005 Profile assesses the situation during school year 2004–2005 (Molnar et al 2004). Leading EMOs tend to focus on managing charter primary schools (cheaper to run than secondary schools) and on enrolling relatively large numbers of students. Above-average enrollments are found essentially in schools managed by the fourteen largest EMOs. These large EMOs manage nearly two thirds of all the charter schools. They account for 81 per cent of the charter schools and 89 per cent of the students enrolled. Fifty-nine EMOs are profiled in the report. They manage a total of 535 schools, attended by approximately 239,766 students. These figures represent an increase from the previous school year of eight firms and 39,363 students. Of the EMO-managed schools reviewed, 86 per cent are charter schools, up from 81 per cent in 2003–2004 and 74 per cent in 2002–2003. These trends and figures are confirmed by the Eighth Annual profile, which stresses that there is no decline but a transition which seems to benefit the larger organizations. Even though EMOs occupy only a very small niche in public education today, these companies generate some interest and hope for solutions to the problems of some public establishments.

To conclude from the still little evidence we have, we can say with a fair amount of certainty that in the future some school districts, especially urban school districts, because of their facing chronic under funding, will continue to be attracted by privatization schemes. Ultimately, the future of for-profit companies naturally lies in their ability to generate profits. This future is still not very clear, but it seems safe to say that if Edison, because it is the number one EMO today, manages to pull through and expand, others will certainly follow. Then the education industry might truly take off, simply because, as commonly happens, they will follow the market leader.

References

Clowes, G. (2000), 'Education and Choice: What Does America Think?', *School Reform News*, March.

Gerstner, L. (1994), *Reinventing Education: Entrepreneurship in America's Public Schools* (New York: Dutton).

Hirsch, E. (1987), *Cultural Literacy: What Every American Needs To Know* (Boston: Houghton Mifflin).

Hirsch, E. (1996), *The Schools We Need and Why We Don't Have Them* (New York: Doubleday).

Lipps, C. (2000), '*Edupreneurs': A Survey of For-Profit Education, Policy Analysis, No. 386*, 26 November (Washington, DC: Cato Institute).

Mathews, J. (2000), 'New Schools of Thought: Making Education Pay: For-Profit Initiative Has Backing', *Washington Post*, 19 April.

Moe, M., Bailey, K. and Lau, R. (1999), *The Book of Knowledge: Investing in the Growing Education and Training Industry* (Merrill Lynch & Co., Global Securities Research and Economics Group, Global Fundamental Equity Research Department), Report 1400 (9 April).

Molnar, A. (2002), 'What's in a Name? The Corporate Branding of America's Schools: 2001–2002' (Tempe: CERU, University of Arizona).

Molnar, A., Morales, J. and Wyst, A. (2000), 'Profiles of For-Profit Education Companies, 1999–2000', Center for Research, Analysis, and Innovation, University of Wisconsin-Milwaukee (6 March).

Molnar, A., Garcia, D., Sullivan, C., McAvoy, B. and Joannou, J (2005), *Seventh Annual Profile in For-Profit Education Management Companies, 2003–2004* (Tempe: CERU, University of Arizona).

Molnar, A., Wilson, G., Allen, D. (2004), *Sixth Annual Profile in For-Profit Education Management Companies*, 2003-2004 (Tempe: CERU, University of Arizona).

Perelman, L. (1992), *School's Out: Hyperlearning, The New Technology, And The End Of Education* (New York: William Morrow).

'Private Management of Public Schools: early Experiences in Four School Districts' (1996), (Washington, DC: GAO/HEHS-96-3), 19 April.

'Report to the Ranking Minority – Public Schools – Insufficient Research to Determine Effectiveness of Selected Private Education' (2002), (GAO-03-11: Washington, DC), 29 October.

Symonds, W., Palmer, A. and McCann, J. (2000), 'For-Profit Schools', *Business Week*, 7 February.

US Department of Education, National Center for Education Statistics (2000), *Digest of Education Statistics, 1999* (Washington, DC: Government Printing Office).

Chapter 10

'We Pay the Rates!' Catholic Voluntary Schools and Scottish School Boards (1872–1918)

Geraldine Vaughan

> We [the Catholics] have paid school rates for Protestant education in Scotland for 34 years without becoming passive resisters.
>
> (SCA 1907)

With the passing of the Education (Scotland) Act in 1872, the former parish and burgh schools were transferred to a more coherent and centralized system of local government. Under this new system, Scottish schools were to be administered by local elected school boards under the supervision of the Scotch Education Department. As opposed to England, where a large voluntary sector survived the 1870 Education Act, in Scotland, the vast majority of schools decided to join the state system in order to receive rate aid. Most of those who remained outside were Episcopalian and Roman Catholic. The development and growth of Catholic education was a consequence of the massive Irish immigration which followed the Famine years (late 1840s) – the Irish Catholic newcomers mainly settled in industrial towns of the Central Belt. In the second half of the nineteenth century, the Irish community formed up to 30 per cent of the population of these Western towns. We shall focus in this paper on the Monklands, a region lying 20 miles east of Glasgow, and in particular on its two main coal-mining and ironworks towns, Airdrie and Coatbridge.

As ratepayers, Catholics, although they did not benefit from the public rate-aided schooling system, wished to control the spending of their local taxes. Accordingly they, with the advantages of the cumulative vote system, became members of school boards in both towns. They thus offer a paradoxical example of voluntary participation in local government structures.

In the first part of this chapter, the reasons for and the reality of Catholic participation on local school boards (election campaigning and results, presence of clergymen, etc.) will be examined. Secondly, the attitude of Catholic members on these boards will be considered. What committees were they most active on? Did they play a greater role by the early 1910s? Was the experience, for instance, of Catholic priests as managers of voluntary schools, useful to boards? Thirdly, the reactions of the other (Protestant) members of boards and of the Scottish citizens in general will be analysed – particularly the numerous conflicts which arose between staunch Protestants and Catholic board members.

Voluntary Bodies Represented on School Boards

Irish Catholics refused to participate in the new educational system for one main reason: they considered it as 'denominational' – whereas in the 1870 Education (England) Act, no religious education was to be given in public schools, in Scottish burgh schools, religious education could be administered to children. In the overwhelming majority of schools, the Shorter Catechism (Presbyterian) was adopted – even though parents who objected could withdraw their children during the religious education hours (which where scheduled to take place before or after school hours). In the Catholic view, the whole school board system was 'Protestant': as a Catholic newspaper explained in 1895, board schools were Protestant schools, staffed with Protestant teachers, and studying Protestant textbooks (*The Glasgow Examiner* [GE] 1895, 28 September). This Protestant orientation of schools, along with the fact that the Catholic Church could have no control over the recruiting and managing of staff and curriculum in Catholic schools, in effect prevented Catholics to join in the new system.

As already pointed out, the involvement of (Irish) Catholics was paradoxical: they engaged in a structure which had virtually no power over Catholic schools, but whose objective was solely to control public expenditure. Indeed, the financial incentive was a trigger to their participation: as ratepayers, the Catholics wanted public money to be cautiously spent. This, in effect, was a major electoral argument: Catholics boasted of their thrifty attitude – as the Catholic paper *The Glasgow Observer* put it in 1888: there was nobody 'more careful and economising than the Catholic members' (*The Glasgow Observer* [GO] 1888, 7 April). For Catholics, in addition to paying rates for the public system, had to support their own schools (building, salaries of teachers, maintenance, books etc.): this thus represented 'double taxation' system for them.[1] This led to numerous grievances, as James McGovern, the headmaster of one of the local Monkland Catholic school, explained in a 1907 letter:

> Paying our equal share of the rates ... in maintaining in an efficient manner all the Public schools ... For our own [Catholic] children ... [we] pay for them out of our own pockets without receiving a fraction of farthing from the rates to help us ... We relieve the rates, but the rates do not relieve us. (*The Airdrie and Coatbridge Advertiser* [AC] 1907, 9 February)

In several cases, some Catholics were even paying triple rates: Catholic schooling, school board rates and Works schools' fees. This occurred in 1878, and James McAuley, the Catholic member, read out to the Old Monkland School Board a list of 62 children whose parents had to pay extra fees (AC 1878, 30

---

1 Catholic schools, however, did receive government grants, as did board schools.

March). This was the case at the Summerlee Ironworks, where 'a deduction of school pence' was made on all wages, even on those of Catholic workers who sent their children to the local Catholic school (SRA 1878). Thus, the board unanimously agreed that this state of affairs was most unjust to Catholic workers and that it should stop.

In 1873, there were two Catholic schools in Airdrie and Coatbridge, and by 1889 an additional school was built: the three educating an average total of 1186 children (GO 1889, 7 September). For instance, the building of Saint Augustine's school, Coatbridge, in 1882, cost over £2174. The financial cost of maintaining schools was very high, and especially difficult to sustain for parishes where the congregation was chiefly composed of Irish labourers: the Catholic priests' correspondence of this period is filled with references to the money needed for schools, debts, etc. Special collections for the purpose of financing schools often had to be arranged: for instance, when Father McIntosh, of Saint Margaret's, Airdrie, wrote to the Bishop in November 1873, the school at that time accommodated 300 (with 500 on the roll). However, additional room for 120 children was needed, at an estimated cost of £300 (a male worker's weekly wage ranged in the second half of the nineteenth century from 12s to 22s weekly) (GAA 1873). In 1882, for example, the building of Saint Augustine's school, Coatbridge, cost over £2,174 (GAA 1882). The Catholic argument was that they knew how to manage education in the most economical way: in 1895, a Catholic newspaper reported that a child in a Catholic school cost £1.6s.3d annually to educate, whereas a child in a board school cost double: £2.8s.3d (GE 1895, 28 September).

Catholics had other incentives to participate in the new educational authorities. The new Act imposed school attendance on all children aged between 5 and 13: thus local school boards had the power to prosecute defaulting parents, whether the children were going to public or voluntary schools. For instance, in 1874, an Irish miner, Patrick Callaghan, was prosecuted by the clerk of the Airdrie School Board and appeared in front of the Sheriff Court, for failing to send his two children, Patrick and Daniel, to school (AC 1883, 6 January). Certificates of exemption from school attendance were delivered by school boards: in 1905, the Airdrie board delivered two exemptions for John Carr and Letitia McGhee, both attending Saint Margaret's school (SRA 1905). Furthermore, the school boards could 'prescribe the hours of employment of Catholic as well as non Catholic children of school age', and provide the education of 'the poor, the blind ... and the truant of all denominations' (*Glasgow Star and Examiner* 1906, 24 March). Lastly, there was another reason that motivated Catholic presence on boards: although they were reluctant to admit it, and besides the fact that it was very seldom mentioned, some Catholic children did attend board schools (however these children were mainly those of the Poorhouse and those coming from mixed backgrounds). This can be seen in 1873, at an Old Monkland School board meeting, when James McAuley, the Catholic member, asked that in board schools, before the hour of religious instruction (Presbyterian Shorter Catechism) there should be a five minutes' interval so that Roman Catholics children could leave the school before such lessons were given. However, no one seconded his proposition (AC 1873, 1 November).

Catholics had to organize, by 1873, for the first triennial elections, in order to have representatives on the three Monkland Boards – which each comprised around nine members (Old Monkland, New Monkland and Airdrie School Boards).[2] In Airdrie, the debate focused on clerical participation: should priests and ministers (as managers of schools, and in charge of educational issues) contest the elections? This issue was apparently specific to the Monklands, as in other Scottish towns, members of clergy ran for election. Saint Margaret's Catholic priest, James McIntosh, publicly declined to participate in the contest, as he declared: 'It has been said that the ministers should not go upon the Board: and [I] made up [my] mind to decline doing so' (AC 1873, 8 March). Indeed, the local (Protestant) Liberal press had been campaigning against clerical candidates in the months preceding the election. However, priests became involved in Monkland school board elections from the early 1880s: in 1881, Father O'Reilly, of Saint Patrick's, Coatbridge, was elected a member of the Old Monkland School Board. As the Catholic newspaper the *Glasgow Observer* remarked in 1889: 'We can return our representatives to the Boards where they will be useful in many ways. In most cases the Catholic representative is the Reverend manager of the schools in the district' (GO 1889, 3 March). In effect, the Catholic clergy became more and more involved in organizing the elections: for instance, in 1891, Michael O'Keefe, senior priest of Saint Patrick's, gave the use of his schoolroom to the Catholic electoral committee, and attended its meetings every night. In May 1906, a mass meeting of Saint Augustine's (Coatbridge) congregation was conveyed by the clergy one Sunday after mass in Saint Augustine school, and presided by Frs. Müller and O'Herlihy (*The Coatbridge Express* [CE] 1906, 29 May). Some priests went as far as to oppose certain Catholic candidates in order to impose on their flock the man they had chosen. In April 1897, at the Old Monkland School Board elections, John Hughes, senior priest of Saint Augustine's, in opposition to Arthur Malone, an Irish Catholic candidate, on the grounds that the latter was a spirits merchant, put forward John Donaldson, a miner's agent (GAA 1897). Malone lost the election, and Donaldson was elected, along with two other Catholics.

The Catholic Church played an active role through its clergymen, with their lending of parochial schools and halls to hold the meetings, their approval of candidates, etc. The voting system instituted by the Act was the cumulative vote, by which 'minorities' such as Catholics and Episcopalians were favoured. Every elector was allowed to accumulate an allocation of votes on one candidate if they wished: this introduced some degree of proportional representation, fairer to minorities (Machin 2000: 48, 75). This voting system was a recurrent source of controversy: for instance, in May 1889, a bill opposing the cumulative vote was examined by the Old Monkland School Board. A Catholic member, Hugh O'Hear, protested that the Catholic community had never abused its voting powers (AC

---

2   The Old Monkland School Board managed Coatbridge schools; the New Monkland and Airdrie School Boards dealt with Airdrie and its surroundings.

1889, 4 May). The cumulative vote, added to a thorough electoral organization, resulted in a consistent representation of the Catholic body on school boards. The voting franchise (£4 per annum) ensured a large number of the Irish flock, consisting mainly of labourers, could go to the poll. On polling day, Catholics revealed their well-thought out organization: in 1891, the committee in charge of the Catholic vote ensured that one of its members, to avoid the loss of a voter, 'took his place at one of the iron furnaces ... while the voter went off to the polling station, which was quite far away' (GO 1891, 18 April). The energy spent in canvassing was acknowledged by the Protestant citizens, as is evidenced in a 1900 newspaper commenting on the high scores of the Catholic candidates in the Old Monkland School Board Election: 'the spoils of the election are to those who canvass hardest' (AC 1900, 7 April).

How many Catholics managed to get represented on boards? In the three boards under examination, during the first twenty years of their existence, at least one member represented this voluntary body. In 1900, the Old Monkland School Board had four Catholic representatives (of which two were priests). Thanks to the cumulative vote, Catholics often topped the poll: in 1882, at the Old Monkland School Board elections, Father O'Reilly, of Saint Patrick's, came first with 7,428 votes (4,001 electors voted) (AC 1882, 8 April). By 1918, Catholics on the Old Monkland School Board even claimed that 'the Catholic body has always returned four members to the Old Monkland School Board' (CE 1918, 20 February). This observation was made by one of its Catholic members, Father Geerty, on the matter of the vacancy caused by the death of one of its Irish members, Charles O'Neill.

What happened when a Catholic member had to retire from the board during his mandate? As early as 1881, when James McAuley, Catholic member of the Old Monkland and Airdrie School Boards died, Catholics were adopted by the boards in place of the late Irishman. The Old Monkland School Board received in October 1881 a letter written by Michael O'Keeffe, Saint Patrick's priest, stating that at a meeting of Catholic ratepayers it was resolved that Father O'Reilly should be co-opted in place of McAuley (SRA 1881b). The board unanimously agreed to it; and at the meeting of the Airdrie School Board, one of its Protestant Scottish members, Mr Adamson, resolving to appoint Alexander McKillop, a Catholic, remarked 'that it was right that there should always be a member of the Roman Catholic denomination on the School Board of Airdrie' (AC 1881, 8 October). This attitude seemed to remain general practice during this 1873–1918 period: however, things did not always go so smoothly, as will be seen in the last part of this chapter.

Catholics on School Boards: Participation, Committees, Disputes

School boards were divided into various committees, dealing with attendance, finances, management, etc. As elected members, Catholics were chosen to attend or chair different committees except of course that of the (Protestant) religious instruction committee. As one Catholic member of the Old Monkland School

Board, Hugh O'Hear, jokingly remarked in April 1900, when the 'religions teaching committee' was formed, amongst whose members there were one Protestant minister and one Orangeman: 'That's a committee of good Protestants [laughter]' (CE 1900, 18 April). The matter became a source of amusement on different boards: for instance, in April 1906, at the Old Monkland School Board meeting, the chairman provoked general hilarity by proposing that Father Hackett be on the Religious Instruction Committee (AC 1906, 21 April). Often Catholic clergymen were appointed to the committee of management of a specific school, because of their experience as school managers. For instance, in April 1882, Father Thomas O'Reilly was assigned to the committee of Faskine school, one of the public schools managed by the board. Another member, Mr Allan, commented that he 'also thought that Mr O'Reilly would make an efficient member of school committee, as the Catholic schools were conducted on a much cheaper scale ... [This would] give the members of the Old Monkland School Board a lesson' (AC 1882, 22 April). Here follows an example of the Catholics (four members) appointed on committees at the Old Monkland School Board in April 1906: they were present on the 'Technical and Continuation schools'; the 'Coatbridge and Gartsherrie Academy Schools' (as well as all the other schools committees); the 'Finance and Law'; and the 'School Attendance and Drill' committees (AC 1906, 21 April). In the opinion of some Protestant members, Catholics were even given too many crucial positions: in 1911, a Baptist minister, Samuel Lindsay, of the Old Monkland School Board, complained that two of the latter denomination had been appointed to key convenerships, respectively the 'Staffing and Attendance Committee' and the 'Technical and Evening Continuation Schools Committee' (*The Coatbridge Leader* [CL] 1911, 8 April).

Although Catholics appear to have been fairly well represented on committees, however, it seems that their appointment was not always unanimous, and on several occasions, Catholics complained of being left aside or being deprived of chairmanships for sectarian reasons. On the occasion cited above (April 1906) occurred a dispute as to whether Catholics should be given chairmanships of committees. Father Hackett declared that some of the members seemed to be 'left aside', adding: 'I don't want a convenership but I want an explanation' (CL 1911, 8 April). Overall, Catholic members, and in particular priests, gave their experience as school managers as a justification of their participation on school committees and in teacher recruiting. At a school board meeting in Coatbridge in 1913, Father Patrick Hackett recommended his colleague Father Geerty to act on a committee choosing certificated teachers: 'Father Geerty was a man of experience; he had been conducting a school for twenty years and he knew a teacher when he saw one. [He was] the best man for the business' (CL 1913, 19 April).

In a attempt to evaluate the work achieved by Catholics on school boards, let us observe positive comments made by Scottish Protestants on their coreligionists' work. In a letter written by 'A Protestant' to the local newspaper, *The Airdrie Advertiser*, in 1900, the author states:

> The Roman Catholic members of the Board ... take a fair share of the work of the board ... [I am] impressed by the fairness, as well as the common sense of the Roman

Catholic members ... All seem to have at heart the best educational interest of the parish. (AC 1900, 21 April)

Furthermore, the other members of school boards were willing to acknowledge the work accomplished by Catholic members – in September 1881, the chairman of the Old Monkland School Board, John Alexander, on the subject of the late Catholic Irishman, James McAuley, lauded his:

> ...most regular attendance and intelligent part in all the business and arrangements necessary for carrying on the work of the Board. In all his intercourse Mr. McAuley's conduct was marked by a gentlemanly and courteous bearing towards his colleagues and his counsel and services were highly appreciated and will be greatly missed by the Board. (SRA 1881a)

Of course, one must not be fooled by the laudatory dimension of obituaries of this kind: but careful attention paid to all the school board reports in the local press and minute books reveal that, as a rule, Catholics were quite regular in their attendance at the general and committee meetings, and willing to collaborate, give advice or oppose other members.

Controversies between Irish Catholic and Scottish Protestant members of the boards did arise, over a wide range of issues. The first sensitive debate that cropped up with the forming of school boards was that of the opening prayer. This was an issue in several school boards in Scotland:[3] at the Old Monkland School Board, strangely, the motion in favour of a prayer was defeated at the first ever meeting held, by James McAuley, the Catholic member, along with four other (Protestant) members (AC 1873, 26 April). The situation was different in Airdrie: in January 1876, at a New Monkland School Board meeting, it was resolved to open the meetings with a prayer, and as a member, J. Wilson, put it: 'Us Scotch people like to commence proceedings of this kind with a prayer' (AC 1876, 29 January). The debate occurred again later, in 1909: the Coatbridge Baptist minister, Samuel Lindsay, newly elected member, opened the first meeting of the Old Monkland School Board by engaging in prayer (CL 1909, 24 April). The four Catholic members present strongly protested against this practice forced upon them: at a subsequent meeting, one month later, Hugh O'Hear, one of the Catholic members, gave a speech as to why Catholics were opposed to (Protestant) opening prayers. After a very heated discussion and debate, the motion in favour of opening prayers was defeated (four votes to five) (CL 1909, 29 May).

With their electoral platform advocating the reduction of the boards' expenses, one might expect to find Catholic members constantly promoting the trimming of costs. In reality, school board reports offer few relevant examples. The following case is one of the rare episodes: in August 1885, the Catholic member of the

---

3 See for instance, the Renton School Board case (Alexandria), where a Catholic clergyman attempted to move that meetings should not start with prayers, as they were dealing with secular issues. His motion was defeated, and meetings started with a ten minute opening prayer (GO 1888, 19 May).

Airdrie School Board, Alexander McKillop, proposed an amendment against the reduction of fees in Albert School, as he exposed that this would cause the rates to increase. His amendment, supported only by one other member, was defeated (AC 1885, 1 August). On some occasions, Catholic members tried to obtain 'their fair share' of the rates, by moving measures in favour of voluntary schools. During the discussions previous to the Education Bills in the early 1900s, Catholic members of the Old Monkland School Board (in 1904 and 1905) 'recommended that school boards have the power to pay pensions or retiring allowances to teachers in Voluntary Schools' (AC 1905, 22 April). The Catholic member, Charles O'Neill, went on arguing that Catholics were 'saving an enormous amount of rates to the public by having schools of their own built, while all the time they had to pay rates to maintain pensions and build schools for Board purposes' (CL 1908, 2 May). This principle was admitted by the board.

One particularly heated point of contention discussed on the various boards was the question of free books: the controversy lasted from 1908 to 1910. This issue first came under examination when the new Education Act for Scotland (1908) made provision for the free supply of books, food and clothing to necessitous children. This act conferred power on the school boards to extend measures of help to voluntary schools, but these powers were permissive, not mandatory (Handley 1947: 236). Catholic members of the Old Monkland School Board argued in favour of voluntary school children getting free books, but Protestant members objected, as Mr Carter put it, in May 1908: 'where public money was being spent there should be some public control' – no free books should be distributed to schools that had chosen to remain independent (CL 1908, 2 May). The Catholics' main argument was that, by keeping their schools 'off the rates' they were saving the ratepayers '£4000 per annum' (CL 1910, 19 February). The irony of it all is that when Catholics finally won the battle of free books for necessitous children attending Catholic schools in 1910 (CL 1910, 12 December), they realized that the books sent were school board books (the words used in the motion led to confusion)! During World War I, another controversy arose on the matter of providing boots to necessitous children: in early 1915, the members of the Old Monkland Board disagreed as to whether the funds were directed to all 'necessitous children of school age' or solely to 'children attending Board schools' (CL 1915, 23 January). When this issue first arose in late 1914, Catholic members of the board used very firm language: Father Patrick Hackett declared: 'We want fair play and justice. We are entitled to that and we will have it' (CL 1914, 19 December). In 1917, at the Airdrie School Board, the Catholic members advocated the payment by the board of a war bonus for teachers of voluntary schools (as was the case for board school teachers) on the grounds that Catholic teachers were getting lower pay than their Public school colleagues and that the Catholic community was significantly participating in the war effort ('sending their sons and daughters out to assist in defending the country') (AC 1917, 28 April). Interestingly, this last argument would be one of the key factors leading to the concessions to voluntary schools in the 1918 Education (Scotland) Act.

'Papists Looking After the Education of our Protestant Children!'[4]

When the Church of Scotland pastor, Joseph Primmer,[5] well-known for his anti-Catholic views, during one of his legendary summer speaking tours, addressed a Coatbridge audience in July 1901, he thundered: 'It is a disgrace ... that in Coatbridge there should be four Papists looking after the education of their Protestant children' and added: 'while Protestants vote for them!' (CE 1901, 10 July). Primmer was certainly always very extreme in his perception of Catholics, but nonetheless it can be said that many Protestant citizens tended to think that Catholics were not fit nor able to work on school boards, and that their numbers on boards were certainly too great. What were the accusations levelled by Protestant citizens at the Catholics on school boards? One essential reproach was that, in Protestant eyes, Catholics, in general, were less concerned by education. In 1875, a letter addressed to the local newspapers, signed 'Pat' and written in a simulated Irish brogue, entitled 'Paddy's opinion of schoolmasters and school boards', summed up the opinion Protestants had of Irish Catholic interest in education. In his letter, 'Paddy' pleaded against those '*skool boords*', wondering why children had to be sent to school, when they should be at work, bringing back some money to allow their parents to '*have a drop of the crathur*' – or, in other terms, to indulge in some drink (AC 1875, 6 March).

This low opinion of Catholic educational prospects was linked to general prejudice against Roman Catholicism, commonly associated with ignorance, superstition, anti-Bible reading etc. Moreover, why would Catholics care in the least for the education of Protestant children? For Catholics were supposedly on school boards only to 'keep the rates low' and why should they care when they did not send their children to board schools (CE 1896, 29 January)? As a correspondent to the local newspaper wrote in 1900: 'four Roman Catholics elected, whose prime object ... is keeping down taxation, and when it comes to touching the local purse, not to further education but to prevent it' (AC 1900, 14 April). Complaints as regards the Catholic attitude on boards were of a great variety: in one case, Catholics were even accused of being too generous. In 1912, a debate occurred as to whether a new school should be built or the old one rearranged at Langloan (Coatbridge). The Catholic members of the Old Monkland School Board were in favour of a new school being built, as Father Hackett put it 'for the children of Langloan they claimed to have a good school erected. He had had an experience of patching up schools and building schools for the past 25 years ... They should give the children, good fresh air, beautiful surroundings' (CL 1912, 30 March). Protestant citizens immediately reacted to this position, and an editorial in the local Liberal newspaper *The Coatbridge*

---

  4   See Joseph Primmer's speech pronounced at Coatbridge in July 1901 (CE 1901, 10 July).

  5   Joseph Primmer (1842–1914) toured Scotland every summer from 1890 to 1903, defending the reformed faith and attacking the Roman Catholic Church (see Gallagher 1987: 35–6).

Leader protested against this 'dispendious attitude' of the Catholic members (CL 1912, 29 May).

Thus, some Protestants were persuaded that Catholics were over-represented on school boards. In the opinion of the staunch Protestant Orangemen, Catholics should not be there in the first place: as John Carter, Master of one of the Coatbridge lodges, put it in 1902, Catholics could have their own school boards and stop what he qualified as the 'impudence of Romanist meddling' (CE 1902, 6 November). Of course these were extreme, though not infrequent, views. A good majority of citizens simply thought that the Catholics were over-represented – as a correspondent of the local paper put it in 1900: 'I do not wish to say a word against our local Catholics, or to imply that we should not have some of them on Board ... I would have supported one or two of them' (AC 1900, 14 April). The main reason for this over-representation, in the minds of Protestant citizens, was the cumulative vote system. This was a recurrent subject, as can be seen in letters addressed to the local press in the period 1873–1918. One correspondent explained in 1900 that in school board elections the 'One man, One vote' principle should be applied: the cumulative vote was experimental at first, '... out of date now. Minorities should scramble on to school boards by ordinary means same as they do on other boards' (AC 1900, 21 April).

Another policy was to protest against Catholics being co-opted to replace retiring board members. In September 1900, one of the Catholic members of the Old Monkland School Board, Father John Hughes, died. Thus a vacancy occurred, and discussions as to which new member would be co-opted entailed. At the next meeting of the board, a petition signed by electors, in favour of the nomination of a Protestant candidate, Mr Wotherspoon, was brought by a deputation of ministers, headed by the Reverend William Winter (CE 1900, 26 September). This deputation presented a memorial signed by 1150 electors, urging the board to nominate the Protestant candidate. Their arguments were that Protestants should be in charge of the education of their own children and 'that the Board had the precedent set before them by themselves in times gone past of a Catholic leaving the Board and being supplanted by a Protestant'.[6] But this protest failed: during this school board meeting, Arthur Malone, the Catholic candidate, was appointed by a majority of six to three (CE 1900, 26 September). In the opinion of some Protestant citizens, certain Protestant members on boards were being too partial to voluntary bodies: in 1909, a correspondent, 'Rip Van Winkle' addressed a letter to the local newspaper, stating that 'the Chairman [Reverend Andrew, a Protestant pastor] is a partisan to voluntary schools, and joins in sending to the County Secondary Committee a [Catholic] representative ...' (AC 1909, 18 September).

If Protestant citizens felt compelled to oppose what they resented as Catholic interference with Protestant education matters, so did certain Protestant elected members of boards. Some of them were very reluctant to grant any advantage to Catholic ratepayers: for instance, in 1879, the New Monkland School Board

---

6   This occurred in 1896, when Mr Donaldson, a retiring Catholic member, was supplanted by Mr Goodman, a Protestant.

refused to lease one of its public schools (Glenboig school) to Father O'Keefe for religious purposes on Sunday mornings. Members of the board argued that it wasn't empowered to grant the school for this purpose (AC 1879, 8 January). The number of Catholic representatives was also a matter of controversy – as the pastor Samuel Lindsay, campaigning for the 1909 school board Elections, stated:

> He did not seek to deprive them [Roman Catholics] wholly of a seat on Board, although he had always held that they were over-represented thanks to the cumulative vote and the apathy of Protestant electors. (CE 1909, 7 April)

The role of Catholics on school boards was an issue: hard-line Protestant members were careful to avoid that the former should not be appointed to important positions. Samuel Lindsay, the Baptist minister, protested in 1911 against the nomination of two Catholic members on school committees, and declared that these two gentlemen, '… in the nature of their relationship to the public schools, had the smallest interest in the success of Protestant teachers and pupils' (CL 1911, 8 April). He contrasted this attitude with that of another school board, the Dalziel board, which had refused to appoint Roman Catholics as members of school committees. From the early 1900s, school board elections started to be fought, to some degree, on sectarian lines: in 1914, on the subject of the Old Monkland School Board elections the *Coatbridge Leader* stressed that 'as usual, of course, the contest was conducted to some extent along well marked party lines', with three Protestant candidates (Lindsay, Chalmers and Neilson) appealing for the Protestant vote.

However, discord along religious lines on school boards seemed to have been triggered in Coatbridge by the arrival of a man cited earlier, the Rev. Samuel Lindsay. From the moment he was first elected to the Old Monkland School Board in April 1909, religious tensions grew strong. As a Catholic member, Hugh O'Hear declared at a subsequent meeting in May 1909, before Lindsay's arrival: 'They had never had any discord amongst themselves yet; they had got along wonderfully well' (CL 1909, 1 May).

Dissension amongst Catholics and Protestants on school boards has been examined so far: however, was the Catholic voluntary body always united? The 1897 controversy over Father John Hughes' choice of contestant has already been referred to earlier – what was not mentioned was that the priest chose a trade-union man, a miners' agent, Donaldson, as candidate. Some debate occurred on the choice of such an applicant to represent Catholics on board: this foreshadowed Labour/Catholic disputes in local elections that took place in the 1900s. When Donaldson left the board one year later in 1897, a non-Catholic was appointed in his place. A member of the Old Monkland School Board, Dr Marshall, argued that Donaldson, although a Catholic, had been returned as a Labour candidate, declaring that 'his Catholic colleagues at the Board had repudiated him as their nominee' (CE 1896, 29 January). In educational affairs, it seemed as a rule that the interests of the Catholic Church came first – thus, the editor of the Scottish Catholic newspaper, *The Glasgow Observer*, D.J. Mitchel Quin, wrote in 1913:

In both these cases [parliamentary and municipal elections] the Irish vote goes solidly for Labour. But at the School Board Election the Irish vote goes for the Catholic members, naturally and properly, and Labour is left to its own resources. (GAA 1913)

However, this was not always the case in the Monklands: some Labour candidates were elected for their political credo in the first place and for their Catholicism in the second instance. For example, Paul McKenna, a miners' agent of Irish descent, ran for elections as a Labour candidate for the Airdrie School Board in April 1914 (one of his electoral slogans was: 'Workers vote for McKenna') (AC 1914, 11 April). He was elected and even topped the poll with 3047 vote papers (CL 1914, 11 April). Of course, this was possible thanks to the Catholic vote: he was supported by Saint Margaret's parishioners, parish to which he himself belonged.

The 1918 Education (Scotland) Act

As the years went by, the voluntary sector's complaints became more vociferous: the financial burden was considered too heavy, and Catholic schools wanted transfer, but only under certain conditions. Father Hackett, one of the members of the Old Monkland School Board in 1914, declared:

> It was only a question of time when they [Catholics] would have their rights in spite of everything because they must insist on fair play, and if they helped to collect £22,500 to educate 8,000 children, the other [Catholic] 4,000 children should get part of the money. They had the same inspectors, the same codes, the same books, the same timetable, but because they taught their children a different Catechism they were deprived of a share of the grant. (CL 1914, 20 June)

In fact, Catholics had to be patient during only four more years, for the Education Act of 1918 would answer their grievances. It is necessary therefore to briefly expose events leading up to this Act.

Numerous pamphlets were published within the first years of the new century, as for instance the one written by Lord Skerrington in 1914, entitled *The Educational Grievance of Scottish Catholics*:

> On the establishment of a truly national system of education, which should include Catholics instead of excluding them at present, we will guarantee, as we already do, that all public monies paid to Catholic schools shall be spent on education and on nothing else. (SCA 1914)

In fact, discussions over the transfer of voluntary schools to the board system occurred several times from the late 1890s. The first time such a transfer was considered by the Catholic authorities was in 1896: the Diocesan Board of Education sent a Memorandum to the Scotch Education Department stating that Catholic schools of Glasgow and district were willing to submit to the school board, provided they remained proprietors of the school buildings with control of staff and school management (Skinnider 1967: 41). Similar conditions were given to voluntary schools in England in the 1902 Education Act: managers of schools, a third of whom were nominated by the newly elected Local Education Authorities, appointed teachers with the consent of the board (the managers retained a veto on religious grounds). However, the 1896 Memorandum received no positive response from the Educational Authorities. Further attempts were made on behalf of voluntary schools before the vote of the 1908 Education Act: the benefits Catholics gained from this new legislation were the permissive powers given to school boards on social benefits (free books, etc.) and ampler support for Catholic secondary education through the new distribution of funds (SCA 1914). Further discussions between the Catholic hierarchy and Scottish authorities were not successful before the passing of the 1918 Education Act. Apparently, section 18 was one way of acknowledging Catholic effort during the war – as the Catholic Education Committee for Scotland reported on the 1918 Bill in February:

> [They] attributed this generous appreciation of the educational needs of the Catholics to the change of feeling brought about in a war in which Catholics had shown themselves as patriotic as the rest of the nation. This, they were afraid, might be forgotten when the war was over. (SCA 1914)

Section 18 of the Act provided for the transfer of voluntary schools, which would now be managed as public schools. Moreover, in the same section, the denominational Church to which the school belonged retained power in the nomination of the teaching staff as can be seen in the third part of Section 18:

> All teachers appointed to the staff of any such school by the education authority shall in every case be teachers who satisfy the Department as to qualification, and are approved as regards their religious belief and character by representatives of the church or denominational body in whose interest the school has been conducted. (Strong 1919: 50–57)

Thus the Education Authority had to select teachers who could exhibit an approval as to the religious belief and character by the authorities in the Churches to which they belong (bishops in Roman Catholic and Episcopalian churches).

In the Monklands, over 40 years of Catholic experience on school boards helped Scottish Protestants to become familiar with their Irish Catholic counterparts. The tenacity of Catholic members on boards, the increase of their numbers and of their claims were factors that helped see the 1918 Act as a fair and/or inevitable issue. For Irish Catholics in Scotland, the Act had very important consequences, as Tom Devine puts it:

> The 1918 Act had a more positive effect, becoming in the long run a key factor in the promotion of Catholic assimilation. Without it, the Scoto-Irish might have been unable to grasp the educational opportunities of the twentieth century and as a result be condemned to the enduring status of an underprivileged and alienated minority. Instead, 1918, and the later changes promoting access to higher education after 1945,

enabled the eventual growth of a large Catholic professional class, fully integrated into the mainstream of Scottish society. (Devine 2000: 497)

What we would like to stress here, is that Catholic participation to local political/educational life in the Monklands, from the 1870s to 1918, was probably a key factor of the integration of Irish Catholics into Scottish society – a path that opened the way to post-1918 effects.

References

Unpublished Sources (Archives, Pamphlets)

Glasgow Archdiocese Archives [GAA]:
  GAA (1873), GC5/1/6: Letter from James McIntosh to Vicar General, 28 November 1873.
  GAA (1882), GC14/4/1–2.
  GAA (1897), GC/29/95: Letter from Charles O'Neill to Archbishop, 15 December 1897.
  GAA (1913), GC45/68: Letter from D.J. Mitchel Quin to George Barns, MP, 15 April 1913.
Scottish Catholic Archives [SCA]:
  SCA (1907), SM13/43: Charles Byrne, *The School Board of Glasgow and the Education of Catholic Defective Children – The Catholic Position explained* (Glasgow: P. Donegan and Co. printers) 5.
  SCA (1914), SM13/43: Lord Skerrington, *The Educational Grievance of Scottish Catholics* (Glasgow).
Scottish Regional Archives [SRA]:
  SRA (1878), CO1/5/1/8/1: *Minute Book of Old Monkland School Board 1873–1879*, Meeting on 25 March 1878.
  SRA (1881a), CO1/5/1/8/2, *Minute Book of Old Monkland School Board 1880–1884*, Meeting on 26 September 1881.
  SRA (1881b), CO1/5/1/8/2: *Minute Book of Old Monkland School Board*, 1880–1884, Meeting on 31 October 1881.
  SRA (1905), CO1/5/5/1: *Airdrie School Board Minutes 1905*, 61.

Contemporary Newspapers

The Airdrie and Coatbridge Advertiser [AC].
The Coatbridge Express [CE].
The Coatbridge Leader [CL].
The Glasgow Examiner [GE].
The Glasgow Observer [GO].

Books and Articles

Bone, T.R. (ed.) (1967), *Studies in the History of Catholic Education 1872–1939* (London: University of London Press).

Devine, T.M. (2000), *The Scottish Nation 1700–2000* (London: Penguin Books).
Gallagher, T. (1987), *Glasgow: The Uneasy Peace. Religious Tension in Modern Scotland* (Manchester: Manchester University Press).
Handley, J.E. (1947), *The Irish in Modern Scotland* (Cork: Cork University Press).
Machin, I.G.T. (2000), *The Rise of Democracy in Britain, 1830–1918* (London: Macmillan Press).
Skinnider, M. (1967), 'Catholic Elementary Education in Glasgow, 1818–1918', in Bone (ed.).
Strong, J. (ed.) (1919), *Education (Scotland) Act, 1918, with Annotations* (Edinburgh: Oliver and Boyd).

PART 6
Citizenship

Chapter 11

'To Serve and to Elect':[1] The Women's Local Government Society, Britain 1888–1918

Myriam Boussahba-Bravard

> The battle for London had been fought by the Women's Local Government Society. It is one of the least known, yet was one of the most effective women's organizations in the late nineteenth century. (Hollis 1987: 317)

Thus writes Patricia Hollis in her opening paragraph on the Women's Local Government Society (WLGS) in the now classic *Ladies Elect* (1987). In the field of local government, the WLGS was part of the complex debate about its organizing principles, duties and elected representatives: who should be in charge of what? Who should be electors?

On 17 November 1888, this group defined its main objective as 'to promote the return, independently of party politics, of women as county councillors'. On 22 November 1888, on the suggestion of Eva McLaren, they adopted the 'Society to Promote the Return of Women as County Councillors' as a name (Minutes of the Executive Committee [MEC], 1888, 17 November); in early 1893, the 'Women's Local Government Society' (WLGS) was durably adopted.[2] The object of the society became 'to secure that women shall be equally with men eligible to be elected and serve on local governing bodies'. Thus they spelt out three claims that the law did not then sanction: *equally* with men, *married* women and spinsters alike should have access to *all* types of local administration (see Annex 1).

What looked like a short-term *ad hoc* London society, even for its founding members, was to structure into a principled, long-term national organization. Faced immediately with legal opposition from unhappy Tory candidates (at the 1889 London Council election), the group decided on fighting legal suits. They realized that the law had to be changed if women were to play their (still restricted) role of elected representatives. To defend their two (elected) female councillors[3] and support the one (co-opted) alderwoman on the London County

---

1 This was the motto of the Women's Local Government Society.
2 The acronym WLGS will be used for the whole period 1888–1918.
3 After the January 1889 London Council election of Margaret Sandhurst and Jane Cobden, unsuccessful Conservative candidates contested their elected mandates. Emma Cons was co-opted.

Council, they established long-term cooperation with male legal professionals, an aspect which was to be one of the strongest points of the WLGS in the following decades. While the WLGS hardened into a service society for grass root activists offering up-to-date and free legal expertise, the Liberal profile of its Executive Committee remained quite stable. From the start their upper-middle-class and Liberal lobbying networks proved extremely fruitful, which is why they stuck to this strategy until the 'civic and imperial' suffrage was granted to women – partially in 1918, then on the same terms as men in 1928. The WLGS was not a suffrage society as it did not ask for women's parliamentary vote; they wanted to extend women's rights to local participation and administration through full local citizenship, equally with men.

Once established they slipped into easy cooperation with sister national organizations whose objectives were compatible when not identical; hence, the Society to Return Women as Poor Law Guardians (1881–1904), the National Union of Women Workers (NUWW) (1888–1917) or the British Women's Temperance Association (BWTA), set up in 1876, worked with the WLGS. They exchanged speakers and meeting halls and had many common members both at grass roots and executive levels.[4] Their common ground was that women played a front-line part in social action, which was axiomatically local, and, for the sake of efficiency, women should reach local decision-making levels. These umbrella organizations surfed on the demand for, and the granting of, increasing powers and duties attributed to local government; electing women on Poor Law and school boards and on town councils (in the future) was the objective of WLGS political literature.

From an Ad Hoc Local Committee to a National Lobby Group, 1888–1893

The founding meeting took place in November 1888, at Mrs Sheldon Amos's house 'for the purpose of ascertaining the most eligible and likely ladies who would consent to put in nomination for election as members of the new county councils' (MEC 1888, 9 November). The 12 persons present, nine women and three men, belonged to the educated upper-middle-class circles with an interest in 'civic and imperial' politics. Sarah Amos, sister of Percy Bunting,[5] was then a widow and sat 'on the Executive Committee of the Women's Liberal Federation, was active in music-hall reform, the National Union of Women Workers and the Salvation Army' (Levine 2005a). She supported suffrage. Her sister-in-law, Mrs Bunting, née Mary Lidgett, came from a Methodist family involved in reforming circles. She supported her husband Percy's involvements in social reform, political

---

  4 The Society to Return Women as Poor Law Guardians (WGS) will be examined along with the WLGS. For the WGS, see Hollis 1987: 195–246. For the National Union of Women Workers, see Bush 2007: 105–31. For the British Women's Temperance Association, see Barrow 2000: 69–89.
  5 Percy Bunting was the editor of the *Contemporary Review* from 1888 until his death in 1911.

Liberalism and the welfare of modern Methodism. Her sister, Miss Elizabeth S. Lidgett (1843–1919) was a Poor Law guardian (she would remain so for 40 years in St Pancras ward) and a suffragist; she declined to stand for election to the London County Council in 1889 but remained a lifelong supporter of the WLGS (Martin 2005c, Montmorency 2005d, WLGS 1920: 29).

From its inception to its end, the key personality in the WLGS was Annie Leigh Browne (1851–1936) who started this society, used her contacts and money for policy developments as the Honorary Secretary of the WLGS (1888–1917).[6] She was born in Bristol in a philanthropic and social reformist family. Once in London, she became involved in girls' education and accommodation. At the same period she became the Honorary Secretary of the Paddington Women's Liberal Association. After 1888 she devoted most of her time to the Society for Promoting the return of Women as County Councillors which became in 1893 the WLGS.

The WLGS played a prominent part in the feminist campaign against the education acts of 1902 and 1903, under which the directly elected school boards on which women had been elected members since 1870 were replaced by local education authorities, on which women were disqualified from serving. Although as a concession to the agitation, the new education committees included co-opted members who were chosen for their involvement in education they lacked the authority of public support of elected members. Hence Annie Leigh Browne continued to organize and fund the campaign to secure access to local politics, and in 1907 her persistence was rewarded with the qualification of Women (County and Borough councils) Act (Martin 2005b).

Both Annie Leigh Browne and her friend Mary Kilgour (1851–1955) were convinced suffragists and quite impatient with the inconsequence of the Liberal party on women's suffrage. Mary Kilgour, a university graduate, supported herself through her maths teaching in advanced institutions for girls. She was part of the Executive Committee of the WLGS from December 1888 until 1918 and wrote much of its political literature in the 1890s. Many WLGS founding members sat on the National Executive of the Women's Liberal Federation (WLF) set up in 1886: Louisa Mallet and Emma Cons, Countess Aberdeen as President and Eva McLaren as Honorary Treasurer of both societies.[7] Louisa Mallet and Emma Maitland, Liberals, were Progressive party candidates for the 1891 London school board election. Both Emma Cons and Eva McLaren had worked with Octavia Hill and were prominent in the temperance movement just like Louisa Twining, a famous reformer of the workhouse system (Banks 1985: 216–17).

---

6 'Miss Browne guaranteed £200 in the event of insufficient subscriptions not coming into the defence case' (MEC 1890, 13 March). The defence case referred to is *De Souza v. Cobden*. See below note 9.

7 Honorary Treasurers of the WLGS: Eva McLaren 1888–1892; Mary Kilgour 1892–1900; Lady Lockyer (sister of Browne) 1900–1918. Presidents of the WLGS: Countess of Aberdeen 1888–1902; Louisa Twining 1903–1904; Lady Strachey: 1905–1918.

The two candidates who accepted to stand in the 1889 London election had to be unmarried;[8] Lady Sandhurst (a widow, founded the Marylebone Women's Liberal Association in 1887) stood successfully in Brixton. Miss Jane Cobden (then a spinster, and a promoter of women's suffrage within the Women's Liberal Federation) was also elected in the Bow and Bromley ward. Both had strong Liberal connections and were duly supported by the London Liberal and Radical clubs. Among the potential female candidates shortlisted by the WLGS but who declined to stand, some were avowedly Conservative. Octavia Hill declined because she remained opposed to the enlarged duties of local government; she also opposed parliamentary women's suffrage as did Lady Jessel (Conservative) and Lady Jersey, Countess of Jersey, Chairman of the anti-suffrage league (MEC 1888, 22 November). They thought it obvious that women's local participation would lead to a national one. However, some anti-suffragists such as Mary Ward welcomed women's local participation while opposing their parliamentary enfranchisement.

The three men present at the first meeting were barristers-at-law or elected to the London County Council (LCC) or both. Was this a sign that legal advice would be immediately needed?[9] Walter McLaren, a Liberal MP and dedicated suffragist, joined the Executive Committee on 17 December 1888 and on 20 December wrote to them urging the appointment of a solicitor. This combination of male legal professionals and local or parliamentary representatives was to be characteristic of the WLGS for years to come. Most were Liberals or 'Progressives' such as the Fabian solicitor Costelloe. However some Conservatives did work for the cause of women as county councillors. Lord Meath, a Conservative peer and philanthropist, an alderman on the London County Council (1889–1892; 1898–1901), was still a Vice-president of the WLGS in 1912. In the Lords, he introduced a private bill on women's qualification for local representation in May 1889 while Mr Channing did the same in the Commons. The Minutes of the corresponding 1889 Executive Committee of the WLGS detailed the preparation and strategic lobbying thus:

> The date for the second hearing being fixed for July 20th the question of the best means of obtaining support was considered. It was thought that information should be supplied to Lord Meath and the advice to friendly peers might be obtained from the Earl of Aberdeen. It was resolved that the secretaries be requested to see Lord and

---

8   See Annex 1 for a chronology of women and local governing bodies.

9   'In 1889 [Margaret Sandhurst] was a member of the council of the Women's Franchise League and ... in January was elected to the London County Council, returned by Brixton. Her election was in March declared void because she was a woman, on the petition of Beresford Hope the Conservative losing candidate' (Crawford 2001: 617). 'Jane Cobden [later Mrs Unwin] held on her seat because her defeated opponent declined to take legal action against her. ... However, once she began actively to participate in committee work, a writ was filed and in 1891 *De Souza* v. *Cobden* was heard in the Court of Appeal. Her membership of the council was held valid but her participation invalid' (Crawford 2001: 695). This paradox comes from the fact that legislation was passed ignoring women and the legal restrictions they suffered from.

Lady Aberdeen and Lord Meath. ... It was decided not to petition in favour of the bill but to get up memorials to individual members in both houses and to obtain an influentially signed memorial to Lord Salisbury, of which copies might be circulated to MPs. (MEC 1889, 1 May).

In 1889 the WLGS gave priority to influence and personal lobbying, perhaps because their small membership made it impossible to adopt another strategy. Although WLGS women were mostly Liberals, they met Conservatives sympathetic to their objective in their social circles. Conservatives could collaborate, and even support, the WLGS. Lady Strachey, a Conservative suffragist, joined the Executive Committee in 1900 and became its third president in 1905.

The same cannot be said about the Primrose League which had banned any involvement of its members in the Parliamentary suffrage campaign and debarred its branches from affiliating to other organizations. They were not likely either to support a female candidate if she was not a Conservative as their remit was exclusively to support the Conservative party (Vervaecke 2007: 180–202). In practice, this meant that the WLGS could expect no formal participation from Primrose League women, which singularly weakened their non-party stance (MEC 1888, 13 December).

The WLGS consisted of reformist women (with a few men) who may have had front-line experience but also possessed several qualities essential to national propaganda: they had money; ladies of their class did not have jobs; they knew publishers, could write about their individual experience and beliefs and were read by their peers. By birth and education, they were involved in existing networks and practices, which eased their access to each other's address books. The WLGS was from the start overwhelmingly Liberal, first through the individual affiliation of its members and their family circles. Besides, their method – lobbying influential males in power, in a discreet way – was another illustration of the Liberal tradition applied by and to women. Its non-party stance was in keeping with the wish of well-meaning individuals, males and females, for public service and general good within a prescriptive dynamics of structural change: this was more akin to the Liberal idea of 'progress' than to the Conservative vision of society, even when the latter was reformist.

The Development of an Umbrella Organization: The Fieldwork of Sister Groups Fed WLGS Propaganda

The Society for Promoting the Return of Women as Poor Law Guardians (also Women Guardians' Society, WGS) was founded in 1881 by Miss Ward Andrews (later Mrs Heberden), Caroline Ashurst Biggs, Laura Ormiston Chant and Eva Muller (later Mrs Eva McLaren), all of them suffragists and Liberals. Chant and Muller were also temperance activists. The remit of the WGS was 'to promote the election or appointment of properly qualified and suitable women as Guardians of the Poor' (Crawford 2001: 105, 397–9, 642, WGS 1890: 2). This society was undoubtedly a forerunner to the WLGS which promoted women's participation first to county councils and after 1893 to all local governing bodies, making the Women Guardians' Society (WGS) somewhat redundant. Besides, Annie Leigh Browne had previously set up a Local Electors' Association (1886–1888) with Eva Muller (Mrs McLaren) and Caroline Biggs (d. 1889): connections between these groups were obvious. After 1893, the WLGS provided the Women Guardians' Society with literature and speakers, shared its premises, sold its literature and after the national WGS disbanded in 1904 sent the requested information, usually of a legal nature, to isolated Poor Law guardians or local groups. The WLGS even organized a nationwide inquiry on women Poor Law guardians and published a 34-page pamphlet entitled the *List of Women Poor Law Guardians and Rural District Councillors in England and Wales 1904*. As usual with these political women,[10] this publication had a double objective: to show the high number of women involved and at the same time the low ratio of female to male representatives. The second aim was to protest against the abolition of school boards (1902; 1904 in London) and the consequent disqualification of women (see Annex 1).

Lists of members of both societies clearly show how valuably connected the two societies were from the early beginnings of the WLGS in 1888. Comparing the directing committees and membership of the 1889 WGS and of the 1903 Women's Local Government Society highlights how closely the two groups were related. Their structure and membership were also remarkably stable through time. Many of the 1889 WGS members belonged to the 1903 WLGS (WGS 1890: 2–3, WLGS 1904a: 2–3, 27–38).

Table 11.1 Women Guardians' Society members 1889 compared with Women's Local Government Society members 1903

1889 Women Guardians' Society	1903 Women's Local Government Society
President (Lord Meath)	One (out of 4) Vice-President (Lord Meath)
10 Vice-Presidents	–
20 Council Members	9 (out of 20) belonged to the WLGS of whom 3 sat on the Executive Committee (out of WLGS 25) 6 were ordinary members
9 on the Executive Council	2 (out of 9) were ordinary members
60 Lady Guardians ex officio members of the Executive Council	17 (out of 60) belonged to the WLGS of whom 2 sat on the Executive Committee (out of 25)

---

10 These activists may have objected to such an adjective, but involved in women's political emancipation as they were, they were undoubtedly 'political' women.

This did not prevent the subscription of ordinary WGS members to the WLGS, nor did it deter the increasing number of individuals convinced of the need for female representation locally and nationally. WGS branches were clearly asked to affiliate to the WLGS and it was more likely than not that locally they would share premises, local information and speakers as well as members. Obviously the Poor Law guardians naturally had their place in the WLGS, even more so after the Women Guardians' Society folded in 1904 (Hollis 1987: 205–35). Would the increasing number of ladies Poor Law guardians subscribe to the official successor of the WGS?

The 1894 Local Government Act introduced a residence qualification instead of a property one. This allowed for the massive arrival of working-class candidates, including women, and the nomination and election of women, including married women. 'One hundred and fifty nine women were guardians in 1893, eight hundred and seventy five in 1895' (five and half times more). 'But by 1897 its [WGS] Annual Report sadly noted that only a hundred of the country's nine hundred women guardians were members of the society. It lacked the money to contact the hundreds of newly elected women in the provinces.' By 1897 only 11 per cent of the women guardians subscribed to the WGS; these subscribers may have been the same or the predecessors of those who transferred to women's umbrella organizations such as the WLGS after 1904.

This snowball effect (or the critical mass effect) discredited the traditional 'reflex hostility of many guardians and Poor Law officials to women joining their boards' (Hollis 1987: 208–9, 236). Party politics which had been rebuked by many female guardians in the past came back to the fore as the legitimate way to select a candidate. If female empowerment had been of use for a transitional period before the 1894 Act, the 1894 parish legislation made the WGS less significant: its sponsoring became less valuable because it was now less effective than party sponsoring. Besides backing female candidates as 'women' at election times, there was now the WLGS.

The first annual report of the Women's Local Government Society (1893) indicated 96 individual subscribers and donors; this figure increased steadily each year to 176 in 1897 (+ 83 per cent since 1893), 253 in 1900 (+44 per cent since 1897) and 483 in 1904 (+90 per cent since 1900). Until 1907,[11] the society remained small in terms of numbers despite its growth. Interestingly, bigger numbers meant more influential subscribers all over the country. And yet the increased budget of the early 1900s did not match the increase in numbers. This could mean that the new subscribers' wealth did not match the original ones' (budget increases: 1893–1897: +150 per cent; 1897–1900: +99 per cent; 1900–1904: +17 per cent). The affiliated groups numbered 21 in 1894, and 26 in 1904; nearly all of them (respectively 90 per cent and 92 per cent) were Women's Liberal Associations. After 1907 the demand and conditions of affiliations varied so much (see Annex 1) that the WLGS set up a subcommittee to deal with them. Suffrage activity was then intense in the country and women's local franchise had been achieved. In

---

11 The Qualification of Women (County and Borough Councils) Act was passed in 1907.

1908–1909, the minutes of their Executive Committee mentioned the following applications:

Group	Affiliation	Date
The York branch of the NUWW	Agreed	13 November 1907
Registration of Nurses Committee (because 'Out of scope')	Rejected	11 December 1907
Birkenhead WLGS (only if it became a WLG Association)	Agreed	8 January 1908
Oxford WLGA (only once financial agreement reached)	Agreed	8 January 1908
The Herbert Road branch of the Woolwich Women's Cooperative Guild	Agreed	12 February 1908
Bath Association for the Return of the Women Guardians ('The Committee expressed the hope that the Association would extend their scope of work, so as to include the return of women to all local government bodies.')	Agreed	13 May 1908
Chelsea WLG A	Agreed	22 July 1908
The local government Sectional Committee of the (new) Bromley branch of the NUWW	Agreed	7 October 1908
Anerley Women's Meeting (as it was not a structured group, it could only be affiliated under the name of their secretary)	Agreed	9 December 1909
Synemouth Women's Local Government Association	Agreed	15 January 1909
St Marylebone WLGA The local government Sectional Committee of the Brighton branch of the NUWW	Agreed	10 March 1909

Interestingly, in their first years most of their work was in and about Parliament. What mattered was lobbying: going to Parliament and meeting MPs and Lords, sending deputations to members of the government. Writing letters, networking and taking well-informed advice did not need high numbers to be effective either. This must be the reason why little literature can be traced from the earlier period: lobbying was more important than propaganda. With their first success in 1894 and their setbacks in 1899 and 1902,[12] the WLGS realized that they should be working on both fronts. The problem in 1894 had been to find women willing to

---

12 When London vestries became boroughs (1899), women lost their electoral qualification (see WLGS 1899). In 1902 school boards were abolished; town councils directly managed education authorities instead, thus disqualifying women who had sat on school boards since 1870 (see WLGS 1901, WLGS 1902b).

go through the electoral process of nomination, campaigning and election. The small numbers of nominees and eventually elected women could be used by anti-suffragists to prove their point, that women wanted neither the vote nor the job. Although this was an argument used against female parliamentary suffrage, it was raised for local elections too. The second argument used by the antis (or the indifferent) was that election was not the best way to get the best suited women into local government: co-option was seen by many as the way to ensure women's service without any recognition of their potential political weight. With the 1899 and 1902 changes (see Annex 1) the same problem arose; if co-option was a way to obtain women's participation in local duties, why bother about reforming the law (WLGS 1902a)? As the WLGS was well aware, apathy was the next danger after stark opposition. Hence informative propaganda from the WLGS to wider and wider circles became a necessity not only because of their success in recruiting members and affiliating groups but also as one weighty component of successful parliamentary lobbying.

Pamphlets directly published by the WLGS, sold to branches or sister organizations, project the image of a society whose tone had to be self-controlled and whose contents aimed at exhaustive information. The pamphlets were densely informative, sold by the hundred or the dozen from the WLGS office. Although the WLGS usually called them 'leaflets', the standard pamphlet numbered four pages. No pamphlet prior to 1894 could be traced either because they did not publish any[13] or because they used available literature from the Women Guardians' Society.[14] The 1894 success vindicated the WLGS; it produced and distributed 37 different items over the period 1894–1918. In the post 1907 Qualification of Women Act period, publication was scarcer and consisted of long annual meeting speeches. By contrast, hard facts dominated the pamphlets issued between 1894 and 1907. The peak years' new production corresponds to four items per year in 1894, 1902, 1904 and five in 1907, all of them answering major changes in the law (see Annex 1). Besides reprints, WLGS members could use the platform of other organizations. In 1903, Mrs Bamford Slack (WLGS and Liberal member) wrote a suffragist pamphlet *A Menace to Liberty* published by the Women's Liberal Federation, in which she based her suffragist arguments on women's contribution to local government and their disqualification from town and borough councils.

The Local Government Act of 1894 was good news 'for on the new local governing Bodies it is expressly provided that women may serve, and in the

---

13 The hypothesis that there was none seems acceptable if one remembers that the first annual report is for the year 1893. Pamphlets that have been traced are in the pamphlet collection of the London School of Economics.

14 The Society for Promoting the Return of Women as Poor Law Guardians published in 1887 *Some Notes upon the Election of the Guardians of the Poor* by Caroline Ashurst Biggs, a 14-page reprint from the *Englishwoman's Review*, 15 March 1887. The nine first pages deal with election law and processes and the importance of women's participation in local government. The final pages turned into Biggs's vision of good management of Poor Law and her analysis of pauperism. The *Englishwoman's Review* backed the WGS (Hollis 1987: 234).

electorate married women have their rightful place' (WLGS 1894c: 1–2). This pamphlet entitled *Women's Work in England and Wales (not including London) under the Government Act, 1894, popularly known as the Parish and District Councils Act* was first published that same year and dealt with changes:

> But although it is the duty of women to see that the men elected are fit and proper persons, their duty does not end there. Not only must women offer themselves as Guardians as heretofore, but for the Council in every parish and in every District (other than borough) one or more suitable women should be induced to let themselves be nominated as candidates, – women of some firmness of character, determined to learn the new work patiently, to co-operate with their colleagues with good will and tact, and capable when principle is involved of making a stand even if unsupported by others. (WLGS 1894c: 1–2)

This pamphlet belonged to the (likely) first series published by the WLGS. Women were informed of their new rights which typically implied new duties. Contemporary women could not misunderstand the modal phrases: they had to take part through their vote, candidacy and election. The language of duty and moral qualities drew the ideal picture of a paragon woman (a language targeting a female audience) which may have been deterring to some would-be female candidates. On the other hand the contemporary tone and writing style – systematic then in women's political literature – stemmed from moral common place convention and softened such righteous overtones. Once women were ready for the contest, they were told what work was about in each administrative unit (parish councils, rural district councils now including Poor Law, urban district councils which were not boroughs). 'But as the Act does not deal with the constitution of town councils, women remain ineligible for these councils owing to the disability imposed on them by the Municipal Corporations Act.' There they could only stand for the separate Poor Law board election and serve as guardians. The short conclusion hoped women would

> (1) poll in large numbers for the best candidates;
> (2) offer themselves for election. For the former active work in registering qualified women is a necessary preliminary; and, as preparation for the latter careful study of the needs of localities is strongly recommended. (WLGS 1894c: 4)

Duties were clear and methods too. Women's group work was emphasized. Neither should women believe that local politics was open to them by right: they would have to fight for their election, a step which in the past had debarred many qualified women from standing, especially on the much sought after school board – hence the former 'genteel' tactics of standing where none was willing to stand or negotiating to be the only candidate (Hollis 1987: 221–7). Obviously this was foregone history already in 1894 when women and working-class citizens could and did stand thanks to the new residence qualification. This widening democratic basis is indicated by the numbers who stood as well as the choice of candidates, usually endorsed by a political party or one or several support groups, sometimes both (Hollis 1987: 224–6).

The second 1894 pamphlet, *Women's Work in London*, adopted the same format. Changes were stated and the duties of London local bodies were listed:

> Their constitution is changed in the following way: – 'The Ballot Act and the Corrupt Practices Act are applied for the first time; the property qualification is abolished; and the principle of one person, one vote is established.' Further it is now made clear by the Act that women can serve on the London vestries and the Woolwich Board of health, and that married women ratepayers can be parochial electors.

The change is soberly acknowledged as 'making democratic the constitution of the Vestries and Board of Guardians'. More unusual in a pamphlet is the paragraph devoted to the vital role of the overseers described in this way:

> ... the most important vestry officials, the Overseers, whose chief duty it is to make and levy the poor rate, and also to make out the lists of parliamentary and local electors. The Overseers must be householders, and are usually nominated by the vestry. It is amusing to read: 'Even a woman may be appointed though men of discretion and substance are usually preferred!' (*Instructions and Explanations for the assistance of Overseers*, published by Shaw & Sons, Fetter Lane) ... Meanwhile it is likely that women occupiers would have fewer complaints to make of being omitted from the register if one of the overseers were a woman. The accounts of the Vestries are audited by elected Auditors. Women can be elected. (WLGS 1894b: 1–2)

The amusement mentioned is a small revenge compared to the permanent problems women had with overseers. Even if the law was far from being clear, overseers usually took no risk and/or thought they were doing public good by systematically excluding women from the register. Of course, in practice the overseer could not be a woman as no vestry would appoint a woman in such a vital office. The above quotation illustrates the common stereotype about women being without 'discretion' or 'substance'. How contemporaries reconciled this shallow superficial vision with the one of the (too) stern (too) dutiful (remarkably) effective lady guardian probably lies in the inconsistencies of the human mind backed by contemporaries' ideological perception of women.[15] The final page of the pamphlet lists local authorities in London 'with names of clerks and addresses of offices' and suggests women should read their local 'annual reports, which contain important information'. Ladies dutifully poring over reports and checking that reality matched the book were not uncommon as the numerous testimonies accounted (Hollis 1987, 303–354).

The pamphlet entitled *The Position of Women under the Local Government Act, 1894*, issued in 1894 explained the rights of women which were 'large, but not equal to those secured to men':

---

15 The ideological vision of women was that they were light and inconsistent, that is 'feminine'. If they were of the serious type, for instance lady guardians, they became 'unfeminine'; in both cases they were objects of ridicule in their contemporaries' eyes.

[Marriage no longer disqualified a woman] for voting in elections under this Act, provided that husband and wife not be qualified in respect of the same property. ... The inequality between the electoral rights of men and women under the Act is introduced by the inclusion of the Parliamentary register. This inclusion newly confers full parochial rights on three classes of men, without conferring them on the same classes of women: the three classes referred to are male owners, male lodgers, and men enjoying the service franchise. *In respect to elections of poor law guardians, women owners are actually deprived of the right to vote which they have hitherto had.*

All parochial electors or alternatively all the residents for at least 12 months could be candidates. This WLGS pamphlet went on:

It is easier for a man to qualify as a parochial elector than for a woman, but the residential qualification is equal between men and women, married and single, and will be invaluable as enabling many married women to give their services as Guardians, as District and Parish Councillors and as members of London vestries. (WLGS 1894a: 1–4)

Making the local franchise dependent on the parliamentary one could simplify male registration; on the other hand it increased electoral discrimination facing women at the local level as no woman could be on the 'parliamentary register'. However the WLGS could be satisfied that residence instead of rate-paying and matrimonial status placed women on the local register, even if unmarried women became disqualified as 'householders' and qualified as residents like married women.

Service and Citizenship

To serve was indeed easier than to elect. By 1894 the ideal of public work and public good in which women *gave* service to the community was hardly ever questioned. Their granted participation was objectified into another avatar of the feminine domestic role where sacrifice and one-way service were the rules. Women's groups (including the WLGS) would use these arguments to safeguard female involvement at local levels. They may have genuinely believed it; but they also understood that once their mandates and work was acknowledged, once their cautious speeches were common place, once their self-restraint was properly understood as determination, they could demand more. The gradual transfer from philanthropic to civic work, from service to citizenship, echoes the debate on pauperism versus poverty in the sense that contemporary thinking gradually took in the status of the individual not as an aggregate of the many making up the community but as a person endowed with rights, whether the individual was working-class, a pauper or a woman. Thus 'the class of women' does make sense as a group reaching for political emancipation; the more emancipated the less relevant the grouping.¹⁶ The implicit contention women had to face (and perhaps fight) was their equivalence to 'family', denying them their individuality.

Jane Lewis's *Women and Social Action in Victorian and Edwardian England* (1991) addresses 'social action' through the writings and campaigns of five well-known females, Octavia Hill, Beatrice Webb, Helen Bosanquet, Mary Ward and Violet Markham to conclude on 'the possibilities and limitations of women's social action' (Hollis 1987: 247–302, Lewis 1991: 302). These women activists grounded their action in 'charity' which, towards the end of the century, gradually melted into the scope and duties of local government. These first-rank women objectified 'local involvement' as a stepping stone to national debates. They drew their national roles from their first-hand experiences in social action which led them to campaign for social reform principally concerned with 'family' management, a concept however which dissolved women as individuals. In her article on 'Gender, the Family and Women's Agency in the Building of the 'Welfare State:' the British Case', Jane Lewis (1994) shows how

> Family and gender were neglected, notwithstanding the fact that the rules concerning eligibility and entitlements have always been saturated with gendered assumptions about family relationships. …The classic texts ignore gender, the family and indeed the voluntary sector. Most texts have considered welfare only in terms of state welfare. (Lewis 1994: 37 fn. 1)

Still today, the relative neglect of local and women's issues – not to say local women's issues – seems to be the corollary of highlighting state and family, easier-to-deal-with units than 'women' even though they may be wives and mothers. Lewis states that 'family' is both a consumer and a provider of welfare and stands as a convenient euphemism for caring unpaid roles assumed by female members of the family. She also remarks that 'the study of women and poverty, for example, has remained largely separate, notwithstanding the concern about lone mother families' (Lewis 1994: 38 fn. 4).

In the period when the WLGS was active, women involved in local social action were already seen as demonstrating their traditional and respected abilities as 'carers', an activity which they could not be blamed for. Local care was traditionally organized at two levels; philanthropic ladies organized charity for poorer women. Whether actors or recipients of help, these women partook of their 'caring role'. That is why the WLGS deliberately excluded anything which was not 'local' and which was not about 'local governing bodies'. Such a strategy breathed caution to better maintain consensus about the caring role of women in their families, the natural extension to the children in need and – euphemistically

---

16 Here is a description of Women Guardians before 1894: 'In so far as [women guardians] continued to read pauperism as moral degeneracy rather than as economic or social dislocation (which under COS [Charity Organization Society] influence they largely did), then they [were] among the most conservative members of their boards, the most judgemental, and the most unpopular' (Hollis 1987: 238). The post 1894 increasing participation in local government of females from various class and political backgrounds made it impossible to see any longer women guardians as such a homogeneous group.

again – the 'children-like' destitute and paupers. By arguing that women had to be on local governing bodies because of their expertise in 'female' fields, that they had to elect and to serve because they did better jobs, the WLGS integrated the contemporary discourse on women's nature. In turn this served two objects: it did not battle in a frontal attack with the more conservative views on women and women's roles. For instance, some anti-suffragists (and suffragists too) supported the local female franchise through arguments based on female essence. Secondly it tried to set men and women not in stark rivalry but in two complementary fields, politics and care. However such a low argumentative profile (about why women should have the local vote) could not cast a shadow over the WLGS target of the *technical* enfranchising of women.

Besides, women's political presence still had to be neutralized, even though, by the end of the nineteenth century, local government politics was a *passage obligé* for women as recipients of local welfare, as social activists or political 'community' contestants. What was at stake, in fact, in the late decade of the nineteenth century was the normalization of single women in local politics and the arrival of married women on the same stage. Playing low key allowed the WLGS to have 'family women' enfranchised, even if officially it was for the sake of the same 'family' these wives had to be extracted from to give them political existence (Boussahba 2003: 42–53). However, it would be hasty to conclude that the WLGS women members were 'maternalists' or exclusively devoted to the welfare of mothers and children, especially as their remit, 'women to elect and to serve on all governing bodies', was geared towards all women becoming electors and getting elected, including working-class activists. After 1894 the WLGS and the WGS organized talks to increase the number of married working-class female candidates and backed them. Indeed, the latter vindicated the WLGS years of lobbying for women as a group, whatever their class and party affiliation. The WLGS agenda was to end sex discrimination in local politics, and it never abandoned its non-party stand. The fact that the WLGS was non-party – despite its members being Liberal and middle class – was also soothing for many of these newcomers who took their first steps in politics and supported labour groups.

The WLGS was truly involved in political work, even if it was officially to help women reach decision levels for the sake of social policies. Their remit was about empowerment of women beyond class; their means was electioneering and there was no stigma of social origins if women were 'suitable'; as long as women were elected it became a victory because gender superseded class. Their approach was based on the idea that all types of women were capable of service; their (mainly) Liberal individual affiliations made them believe in improvement through time of systems and individuals with potential. Their main concern was having female candidates standing at local elections. The WLGS moralistic tone illustrated the widespread idea that, by essence, women were morally superior to men, which meant that they should be rewarded with the vote. The lower-key phrase 'equally with men' suggested that, by right, women too should be part of the electoral process.

With such a vision of the role women had to play in local government, a vision which included women in and worked for the democratization of local politics, it became difficult to obliterate the role women could play in national politics. If, according to the WLGS, they were capable of so much locally, they could not but be expected to be capable nationally. The WLGS as a group never varied from its non-party non-suffragist position, but individual members were overwhelmingly – and logically – suffragists.

Annex 1: A Chronology of Women in Local Government

Poor Law Boards remained independent from Local Government structure up to 1914; this guaranteed that women (first unmarried female householders then all female residents) retained the vote and eligibility as guardians from 1875. From 1894 residents made up parochial electors instead of ratepayers and owners (WLGS 1894a, b, c, Graham and Brodhurst 1894: ix–x).

In the Edwardian period, female householders, single or widowed women and owners or tenants of property, may have represented 16 per cent of the municipal electorate; determining their class remains difficult (Tanner 1990: 124–7). From 1894, outside municipal elections, married women could qualify as residents or as owners (if it was not for the same property as their husbands).

1835 local representation	Municipal Reform Act. Town councillors elected for two and a half years by ratepayers, males over 21 owners or tenants of property. Wards for voting in towns over 6,000.
1844 social reform	Poor Law Amendment Act. Owners and ratepayers were allowed to vote for the election of guardians.
1867 Representation of the People Act	Borough franchise extended to all *male* ratepayers and lodgers paying rental of £10, and one-year residence qualification
1870 education reform	School boards set up. *All women could be candidates. All ratepayers including women could vote.*
1870 status of women	Married Women's Property Act allows women to retain £200 of their own earnings
1875 status of women	Women householders eligible for election to local Boards of Guardians.
1882 status of women	Married women's Property Acts allows women to own and administer their property.
1884 Representation of the People Act	Uniform male parliamentary franchise in boroughs and counties on the basis of the 1867 Act.
1884 status of women	Married Women's Property Act makes a woman no longer a 'chattel' but an independent and separate person.
1888 Local Government Act	County councils set up, elected by ratepayers *including (unmarried) women householders*.
1889 Local Government, London	Establishment of London County Council. *Unmarried women householders could vote but could not sit on councils.**

1894 Local Government Act	All parliamentary electors given the vote in local elections, *means no women*. Rural and urban district councils set up. Vestries abolished and new parish councils set up. Poor Law boards remained independent bodies. *All female ratepayers, including married women, eligible to vote for and sit on parish and district councils, London vestries and to sit on Poor Law and school boards. Still debarred from sitting on county and borough councils.*
1899 Local Government Act, London	London vestries converted into borough councils. *All Women lost the parochial franchise based on residence. Only unmarried women householders could vote.*
1902 education reform	School boards abolished and replaced by new local education authorities; county and borough councils in charge of them. *All women lost their standing qualifications, could only be co-opted. Unmarried female householders could vote.*
1904 London	London school boards abolished. *Women could only be co-opted.*
1907 status of women	Qualification of women (County and Borough Councils) Act. *All Women allowed to vote and become town councillors.*
1918 Representation of the People Act	Common franchise for county councils, boroughs, rural and urban districts on the basis of the parliamentary register (*women allowed to become MPs*): universal male (over 21) qualification; female (over 30) property-based qualification.
1925 status of women	Married Women's Property Act requires husband and wife to be treated as separate individuals in any property transaction.
1928 Representation of the People Act	Women and men on the same terms on Parliamentary and local registers: universal suffrage for men and women over 21.
1929 Local Government Act	Boards of Guardians abolished and their functions transferred to county councils and county boroughs.

* (Parker 1888, 11, 25). See note 9.

Sources: Parker 1892, 1894; WLGS 1894a, b, c, 1899, 1901, 1902a, b; Lauder 1907; Wright and Hobhouse, 1914; Cook and Stevenson 1983; Graham and Brodhurst 1894; Hollis 1987.

References

Unpublished Sources

Graham, H. and Brodhurst, S. (1894), *A Practical Guide to the Parish Council Act, 1894* (London).
Lauder, A.E. (1907), *The Municipal Manual, a Description of the Constitution and Functions of Urban Local Authorities* (London).
Parker, F.R. (1892), *The Local Government Act, 1888*, 2nd edn (London).
Parker, F.R. (1894), *The Election of Parish Councils under the Local Government Act, 1894* (London).
Wright R. S. and Hobhouse, H. (1914), *An Outline of Local Government and Local Taxation in England and Wales (excluding London)*, 4th edn (London).

Women Guardians' Society (WGS)

Biggs, C.A. (1887), *Some Notes upon the Election of the Guardians of the Poor* (London: WGS), a 14-page reprint from the *Englishwoman's Review* (15 March 1887), London School of Economics.
Society for Promoting the Return of Women as Poor Law Guardian (1890), *Ninth Annual Report* (London: WGS), London School of Economics.

Women's Local Government Society (WLGS)

MEC, 'Minutes of the Executive Committee' 1888–1907, Women's Local Government Society Papers, London Metropolitan Archives.
WLGS (1894a), *The Position of Women under the Local Government Act* (London: WLGS), London School of Economics Pamphlet Collection.
WLGS (1894b), *Women's Work in London under the Government Act, 1894, popularly known as the Parish and District Councils act* (London: WLGS), London School of Economics Pamphlet Collection.
WLGS (1894c), *Women's Work in England and Wales (not including London) under the Government Act, 1894, popularly known as the parish and district councils Act* (London: WLGS), London School of Economics Pamphlet Collection.
WLGS (November 1899), *The London Government Act, the Latest Disqualification of Women* (London: WLGS), London School of Economics Pamphlet collection.
WLGS (October 1901), *Local Education Authorities and the Need for Women as Members* (London: WLGS), London School of Economics Pamphlet Collection.
WLGS (April 1902a), *Election versus Co-option* (London: WLGS), London School of Economics Pamphlet Collection.
WLGS (October 1902b), *Opinions of Chairmen and Other Eminent Members of the London School Board on the Work of Women Members* (London: WLGS), London School of Economics Pamphlet Collection.
WLGS (1904a), *Annual 1903 Report* (London: WLGS), London School of Economics.
WLGS (1904b), *List of Women Poor Law Guardians and Rural District Councillors in England and Wales 1904* (London: WLGS), London School of Economics Pamphlet Collection.
WLGS (1920), *Annual Report 1919–1920* (London: WLGS), London School of Economics.

Biographical Sources

Banks, O. (1985), *The Biographical Dictionary of British Feminists* (Brighton: Wheatsheaf Books).
Crawford, E. (2001), *The Women's Suffrage Movement* (London: Routledge).
Levine, P. (2005a), 'Amos, Sarah McLardie (1840–1908)', in *ODNB*.
Martin, J. (2005b), 'Browne, Annie Leigh (1851–1936)', in *ODNB*.
Martin, J. (2005c), 'Lidgett, Elizabeth Sedman (1843–1919), in *ODNB*.
Montmorency, J.E.G. de, revised by Macquiban, T. (2005d), 'Bunting, Sir Percy William (1836–1911)', in *ODNB*.
Oxford Dictionary of National Biography (ODNB) (2005e), <http://www.oxforddnb.com/> (home page), accessed 15 April 2005.

Books and Articles

Barrow, M. (2000), 'Teetotal Feminists: Temperance, Leadership and the Campaign for Women's Suffrage', in Eustance, C. et al. (eds).
Boussahba-Bravard, M. (2003), 'Vision et visibilité: la rhétorique visuelle des suffragistes et des suffragettes britanniques 1907–1914', *LISA/ LISA e-journal*, 1:1, 42–53 (published online 2003) <http://www.unicaen.fr/mrsh/lisa/publications/001/table001fr.pdf.>, accessed 15 April 2005.
Boussahba-Bravard, M. (ed.) (2007), *Suffrage Outside Suffragism, Women's Vote in Britain 1880–1914* (London: Palgrave).
Bush, J. (2007), 'The National Union of Women Workers and Women's Suffrage', in Boussahba-Bravard (ed.).
Cook, C. and Stevenson, J. (1996), *Modern British History 1714–1995*, 3rd ed. (London: Longman).
Eustance, C., Ryan, J. and Ugolini, L. (eds) (2000), *A Suffrage Reader, Charting Directions in British Suffrage History* (London: Leicester University Press).
Hollis, P. (1987), *Ladies Elect: Women in English Local Government, 1865–1914* (Oxford: Clarendon).
Lewis, J. (1991), *Women and Social Action in Victorian and Edwardian England* (Aldershot: Edward Elgar).
Lewis, J. (1994), 'Gender, the Family and Women's Agency in the Building of the "Welfare State": The British Case', *Social History* 19:1, 37–55.
Tanner, D. (1990), *Political Change and the Labour Party 1900–1918* (Cambridge: Cambridge University Press).
Vervaecke, P. (2007), 'The Primrose League and Women's Suffrage', in Boussahba-Bravard (ed.).

Chapter 12

The 'Third Way' and the Governance of the Social in Britain

Jérôme Tournadre-Plancq

Regardless of the 'world of Welfare' in which it functions – to use the term coined by Gøsta Esping-Andersen (1990) – the state has, during a large part of the twentieth century, come to play an essential role in the handling of welfare in liberal democracies. This does not mean that its role amounts to exercising a monopoly. Providing a counterweight to the market in the social-democratic 'compromise', the Welfare State often emerges, in the political thought of the majority of the post-war centre-left, as the most reliable guarantor of the common good. The 'social' (Donzelot 1984) is then considered as the best way to reinforce this idea. The 'welfare backlash' (Merrien 2005: 253) which marked the 1980s and 1990s has reversed this belief. Sustaining and feeding on the premise of a 'crisis' of the Fordist Welfare State, this backlash constituted, above all, an ideological attack on an institution accused of 'inefficiency' to which there was only one possible solution: retrenchment. Particularly widespread in Great Britain during the Thatcher years, this offensive takes as its model the ideal of the 'Hollow State' (Peters 1993). It is given substance in various movements running concurrently: a wave of privatizations affecting certain public services, liberalization leading to the fragmentation of welfare between several bodies (private and 'para-public') deregulation of the Social through the emergence of internal markets in some public services, and the abandonment of universalism in favour of a better targeted, residual social assistance. Nevertheless, as Colin Crouch (Crouch 2004: 103) remarks, the free market economy thus promoted by neoliberalism does not exist in the state of nature. The apparent withdrawal of the British Welfare State is only made possible by strengthening the power of a centralized state in order to guarantee the best framework for privatization and the *commodification of welfare* (see Gamble 1988).

Whatever form it might take, the questioning of the state's primacy has led to a 'change of style' in the handling of the Social, evident even within the left. Traces of this change can be found more precisely in the theorization of the Third Way, a political project elaborated at the heart of intellectual and political 'left-wing' groups in the early nineties. Dissatisfied with the traditional ways of apprehending the relationship between public and private initiatives, a number of advocates of this 'new progressivism' (see Gamble and Wright 2004: 1–10) have set out to redefine the new shape of welfare, a step which should lead to a conception of the role of the institution as no longer exclusively that of a 'proprietor or an employer'. The state must, above all, assert itself as a 'partner, an enabler, a catalyst, a coordinator' (Brown 1995: 4). Its principal role (enabling each individual to have access to the resources necessary for his personal development) thus amounts to directly ensuring distribution of its goods and services.

The stance adopted by Third-Wayers as regards the duties of the state can be read as an indictment of the 'interventionism' associated with Old Labour and of a vision of the state – the 'nanny state' – mainly influenced by mid-century Fabianism. Douglas Jay's now famous words 'The men of Whitehall know best' best sum up the interventionist, *dirigiste* attitude of which Old Labour is accused. According to the Third Way, it is essential to allow agents other than the state to participate in the domain of welfare and to ensure the distribution of certain goods and services. Third-Wayers thus hope to pave the way for 'social governance' by proposing the development of partnerships in social protection. This will to reconfigure the domain of welfare has found expression within the framework of a 'New Localism'[1] which includes characteristic notions such as the community, mutualism and also that ideal local *leader* – the social entrepreneur.

Finally, it is essential to emphasize that this discussion will focus only on the ideas put forward to legitimize this form of 'governance' and the way these ideas have been circulated in the politico-intellectual debate surrounding the Third Way.[2]

The Return of the Community

One of the characteristics of the 'space of theorization' of the Third Way has been to encourage, within its midst, a confrontation between various currents of thought, going from 'Christian socialism' to 'left-wing liberalism' or, then again, 'Keynesian social democracy'. Despite this pluralism, the main theoreticians

---

1 'A strategy aimed at devolving power and resources away from central control and towards front-line managers, local democratic structures and local consumers and communities, within an agreed framework of national minimum standards ...' (Stoker 2004: 117).

2 A definition should be given here of what is intended by the 'Third Way' in these pages. Convinced that any domination in a debate is the result of a hegemony in the British market of ideas, in the early 1990s the 'modernizing' wing of *Labour* undertook to mobilize various thinkers (academics, think tanks, experts, etc.) to elaborate a 'new' doctrine. This call for intellectual mobilization has contributed to the emergence of a specific social space: *the space of theorization of the Third Way*. Built on a fabric of formal and informal relationships, areas of research and all manner of social exchanges, the space of theorization has as its sole purpose the elaboration of a 'new progressivism'. The 'Third Way' referred to here is, therefore, not a mere reference to neo-Labour, that is to say to the policies, beliefs and practices of the 'modernizers' but an amalgam of the different contributions made within the space aforementioned, acknowledged by its participants as well as those outside. It can be likened to a sort of *maximal agenda* from which can be lifted certain theoretical elements necessary for the foundation of 'New Labour'.

of the Third Way have identified two major traits allowing a definition of the social order: the emergence of a new form of individualism[3] and the growing interdependence of individuals. The tensions which arise from the interaction of these two phenomena can be overcome, according to a majority of Third-Wayers, by emphasizing the 'virtues' of the community. The central position occupied by the community in the theoretical corpus of the Third Way can be explained in several ways. One of the first reasons might be the influence on the British centre-left of United States political doctrine concerning the community. This philosophy, pivotal to the speeches of the New Democrats of Bill Clinton and Al Gore, has received the attention of influential members of the space of theorization, especially that of the think tank Demos, co-founded by Geoff Mulgan, one of Tony Blair's principal advisors. Another reason could be the taking into consideration of the power struggle characterizing the Labour Party during the 1980s. Faced with a powerful neo-Marxist or Bennite 'left', presented as the main culprit for Labour's fall from favour, the 'right' and 'centre' of the partisan organization elaborated a philosophical project likely to change the way the party was perceived in the political arena (Foote 1997). Academics and some members of the party leadership, well-versed in intellectual debate, set out to rediscover the Idealistic, Christian and Liberal roots of the Labour movement. This produced a discourse dominated by notions of 'individual responsibility', 'civic commitment', and, above all, 'community' which rapidly became a source of inspiration for Neil Kinnock and the 'modernizers'. Finally, the notion of 'community' took clear shape in the political rivalry of the 1990s. In opposition to an insubstantial vision of the market, accused of encouraging social fragmentation, the notion of community is compatible with the leftist value of solidarity while at the same time reassuring Conservative voters attached to a cohesive social order. Coveted across the political board, both sides eager to appropriate the idea, 'community' has slowly emerged as the 'new territorialisation of political thought' (Rose 1999: 475).

The recourse to the discourse of community by the Labour 'modernizers' is somewhat ambiguous. If the community can be defined as a social space within which the individual is encouraged to develop, this approach does not inform us completely about where the limits of this concept lie. The various advocates of the Third Way have thus attributed to it in turn a national, local or international dimension. It has become an amalgam of Great Britain, the family, the neighbourhood, ethnic and social associations and civil society. This confusion comes from the fact that, more than a 'structure' within which individuals evolve, the community represents a way of perceiving the individual in their environment.

---

3   According to Anthony Giddens, 'New Individualism does not signal a process of moral decay. Rather to the contrary, surveys show that younger generations today are sensitized to a greater range of moral concerns than previous generations. They do not, however, relate these values to tradition, or accept traditional forms of authority as legislating on questions of lifestyle. Some such moral values are clearly post-materialist in Ingelhart's sense, concerning for example ecological values, human rights or sexual freedom' (Giddens, 1998).

It claims the existence of both a social and moral interdependence between people which can operate in the different spheres already mentioned and which should give rise to the *good society* embodied by the 'cohesive society'. Consequently, the community is supposed to demolish the stance adopted by the neoliberal wing of the Conservative party, summed up by the famous words, uttered by Margaret Thatcher in 1987: 'There is no such thing as society.' It provides a timely opposition to market individualism in a British society characterized by the fear of social disintegration.

Whereas Thatcherite neoliberalism had turned the market into an ideal 'partner', the Third Way – or at least part of it – aims to involve the community in the responsibility for the Social, thus bestowing on it the characteristics of civil society. For Third-Wayers, civil society emerges as the long-lost child of the politics of the second half of the twentieth century, ignored by a left too busy reinforcing the power of the state in its relationship to the individual and by a right striving, for its part, to give greater importance to the latter. Long neglected, the civil society referred to by the Third-Wayers brings together all those elements which fall outside the remit of the state or the market. Some Third-Wayers envisage it as a flourishing of local communities, attracting in their orbit different associations and organizations. Civil society sometimes emerges as an idyllic space. Ian Hargreaves describes it as 'a place where citizens freely act together to consolidate and express their freedoms, to solve problems, to provide services to each other or simply enjoy each other's company' (Hargreaves 1999).

The Third-Wayers maintain that, after two decades of market assaults and a weakened local democracy due to Conservative policies, civil society, long disdained by a left partisan of state control, is in dire need of 'renewal'. It must assert itself in order to protect the individual from a state judged over-powerful and from a potentially disintegrating market. Given that civil society is not the state of natural harmony the Tories believed it to be, its regeneration might imply government intervention. The public authorities would then be encouraged to organize the mobilization of the members of the civil society for the common good. Therefore, it is once again thanks to the civic argument that the Third Way seeks to assert its difference. Traces of this Republican stance can be found in the principle of 'community involvement', for example, which influences the granting of government funds to local programmes set up to fight social exclusion.

Some Third-Wayers are now starting to look for the best tools which will enable them to lay down the civic foundations for the civil society. Charles Leadbeater thus suggests that the club could serve as a model for the institutions which the state must encourage to exist at the heart of the civil society (Leadbeater 1997). Such a structure would engender a strong feeling of belonging and would have the merit of combining 'citizenship' and 'modernity'. Indeed, it reconciles a sense of reciprocity with individual choice. The ambitions of the Third Way as expressed here by one of its 'experts', cannot be more explicit. They consist in encouraging autonomous individuals to participate actively (whatever form that might take), a consequence of which will be the production of social capital. Thus reconfigured, the civil society is transformed into a 'strong civic society' (Blair 2001), within which every individual, by virtue of common shared values, can express a 'civic patriotism' (Brown 2000). The state must acknowledge this emerging 'reality' by delegating a substantial part of its power and its prerogatives in the domain of welfare. It is partly on this standardized vision of society that rests the theory of 'new mutualism', the logical outcome of a collective exercise in active citizenship.

The Emergence of a 'New Mutualism'

In 1995 Geoff Mulgan and Charles Landry took the defence of a rather curious thesis (Mulgan and Landry 1995). By reading too much Adam Smith without trying to understand him, the Thatcherites and their adversaries seemed to have forgotten the existence of 'another invisible hand', other than the one striving to achieve economic prosperity through market mechanisms. A force for 'generosity, assistance and moral commitment', such an entity could incite individuals to gather around a common project (Mulgan and Landry 1995: 2). In a society where government control had 'run out of steam' and the market had become 'devalued', the future of a 'modern' left depends inevitably on an understanding of the mechanisms of this 'other invisible hand', according to Mulgan and Landry. These two political thinkers suggest that one of these mechanisms is a reassertion of the value of mutualism.

As from the late 1980s, mutualism has become a recurring theme in the debates of the British left and the subject of much theoretical investment within the space of theorization (Hargreaves 1999), eventually giving rise to a discourse proposing the rehabilitation of 'cooperative socialism' or even 'socialism without the state'. Consequently, what is paradoxical is the fact that the 'modernity' which 'New Mutualism' purports to embody finds its legitimacy in the continuous references to the history of the working-class movement. The type of socialism represented here is thus a 'grass-root' socialism, anchored in civil society and steeped in moral values, almost legitimist insofar as it is imbued with what are presented implicitly as the 'eternal values of the left'. In 1994, certain 'modernizers' evoked pre-war socialism thus:

> Long before the age of post-war State planning, and even Clause IV, British Socialists were probably acclaimed for their identification with the principles of communitarian fraternity, mutual co-operation, individual responsibility and self-help. Co-operative, friendly societies and trade unions all formed an increasingly successful welfare network dedicated to the provision of ... efficient ... health and welfare services for their members. (Pollard et al. 1994: 1)

Although the picture painted here is a somewhat idealistic one, it refers to proven facts. Indeed, the historian Edward P. Thompson has evoked the importance of 'mutual assistance groups' in the constitution of the British working-class movement (Thompson 1963). These corporatist associations – the friendly societies and self-help groups – brought together more than six and a half million individuals at the beginning of the twentieth century. Combining religion, politics, social issues, Methodism, Chartism and Owenism, they provided a burgeoning working class with the means to achieve 'collective independence' as early as the eighteenth century by mutualizing the risks linked to illness and unemployment. The autonomous social system set up by these mutualist organizations was, however, marginalized by the social assistance offered by the state in the National Insurance Act voted in 1911 and then by the setting up of the Welfare State in the 1940s. The 'cooperative socialism' they embodied was then slowly replaced by a more state-controlled progressivism. Yet, it is to the former that Tony Blair, amongst others, referred to at length as early as 1994:

> The history of workers' cooperatives, the friendly societies and the unions from which the Labour Party sprang is one of individuals coming together for self-improvement and to improve people's potential through collective action. We need to recreate for the twenty-first century the civil society to which these movements gave birth. (Blair 1994)

The allusion to this 'forgotten patrimony' signals the outcome of a period of rehabilitation begun at the end of the 1980s. Individuals caught up in the 'modernizing' current set out to evoke the importance of the cooperative and mutualist movement in the Labour constitution at a time when the Labour Party was completing its policy review. Frank Field, the minister for Welfare Reform after May 1997, has emerged as the pioneer of this rehabilitation process. Aware of his marginality within the Labour Party due to his opposition to a certain partisan orthodoxy, Frank Field has participated actively in public debate thanks to his numerous contributions to the mainstream press. True to his reputation as a 'freethinker', he has rebuked a Labour Party which he believes has lost sight of its roots. He has thus enjoined the Party to stand up for the values of cooperation and to renounce an inclination towards state control, a tendency discredited and undermined, in his opinion, by the standard-bearers of neoliberalism. The works subsequently published by the Parliamentarian herald much of the social discourse of neo-Labour's first mandate, referring explicitly to the experiment of friendly societies and mutualism. Taking advantage of his presence in different social worlds (think tanks, press, etc.), Field has been one of the principal agents of reconversion within the space of theorization as regards this aspect of the history of British socialism.

David Green, a character as unorthodox as Field can be but not part of the 'modernizing' current, has also had a role to play in this process of rehabilitation. A former Labour councillor, strongly influenced by ethical socialism, Green is nonetheless a member of the Institute of Economic Affairs (IEA) a neoliberal think-tank of which he chairs the Health and Welfare Unit. Since the early 1980s, he has also written several essays on the subject of working-class mutualism and its possible applications in today's society.[4] His work has been widely circulated thanks to the strong influence of the IEA on the media. Moreover, it can be

---

4   Green is the author of *Mutual Aid or Welfare State* (1984), *Working-Class Patients and the Medical Establishment: Self-Help from the Mid-Nineteenth Century to 1948* (1985) and *Reinventing Civil Society* (1993).

added that David Green has in a certain way contributed to strengthening Frank Field's position and therefore his ideas in the space of theorization by allowing him, on numerous occasions, to express himself and to publish his work in the framework of the IEA.

The ideas put forward by Field and Green, increasingly evident in the market of ideas as New Labour was coming closer to power, fall into the same mould: they criticize a 'Statist left'. Yet the two men diverge when it comes to their respective ambitions. The former wants to allow the modernizers to make a definitive break from Old Labour whereas the latter aims to prove, without resorting to the neoliberal phraseology which little by little fell from favour during the 1990s, that the Labour movement has become a 'bureaucratic' ideology. Despite the relatively marginal positions occupied by their authors in their respective political camps, the broad reception given to Field and Green's ideas by the political world is an indication of the strong rise, both on the left and on the right, of the feeling that it has become electorally unviable to build a political project taking as the sole point of reference either the state or the market. On the left, this feeling is quite clearly at the heart of the reflection elaborated by certain elements of the 'modernizing' current. As well as the return to favour of a 'socialism without the state', its existence could be perceived as early as the second half of the 1980s when, following the popular 'success' of Thatcher's privatizations, the Labour Party felt constrained to opt for the notion of social ownership over state ownership. The 'new ideal' of the left-wing party thus became:

> ... an economy in which enterprises are owned and managed by their employees –or, where appropriate, by consumers or local communities– and thereby serve the wider interests of their consumers and the community. (Shaw 1994: 87)

These reorientations in Labour doctrine manifest the will to disengage the state which can be justified in 'progressive' terms. Furthermore, these changes rest on values dear to 'new social democracy:' a sense of duty towards the community, civic commitment, etc. In concrete terms, this 'redefinition of the frontiers between the state and individual responsibility' (Field 1997) favours the development of the third sector, a space belonging neither to the public nor the private sectors. Gathering mainly mutualist groups, corporatist or voluntary associations as well as other non-profit-making organizations, the third sector emerges as the successor of the working-class cooperative movement. Thanks to the values it claims to represent, this sector offers a practical application of the discourse on community; it seems to crystallize social interdependence while at the same time preserving the individual's desire for autonomy. Thus, Frank Field, in a document published in 1996, proposes the setting up of a *stakeholder welfare*, built on what might be the 'emerging values' of contemporary British society: property and control (Field 1996). The 'voters', demanding that their 'growing social autonomy' be acknowledged, now wish to benefit from personalized social benefits, according to Frank Field. In order to do so, they can resort to free association. The government must, therefore, provide them with the means to set up their own institutions for social protection outside the influence of the state.

The renewed interest in mutualism does not end with a reappraisal of the long forgotten roots of the Labour movement. It can also be interpreted as a questioning of a trade union movement judged incapable of meeting the new expectations of the workers. The diversification and unpredictability of the working experience, the spread of self-employment, the growing flexibility of the workplace and the more personal relationships which now exist between employer and employee are all arguments put forward by a majority of Third-Wayers to denounce the ineffectuality of the 'traditional' trade union structures. Particularly widespread in the industrial and public sectors, trade unions seem to be less popular with younger workers and with those employed in highly flexible professional fields such as the tertiary sector or small companies. Researchers from Demos have outlined a new structure, based on the principles of mutualism, able to appeal to millions of salaried workers: the *employee mutual*. The employee mutual is a local structure aiming to help people 'find work, improve their qualifications and organise their professional life' (Leadbeater and Martin 1999: 9). It caters for both salaried workers and the unemployed. Claiming to offer a framework for the individual to participate actively in democracy, the employee mutual is controlled by its members, providing them with training, childcare and jobseekers' allowances. It aims, above all, to remain in direct contact with employers, selling them the 'services' of its members to whom it offers the best adapted workforce for the jobs proposed.

Although not openly presented as a direct rival of the trade unions, the employee mutual is nevertheless an indication that trade union representation seems to find itself at a dead end. Built as a counter-model to the 'monolithic' structure (a criticism levelled at the trade unions by Third-Wayers) the employee mutual contains, more importantly, all the paths of reconversion which these same individuals attribute to the trade unions. Weakened by the Conservative governments of the 1980s, the trade unions appear in the literature of the Third Way as the relics of the Fordist era. As a result, they have no alternative but to change (Mandelson and Liddle 1996: 226). The rebirth of mutualism can, therefore, be a solution, coming at an opportune time. Such a reconversion seems all the more logical as the trade unions are the direct heirs of the friendly societies. Weary of the 'ideological' stance adopted by the unions, their members demand, first and foremost, that they move towards the provision of health and insurance services, management of pension funds and counselling.

Such 'suggestions' are not necessarily devoid of all ulterior motives. The future of the trade union movement, outlined by some entrepreneurs of the Third Way, must be placed in the context of the repositioning of the Labour Party, begun during the 1980s. By limiting the sphere of activity of the trade unions to a social one, the Third Way has diverted them from political activity which in the past might have been responsible for thwarting the electoral ambitions of the British 'governmental left'. Indeed, in 1984, a year-long National Union of Mineworkers' strike ended with the capitulation of the miners. Hostile to the wave of strikes which led, in the late 1970s, to the Winter of Discontent, 'public opinion' was overwhelmingly against this new movement. The rejection of the trade unions by what would seem to be the bulk of voters consequently forced Kinnock's

Labour Party to distance itself from those very people who founded it a century earlier. In 1999 Tony Blair was to make this position 'official' by declaring that the trade unions should not expect to receive 'any favours' but 'fair treatment' from a Labour government.

Interested in a mutualism in harmony with its discourse on community, the Third Way has also revealed its individualistic inclination by turning to a new figure in the framework of the renovation of civil society and of the management of welfare: the social entrepreneur.

The Social Entrepreneur or the Ideal Local Leader

Embodying the ideal local leader in the field of welfare and epitomizing the perfect citizen promoted by the Third Way, the social entrepreneur can be situated at the intersection of the public, private and third sectors, combining their respective values. He is characterized by a 'creative individualism', nurtured by a sense of the common interest, by an enlightened opportunism and an innovatory mind (Leadbeater 1997a: 11). The social entrepreneur has swiftly become a recurring figure in the imaginary world created by the space of theorization of the Third Way. A few weeks after his arrival at Downing Street, Tony Blair vowed that his government would support 'the thousands of social entrepreneurs ... who bring to social problems the same enterprise and imagination business entrepreneurs bring to wealth creation' (Blair 1997).

Individualistic while fighting for the interests of the community, charismatic, endowed with local expertise, breaker of rules and flouter of stifling conventions, quick to create alliances, the social entrepreneur is presented as the antithesis of the civil servant (Coote 1999: 126). He is an indictment of a Welfare State judged excessively bureaucratic. According to Charles Leadbeater, the autonomy and the spirit of initiative which characterize the social entrepreneur signal him out as a natural member of the movement set in motion by 'new individualism' and destine him to become the agent 'of a modern type of welfare for the twenty-first century' (Leadbeater 1997b: 8). To fulfil this role, the social entrepreneur must answer local needs left unsatisfied until now by traditional social structures. Indeed, he distinguishes himself thanks to a capacity to mobilize, at the local level, the resources unexploited or underexploited by the state or by any other authority. Leadbeater gives the example of Andrew Mawson, a pastor who, in the 1980s, succeeded in uniting the inhabitants of an underprivileged neighbourhood in east London in a project which consisted in refurbishing dilapidated buildings belonging to the Reformed Church. From abandoned premises there swiftly rose a nursery, a crèche, various art centres and a health centre.

The social entrepreneur is, moreover, at the centre of what Leadbeater describes as the 'virtuous circle of social capital' (Leadbeater 1997b: 67). Inspired by Robert Putnam, the notion of 'social capital' implies shared values, norms of reciprocity, mutual obligations and expectations which characterize social relationships and encourage cooperation between individuals, leading to the birth of a sense of common interest. Since it is mainly built on 'trust', social capital also dons the democratic mantle by facilitating discussion between individuals. Stronger social ties have an impact on the market and consequently, contribute to economic growth. Social capital thus reconciles opportunely the concerns of the individual and the interests of society. For the new agent of welfare, social capital is the primary weapon in the fight against social exclusion, crime and the different causes of 'community decline'. The capital comes from the various social networks and contacts established by the social entrepreneur to achieve his ends. Gradually, he becomes involved in the setting up of new local services, the rehabilitation of certain public places, etc. These investments, uniting individuals mobilized by the social entrepreneur, will produce dividends by reviving collaboration and social ties at the heart of the community. This new social fabric will, in its turn, encourage the setting up of new community projects and will subsequently unite individuals around the same shared values.

*

Does the distribution of tasks sketched out here mean a simple privatization of 'the Social?' This premise appeals to the left insofar as it transforms British 'new progressivism' into the avatar of neoliberalism. The answer is more complex and less clear-cut. Although this kind of 'governance' transfers part of the state's responsibilities to non-state entities, it is nonetheless clear that the state retains its role as social regulator and has the monopoly on deciding who the new participants should be. It is also the state's role to bestow legitimacy on their new status. The state thus becomes the sole centre of gravity of 'governance of governance' (Jayasuryia 2004: 490). Its 'partners', whether they be social entrepreneurs, mutualist groups or community leaders are like satellites revolving in its orbit. This can explain Janet Newman's suggestion that, paradoxically, the main consequence of the 'privatization of the Social' is to make it easier for the state to impose its values:

> The spread of an official and legitimated discourse of partnership has the capacity to draw local stakeholders, from community groups to business organisations, into a more direct relationship with government's agenda. ... From the perspective of the voluntary and community sectors, partnerships may represent 'dangerous liaisons,' implying a process of incorporation into the values of the dominant partner. (Newman 2001: 125–6)

Finally, one may add that, in a different context, Vivien Schmidt has shown how the fact that the state delegates some of its functions and duties to other agents does not mean a loss of power or the choice of a policy of 'non-interference'. In fact, such a movement should be read as a shift from 'doing' to 'having done' or 'doing with', for the state continues to set the targets, to lay down directives and, above, all to demand that its partners be held accountable for the activities delegated to them (Schmidt 2005).

References

Blair, T. (1994), quoted in *The Guardian*, 25 May.
Blair, T. (1997), 'Will to Win', *Speech at Aylesbury Estate*, 2 June.
Blair, T. (2001), 'The Strong Society: Rights, Responsibilities and Reform', speech at Newport, 30 May.
Brown, G (1995), 'Foreword', in Crouch, C. and Marquand, D. (eds).
Brown, G. (2000), *Speech at the NCVO Conference*, 9 February.
Coote, A. (1999), 'The Helmsman and the Cattle Prod', in Gamble, A. and Wright, T. (eds).
Crouch, C. (2004), 'The State and Innovations in Economics Governance', in Gamble, A. and Wright, T. (eds).
Crouch, C. and Marquand, D. (eds), *Reinventing Collective Action* (Oxford: Blackwell/ The Political Quartely).
Donzelot, J. (1984), *L'invention du Social. Essai sur le déclin des passions politiques* (Paris: Fayard).
Eliassen, K.A. and Kooiman, J. (eds) (1987), *Managing Public Organizations* (London: Sage).
Esping-Andersen, G. (1990), *The Three Worlds of Welfare Capitalism* (Cambridge: Polity Press).
Field, F. (1996), *Stakeholder Welfare* (London: IEA).
Field, F. (1997), 'The Welfare and the Third Way', speech at the Victoria and Albert Museum, 24 September.
Foote, G. (1997), *The Labour Party's Political Thought. A History* (New York: St Martin's Press).
Gamble, A. (1988), *The Free Economy and the Strong State. The Politics of Thatcherism* (Basingtoke: Macmillan).
Gamble, A. and Wright, T. (eds) (2004), *Restating the State* (Oxford: The Political Quarterly Publishing).
Giddens, A. (1998), *The Third Way. The Renewal of Social Democracy* (Cambridge: Polity Press).
Hargreaves, I. (1998), 'A Step Beyond Morris Dancing: The Third Sector Revival', in Hargreaves, I. and Christie, I. (eds).
Hargreaves, I., and Christie, I. (eds) (1998), *Tomorrow's Politics. The Third Way and Beyond* (London: Demos).
Hargreaves, I. (1999), *New Mutualism. In from the Cold. The Co-operative Revival and Social Exclusion* (London: The Co-operative Press).
Jayasuriya, K. (2004), 'The New Regulatory State and Relational Capacity', *Policy and Politics* 32:4,493–508.
Leadbeater, C. (1997a), *Civic Spirit. The Big Idea for a New Political Area* (London: Demos).
Leadbeater, C. (1997b), *The Rise of the Social Entrepreneur* (London: Demos).
Leadbeater, C. and Martin, S. (1999), *The Employee Mutual. Combining Flexibility with Security in the new World of Work* (London: Demos).
Mandelson, P. and Liddle, R. (1996), *The Blair Revolution. Can New Labour Deliver?* (London: Faber and Faber).
Merrien, F.-X., Parchet, R. and Kernen, A. (eds) (2005), *L'État social. Une perspective internationale* (Paris: Armand Colin).
Mulgan, G. and Landry, C. (1995), *The Other Invisible Hand. Remaking Charity for the 21st Century* (London: Demos).

Newman, J. (2001), *Modernising Governance* (London: Sage).

Peters, G. (1993), 'Managing the Hollow State', in Eliassen, H. and Koiman, J. (eds).

Pollard, S., Liddle, T. and Thompson, B. (1994), *Towards a more Co-operative Society: Ideas on the Future of the British Labour Movement and Independent Healthcare* (London: Independent Healthcare).

Rose, N. (1999), 'Inventiveness in Politics', *Economy and Society* 28:3, 467–93.

Schmidt, V. (2005), 'L'État, l'économie et la protection sociale aux États-Unis et en Europe', *Critique internationale* 27:2, 83–107.

Shaw, E. (1994), *The Labour Party since 1979. Crisis and Transformation* (London: Routledge).

Stoker, G. (2004), 'New Localism, Progressive Politics and Democracy', in Gamble, A. and Wright, T. (eds).

Thompson, E.P. (1963), *The Making of English Working Class* (New York: Vintage Books).

Conclusion

Jane Jacobs Revisited?

Sophie Body-Gendrot, Jacques Carré and Romain Garbaye

More than 40 years ago, Jane Jacobs set forth an influential set of recommendations for urban planners in her book *The Death and Life of Great American Cities* (Jacobs 1961, Body-Gendrot 2000: 414–15). A mother, community activist and reporter, living in Greenwich Village in New York, she showed in her book how a wide diversity of peoples and activities made urban life vibrant. Her description of her neighbourhood streets focused on the roles played by the bookstore owner, the barber, the meat-market workers interacting with people traveling to and from work and stopping on the streets to exchange daily information or to shop (Beauregard 2006). The encounters gave a democratic vibrancy to the streets. Not only did they make people more familiar to each other, more helpful and more tolerant, but they created a sense of civility and of 'community' in the long term. It implied that collective goals were shared.

Jacobs' bottom up approach, ahead of her time, carried a vigorous denunciation of what she called 'orthodox' city-planning in the twentieth century. Urban planners as viewed by Jacobs tackled problems of decaying centres, and the management of regeneration projects, in a deductive light, that is to say they started from general and abstract premises about what constitutes the good city, and how it should be built and managed, and then sought to apply these ideas to the real world.

The result was epitomized by the Garden Cities of turn-of-the-century Britain. Designed to address over-population in London, these small cities were to be kept under 30,000 inhabitants. Good housing was essentially suburban or small town style, the commercial needs of new cities were standardized and limited and the whole design failed to anticipate any sort of evolution once the cities would be built. This approach was vigorously condemned by Jacobs as not only paternalistic, but even authoritarian. She applied a similar criticism to twentieth-century American planners such as Lewis Mumford or Clarence Stein – the 'Decentrists' – whose vision of the city was based on similar principles: the needs of neighbourhoods for goods and commerce should be evaluated 'scientifically,' the privacy and even the isolation of homes should be searched for, as a means to escape from the evils of the crowded streets of the big city. As with the Garden City, all aspects of the new, ideal city had to be controlled by the founding authority and evolution diverging from the original plan was not allowed.

These types of utopias, although seldom put into practice, permeated the understanding that urban planners and more broadly economic and political elites have of the city in Jacob's time, and revealed their negative effects. For Jacobs, these ideas amounted to imposing a ready-made, one-size-fits-all project to cities, overlooking their inherent complexity and singularity, and essentially solving the city's problems by getting rid of many of the elements that precisely make a city a city. According to Jacobs, cities should be understood as examples of 'organized complexity' because they are constituted of a large number of elements, whose interactions are not random but follow precise patterns. In other words, they can be compared to living organisms. This is why abstract generalizations are not sufficient to make sense of them, and why students of cities should work inductively, starting from empirical observations to gain an understanding of the logics of social, economic and political interactions that take place on urban territories and form the fabric of cities.

The issue of urban safety closely linked to urban planning, illustrates Jacobs' point. Urban decay is not only caused by delinquency but by fear of crime and of violent incidents. Streets should be under the watch of all. Not only could store owners, bar tenders, street peddlers, park attendants be involved, but the residents could spot out strangers or unusual events more easily because in richer or poorer areas, they knew each other. They thus could become the 'ears and the eyes' of the streets – providing there was good street lighting – just as efficiently as law enforcers patrolling the neighbourhoods, familiar figures to whom they could relate:

> We seem to have simple goals here: trying to secure streets where public space is clearly public, not physically mixed with private or undetermined space so that the area that need to be watched is clearly circumscribed and easy to respect; making sure that these public streets have eyes focused on them as continuously as possible. (Quoted in Beauregard 2006: 36)

Parks would attract crowds if a large display of events and uses occurred while they would be dangerous, if they remained open. Public housing made of high towers concentrating the poor would be avoided by those who had the resources to do so. Long corridors, with no guards, lifts, stairs, roofs and backyards with no guards and surveillance provided would inspire fear. But as Jacobs suggested, if human resources were encouraged, such as stores and workshops in the buildings, mixed income tenants some of them collectively filling surveillance jobs, the feeling of insecurity would alleviate, especially among women and minorities (Wekerlé 1999).

That social scientists should focus on the logics and dynamics of the cities' 'workings' implies an attention to particular cases. For Jacobs, the locality factor – place matters – and the daily experience of residents and all users of space were crucial because it is only by paying attention to them that specific, idiosyncratic elements appear, explaining why a given neighbourhood or area is presenting features which statistical or theoretical models failed to predict. Cities must then be understood as processes, rather than fixed situations.

The authors of this volume have worked with similar principles in mind. By focusing on a variety of specific policy sectors, they have sought to illustrate the complexity of the city: fields as diverse as housing development, social housing policy, the management of prisons or self-defence communities, all make a part of the city. And, as diverse as they are, they tell similar stories, revealing the complexity of the city's geographical, social and political fabric, and of the private/public boundaries.

With respect of city government and politics, Jacobs' desire to leave aside top down, bureaucratic, abstract and centralized projects and decisions in favour of better informed, locality-sensitive approaches finds historical and contemporary significance. In terms of actors, Jacobs advocates a shift of focus, from the planners, or more generally from the political and economic elites, to a wider range of actors. Since cities are self-regulated, attention must be paid to the diversity of agents that contribute to its daily life. The notion of governance as defined at the beginning of this volume similarly manifested an interest in the diversity of actors, public, private, or third sector, who participate in the government of the city. The advocates of the Third Way studied by Tournadre-Plancq, and their interest in local leadership and social entrepreneurs, reflect Jacob's insistence on displacing power from planning agencies and placing it in the hands of the participants of the daily economic and social life of the city. The chapters on diverse policy sectors in the current period, by Fée on housing associations policy in Britain, Combeau on self-defence groups, and Vindevogel on the privatization of prisons in the United States, all confirm the growing role of diverse types of actors in local affairs.

This volume has also shown that a sensitivity to the urban fabric has predated the twentieth-century bureaucratic and top down models of urban planning. Renaud Le Goix has revealed how the concept of the privatization of the public space, found in the contemporary American gated community, appears much earlier, for instance in some French developments in the nineteenth century. Geraldine Vaughan and Myriam Boussahba-Bravard have unveiled how religious or civic groups were influential actors in British local politics in the 1880s. In this sense this book has shown how the idealistic, but abstract and dehumanizing culture of planning which, according to Jacobs becomes pervasive the early twentieth century onward, should now be viewed as situated in a bounded historical period, ranging roughly from 1900 to the 1970s. The rise of third-sector and for-profit actors in local affairs since then, and the concomitant academic interest in them, should not be conceptualized as a new beginning but as a return to earlier modes of social and political organization. According to David Fée, the mid-twentieth century era of 'big government' and planning should be viewed as a 'parenthesis.' Thus this volume nuances the importance of the decentralists and American New Urbanism, construed by Jacobs as a pervasive common sense of the twentieth century, and shows instead how limited in time they were. Further, it shows how these movements were not as 'authoritative' as Jane Jacobs makes them, but in fact sought to cater for the needs of city dwellers in given contexts. On the whole, however, this volume concludes to the enduring relevance of Jacob's interpretation of the city, and in fact reveals the premonitory nature of her insights: today more than ever, cities should be understood as complex balances between a variety of social and economic interests.

References

Beauregard, R. (2006), *When America Became Suburban* (Minneapolis: University of Minnesota Press).
Jacobs, J. (1961), *The Death and Life of Great American Cities* (New York: Vintage).
Paquot, T., Lussault, M. and Body-Gendrot, S. (eds) (2000), *La Ville et l'urbain: L'état des savoirs* (Paris: La Découverte).
Wekerlé, G. (1999), 'De la coveillance à la ville sûre', *Les Annales de la recherche urbaine* 83–84, 164–9.

Index

9/11 3, 7, 25, 31, 106–7, 125

actors
  for-profit 3, 215
  non-elected 2
  private 2
  public 2, 120
  third sector 3, 215
Austin, J. 118–21
Australia 77, 115–17, 120–21
Austria 60

Balchin, P. 41–2, 46, 51
Beck, A. 118, 124, 126
Bellamy, Edward 64, 68
Blair, Tony 4, 50, 53, 203–4, 206, 209
Blakely, E.J. 77, 81, 88
board schools 163–76
Booth, Charles 57–8, 64
Bowser, Benjamin P. 7, 133, 135, 139
Britain, Great *see* United Kingdom
British Women's Temperance Association (BWTA) 182
Brower, T. 87, 95
Brown, Gordon 53, 202, 205
Brown Maxwell, R. 5, 6
Browne, Annie Leigh 183, 186
Bush, George W. 106, 140
business interests 1, 2, 116, 126, 160

Caldeira, T. 26, 77, 81, 84, 90
California Prevention Education Project (Cal-Pep) 7–8, 95, 133–6, 138–42
Campbell, Colen 18, 21
Cantaroglou, Frédéric 4, 57, 60
Carvalho, M. 77, 84
Cheung, A. 117, 122, 126
China 77
citizenship 1–2, 9, 49, 64, 77, 81, 88, 182, 192, 204–5
civil society 136, 203–6, 209
Clinton, Bill 203
Cold War 126

commodification 26–7, 36, 201
Common Interest Developments (CIDs) 86–7
communities
  affinity-based 82
  black 135
  cultural 116
  ethnic 135
  gated 5–6, 26, 77–97, 103
  'new' 57–71, 108
  Owenite 60–61
  private 95
  rural 127, 133
Compulsory Competitive Tendering 47, 51
Cons, Emma 181, 183
Corrections Corporation of America (CCA) 115, 117, 120–22, 125–7
corruption 116, 119
council housing *see* public sector housing
Coventry, G. 119–21
Crary, D. 125–6
crime 79–81, 90–91, 93–4, 103–7, 109, 111, 116, 118–19, 122–3, 126, 210, 214
criminal justice system 6, 115–16, 126

Davis, M. 80, 84–5
Defoe, D. 14, 16, 22
democracy 27, 31, 45, 49, 62–3, 65, 67, 202, 204, 207–8
  social 202, 207
Devine, Tom 175–6
Donzelot, J. 81, 82, 84, 201
Donziger, S.R. 118, 119, 126

Eastern Europe 5, 77
Eden, Anthony 44, 45
education
  for-profit 149–61
  edupreneurs 150, 152–4, 160
  K-12 152–4
  sexual 140
Education Management Organizations (EMOs) 8, 149–61

Engels, Frederick 51, 57
ethnicity 7, 8, 30, 88, 133, 134, 138, 142
Euchner, C.C. 63, 64
exclusion 6, 80–82, 158, 204, 210
exclusivity/exclusiveness 65, 85–6, 87–90

Fainstein, S. 4, 31, 33
Fassin, D. 133, 138
Federal Bureau of Prisons (FBOP) 124–5, 127
Field, Frank 206–7
Fischer, C.S. 65, 66
France 2, 5–8, 57–71, 78, 82–4, 86, 91, 93, 97, 103–4, 107, 109–11, 113, 133–4, 136–8, 141–4

Garden Cities 4–5, 58–70, 213
  Garden Cities Association 58–9
Garnier, Tony 60
gender 30, 193–4
Lloyd George, David 42, 43
Gerstner, L. 150, 151
ghettoes 82, 135
Glasze, G. 77, 81, 84
Gloor, Audrey 4, 57
Goldberger, Paul 31–4
governance
  decentralized 57
  of new communities 57–71
  local 1, 86, 91
    see also local government
  participative 61
  private 85–7, 91–2, 97
  urban 1–2, 15, 23, 52, 58–9, 85–7, 91–2, 97
Green, David 206, 207
Greene, J. 121–2, 124–5
Grosvenor, Sir Richard 13, 15–16, 20–22
Gwynn, John 13–14, 17

Hall, David 66, 71
Hall, Peter 58, 60, 63, 67–8
Hanson, A.E. 89–90, 95
Hardy, Dennis 66
Hargreaves, Ian 204, 205
Harrison, P. 115, 124, 126
health care 26, 115, 118, 121, 128, 136
Heseltine, Michael 45, 46
Hill, Octavia 183–4, 193
Hirsch, E. 136–7, 155

HIV/AIDS 7–8, 133–44
Hobson, L. 7, 133, 134, 137
Hollis, Patricia 181–2, 187, 188–91, 193, 197
housing trusts
  Guiness 52
  Housing Action 47
  Peabody 4, 52
Howard, Ebenezer 1, 58–60, 63–71, 86, 94

immigrants 7, 82, 124, 133–4, 142
individualism 23, 80–81, 203–4, 209
inequality 2, 26, 138, 142
infrastructure 88, 91
Ireland 35
Israel 35

Jackson, K. 27, 85, 86
Jacobs, Jane 3, 27, 213–15
Jaillet, M.-C. 83–4

Kahn, B. 28, 29
Kennedy, D.J. 81, 87
Kilgour, Mary 183
King, R.S. 124, 127
Kinnock, Neil 203, 208
Kleinman, M. 41, 46
Kohn, M. 26, 28, 31, 33

Lacour-Little, M. 88, 95
landlordism 47, 64
law and order 5–6, 103–13
law enforcement 6, 105, 106, 111
Leadbetter, Charles 204, 208–9
Lebanon 84
Le Corbusier 27, 59
Lefebvre, H. 3, 27
liberalism 20, 202
Lips, Carrie, 152–3
local government 2, 9, 15, 23, 50, 53, 116, 139–40, 163, 181–2, 184, 188–9, 193–4
Lockett, Gloria 7, 133, 134
Lopez, R. 80–82
Low, S.M. 80, 90–91
Lowe, R. 43–5

Macmillan, Harold 41, 50
Major, John 4, 118
Malpass, Peter 4, 41, 43, 45, 51–2, 118

Malpezzi, S. 88, 95
March, A. 62, 63, 65, 66
Marchand, B. 83, 92
Marcuse, P. 26, 80
Martin, J. 183, 208
Mattera, P. 117, 120–21, 125, 127
McCauley, James 164–5, 167, 169
McDonald, Douglas 117, 121, 122
McGovern, S. 63, 64
McKellar, Elizabeth 15, 19
McKenzie, E. 86–7, 90–91
McLaren, Eva 181, 183, 185
modernism 3, 25, 27, 30, 32–6, 59, 61–2, 64
Molnar, Alex 152, 158–61
Montagutelli, Malie 5, 149
Montmorency, J.E.G. 5, 94–5, 183
Moroni, S. 2, 63
Mulgan, Geoff 203, 205
Mumford, Lewis 5, 58, 60, 64, 213
Murie, A. 41, 46
mutualism 9, 202, 205–6, 208–9

National Union of Women Workers (NUWW) 182, 188
neoliberalism 26, 115, 201, 204, 206, 207, 210
networks 2, 31, 61, 182, 185, 210
Newman, Janet 80, 88, 90–91, 94, 210
New Zealand 35
non-governmental organizations (NGOs) 8, 133–44
non-profit organizations 4, 32, 139, 152, 207

Owen, Robert 1, 60–61, 65
 Owenism 206
owner-occupation 43, 47

Parnes, B. 88–9
Patten, C. 121, 122
Pen, Jean-Marie Le 93, 138
philanthropy 2, 4, 51, 58, 183, 192–3
Pinçon, M. and Pinçon-Charlet, M. 83, 94–5
planning
 democratic 62
 neo-traditional 30
 public 19
 urban 2–4, 58–61, 64, 68, 71, 214–15

policing 7, 80, 91, 113, 115
 community 80, 91
 private 7
political parties
 France
  Front National 93, 138
 United Kingdom
  Conservative 42–53, 181, 184–5, 204
   New Right 45–6, 50
  Labour 9, 44–5, 51, 203, 206–9
   New 9, 53, 202, 207
   Old 202, 207
  Liberal 166, 171, 182–5, 189, 194, 203
  Liberal Democrats 69
 United States of America
  Democrat 62, 203
   New 203
  Republican 7, 125, 204
Pollak, M. 136, 141
Poor Law 182–3, 185–7, 189–90, 196–7
postmodernism 4, 27, 33, 59, 63, 71
private prisons 7–8, 115–18, 120–21, 124, 128
privatization 1–4, 7–9, 19, 25–6, 28, 31, 36, 42, 46–50, 112, 115–20, 122, 124, 126–8, 158–9, 161, 201, 207, 210, 215
 prison 7, 115–28
 school 159
public health 7, 51, 133–5, 138–41
public interest 2, 3, 13–15, 19, 22–3, 26–4, 55–71, 81, 109, 119
public safety 91, 103, 119
public spaces 25–6, 28, 29, 31, 33–4, 81, 85, 91. 103
punishment 6, 116, 126
public sector housing 4, 41–53
Putnam, Robert 64, 209

race 8, 87, 134, 136, 138, 142
Ralph, James 13, 14, 18
Reagan 7, 116, 119, 125, 143
regulations 26, 89, 92, 97, 112, 154–5, 157
religion 30, 88–9, 138, 205
religions/religious affiliations
 Catholic 8, 136, 163–76
 Christian 22, 156, 202, 203
 Episcopalian 163, 175
 Methodist 88, 182–3, 206
 Presbyterian 164–5
 Protestant 8, 86, 163–4. 166–73

Ridley, Nicholas 45, 46
riots 80, 82, 121

Sandercock, Leonie 31, 71
school boards 8, 155, 163–76
schools
  charter 150–57, 159–61
  privatized 154
  public (USA) 8, 26, 105, 149–55, 157, 159–60, 164, 168, 173, 175
security 2, 5, 33–4, 41, 75, 77–80, 82, 84, 90, 92–3, 107–9, 113, 116, 120–21, 124, 125
self-defence 6, 80, 103–13, 215
self-help 5, 6, 136, 205
Sennett, R. 27, 29, 31, 34, 64
Shaw, E. 191, 207
Shephard, Edward 15, 18, 21, 22
shopping malls 26–8
Simon, J. 6, 7
Smith, Carla Dillard 7, 133
Snyder, M.G. 77, 81, 88
socialism 1, 23, 48, 50, 94, 202, 205–7
  Christian 202
  cooperative 205, 206
social justice 3, 6, 31
South Africa 77, 81, 84, 117
Spain 60
Steffen, M. 137, 138, 14
suburbs 26, 77–97, 133
Summerson, John 3, 13, 16
surveillance 26–8, 80, 116, 214

Tabbarok, A. 117, 124
Tenants Management Organizations (TMOs) 47, 49
Thatcher, Margaret 4, 41, 42, 45–7, 201, 204, 207
third sector 2, 50, 53, 207, 215
Third Way 9, 201–10, 215
Thompson, E.P. 205
Town and Country Planning Association 58, 66
Turner, N.R. 123, 124

United Kingdom (UK) 2, 5, 13–23, 41–53, 57–71, 86, 105, 120, 181–97, 201–10, 213, 215
United States of America 5, 7, 25–36, 57–71, 103–13, 115–28, 133–44, 149–61
urbanism
  counter- 36
  high modernist 3, 27, 30, 32, 36
  inclusive 31–2, 34–5
  neo-traditional 27
  new 4–5, 28, 58–9, 61, 63–5, 71, 215
  postmodern 27, 33
  privatized 77
  security-oriented 78–80
urbanization 81, 84
utopianism 1, 4, 30–31, 36, 57–60, 64–5, 70–71, 85–6, 90–91, 94, 213

Vaughan, Geraldine 8, 163, 215
violence 6, 80, 103, 120–21, 214
voluntary ation 2, 49

Waldo, D. 67, 68
Ward, Mary 184, 193
Ward, S.V. 57, 60, 63, 67
Warren, Roland 67, 70–71
Webb, Beatrice 193
Weber, Max 1
Webster, C.J. 77, 87–8, 95
Welfare State 41, 43, 45–6, 48, 50, 52, 193, 201, 206, 209
Women Guardians' Society (WGS) 182, 185–7, 189, 194
Women's Liberal Federation (WLF) 182–4, 289
Women's Local Government Society (WLGS) 181–97
World Trade Center 3, 25–36
World War I 48, 52, 170
World War II 4, 27, 42, 43, 48, 49, 78
Wright, T. 197, 201

Zecchini, L. 80, 82, 84

Temperature Control Principles
for Process Engineers

Temperature Control Principles for Process Engineers

Edited by
Eugene P. Dougherty

Hanser Publishers, Munich Vienna New York
Hanser/Gardner Publications, Inc., Cincinnati

The Editor:
Dr. Eugene P. Dougherty, Senior Research Engineer, Rohm and Haas Co., Bristol, PA 19005, USA

Distributed in the USA and in Canada by
Hanser/Gardner Publications, Inc.
6600 Clough Pike, Cincinnati, Ohio 45244-4090, USA
Fax: +1 (513) 527-8950

Distributed in all other countries by
Carl Hanser Verlag
Postfach 86 04 20, 81631 München, Germany
Fax: +49 (89) 98 48 09

The use of general descriptive names, trademarks, etc., in this publication, even if the former are not especially identified, is not to be taken as a sign that such names, as understood by the Trade Marks and Merchandise Marks Act, may accordingly be used freely by anyone.

While the advice and information in this book are believed to be true and accurate at the date of going to press, neither the authors nor the editors nor the publisher can accept any legal responsibility for any errors or omissions that may be made. The publisher makes no warranty, express or implied, with respect to the material contained herein.

Library of Congress Cataloging-in-Publication Data
Temperature control principles for process engineers / edited by
  Eugene P. Dougherty.
    p.   cm.
  Includes index.
  ISBN 1-56990-152-X
  1. Chemical process control.   2. Temperature control.
I. Dougherty, Eugene P.
TP155.75.T46   1993
660'.2815—dc20   93-34840

Die Deutsche Bibliothek - CIP-Einheitsaufnahme
Temperature control principles for process engineers / ed. by
Eugene P. Dougherty. - Munich ; Vienna ; New York : Hanser 1993
  ISBN 3-446-15980-0
NE: Dougherty, Eugene P. [Hrsg.]

All rights reserved. No part of this book may be reproduced or transmitted in any form or by any means, electronic or mechanical, including photocopying or by any information storage and retrieval system, without permission in writing from the publisher.

© Carl Hanser Verlag, Munich Vienna New York, 1994
Typesetting in the USA by Agnew's Electronic Manuscript Processing Service, Grand Rapids, MI
Printed and bound in Italy by Editoriale Bortolazzi-Stei s.r.l., Verona

Preface

Ordinarily, temperature control is pretty trivial for most process engineers. But, for certain processes, precise control of temperature is imperative, and not at all easy to accomplish. Temperature control of highly exothermic chemical reactions, reactive extruders, or batch sterilization units—all very different—can be crucial, but difficult.

Fortunately, there have been some major developments in the past few years—in temperature measurement, statistical analysis, computer technology equipment design, and control theory. These have made the life of a process engineer in some ways easier, in some ways harder. One must understand what these technologies have to offer (and perhaps more important, what they are *lacking*) and how to implement them as well. A proper understanding and proper implementation of the new technologies can have tremendous payoffs: better temperature control may mean greater safety, greater efficiency, higher quality products, and a better bottom line.

This book attempts to familiarize the process engineer with some of the new technologies and disciplines. First, it includes chapters by experts in various fields explaining why temperature control is important in certain, very different processes. Next, it teaches the process engineer about the equipment—new and old—used in temperature control. Topics such as temperature measurement, heat exchanger design, steam injection heating systems, etc. are covered. Third, the book treats the problem of analysis in temperature control. How the statistical techniques meld with older, more traditional process control technologies is especially intriguing.

Finally, there is a concluding chapter in this book on the benefits of better temperature control—safety, quality, productivity, and economics.

Enjoy the book!

Eugene P. Dougherty

Contents

1 Introduction and Plan 1
  Eugene P. Dougherty

  1.1 Purpose and Scope of the Book 1
  1.2 Overview/Plan of the Book 2

2 The Importance of Temperature Control in Biochemical
  Process Engineering 5
  Stephen J. Lorbert and James P. Pike

  2.1 Introduction 5
  2.2 Temperature Control for Fermentation Based Production 6
      2.2.1 Effect of Temperature on Microbial Systems 6
      2.2.2 Temperature Control Systems for Fermentation 8
      2.2.3 Temperature Control for Media and Equipment
            Sterilization 9
  2.3 Importance of Temperature for Product Purification Processes 10
      2.3.1 Effect of Temperature Product Stability and Purity 10
      2.2.2 Effect of Temperature on Protein Purification Technology ... 12
  References 16

3 Nonisothermal Effects in Polymer Reaction Engineering 19
  Donald H. Sebastian

  3.1 Introduction 19
  3.2 Basic Transport Theory 19
  3.3 Characteristic Times 21

       3.3.1   Characteristic Times for Chemical Reaction 22
       3.3.2   Characteristic Times for Heat Conduction 23
       3.3.3   Characteristic Times for Heat Conduction with Surface
               Convection 25
       3.3.4   Characteristic Times for Heat Generation by Viscous
               Dissipation 28
       3.3.5   Characteristic Times for Thermal Profile Development 31
   3.4 Polymerization Kinetics 32
       3.4.1   Random Propagation 34
       3.4.2   Step Propagation 35
       3.4.3   Addition Propagation 36
   3.5 Reactor Analysis 37
       3.5.1   Batch Reactors 37
       3.5.2   Plug Flow Reactors 38
       3.5.3   Ideal Mixers 38
       3.5.4   Unmixed Batch Reactor 39
       3.5.5   Continuous Tubular Reactor 39
   3.6 Temperature Effects in Polymerization Reactors 40
       3.6.1   Lumped Parameter Runaway 41
               3.6.1.1   Thermal Ignition Theory 42
               3.6.1.2   Effect of Reactant Consumption 46
               3.6.1.3   Computational Studies 47
               3.6.1.4   Experimental Studies 50
               3.6.1.5   Thermally Complex Systems 53
       3.6.2   Distributed Parameter Runaway 55
       3.6.3   Stability Analysis 58
   3.7 Conclusion 68
   References 70
   Notation 70

4 **Temperature-Dependent Effects in Polymer Processing** 73
   David Roylance

   4.1 Introduction 73
   4.2 Polymer Properties 74
       4.2.1   Effect of Temperature on Viscosity 74
       4.2.2   Effect of Temperature on Chemical Reactions 76
               4.2.2.1   Reaction Rates 76
               4.2.2.2   Effect of Cure in Thermosets 76
   4.3 Thermal Effects in Polymer Processing Flows 78
       4.3.1   Governing Equations 79
       4.3.2   Dimensional Analysis and Scaling 80
       4.3.3   Example: Extruder Channel Flow 82

		4.3.4	Numerical Simulation Methods	83
			4.3.4.1 The Galerkin Finite Element Method	84
			4.3.4.2 Some Numerical Examples	87
	4.4	Practical Consequences in Processing		89
		4.4.1	Chemical Reaction Mechanisms—An Example	89
		4.4.2	Kinetic Thermal Analysis	90
		4.4.3	Laminate Cure Analysis	94
	4.5	Summary		95
	References			96

5 Temperature Measurement Fundamentals ... 99
E. Marcia Katz

	5.1	Introduction		99
		5.1.1	General Concept of Temperature	99
		5.1.2	International Temperature Scales	100
	5.2	Basic Considerations for Temperature Measurement		100
	5.3	Thermoelectric Thermometry, the Basis of the Thermocouple		101
		5.3.1	Background	101
		5.3.2	Principles of Thermoelectric Circuits	103
		5.3.3	Industrial Thermocouples	104
		5.3.4	Thermocouple Calibration, Accuracy, and Standards	106
	5.4	Resistance Thermometry		107
		5.4.1	Background	107
		5.4.2	Industrial Applications of Resistance Thermometry	108
			5.4.2.1 Resistance Temperature Devices	108
		5.4.3	Thermistors	109
	References			110

6 Process Control Theory: Overview and Fundamentals ... 111
F. Greg Shinskey

	6.1	Introduction	111
	6.2	Regulation by Negative Feedback	112
		6.2.1 Influences: Set Point and Load	113
		6.2.2 Performance Criteria: Area and Peak Height	114
		6.2.3 Best-Possible and Actual Performance	117
	6.3	PID Controllers	117
		6.3.1 Proportional and Derivative Modes	118
		6.3.2 Integral Action and Windup	119
		6.3.3 Digital Control	120
	6.4	Model-Based Controllers	121
		6.4.1 PID τd Controller	122
		6.4.2 Performance and Robustness	123

6.5 Nonlinear Elements 124
    6.5.1 On–Off Controllers 124
    6.5.2 Valve Characteristics 126
    6.5.3 Flow-Variable Process Parameters 127
    6.5.4 Cascade Configurations 127
6.6 Feedforward Control 129
    6.6.1 Steady-State Models 130
    6.6.2 Dynamic Compensation 131
    6.6.3 Adding Feedback 132
    6.6.4 Decoupling Methods 132
References 133
Notation 133

7 Recursive Identification, Autotuning, and Adaptive Control 135
Guy A. Dumont

7.1 Introduction 135
    7.1.1 What Is Adaptive Control? 135
    7.1.2 Why Use Adaptive Control? 136
7.2 The Tuning Problem 136
    7.2.1 Classical Methods 137
    7.2.2 Model-Based Methods 137
7.3 Recursive Identification 139
    7.3.1 Identification Methods 139
        7.3.1.1 Least-Squares Method 139
        7.3.1.2 Maximum-Likelihood Method 140
    7.3.2 Recursive Identification Methods 142
        7.3.2.1 Recursive Least-Squares (RLS) 142
        7.3.2.2 Recursive Extended Least Squares, and Recursive Maximum-Likelihood 143
    7.3.3 Tracking Time-Varying Systems 144
7.4 Adaptive Control 146
    7.4.1 Indirect Adaptive Control 147
    7.4.2 Direct Adaptive Control 148
    7.4.3 Adaptive Predictive Control 148
    7.4.4 Implementation Issues 150
    7.4.5 Another Parameterization 151
7.5 Autotuning 151
    7.5.1 The Relay Method 152
    7.5.2 Pattern Recognition 155
    7.5.3 Model-Based Methods 155
    7.5.4 Commercial Products 156

7.6	Applications		156
	7.6.1	Glass Furnace Bottom Temperature Control	156
	7.6.2	Lime-Kiln Cooler-Feeder Control	158
7.7	Conclusions		159
References			160

8 Methodologies for Temperature Control of Batch and Semi-Batch Reactors ... 163
Richard S. Wu and Eugene P. Dougherty

8.1	Introduction		163
8.2	Time Series Analysis		163
	8.2.1	Model Identification	163
	8.2.2	Model Structure	166
	8.2.3	Controller Design	167
8.3	Dynamic Process Modeling		170
	8.3.1	The Philosophy of Computer Modeling and Simulation	170
	8.3.2	Building and Using Dynamic Process Models	171
	8.3.3	A Simple Dynamic Process Model for Temperature Control	173
	8.3.4	The SCOPE Model: A Sophisticated Dynamic Process Model	176
8.4	Feedforward and Feedback Temperature Control		179
	8.4.1	Why Feedforward?	179
	8.4.2	A Simple Form for the Feedforward Controller	179
	8.4.3	Simulation Example	182
	8.4.4	Generic Model Reference Control	187
8.5	Statistical Process Control and Engineering Process Control		188
	8.5.1	Deming Philosophy of Continual Improvement	188
	8.5.2	Statistical Charting Techniques, Autocorrelation, and Process Control	188
	8.5.3	Closed-Loop Controller Performance Assessment	190
	8.5.4	Special Clause Identification under Autocorrelation	193
	8.5.5	Determination of Process Disturbances Under Feedback Control	193
References			195

9 Integrated Temperature Control Applications in a Computer Control Environment ... 197
Martin Dybeck

9.1	Introduction	197
9.2	Integrated Temperature Control through Distributed Process Computers	197

	9.2.1 Temperature/Pressure Verification 198

        9.2.1 Temperature/Pressure Verification 198
        9.2.2 Predictive Maintenance on a Heat Exchanger 199
  9.3 Process Optimization: The "Hyperplane" Technique 199
  Reference 202

10 Servo Temperature Control of a Batch Reactor 203
Thomas W. Campbell

  10.1 Introduction 203
  10.2 Plant Description 205
  10.3 The Linearity and Stationarity Assumptions 205
       10.3.1 Effect of Valve Characteristic on Plant Stationarity 206
       10.3.2 Effect of Gain Balance on Plant Stationarity 208
       10.3.3 Effect of Valve Deadband and Crossover on Plant Stationarity 209
       10.3.4 Effect of Valve Crossover on Stationarity 210
       10.3.5 Effect of Temperature on Plant Stationarity 210
  10.4 Plant Identification 211
  10.5 Control Objectives 213
  10.6 Controller Optimality 214
  10.7 Theoretical Development 214
  10.8 Results 219

11 Modifications of a 500-Gallon Batch Reactor to Provide Better Data Acquisition and Control 221
R. J. Sadowski and C. G. Wysocki

  11.1 Introduction 221
  11.2 Functional Requirements of the Control and Data Acquisition System 222
  11.3 The Control and Data Acquisition System 223
  11.4 Process Calculations and Graphics 226
  11.5 On-Line Energy Release Calculations to Estimate Reactor Conversion 227
  11.6 Choice of Instruments 231
  11.7 Project Planning and Costs 232
  11.8 Summary of Our Results and Experiences 235

Index 237

CHAPTER 1

Introduction and Plan

Eugene P. Dougherty

1.1 Purpose and Scope of the Book

As an industrial process research scientist, I have worked on many projects in which temperature control was of critical importance. In fact, very recently, I was given the responsibility to scale up a new polymer product that had to adhere to very strict specifications. The key to meeting these specifications was — you guessed it — temperature control. Ironically, when I agreed to edit this book, I had originally thought that my activity would cost my company money, as I had to spend time away from my "real work." In reality, what I learned about temperature control from editing this book saved my company money. Poor temperature control would have most certainly led to production of polymer that was out of specification. Instead, through careful temperature control, we were able to make product within specification, to keep the business of a key customer, and to get some new customers as well.

Is this experience unique? I think not. Consider a hypothetical process whose rate-determining kinetic rate constant has an activation energy of −20 kcal/mol. If this (moderately temperature-dependent) process is run at 60 deg C rather than 62 deg C, the rate will be about 20% slower! An error of 2 deg C may sound innocuous, but not if you are the engineer trying to explain to your production manager why the plant was running consistently 20% below capacity.

Thus *Temperature Control Principles for Process Engineers* is written primarily for people like me: engineers and scientists who need to know about the power and techniques of temperature control. Such process engineers and scientists are usually already familiar with the processes they are responsible for and know that temperature can affect product and process performance. What they may not know is

---

Eugene P. Dougherty, Rohm and Haas Company, P. O. Box 219, Bristol, PA 19007, USA

how accurately temperature can be measured, what a proportional-integral-derivative (PID) algorithm can do, how their well-established models of the process can be used in feedforward control algorithms to control temperature better, and what sort of benefits can accrue from good temperature control. These are the topics covered in this book.

This book also has a second audience — process control engineers who need to familiarize themselves with the kinds of processes that they have to control. Such engineers generally already know a lot about thermocouples, computerized data acquisition systems, and PID algorithms. But, what they need to acquire is the knowledge and language of biochemical process engineering, polymer reaction engineering, polymer processing, and so on. Armed with this knowledge, process control experts can translate models for such processes directly into model-based, feedforward control algorithms to obtain better temperature control than simple feedback controllers will allow. Indeed, with better knowledge of the language and familiarity with the processes, the process control engineer will become a much better and more highly valued process consultant. Communication with the process designers will be improved with a common language base; and process control systems will be designed with intelligence and sensitivity to what the "real" problems are.

1.2 Overview/Plan of the Book

This book consists of three major sections. Chapters 2, 3, and 4 concern themselves with why we need to do temperature control. Three very different process disciplines are chosen to illustrate how temperature can be very important in a wide variety of areas. Although there are other disciplines where temperature can be a critical parameter, these three disciplines have significant industrial importance and are sufficiently well studied that at least semiquantitative process models exist. What links these disciplines together is that temperature is a central parameter in all three. For, as Prof. Roylance points out in Chapter 3, temperature controls a material's ability to flow and to react. It is absolutely vital that temperature effects be understood by the designer, so that suitable controls can be put into place. The authors of these chapters — Lorbert and Pike, Roylance, and Sebastian — all provide and use analytical theory, which can be put to use by the process control experts to make intelligent choices for feedforward and feedback control algorithms.

In Chapter 2 Steve Lorbert and Jim Pike show how critical temperature control is to biotechnology, not only in the fermentation processes to manufacture biotechnology products, but also in the downstream purification processes to produce these products in high yields at high purity levels.

Professor Sebastian's highly mathematical treatment of polymerization processes in Chapter 3 keynotes the important role temperature can play in both chain growth and step growth polymerizations. The equations for polymerization technology are, in general, better known than those governing biotechnology. Professor Sebastian explores the parametric sensitivity of these nonlinear equations, showing how even slight changes in temperature can produce difficult-to-control — or worse yet, runaway or explosive — polymerizations.

Professor Roylance explores the effects of temperature in polymer processing, both for viscosity effects and reactive effects. He explores the molecular mechanisms responsible for these effects. Finally, he provides a real-life application of these concepts to laminate cure analysis. Quite honestly, the book would have been even better if information had been provided for other process disciplines in which temperature is a central parameter. For example, petroleum engineering processes such as distillation and cracking are critically dependent on temperature control. Although petroleum process control engineering is not explored in depth, examples from other chapters (e.g., the examples given in Chapter 7 by Professor Dumont) are explored.

The key point is that there are many processes where temperature is crucial; the three process types explored here are commercially significant, fairly representative, and — finally — eloquently and lucidly described by the chapter authors.

The second section of the book — Chapters 5–8 — represents "tools of the trade" for obtaining good temperature control. Chapter 5, written by Dr. Marcia Katz, is included in this book for a very simple reason: you can't control what you can't measure. So Dr. Katz's chapter discusses both the principles and the practice of temperature measurement, focusing most heavily on the most popular devices — thermocouples and resistance thermometers. Accuracy, precision, and selection criteria for these devices are discussed, so that the process (or control) designer will make the right field instrumentation choice.

Chapter 6, written by Dr. Greg Shinskey (Foxboro), discusses process control fundamentals. Dr. Shinskey's lucid, no-nonsense chapter is where you will find what all the words that the process control experts are fond of using mean. Shinskey tells us what words such as feedback, feedforward, nonlinearity, antireset windup, and interacting really mean and why it is worth knowing about these concepts. In addition, at the end of this chapter, Dr. Shinskey shows some real-world case studies that you will definitely want to read about.

Chapter 7, written by Prof. Dumont, focuses on some newer, rather advanced notions of process control: self-tuning, autotuning, gain-scheduling, and so on. The newer, "smarter" controllers now out on the market are using these concepts routinely, as microprocessors and computer chips get increasingly smaller and more powerful. Chapter 7 is included for those of us who need to know what the controllers are really doing; this should help us make more intelligent decisions for determining what sort of controller to buy. Like Professor Roylance, Prof. Dumont also includes some application areas where these concepts are useful; in particular glass furnace bottom temperature control and lime kiln cooler-feeder control.

Chapter 8, co-authored by my colleague at Rohm and Haas, Dick Wu, presents some methodologies that, although conceptually rather simple, have proven to be effective for us at Rohm and Haas in achieving better temperature control. Time series analysis, dynamic process modeling, feedforward/feedback control, and statistical quality control (SQC) techniques have all been used by us in one project or another. We know they work; we've seen it happen. For proprietary reasons we cannot go into further detail on some of our applications, but knowledge of these methodologies should be particularly useful to the industrial problem-solver.

The final three chapters of the book — Chapters 9–11 — discuss some real-life temperature control applications. In Chapter 9, Martin Dybeck, a temperature control consultant, describes some generic techniques that he has found useful to solve process control problems in areas as diverse as polyvinyl chloride polymerization technology and control of batch brewery operations. One such technique, the so-called "hyperplane" technique, should prove useful in multivariable process control applications requiring tradeoffs among the variables to be controlled.

As an industrial researcher, I found Mr. Tom Campbell's reactor temperature control application, described in Chapter 10, particularly impressive. Mr. Campbell shows step by step how the heating and cooling of a reactor observe different process dynamics (i.e., he applies some analytical theory to the problem), he describes experiments used to identify process gains and delay times, and he then describes how the process controller was designed using a few heuristic, practical rules. Finally, the "bottom line" is shown in Figure 10.12: excellent temperature control of a difficult batch reactor in about 90 seconds. Not bad at all!

Finally, Chapter 11 details the kind of effort and planning needed for retrofitting a 500 gallon reactor to accommodate a new distributed system for temperature control. Messrs. Sadowski and Wysocki briefly show some of the calculations used to do on-line heat balances for their retrofitted reactor. In addition, they describe in some detail the planning required for a supervisory control system, together with a discussion of the all-important costs to be incurred. Anyone planning a project to use the tools for temperature control described in Chapters 5–8 will want to read Chapter 11 to see how these ideas can be reduced to practice in the 1990s. Clearly the infrastructure must be in place to use the temperature control tools; Messrs. Sadowski and Wysocki show us how to build that infrastructure.

CHAPTER 2

The Importance of Temperature Control in Biochemical Process Engineering

Stephen J. Lorbert and James P. Pike

2.1 Introduction

Temperature control systems are an integral part of biochemical manufacturing processes that regulate both the quality and the rate at which products can be produced. This is particularly true for the broad range of commercially important biochemical compounds that are produced by fermentation processes — important enzymes, pharmaceuticals,and food-related compounds. The production technologies for these products have been extensively reviewed [1,2]. In these processes the products are synthesized by living microorganisms that require carefully controlled conditions for growth and product expression. Temperature is a fundamental parameter regulating organism growth, kinetics, and overall product yields. As such the temperature of the fermentation process is usually maintained within a very tight range to maximize the production of cells and product during the batch.

Likewise, rigorous control of process operating temperatures is essential in ensuring rate and quality from downstream product purification operations. Temperature is a key factor controlling product physical properties and is often manipulated to effect further purification of the product. Sometimes a post fermentation modification of a compound can be required for "activation" of the product. Temperature is a major factor regulating the rate and extent of these chemical reactions. When working with many biologically active compounds such as proteins, the temperature of the

---

Stephen J. Lorbert, Novus International, Inc., 530 Maryville Centre Drive, St. Louis, MO 63141, USA; James P. Pike, Monsanto Company, 700 Chesterfield Parkway North, St. Louis, MO 63198, USA

purification process must be carefully controlled to preserve the integrity of the compound and prevent product degradation.

In general then, biochemical manufacturing processes depend heavily on the implementation of well-designed temperature control systems for both the product synthesis and product purification phases of the process. This chapter expands on the importance of temperature control for biochemical production processes, focusing specifically on fermentation-based products.

2.2   Temperature Control for Fermentation Based Production

2.2.1   Effect of Temperature on Microbial Systems

Temperature is one of the better understood parameters affecting fermentation-based production processes. There are numerous references which discuss the relationship between temperature and microbial growth [3–5]. The simple microbial systems that are the focus of commercial fermentation processes are really dependent on a multitude of complex chemical reactions that effect cell reproduction and product synthesis. Temperature is a primary variable affecting chemical reaction rates, and as such it serves as one of the fundamental parameters regulating cell growth.

One of the simple mathematical models describing cell growth was developed by Monod [6]. He observed that cell numbers increase in proportion to the number of cells that are present at a given time. This results in the following first-order expression:

$$dX/dt = uX \tag{2.1}$$

where X is the number of cells, t is time, and u is the growth rate constant. The integrated form of the equation is

$$\ln(X/X_0) = u\,(t - t_o) \tag{2.2}$$

In the equations above the growth rate constant is temperature dependent and generally follows an Arrhenius type relationship:

$$u = K\,\exp(-E_a/RT) \tag{2.3}$$

where K is a constant, E_a is the activation energy, R is the gas constant, and T is the absolute temperature. The constants K and E_a must be determined empirically and are characteristic of the specific organism of interest. These data can be used to predict a general relationship between organism growth and fermentation temperature.

Optimizing the temperature control strategy for product manufacture is usually much more complex and must be determined through experimentation. Optimizing the production of a particular metabolite very often involves changing environmental conditions inside the fermentor to exploit the particular enzyme system responsible for product production. As expected, these conditions may be slightly different than those required for global optimization of the machinery required for cell growth. The concept of separate temperature optima for cell growth and product production is illustrated most dramatically by the temperature induced product expression systems that have been developed using recombinant DNA technology. This technology has allowed the microbiologist to insert into a host microorganism, usually *Escherichia coli* (*E. coli*), foreign DNA which codes for the product of interest. These expression systems have been described in considerable detail elsewhere [7–9]. Typically the bacteria are first grown in a cell-producing mode at a lower temperature. Later in the batch the temperature is increased to induce the production of the desired product. At the lower temperature (usually 30–33 deg C) the cells reproduce without significant product yield. When the cells have been propagated to the desired density in the fermentor, product yield is increased by raising the temperature in the fermentor to 40–45 deg C. At this temperature, the cells no longer reproduce. Instead the cell's synthesis machinery is redirected toward product manufacture. These systems can be very efficient: up to 20–30% of total cell protein is expressed as the product of interest.

Although these systems can be very efficient with respect to product yield, they tend to be very inefficient with respect to nutrient consumption. Typically, a large amount of the carbon source consumed during the fermentation is converted directly to heat. Cooney et al. [10] have related heat evolution rate to oxygen uptake rate for a broad range of microorganisms grown aerobically on various carbon sources. The following relationship was developed:

$$\mathrm{HER} = 0.12\,\mathrm{OUR} \qquad (2.4)$$

where HER is the heat evolution rate in kcal/L-h and OUR is the oxygen uptake rate in millimoles of O_2/L-h. The oxygen uptake rate is directly dependent on cell density and growth rate and thus is indirectly related to the rate at which nutrients are consumed.

Figure 2.1 shows a profile of cell density, oxygen uptake rate, and heat evolution rate during a batch fermentation of *E. coli*. For fast-growing bacteria such as *E. coli*, heat evolution rates can approach 250–300 kcal/L-h when high cell densities are achieved in the reactor. This is very near the limit of the heat transfer capability of most conventional pilot scale fermentors. Interestingly, in these same fermentations, heat may actually have to be put into the fermentor at the beginning of the batch when cell densities are initially very low. Heat evolution rates often change very dramatically because cell densities will increase many orders of magnitude during the course of the fermentation. The dynamics in heat evolution rates that occur during the course of the batch, along with the actual quantity of heat that must be removed to keep a constant temperature, present a significant challenge in developing the design of a temperature control system.

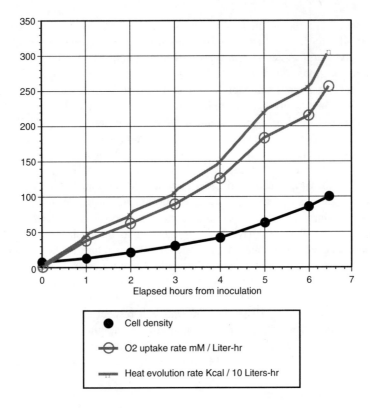

Figure 2.1 Batch fermentation of *E. Coli*. Cell density, heat of evolution, and O_2 uptake rate (1500-L, scale).

2.2.2 Temperature Control Systems for Fermentation

A typical fermentor and temperature control system is pictured in Figure 2.2. As can be seen from the diagram, hot water or steam is provided for heat input during the early portions of the fermentation. During the early phases of a batch, heat losses from the reactor may be greater than the rate at which heat is evolved from the fermenting microorganisms. A source of chilled water is provided to take care of the need for heat removal during the later phases of the batch. A split range control system is provided to control the operation of the two control valves which depend on the needs of the reactor during a given time period. The reactor itself is usually fully jacketed to maximize heat transfer surface area. The fermentor is also well agitated, resulting in heat transfer coefficients in the range of 100–150 Btu/Hr/ft²/F. The high level of agitation required for high-density bacterial fermentations, 3–40 Hp/1000 gallons, also results in significant amounts of heat input into the fermentor.

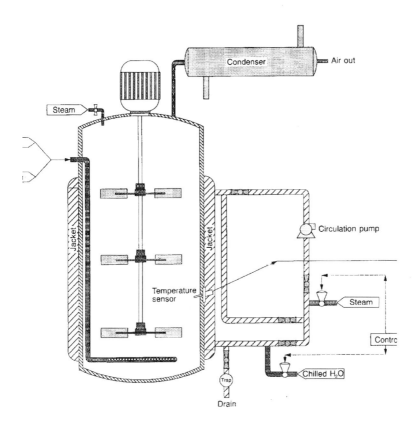

Figure 2.2 Typical fermentor and temperature control system.

2.2.3 Temperature Control for Media and Equipment Sterilization

One of the primary concerns in any fermentation process is maintaining the homogeneity of the culture during the course of the batch. Microorganisms are ubiquitous and opportunistic. The fermentation media is not only a perfect substrate for the organism of interest, but it is probably perfect for hundreds of other organisms as well. Contaminating microorganisms must be kept out of the batch through effective sterilization of media and equipment. In commercial processes, this is almost always accomplished through the application of moist heat, steam.

Sterilization of media and process equipment is covered in considerable detail elsewhere [3,11]. Basically, killing contaminating cells in fermentation media or equipment is accomplished by heating the materials to a sufficient temperature for a sufficient period of time. For most organisms, cell death is logarithmic once a threshold temperature has been surpassed.

Some microorganisms have the ability to form spores. Spores are heat resistant bodies that have the ability to germinate into a new microorganism once conditions have become more favorable for growth. Typically, media are sterilized at 121 deg C for 30–60 min to kill both vegetative cells and spores.

Temperature control systems for biological reactors must be designed to meet the requirements for equipment sterilization as well as provide effective cooling during the fermentation process itself. Steam is applied to the jacket of the fermentor and is sometimes sparged into the media to provide sterilizing conditions. The temperature sensing instrumentation must be selected and calibrated to measure across a range that can span 10–150 deg C. The instrumentation and control system must provide a reliable and reproducible means of sterilizing the system. This is very important to the regulatory agencies that review the operation of manufacturing processes for pharmaceutical and health-care-related products.

2.3 Importance of Temperature for Product Purification Processes

Temperature control concerns in processing of proteins and biomolecules can be considered in two different categories. First, there are concerns involving the stability of the protein or biomolecule in relation to temperature. Changes in the conformation and structure of the protein including irreversible denaturation, dimerization, attack by contaminating enzymes, or attack by contaminating bacteria in the process stream can lead to direct losses of product or biological inactivity of the desired molecule. Direct contamination of the product streams by bacteria can contribute extraneous protein and endotoxin in the case of certain recombinant bacterial systems. Temperature has a marked impact on all of these. The other category of concerns involves temperature and how it impacts the production process itself. This can include reaction kinetics and effects on the physical properties of process reagents and their interaction with processing equipment and the molecule and contaminants.

2.3.1 Effect of Temperature on Product Stability and Purity

Temperature plays an important role in the quality of protein products that are produced through recombinant systems or extracted from biological tissues. Protein containing processing streams can provide growth media for a number of organisms that can originate from upstream process steps. This is the case with protein products produced recombinantly or by the introduction of organisms through process stream additions. Contaminating bacteria can directly reduce product yields by utilizing product proteins as a carbon source in an environment that provides minimal media. These bacteria can also contribute product-degrading enzymes and extraneous nonproduct proteins.

Depending on the bacterial system used to produce some recombinant products, the host organism can contribute endotoxins, as is the case with recombinant *E. coli* systems. Many products such as antibiotics and injectables are required to be low bioburden or sterile. In a protein purification process it must be decided at which point the process should be run under low bioburden or sterile conditions to ensure product quality. Even though viable upstream organisms can be eliminated through sterile filtration, their impact on downstream quality can be dramatic. With endotoxin producing bacteria, contamination of less than 10 colony-forming-units (cfu)/ml in upstream process steps can cause pyrogenicity in a sterile product. Many sterile products are required to have endotoxin levels ¡1 EU/mg of protein. Endotoxins produced by the bacteria may not be removed through sterile filtration and can be carried forward to sterile portions of the process. For this reason it is important for bioburden to be minimized in process steps directly preceding sterile process steps.

Many times organisms are contributed to processing streams through addition of reagents introduced with deionized water as a diluent. Unfortunately, deionized water systems very often contain *Pseudomonas* bacteria. Bacterial contaimination may be small, but if low temperatures are not maintained, these organisms may bloom, providing unacceptable levels of contamination that may be carried forward to sterile segments of the process. Bacteria and the impact of bacterial contaminants on the product may be magnified if the process involves successive ultrafiltration and concentration steps where contaminants are concentrated in conjunction with the product.

By the exponential (i.e., Arrhenius) dependence of cell growth rate constants on temperature, it is clear that by maintaining low process stream temperatures, bioburden in these streams can be kept to a minimum. Because of this relationship many downstream processing steps are performed at temperatures below 10 deg C.

Process reagents and conditions, such as pH, can provide an environment that is not suitable to cell growth. However, when these reagents are removed or conditions changed, spores may be able to bloom if low temperature is not maintained. This is the case in protein refolding, which is a common step in the processing of recombinant proteins. In many recombinant bacterial systems the desired protein is produced in a reduced state and needs to be folded into the active form in which the oxidation of sulfhydryl groups creates disulfide bridges. These reactions are accomplished with the protein solubilized in a kaotrope solution, generally at high pH. The refold solution is not a favorable environment for cell growth and can kill recombinant cells carried forward to this process step. Once the refold is complete the kaotrope may be removed by diafiltration. At this point if low temperature is not maintained, contaminating cells and spores that might survive the kaotrope environment are able to bloom. As stated earlier the dependence of the growth constant and enzyme activity on temperature allows for the effects of these contaminants to be minimized.

Direct stability of protein products is also dependent on temperature. This is important from the aspects of product efficacy and regulatory purity. In protein products such as somatotropins the secondary structure or conformation of the protein determines the activity of the molecule. The native conformation of bovine somatotropin involves two covalent disulfide bonds. In bovine somatotropins the reduced primary structure is not biologically active. The activity of this molecule depends on the oxidized secondary structure, so it is important that the integrity of this structure is maintained throughout the purification process. Each product must be considered individually with respect to temperature stability. Even within a specific class of molecules such as the somatotropins there are significant differences in the stability of the molecule. A concern with regard to somatotropins is the formation of dimers. Even though these dimers may be biologically active it is hard to determine their impact on efficacy. Moreover, from a regulatory standpoint, dimers may be considered to produce a nonhomogeneous product. Somatotropins as a class, produced recombinantly, show differing rates of dimerization at a standard temperature. Even though they can be very similar in primary structure and secondary conformation they have significant differences in processing requirements with respect to temperature. In general the stability of the molecule can be increased by maintaining low temperatures throughout the purification process.

Because of the overall requirements for product stability of proteins, most processing steps are carried out at temperatures below 10 deg C, with many pilot scale and production scale processes being performed in cold room environments. Cold room environments are most conducive to processes that do not contain steps that have high energy input or require very large scale. As scale increases, the ratio of exchange surface area to the tank volume decreases. This makes cold rooms less viable as an option for maintaining low process temperatures because air has a minimal heat capacity. In processes that have steps that require high mechanical energy input, additional temperature control may be necessary. This may be accomplished with jacketed vessels or in-line heat exchanger loops. Jacketed vessels and heat exchangers may be used together with cold room environments.

2.3.2   Effect of Temperature on Protein Purification Technology

Downstream processing of proteins and large biomolecules involves a great diversity of technology. Temperature can impact reaction kinetics directly and the physical properties of reagents used in a process. In a single purification stream a multiple technologies can be involved, including: protein refolding, membrane filtration, ultrafiltration and molecular partitioning, liquid chromatography, selective precipitations, and liquid/liquid extraction. Figure 2.3 depicts what might be a general process flow diagram for the purification of an intracellular precipitated recombinant protein. Within this process many different technologies are being used, each being impacted by temperature, in terms of kinetics or equipment performance. Within each of these general methods there are many variations available to apply to specific molecules and contaminants. In all these technologies temperature can play an important role in the success of their implementation. Good temperature control is critical in developing consistent product throughput. This becomes very critical in being able to accurately scale up a process for plant design and capacity.

2. Importance of Temperature Control in Biochemical Process Engineering 13

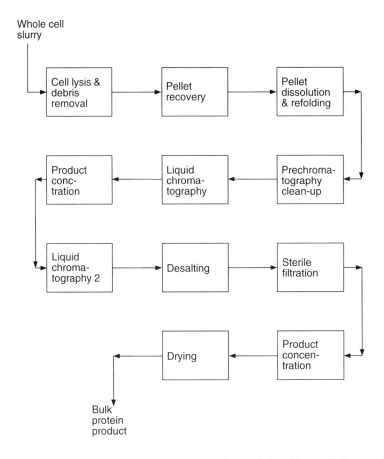

Figure 2.3 Typical downstream process for precipitated intracellular protein.

In the downstream processing of proteins, particularly recombinant proteins, the initial step may involve refolding the protein to the biologically active oxidized form. Temperature is critical in determining the rate at which the refold proceeds. The refold reaction is a non-zero-order reaction with rate dependent on the concentration of reduced protein in the reaction solution:

$$r_a = k\, C_A^a \tag{2.5}$$

In the above equation r_a is the rate of conversion of the reduced protein form to the oxidized form. C_A is the concentration of the reduced protein and k is a temperature dependent rate constant that can be expressed through the Arrhenius equation

$$k = A\, e^{-E/RT} \tag{2.6}$$

Ideally the refold should be carried out at the highest temperature possible without impacting protein quality and by maintaining efficiency in terms of percentage of reduced monomer converted to oxidized monomer. There can be a tradeoff between reaction efficiency and rate to achieve the highest throughput in a process. The importance of either consideration may be determined by evaluating upstream capacity, required tank scale and resultant cost.

As demonstrated in Figure 2.3, the purification process for a recombinant protein molecule may involve many dissimilar technologies. The majority of processes for the purification of a protein involve a packed column liquid chromatography step and may include several chromatography steps. The exchange resins used in these processes can be adversely affected by excessive pressure. It is also important to maintain flow rate properties of the column to ensure consistent separations and to maintain throughput for manufacturing situations. Compaction of the resin bed can lead to loss of flow rate and destruction of resin morphology. This may require time-consuming repacking of the column, forcing it to be taken off-line. The role temperature plays in effecting the pressure drop across a packed column can be seen by the correlation given by Leva for fixed beds of granular solids [12]:

$$\Delta p = 2 f_m G^2 L (1 - e)^{3-n} / D_p g_c p \emptyset_s^{3-n} e^3 \qquad (2.7)$$

In the equation Δp is the pressure drop; L is the length of gbed; g_c is the dimensional constant; D_p is the average particle diameter; e is the voidage; $\emptyset_s$ = shape factor; G = superficial mass velocity; p = fluid density; and f_m = friction factor, which is a function of the Reynolds number. The friction factor is inversely proportional to the Reynolds number.

$$N_{re} = D_p G / \mu \qquad (2.8)$$

In this equation, the Reynolds number is inversely proportional to μ, fluid viscosity, which increases with decreasing temperature. Overall decreases in temperature can increase the predicted pressure drop across a packed bed column by increasing the friction factor number. Ideally the impact temperature has on pressure drop and resin condition as seen in the column's performance should be determined empirically for successful scaleup of the process to achieve the required separation and throughput for a manufacturing process. Good temperature control is also important in maintaining an accurate gradient in the operation of the column. Both pH and salt gradients can be monitored and controlled based on conductivity. Temperature fluctuations of the gradient feed to a column can cause gradient irregularities as the monitored conductivity and pH change with the temperature. Overall, good temperature control is required to maintain consistent column performance in terms of column longevity and quality of the separation. Thus, while we have seen that temperature control is critical in the reaction kinetics of protein refolding, maintaining consistent temperatures is equally vital to a successful scaleup for manufacturing for packed column processes.

2. Importance of Temperature Control in Biochemical Process Engineering

Another technology that is widely used in the purification of proteins is membrane separation processes [13,14]. This technology can be used for diafiltration of protein solutions to remove unwanted reagents, concentrating protein solutions, or doing molecular partitioning of proteins and contaminants of different molecular weights, just to name a few applications. Materials of construction for separation membranes vary widely, including cellulosic systems, ceramic systems, etc. In all these systems temperature plays an important role in process performance.

If we examine Darcy's Equation for flow through a porous media,

$$(p_1 - p_2)/L = a\mu V/g_c \tag{2.9}$$

where p_1 is the absolute upstream pressure; p_2 is the absolute downstream pressure; L is the porous media thickness; V is the superficial velocity of fluid; μ is the fluid viscosity; and g_c is the dimensional constant, we can see that temperature can directly affect transmembrane pressures and permeate flux rates caused by changes in fluid viscosity with changes in temperature [12,15]. Figure 2.4 demonstrates this relationship as seen in a cellulosic microfiltration system. These effects can be seen both in micro- and ultrafiltration systems. By raising temperatures, increases in permeate flux rates can be realized, and this would seem appropriate for increasing process throughput and decreasing capital costs for manufacturing scaleup. But the impact temperature plays in protein stability must also be considered and will limit operating temperatures for these systems. Temperature can also affect the performance of these systems

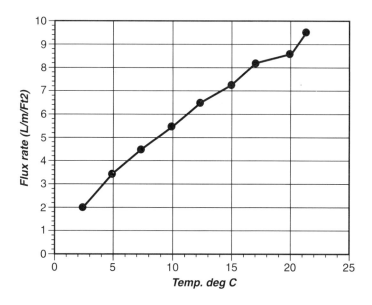

Figure 2.4 D.I. water flux data (0.22 μm cellulosic membrane).

by indirectly affecting the physical condition of the membrane and molecule. Many ultrafiltration membranes are pressure sensitive and will show irreversible compaction at elevated pressures, reducing flux rates and the life of the membrane. As Darcy's equation shows, decreasing temperature and keeping flux rates constant for a particular throughput requirement will require operating pressure to be increased, either by increasing back pressure on the retentate cross flow or by increasing the retentate crossflow rate. Membrane replacement is costly: the rate of irreversible compaction can largely determine the replacement frequency and life of a membrane. Membrane flux may also be decreased by a condition known as membrane polarization, whereby particles in the retentate stream may become deposited on the membrane surface or precipitated in the membrane structure. Elevated temperatures may cause proteins to be susceptible to shear or cause soluble protein contaminants to precipitate out of solution. These protein fragments or precipitated contaminants may be small enough to embed within the membrane because of their smaller nominal size than the protein for which the membrane was selected. This fouling can reduce membrane fluxes over time and can become irreversible, reducing the life of the membrane and causing membrane rejection. It should also be noted that many crossflow membrane processes involve high heat input to the system from the high pumping rates that are required to operate these systems. When designing and scaling up membrane processes, consistent temperature control is again critical in determing performance and throughput. Porous membranes cannot be described in the way fixed beds of solids can be and vary widely in terms of resistance to compaction and morphology. This requires the engineer to determine optimum temperatures for each individual system and product empirically in the laboratory and pilot plant to be assured of adequate performance and scaleup for manufacturing.

With the plethora of protein and biomolecule products in commercial use and the wide range of technology for the purification of these products, it must be stressed that the impact of temperature on the stability of the product and on process performance must be empirically determined in the lab and pilot plant. Temperature impact on product quality and process throughput make this critical to proper scaleup of downstream processes for manufacturing.

References

1. Moo-Young, M., *Comprehensive Biotechnology, Vol. 3: The Practice of Biotechnology: Current Commodity Products.* Pergamon Press (1985).
2. Moo-Young, M., *Comprehensive Biotechnology, Vol. 4: The Practice of Biotechnology, Specialty Products and Service Activities.* Pergamon Press (1985).
3. Wang, D.I., Cooney, C.L., Demain, A.L., Dunnill, P., Humphrey, A.E., and Lilly, M.D., *Fermentation and Enzyme Technology.* John Wiley & Sons (1979).
4. Stanier, R.Y., Adelberg, A., and Ingraham, J.L., *The Microbial World.* Prentice-Hall, Inc. (1976).
5. Bailey, J.E. and Ollis, D.F., *Biochemical Engineering Fundamentals.* McGraw-Hill (1977).
6. Monod, J., The growth of bacterial cultures. *Annu. Rev. Microbiol.* **3**, 371 (1949).

7. Khosrovi, B. and Gray, P., Products from Recombinant DNA, in *Comprehensive Biotechnology, Vol. 3* (Moo-Young, M. ed.). Pergamon Press (1985).
8. Zabriskie, D.W. and Arcuri, E.J., Factors influencing productivity of fermentations employing recombinant microorganisms. *Enzyme Microbiolol. Tech.* **8**, 705 (1986).
9. Yang, R.D. US Patent 4 705 848 (1987).
10. Cooney, C.L., Wang, D.I., and Matels, R.I., Measurement of heat evolution and correlation with oxygen consumption during microbial growth. *Biotechnol. Bioengin.* **11**, 269 (1968).
11. Olson, W.P. and Groves, M.J., *Aseptic Pharmaceutical Manufacturing.* Interpharm Press (1987).
12. Sakiadis, B.C., Fluid and particle mechanics, in *Perry's Chemical Engineers' Handbook*, 50th edit. (Green, D.W. ed.). McGraw Hill (1984).
13. McGregor, W.C., Selection and use of ultrafiltration membranes, in *Membrane Separations in Biotechnology, Vol. 1,* (McGregor, W.C. ed.). Marcel Dekker (1986).
14. Rautenbach, R. and Albrecht, R., *Membrane Processes.* John Wiley and Sons (1989).
15. Le, M.S. and Howell, J.A., Ultrafiltration, in *Comprehensive Biotechnology, Vol. 2* (Moo-Young, M., ed.). Pergamon Press (1985).

CHAPTER 3

Nonisothermal Effects in Polymer Reaction Engineering

Donald H. Sebastian

3.1 Introduction

Polymer reaction engineering represents the interface between the studies of transport phenomena and reaction kinetics. The interaction among fluid dynamics, mixing, heat transfer, and chemical reaction path uniquely shape a polymerizer's ability to transform a feed stream of low molecular weight material into a high polymer of specific chain length and chain length distribution. Polymer reactions are generally accompanied by a large heat effect coupled with a strong temperature sensitivity in the rate of reaction; therefore, heat transfer becomes a paramount consideration for the maintenance of product quality when designing and operating reactors. The purpose of this chapter is to present the fundamentals through which one can understand, predict, and ultimately control the nonisothermal behavior of polymer reaction vessels.

Throughout this chapter, simplified models of reaction kinetics and reactor behavior will be used to illustrate basic concepts. The reader should not be deceived by the apparent simplicity. These models do not trivialize the results but rather capture the essence that distinguishes principal classes of reaction and reactor behavior without obscuring the principles in intractable mathematics.

3.2 Basic Transport Theory

Transport phenomena provide the mathematical framework within which one can describe the complex interactions of fluid dynamics, chemical reaction, and heat

---

Donald H. Sebastian, Co-Director, Design & Manufacturing Institute & Professor of Chemical Engineering, Stevens Institute of Technology, Castle Point on the Hudson, Hoboken, NJ 07030, USA

transfer that combine to determine a reactor's performance. The toolset derived from this body of study is a set of balance equations, often referred to as the Equations of Change [1]. These represent mathematical statements of the principle of conservation of mass, momentum, and thermal energy applied to a region in space often called a control volume. Simple stated, they prescribe that for any volume, the time rate of change, or accumulation, of any extensive property is created by the net difference between the rate of exchange with the surroundings due to flows across the control volume's surface, and the rate of production within the volume due to internal sources.

$$\left\{ \begin{array}{c} \text{Rate} \\ \text{of} \\ \text{Accumulation} \end{array} \right\} = \left\{ \begin{array}{c} \text{Rate} \\ \text{of} \\ \text{Flow} \end{array} \right\} + \left\{ \begin{array}{c} \text{Rate} \\ \text{of} \\ \text{Production} \end{array} \right\} \quad (3.1)$$

Furthermore, flows across the control volume's boundaries can arise from either of two different mechanisms, convection and conduction. Convection is bulk flow and requires a material (mass) exchange with the surroundings, whereas conduction is a molecular process. Diffusion, shear transmission of force, and heat conduction are examples of the latter, and do not require a net mass flow across boundaries to transport the property in question. Because their physical origins are different, the mathematical representations of convection and conduction are sufficiently different to warrant separate designations in our balance statement. Thus Eq. (3.1) becomes:

$$\left\{ \begin{array}{c} \text{Rate} \\ \text{of} \\ \text{Accumulation} \end{array} \right\} = \left\{ \begin{array}{c} \text{Rate} \\ \text{of} \\ \text{Conduction} \end{array} \right\} + \left\{ \begin{array}{c} \text{Rate} \\ \text{of} \\ \text{Convection} \end{array} \right\} + \left\{ \begin{array}{c} \text{Rate} \\ \text{of} \\ \text{Production} \end{array} \right\} \quad (3.2)$$

Two different forms of the balance arise naturally in reaction engineering applications. The first is a macroscopic balance in which the control volume is essentially the entire region of interest (i.e., the entire reactor volume).

$$\underbrace{\iiint \tfrac{dE}{dt} dV}_{r_{\text{acc}}} = \underbrace{\iint \bar{\Phi} \cdot \bar{n} dA}_{r_{\text{cond}}} + \underbrace{\iint e\bar{v} \cdot \bar{n} dA}_{r_{\text{conv}}} + \underbrace{\iiint s dV}_{r_{\text{gen}}} \quad (3.3)$$

The second is the microscopic balance in which the control volume is a differential element located at some arbitrary position within the solution domain.

$$\underbrace{\tfrac{\partial i}{\partial t}}_{r_{\text{acc}}} = \underbrace{-\nabla \cdot \bar{\Phi}}_{r_{\text{cond}}} - \underbrace{\bar{v} \cdot \nabla i}_{r_{\text{conv}}} + \underbrace{s}_{r_{\text{gen}}} \quad (3.4)$$

The full set of microscopic balance equations, with the vector operators expanded in various coordinate systems, can be found in any text on the subject [1–3]. It should be apparent that the integration of the microscopic balance over the entire solution space will give rise to the corresponding macroscopic balance.

3.3 Characteristic Times

Although the transport balances provide the means to describe the most complicated of reactor environments, the solution of those equations can be daunting. In some instances, closed form, analytical solutions can be achieved. Solutions in this form are highly desirable because they tend to reveal global forms of behavior, limiting extremes of performance, and give rise to natural clustering of pertinent variables. Unfortunately, analytical solutions are generally limited to problems where properties vary in only one spatial dimension, and where the effects of heat, mass, and momentum transport can be decoupled. Alternatively, the equations can be solved numerically using techniques of digital computation. This approach greatly extends the range of problems that can be tackled but there is an associated cost. Numerical solutions provide only local information. That is, one set of input conditions can lead to only one set of output conditions. Attaining global information requires a tedious process of iterative solution coupled with the implementation of some strategy for selecting appropriate permutations of the input parameter values.

The method of characteristic times is a powerful technique for generalizing behavior of transport-related processes. Without solving the explicit equations of change, it is still possible to deduce global system behavior and to identify the naturally occurring groupings that exist among system parameters.

A characteristic time evolves from the simplest of algebraic relationships: distance equals rate times time. Extended to transport parlance, the amount of an extensive quantity transported (distance) is equal to the transport rate times some characteristic time scale. Rearranged to define the time scale:

$$\text{Time} = \frac{\text{Extensive Property}}{\text{Rate}} \qquad (3.5)$$

Realizing that source and flux expressions represent rate of transport per unit volume and area, respectively, of an extensive property, it suggests that approximation to the various differential operators on those expressions will provide the rate term needed in Eq. (3.5).

$$\text{Time} = \left\{ \begin{array}{l} \dfrac{(\text{Ext. Prop/Vol}) \text{ Volume}}{\text{Flux Area}} = \dfrac{eL}{\Phi} \\ \dfrac{(\text{Ext. Prop/Vol}) \text{ Volume}}{\text{Source Volume}} = \dfrac{e}{s} \end{array} \right\} \qquad (3.6)$$

Using initial and boundary values for the parameters in the characteristic times, and using differences to approximate gradient terms in the flux expressions, characteristic times can be evaluated without solving the related transport balance equations. What remains to be demonstrated is the fact that semiquantitative behavior predicted by these entities is wholly consistent with the detailed solutions to those balances.

One additional, general concept must be introduced, the dimensionless number. Dimensionless quantities are known to most engineers as scaling parameters, or correlating factors for experimental data. What is remarkable is the notion that all of the classic dimensionless parameters can be represented as the ratio of characteristic times for two relevant and competing transport phenomena. It should be clear that the ratio of any two characteristic times is a naturally unitless quantity. Furthermore, when the ratio has a value close to unity, then the two characteristic times are on the same order of magnitude and should be equal in importance when considering overall system dynamics. If, however, the ratio is very large or very small, then one of the two processes may be viewed as dominant and rate controlling. In subsequent sections this concept will be demonstrated, and it will be shown that most major changes in system behavior occur when characteristic time ratios are between 1:10 and 10:1.

3.3.1 Characteristic Times for Chemical Reaction

Characteristic times arise naturally in the discussion of chemical reaction kinetics. The concept of the half-life is a familiar measure of the intrinsic time scale for a reaction. We shall demonstrate that this is a special instance of the characteristic time that arises from simple second-order kinetics. To begin, realize that the extensive property relevant to the material balance for a reactor can be thought of as the initial number of moles of a key reactant. The total rate of consumption is the chemical reaction rate times the volume of the system. Because the rate of reaction changes continuously during the course of reaction by virtue of composition and temperature change, some metric is required to represent the typical reactor characteristics. It is suggested that feed or initial conditions represent a choice that captures order of magnitude behavior and can be evaluated without solving any equations. Thus:

$$\tau_r = \frac{n|_0}{r|_0 V} = \frac{c|_0}{r|_0} \tag{3.7}$$

For simple nth order kinetics, the characteristic time can be found to be:

$$\tau_r = \frac{1}{kc^{n-1}|_0} \tag{3.8}$$

Thus, for a first-order reaction scheme the characteristic time is just the reciprocal of the kinetic rate constant, whereas for a second-order reaction it is the reciprocal of the rate constant times the feed concentration. The reader may recognize the latter as the formal definition of the half-life.

The unifying ability of the characteristic time becomes evident in Figure 3.1. The solution to the kinetic expressions for both batch rectors and ideal mixer reactors employing half-, first-, and second-order kinetics are shown on a common plot. The

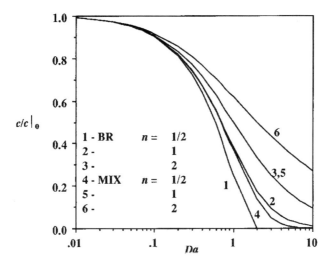

Figure 3.1 Dimensionless concentration histories for nth order kinetics in batch and ideal mixer reactors.

time scale, elapsed time for a batch reactor and average residence time for the mixer, has been normalized by the appropriate characteristic time for reaction in each instance. This forms a dimensionless quantity, known as the Damkohler Number, Da, which is the ratio of reactor time scale (average residence time) to reaction time scale.

$$Da = \frac{\tau_F}{\tau_r} = \frac{Vr|_0}{Vc|_0} \tag{3.9}$$

Note that although the details of the concentration history vary from case to case, one can approximate conversion to be roughly half complete at one characteristic time value, and completion of the reaction by 10 times the characteristic value. In essence, the conclusion is that the reactor holding time should be an order of magnitude greater than the reaction time to allow for complete conversion. Thus, the Damkohler Number provides a simple heuristic for estimating critical reactor parameters. Using the relationship $Da = 10$, one can solve for any parameter in the group given values of the others, providing a simple linearization of a potentially complicated kinetic analysis. As shown in subsequent sections, this approach remains legitimate even when the kinetic scheme is extended to multiple reactants, and parallel and series reaction elements.

3.3.2 Characteristic Times for Heat Conduction

In the case of batch reactor chemical kinetics, the time scale for a transport source term was developed and compared against elapsed time to draw performance generalizations. The same approach can be used to characterize behavior of a system dominated by transport flow terms. Consider heat conduction through a solid slab with each face maintained at some uniform temperature that is different from the initial temperature of the slab. The extensive property in question is the sensible heat content that must be removed to equilibrate the slab with its surroundings. The transport rate is the product of the heat flux and the surface area transverse to the heat flow direction.

$$\tau_H = \frac{mC_p\Delta T}{qA} \qquad (3.10)$$

This requires some approximation because the heat flux may vary from point to point in the cross-section as dictated by the Fourier's Law relationship between flux and local temperature gradient. Using an approximation to the gradient based on placing the maximum temperature at the slab centerline, and using a linear temperature profile, one can reduce the characteristic time expression to the following form:

$$\tau_H = \frac{\rho C_p \Delta T W H L}{k \frac{\Delta T}{H/2} 2WL} = \frac{\rho C_p (H/2)^2}{k} = \frac{R_H^2}{a_T} \qquad (3.11)$$

where α_T is the thermal diffusivity, $k/\rho c_p$. The same procedure can be applied to a cylinder and an annulus to arrive at the formulae

$$\tau_H = \frac{\rho C_p \Delta T \pi R^2 L}{k \frac{\Delta T}{R/2} 2\pi R L} = \frac{\rho C_p (R/2)^2}{k} = \frac{R_H^2}{a_T} \qquad (3.12)$$

$$\tau_H = \frac{\rho C_p \Delta T \pi (R_2^2 - R_1^2) L}{k \frac{\Delta T}{(R_2-R_1)/2} 2\pi (R_2 + R_1) L} = \frac{\rho C_p (R_2 - R_1/2)^2}{k} = \frac{R_H^2}{a_T} \qquad (3.13)$$

from which it can be generalized that the hydraulic radius, R_H, defined as the ratio of volume to exposed surface area, is the geometric scaling parameter that relates diverse shapes in a single relationship.

$$\tau_H = \frac{R_H^2}{a_T} \qquad (3.14)$$

Plotting the solution to the thermal energy balance equations for transient heat conduction illustrates the significance of τ_H as a yardstick for the time needed to reach thermal equilibrium. Cooling curves for a slab of uniform initial temperature, subjected to a step change in surface temperature, are shown in Figure 3.2. Once again, normalizing elapsed time by the characteristic time for conduction (which forms the dimensionless Fourier Number, F_o) places all thermal histories on the same set of axes. Furthermore, as with chemical reaction, equilibrium is attained when the critical dimensionless number exceeds a value of 10.

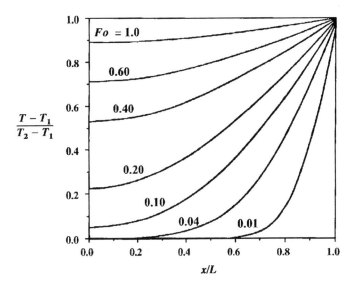

Figure 3.2 Transient temperature distributions in a rectangular slab of constant wall temperature.

3.3.3 Characteristic Times for Heat Conduction with Surface Convection

Thus far, characteristic times have been shown in relatively simple settings: ones in which only one transport process was operative. The next question to be addressed is the utility of the technique when multiple processes exist, both in series and in parallel. Consider a variation of the analysis in the previous section which deals with the serial process of heat transfer through a solid, and then through the "thin film" associated with convective heat transfer from a solid surface to a surrounding fluid. The first step is a molecular conduction through the solid, and is described by τ_H as derived previously. The second step can be described by Newton's Law of Cooling which relates the flux at the fluid–solid interface to the driving force temperature difference and a heat transfer coefficient.

$$q|_{Surface} = h(T|_{Surface} - T|_{Surroundings}) \qquad (3.15)$$

Using Eq. (3.15), and applying it to a rectangular slab,

$$\tau_R = \frac{\rho C_p \Delta T W H L}{h \Delta T 2 W L} = \frac{\rho C_p (H/2)}{h} = \frac{\rho C_p R_H}{h} \qquad (3.16)$$

one arrives at the intrinsic time scale for heat removal through the hydrodynamic film at the solid surface. Note, once again, the presence of the hydraulic radius as the key geometric factor consolidating a wide variety of shapes.

Straightforward application of the thermal energy balance, at steady state, yields:

$$0 = k\frac{d^2T}{dx^2} \tag{3.17}$$

with boundary conditions:

$$-k\frac{dT}{dx}\bigg|_{x=0} = h(T_{C1} - T|_{x=0}) \tag{3.18}$$

$$-k\frac{dT}{dx}\bigg|_{x=H} = h(T|_{x=H} - T_{C2}) \tag{3.19}$$

This yields to analytical solution:

$$\hat{T} = \frac{Nu\,\hat{x} + 1}{Nu + 2} \tag{3.20}$$

where:

$$\hat{x} \equiv \frac{x}{H} \tag{3.21}$$

$$\hat{T} \equiv \frac{T - T_{C1}}{T_{C2} - T_{C1}} \tag{3.22}$$

and the Nusselt Number is readily defined by the ratio of the characteristic times for heat conduction to surface heat convection:

$$Nu = \frac{\tau_H}{\tau_R} = \frac{\rho C_p R_H^2/k}{\rho C_p R_H/h} = \frac{hR_H}{k} \tag{3.23}$$

Large values of the Nusselt Number, Nu, indicate that heat conduction is the rate-limiting step, and thus one would expect a linear temperature profile ranging from the left-side coolant temperature at $x = 0$ to the right-side coolant temperature at $x = L$. Conversely, when Nusselt is small, heat transfer through the surfaces is rate controlling, and one would expect a flat temperature in the part with discontinuous changes at each surface. The limiting instances of Eq. (3.23) show that the Nusselt Number does indeed characterize the extremes of thermal behavior.

$$\lim_{Nu\to\infty}\hat{T} = \lim_{Nu\to\infty}\frac{\hat{x} + 1/Nu}{1 + 2/Nu} = \hat{x} \tag{3.24}$$

$$\lim_{Nu\to 0}\hat{T} = \lim_{Nu\to 0}\frac{Nu\,\hat{x} + 1}{Nu + 2} = 1/2 \tag{3.25}$$

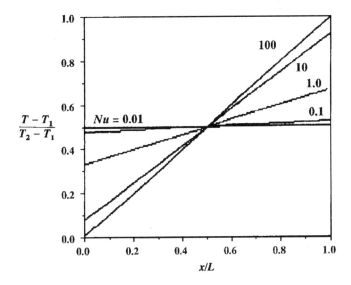

Figure 3.3 Steady-state temperature profiles for various values of Nu.

Not only do the formal limits demonstrate this behavior, but plots of $\hat{T}$ versus $\hat{x}$ shown in Figure 3.3 illustrate the families of thermal behavior resulting from variation in Nu. More importantly, the transition from one extreme of behavior to the other is not a slow and continuous process. The plot in Figure 3.4 shows the slope of the temperature

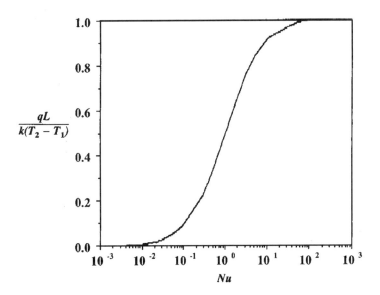

Figure 3.4 Dimensionless heat flux as a function of Nu.

profile as a function of the Nusselt Number. It is apparent that the transition from adiabatic to isothermal wall behavior all takes place in the region one decade above and one decade below $Nu = 1$. It is intuitively satisfying that the empirically derived characteristic time ratio quantitatively captures this important transition.

3.3.4   Characteristic Times for Heat Generation by Viscous Dissipation

In laminar flows, a certain portion of the energy input intended to create motion is irreversibly lost as heat. This is referred to as viscous energy dissipation (VED). It appears in the thermal energy balance as an apparent source term, and is the product of a stress tensor component and a shear rate. Consider the flow of a viscous fluid through a cylindrical tube. At some point downstream from the inlet, the system will attain fully developed conditions — that is, there will be no further variations in the transverse profile with respect to downstream position. Subject to the fully developed flow assumption, the transient and axial dependencies vanish. If cooling is provided at the tube surface, according to Newton's Law of Cooling, as described in the previous section, the pertinent equations are for momentum:

$$0 = -\frac{dp}{dz} + \frac{1}{r}\frac{d}{dr}\left(\eta r \frac{dv_z}{dr}\right) \tag{3.26}$$

with boundary conditions:

$$\left.\frac{dv_z}{dr}\right|_{r=0} = 0 \tag{3.27}$$

$$v_z|_{r=R} = 0 \tag{3.28}$$

and for thermal energy:

$$0 = \frac{1}{r}\frac{d}{dr}\left(kr\frac{dT}{dr}\right) + \eta\left(\frac{dv_z}{dr}\right)^2 \tag{3.29}$$

with boundary conditions:

$$\left.\frac{dT}{dr}\right|_{r=0} = 0 \tag{3.30}$$

$$\left.\frac{dT}{dr}\right|_{r=R} = -\left(\frac{h}{k}\right)(T|_{r=R} - T_C) \tag{3.31}$$

Since the heat removal mechanism is identical to that posed in the previous section, one expects that both the characteristic time for heat conduction and surface convection will be important. In addition, there is the need to characterize the heat generation rate. Following the procedure already described:

3. Nonisothermal Effects in Polymer Reaction Engineering

$$\tau_V = \frac{\rho C_p T_C WHL}{\eta \left(\frac{\langle v \rangle}{R_H}\right)^2 WHL} = \frac{\rho C_p R_H^2 T_C}{\eta \langle v \rangle^2} \quad (3.32)$$

One can gain insight as to the important parameter groupings by assuming the viscosity is weakly dependent on temperature, thus leading to an analytical solution to Eq. (3.26) and (3.27). The solution for the temperature profile in the tube is:

$$\frac{T - T_C}{T_C} = Br\left(1 - \left[\frac{r}{R_H}\right]^4 + \frac{4}{Nu}\right) \quad (3.33)$$

where the Brinkman Number, Br, is the ratio of the characteristic time for heat conduction to that of heat generation by VED.

$$Br = \frac{\tau_H}{\tau_V} = \frac{\rho C_p R_H^2 / k}{\rho C_p R_H^2 T_C / \eta \langle v \rangle^2} = \frac{\eta \langle v \rangle^2}{k T_C} \quad (3.34)$$

Consider two separate cases, one where heat removal from the surface is highly effective ($Nu \gg 1$), and a second where heat removal from the surface is rate controlling relative molecular conduction ($Nu \ll 1$).

In the first case, if Br is small, then the steady-state temperature profile reduces to that of the coolant temperature. This is consistent with the characteristic time definition which suggests that small values of Br mean that the heat removal time is much less than the generation time. If Br is very large, then temperatures will be distributed from a maximum at the centerline (roughly equal to Br if Nu is large), decaying to zero at the wall (again, if Nu is sufficiently large relative to Br). Figure 3.5,

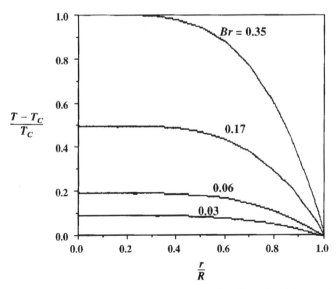

Figure 3.5 Temperature distributions for tube flow as a function of Brinkman Number, with large Nusselt Numbers.

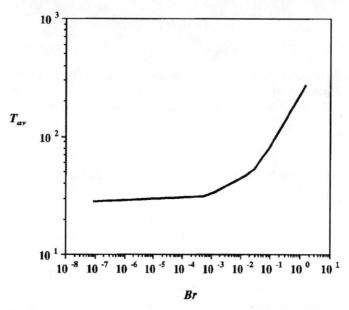

Figure 3.6 Maximum temperature for tube flow as a function of Brinkman Number, with large Nusselt Numbers.

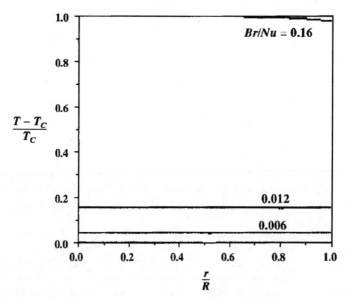

Figure 3.7 Temperature distributions for tube flow as a function of Brinkman Number, with small Nusselt Numbers.

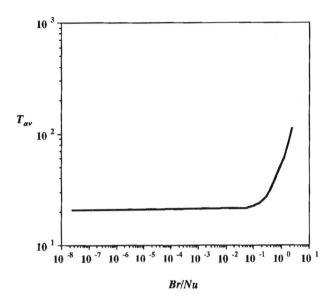

Figure 3.8 Maximum temperature for tube flow as a function of Brinkman Number, with small Nusselt Numbers.

which is based on numerical solution of the balance equations without the assumption of temperature independence of viscosity, confirms this behavior, demonstrating the growth in the temperature maximum as Br is increased. Furthermore, plotting the maximum temperature versus the value of Br, as in Figure 3.6, it is clear that quasi-isothermal behavior prevails as long as $Br < 0.1$.

If the Nusselt Number is set to a very small value, it should be apparent that Br is not a relevant parameter. It compares heat removal by conduction to generation by VED, but when Nusselt is small, heat removal by conduction is not rate controlling. A more insightful comparison would contain the characteristic time for heat removal from the surface to that of generation, which can be formed by dividing Br by Nu. Examining the analytical solution shows that under these assumptions, the temperature profile is flat, and equal to $4Br/Nu$. The numerical solutions shown in Figures 3.7 and 3.8 confirm the trends in the detailed thermal behavior as well as the maximum temperature values in response to variations in Br/Nu. As with the first case, transitions in system behavior are keyed to the operative characteristic time ratio exceeding a value of 0.10.

3.3.5 Characteristic Times for Thermal Profile Development

As a final example, reconsider the previous example without the restriction of fully developed flow. Let the material enter the tube at some temperature different from that of the coolant. Since the momentum transport time scale to reach steady state is always quite short for polymer flows, the steady-state momentum balance, Eq. (3.26), still applies. The thermal energy balance with boundary conditions reduces to:

$$\rho C_p v_z \frac{\partial T}{\partial z} = \frac{1}{r}\frac{\partial}{\partial r}\left(kr\frac{\partial T}{\partial r}\right) + \eta\left(\frac{dv_z}{dr}\right)^2 \quad (3.35)$$

$$\left.\frac{\partial T}{\partial r}\right|_{r=0} = 0 \quad (3.36)$$

$$\left.\frac{\partial T}{\partial r}\right|_{r=R} = -\left(\frac{h}{k}\right)(T|_{r=R} - T_C) \quad (3.37)$$

$$T|_{z=0} = T_0 \quad (3.38)$$

A new comparison is needed, one that contrasts the operative heat transfer mechanism with the residence time (which is the time for bulk convection of any quantity). Thus, if Nu is large, the ratio of heat conduction time to residence time should characterize the approach to fully developed flow. If Nu is small, then it should be the ratio of surface convection time and residence time. The former is the Peclet Number (Pe), whereas the latter is the inverse of the Stanton Number, St. These dimensionless numbers are defined as follows:

$$Pe = \frac{\tau_H}{\tau_F} = \frac{\rho C_p R_H^2/k}{L/\langle v \rangle} \quad (3.39)$$

$$St = \frac{\tau_F}{\tau_R} = \frac{L/\langle v \rangle}{\rho C_p R_H/h} \quad (3.40)$$

Figures 3.9–3.11 establish the parametric dependence of the thermal profile development for both large and small Nusselt Numbers, and with and without VED. It should be evident that fully developed conditions are attained when the critical dimensionless grouping passes through 0.10.

3.4 Polymerization Kinetics

In spite of the myriad of chemical components and reaction mechanisms that exist in commercial polymerization systems, it is possible to reduce these to three fundamental classes of reaction: random propagation, step propagation (addition propagation without termination), and addition propagation with termination. Each has fundamentally different characteristics that distinguish the associated rates of consumption of principal reactants and production of polymer, as well as the evolution of chain length statistics. Each following section discusses some of the variations on model behavior but detailed analysis of these effects will not be carried through the text. The reader is referred elsewhere [4] for extended discussion of such topics.

3. Nonisothermal Effects in Polymer Reaction Engineering 33

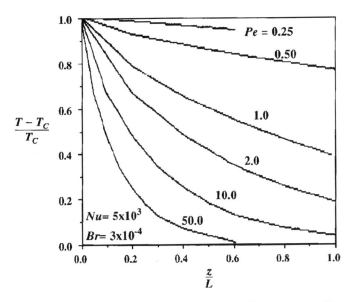

Figure 3.9 Cup average axial temperature profiles for large Nu and small Br, with Pe as parameter.

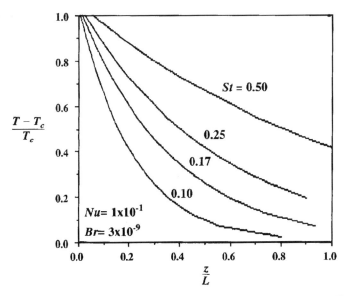

Figure 3.10 Cup average axial temperature profiles for small Nu and small Br, with St as parameter.

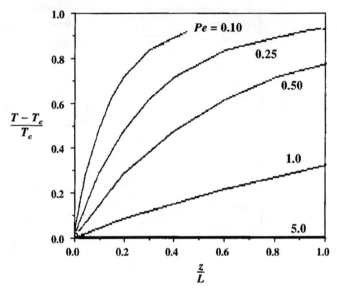

Figure 3.11 Cup average axial temperature profiles for large Nu and large Br, with Pe as parameter.

3.4.1 Random Propagation

Random propagation derives its name from the fact that at any given moment in the reaction history, chain building reactions may occur between any two species drawn randomly from all possible chain lengths. This mechanism includes many commercially important reactions including those for the production of polyesters, polycarbonates, polyamides, polysulfones, and polyurethanes. Often, these reactions produce a low molecular weight byproduct such as water or hydrochloric acid that needs to be removed to promote the reaction, and hence they are sometimes referred to as condensation polymerizations. A consequence of the kinetic scheme is that average chain lengths remain short until the highest levels of conversion are attained, at which point reaction among predominantly long-chain molecules results in a rapid growth in the degree of polymerization.

A general kinetic mechanism for reversible random propagation would be:

$$m_x + m_y \leftrightarrow m_{x+y} + m_0 \qquad (3.41)$$

where m_i is a polymer chain containing "i" number of repeat unit and m_0 represents the byproduct molecule. If, for simplicity we consider the reaction to be far from the equilibrium point, then the byproduct plays no role in the forward reaction kinetics, and we can reduce the above sequence to the simple random propagation mechanism:

$$m_x + m_y \rightarrow m_{x+y} \tag{3.42}$$

With the assumption of the Principle of Equal Reactivity, that is, the rate of the above reaction is independent of the degree of polymerization of the reacting molecules, the rate of the polymerization can be determined to be a simple second-order process:

$$r_p = kc_p^2 \tag{3.43}$$

where:

$$c_p = \sum_{x=1}^{\infty} c_x \tag{3.44}$$

Using the analysis developed earlier, it follows from Eq. (3.8) that a characteristic time for this class of polymerization reaction is given by:

$$\tau_r = \frac{1}{kc_0} \tag{3.45}$$

where c_0 is the initial concentration of reactive functional groups.

3.4.2 Step Propagation

Step propagation is one of two addition-type mechanisms. In contrast to the random propagation, chain building can take place only in reactions that involve the monomer. Growing chains are built one repeat unit at a time by adding monomer to the end of the active polymer chain. Ionic polymerizations typically follow this mechanism, but some heterogeneously catalyzed reactions as well as the ring opening caprolactam polymerization to produce Nylon 6 show step propagation characteristics. This mechanism usually requires an additional reagent, called an initiator, to activate monomer creating a polymer chain of length one. Thereafter, monomer successively adds to the active polymer increasing the degree of polymerization in unit steps.

$$\begin{cases} m_0 + m \rightarrow m_1 \\ m_x + m \rightarrow m_{x+1} \end{cases} \tag{3.46}$$

However, in many instances, the initiation step is quite rapid. Essentially, all of the initiator is consumed prior to any significant amount of chain growth. Under this assumption, a fixed number of active chains are formed equal to the amount of initiator introduced.

The chains that are initially formed then grow in tandem, each with an equal probability of propagation. This leads to the very narrow molecular weight distributions that are characteristic of the mechanism.

$$m_x + m \rightarrow m_{x+1} \qquad x = 1, \infty \tag{3.47}$$

The rate of the polymerization is given by:

$$r_p = k c_p c_m \tag{3.48}$$

Noting that the concentration of polymer is a constant, equal to the initial concentration of initiator. This mechanism results in a first-order rate of reaction:

$$r_p = k c_i|_0 c_m = k_{ap} c_m \tag{3.49}$$

As a pseudo-first-order reaction, the step reaction has a characteristic time scale that is given by the reciprocal of the lumped rate constant:

$$\tau_r = \frac{1}{k_{ap}} \tag{3.50}$$

3.4.3 Addition Propagation

Addition propagation shares the basic chain building process of the step growth mechanism, but adds a kinetic step that terminates a chain's growth prior to complete consumption of reactants. The dynamics are such that chains are continuously initiated, grown, and terminated throughout the reaction process. Chain growth is generally so fast that the growing chains are considered reaction intermediates. The free radical processes for production of acrylic, olefinic, and vinyl polymers are all chain addition propagations with termination.

$$\begin{cases} m_0^* + m \rightarrow m_1^* \\ m_x^* + m \rightarrow m_{x+1}^* \\ m_x^* + m_y^* \rightarrow m_{x+y} \text{ or } m_x + m_y \end{cases} \tag{3.51}$$

$$r_p = k_p \sqrt{\frac{2 f k_d}{k_t}} c_i^{1/2} c_m = k_{ap} c_i^{1/2} c_m \tag{3.52}$$

Frequently, the kinetic constants associated with the initiator decay render the process much slower than that of monomer consumption. Under such conditions, the initiator concentration remains at or about its initial value throughout the reaction. This reduces the overall rate to a simple first-order process, much like the step propagation reaction.

$$r_p \cong k_{ap} c_i^{1/2}|_0 c_m = k c_m \tag{3.53}$$

Unlike the previous two reaction mechanisms, this process creates high polymer from the outset. One may view the reaction environment as one of increasing concentrations of polymer diluted in its own monomer. Like the step addition mechanism, the time constant for the chain addition mechanism is that of a pseudo-first-order process:

$$\tau_r = \frac{1}{k_{ap} c_i^{1/2}|_0} \tag{3.54}$$

3.5 Reactor Analysis

One can view all chemical reactors as being one of three types: batch, semi-batch, or continuous. The batch reactor is a closed system; no material enters or leaves during the course of the reaction, although heat may be exchanged with the surroundings. Batch reactors do not have a steady state, per se. They may, however, proceed to an equilibrium point if the thermodynamics of the reaction admit one. In a semi-batch system material is added or removed during the course of reaction. Makeup feed of a reactant or removal of a volatile byproduct are examples of instances where semi-batch operation is used. In these cases, equilibrium is never achieved. In continuous operation, product is withdrawn at the same rate as fresh feed is introduced. These factors are generally operated under dynamic steady-state conditions.

The mathematical description of chemical reactors involves the application of the transport balance equations to describe the conservation of mass for each chemical component, and the conservation of thermal energy. The preceding discussion of chemical kinetics has laid the foundation for establishing expressions for the rate of consumption of the principal reactants as well as for the production of polymer product. These rate expressions, when inserted in the reactor balance equations given below, provide the framework for analyzing the nonisothermal behavior of polymerization reactors.

3.5.1 Batch Reactors

The batch reactor is classified as a closed system, with no material exchange with the surroundings. It is well mixed so that there are no spatial dependencies in temperature or composition. Heat exchange is provided through jacket cooling or cooling coils, and is characterized by an overall heat transfer coefficient expression. The pertinent equations of change reduce to:

$$\frac{dc_k}{dt} = r_k \quad k = 1, 2, 3 \ldots N \tag{3.55}$$

$$\rho C_p \frac{dT}{dt} = \sum_{k=1}^{N} -\Delta H_k r_k - h \frac{A}{V}(T - T_C) \tag{3.56}$$

3.5.2 Plug Flow Reactors

The plug flow reactor is an open flow system in which there is no material exchange in the flow direction, but complete uniformity of temperature, composition, and velocity transverse to the flow direction. Typically, it is a tubular reactor with no radial velocity profile, perfect radial uniformity of temperature and concentration, but no axial diffusion or dispersion. The plug flow reactor is a continuous flow system that has the same dynamics as the batch reactor if one regards axial position normalized by velocity as equivalent to time in the batch system. This quantity is sometimes referred to as space time ($t = z/v_z$) and represents the time needed to reach the given axial position. The material balance for each component takes the form:

$$v_z \frac{dc_k}{dz} = r_k \quad k = 1, 2, 3 \ldots N \tag{3.57}$$

The thermal energy balance takes the form:

$$\rho C_p v_z \frac{dT}{dz} = \sum_{k=1}^{N} -\Delta H_k r_k - h\frac{A}{V}(T - T_C) \tag{3.58}$$

where it is assumed that heat transfer is by convective cooling to a constant temperature surroundings at T_c, and is characterized by an overall heat transfer coefficient, h, that reflects film and wall resistances to heat transfer.

3.5.3 Ideal Mixers

The ideal mixer is a generalization of the Continuous Stirred Tank Reactor (CSTR) common to chemical engineering analysis. Any open flow system with internal mixing characteristics such that all particles in the reactor have an equal probability of exit can be viewed as an ideal mixer. If the inflow of feed material matches the withdrawal rate, steady-state conditions will prevail. Furthermore, if the mixing process extends to the molecular level, the reactor can be characterized by a lumped parameter model. To meet this requirement, the time scale for molecular diffusion across a turbulent eddy must be shorter than the time scale for chemical reaction. For completeness, the transient terms are shown, although steady-state conditions are generally presumed. For each component there is a material balance where the volume and area integrals of Eq. (3.3) reduce to the scalar products shown since concentration and temperature are assumed to be position independent.

$$V\frac{dc_k}{dt} = 0 = \dot{V}(c_{fk} - c_k) + r_k V \quad k = 1, 2, 3 \ldots N \tag{3.59}$$

Similarly, the thermal energy balance is given by:

$$\rho C_p V \frac{dT}{dt} = 0 = \sum_{k=1}^{N} -\Delta H_k r_k V - hA(T - T_C) + \rho C_p \dot{V}(T_f - T) \quad (3.60)$$

3.5.4 Unmixed Batch Reactor

When there is no agitation to remove the spatial variations in temperature and concentration, the reactor balances must include the flux terms for mass and thermal energy conditions. Equations (3.55) and (3.56) are thus modified to give the following:

$$\frac{dc_k}{dt} = \nabla D \nabla c_k + r_k \quad k = 1, 2, 3 \ldots N \quad (3.61)$$

$$\rho C_p \frac{dT}{dt} = \nabla k \nabla T + \sum_{k=1}^{N} -\Delta H_k r_k \quad (3.62)$$

The unmixed or stagnant batch reactor provides a "worst-case" estimate of reactor performance with respect to temperature control. Note that thermal homogeneity may still result in the absence of mixing when the heat transfer to surroundings is sufficiently poor ($Nu < 0.1$) as demonstrated in Section 3.2.3 through 3.2.5.

3.5.5 Continuous Tubular Reactor

Strong diffusion, either radially or axially, as well as the presence of a radial distribution in axial velocity, necessitate a more complete model for tubular reactor dynamics. As for the unmixed batch reactor, flux terms are added, and the convective transport is also added:

$$v_z \frac{\partial c_k}{\partial z} = \nabla D \nabla c_k + r_k \quad k = 1, 2, 3 \ldots N \quad (3.63)$$

$$\rho C_p v_z \frac{\partial T}{\partial z} = \nabla k \nabla T + \sum_{k=1}^{N} -\Delta H_k r_k \quad (3.64)$$

Note that viscous energy dissipation may also be a source term linking the thermal energy balance to the momentum equation. It is important to realize that for polymerizers operating at high concentrations of polymer, the coupling of mass, energy, and momentum transport is extremely important. The extent of reaction affects the viscosity which in turn alters the heat transport characteristics. Temperature variations profoundly affect the rate of reaction, and thus local conversion and chain length characteristics so that the interactions among these effects can be profound and self aggravating.

3.6 Temperature Effects in Polymerization Reactors

Understanding the control of thermal effects in polymerization reactors requires an appreciation of the source of nonisothermicity and its consequences with respect to polymer properties. There are some ionic (step-addition) reactions that are endothermic, but as a general rule, polymerizations are exothermic reactions. In fact, most polymer reactions have a large heat effect, on the order of 20 kcal of thermal energy produced per mole of monomer consumed. Because the heat of reaction is produced at every point within the reactor domain, but heat removal can occur only at reactor surface locations such as jacketed walls or coiling coil surfaces, there is a natural imbalance between the two mechanisms. The formation of polymer leads to a product that is high in viscosity and low in thermal conductivity so that classic heat transfer approaches that depend on turbulent transport from the reacting medium are limited in effectiveness. These adverse effect may be mitigated through use of diluents that reduce the viscosity of the product mix, and act as a thermal sink. The drawback of such an approach is that solvents must be removed in a post-reactor finishing step, and toxicity constraints posed by end-use applications may limit the range of solvents that can be used.

Generally, nonisothermal problems in polymerization reactors are distributed parameter phenomena. A local hot spot may develop, and then propagate throughout the reaction environment. Such a rapid, uncontrolled rise in temperature is referred to as *thermal runaway*. When thermal runaway leads to an accelerating temperature rise it is termed *thermal ignition*. This phenomenon of auto-acceleration can occur exclusively from kinetic mechanisms that produce chain branching, but there may also be a purely thermal cause. When temperature rises, the rate of most chemical reactions increases exponentially with respect to the temperature change. If the reaction is exothermic, the rate of heat production rises in direct proportion to the increase in reaction rate. The heat removal rate is generally in linear proportion to the difference in temperature between the reactants and the coolant medium. Consequently as temperatures rise, heat removal rate increases at a rate that lags the heat production rate and so temperature continues to rise. The exponential nature of the heat production rate thus leads to an accelerating temperature rise that is bounded only by the availability of reactants to sustain the reaction. The mathematics that describe this process are based on analysis of explosions, although the thermal ignition process may not have such a dire outcome. Uncontrolled temperature rise may merely produce severely off-spec product, but the effect of several hundred degrees temperature rise can produce explosive side effects and should not be taken lightly.

The situation described above is formally termed *parametric sensitivity*. This refers to a system response in which small changes to any parameter (such as heat transfer coefficient or initial conditions) are amplified into large changes in the system's *state variables* (e.g., conversion or temperature). This is often confused with the concept of *stability*. Stability analysis can apply only to those systems that exhibit steady-state behavior, and thus cannot be applied to batch reactors. The term refers to the tendency of the state variables to return to their steady-state values in the face of perturbations in those values, while parameter values are held constant. If small deviations are tolerated, then the system is said to exhibit local stability. If any magnitude of deviation can be sustained, then global stability is exhibited. Stability analysis will be discussed in the context of Ideal Mixer reactors.

3.6.1 Lumped Parameter Runaway

The basic concept of thermal runaway can be understood through the examination of thermally simple reactions in ideal batch reactors. A thermally simple reaction is one in which the heat of reaction can be attributed to a single kinetic step. This is generally applicable to polymerization reactions, where the primary source of the heat of reaction is the propagation step. Thus for addition propagation kinetics the heat generation rate is given as:

$$r_G \cong -\Delta H r_p = -\Delta H k_{ap} c_i^{1/2} c_m \tag{3.65}$$

Referring to the general batch reactor thermal energy balance, Eq. (3.56), it follows that for thermally simple reactions in a batch reactor the time rate of change of temperature must obey the following equation.

$$\frac{dT}{dt} = \frac{-\Delta H}{\rho C_p} k_{ap} c_i^{1/2} c_m - h \frac{A}{\rho C_p V}(T - T_c) \tag{3.66}$$

Using initial concentration to make composition dimensionless, and adopting the following format for making temperature dimensionless,

$$\hat{T} \equiv \frac{T - T_{ref}}{T_{ref}} \tag{3.67}$$

Equation (3.66) becomes

$$\frac{d\hat{T}}{dt} = \frac{-\Delta H (r_p)_{ref}}{\rho C_p T_{ref}} \hat{r}_p - \frac{hA}{\rho C_p V}(\hat{T} - \hat{T}_c) \tag{3.68}$$

Recognizing that the rate can be expressed as the product of a kinetic constant having an Arrhenius dependence on temperature and reactant concentrations raised to some power, the dimensionless heat generation rate is given as:

$$\hat{r}_p \equiv \frac{r_p}{(r_p)_{ref}} = \frac{r_p(c_k, T)}{r_p(c_{k0}, T_{ref})} = \exp\left(\frac{\hat{E}\hat{T}}{1+\hat{T}}\right) \hat{c}_i^{1/2} \hat{c}_m \tag{3.69}$$

It should be apparent that the parameter groupings that form the coefficients of the dimensionless generation and removal terms in Eq. (3.68) must have units of reciprocal time to maintain dimensional consistency with the left hand side of the equation. In fact, they are the inverse of the characteristic times for their respective processes, and could be synthesized a priori using Eq. (3.6).

$$\tau_G = \frac{\rho C_p T_{ref} V}{-\Delta H (r_p)_{ref} V} = \frac{\rho C_p T_{ref}}{-\Delta H (r_p)_{ref}} \qquad (3.70)$$

$$\tau_R = \frac{\rho C_p T_{ref} V}{h A T_{ref}} = \frac{\rho C_p}{h R_H} \qquad (3.71)$$

and so the partially dimensionless thermal energy balance becomes:

$$\frac{d\hat{T}}{dt} = \tau_G^{-1} \exp\left(\frac{\hat{E}\hat{T}}{1+\hat{T}}\right) \hat{c}_i^{1/2} \hat{c}_m - \tau_R^{-1}(\hat{T} - \hat{T}_C) \qquad (3.72)$$

Thus it is apparent that thermal behavior is going to be uniquely characterized by the relative values of the two characteristic times τ_G and τ_R.

The subsequent analysis will be facilitated by adopting a modified definition of dimensionless temperature suggested by Semenov [5]. It is the product of the dimensionless temperature as defined in Eq. (3.67) with the dimensionless activation energy:

$$\theta \equiv \frac{E}{R_g T_{ref}} \left(\frac{T - T_{ref}}{T_{ref}}\right) = \hat{E}\hat{T} = \frac{\hat{T}}{\varepsilon} \qquad (3.73)$$

so that the thermal energy balance becomes:

$$\frac{d\theta}{dt} = \tau_{AD}^{-1} \exp\left(\frac{\theta}{1+\varepsilon\theta}\right) \hat{c}_i^{1/2} \hat{c}_m - \tau_R^{-1}(\theta - \theta_C) \qquad (3.74)$$

The meaning of the new characteristic time, $\tau_{AD} = \varepsilon \tau_G$, will be made apparent in the ensuing discussion.

3.6.1.1 Thermal Ignition Theory

The theoretical treatment of explosions was developed by Semenov through approximation to Eq. (3.74). If one assumes, for the moment, that the initial temperature and the coolant (ambient) temperature are the same, then $T_{ref} = T_0 = T_c$, and thus $\theta_c = 0$. Furthermore, noting that explosions are an *early phenomenon*, that, is they occur before there is any appreciable consumption of reactants, it then follows that all dimensionless concentrations are approximately equal to one. This is called the *Early Runaway Approximation*, and leads to:

$$\frac{d\theta}{dt} \cong \exp\left(\frac{\theta}{1+\varepsilon\theta}\right) - a\theta \qquad (3.75)$$

3. Nonisothermal Effects in Polymer Reaction Engineering 43

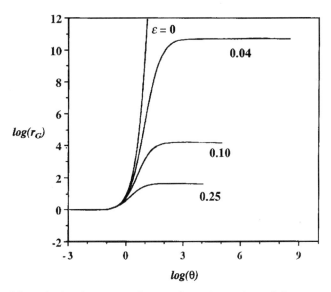

Figure 3.12 Dimensionless heat generation rate for various values of dimensionless activation energy.

where the dimensionless ignition parameter, a, is the ratio τ_{AD}/τ_R. Semenov additionally assumed large activation energies, and thus $\varepsilon \sim 0$, but this restriction is not necessary to complete the analysis.

A graphical analysis is helpful in understanding the dynamic behavior produced by systems described by Eq. (3.75). Figure 3.12 shows the temperature dependence of the first term, the dimensionless generation term, for various values of the inverse dimensionless activation energy, ε. Note, first, the ε has the effect of steepening the ascent of the generation function, moving its high-temperature plateau to increasingly large values as the activation energy increases (i.e., $\varepsilon \to 0$). By way of reference, chain addition polymerizations typically have a value of $\varepsilon \sim 0.04$. the removal function is a straight line whose slope has a value of a. When plotted on log–log coordinates, a shifts the y-intercept of the removal function line.

It should be clear that solutions to Eq. (3.75) are represented by intersection points between the generation curve and the removal curve for any fixed set of values of ε and a. Focusing attention on the generation curve with $\varepsilon \sim 0.04$, as shown in Figure 3.13, it is apparent that three regions of behavior can be delineated: one, where there is only one, low-temperature intersection; a second where three intersections occur; and a third where a single high-temperature intersection occurs.

Consider the first case. The system begins at zero temperature (or $-\infty$ on the log–log plot). Because the generation curve is above the removal curve, the value of Eq. (3.75) must be greater than zero, and temperature will rise, moving the system forward along the horizontal axis. In so doing, the gap between the generation and

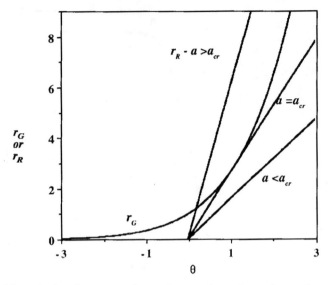

Figure 3.13 Dimensionless heat generation and removal rate for various values of runaway parameter a.

removal curve diminishes, producing a slowing in the rate of temperature rise until the intersection point θ_{s11} is attained whereupon temperature will stay at this quasi-steady-state value. Should parametric fluctuations push the temperature higher than this value, the removal curve is above the generation curve and thus the temperature will be forced to decrease until the quasi-steady-state value is re-attained.

The second case has both the lower and upper temperature regimen intersections of cases one and three. In addition, there is a third intersection point with a different character from the other two. However, because the system is constrained to start at $\theta = 0$, these additional intersection points have no bearing on the dynamics.

The third juxtaposition produces dynamics similar to the first: an increasing temperature that stabilizes at a quasi-steady-state value. The significant difference is the magnitude of this value. For $\varepsilon = 0.04$, the minimum value of $\theta_{s13} > 10^{10}$ corresponding to an inconceivably large temperature. Clearly, the transition from case two to three, which occurs when the generation and removal curves are tangent and equal at the "elbow" in the generation curve, represents a critical threshold for the onset of runaway conditions. The parameters ε and a uniquely determine this location, with a showing the strongest influence.

Mathematically, the conditions described above are met when

$$\exp\left(\frac{\theta}{1+\varepsilon\theta}\right) = a\theta \tag{3.76}$$

and

$$\frac{1}{(1+\varepsilon\theta)^2} \exp\left(\frac{\theta}{1+\varepsilon\theta}\right) = a \qquad (3.77)$$

which can be solved to find a critical value of θ that represents the tangent point.

$$\theta_{cr} = \frac{1 - \sqrt{1 - \left(\frac{2\varepsilon}{1-2\varepsilon}\right)^2}}{\frac{2\varepsilon^2}{1-2\varepsilon}} \cong \frac{1}{1-2\varepsilon} \qquad (3.78)$$

Substituting this value back into Eq. (3.76) yields a relationship for the dimensionless parameter a:

$$a > (1 - 2\varepsilon) \exp\left(\frac{1}{1-\varepsilon}\right) \qquad (3.79)$$

When this inequality is honored, a low-temperature solution exists, and runaway is averted. Larger values should result in effectively unbounded temperature rises. Noting that ε is generally small, we can further approximate that $a \sim \exp(1) = 2.72$.

At this point, it is worth reflecting on the characteristic times that comprise the parameter a. The characteristic time for adiabatic reaction, τ_{AD}, arose from the mathematics of the runaway analysis, but has not been rationalized according to the general definition of characteristic times posed earlier in this chapter.

It has been demonstrated that the initial value of the heat generation function is always greater than that of removal. The slope of the removal curve dictates whether or not a stable intersection point will be reached before runaway temperatures are reached. Recognizing the importance of not just the relative value of the generation and removal curves, but of the slopes of each of theses functions, it is interesting to note that:

$$\tau_{AD} = \left(\frac{dr_G}{d\theta}\right)^{-1} \qquad (3.80)$$

$$\tau_R = \left(\frac{dr_R}{d\theta}\right)^{-1} \qquad (3.81)$$

Thus the condition in Eq. (3.79) suggests that the temperature sensitivity of the removal function has to be two to three times greater than that of generation if runaway is to be averted. Equation (3.80) also suggests a possible generalized mechanism for synthesizing τ_{AD} for more complex reaction schemes. Although valid, this form for defining τ_{AD} lacks consistency with the approach used for all other characteristic times. Realizing, however, that this time constant deals with an "acceleration" in the heat production rate, rather than with its magnitude, it can be demonstrated that this time constant can be formally defined as the rate of generation divided by its rate of change:

$$\tau_{AD} = \left(\frac{r_G V}{\left. \frac{dr_G}{dt} \right|_{AD} V} \right) \qquad (3.82)$$

Furthermore, the relationship to adiabatic conditions can be established by analytical solution to a simplified set of equations for adiabatic, first-order kinetics:

$$\frac{d\hat{c}}{dt} = \tau_r^{-1} \hat{c} \exp(\theta) \qquad (3.83)$$

$$\frac{d\theta}{dt} = \tau_{AD}^{-1} \hat{c} \exp(\theta) = -b \frac{d\hat{c}}{dt} \qquad (3.84)$$

Eliminating $\hat{c}$ via the above and solving the resulting differential equation for temperature as a function of time:

$$\frac{d\theta}{dt} = \tau_{AD}^{-1} \frac{\exp(\theta)}{(1 - \theta/b)} \qquad (3.85)$$

yields the following solution for the time needed to reach the maximum temperature prior to the onset of runaway ($\theta = 1$):

$$\frac{t}{\tau_{AD}} = -b \exp\left(-\ln\left(\frac{b}{b-1}\right)\right) + \sum_{i=1}^{\infty} \frac{b^i}{ii!} \left[1 - \left(1 - \frac{1}{b}\right)^i\right] \qquad (3.86)$$

For large values of b, this sum converges to a value of one, confirming τ_{AD} as the measure of the prerunaway induction period, and the time scale for the fastest possible reaction.

3.6.1.2 Effect of Reactant Consumption

With the aid of numerical analysis, the restriction of the Early Runaway Approximation can be removed, and the effect of reactant conversion quantified. The process requires the simultaneous solution of the material and energy balances, that can be represented in dimensionless form for a single reactant system, with nth order reaction kinetics as:

$$\frac{d\hat{c}}{d\hat{t}} = -b^{-1} \hat{c}^n \exp\left(\frac{\theta}{1 + \epsilon\theta}\right) \qquad (3.87)$$

$$\frac{d\theta}{d\hat{t}} = \hat{c}^n \exp\left(\frac{\theta}{1 + \epsilon\theta}\right) - a(\theta - \theta_C) \qquad (3.88)$$

3. Nonisothermal Effects in Polymer Reaction Engineering   47

where time has been normalized by the adiabatic reaction time τ_{AD}, and a new dimensionless parameter, b, appears in the material balance. Defined as:

$$b \equiv \frac{\tau_r}{\tau_{AD}} \tag{3.89}$$

it compares the time scale for an isothermal reaction to that of the adiabatic case. Intuitively, one would expect very large values of b to indicate reactions that conform to the Early Runaway Approximation since reactant consumption in the nearly isothermal period before a runaway would be quite small. This is consistent with the mathematics, which indicate the large values of b would render the time rate of change of concentration via Eq. (3.87) to be nearly zero, and thus concentration would remain at its initial value.

3.6.1.3 Computational Studies

The case of nonisothermal nth order kinetics has been solved by Barklew [6]. As his results are consistent with the more general treatment of chain addition polymerization [7], the latter will be used to demonstrate applicability of the Semenov type runaway analysis to polymerization reactions. Recall that when initiator decay rate is very slow relative to monomer consumption rate, chain addition polymerization is pseudo-first-order. Using the characteristic time scales for each component, several criteria for such behavior can be established. First, the time scale for initiator disappearance must be much greater than that of monomer, so:

$$\frac{\tau_i}{\tau_m} \gg 1 \tag{3.90}$$

Furthermore, early runaway criteria necessitate that each time scale must be much greater than that of the adiabatic reaction, so:

$$b_i \equiv \frac{\tau_i}{\tau_{AD}} \gg 1 \tag{3.91}$$

$$b_m \equiv \frac{\tau_m}{\tau_{AD}} \gg 1 \tag{3.92}$$

where the general definition of b, Eq. (3.89), has been extended to apply to the individual reactants. Thus, one expects good agreement between chain addition reaction behavior and a Semenov model when b_i and b_m are very large, and the ratio b_i/b_m is also large. Figure 3.14 shows some simulated thermal histories for just such a set of conditions. Notice that there are two distinctly different classes of thermal behavior. One, at large values of a, would be classified as quasi-isothermal. That is, the temperature rise is small and changes in temperature are gradual. The second, occurring at small values of a, is adiabatic and characterized by a rapid rise in

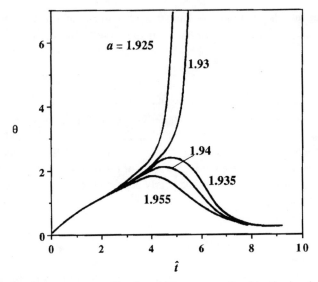

Figure 3.14 Simulated temperature profiles for addition propagation kinetics in a batch reactor demonstrating parametric sensitivity (large b_i and b_m).

temperature that accelerates until all reactants are consumed. Furthermore, the reaction behavior changes abruptly with respect to a very small change in the parameter a — thus demonstrating the "parametric sensitivity" required of thermal ignition.

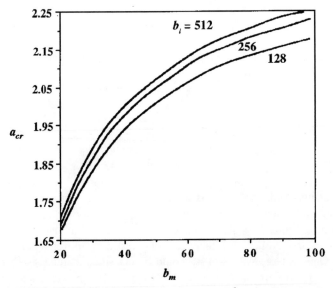

Figure 3.15 Thermal runaway boundary as a function of b_m for a fixed value of b_i.

The abruptness of the transition suggests that the full parameter space of b_i and b_m could be examined to determine the critical value of a that produces the transition from well-behaved, quasi-isothermal behavior to runaway conditions. Figures 3.15 and 3.16 illustrate two such bounding curves. It is apparent from each, that when either b_i or b_m is fixed, at sufficiently high values of the other, the critical value of a for the onset of runaway remains relatively constant. Furthermore, that critical value decreases as the associated b value decreases. This is attributable to the effect of rapid reactant consumption in the prerunaway induction period extinguishing conditions that were runaway prone at the outset. One can think of the effect of concentration decay as serving to displace downwards, the generation curve shown in Figure 3.12. As a result, the removal curve can intersect the displaced generation curve when no such intersections were possible under initial conditions.

The thermal characteristics of reactions with rapid composition decay are noticeably different from those of the parametrically sensitive cases shown previously in Figure 3.14. By way of contrast, examine the temperature trajectories shown in Figure 3.17, where the value of b_i has been decreased to a relatively small value. It is now much more difficult to clearly distinguish the runaway transition. There appears to be a continuous blend from nearly isothermal behavior to adiabatic, and much larger changes in the magnitude of a are required to effect such changes than were necessary for the case of large b values. That is, the parametric sensitivity of the runaway has disappeared and thus, controllability issues are much less severe to deal with.

Given the beneficial effects of temperature rise from the standpoint of increased reaction rates, one is led to seek criteria that might identify regions of runaway where parametric sensitivity is absent. Figures 3.18 and 3.19 attempt to provide such

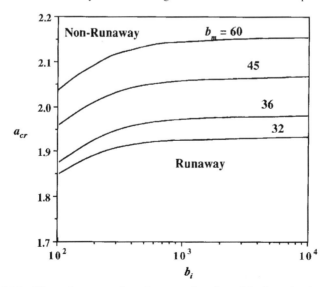

Figure 3.16 Thermal runaway boundary as a function of b_i for a fixed value of b_m.

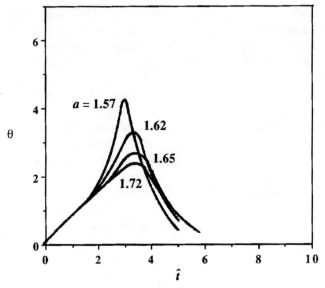

Figure 3.17 Simulated temperature profiles for addition propagation kinetics in a batch reactor demonstrating loss of parametric sensitivity (small b_i).

information. At fixed values of b_i and b_m, the runaway parameter a was varied continuously, and the maximum temperature observed in the computed behavior was plotted versus the parameter. When parametric sensitivity is present, such a curve should show an abrupt, almost discontinuous rise as the critical value of a is reached. Figure 3.18, for example, shows just this sort of behavior for values of $b_m > 23$, while in Figure 3.19 the curves for $b_i > 70$ show the same characteristics.

3.6.1.4 Experimental Studies

The phenomena of thermal runaway and parametric sensitivity have been demonstrated experimentally for addition propagation polymerizations and copolymeriations [8,9]. Batch polymerizations were conducted in bulk (no solvent added) in a bench-scale reactor with heat transfer to a constant temperature bath. The dimensionless runaway parameters were manipulated by adjusting the feed and coolant temperatures or by varying the feed initiator concentration. Figures 3.20 and 3.21 illustrate typical runaway transitions with and without parametric sensitivity. Notice in Figure 3.20 the relatively abrupt transition from quasi-isothermal behavior to the rapid ascent of runaway as parameter a goes through a small change in magnitude. At higher temperatures, the decay rate of initiator becomes more pronounced and the value of b_i drops to a sufficiently small value so as to preclude a sensitive runaway. The temperature peaks slowly increase in maximum value as parameter a is decreased, but there is no sharp dividing line between quasi-isothermal and adiabatic-like behavior.

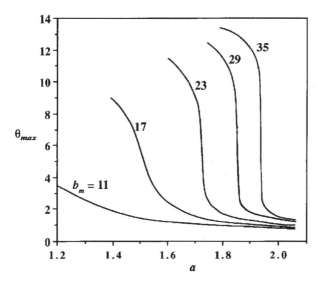

Figure 3.18 Maximum temperature as a function of runaway parameter a, for decreasing values of b_m.

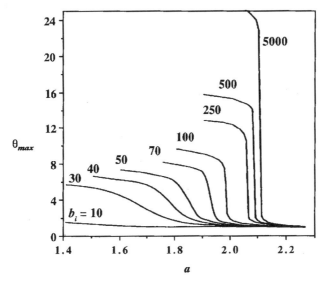

Figure 3.19 Maximum temperature as a function of runaway parameter a, for decreasing values of b_i.

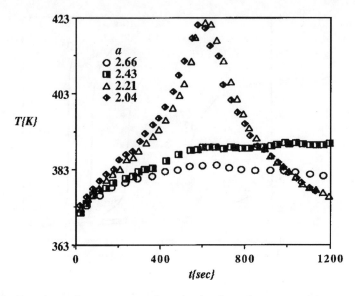

Figure 3.20 Experimental temperature trajectories for thermal runaway with parametric sensitivity.

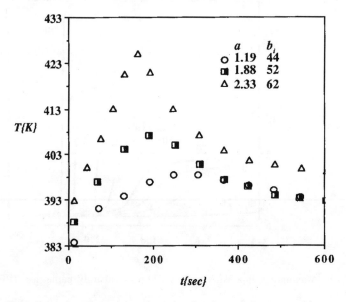

Figure 3.21 Experimental temperature trajectories for thermal runaway with no parametric sensitivity.

These conditions offer the positive benefits of improved reaction rates while removing the danger of uncontrollable and unbounded temperature rise. Similar observations were drawn from experimental studies in tubular polymerizers [10].

3.6.1.5 Thermally Complex Systems

The foregoing analysis pertained to thermally simple systems, those in which a single kinetic step was responsible for the production of the heat of reaction. The resulting characteristic time-based dimensionless parameters, however, form a basis for extension to more complicated schemes. Consider, for example, the kinetics of chain addition copolymerization. In such a reaction there are four discernible propagation steps, one for each of the possible pairings of comonomer and chain end radical type.

$$
\begin{aligned}
m_A + m^*_{Ax} &\xrightarrow{k_{pAA}} m^*_{Ax+1} \\
m_A + m^*_{Bx} &\xrightarrow{k_{pBA}} m^*_{Ax+1} \\
m_B + m^*_{Ax} &\xrightarrow{k_{pAB}} m^*_{Bx+1} \\
m_B + m^*_{Bx} &\xrightarrow{k_{pBB}} m^*_{Bx+1}
\end{aligned}
\tag{3.93}
$$

The heat of reaction is different for each of these steps, so the rate of heat generation is the sum of four separate contributions which cannot be factored to make a simple product of a lumped heat of reaction, a concentration forcing function, and the explicitly temperature-dependent terms. Nevertheless, using the generalized forms, an overall characteristic time for reaction, heat generation, and adiabatic reaction can be formulated for such a scheme:

$$\tau_m = \frac{(c_A)_0 + (c_B)_0}{\sum\sum (r_{pij})_0} \tag{3.94}$$

$$\tau_G = \frac{\rho C_p T_{ref}}{\sum\sum (-\Delta H_{ij} r_{pij})_0} \tag{3.95}$$

$$\tau_{AD} = \frac{\sum\sum (-\Delta H_{ij} r_{pij})_0}{\sum\sum \frac{d}{dt}(-\Delta H_{ij} r_{pij})_0} \tag{3.96}$$

Figure 3.22 illustrates computed temperature profiles for a styrene-acrylontrile copolymerization, and Figure 3.23 shows experimental evidence that confirms the utility of these parameters for defining runaway behavior. Note the similarity of these to the thermally simple systems in Figures 3.14 and 3.20. In both instances, parametric sensitivity with respect to parameter a is demonstrated, and the magnitude of a at the runaway transition point is of the same order.

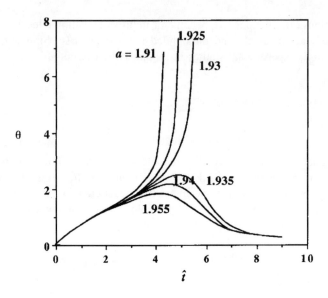

Figure 3.22 Simulated temperature profiles for styrene acrylonitrile addition copolymerization in a batch reactor demonstrating parametric sensitivity (large b_i and b_m).

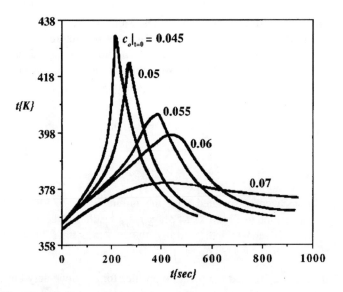

Figure 3.23 Simulated temperature trajectories for profiles for styrene acrylonitrile addition copolymerization thermal runaway with parametric sensitivity.

3.6.2 Distributed Parameter Runaway

When the resistance to heat transfer is heat conduction through the fluid itself, the preceding analysis must be modified. The governing equations no longer lend themselves to simple analytical solution via a Semenov analysis. Even when there is only one gradient direction for heat transport, the thermal energy balance is a partial differential equation in temperature that reflects the temporal and spatial dependence of temperature. Consider unidirectional heat transfer in the presence of an exothermic chemical reaction. The material balance can be simplified for polymerizing systems by eliminating molecular diffusion owing to the relative immobility of polymer chains. The resulting equations are:

$$\frac{dc}{dt} = r \tag{3.97}$$

$$\rho C_p \frac{dT}{dt} = k\left[\frac{d^2T}{dx^2} + \frac{\lambda}{x}\frac{dT}{dx}\right] + -\Delta H r \tag{3.98}$$

where $\lambda = 0$ for rectangular, 1 for cylindrical, and 2 for spherical geometry. Frank-Kamenetskii proposed an approach that involved solving the steady-state thermal energy balance subject to the early runaway approximation, and assuming a very large activation energy and perfect heat transfer at the walls [11]. The resulting equation, in dimensionless form is:

$$\frac{d^2\theta}{dx^2} = -\frac{\tau_H}{\tau_{AD}} \exp\theta \tag{3.99}$$

subject to the boundary conditions:

$$\left.\frac{d\theta}{dx}\right|_{center} = 0 \tag{3.100}$$

$$\theta|_{wall} = 0 \tag{3.101}$$

Runaway conditions were associated with the failure if Eq. (3.99) to show a real valued solution. The plot in Figure 3.24 shows the result for rectangular geometry, where once again it is seen that the ratio of the two important characteristic times forms the critical determinant of system behavior. The grouping $\Delta \equiv \tau_{AD}/\tau_H$ is directly analogous to a except that the characteristic time for heat conduction through the fluid substitutes for the characteristic time for heat removal through the walls. Using numerical analysis, the restriction of large activation energy can be removed, and the resulting values for critical Δ are shown for each of the principal geometries in Figure 3.25.

Removing the assumption of the early runaway approximation calls for simultaneous solution of the component balances and the thermal energy balance. Figure 3.26 is the

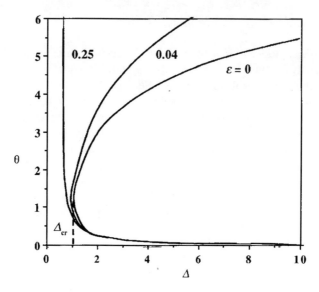

Figure 3.24 Steady-state temperature solutions for a rectangular slab with heat production.

distributed parameter counterpart to the runaway sensitivity plot for lumped parameter polymerization given in Figure 3.19. Note that the behavior is both qualitatively and quantitatively similar. These solutions for chain addition polymerization show that increased monomer consumption rate, as characterized by decreasing values of b_m,

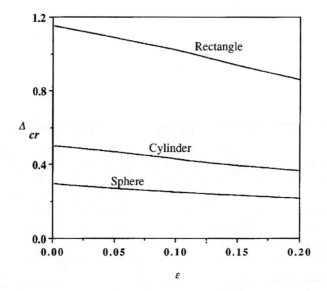

Figure 3.25 Critical values of Δ as a function of ε for different geometries.

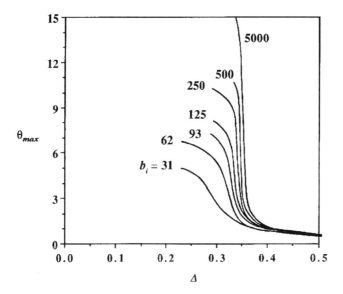

Figure 3.26 Maximum temperature as a function of runaway parameter Δ, for decreasing values of b_i.

lead to a depression in the critical value of the runaway parameter, and ultimately eliminate the sensitivity of runaway as b_m drops below 75.

Finally, the restriction of isothermal walls can be removed. When the heat transfer resistance is shared by both the fluid and the transfer to the surroundings, heat removal is a series process. Thus, a composite characteristic time for total heat removal should be the simple sum of the two component times:

$$T_R = \tau_R + \tau_H \qquad (3.102)$$

Using this composite time, one can generalize on the dimensionless runaway parameter a, as:

$$a = \frac{\tau_{AD}}{T_R} \qquad (3.103)$$

and

$$Nu = \frac{\tau_H}{T_R} \qquad (3.104)$$

In the limit of very small or very large values of Nusselt Number (which correspond to lumped parameter and isothermal wall distributed parameter conditions), the parameter a reduces to a and Δ respectively.

When thermal behavior is tracked for chain addition polymerization in a cylinder, the runaway transition is shown in Figure 3.27. Note that for values of the Nusselt

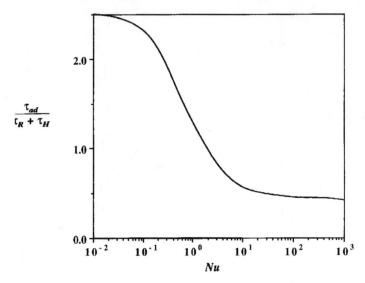

Figure 3.27 Runaway boundary as a function of Nu.

Number > 10, the characteristics asymptotically approach that of distributed parameter behavior, while for $Nu > 0.10$ the behavior converges to that of the lumped parameter model. In all instances, the transitions occur when the adiabatic reaction time and the composite heat removal time are on the same order of magnitude. To complete the picture, detailed, transverse temperature profiles are given in Figures 3.28 and 3.29 to show the nature of runaway at the extremes of heat removal behavior.

3.6.3 Stability Analysis

Heat transfer effects in lumped parameter, open flow systems have been widely studied and characterized for conventional reaction kinetics. The transient equations that describe these systems do possess steady-state solutions, and thus are amenable to the wealth of techniques that exist for stability analysis. It is not in the scope of this chapter to review all such techniques, but rather, the basic consequences of steady-state multiplicity, and dynamic stability will be examined using accepted techniques.

Consider first the basic equations for nonisothermal behavior in well-mixed reactors, recast in dimensionless form:

$$\frac{d\hat{c}_k}{d\hat{t}} = b_k^{-1}[Da_k^{-1}(1 - \hat{c}_k) + \hat{r}_k] \tag{3.105}$$

$$\frac{d\theta}{d\hat{t}} = \hat{r}_G - a\theta \tag{3.106}$$

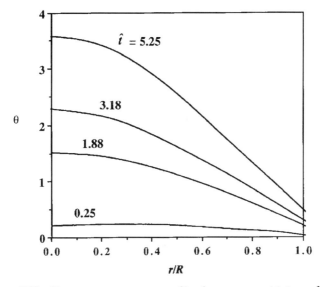

Figure 3.28 Tranverse temperature profiles for runaway with large Nu.

Note that choice of an unusual reference temperature, defined below, results in the flow term and the coolant heat removal term collapsing into a single linear function of temperature.

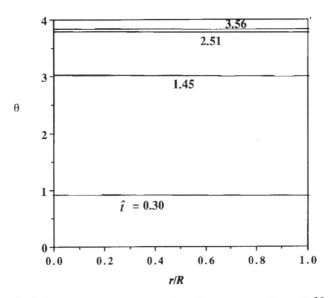

Figure 3.29 Tranverse temperature profiles for runaway with small Nu.

$$T_{ref} = \frac{\tau_F^{-1} T_f + \tau_R^{-1} T_C}{\tau_F^{-1} + \tau_R^{-1}} \tag{3.107}$$

This temperature is actually the value of the steady-state temperature that would be attained in the absence of any reaction exotherm, and is thus a better metric of reaction behavior than either the feed of coolant temperature. Also, a new characteristic time has been introduced to represent the combined effects of flow and heat removal to the coolant. Because these processes occur in parallel. unlike the sequential juxtaposition of conduction and wall removal presented in distributed parameter systems, the composite characteristic time takes the form of a sum of reciprocals:

$$T_R^{-1} = \tau_F^{-1} + \tau_R^{-1} \tag{3.108}$$

and thus the ratio of τ_{AD} to T_R appears as a critical parameter in the dimensionless thermal energy balance. Using chain addition polymerization as a model of the multireactant, thermally simple system, the above equations reduce to:

$$\frac{d\hat{c}_i}{d\hat{t}} = b_i^{-1} \left[Da_i^{-1}(1 - \hat{c}_i) - \hat{c}_i \exp\left(\frac{\varepsilon E_d \theta}{1 + \varepsilon \theta}\right) \right] \tag{3.109}$$

$$\frac{d\hat{c}_m}{d\hat{t}} = b_m^{-1} \left[Da_m^{-1}(1 - \hat{c}_m) - \hat{c}_i^{1/2} \hat{c}_m \exp\left(\frac{\theta}{1 + \varepsilon \theta}\right) \right] \tag{3.110}$$

$$\frac{d\theta}{d\hat{t}} = \hat{c}_i^{1/2} \hat{c}_m \exp\left(\frac{\theta}{1 + \varepsilon \theta}\right) - a\theta \tag{3.111}$$

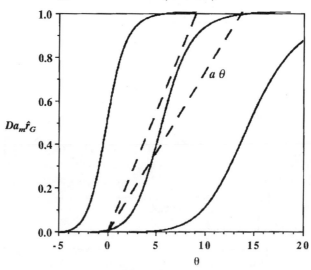

Figure 3.30 Generation and removal functions for addition propagation in a CSTR.

3. Nonisothermal Effects in Polymer Reaction Engineering

These equations can be reduced to a single equation in temperature under steady-state conditions by setting the right hand side of each to zero, and eliminating the explicit concentration dependence. The resulting expression for $\hat{r}_G$ [the first term on the right hand side of Eq. (3.11)] is:

$$\hat{r}_G = \frac{\left[1 + Da_i \exp\left(\frac{1}{2}\right) - \frac{Da_m}{(v_N)_0} \exp\left(\frac{\varepsilon \hat{E}_d \theta}{1+\varepsilon\theta}\right)\right] \exp\left(\frac{\theta}{1+\varepsilon\theta}\right)}{\left[\left(1 + Da_i \exp\left(\frac{\varepsilon \hat{E}_d \theta}{1+\varepsilon\theta}\right)\right) + Da_m \exp\left(\frac{\theta}{1+\varepsilon\theta}\right)\right]\left(1 + Da_i \exp\left(\frac{\varepsilon \hat{E}_d \theta}{1+\varepsilon\theta}\right)\right)} \quad (3.112)$$

When plotted versus temperature, the generation curve is sigmoidal, as shown in Figure 3.30, while the removal curve is linear, with a slope of a. Thus, there is a striking similarity to the Semenov type analysis for batch reactors subject to the early runaway approximation. Figures 3.31 and 3.32 demonstrate the effect of initiator decay rate parameters on the rate of heat generation. In all cases, the curves show a decreasing maximum temperature as the value of Da increases. This is due to the relatively high levels of conversion that are present at the lowest temperatures, when large values of Da indicate residence times in excess of the reaction time scale.

Intersection of the removal and generation curves represent steady-state solutions to the reactor balance equations (3.109–3.111). As was the case for the Semenov analysis, sigmoidal generation curves and linear removal curves have a maximum of three intersection points, one of which (the middle of three) will always be an unstable solution. Figure 3.33 illustrates the effects of Damkohler Number and runaway parameter a on the relative juxtaposition of these two curves. Note that each generation curve is normalized by the maximum value of the function, Da_m^{-1}, so that a value of one is the largest and zero is the minimum for all. Plotted in this fashion, the generation curves steepen and shift to the left as the Damkohler Number is increased. The most important observation is that for values of $Da < 0.01$, the inflection in the generation curve lies to the left of the origin. This means that for larger values of Da, only one intersection is possible between the linear removal curve (which it must pass through the origin), and the generation curve. Multiplicity of steady states requires relatively small values of Da.

A great deal of research has been done on the dynamic nature of steady-state solutions [12–16]. It is well established that the steady-state solutions that appear to be stable by virtue of the simple slope criteria demonstrated above graphically are necessary but not sufficient conditions to ensure either local or global stability. A more formal approach to examining stability involves the analysis of the balance equations, linearized about the steady-state solutions. Expressed in terms of small displacements from the steady state, the linearized equations take the form:

$$\frac{d\bar{x}}{dt} = \bar{\bar{F}} \bar{x} \quad (3.113)$$

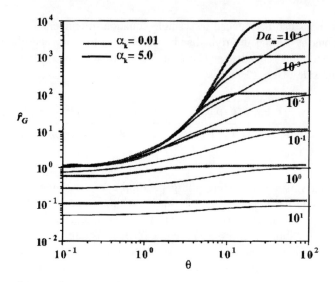

Figure 3.31 Effect of relative initial rate of initiator and monomer consumption on generation function for addition propagation in CSTR, where $\alpha_K = \tau_i/\tau_m$.

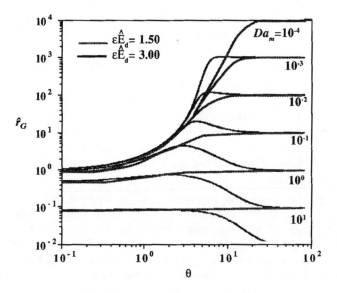

Figure 3.32 Effect of relative initiator and monomer activation energies on generation function for addition propagation in CSTR.

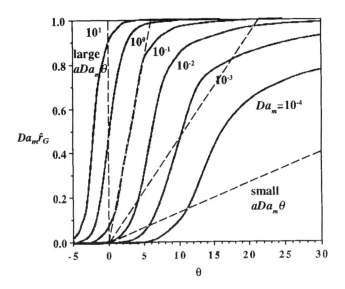

Figure 3.33 Normalized generation rate and removal curves for CSTR showing influence of Da_m and aDa_m.

where

$$x_k = (\hat{c}_k - \hat{c}_k|_{SS}) \quad 1 \leq k < N \quad (3.114)$$

$$x_N = (\theta - \theta|_{SS}) \quad k = N \quad (3.115)$$

and

$$F_{ij} \equiv \left.\frac{\partial f}{\partial x_i}\right|_{SS} \quad (3.116)$$

Stable behavior requires that all of the eigenvalues of F must be negative, or have negative real parts; otherwise any deviation from steady state will grow with time rather than following a trajectory that returns directly to the steady state. The Routh–Hurwitz criteria provide a convenient means for assessing the sign of the eigenvalue real parts. For a system of N equations, the criteria are:

$$C_1 = a_1 > 0$$

$$C_2 = \begin{vmatrix} a_1 & a_3 \\ 1 & a_2 \end{vmatrix} > 0$$

$$C_3 = \begin{vmatrix} a_1 & a_3 & a_5 \\ 1 & a_2 & a_4 \\ 0 & a_1 & a_5 \end{vmatrix} > 0$$

$$C_N = \begin{vmatrix} a_1 & a_3 & a_5 & \cdots & 0 \\ 1 & a_2 & a_4 & \cdots & 0 \\ 0 & a_1 & a_3 & \cdots & 0 \\ 0 & 1 & a_2 & & \vdots \\ \vdots & \vdots & \vdots & & a_N \end{vmatrix} > 0 \tag{3.117}$$

where

$$a_j = (-1)^j I_j \tag{3.118}$$

and the I_j are the invariants of F. It can be shown [17] that the first criterion always reduces to:

$$\text{Trace}\,(F) < 0 \tag{3.119}$$

while the last (Nth) criterion is:

$$(-1)^N \, Det(F) > 0 \tag{3.120}$$

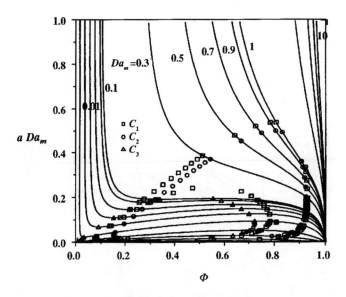

Figure 3.34 Stability envelopes for addition propagation in CSTR.

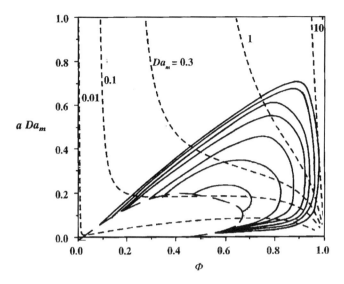

Figure 3.35 Effect of b_m on stability envelopes for addition propagation in CSTR.

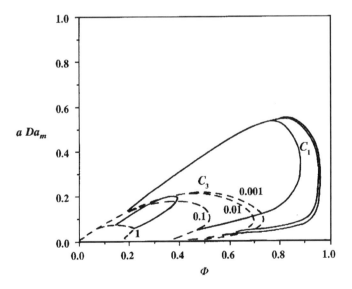

Figure 3.36 Effect of b_i/b_m on stability envelopes for addition propagation in CSTR.

Furthermore, the determinant criterion, when expanded becomes:

$$\frac{d\hat{r}_R}{d\theta} - \frac{d\hat{r}_G}{d\theta} > 0 \qquad (3.121)$$

which is the mathematical statement of the slope criterion shown graphically in the previous section.

Adapting the approach of Hugo and Wirges [15], one can gain an insight to the regions of stability delimited by each of the stability criteria. Figure 3.34 shows a typical plot of parameter group aDa_m versus monomer conversion with Da_m as parameter for chain addition polymerization. The symbols indicate regions where each of the stability criteria are violated. It is apparent from the plot that only those instances for which $Da_m < 0.10$ violate the slope criterion, thus confirming the conclusions drawn above from Figure 3.30. Figures 3.35–3.37 summarize the effect of key parameter groupings in altering the appearance of these stability plots. It is apparent that regardless of parameter values, one can ensure that a single globally stable steady state exists when $aDa_m > 1.0$.

Ray et al. [13] showed that first-order irreversible reactions in well-mixed reactors possessed as many as 12 distinctly different classes of stability ranging from a single globally steady state to three globally unstable steady states. Although he was unable to find a similar richness of dynamic behavior when examining free radical chain addition polymerization [14], Sebastian [16] did uncover a variety of instabilities. Figure 3.38 shows several trajectories in phase space (initiator and monomer conversion, and temperature) for the classic case, three steady states, with the central one violating the

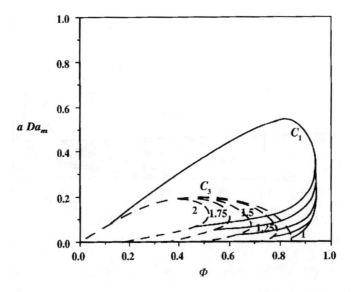

Figure 3.37 Effect of E_d on stability envelopes for addition propagation in CSTR.

3. Nonisothermal Effects in Polymer Reaction Engineering   67

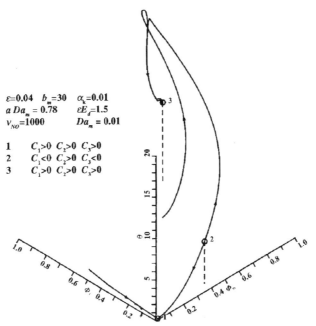

Figure 3.38 Phase space trajectories for addition propagation in CSTR with three steady states, two of which are globally stable.

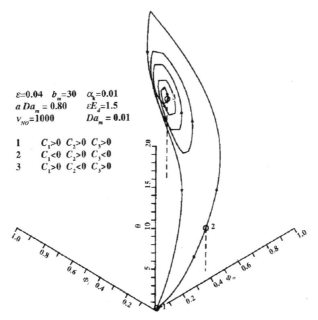

Figure 3.39 Phase space trajectories for addition propagation in CSTR with three steady states, only one of which is globally stable.

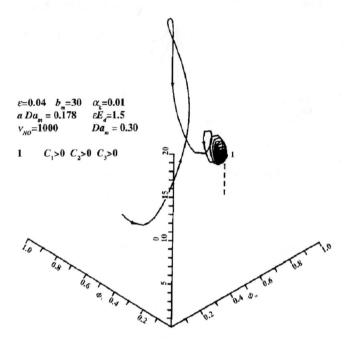

Figure 3.40 Phase space trajectories for addition propagation in CSTR with one globally stable state.

slope criterion. Notice that small displacements from steady state number two result in the immediate decay to one of the other steady states. Figure 3.39 demonstrates the effect of violating an additional criterion for the upper steady state. It now shows an outwardly spiralling trajectory that leads all displacements back to steady state number one.

Figures 3.40–3.42 demonstrate the transformation of a single, globally steady state to one that shows continued oscillatory behavior called a limit cycle. The parameter group aDa_m is varied to produce this behavior, and it is clear that the onset of dynamic instability is a parametrically sensitive phenomena, because the onset of violating the Routh–Hurwitz criteria happens in a discontinuous fashion.

3.7 Conclusion

The thermal characteristics of polymer reactors can be understood within the framework of classic reaction engineering concepts. Polymer reactors show pronounced

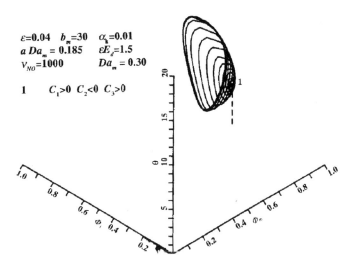

Figure 3.41 Phase space trajectories for addition propagation in CSTR with one globally unstable steady state violating a single stability criterion.

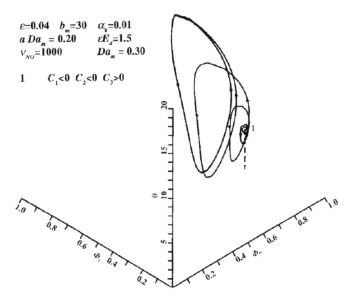

Figure 3.42 Phase space trajectories for addition propagation in CSTR with one globally unstable steady state violating a two stability criterion.

heat effects owing to their strongly exothermic character coupled to the inability to effectively agitate the highly viscous product of reaction. Understanding the dynamics of heat production and removal mechanisms, however, can reduce the need for overdesign to avoid dangerous operating conditions. The characteristic time analysis outlined in this chapter is a deceptively simple but powerful technique for analyzing the relative importance of competing transport phenomena in the reaction environment, and for making design decisions to keep these in balance.

References
1. Bird, R.B., Stewart, W.E., and Lightfoot, E.N., *Transport Phenomena*. John Wiley & Sons (1960).
2. Welty, J.R., Wicks, C.E., and Wilson, R.E., *Fundamentals of Momentum, Heat, and Mass Transfer*. John Wiley & Sons (1969).
3. Fahien, R.W., *Fundamentals of Transport Phenomena*. McGraw-Hill (1983).
4. Biesenberger, J.A. and Sebastian, D.H., *Principles of Polymerization Engineering*. John Wiley & Sons (1983).
5. Semenov, W.N., *Some Problems in Chemical Kinetics and Reactivity*. Princeton University Press, Princeton, NJ (1958), p. 87.
6. Barkelew, C.R., *Chem. Eng. Symp. Ser.* No. 25, **55**, 37 (1959).
7. Biesenberger, J.A. and Sebastian, D.H., *Principles of Polymerization Engineering*. John Wiley & Sons (1983), p. 418.
8. Sebastian, D.H. and Biesenberger, J.A., *Polym. Eng. Sci.* **16**, 117 (1976).
9. Sebastian, D.H. and Biesenberger, J.A., *Polym. eng. Sci.* **19**, 190 (1979).
10. Valsamis, L. and Biesenberger, J.A., *AIChE Symp. Ser.* 160, **72**, 18 (1976).
11. Frank-Kamenetskii, D.A., *Diffusion and Heat Exchange in Chemical Kinetics*. Princeton University Press, Princeton, NJ (1955), 202–266.
12. Bilous, O. and Amundson, N., *AIChE J.* **1** 513 (1955).
13. Uppal, A., Ray, H., and Poore, A.B., *Chem. Eng. Sci.* **26**, 967 (1974).
14. Jai Singhani, R. and Ray, H., *Chem. Eng. Sci.* **32**, 811 (1977).
15. Hugo, P. and Wirges, H.P., Chapter 41, *Chemical Reaction Engineering-Houston*, ACS Symposium Series 65, American Chemical Society, Washington, D.C. (1978).
16. Biesenberger, J.A. and Sebastian, D.H., *Principles of Polymerization Engineering*. John Wiley & Sons (1983), p. 484.
17. Biesenberger, J.A. and Sebastian, D.H., *Principles of Polymerization Engineering*. John Wiley & Sons (1983), p. 699.

Notation

Symbols

A Area
a Dimensionless runaway parameter τ_{AD}/τ_R
b Dimensionless runaway sensitivity parameter τ_r/τ_{AD}

c	Concentration
C_p	Heat capacity
E	Extensive property, activation energy
e	Extensive property per unit volume
E_r	Activation energy
f	Iniator efficiency factor
H	Thickness
ΔH_r	Enthalpy of reaction
h	Heat transfer coefficient
i	Intensive property
k	Reaction rate constant
k	Thermal conductivity
L	Length
m	Monomer
m^*	Active polymer chain intermediate
N	Moles
p	Pressure
q	Heat flux
r	rate
R	Radius
R_g	Universal gas constant
R_H	Hydraulic radius
s	Transport source term (rate of production/volume)
T	Temperature
t	Time
V	Volume
$\dot{V}$	Volumetric flow rate
v	Velocity
W	Width

Greek Symbols

α_K	Relative rates of initiator to monomer consumption, τ_i/τ_m
α_T	Thermal diffusivity $k/\rho C_p$
ε	Inverse dimensionless activation energy
Φ	Flux
η	Viscosity
θ	Dimensionless temperature
ρ	Density
τ	Time constant

Subscripts

ap	Apparent
AD	Adiabatic
A	Reactant A

B	Reactant B
C	Coolant
d	Decomposition of initiator
f	Feed
F	Convective flow
G	Heat generation
H	Heat conduction
i	Initiator
m	Monomer
p	Polymer, propagation
r	Reaction
R	Heat removal
S	Surface
V	Viscous energy dissipation
x	Polymer or intermediate chain "x" repeat units in length
y	Polymer or intermediate chain "y" repeat units in length
z	Axial (z-axis) direction
0	Initial

CHAPTER 4

Temperature-Dependent Effects in Polymer Processing

David Roylance

4.1 Introduction

Temperature is among the most critical control parameters in polymer processing, as variations in temperature generally produce exponential variations in polymer viscosity and rates of chemical reaction. This chapter outlines the molecular mechanisms responsible for these dramatic effects, and reviews the analytical procedures that are available for modeling them. These models for temperature-dependent material properties are then incorporated into analyses of the overall processing operation, and illustrative closed-form and finite-element procedures are discussed. The chapter ends with a case study of thermal curing in a laminate containing reactive adhesive interlayers.

In polymer processing temperature effects arise from a number of sources. The material being processed may have a strong temperature dependency in its properties; this is true, for example, of the viscosity of a polymer melt. Beyond this, the processing of even a temperature-independent material will generally involve nonuniform temperature fields, corresponding to discrete heater locations, internal heat generation, and other such heat transfer effects. We begin by summarizing the temperature sensitivity of typical material properties, and then expand on the engineering equations relevant to nonisothermal fluid processing in general. Finally, we illustrate the application of these principles by an analysis of processing printed wiring boards containing reactive adhesive interlayers.

Because temperature has such a pervasive effect on polymers and their processing, a complete treatise on this subject would require far more space than is available in this chapter. For that reason, we will emphasize the fundamental principles underlying

---

David Roylance, Massachusetts Institute of Technology, Cambridge, MA 02139, USA

selected important temperature effects, with only an abbreviated coverage of examples and applications. The reader is referred to specialist texts in polymer processing (e.g., [1,2]) for additional detail, and it is hoped this chapter can serve as an introduction.

4.2 Polymer Properties

4.2.1 Effect of Temperature on Viscosity

The viscosity of a polymer melt is perhaps the dominant material property in terms of its processibility, determining the magnitude of force required of the equipment to achieve a given flow rate. The viscosity is a measure of the resistance to shearing molecular segments past one another, and is generally a large value in polymers due to the highly entangled nature of the molecules. Viscous flow is a rate process, with a very strong dependence on temperature. As stated in a number of texts (e.g., [3]), at temperatures well above the polymer's glass transition temperature this dependency can generally be modeled satisfactorily by an inverse Arrhenius expression:

$$\eta = \eta_0 \exp \frac{E_\eta}{R_g T} \qquad (4.1)$$

Here η_0 is a preexponential constant, E_η is the activation energy for viscosity, and $R_g = 8.31$ J/mol-°K is the gas constant. The activation energy is a measure of the molecular barrier to flow, and generally correlates with the degree of complexity in the polymer's molecular architecture. Some typical values for this parameter, listed in order of increasing molecular complexity, are listed in Table 4.1 [3].

When the processing temperature is within $\approx$ 100 deg C of the glass transition temperature, the Arrhenius equation often fails to model the temperature dependence accurately, and in this range the "WLF" equation [4] is usually preferred:

$$\log_{10} \frac{\eta}{\eta_0} = \frac{(-17.44)(T - T_g)}{51.6 + (T - T_g)} \qquad (4.2)$$

Table 4.1 Typical Activation Energies for Viscous Flow

Polymer	E_η, kJ/mol
Polyethylene (high density)	26.3 – 29.2
Polypropylene	37.5 – 41.7
Polyethylene (low density)	48.8
Polystyrene	104.2
Polycarbonate	108.3 – 125

where T_g is the polymer's glass transition temperature and η_0 is the viscosity at this temperature. The numerical constants have been found experimentally to be valid for a wide range of polymers.

The WLF was developed empirically, but can be rationalized in terms of the free volume concepts proposed by Doolittle [5]. This view of polymer kinetics takes the free volume v_f — the volume not occupied by polymer molecular segments — as controlling the rate of viscous flow. Doolittle proposed a relation of the form

$$\eta = A \exp\left(\frac{B}{v_f}\right) \tag{4.3}$$

where A and B are constants. If the free volume is taken to be increased by increases in temperature according to simple thermal expansion, then:

$$v_f = v_{fg} + \alpha_v (T - T_g) \tag{4.4}$$

where v_{fg} is the free volume at T_g and α_v is the difference in coefficient of volumetric thermal expansion between the glassy and rubbery states. From these relations it is easy to show that:

$$\log_{10} \frac{\eta}{\eta_0} = \frac{(-B/v_{fg})(T - T_g)}{(v_{fg}/\alpha_v) + (T - T_g)} \tag{4.5}$$

This expression is of the same form as Eq. (4.2), with $(v_{fg}/\alpha_v) = 51.6$. The value of α_v is nearly the same for many polymers, approximately 5×10^{-4}/ deg C. It then follows that $v_{fg} = (51.6)(5 \times 10^{-4}) \approx 0.025$. This implies that the glass transition occurs when thermal expansion has increased the free volume to be 2.5% of the total.

In addition to its obvious use in predicting the temperature dependence of viscosity, the WLF equation can helpful in constructing master curves for viscosity that cover a wide range of temperatures and shear rates. This technique, known as "time–temperature superposition," is also used in solid viscoelasticity for relating time and temperature in "thermorheologically simple" materials.

The viscosity ratio $\log_{10}(\eta/\eta_0) = \log \eta - \log \eta_0$ in Eq. (4.2) indicates how much the viscosity η "shifts" relative to a reference value η_0 when the temperature is varied. In its usual application, the shifting procedure is used to combine a number of experimental curves in which viscosity η is plotted against logarithmic shear rate $\log \dot{\gamma}$, each curve having been obtained at a different temperature and being limited by experimental necessity to a restricted range of shear rate. One of these curves is chosen as a reference, and the others shifted horizontally along the $\log \dot{\gamma}$ axis by an amount given by Eq. (4.2). This will produce a single curve spanning a much larger range of shear rates than was available in the original data. This master curve will be valid only for the temperature of the reference curve, but it can be adjusted easily for other temperatures, again by using Eq. (4.2).

4.2.2 Effect of Temperature on Chemical Reactions

A number of polymer processing operations involve deliberate or inadvertent chemical reaction, and these take place at rates that, like viscosity, vary strongly with temperature. Thermosetting resins are important examples of deliberate chemical reactions, in which chemical crosslinking is used to connect initially low molecular weight prepolymers. Thermal degradation is an example of an inadvertent, and generally unwelcome, chemical reaction. This is one reason the use of regrind or recycled material must usually be limited in polymer processing, as this material will already have experienced previous molding cycles during which some degradation will generally have occurred. In the following sections, we outline some of the analytical techniques used to model these important effects.

4.2.2.1 Reaction Rates

As described in standard texts in physical chemistry (e.g., [6]) the rate of chemical reaction is naturally dependent on the concentration of chemical species taking part in the reaction. In many cases, this dependency takes a simple power-law form:

$$R = kC^n \tag{4.6}$$

where C is the concentration of reactive species, for instance in mol/m^3, k is the rate constant, and n is the reaction order. The reaction rate R would have consistent units, for instance mol/m^3·s. The temperature dependence of the reaction rate is contained in the rate constant k, and this can often be taken as an Arrhenius relation:

$$k = Z \exp\left(\frac{-E_C}{R_g T}\right) \tag{4.7}$$

where Z is a preexponential constant and E_C is an activation energy for chemical reaction. Combining these relations:

$$R = Z \exp\left(\frac{-E_C}{R_g T}\right) C^n \tag{4.8}$$

The adjustable parameters in this expression must be chosen by reference to suitable experiments, and an example of such a procedure is given in a later section.

4.2.2.2 Effect of Cure in Thermosets

The course of chemical reaction is strongly dependent on molecular mobility, as the reactants must be able to "find each other" in order to react. Temperature has a strong effect on mobility, but in many thermoset cure cycles the degree of reaction itself may be equally important. On initial heating of an uncured thermoset, the viscosity will fall, just as in most fluids. However, chemical reaction will eventually overshadow this thermal thinning, and the viscosity will rise as the mobility of the resin is increasingly restricted by intermolecular crosslinking. When enough crosslinking has occurred to cause incipient gelation (some molecules having become large enough to span the entire specimen), the viscosity will become indefinitely large. The resin has now passed technically from a liquid to a solid, and will no longer permit unrestricted deformations. Many processing operations, such as molding or void suppression, must be completed before gelation has occurred.

The resin glass temperature T_g will also rise as the curing reaction proceeds, as crosslinking serves to reduce molecular mobility for a given temperature. If T_g rises enough to equal the cure temperature, the resin will by definition have vitrified. The reaction will then become largely diffusion limited, with a substantial reduction in its rate.

The work of J. K. Gillham [7,8] provides a convenient means of visualizing the transformations which take place during cure of a thermosetting resin. Gillham used torsional braid analysis (TBA) and other methods to measure the times to gelation and vitrification at various isothermal cure temperatures. Figure 4.1 [8], termed by Gillham a Time–Temperature Transformation (TTT) diagram, provides a schematic illustration of the major features of such data.

The TTT diagram shows that the time to gelation, which is a point of fixed conversion calculable from statistical theory, increases as the cure temperature is lowered; this is expected for a thermally activated rate process. The S-shaped vitrification curve reflects the competition between the usual tendency of rising temperature to soften the material, and the role of increasing reaction rate to accelerate the curing

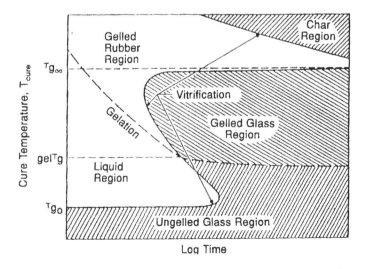

Figure 4.1 The time–temperature transformation diagram for isothermal cure.

reaction and harden the material by crosslinking. T_{g_0} is the temperature at which even the completely uncured resin vitrifies, and T_{g_∞} is the glass temperature of the fully cured resin. The vitrification curve must obviously remain between these limiting temperatures.

The TTT diagram is very useful for visualizing what otherwise is a confusing interplay of phenomena, notably the dual role played by temperature. The diagram is also valuable as a processing aid. The temperature $_{\text{gel}}T_g$ at which the gelation and vitrification lines cross indicates the upper temperature at which the resin can be stored. Once the resin has "gelled," that is, has developed a three-dimensional network that prevents unbounded deformation, the material cannot be processed further. At temperatures less than $_{\text{gel}}T_g$ vitrification occurs before gelation. As vitrification quenches the crosslinking reaction, gelation will be avoided and the material will remain processable.

The previous discussion assumes isothermal curing, but can be extended to include "scanning" experiments in which the temperature is increased according to an arbitrary cure cycle. During the scanning thermal experiment sufficient crosslinking may occur such that the resin T_g will catch up to the cure temperature. From that time on, the resin may be reacting in a diffusion-controlled manner, with the T_g keeping a few degrees ahead of the steadily increasing cure temperature. Gillham reports [9] that this effect can be modeled satisfactorily by adopting a relation between T_g and the extent of reaction α of the form:

$$\frac{T_g - T_{g0}}{T_g} = \frac{(C_1 - C_2)\alpha}{1 - (1 - C_2)\alpha} \tag{4.9}$$

When the glass temperature T_g as given by Eq. (4.9) is greater than the current cure temperature, the reaction rate equation [Eq. (4.35)] is then replaced by one due to Kaeble [10] which modifies the preexponential constant Z as follows:

$$\ln Z(T) = \ln Z(T_g) + \frac{C_1(T - T_g)}{C_2 + (T - T_g)} \tag{4.10}$$

The $Z(T_g)$ is the frequency factor at T_g, and is assumed to have the same value as in the rubbery or liquid state. The second term is a WLF-type expression that attempts to account for the reduced free volume and molecular mobility at temperatures below T_g.

4.3 Thermal Effects in Polymer Processing Flows

The above discussion dealt with the idealized case in which a small specimen is subjected to a simple thermal or mechanical stimulus, and the response of the material measured. In actual processing, the temperature and stress fields will be nonuniform both spatially and temporally, and the process engineer must allow for this more complicated situation. In the sections to follow, we will outline how closed-form or computational mathematical approaches can be used to combine the materials response with an overall model of the process geometry so as to obtain a realistic view of the actual process. As mentioned previously, this presentation cannot provide more than a brief introduction to the very broad field of transport phenomena in general and polymer processing in particular.

4.3.1 Governing Equations

The dominant variables in processing problems are governed by well-known conservation equations, developed in standard texts in transport theory (e.g., [11]). These can be written in a number of different formats, but for our purposes the following concise listing will suffice:

$$\rho \left[\frac{\partial u}{\partial t} + u \nabla u \right] = -\nabla p + \nabla (\eta \nabla u) \tag{4.11}$$

$$\rho c \left[\frac{\partial T}{\partial t} + u \nabla T \right] = Q + \nabla (k \nabla T) \tag{4.12}$$

$$\left[\frac{\partial C}{\partial t} + u \nabla C \right] = R + \nabla (D \nabla C) \tag{4.13}$$

Here u, T, and C are fluid velocity (a vector), temperature, and concentration of reactive species; these are the principal variables in our formulation, though other choices are possible as well. Other parameters are density (ρ), pressure (p), viscosity (η), specific heat (c), thermal conductivity (k), and species diffusivity (D). The ∇ operator is defined as $\nabla = (\partial/\partial x, \partial/\partial y)$. The similarity of these equations is evident, and leads to considerable efficiency in the coding of their numerical solution. In all cases, the time rate of change of the transported variable (u, T, or C) is balanced by the convective or flow transport terms (e.g., $u \nabla T$), the diffusive transport (e.g., $\nabla [k \nabla T]$), and a generation term (e.g., Q).

The units must be given special attention in these equations, especially as material properties obtained from various handbooks or experimental tests will usually be reported in units that must be converted to obtain consistency when used in the above equations. The governing equations are volumetric rate equations. For instance, the heat generation rate Q is energy per unit volume per unit time, such as N-m/m^3-s if using SI units. The user must select units for all parameters so that each term in the energy equation will have these same units.

Q and R are generation terms for heat and chemical species respectively, whereas the pressure gradient ∇p plays an analogous role for momentum generation. The heat generation arises from viscous dissipation and from reaction heating:

$$Q = \tau : \dot{\gamma} + R(\Delta H) \tag{4.14}$$

where τ and $\dot\gamma$ are the deviatoric components of stress and strain rate, R is the rate of chemical reaction, and ΔH is the heat of reaction. R in turn is given by a kinetic chemical equation, such as was discussed earlier in Eq. (4.8).

The viscosity η is a strong function of the temperature and the shear rate for many polymer melts. The effect of increasing temperature in lowering ("thinning") the viscosity has been discussed previously. Increasing the shear rate also leads to thinning for many polymers, as it tends to straighten and orient the molecular chains, reducing their entanglement density. A convenient viscosity model is obtained by combining a Carreau power-law formulation for shear thinning and an Arrhenius expression as in Eq. (4.1) for thermal thinning. The formal equation is:

$$\eta = \eta_0 \exp\left(\frac{-E_\eta}{R_g T}\right) \left[1 + (\lambda\dot\gamma)^2\right]^{\frac{m-1}{2}} \tag{4.15}$$

Here η_0 is the "zero-shear" viscosity limit, E_η is the activation energy for thermal thinning, λ is a shape parameter, and m is the power-law exponent. This formulation is not suitable for all cases, such as liquids exhibiting strong elastic effects, but it is useful for a number of analyses in viscous flow rheology.

The boundary conditions for engineering problems usually include some surfaces on which values of the problem unknowns are specified, for instance points of known temperature or initial species concentration. Some other surfaces may have constraints on the gradients of these variables, as on convective thermal boundaries where the rate of heat transport by convection away from the surface must match the rate of conductive transport to the surface from within the body. Such a temperature constraint might be written:

$$h(T - T_a) = -k\nabla T \cdot \hat{n} \quad \text{on} \quad \Gamma_h \tag{4.16}$$

Here h is the convective heat transfer coefficient, T_a is the ambient temperature, and $\hat{n}$ is the unit normal to the convective boundary Γ_h.

4.3.2 Dimensional Analysis and Scaling

Each of the terms in Eqs. (4.11)–(4.13) represents a mode of transport: the first term is the time rate of change of the variable in question (momentum, thermal energy, or mass species in each equation, respectively), and the remaining three state the contributions to that rate of change by flow advection, local generation, and diffusive flux. In certain cases one or more of these terms may vanish identically due to the nature of the geometry of other factors. In other cases it may be possible to neglect certain terms as being small in comparison with the others, and in these cases enough simplification may be introduced to permit a solution to the problem which would not be possible otherwise. In addition, examination of the magnitudes of the various terms is of great value to the process analyst, as this helps identify which physical mechanisms are important and which are not.

The magnitudes of the terms are generally expressed as a group of ratios, made nondimensional and usually carrying the name of a pioneer in transport theory. For instance, the *Reynolds' Number* is the ratio of the convective term in the momentum equation ($\rho u \nabla u$) to the viscous term ($\nabla(\eta \nabla u)$), which the rheologist knows as the diffusive "momentum flux"), made dimensionless by dividing by a characteristic length L:

$$Re = \rho U L/\eta \qquad (4.17)$$

where U is a characteristic velocity. Such dimensionless groups are important in scaling: if a scaled-down laboratory prototype is to be constructed of an actual process, the Reynolds' Numbers of both devices must be kept the same if dynamic similitude is to be achieved. Because the characteristic length L is to be reduced, there must corresponding increases in ρ or U, or an increase in η.

The Reynolds' Number is usually very small in melt polymer processing, mainly due to the high viscosity η. As a consequence, the convective term $u\nabla u$ can normally be neglected. This is "creeping" or "Stokes" flow, and is usually much easier to solve than flows with strong convective influences. However, the small Reynolds' Number should not be taken to mean that the corresponding advective terms in the energy and species equation can be neglected as well. In the energy equation, the ratio of the advective ($\rho c u \nabla T$) and diffusive ($\nabla(k \nabla T)$) components is the *Peclet Number*, defined as

$$Pe = \rho c U L/k \qquad (4.18)$$

This number can be large, on the order of 10^4 for many processing situations, due to the low thermal conductivity k. The energy and mass equations typically have large or even dominating contributions from the advective terms, and these often require special handling in numerical solutions [12].

The low thermal conductivity generally exhibited by polymers can have another important heat transfer effect: when the polymer is generating heat internally by exothermic chemical reaction or by viscous dissipation, internal temperatures can rise above acceptable values due to the inability of the polymer to remove the heat by thermal conduction. The relevant parameter here is the ratio of the heat generation rate to the conductivity, made dimensionless in the *Brinkman Number*, Br:

$$Br = \frac{QL}{kT} \qquad (4.19)$$

where L and T are a characteristic length and temperature, respectively. Consideration of this parameter illustrates the difficulty in processing articles having thick sections: it is difficult to get heat to the central regions to melt or react the material, and it is difficult to remove heat when that becomes necessary. This in turn leads to high cycle times in processing of polymeric articles, which can make the choice of material uneconomic.

4.3.3 Example: Extruder Channel Flow

The melt extruder, in which molten polymer is dragged toward a die by the relative motion of the extruder barrel relative to the screw, is an important processing method in polymer technology, and is also well suited for illustrating the application of the mathematical formalism stated above. The flow channel is of a sufficiently simple shape to permit theoretical solutions for comparison purposes, but the flow is of a general mixed-boundary-value nature so that the general applicability of computational approaches may be demonstrated as well.

As described in several texts (e.g., [1,2]), the helical flow path in a screw extruder may be idealized as a straight, rectangular channel covered by a plate that moves tangentially to the channel as shown in Figure 4.2. Due to the tangential motion of the top plate, fluid flow is established in the the axial (down-channel) and transverse (cross-channel) directions. In addition, the axial flow in inhibited by the development of pressure by the die. In the case of Newtonian melts, these two flow fields are uncoupled and may be treated separately.

The down-channel flow can be treated as a standard textbook problem in fluid mechanics, that of an incompressible viscous fluid constrained between two boundaries of infinite lateral extent. (The coordinate axes will now take x as being in the down-channel direction, with y being the coordinate measured upward from the base of the channel to the barrel surface.) A positive pressure gradient is applied in the x-direction corresponding to the increasing pressure as the die is approached, and the upper boundary surface at $y = H$ is displaced to the right at a velocity of $u(H) = U$. The drag velocity is in turn related to the screw speed as $U = \pi D_s N$, where D_s is the screw diameter and N is its rotational speed (in rad/s). The solution for the x-direction velocities requires only the x-direction momentum equation, which after dropping terms that are identically zero becomes:

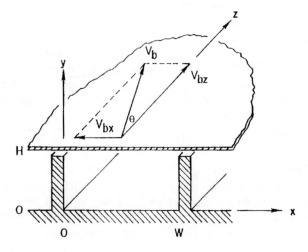

Figure 4.2 Straight-channel idealization of single-flight melt extruder.

$$\frac{d^2u}{dy^2} = \frac{1}{\eta}\left(\frac{\Delta p}{\Delta x}\right) \tag{4.20}$$

Integrating this twice, and applying the boundary conditions $u(0) = 0$, $u(H) = U$, the velocity is given as

$$u(y) = \frac{1}{2\eta}\left(\frac{\Delta p}{\Delta x}\right)\left(Hy - y^2\right) + U\left(\frac{y}{H}\right) \tag{4.21}$$

The first term above is the "Poiseuille" parabolic distribution produced by the pressure gradient; the second term in the linear "Couette" distribution caused by the drag.

The fluid velocity is an important variable in its own right, but it can be used to calculate other important processing parameters as well. For instance, the total flow rate — the volumetric output from the extruder — can be computed by integrating the velocity over the channel's cross-sectional area. The power required of the screw drive can be computed by evaluating the velocity gradient at the barrel surface, using this to compute the corresponding shear stress, and integrating the stress over the barrel surface to obtain the total force. The power is then the force times the barrel surface velocity.

One important means by which temperature effects can enter this problem is via the fluid's viscous dissipation. Considering for illustration the case in which only the drag component of velocity is present (this is "open-channel" flow, in which the die is removed and pressure is not allowed to increase along the screw), the shear rate is $\dot{\gamma} = (\partial u/\partial y) = U/H$. The associated stress is $\tau = \eta\dot{\gamma}$, and the thermal dissipation is then $Q = \tau\dot{\gamma} = \eta(U/H)^2$. The energy equation then becomes:

$$\frac{d^2T}{dy^2} = -\left(\frac{\eta}{k}\right)\left(\frac{U}{H}\right)^2 \tag{4.22}$$

This can be solved easily by integrating twice and imposing fixed thermal boundary conditions at the top and bottom of the flow channel; this solution will be compared with numerical prediction in a later section.

4.3.4 Numerical Simulation Methods

In practical problems, it is often impossible to solve the set of nonlinear and interrelated transport equations in closed form, especially in light of the irregular boundary conditions often encountered in engineering practice. However, the equations are amenable to discretization and solution by numerical techniques such as finite differences or finite elements. At present, a number of computer codes are commercially available to assist in process analysis and development, and in this section we will expand somewhat on the methods underlying their operation.

The finite element approach is attractive due to its flexibility with regard to geometry and complex material property relations, and has become the dominant technology in this field. The following overview of this method will be somewhat terse in light of space requirements in this chapter, and the reader is referred to standard texts such as that of Zienkiewicz [13] or Baker [14] for a more complete description. Recent work by the author [15] provides an example of the application to nonisothermal and reactive polymer processing. Finally, the popularity of finite element codes should not be taken to mean other approaches are not often just as effective; for instance, Guceri [16] has combined finite difference approaches with powerful geometrical mapping techniques to achieve many of the same advantages claimed by finite elements.

4.3.4.1 The Galerkin Finite Element Method

As an illustrative example of the numerical principles underlying the finite element approach, consider the specialization of the thermal transport equation to a two-dimensional problem in steady conductive heat transfer with internal heat generation and constant conductivity:

$$0 = Q + k\nabla^2 T \tag{4.23}$$

If a closed-form solution were being attempted, we would use successive integration or other mathematical techniques to determine a function $T(x, y)$ that satisfies this equation and also the boundary conditions of the problem. This can be done when the boundary conditions are sufficiently simple.

Considering the important case when no closed-form solution can be found, let us postulate a function $\tilde{T}(x, y)$ as an approximation to T:

$$\tilde{T}(x, y) \approx T(x, y) \tag{4.24}$$

Many different forms might be adopted for the approximation $\tilde{T}$. The finite element method discretizes the solution domain into an assemblage of subregions, or "elements," each of which have their own approximating functions. A number of discrete points, called "nodes," are also defined within the solution domain, usually at the corners of the elements. The approximation for the temperature $\tilde{T}(x, y)$ within an element is written as a combination of the (as yet unknown) temperatures at the nodes belonging to that element:

$$\tilde{T}(x, y) = N_j(x, y) T_j \tag{4.25}$$

Here the index j ranges over the element's nodes, T_j are the nodal temperatures, and the N_j are "interpolation functions." These interpolation functions are usually simple polynomials (generally linear, quadratic, or occasionally cubic polynomials) which are chosen to become unity at node j and zero at the other element nodes. The interpolation functions can be evaluated at any position within the element by means of standard subroutines, so the approximate temperature at any position within the element can be obtained in terms of the nodal temperatures directly from Eq. (4.24).

Because $\tilde{T}$ is an approximation rather than the true solution, we would expect that for a given set of approximate nodal temperatures Eq. (4.23) would not be satisfied exactly:

$$Q + k\nabla^2 \tilde{T} \neq 0 \qquad (4.26)$$

One powerful method for selecting the nodal temperatures so as to achieve a form of global accuracy is to ask not that the governing equation be satisfied identically everywhere within the element, but only that its integral over the element volume be as small as possible:

$$\int_V (Q + k\nabla^2 \tilde{T}) \, dV = \mathcal{R} \approx 0 \qquad (4.27)$$

Here $\mathcal{R}$ is the "residual" of the approximation; it would clearly be zero if $\tilde{T}$ happened to equal the true solution T.

Equation (4.27) provides only a single equation for each element, which would not be sufficient to determine all of the nodal temperatures in the approximation. However, we can obtain a number of such residual equations by premultiplying the integrand by a "weighting function" which might, for instance, be chosen to enforce accuracy at a number of different points in the solution domain. This might involve choosing a weighting function that is unity in the vicinity of a point at which the approximation should be accurate (i.e., have a zero residual), and zero elsewhere. This is just what the interpolation functions do, and the "Galerkin" weighted residual method takes the weighting functions and the interpolation functions to be the same. The set of weighted residual equations then becomes:

$$\int_V N_i (Q + k\nabla^2 \tilde{T}) \, dV = \mathcal{R} \approx 0 \qquad (4.28)$$

It is convenient to integrate Eq. (4.28) by parts to reduce the order of differentiation; this also introduces the thermal boundary conditions in a natural way. The second-order term is expanded as:

$$\int_V N_i k \nabla^2 \tilde{T} \, dV = \oint_\Gamma N_i k \nabla \tilde{T} \cdot \hat{n} \, d\Gamma - \int_V \nabla N_i k \nabla \tilde{T} \, dV \qquad (4.29)$$

Here Γ is the element boundary, and $\hat{n}$ is the unit normal to the boundary. Using Eq. (4.11) for the boundary convection condition, Eq. (4.28) becomes:

$$\int_V \nabla N_i k \nabla \tilde{T} \, dV = \int_V N_i Q \, dV + \oint_\Gamma N_i k \nabla \tilde{T} \cdot \hat{n} \, d\Gamma$$

$$= \int_V N_i Q \, dV - \oint_\Gamma N_i h(\tilde{T} - T_a) d\Gamma \qquad (4.30)$$

Now using expression for $\tilde{T}$ from Eq. (4.25) and factoring out the nodal temperatures that are not functions of x and y, we obtain a relation in which the nodal temperatures are related to the nodal heat fluxes:

$$k_{ij}T_j = q_i \tag{4.31}$$

where

$$k_{ij} = \int_V \nabla N_i k \nabla N_j \, dV + \oint_\Gamma N_i h N_j \, d\Gamma \tag{4.32}$$

and

$$q_i = \int_V N_i Q \, dV + \oint_\Gamma N_i h T_a \, d\Gamma \tag{4.33}$$

Of course, the integrals in the above equations must be replaced by a numerical equivalent acceptable to the computer. Gauss–Legendre numerical integration is commonly used in finite element codes for this purpose, as that technique provides a high ratio of accuracy to computing effort. Stated briefly, the integration consists of evaluating the integrand at optimally selected integration points within the element, and forming a weighted summation of the integrand values at these points. In the case of integration over two-dimensional element areas, this can be written:

$$\int_A f(x,y) \, dA \approx \sum_l f(x_l, y_l) w_l \tag{4.34}$$

The location of the sampling points x_l, y_l and the associated weights w_l are provided by standard subroutines. In most modern codes, these routines map the element into a convenient shape, determine the integration points and weights in the transformed coordinate frame, and then map the results back to the original frame. The functions used earlier both for interpolation and residual weighting can be used for the mapping as well, achieving a significant economy in coding. This yields what are known as "numerically integrated isoparametric elements," and these are a mainstay of the finite element industry.

Equations (4.31)–(4.33), with the integrals replaced by numerical integrations of the form in Eq. (4.34), are the finite element counterparts of Eq. (4.23), the differential governing equation. The computer uses these by looping over each element, and over each integration point within the element. At each integration point, the integrands for the various terms, such as k_{ij} as given in Eq. (4.32) must be computed. Equations (4.31)–(4.33) provide relations between for a single element only, but the thermal conductivity matrix k_{ij} and heat flux vector q_i can be generated in turn for every element in the problem. The contribution of each element's conductivity and flux arrays can then be added ("assembled") into a large "global" set of simultaneous algebraic equations that relate all of the problem's nodal temperatures and externally applied heat fluxes. This system of equation can then be solved by the computer using Gaussian elimination or other schemes to obtain the nodal temperatures T_j.

The description above treats only two terms of one of our governing equations; similar procedures were used in the flow code to treat all of the terms in Eqs. (4.12) and (4.13). Certain special techniques are needed occasionally to handle such features as enforcement of fluid incompressibility and stability of advection-dominated flows; in the interest of space, for these the reader is referred to the literature cited previously. The contributions of all needed terms are computed by a single element routine, and are added to the locations in the stiffness matrix associated with the degree of freedom number for the variable under consideration. One additional element type is used for boundaries on which convective heat transfer occurs.

In conventional closed-form analysis, one generally seeks to simplify the governing equations by dropping those terms that are zero or whose numerical magnitudes are small relative to the others, and then proceeding with a mathematical solution. In contrast, finite element codes can be written to contain all of the terms, with the particularization to specific problems being done entirely by selection of appropriate numerical parameters in the input dataset.

4.3.4.2 Some Numerical Examples

Figure 4.3 shows a simple 10×3 mesh of 4-node quadrilateral finite elements that can be used to simulate the down-channel flow in the melt zone of a screw extruder. A positive pressure gradient is applied in the x-direction, and the upper boundary surface at $y = H$ is displaced to the right at a velocity of $u(H) = U$. The y-velocities are all set to zero; the problem is underconstrained otherwise. Numerical parameters such as η and H are set to unity in this example problem. When the problem is linear, numerical results for other problem parameters can be obtained by suitable scaling; nondimensionalized units are used in Figure 4.4 to emphasize this point.

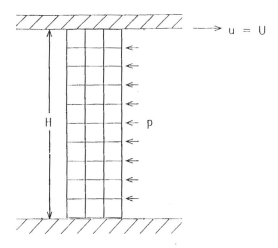

Figure 4.3 Simulation of drag/pressure plane flow.

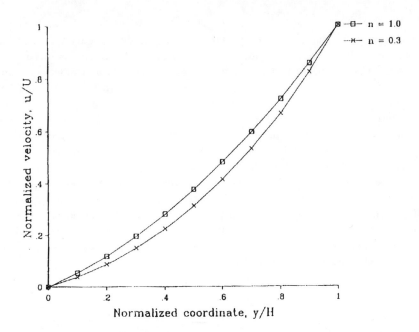

Figure 4.4 Finite element prediction of plane flow velocity profile.

Figure 4.4 shows the finite-element prediction of this velocity profile for two cases: a Newtonian fluid (power-law exponent $m = 1$) and a shear-thinning fluid ($m = 0.3$). The shear-thinning analysis is nonlinear, and was accomplished by cycling the finite element code to perform a Newton–Raphson iteration.

The influence of internal heat generation due to viscous dissipation can be illustrated using the same grid as Figure 4.3; the dimensionless temperature results are shown in Figure 4.5. Here no pressure gradient is imposed, so the numerical results can be compared with those predicted by Eq. (4.22). Figure 4.5 also shows the temperature profile which is obtained if the upper boundary exhibits a convective rather than fixed condition, using the convective boundary element discussed earlier. The convective heat transfer coefficient h was set to unity; this corresponds to a "Nusselt Number" $Nu = (hH/k) = 1$. The specific numerical values, of course, reflect the values used as input parameters; the unit values used in this simulation give a Brinkman Number $Br = (QH^2)/(kT)$ of unity, if the characteristic temperature in this definition is also taken as unity.

To illustrate the application of the method to a somewhat more complex practical problem, Figure 4.6 shows a mesh used to simulate the upper symmetric half of a 4:1 entry flow from a reservoir into a capillary. Also included in Figure 4.6 are the streamlines resulting from a Newtonian solution, and the associated temperature contours which correspond to internal heating by viscous dissipation and heat transfer which in this simulation is dominated by conduction rather than advection ($Pe = 0$).

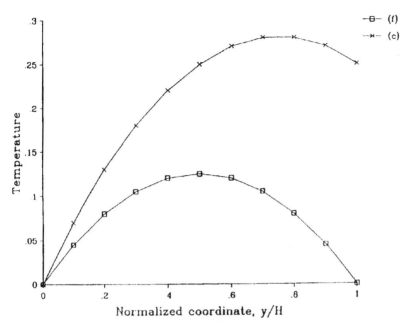

Figure 4.5 Finite element simulation of plane Couette flow with thermal dissipation and conductive heat transfer. f fixed temperature condition; c convective boundary condition.

4.4 Practical Consequences in Processing

4.4.1 Chemical Reaction Mechanisms — An Example

Thermosetting resins can achieve chemical crosslinking by a variety of mechanisms, provided only that functionality exist which can produce covalent bonding between

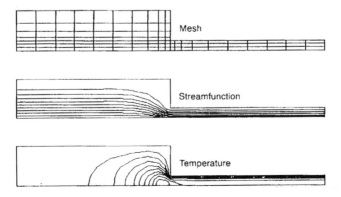

Figure 4.6 Finite element simulation of 4:1 entry flow with coupled conductive heat transfer.

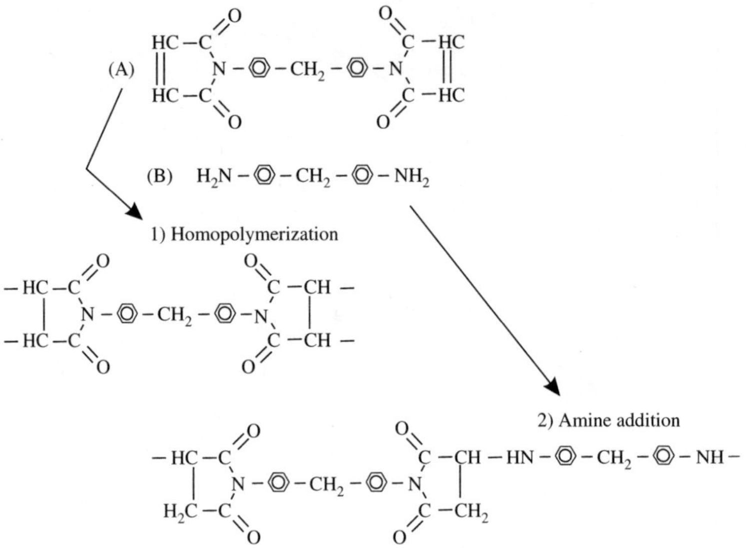

Figure 4.7 Cure chemistry of Kerimid 601 polyimide resin.

either the resin entities themselves or between resin and a crosslinking agent (a hardener). A functionality of at least two in one constituent and three in the other will be needed to form three-dimensional networks. Labana [17] has provided a recent review of the various types of resins and hardeners in current use. Rather than repeat such a list here, it may be sufficient to present a single example that illustrates two of the crosslinking mechanisms found in many systems.

Kerimid 601 (Rhone-Poulenc Company, France) is a bismaleimide resin based on short, linear, polymerizable monomers containing the imide group [18], and was developed to overcome the problems associated with off-gas generation in conventional polyimides. At elevated temperatures, the preimidized segments polymerize at the end groups without producing any volatiles [19]. It can be crosslinked by mixing 2.5 mol of the 4,4'-bis(maleimide diphenyl methane) with 1 mol of 4,4'-diaminodiphenyl methane. The reaction may proceed by homopolymerization at the maleimide double bonds, or by addition of the diamine at the maleimide double bonds as shown in Figure 4.7 [20]. During cure, both reactions can occur simultaneously.

4.4.2 Kinetic Thermal Analysis

In stoichiometric mixtures of resin and hardener, it is often possible to model the kinetics of thermoset cure by relatively simple nth order rate expressions such as were described earlier. Rewriting Eq. (4.8) in terms of the fractional extent of reaction $\alpha = (C_0 - C)/C_0$, we have:

$$\frac{d\alpha}{dt} = Z \exp\left(\frac{-E_C}{RT}\right)(1-\alpha)^n \qquad (4.35)$$

The material-dependent parameters in this expression (Z, E_C, and n) must be determined by experimentation which is able to monitor the reaction as a function of time and temperature. With these $\alpha(t, T)$ data in hand, numerical methods must be used to fit Eq. (4.35) to the data by suitable choice of the parameters.

Differential scanning calorimetry (DSC) can be used to measure the rate of heat absorption or evolution by a specimen as the temperature is raised at a constant rate. In these scanning experiments the data are recorded on a thermogram as a trace of the heat flow (or rate of heat evolution), dH/dt, given as a function of the temperature T. Positive deviation from the baseline in the thermogram indicates an increase in the specific heat of the specimen, or that an exothermic reaction is occurring in the specimen. The thermoset curing reaction is usually exothermic, and can be observed easily using DSC.

The use of DSC in preliminary kinetic analysis of thermoset cure can be illustrated using a recent study [21] of the Kerimid 601 bismaleimide resin discussed earlier. The material used in this research was supplied in the form of B-staged prepreg, with an unspecified quantity of glass fibers in the reactive polyimide resin. All of the specimens were taken from the same sheet of prepreg to avoid the possibility of inconsistency between lots. The prepreg was stored in a sealed bag at 0°F until the specimens were prepared to prevent exposure of the material to heat and moisture, and specimens were not prepared until the time of each individual run. Using the earlier work by Pappalardo [22] as a guideline, the DSC was set to heat the specimen from room temperature to 350 deg C to ensure that the entire reaction exotherm would be recorded. A typical thermogram is shown in Figure 4.8.

Thermograms of the sort shown in Figure 4.8 are valuable in providing an intuitive guide to the range of temperatures and energies expected in curing reactions. In addition, the thermograms can provide an experimental means of determining the numerical parameters in hypothesized kinetic models, and this model fitting procedure can yield analytical means of studying and optimizing the fabrication of complex items containing the reactive polymer. Several procedures have been proposed during the past several decades to perform model fitting using thermal analysis data [23–27], and recently Dhar [28] has provided a useful review that includes a numerical program for comparing the results of several methods.

To illustrate the general nature of the process, the nth order kinetic model of Eq. (4.35) is assumed, and the method of Freeman and Carroll [29,30] is employed to fit the model to the thermogram. The method of Freeman and Carroll is one of the most convenient available, in that only a single scanning DSC experiment is needed to obtain all of the kinetic parameters. However, one might expect that this convenience could be accompanied by a loss of accuracy, and a number of workers feel this to be true [31]. Further, we must keep in mind that the assumption of thermally activated nth order kinetics might be incorrect as well. The Kerimid cure is thought to consist of simultaneous addition and crosslinking reactions as shown in Figure 4.7, and the

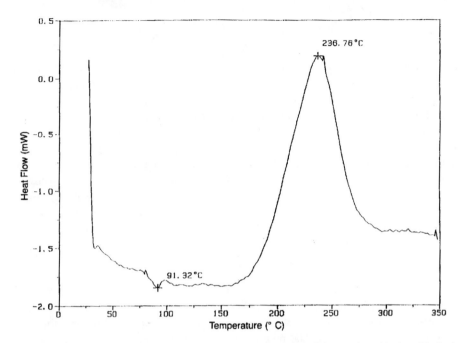

Figure 4.8 DSC thermogram of Kerimid 601 prepreg material tested at 10 deg C/min in nitrogen atmosphere. (14.1 mg specimen mass, including glass fibers.)

combination of these reactions might not be describable with a single nth order model. Finally, Sichina [32] notes that curing reactions that exhibit autocatalyzing effects may not obey the simple kinetic scheme used here.

While the above concerns should be kept in mind, the results to be shown below are useful in illustrating a general approach. Of course, a more exhaustive study would be required to assess fully the validity of the underlying assumptions. The extent of reaction α and the rate of reaction $d\alpha/dt$ can be measured directly from the DSC thermogram, assuming each reaction event to liberate the same quantity of heat:

$$\frac{d\alpha}{dt} = \frac{1}{H_0} \cdot \frac{dH}{dt} \qquad (4.36)$$

$$\alpha = \int \frac{d\alpha}{dt} \, dt$$

Here dH/dt, the rate of heat evolution, is just the ordinate of the DSC thermogram, and H_0 is the area between the DSC baseline and the ordinate over the range of temperatures comprising the reaction. H_0 is the total heat evolution of the cure reaction; in our case this quantity is not that of the resin alone, since the specimen also contains an unmeasured quantity of glass fibers.

The Freeman–Carroll approach linearizes Eq. 4.35 by taking logarithms:

$$\log \frac{d\alpha}{dt} = \log Z + \frac{E}{2.303RT} + n\log(1-\alpha) \qquad (4.37)$$

This equation is then evaluated at various temperatures spaced at equal increments of $1/T$, and the corresponding experimental values of α and $d\alpha/dt$ are used in a difference equation obtained from Eq. (4.37):

$$\Delta \log \frac{d\alpha}{dt} = \Delta \log Z + \frac{E}{2.303R}\Delta\left(\frac{1}{T}\right) + n\Delta\log(1-\alpha) \qquad (4.38)$$

This equation predicts that a plot of the differences of the logs of the rates of reaction at various temperatures, spaced at equal increments of reciprocal temperature, versus the corresponding differences of logs of the extent of reaction at those temperatures, should be a straight line whose slope is the reaction order n and whose intercept can be used to compute the activation energy E. (Of course $\Delta \log Z = 0$, since Z is a constant.) Once E and n are known, Z can be found by evaluating Eq. (4.37) at any selected temperature. This procedure can be performed using spreadsheet software on personal microcomputers. Figure 4.9 shows a typical Freeman–Carroll plot for the Kerimid material.

Three such plots were made in this study, each from separate DSC experiments. (Each experiment, however, used specimens from the same batch of Kerimid prepreg.)

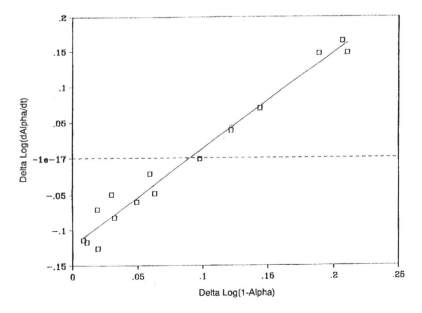

Figure 4.9 Freeman–Carroll plot.

Table 4.2 Kinetic Parameters for Kerimid 601

Test	1	2	3
Reaction order	1.35	1.40	1.31
Activation energy, kJ/mol	116.3	115.9	112.6
Log (Z, 1/s)	11.2	10.6	10.2
Correlation coefficient	0.97	0.94	0.95

The listing of numerical parameters obtained from these three plots, shown in Table 4.2, shows that the analysis appears reproducible.

4.4.3 Laminate Cure Analysis

The BMI resins are natural candidates for adhesive and encapsulation applications requiring good resistance to elevated temperature. As an example, consider the curing of a multilayer printed wiring board consisting of symmetric outer layers of copper-clad laminate and one central copper-clad layer, bonded by the Kerimid adhesive prepreg material. Noting that the thermal and reactive species gradients are much larger in the board through-thickness direction than in the plane of the board, we place a single strip of finite elements running from the board centerline to the outer edge as shown in Figure 4.10. The time–temperature program of the press cure cycle is imposed on the topmost nodes as a boundary condition, and the code is operated in a time-stepping fashion to compute the internal temperatures and degrees of reaction as the cure proceeds.

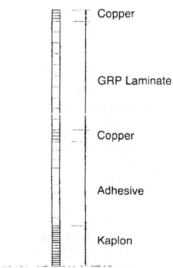

Figure 4.10 Finite element grid for one-dimensional simulation of wiring board cure.

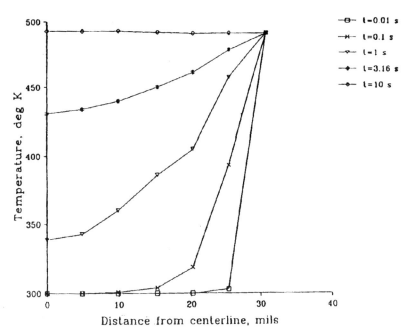

Figure 4.11 Predicted temperature profiles at various times for cure program in which outer surfaces of wiring board are brought suddenly to 425 deg F (491 K).

Figure 4.11 shows the temperature profiles which are predicted within the board at various times when the board is placed in a heated mold and the outer surfaces brought suddenly to the curing temperature of 425 deg F (491 K). The temperatures equilibrate in times on the order of 10 s, and in this time the reaction proceeds to completion as well. Processing time is obviously minimized by such a cure cycle, but the thermal strains produced by the nonuniform temperatures at early times may be problematic in terms of board warpage and interlayer delamination.

Figure 4.12 shows the results of heating more gradually at 10 deg F/min until 425 deg F is reached, and then holding at that temperature. In this case the heating rate is slow enough compared to the thermal equilibration time that the board is at essentially uniform temperature and degree of reaction during the process, and the reaction proceeds to completion during the heat-up phase of the cure cycle. The high-temperature hold following the heat-up is unnecessary with regard to chemical reaction in the adhesive.

4.5   Summary

This chapter has shown that temperature is a central parameter in polymer processing, controlling the material's fluidity and its chemical reactivity. It is clearly vital that temperature effects be understood by the process designer, and that suitable controls

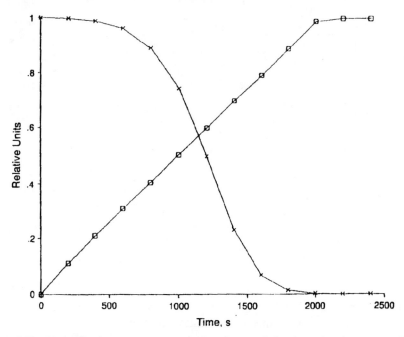

Figure 4.12 Normalized temperature (ascending line) and fraction of resin unreacted (descending curve) for cure program consisting of heating at 10 deg F/min to 425 deg F followed by hold at 425 deg F.

be incorporated into the process that ensure appropriate temperatures throughout the process cycle. Feedback temperature control, often microprocessor-based, is now common in polymer processing equipment. The selection of correct controller settings is often made by trial and error, but increasing use is being made of analytical theory as was outlined above in helping make these choices. Ultimately, the analytical models will be made part of the control scheme, leading to an intelligent and optimal process.

References

1. Middleman, S., *Fundamentals of Polymer Processing*. McGraw-Hill (1977).
2. Tadmor, Z. and Klein, I., *Engineering Principles of Plasticating Extrusion*. Van Nostrand-Reinhold (1970).
3. Nielson, L.E., *Polymer Rheology*. Marcel Dekker (1977).
4. Williams, M.L., Landel, R.F., and Ferry, J.D., The temperature dependence of relaxation mechanisms in amorphous polymers and other glass-forming liquids. *J. Am. Chem. Soc.* **77**, 3701–3707 (1955).
5. Doolittle, A.K., Studies in Newtonian flow. II. The dependence of the viscosity of liquids on free-space. *J. App. Phys.* **22**, 1471–1475 (1951).
6. Castellan, G.W., *Physical Chemistry*. Addison-Wesley, 1983.
7. Enns, J.B. and Gillham, J.K., Time temperature transformation (TTT) cure diagram: modeling the cure behavior of thermosets. *J. of App. Polymer Sci.* **28**, 2567–2591 (1983).

8. Gillham, J.K., Curing, in *Encyclopedia of Polymer Science and Engineering, Vol. 4.* John Wiley & Sons, (1986), pp. 519–524.
9. Gillham, J.K., Modeling reaction kinetics of an amine-cured epoxy system at constant heating rates from isothermal kinetic data. *Polymer Mat. Sci. Eng.* **57**, 87–91 (1987).
10. Kaeble, D.H., *Computer-Aided Design of Polymers and Composites,* Chap. 4. Marcel Dekker (1985).
11. Bird, R.B., Stewart, W.E., and Lightfoot, E.N., *Transport Phenomena.* John Wiley & Sons (1960).
12. Hughes, T.R.J. and Brooks, A., A multidimensional upwind scheme with no crosswind diffusion *Finite Element Methods in Convection Dominated Flows.* American Society of Mechanical Engineers (1979), pp. 19–36.
13. Zienkiewicz, O.C., *The Finite Element Method.* McGraw-Hill (1977).
14. Baker, A.J., *Finite Element Computational Fluid Mechanics.* McGraw-Hill (1983).
15. Roylance, D., Reaction kinetics for thermoset resins, in *The Manufacturing Science of Composites.* American Society of Mechanical Engineers, (1988), pp. 7–11.
16. Coulter, J.P. and Guceri, S.I., Resin transfer molding: process review, modeling and research opportunities, in *The Manufacturing Science of Composites.* American Society of Mechanical Engineers (1988), pp. 79–86.
17. Labana, S.S., Crosslinking, in *Encyclopedia of Polymer Science and Engineering, Vol. 4.* John Wiley & Sons (1986), pp. 349–395.
18. Darmory, F.P., *Kerimid 601 Polyimide Resin for Multilayer Printed Wiring Boards.* Rhodia
19. Kumar, D., Fohlen, G.M., and Parker, J.A., High-temperature resins based on aromatic amine-terminated bisaspartimides. *J. Polymer Sci. Polymer Chem. Edit.* **21**, 245–267 (1983).
20. DiGiulio, C., Gautier, M., and Jasse, B., Fourier transform infrared spectroscopic characterization of aromatic bismaleimide resin cure states. *J. Appl. Polymer Sci.* **29**, 1771–1779 (1984).
21. Fullerton, R., Roylance, D., Acton, A., and Allred, R., Cure analysis of printed wiring boards containing reactive adhesive layers. *Polymer Eng. Sci.* **28**, 372–376 (1988).
22. Pappalardo, L.T., DSC evaluation of epoxy and polyimide-impregnated laminates (prepregs). *J. Appl. Sci.* **21**, 809–820 (1977).
23. Borchardt, H.J. and Daniels, F., The application of differential thermal analysis to the study of reaction kinetics. *J. Am. Chem. Soc.* **79**, 41–46 (1957).
24. Watson, E.S., O'Neill, M.T., Justin, J., and Brenner, N., The analysis of a temperature controlled scanning calorimeter. *Anal. Chem.* **36**, pp. 1238–1245 (1964).
25. Fava, R.A., Differential scanning calorimetry of epoxy resins. *Polymer* **9**, 137–151 (1968).
26. Abolafia, O.R., Application of differential scanning calorimetry to epoxy curing studies. *Proc. SPE Annual Technical Conference* **15**, 610–616 (1969).
27. Duswalt, A.A., The practice of obtaining kinetic data by differential scanning calorimetry. *Thermochim. Acta* **8**, 57–68 (1974).
28. Dhar, P.S., "A comparative study of different methods for the analysis of TGA curves." *Comput. Chem.* **10**, 293–297 (1986).
29. Freeman E.S. and Carroll, B., The application of thermoanalytical techniques to reaction kinetics. *J. Phys. Chem.* **54**, 394–397 (1957).
30. Reich, L. and Stivala, S.S., *Elements of Polymer Degradation.* McGraw-Hill (1971).
31. Meeting of the New England Thermal Forum, Newton, Massachusetts, April 1987.
32. Sichina, W.J., *Considerations in Modeling of Kinetics by Thermal Analysis.* Du Pont Co. Publication E-81774, Wilmington, DE.

CHAPTER 5

Temperature Measurement Fundamentals

E. Marcia Katz

5.1 Introduction

This book is intended as a guide for process engineers who need to learn more about temperature control technology, so the emphasis in this chapter is to provide information to enable the process engineer to select the sensors and instrumentation that are appropriate for the application.

The material has been selected so the engineer can understand what options temperature measurement technology offers, what it lacks, and how to implement it. The chapter introduces the concept of temperature, discusses briefly the international temperature measurement standards, and gives a general overview of factors to be considered for industrial temperature measurement.

The most commonly used industrial temperature sensors are those based on thermoelectric principles, thermocouples, and those based on resistance thermometry, resistance temperature devices, and thermistors. A review of the history, the principles, the advantages and disadvantages, and guidelines for selection are presented for each.

A reference list is included for the engineer who wants more information on the topics addressed in this chapter.

5.1.1 General Concept of Temperature

An exact definition of temperature is difficult. It is the property that gauges the ability of matter to transfer energy by conduction or radiation; it is a sense of hotness or

---

E. Marcia Katz, *The Department of Nuclear Engineering, The University of Tennessee, Knoxville, TN 37996-2300, USA*

coldness. But these qualitative definitions are often unreliable. For instance, a very cold body may seem hot, and different materials at the same temperature may seem to be at different temperatures.

Therefore usually the equality of temperature is defined, which does not help when we need to know the temperature of a material or an environment in an industrial process.

We do know that temperature is an intensive property: it is the same for the entire or any part of a homogeneous object. This is contrasted with an extensive property such as length, for which the whole is the sum of its parts. The property of temperature also differs from the property of length in the sense that defining a standard meter is sufficient to define longer lengths but defining the temperature at one thermal condition is not enough to provide values of temperature at other thermal conditions.

5.1.2 *International Temperature Scales*

Temperature is a basic property in science and engineering, so it is necessary to be able to determine if conditions are the same from one laboratory to another or from one industrial site to another. The international series of "Temperature, Its Measurement and Control in Science and Industry" conferences, beginning in 1939 and continuing through the sixth one in 1992, is evidence of the worldwide concern with temperature and its accurate measurement.

The United States cooperates through the National Institute of Standards and Technology, formerly the National Bureau of Standards, in an international agreement to define the International Practical Temperature Scale. The newest version is the recently adopted IPTS-90, which was established by the following process. Temperatures at fixed points are based on physical phenomena, such as the freezing, boiling, and triple points of pure materials. These give stable, reproducible thermal conditions. There is still the problem of assigning numbers, which is done by using established laws of nature (gas law, Planck's radiation law, etc.). Then interpolating thermometers were selected for specific temperature ranges, and their readings at the fixed points determined. Finally functional forms of the behavior between the fixed points were selected.

A precise, reproducible, practical temperature scale is established that closely matches the theoretical thermodynamic temperatures.

5.2 Basic Considerations for Temperature Measurement

In general, absolute thermometers permit calculation of a temperature by measurement of one or more physical properties. An element "senses" the measurand, the physical quantity to be measured, and converts it to a measurable signal. Temperature transducers convert one physical property to another, and they require calibration of some temperature-dependent measurable property versus temperature.

There are several factors to consider when designing or selecting a temperature sensor: accuracy, stability, sensitivity, speed of response, usable life, initial and maintenance costs, reproducibility, linearity of output, range of usability, ease of reading, simplicity, and safety.

Desirable characteristics in the sensing element include the following: an unambiguous response with temperature, high sensitivity at all temperatures, stability, low cost, wide range of applicability, and small mass to be brought up to temperature and small heat capacity for rapid heat conduction so the response is fast.

Thermocouples (TCs), resistance temperature devices (RTDs), and thermally sensitive resistors (thermistors) are the most common industrial temperature transducers. TCs are devices in which the measurand is the voltage produced when an electrical circuit of dissimilar metals experiences a temperature gradient. RTDs and thermistors are applications of resistance thermometry: the measurand is the element's electrical resistance, a function of temperature. In an RTD the sensor is a metal; in a thermistor it is a semiconductor.

The installation of the sensor affects the measured temperature. Factors to be considered are bare sensor versus sensor in a thermowell, a protective sheath; flowing versus static fluid; and fluid versus solid environment. Other considerations are necessary if transient temperature measurements are desired. No instrument responds instantly to a change in its environment or reports a transient perfectly. The rate of response of a temperature sensor depends on the physical properties of the sensor and its environment.

The characteristic time response that is usually reported is based on the first-order approximation of the response to a step change in the temperature of the environment and is the time to reach 63.2% of the final, steady-state temperature. Several things can be done to improve the response (reduce the time response) of an installed sensor: use a bare sensor; reduce the gap between the sensor and thermowell; fill air gap with material that has high thermal conductivity; or choose a thermowell made of material with high thermal conductivity.

If it is important to know the response time of a sensor, it must be measured in situ because so many installation factors affect the response time.

5.3 Thermoelectric Thermometry, the Basis of the Thermocouple

5.3.1 Background

In 1821 Thomas Johann Seebeck, a contemporary of Ohm, discovered thermoelectric currents, the continuous electric current that is induced when the junctions in a circuit of two dissimilar metals are at different temperatures. About 5 years later, Antoine Cesar Becqueral applied Seebeck's discovery to temperature measurement.

Today's industrial TCs, schematically shown in Figure 5.1, consist of two wires of different materials joined at one end, the measuring junction. When the TC is placed in a temperature gradient, a voltage difference is observed across the open ends of the wires, the reference junction. The voltage is approximately proportional to the difference in temperature between the measuring and reference junctions:

$$V \propto (T_M - T_R) \tag{5.1}$$

where
  V is the thermoelectric open circuit voltage, volts
  T_M is the temperature of measuring junction, deg C
  T_R is the temperature of reference junction, deg C.
The proportionality can be replaced by an equal sign and a constant:

$$V = S(T_M - T_R). \tag{5.2}$$

The constant S is called the Seebeck coefficient. It has units of volts/deg C.

The absolute Seebeck coefficient of material A, designated S_A, is a temperature-varying property of the material and is independent of the size, shape, and amount of material present. S_A cannot be measured without connecting material A to some other material so a relative Seebeck coefficient is defined:

$$S_{AB} = S_A - S_B, \tag{5.3}$$

where material B is often platinum.

The relative Seebeck coefficient for a TC formed of material A and material C is

$$S_{AC} = S_{AB} - S_{CB}. \tag{5.4}$$

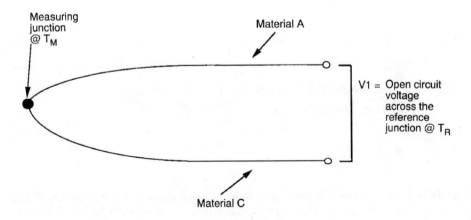

Figure 5.1 Basic thermocouple.

The open circuit voltage V across the reference junction in Figure 5.1 is given by

$$V = S_{AC}(T_M - T_R), \tag{5.5}$$

which represents the sum of voltages around the thermoelectric circuit. Each is the product of the material's Seebeck coefficient and the difference between the far temperature and the near temperature. Beginning at the upper reference junction,

$$V = V_A + V_C \tag{5.6}$$

where

$$V_A = S_A(T_M - T_R) \tag{5.7}$$

$$V_C = S_C(T_R - T_M). \tag{5.8}$$

Equation (5.5) results when Eq. (5.7) and Eq. (5.8) are substituted into Eq. (5.6).

5.3.2 Principles of Thermoelectric Circuits

The thermocouple voltage is produced by temperature gradients along the TC elements. No voltage is produced at the junctions. This basic tenet is expressed in three principles or laws of thermoelectric circuits: the Law of Homogeneous Materials, the Law of Intermediate Materials, and the Law of Successive or Intermediate Temperatures.

The Law of Homogeneous Materials states that a thermoelectric current cannot be induced by the application of heat alone in a circuit of a single homogeneous material, no matter how its cross-section varies. If the TC shown in Figure 5.1 consisted of wires of the same material D, the circuit analysis would be

$$V = S_D(T_R - T_M) + S_D(T_M - T_R) = 0. \tag{5.9}$$

Consequently, at least two different materials are required for a TC circuit.

The Law of Intermediate Material states that the algebraic sum of the thermoelectric forces (voltages) in a circuit composed of any number of dissimilar materials is zero if all of the circuit is at a uniform temperature. If the temperature of the reference junction, T_R, and the temperature of the measuring junction, T_M, are both equal to T_1 Eq. 5.5 becomes

$$V = S_{AC}(T_1 - T_1) = 0. \tag{5.10}$$

The result is that any material in the circuit will have no effect if both ends are at the same temperature. So a thermoelectric measuring device can be introduced and the junction formed in any manner without affecting the temperature measurement as long as the additional junctions are at the same temperature. It also means that inhomogeneities in the thermocouple wires will affect the measurement only when they exist in a thermal gradient.

The Law of Successive or Intermediate Temperature can be stated as follows: if the two dissimilar materials produce a thermal emf E_1 when the junctions are at T_1 and T_2 and a thermal emf E_2 when the junctions are at T_2 and T_3, the emf generated when the junctions are at T_1 and T_3 will be $E_1 + E_2$.

Therefore a TC calibrated for a given reference temperature can be used with any other reference temperature with a simple correction. Standard calibration tables use a reference junction temperature of 0 deg C or 32 deg F, with special tables available for a 150 deg F reference temperature. Table 5.1 is an excerpt from a standard table with a reference of 0 deg C. For other reference junction temperatures follow these steps.

1. Find the voltage in standard tables for the known, non-standard reference temperature.
2. Add this reference junction voltage to the measured TC voltage.
3. Find the temperature in the standard tables for the voltage sum.

Another result of this law is that the ends of extension wires with the same thermoelectric characteristics as the sensing wires can be at different temperatures without affecting the measurement.

5.3.3 Industrial Thermocouples

Thermocouples are simple, inexpensive, versatile, and durable. They are physically small and favored for fast response over a wide temperature range −183 deg C to 2500 deg C, offering the highest working temperature at the lowest cost.

TCs come in a wide variety of styles:

Bare or sheathed;

Absolute or differential;

Intrinsic, the measuring junction is the object for which the temperature is desired;

Thermopile, a series of TCs used to amplify the voltage induced by a temperature difference.

Any conductor can be a TC element, and the Instrument Society of America (ISA) has designated seven standard types by single letters: J, T, K, E, S, R, and B. The materials in these TCs are listed in Table 5.2.

Table 5.1 Standard TC Calibration Table

Deg C	0	1	2	3	4	5	6	7	8	9	10	Deg C
0	0.000	0.059	0.118	0.176	0.235	0.295	0.354	0.413	0.472	0.532	0.591	0
0	0.591	0.651	0.711	0.770	0.830	0.890	0.950	1.011	1.071	1.131	1.192	10
0	1.192	1.252	1.313	1.373	1.434	1.495	1.556	1.617	1.678	1.739	1.801	20
0	1.801	1.862	1.924	1.985	2.047	2.109	2.171	2.233	2.295	2.357	2.419	30
0	2.419	2.482	2.544	2.607	2.669	2.732	2.795	2.858	2.921	2.984	3.047	40
50	3.047	3.110	3.173	3.237	3.300	3.364	3.428	3.491	3.555	3.619	3.683	50
60	3.683	3.748	3.812	3.876	3.941	4.005	4.070	4.134	4.199	4.264	4.329	60
70	4.329	4.394	4.559	4.524	4.590	4.655	4.720	4.786	4.852	4.917	4.983	70
80	4.983	5.049	5.115	5.181	5.247	5.314	5.380	5.446	5.513	5.579	5.646	80
90	5.646	5.713	5.780	5.846	5.913	5.981	6.048	6.115	6.182	6.250	6.317	90
100	6.317	6.385	6.452	6.520	6.588	6.656	6.724	6.792	6.860	6.928	6.996	100
110	6.996	7.064	7.133	7.201	7.270	7.339	7.407	7.476	7.545	7.614	7.683	110
120	7.683	7.752	7.821	7.890	7.960	8.029	8.099	8.168	8.238	8.307	8.377	120
130	8.377	8.447	8.517	8.587	8.657	8.727	8.797	8.867	8.938	9.008	9.078	130
140	9.078	9.149	9.220	9.290	9.361	9.432	9.503	9.573	9.644	9.715	9.787	140
150	9.787	9.858	9.929	10.000	10.072	10.143	10.215	10.286	10.358	10.429	10.501	150
160	10.501	10.573	10.645	10.717	10.789	10.861	10.933	11.005	11.077	11.150	11.222	160
170	11.222	11.294	11.367	11.439	11.512	11.585	11.657	11.730	11.803	11.876	11.949	170
180	11.949	12.022	12.095	12.168	12.241	12.314	12.387	12.461	12.534	12.608	12.681	180
190	12.681	12.755	12.828	12.902	12.975	13.049	13.123	13.197	13.271	13.345	13.419	190
Deg C	0	1	2	3	4	5	6	7	8	9	10	Deg C

Reference junction at 0 deg C.

Table 5.2 Thermocouple Materials

Type K: Chromel and alumel
Type J: Iron and constantan
Type T: Copper and constantan
Type E: Chromel and constatan
Type R: Platinum–13% Rhodium and Platinum
Type S: Platinum–10% Rhodium and Platinum
Type B: Platinum–30% Rhodium and Platinum–6% Rhodium

NOTE: Alumel is an alloy of nickel and aluminum; chromel is nickel and chromium; and constantan is copper and nickel.

5.3.4 Thermocouple Calibration, Accuracy, and Standards

The limits of error, shown in Table 5.3 for premium and regular TCs, are valid only for new, clean TCs prior to calibration or exposure to service conditions. Recalibration

Table 5.3 Limits of Error for Thermocouples

Thermocouple Type	Temperature range, deg C	Limits of error[*]	
		Standard	Premium
T	−59–93	±1 deg C	±0.5 deg C
	93–371	±0.75%	±0.4%
J	0–277	±2.2 deg C	±1.1 deg C
	277–1260	±0.75%	±0.4%
E	0–316	±1.7 deg C	±1 deg C
	316–817	±0.5%	±0.4%
K	0–277	±2.2 deg C	±1.1 deg C
	277–1260	±0.75%	±0.4%
R or S	0-538	±1.5 deg C	±0.6 deg C
	538–1482	±0.25%	±0.1%
B	871–1705	±0.5 deg C	n.a.
Reference junction 0 deg C			

[*] Limits of error are expressed in percentage of Celsius temperature. Limits of error are materials tolerances, not accuracies.

of a used, possibly inhomogeneous, thermocouple has no validity in establishing its in-service accuracy unless the recalibration is performed in the in-service temperature gradient.

In fact the conditions of the calibration operation may affect the properties of the TC. Inhomogeneities might be created, which affect the accuracy of the TC when it is returned to service.

5.4 Resistance Thermometry

5.4.1 Background

Sir Humphrey Davy discovered in 1821 that the conductivity of various metals was inversely proportional to temperature. About 50 years later, Sir William Siemens first outlined the method of resistance thermometry. But modern precision resistance thermometry began in 1887 when Hugh Longbourne Callendar published a scientific paper on the subject in which he followed Siemens's idea and proposed a parabolic relationship between resistance of platinum and temperature that is known as the Callendar Equation. It was valid for temperatures between 0 deg C and 500 deg C. In 1925 VanDusen proposed that an additional term be added to the Callendar Equation so it would also be correct between -182 deg C and 0 deg C.

Resistance thermometers, shown schematically in Figure 5.2, are temperature measuring devices with the following components:

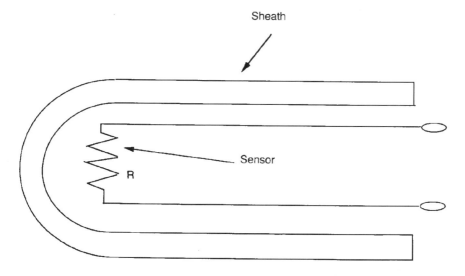

Figure 5.2 Schematic of a resistance thermometer.

A sensor, an electrical circuit element whose resistance varies with temperature

A framework to support the sensor;

A sheath to protect the sensor;

Wires connecting the sensor to a measuring instrument, which indicates the effects of variations in sensor resistance.

Resistance thermometers provide a direct measurement of temperature. Reference junctions or special extension wires between sensor and measuring device (readout) are not needed.

There are two categories of resistance thermometers: resistance temperature devices (RTDs) with metallic sensing elements and thermally sensitive resistors (thermistors) whose sensing elements are semiconductors.

RTDs and thermistors are accurate, linear, and stable; have physical strength; resist corrosion; provide ease of conversion to engineering units; and eliminate many measurement errors caused when a reference temperature is required.

5.4.2 Industrial Applications of Resistance Thermometry

5.4.2.1 Resistance Temperature Devices

The operation of the RTD is based in the Callendar–VanDusen Equation:

$$R/R_0 = 1 + \alpha[T - \delta(T/100 - 1)(T/100) - \beta(T/100 - 1)(T/100)^3] \quad (5.11)$$

where
  R is resistance at temperature T
  R_0 is resistance at the ice point, 0 deg C, typically, 25, 100, 200, or 500 ohms

$$\alpha \text{ (alpha)} = \left\{ \frac{R_{100} - R_0}{100 R_0} \right\}$$

  $= 0.00385$–0.00392, the higher the purity of platinum the higher the value
  R_{100} is resistance at the steam point, 100 deg C
  δ is a constant for a particular sensor, typically 1.4–1.5

$$\beta \text{ is } \begin{cases} 0 \text{ for } T \geq 0 \text{ deg } C \\ \text{Constant for } T < 0 \text{ deg } C, \text{ typically } 0.1 \end{cases}$$

To solve for T given R/R_0, for temperatures greater than 0 deg C, Eq. (5.11) becomes

$$T = \frac{-B - (B^2 - 4C)^{1/2}}{2} \qquad (5.12)$$

where

$$B = \left(\frac{10^4}{\delta} + 100\right) \qquad (5.12\text{a})$$

$$C = \frac{10^4}{\delta} \left\{\frac{(R/R_0 - 1)}{\alpha}\right\}. \qquad (5.12\text{b})$$

RTDs have elements of solid electrical conductors (platinum, nickel, or copper wire) characterized by a positive coefficient of resistivity. That is, the resistivity is directly proportional to temperature.

Platinum is most commonly used for industrial RTDs and exclusively in precision RTDs. It is stable and relatively indifferent to its environment, resists corrosion and other chemical attack, and is not readily oxidized. It can be produced with a high degree of purity for reproducible electrical and chemical characteristics. Platinum is easily workable so it can be drawn into a fine wire, has a high melting point, and a simple, stable R–T (resistance versus temperature) relationship. But it is extremely sensitive to minute amounts of contaminating impurities and to strains, both of which alter the R–T relationship. Therefore care is taken to construct platinum RTDs (PRTs) so the sensing wire is mounted to be free of strains and contaminants. PRTs are certified by the National Institute of Standards and Technology, formerly the National Bureau of Standards, for temperatures up to 1000 deg F (537 deg C).

The R–T relationship of nickel is nonlinear. RTDs with nickel sensors are used up to 900 deg F (482 deg C). Copper has a quite linear R–T relationship, has low resistance, which is an advantage for very accurate measurements, and can be used to 300 deg F (149 deg C).

Below about 700 deg C, the best industrial RTDs are now more accurate and more reliable than any TC.

5.4.3 Thermistors

The electric circuit element in a thermistor is formed of solid semiconducting materials that are characterized by a high negative coefficient of resistivity: the resistivity decreases when the temperature increases. At any fixed temperature it behaves as any ohmic conductor. If the temperature changes, the resistance is a definite reproducible function of its temperature, typically 50,000 ohms at 100 deg F to 200 ohms at 500 deg F. Their characteristic R–T relationship can be approximated by a power function of the form

$$R = ae^{b/T} \tag{5.13}$$

where
R is the thermistor resistance at absolute temperature, T,
a, b are constants of a particular thermistor.

Use of a thermistor is based on the measurement of its resistance, and ordinary copper wire can be used throughout the circuit. So no special extension wires or reference junctions are needed. When properly aged, thermistors are quite stable, with <0.1% drift in resistance over several months. The sensors have a sensitivity to temperature up to 10 times that of usual, metal-based TCs and response times on the order of milliseconds. Their practical range of application is from the ice point to 600 deg F (315 deg C), and if the sensing current is limited, preventing I^2R heating, measurements can be made to within 0.1 deg F.

In the room temperature range, thermistors are excellent for low-cost, precise temperature measurement.

References

1. Benedict, R.P., *Fundamentals of Temperature, Pressure, and Flow Measurements*. John Wiley & Sons (1984).
2. Kerlin, T.W. and Shepard, R.L., *Industrial Temperature Measurement*. Instrument Society of America, Research Triangle Park, NC (1982).
3. Kinzie, P.A., *Thermocouple Temperature Measurement*. John Wiley & Sons (1973).
4. McGee, T.D., *Principles and Methods of Temperature Measurement*. John Wiley & Sons (1988).
5. Quinn, T.J., *Temperature*. Academic Press (1983).
6. Sandborn, V.A., *Resistance Temperature Transducers*. Metrology Press (1972).
7. Wightman, E.J., *Instrumentation in Process Control*. Butterworth & Co. Ltd (1972).
8. *Temperature, Its Measurement and Control in Science and Industry*
    Vol. 1; Ed. Q.C. Wolfe; Reinhold 1941. (Conference in New York City in November 1939)
    Vol. 2; C.M. Herzfeld; Reinhold, 1955. (Conference in Washington, DC, in October 1954)
    Vol. 3; Parts 1, 2, and 3; C.M. Herzfeld; Reinhold, 1962. (Conference in Columbus, Ohio in March 1961)
    Vol. 4; Parts 1, 2, and 3; H.H. Plumb; ISA, 1972. (Conference in Washington, DC in June, 1971)
    Vol. 5; Parts 1 and 2; J.F. Schooley; American Institute of Physics, New York, 1982.

CHAPTER 6

Process Control Theory: Overview and Fundamentals

F. Greg Shinskey

6.1 Introduction

This chapter discusses all major aspects of temperature control, both feedback and feedforward. It begins with a presentation on the purpose and also the limitations of feedback control. Economic performance criteria are presented along with the ability of feedback controllers to meet them. The separate modes of proportional, integral, derivative (PID) controllers are introduced, with recommendations as to where they are best used. Integral windup is presented, along with methods to avoid it. Model-based controllers are proposed for their performance, although robustness is a problem. Tuning recommendations are given for all controllers. Nonlinear elements common to temperature loops are then introduced, beginning with two-state and three-state controllers. Valve characteristics and actuator dynamics are then presented. The variable dynamics of heat exchangers and the steady-state instability of exothermic reactors are also considered. Cascade control can improve linearity if properly installed, or introduce nonlinearity if not; configuration is critical in determining robustness and ease of operation. Feedforward control offers order-of-magnitude improvement over feedback performance, and is widely used to control boilers and distillation columns. Dynamic compensation is an important feature, which requires tuning like a controller. The feedback controller requires careful integration with the feedforward system for optimum performance and windup protection. Decoupling, required in cases of severe loop interaction, is implemented using the methods developed for feedforward control.

F. Greg Shinskey, The Foxboro Company, Foxboro, MA 02035, USA

6.2 Regulation by Negative Feedback

Negative feedback is the principal regulating mechanism for temperature or any other measured process variable. The current value of the controlled variable c is compared with its desired value or set point r as shown in Figure 6.1, and the controller manipulates some output variable m to bring their difference, deviation e, to zero. Two blocks are shown making up the control loop: the controller, and the process block having the manipulated input. The other process block has the load q as an input, and may have steady-state and dynamic properties that differ from the first. Each block has a steady-state gain K that determines how much its output will change relative to its input in the steady state, and a dynamic gain vector $\mathbf{g}$ that determines when and how fast that change appears in the output. The vector has both magnitude and phase angle, which are functions of the frequency or period of the signal passing through.

A rising temperature will be acted on by the controller to reduce it — this is the essence of negative feedback. (The opposite action, positive feedback, will augment a deviation, causing the controlled variable to move farther away from set point.) Most controller-output devices are set to fail-safe, which means that their supply of heat to the process will stop, or supply of cooling will maximize, on loss of the control signal. Therefore, an increase in controller output will raise temperature, i.e., $K_m > 0$, in almost every installation. This requires that the controller respond to a rising controlled variable by reducing its output — the negative sign at the controlled-variable input to the controller in Figure 6.1 indicates the proper action. (Note that this may not be the case with other process control loops such as liquid-level and pH.)

Although negative feedback loops are intended to regulate, they also can develop oscillations. A rising temperature is acted on by the controller to reduce heat flow into

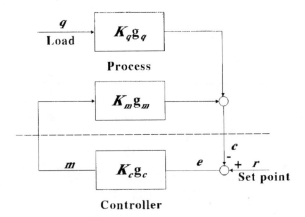

Figure 6.1 The controller tries to keep the controlled variable at set point in the face of changes in load.

the process. This action will tend to reduce temperature, but is not immediately effective owing to delays or lags in the process. If the controller moves its output too much or too fast in response to a rise in temperature, the fall that follows may be excessive, causing the controller to raise heat input again and develop a continuing cycle. The conditions responsible for producing an undamped or expanding cycle are covered adequately elsewhere [1], and so will not be developed here. Instead, this treatise concentrates on the conditions necessary for optimum control-loop performance.

6.2.1   Influences: Set Point and Load

There are two external influences on the control loop in Figure 6.1: set point and load. The set point may be repositioned from time to time on a continuous process, or on a regular basis for a batch process whose state is changed several times during a production run. Special consideration should be given to controlling batch processes to avoid temperature overshoot of large set-point changes, particularly in exothermic chemical reactors which can be inherently unstable. A third possibility is the continuous manipulation of the set point of one controller by another in cascade; the secondary or slave controller must then be responsive to the output of the primary or master controller.

Although set-point response is critical for some control loops some of the time, load response is important for most loops most of the time. Load input q in Figure 6.1 is defined as the heat load on the process that must be matched by manipulated variable m to keep temperature at set point. It can have more than one component; for example, the flow and temperature of fluid entering a heat exchanger are two components of the heat load on the exchanger. There could be more than a single stream entering as well. And its gain K_q could have either sign, as it could represent a cooling load.

Some processes — usually batch — can have states of zero load, where little if any heating or cooling is required to keep temperature at set point. A vessel whose contents are being cooled to ambient temperature prior to discharge will have zero load. A vessel or mass heated to an elevated temperature and held there will have a small load amounting to heat losses to the surroundings. For these processes, the principal demand for heating or cooling is that required to follow set-point changes. If a controller need not contend with significant load changes, then it does not require integral action.

However, if a process must operate at a given temperature under a variety of heat loads, a steady-state deviation or offset will develop proportional to the load unless integral action is used. Integration changes the controller output at a rate proportional to the deviation, and consequently will not allow the output to rest as long as a deviation exists. The particular value that the output reaches at any steady state is an indication of the load, and is ultimately developed by integrating the deviation over the course of time. But integral action has its costs, too. It tends to slow the response of the controller by introducing phase lag, and thereby to extend the period of oscillation of the loop and its settling time following a disturbance. It also is the principal contributor to overshoot of the set point, especially for the large set-point changes common to batch processes. This tendency to overshoot can be limited, as described later, but is better avoided altogether by omitting integral action from the controller where possible. But again, this is typically possible only where the load is always zero or at some other fixed point.

The load may or may not enter the process at the same point as the manipulated variable. In the case of heating or cooling by direct contact of two fluids, one being the load and the other manipulated, there is no difference in their individual temperature responses. Then $\mathbf{g}_q$ and $\mathbf{g}_m$ in Figure 6.1 will be equal, unless the valve manipulated by the controller has some significant dynamic characteristic such as an electric-motor drive (which is an integrator). Quite commonly the load and manipulated variable enter at different points in thermal processes, and therefore produce different temperature responses. In a heat exchanger, for example, a liquid passing through its tube bundle may be heated by steam condensing in its shell. Temperature will tend to respond faster to changes in liquid flow than in steam flow, owing to the extra heat capacity of the shell. Similarly, an air stream heated electrically may cool more quickly on increasing air flow than it can be heated by increasing current flow due to the heat capacity of the element.

Where there are two manipulated variables such as heating and cooling, a difference in their response speeds may be observed. Again, this would be due to differing heat capacities or points of entry into the process; each would have its own K_m and $\mathbf{g}_m$. Some controllers have two separate outputs with separate mode settings to accommodate these differences.

6.2.2 Performance Criteria: Area and Peak Height

Figure 6.2 is a response curve of an optimally tuned PID control loop responding to a step change in load, where load and manipulated variable happen to enter at the same point. Before time zero, controller output m and load q were identical, and a steady state existed. At time zero, the load was stepped downward, but because of delays and lags in the load path, some time elapsed before the temperature began to rise. A feedback controller cannot change its output until a deviation develops, and then response to its action is not immediate because of delays and lags in the path of the manipulated variable. As a result, more time elapses before it can restore the deviation to zero.

The two principal features of this typical response curve are its peak height and the integrated error or area between controlled variable c and set point r. Peak height is important where overtemperature operation could damage product, stress equipment, or start a fire. If independent automatic protection is provided against such an event, then it may shut down the process when the danger point is reached. In either case, it

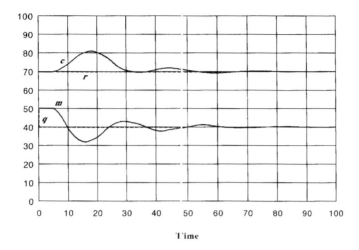

Figure 6.2 Response of a second-order process with deadtime to a step change in load under PID control.

is important that the controller minimize the peak height to avoid the costs associated with using excessive temperatures. The area between the controlled variable and set point is proportional to the excessive fuel or power required to create the excessive temperature over that span of time. Therefore integrated error represents a second important cost factor that should be minimized by proper application and tuning of the controls. Peak height and area are both proportional to the magnitude of the load change.

The response curve shown in Figure 6.2 is optimal from the aspect that the integrated absolute error (IAE) has been minimized for that particular disturbance by appropriate tuning of the controller modes. Although integrated error is the correct cost function, it cannot be minimized by controller tuning without causing oscillations to develop due to excessive loop gain. But when IAE is minimized, oscillations tend to be heavily damped. Also, because almost all of the curve lies on one side of the set point for a step load response, IAE is only slightly higher than integrated error. The ideal load–response curve has but a single, symmetrical peak, with no overshoot. The curve in Figure 6.2 has a slight overshoot, with visible second and third peaks, but its first peak is symmetrical. Yet this is about as close as a PID controller can approach the ideal curve.

The dynamic characteristics of most thermal processes can be modeled as deadtime with a primary and secondary lag. The deadtime in the load path can be observed in Figure 6.2 as the elapsed time from the introduction of the load step to the first indication of the resulting deviation. The controller's derivative action responds to the rate of change of the controlled variable. Its contribution then causes the controller output to depart from the steady state precisely at the point that the load deadtime elapses.

Without any control action at all, that is, in the open loop, the temperature would approach a new steady state at an exponentially decreasing rate, as shown by the dashed curve in Figure 6.3. The trajectory of that curve is described by the following equation:

$$c = c_0 + \Delta q K_q (1 - e^{-(t-\tau_{dq})/\tau_q}) \tag{6.1}$$

The curve is that of a step response of a first-order lag having a time constant τ_q; e is 2.718, the base of the natural logarithms, and t is time. Note that K_q is negative because temperature rises on a decrease in load. The time constant of the lag is the time required for the controlled variable to traverse 63.2% of the distance from its initial to its final steady state, following the elapse of the deadtime. If the only dynamic elements present were deadtime and one lag, the elapse of the deadtime would be featured by the sharp change in temperature shown in Figure 6.3. However, most thermal processes have at least another lag, in the heat capacity of the measuring element or refractory or some other element in the system. These secondary lags produce the smooth departure of temperature from its original steady state toward the exponential curve characteristic of the primary lag as shown in Figure 6.2.

Deadtime is usually produced by transportation of material from the point where one of its properties is changed to the point where that property is measured. It is therefore affected by the location of the temperature measuring element and the velocity of the fluid being measured. The dominant lag has a time constant equal to the heat capacity of the system divided by its maximum heat flow. However, many thermal processes may not have identifiable elements that can be associated with deadtime and two lags.

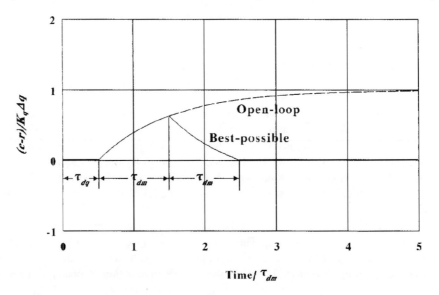

Figure 6.3 The best-possible recovery is accomplished by the second deadtime after the deviation begins.

In some, heat capacity and resistance are *distributed* throughout the process rather than lumped. This is the case with heat exchangers, furnaces, and slabs of metal. Still, these distributed systems can be modeled quite satisfactorily by a deadtime, large primary lag, and secondary lag comparable to the deadtime. This simplifies the characterization of distributed processes, and allows the use of controller tuning rules developed for second-order processes with deadtime.

6.2.3 Best-Possible and Actual Performance

Figure 6.3 shows the best-possible recovery curve for a step load change applied to a first-order process with deadtime. No control action can begin until the load deadtime elapses and a deviation appears. But before the manipulated variable can have any effect on the rising deviation, the deadtime through the manipulated path, τ_{dm}, must elapse. By this time, the deviation will have reached the peak value shown by the solid curve in Figure 6.3. The best that any feedback controller can then do is to return deviation to zero following a second elapse of τ_{dm}. This represents the absolute limit of controller performance [2]. The best-possible IAE for a step load change is the area under this curve:

$$\text{IAE}_b = |\Delta q K_q| \tau_{dm} (1 - e^{-\tau_{dm}/\tau_q}) \tag{6.2}$$

The presence of any secondary lag τ_s has no effect on IAE_b, but it does reduce peak height e_p:

$$|e_p| = \frac{\text{IAE}_b}{\tau_{dm} + \tau_s} \tag{6.3}$$

It also shifts the location of the peak, and makes IAE_b more difficult to approach with real controllers.

The response curve of Figure 6.2 has a peak height 2.2 times the best possible, and an IAE 3.56 times the best possible. If, in a given installation, this level of performance is inadequate, then something better than a PID controller will be required. A higher performance may be achieved using a model-based controller, but even its optimum tuning produces a peak height 1.75 times the best possible, and an IAE 1.91 times the best possible, on this particular process. The limits of e_p and IAE_b to feedback control are absolute. The only route to better load response is through feedforward control.

6.3   PID Controllers

The standard controller for fluid processes is the PID controller. It combines the stability of proportional action, elimination of offset that integral contributes, and the speed of a derivative in overcoming secondary lags. Although its performance cannot be as high as that of some model-based devices, it is easier to tune, and tends to be more robust. Robustness is the ability of a control loop to remain stable as process parameters (deadtime, lag, gain) change.

6.3.1 Proportional and Derivative Modes

The simplest of the PID controllers is the proportional. Its output is related to deviation as

$$m = \frac{100}{P}e + b \qquad (6.4)$$

where P is the proportional band expressed in percent, and b is its output bias, a fixed or manually adjusted setting. Instead of a proportional band, some controllers have a proportional-gain setting, which would be $G = 100/P$.

As the equation indicates, deviation will be zero only when the controller output happens to equal the bias. For a zero-load process, this relationship is acceptable, for setting the bias to zero will produce no offset in the steady state. Some controllers manipulate both heating and cooling from a single output in split range, with the heating valve opening from 50 to 100% output, and the cooling valve opening from 50 to 0% output. In this case, a zero-load process would require the bias to be set at 50%, where both valves are closed.

If the load is variable, then the controller output can be driven from the bias value only by a deviation that represents the required output change multiplied by the proportional band. The proportional-band setting required for stable control is approximately equal to $100 K_m \tau_{dm}/\tau_m$ for lag-dominant processes, where τ_m is the time constant of the primary lag in the path of the manipulated variable. If the deadtime is very short relative to the time constant, the proportional band can be set as narrow as 10% or less, in which case any offset caused by a load change may be acceptably small. For many noncritical applications on lag-dominant processes, proportional control may be adequate.

Secondary lags are quite common to thermal processes due to the distribution of heat capacity among many elements, if not simply the lag in the measuring element. The formula for the proportional band given above does not include an adjustment for a secondary lag, because such a lag exerts more of an effect over the time response of the loop than over dynamic gain. Some thermal processes, however, are characterized by a pronounced secondary lag much greater than any observable deadtime. In this case, changing the proportional band of the controller seems to have very little effect on either stability or set-point overshoot. In practice, proportional control is not particularly suitable for a two-capacity process — derivative action is needed.

A PD (proportional-plus-derivative) controller functions as

$$m = \frac{100}{P}(e + D\frac{de}{dt}) + b \tag{6.5}$$

where D is its derivative time constant. Equation (6.5) applies derivative action equally to the controlled variable and set point because it acts on deviation; some controllers apply derivative action only to the controlled variable, however, to avoid large output excursions caused by set-point adjustments. The two methods will produce different set-point responses.

A derivative function acts as a lead — the inverse of a lag. A derivative function can therefore cancel the effect of a secondary lag in the loop. Applied to two-capacity processes then, a PD controller is very effective, giving a fast response with no set-point overshoot. It is highly recommended for zero-load processes. The optimum setting for the derivative time constant is about $0.4\tau_s$ in the absence of deadtime, and about $0.6\tau_s + 0.5\tau_{dm}$ when the deadtime is comparable in value to the secondary lag. In the absence of deadtime, the proportional band may be set as narrow as 1 or 2%, sometimes even less; in its presence, the formula for setting the proportional controller given previously applies.

An ideal derivative function as shown in Eq. (6.5) would apply an increasing gain to signals of increasing frequency without limit. Because this would amplify noise excessively, derivative gain is limited in all controllers. A filter is used to reduce the high-frequency response to a gain limit typically of 10, which still gives adequate control action. Derivative action is not very useful in controlling processes dominated by deadtime, or when the controlled variable is a noisy signal. But neither of these situations is common to temperature control, so it can and should nearly always be used on temperature loops.

6.3.2 Integral Action and Windup

Adding integral action to a proportional controller produces the PI (proportional-plus-integral) controller:

$$m = \frac{100}{P}\left(e + \frac{1}{I}\int_{t_0}^{t_n} e\, dt\right) + m_0 \tag{6.6}$$

where I is the integral time constant, m_0 is the output at time t_0, and the present time is t_n. Some controllers have their integral setting in inverse time units, $1/I$, expressed in repeats (of the proportional component of output) per unit time. (Although integral-only controllers are available, they are unstable on non-self-regulating processes such as liquid level, and are not recommended for temperature control.)

Integral action is necessary for controlling temperature on variable-load processes requiring a proportional band of more than a few percent. such as heat exchangers, distillation columns, and most reactors. The PI controller is not particularly effective on lag-dominant processes, producing an IAE that is over four times the best possible, and still worse in the presence of a secondary lag. Its proportional band should be set using the same formula as a proportional controller, with integral time set at about $4\tau_{dm}$; both need to increase with any secondary lag.

Adding derivative action to a PI controller can be accomplished in two different ways. The more common PID controller has derivative and integral modes acting in series, in which case they interact with each other's setting. The noninteracting version has these two modes in parallel, so that the functions of the three modes expressed in Eqs. (6.5) and (6.6) simply add. There is not much difference in their performance except in the presence of a large secondary lag, where the noninteracting controller is more effective. Otherwise, both produce an IAE on lag-dominant processes that is about twice the best possible. They are tuned differently, however: optimum settings for the interacting controller on a lag-dominant process are $P = 108 K_m \tau_{dm}/\tau_m, I = 1.6\tau_{dm}, D = 0.6\tau_{dm}$; for the noninteracting controller, $P = 78 K_m \tau_{dm}/\tau_m, I = 1.9\tau_{dm}, D = 0.5\tau_{dm}$. Again, a secondary lag will require all three settings to increase. The response curve of Figure 6.2 was produced by an interacting controller set at $P = 120 K_m \tau_{dm}/\tau_m, I = 1.6\tau_{dm}+0.8\tau_s, D = 0.6\tau_{dm} + \tau_s$.

The principal liability of integral action is "windup," a condition caused by integrating a deviation while the control loop is open. This can take place whenever an overload causes the controller to drive its output to a limit or other constraint, or control is prevented by some obstruction such as a closed stop-valve or empty vessel. The constant of integration m_0 in Eq. (6.6) will reach some limit, and the controller output will not come away from that limit until the deviation reverses sign, that is, as the set point is crossed. Overshoot is therefore unavoidable, unless logic is applied to change the constant of integration during the open-loop condition, or derivative action is applied with a time constant greater than the integral time constant. The former method is described for several different applications in ref. 1. Both methods may require some compromises to the controller settings to prevent overshoot altogether, which may reduce its responsiveness to load changes.

6.3.3 Digital Control

Implementing PID or other control algorithms digitally introduces two features that can interfere with control: sampling and limited resolution. Digital algorithms do not operate continuously but repetitively, their execution separated by regular intervals known as the sample interval. The derivative operator d appearing in Eqs. (6.5) and (6.6) is replaced by the difference operator Δ, with dt becoming the sample interval Δt. During each sample interval, the control loop is open. This adds a delay to the control loop equivalent to half the sample interval (the average age of each sample), which must be added to the process deadtime in estimates of controller preformance and optimum settings. Sampling always detracts from the performance of a temperature controller, and so Δt should be minimized for best results.

Sampling has a further impact over the gain of the derivative mode, which is limited thereby to $D/\Delta t$. Consider the example of PID control of a typical heat exchanger having a deadtime of about 8 s. According to the tuning rules already given, the derivative time constant should be set at about 4.5 s. To provide a derivative gain of 10 then, the sample interval should be < 0.5 s. If the controller already has a derivative filter establishing a gain limit of 10, then the effective gain limit will be reduced to 5 by the sampling interval, for the effective gain limit is the reciprocal of the sum of the reciprocals of sampler and filter gain limits.

Measured temperature is converted to digits in an analog-to-digital converter of some type. A given temperature range is then represented by a discrete number of bits or counts, each of which is the finest gradation that the controller can act on. An 8-bit converter will break up the temperature range into 2^8 or 256 counts; 10 bits equal 1024 counts, and 12 bits are 4096 counts. The zero elevation of a typical signal is 20% (e.g., 4–20 ma representing 0–100%) so that the useful span of a 12-bit converter is 4000 counts.

A 4000-count span gives each count 0.025% of full scale. Although this would appear to be fine enough for smooth control, there are applications where it is not. For a typical stirred-tank reactor with cascade control (as described in more detail later), this level of resolution is inadequate. Given measurement spans of 100 deg C for each temperature, the controllers will be tuned with about a 20% proportional band each, which is a gain of 5. A change in primary temperature will then be acted on by a derivative gain of 10 and two proportional gains of 5 in moving the valves. The smallest measurement change of 0.025% is then multiplied by 250, causing the valves to move a minimum of 6.25% each time the temperature changes. The record of valve motion then becomes a series of 6.25% spikes or multiples thereof, keeping the loop from coming to rest. Dynamic filtering introduced between the controllers to attenuate the spikes also defeats the derivative action. Nonlinear filtering has been used to reduce loop gain for small deviations only, and this is effective. However, the preferred solution is to use a 16-bit converter.

6.4   Model-Based Controllers

A model-based controller is constructed from lags and deadtime, as a model of the process dynamic elements. The theory is that the negative-feedback loop through the process can be canceled by an identical positive-feedback loop through the model, preventing oscillations even with a controller gain that would be high enough to sustain them in a PID loop. Figure 6.4 shows two of many possible ways to implement this strategy: above is a standard interacting PID controller modified by placing a deadtime block in series with the integral time constant in the feedback loop which produces

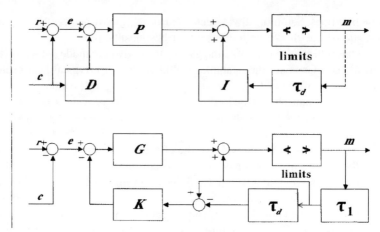

Figure 6.4 The PIDτ_d controller (*above*) is functionally equivalent to the Smith Predictor (*below*).

integral action; below is a variation of a Smith Predictor, which has two feedback loops within it.

In the Smith Predictor, a positive-feedback loop contains deadtime τ_d, lag τ_1, and gain K, conceptually intended to match process parameters τ_{dm}, τ_m, and K_m, thereby cancelling its negative-feedback loop. The only remaining feedback loop is then the negative one in the controller, containing lag τ_1 alone. This allows controller gain G to be set very high, giving performance on deadtime-dominant processes that approaches the best-possible. The PIDτ_d controller devised by the author actually has an identical load response to the Smith if its derivative gain is equal to G. It is preferred over the Smith in being a simple modification to a commercial controller, and being much easier to tune.

6.4.1 The PIDτ_d Controller

The PIDτ_d controller can be matched to the process parameters by setting $\tau_d = \tau_{dm}$, $D = \tau_m$, and $P = 100K_m$, with I set at 0. The load response resulting from these settings with either this controller or the Smith approaches the best possible only for deadtime-dominant processes, however [2]. Although proponents of model-based control do not advocate intentionally mismatching controller and process, this practice can improve performance with careful tuning. Model-based controllers are not configured to match a non-self-regulating or steady-state-unstable process, and so are not ordinarily recommended to control them. Yet the author has found that they can outperform PID controllers on these processes also, if tuned properly. The PIDτ_d controller can therefore be recommended for temperature control of lag-dominant processes, and even exothermic reactors, where its higher proportional gain can extend stability considerably.

Applied to a first-order lag-dominant process, controller and process deadtimes should be matched, with the other settings as follows: $I = 0.17\tau_{dm}$, $D = 1.3\tau_{dm}$, and $P = 100K_m\tau_{dm}/\tau_m$. If a secondary lag is present, I and τ_d should increase directly with its value, with a smaller increase in D; the proportional band may actually be decreased at the same time. A PIDτ_d controller applied to the process of Figure 6.2 would be optimally tuned with the time settings above augmented by about $0.5\tau_s$, and P about one-fourth lower. As mentioned earlier, the PIDτ_d controller can reduce the peak of the response curve in Figure 6.2 from 2.2 to 1.75 times the best possible, and IAE from 3.56 to 1.91IAE$_b$. It is equally effective on multiple-lag and distributed processes, although they have no inherent deadtime.

In the presence of noise on the controlled variable that would preclude the use of derivative action, it may be set to zero, giving a PIτ_d controller. Although considerably less effective without derivative action, it is nonetheless much more effective than the PI controller on a lag-dominant process. It should be tuned as follows: $\tau_d = 1.55\tau_{dm}$, $I = 2.15\tau_{dm}$, and $P = 65K_m\tau_{dm}/\tau_m$. With these settings it will yield an IAE about twice as high as the same controller with derivative action, but still one-third less than a PI controller. It is not particularly effective in the presence of a secondary lag, but noise is not as common there, either.

6.4.2 Performance and Robustness

The performance of model-based controllers is their principal attraction over PID controllers. Reduction in peak height and IAE were noted above. Other benefits include elimination of oscillation and reduced settling time following a load change. Also, any observable oscillation has a noticeably shorter period than with PID control. For example, the period of oscillation of a temperature loop under PI control is about $6\tau_{dm}$, under proportional control $4\tau_{dm}$, PD and PID control $3\tau_{dm}$, and under PIDτ_d control it is only $2\tau_{dm}$.

Set-point response of model-based controllers is also better than that of PID controllers, giving faster response with minimal overshoot. A PID controller specifically tuned to eliminate set-point overshoot will not respond optimally to load changes, but a model-based controller responds equally well to both disturbances.

Improved performance comes at a price, however. Model-based controllers are not as robust as their PID counterparts [2]. Robustness is the property of a closed loop that keeps it stable as process parameters change. A typical PI loop will allow process gain or deadtime to double before the loop reaches its limit of stability, indicated by a uniform oscillation; and no stability limit is encountered with a reduction in gain or deadtime in any amount. A PID controller has a somewhat narrower stability margin, allowing a 40–50% increase in deadtime or gain before going unstable; again, there is no stability limit on the decreasing side.

Model-based controllers will accommodate a similar increase in process gain, but are quite sensitive to a mismatch between process and controller deadtimes, in either direction. A deadtime mismatch places the positive- and negative-feedback loops out of phase, so that a disturbance is not completely cancelled, but leaves a residual pulse passing through both loops. If there is insufficient filtering to overcome the high controller gain, the residual pulse can be replicated each time through the loop, growing into a pulse train and finally a high-frequency oscillation. This is a real danger with first-order and deadtime-dominant processes, which is why filtering is always available in model-based controllers. Fortunately, thermal processes tend to be second-order lag-dominant, and therefore are less likely to fall into high-frequency instability.

However, model-based control of temperature is still somewhat sensitive to deadtime mismatch, again in either direction, so that there is no safe or fallback direction for the controller settings. If oscillations having a shorter period than $2\tau_{dm}$ are observed in the controller output, they are caused by excessive controller deadtime. Too little controller deadtime will result in overshoot and an extended period of oscillation. But the robustness of the PIDτ_d controller on thermal processes is felt to be sufficient to recommend its use, especially in light of the performance improvement it provides over PID control.

6.5 Nonlinear Elements

Most control loops contain one or more nonlinear elements, and temperature loops are no exception. The temperature measuring element is not usually sufficiently nonlinear to pose a problem to the control loop, but valve characteristics can be. Many common thermal processes such as boilers and heat exchangers also have steady-state and dynamic properties varying with flow. Further, the variation of the rate of a chemical reaction with temperature can cause the reactor to be steady-state unstable.

Some of these nonlinear characteristics can be compensated, while the rest must simply be accommodated. But sometimes nonlinear controllers are used not for the purpose of improving control, but of reducing the cost of the control system. This subject with its ramifications is covered first.

6.5.1 On–Off Controllers

On–off controllers are used to manipulate two-state devices such as electric heaters and solenoid valves, and also three-state devices such as motor-driven valves. The last introduce an integrator into the loop (the motor) and are covered after two-state control.

The on–off controller switches abruptly between states, one of which tends to drive the controlled variable up and the other to drive it down. The load must lie somewhere between these two limits for control to be achieved. But because neither output state balances the load, no controlled steady state can be reached. Undamped oscillations will result having a natural period τ_n of at least $4\tau_{dm}$ and an amplitude of about

$K_m\tau_n/2\pi\tau_m$. If the load is not centered between the two output states, then the rising and falling rates will be unequal, increasing the period. The resulting temperature cycle will assume a saw-tooth appearance and will not be centered about the set point.

Any on–off controller requires a measurable deviation to change states, introducing deadband or hysteresis into the loop. This will increase the amplitude of the cycle from the above estimate by an amount equal to the deadband, and the period will also increase proportionately. From this standpoint, it would be desirable to minimize the deadband; however, any noise on the measurement or electrical feedback could cause the controller to chatter between the two states as zero deviation is crossed. As a consequence, enough deadband should be introduced into the controller to overcome this tendency, accepting the accompanying increase in amplitude and period of oscillation.

Derivative action is often added to on–off temperature controllers by connecting a small resistance element to the controller output. In heating faster that the process itself, the element can warm the temperature sensor enough to turn off the heat before the true process temperature reaches set point, thereby avoiding overshoot and also shortening the period and amplitude of the cycle.

If the ratio of process deadtime to time constant is quite small, the amplitude of the temperature oscillation may not be objectionable. If this is not the case, however, a time-proportioning or duty-cycle controller can be used, which switches between the output states at a selected cycle time τ_c that is shorter than τ_n, and with a duty-cycle proportional to the deviation. This will reduce the amplitude of the temperature oscillation by the ratio τ_c/τ_n, if the proportional band is tuned properly. The controller essentially mimics the proportional algorithm of Eq. (6.4), with m being the percent of the time that the output is in the energized state (percent duty). The rules given for tuning a proportional controller apply; offset will result whenever the load does not equal the bias.

A three-state controller can be used for manipulating two two-state devices such as a heater and a fan. A deadzone must exist around zero deviation, where neither device is energized. This arrangement can work well for zero-load processes which must only follow set-point changes. The more common use of a three-state controller is to drive a bidirectional motor stroking a valve or damper. Again, a deadzone is required to avoid energizing both motor windings simultaneously.

A motor is an integrator, as the position of its shaft varies with time while it is energized. If the controller receives a valve-position feedback signal, then it is in effect a valve positioner. But without any such feedback loop, the integrating characteristic of the motor adds 90 degrees of phase shift to the temperature control loop, producing unstable behavior. A time-proportioning controller used to drive a motorized valve becomes in effect an integrating controller, whose integral time is the stroking time of the valve multiplied by $P/100$. This loop will not produce an offset greater than the sum of the deadzone and deadband, with load changes. Although acceptable as a flow controller, it is sluggish and unresponsive in a temperature loop.

A better solution to the motorized-valve problem is the addition of derivative action to the controller. This is accomplished by connecting a first-order lag from the output to the input of the controller in a negative-feedback loop as shown in Figure 6.5. In the absence of an integrating valve motor, the controller becomes a PD device, with the time constant of the lag acting as the derivative setting, and the feedback gain as the proportional-band setting as shown. This configuration can be used for PD control of one or two two-state devices. In the presence of the integrating motor, however, it becomes a PI controller, with integral time I as the lag time constant D; the true proportional band then becomes $(P/100)(\tau_v/D)$, where τ_v is the time for the valve motor to travel full stroke. The device tunes as a standard PI controller (with the above corrections), but its performance is reduced by the deadzone, deadband, and limited valve speed.

6.5.2 Valve Characteristics

Valves, like other elements, have both steady-state and dynamic characteristics. Their steady-state characteristic relates flow delivered to stem position, whereas the dynamics are associated with the actuator, one type of which was described previously.

There are three basic types of steady-state valve characteristic: linear, equal-percentage, and quick-opening, with the last not particularly useful for temperature control. The linear valve has a constant gain (change in flow per increment of stroke), but only under conditions of constant pressure drop. In many installations, pressure drop across the valve is not constant, but varies inversely with flow. This is the case of a gas valve supplying fuel from a header to a burner. As firing rate is increased, the burner backpressure rises, reducing pressure drop across the valve. Each increment in valve opening then produces a smaller increase in fuel flow to the burner. Thus a linear valve may appear to have a nonlinear installed characteristic.

The equal-percentage valve is logarithmic in nature, with its gain (change in flow per increment of stroke) increasing directly proportional to delivered flow. Its rangeability is its ratio of maximum to minimum controllable flow, typically falling between 30 and 100; this also affects the shape of the characteristic curve, as the valve gain is

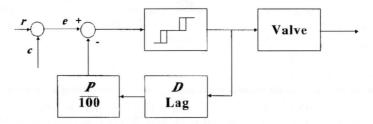

Figure 6.5 The feedback loop adds proportional and derivative action to this three-state controller.

its delivered flow multiplied by the natural logarithm of the rangeability. When an equal-percentage valve is installed in a variable pressure-drop situation such as the fuel-gas valve above, its installed characteristic becomes more linear. Therefore equal-percentage valves are often recommended for throttling fuel. Butterfly and ball valves have inherently equal-percentage characteristics, whereas plug cocks tend to be linear.

Friction in the stem packing of a valve can resist the force of the actuator enough to alter the relationship between the position of the stem and the signal to the pneumatic actuator. Whenever the control signal changes direction, the stem tends to stall until enough force is developed to overcome the friction in the new direction. The deadband produced between increasing and decreasing paths acts as a dynamic lag between the control signal and stem position, but one that is a function of signal size rather than frequency or period. Small reversals of direction may produce no stem motion at all, which can cause the control loop to cycle slowly about set point. In a temperature loop, deadband can cause the period of oscillation to increase as its amplitude falls. The best way to overcome deadband is by closing the loop around the valve, either with a mechanical valve-positioner or a flow controller.

6.5.3 Flow-Variable Process Parameters

A simple energy balance around a steam-heated exchanger reveals the variable-gain nature of heat transfer. Consider a liquid flowing at rate F and specific heat C being raised in temperature from T_1 to T_2 by condensing steam at rate S and latent heat ΔH:

$$T_2 = T_1 + \frac{S \Delta H}{FC} \tag{6.7}$$

The gain of controlled temperature T_2 with respect to manipulated flow S varies inversely with liquid flow F. In other words, the smaller the liquid flow, the greater the temperature rise a given steam flow will produce. This characteristic is common not only to heat exchangers, but also to direct-contact heaters, and boilers as well, which are exceptionally hard to control at low production rates.

Compensation for this gain variation can be as simple as using an equal-percentage steam valve. Its gain varies directly with steam flow to offset the process gain which varies inversely with liquid flow. Any significant variation in temperature rise will, however, alter their flow ratio and affect loop gain.

Process deadtime and time constant also change in inverse proportion to liquid flow. Because the optimum proportional-band setting of the controller is a function of their ratio, it will not be affected. But the integral and the derivative settings should both be proportional to deadtime, and therefore will not be optimally tuned as flow varies. Integral time should be set for the lowest expected flow, and derivative time for the highest, unless the controller settings can be adapted as a function of flow.

6.5.4 Cascade Configurations

Cascade control consists in a primary or master controller setting the set point of a secondary or slave controller, as illustrated by the control system for an exothermic reactor shown in Figure 6.6. Each controller has its own controlled variable, but only the secondary manipulates a valve. Both controlled variables are affected by the manipulated flow, with the secondary having a faster response than the primary. The primary controlled variable is to be held at a fixed set point, whereas the secondary is adjusted as necessary to follow changes in load. Cascade control is used to reject disturbances originating within the secondary loop, and to speed the response of the primary loop by closing a loop around the secondary dynamic elements.

The most common secondary loop is the flow loop. Because its dynamic response is so much faster than temperature, cascading to flow has no noticeable effect on the response of the temperature loop, except in the presence of valve deadband, where it is quite helpful. The flow loop is useful in keeping supply-pressure disturbances from affecting temperature; however, it also removes the effects of the valve characteristic as well, which may or may not be desired. But be certain that the flow measurement is linear — use of an orifice meter without linearization will cause the gain of the temperature loop to vary inversely with load, approaching infinity as the load approaches zero! Temperature controllers on heat exchangers and endothermic (heat-absorbing) reactors sometimes set shell steam pressure in cascade, a very effective configuration.

The temperature-on-temperature cascade system of Figure 6.6 is used primarily on exothermic (heat-producing) reactors because of their difficult nature. They must be

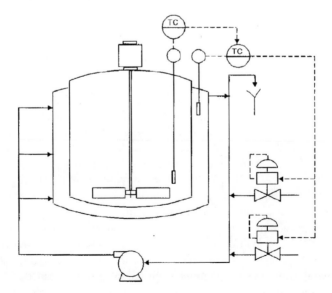

Figure 6.6 Reactor temperature is controlled by setting coolant outlet temperature in cascade.

heated by steam or hot liquid to reaction temperature, and then cooled once the reaction begins, requiring the two valves shown. By using the coolant return temperature as the secondary controlled variable, the cooling system is removed from the primary loop, thereby improving its response — the results are better than when the coolant inlet temperature is used. The primary loop is linear, in that heat-transfer rate is directly proportional to the difference between the two controlled temperatures, regardless of their difference. The gain of the secondary loop is not constant, however, in that the heat-removal rate is proportional to the product of coolant flow and temperature rise, the latter varying with both primary set point and heat load. Neither a linear nor equal-percentage valve compensates correctly for this nonlinearity as it lies between the two valve characteristics. Yet the nonlinearity is better contained in the secondary loop than in the primary, due to its faster response.

A marked improvement in cascade control has been achieved by using the secondary temperature as feedback to the integral function of the primary controller. Examine how integration is achieved in the PIDτ_d controller in Figure 6.4: the output is fed back positively through the deadtime and integral time constant. Without the deadtime, this is the standard structure of many interacting PID controllers. The connection represented by the dashed line in the figure can be broken to stop integration and thereby prevent windup. In the recommended cascade configuration, the secondary controlled variable is connected to this feedback input, rather than using the output of the primary controller. In the steady state, these two signals will be identical, if the secondary controller has integral action, and therefore the primary controller will integrate normally. If the secondary controller cannot respond to set-point changes, however, either because it is in manual or at some limit, the feedback signal will not equal the primary controller output, and it will stop integrating. This protects the primary controller against windup, and allows it to remain in automatic all the time.

An additional benefit is improved response to load changes. The entire secondary loop, including the valve and heat-transfer surface, is now within the integral path of the primary controller. This delays integration until the secondary temperature responds, much like the deadtime provided in the PIDτ_d controller. The primary integral time may be shortened considerably, even shorter than the primary derivative time and the secondary integral time; these settings will reduce the period of oscillation and the overshoot to set-point changes. An added benefit is the insensitivity of this configuration to changes in the process primary lag. During experiments on a batch reactor by the author, neither controller required retuning when the size of the batch or the heat-transfer area was changed by a factor of two.

6.6 Feedforward Control

For processes where temperature must be controlled precisely but load disturbances are frequent, even the best-possible feedback control may not be adequate. This is the case for controlling steam-superheat temperature in boilers, boiling-point rise in evaporators, and product cut-point temperatures in distillation columns. Feedforward control is, in principle, capable of perfect control, bypassing the limitations of feedback control. Load sources are measured and converted into equivalent values of the manipulated variable, and if the calculations are both accurate and timely, load variations can be completely cancelled.

Figure 6.7 shows how this is done: load q is operated on by feedforward steady-state and dynamic gains K_f and $\mathbf{g}_f$ to calculate the cancelling value of m. For cancellation to take place, K_f must equal K_m/K_q, and $\mathbf{g}_f$ must equal $\mathbf{g}_m/\mathbf{g}_q$. Typically the steady-state and dynamic compensators are implemented separately. If the steady-state calculation is in error, then a load change will produce an offset proportional to that error, unless adjustment is made by a feedback controller. (Although Figure 6.7 shows both feedforward and feedback control, the latter may not be present if an on-line measurement of the controlled variable is not available.) If dynamic compensation is inaccurate, the controlled variable may deviate from set point temporarily following a load change, but eventually will return. If the load and manipulated variable enter the process at the same point, dynamic compensation may not be necessary.

6.6.1 Steady-State Models

The heat exchanger described by Eq. (6.7) is a candidate for feedforward control. The steady-state feedforward model is simply the solution of the energy balance in terms of the manipulated variable, steam flow:

$$S = \frac{FC}{\Delta H}(T_2^* - T_1) \tag{6.8}$$

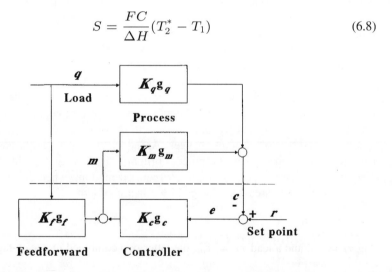

Figure 6.7 The Feedforward block converts measured changes in load into cancelling changes in the manipulated variable.

The asterisk attached to T_2 in Eq. (6.8) designates it as the exit-temperature set point, and *not* the measured variable, which if used in the feedforward calculation would form a positive-feedback loop. There are two components of load here: flow F and inlet temperature T_1. If the latter does not change appreciably or rapidly, it could be left out of the calculation, leaving a ratio system where S is set proportional to F, with their ratio adjusted to produce the desired temperature rise. Any changes to T_1 or T_2^*, however, will require a readjustment to the ratio. If Eq. (6.8) is completely implemented, then adjustment for those inputs is automatic.

Observe that this steady-state feedforward calculation does not fit the mold of the linear representation of Figure 6.7. The controlled process is in fact nonlinear, which was already pointed out. Equation (6.8) is called a *bilinear* equation: steam flow is linear with liquid flow for a constant temperature rise, and linear with temperature rise for a constant liquid flow. The gain K_f for each load input varies with the other load input. For this process, the junction where the load and manipulated variables are combined to produce the controlled variable is not a summing junction, but a divider. For proper feedforward compensation, then, the junction at the output of the feedforward block should not be a summer but a multiplier. Temperature control loops are nearly all nonlinear in some respect; therefore, it is less confusing to stay with the energy-balance model than to try to fit the control system to some preordained mold.

To maximize the accuracy of the feedforward calculation, a steam-flow controller should be used, rather than simply sending the output of the calculation to a valve. In this way, the valve characteristics and variable pressure drop will have no effect on performance. The flow measurement could be a nonlinear orifice meter if the liquid flowmeter is as well, and the temperature input is left out, but they should both be linear for best results.

6.6.2 Dynamic Compensation

If deadtimes τ_{dm} and τ_{dq} are not matched, then simultaneous changes in q and m will produce a temporary deviation, in the direction favored by the shorter deadtime. If lags τ_m and τ_q are not matched, then the velocity with which the deviation begins will be favored by the shorter time constant. The integrated error developed by simultaneous step changes is a function of the difference between the summed dynamic elements on the two sides of the process, that is, $\tau_m + \tau_{dm} - \tau_q - \tau_{dq}$. Feedforward control can produce zero integrated error following a load change by applying a proportional integrated difference between the input and output of the dynamic compensator.

The dynamic-compensating function $\mathbf{g}_q/\mathbf{g}_m$ requires a deadtime $\tau_d = \tau_{dq} - \tau_{dm}$, a lag $\tau_l = \tau_q$, and a lead $\tau_L = \tau_m$, the latter two combined in a lead–lag compensator. Only a positive deadtime difference can be compensated, obviously, and lead–lag ratios should be kept at 10 or less for the same reason given for limiting derivative gain in controllers, as it is the same basic function. In some instances, this may make exact dynamic compensation impossible. However, integrated error may still be driven to zero by setting

$$\tau_d + \tau_l - \tau_L = \tau_{dq} + \tau_q - \tau_{dm} - \tau_m \qquad (6.9)$$

Once settings have been found producing an integrated error of zero, further adjustments may be made to reduce the peak height and IAE. A detailed set of tuning rules is provided in Chapter 7 of ref. 1.

The individual load components may each have their own particular dynamic response. Therefore, it is advisable to locate a dynamic compensator at each load input, before combination with other components or feedback.

The lags and deadtime in the heat exchanger vary inversely with flow. This will make it impossible to tune the dynamic compensator perfectly for all loads, unless its settings can be programmed as a function of measured flow. However, the dynamic gain of the lead–lag unit, which is equal to the ratio of the settings, will remain correct for all loads.

6.6.3 Adding Feedback

Most feedforward compensators will be coordinated with a feedback loop as indicated in Figure 6.7. This eliminates the possibility of offset due to the inevitable errors in the steady-state calculation. The combination of both flowmeter errors and neglected heat losses could be 2% or more. Without feedforward compensation, the feedback controller would have to move its output the full extent of the load change, but with it, only the extent of the error in the feedforward calculation. Thus feedforward is capable of reducing the integrated error resulting from load changes by a factor of 50.

If there is no steady-state error in the calculations, the output of the feedback controller need not change at all, which means that integrated error will be zero, even without dynamic compensation. A dynamic imbalance without compensation would produce a large transient deviation on one side of set point, which the feedback controller would integrate, producing an equal-area transient on the other side. Proper dynamic compensation can reduce both to nearly zero.

It is important to connect the feedback controller to the proper point in the feedforward calculation. Generally the best point to introduce feedback is the place where the controlled variable (set point) appears in the equation. Thus, the output of the feedback controller should take the place of T_2^* in Eq. (6.8). In this location, it is multiplied by liquid flow, which compensates exactly for the inverse variation of process gain with flow pointed out in Eq. (6.7). Again, use the energy-balance model rather than trying to fit the system into an arbitrary linear configuration. In addition, dynamic compensators should be kept out of the feedback loop.

Windup protection for the feedback controller is provided by a method similar to that used for cascade systems. However, the secondary controlled variable (here steam flow) cannot be fed back directly to the temperature controller, because its output does not represent steam flow. These two signals are not the same in the steady state, and integration will not proceed properly unless the controller has a signal equal to its own output fed back. The proper feedback signal must be calculated by solving the feedforward equation backwards. The controller output would take the place of T_2^* in Eq. (6.8). Then that equation must be solved for the same term as a function of measured steam flow and the load components. The equation that would be used in this application is Eq. (6.7). In the case where T_1 is left out of the feedforward calculation, liquid flow F would simply be multiplied by the output of the feedback controller to set steam flow. Then the backcalculation is just as simple: measured steam flow would be divided by F to produce the feedback signal.

6.6.4 Decoupling Methods

Many temperature loops exist in a multivariable setting such as a boiler. One manipulated variable may then affect more than one controlled variable, resulting in loop interaction. Each controller should manipulate that variable that has most influence over its controlled variable, and controllers must be tuned when all are in automatic for multiloop stability.

Even when these rules are followed, however, loop interaction could still be severe, for example, in the case where two manipulated variables exert equal influence over a controlled variable. The best remedy for this level of interaction is decoupling — combining manipulated variables in such a way that cancels their natural interaction.

Decoupling can actually be implemented following the same method as feedforward control. Their only difference is that in the typical feedforward application, the disturbing variable is an independent load variable, whereas in the case of loop interaction, it is manipulated by another controller. But the cancellation of a disturbance introduced by another controller is no different than cancelling the effect of a load change. The same steady-state modelling and dynamic compensation should be used as described for feedforward control. For best results, the disturbance input to a decoupler should be a measured process variable rather than a controller output. In this way, the decoupler will work even if the disturbing controller is in manual or constrained. Initialization is far easier then, too.

References
1. Shinskey, F.G., *Process Control Systems*, 3rd edit. McGraw-Hill (1988).
2. Shinskey, F.G., *Chemical Eng.* **97**, 12, 99 (1990).

Notation

Symbols:

b Output bias
c Controlled variable

C — Heat capacity
d — Derivative operator
D — Derivative time constant
e — Deviation, 2.718
e_p — Peak deviation
F — Flow rate
g — Dynamic gain vector
G — Proportional gain
H — Enthalpy
K — Steady-state gain
m — Manipulated variable
P — Proportional band
q — Process load
r — Set point
S — Steam flow
t — Time
T — Temperature
Δ — Difference
τ — Time constant
τ_c — Cycle time
τ_d — Deadtime
τ_n — Natural period
τ_s — Secondary lag
τ_L — Lead
τ_l — Lag
τ_1 — Lag in Smith Predictor

Subscripts:

b — Best possible
f — Feedforward
m — Manipulated
n — Now
p — Peak
q — Load
0 — Initial
1 — Inlet
2 — Outlet

Superscripts:

$*$ — Set point

CHAPTER 7

Recursive Identification, Autotuning, and Adaptive Control

Guy A. Dumont

7.1 Introduction

This chapter is a brief introduction to the techniques of recursive identification and adaptive control. We first discuss the tuning problem. This leads to the introduction of adaptive controllers as a combination of a recursive identifier and a fixed structure controller. We then present the principles of least-squares and maximum-likelihood parameter estimation. Recursive versions of those methods are then introduced. Adhoc modifications for tracking time-varying parameters are presented. Both indirect and direct adaptive control strategies are then reviewed. Because of their industrial applicability, we then dwell on adaptive predictive controllers. Next we discuss various parameterization problems, particularly in the presence of varying time delays. Various automatic tuning techniques for proportional, integral, derivative (PID) controllers are then discussed, some of which form the basis of successful commercial products. The latter are then briefly reviewed, together with some typical industrial applications. Finally, we draw conclusions and highlight some of the future potential developments in this field.

7.1.1 What Is Adaptive Control?

An adaptive controller is able to change its behavior in response to changes in the process dynamics, by automatically adjusting its parameters. This definition implies a

---

Guy A. Dumont, Department of Electrical Engineering, University of British Columbia, 2385 East Mall, Vancouver, B.C. Canada V6T 1Z4

fixed-structure controller, with variable parameters. In this sense, adaptive control is one way of dealing with parametric uncertainty. Adaptive control theory essentially deals with finding parameter adjustment algorithms that guarantee global stability and convergence.

7.1.2 Why Use Adaptive Control?

There are essentially two main situations that may call for the use of adaptive control. The first is the control of systems with unknown dynamics. The second is the control of systems with time-varying dynamics. If, however, the dynamics change with the operating conditions in a known fashion, then one should use *gain scheduling*, as shown in Figure 7.1.

If the use of a fixed or a gain-scheduled controller cannot achieve a satisfactory compromise between *robustness* and *performance*, then, and *only then*, adaptive control is an attractive alternative. *In any event one should always use the simplest technique that satisfies the specifications!*

7.2 The Tuning Problem

The typical PID controller requires the setting of three parameters. This is the *tuning* problem. The right tuning constants depend on:

1. The process dynamics.
2. The disturbance dynamics.

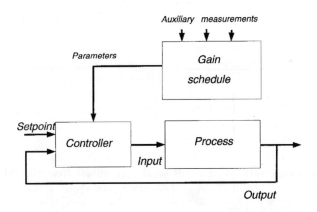

Figure 7.1   Gain scheduling scheme.

3. The control objective.
4. The modelling uncertainty.

7.2.1 Classical Methods

All controllers are described by a set of gains whose numerical values have to be set. The setting of these values is called the *tuning problem*, and is of fundamental practical importance. For controllers such as the minimum-variance and the Dahlin controllers, once a model for the process has been identified, the design procedure gives the controllers and its parameters values. Thus, in practice, the main tuning problem encountered by control engineers is for the PID controller, for which there exists a plethora of methods. The primary method for tuning PID controllers is due to Ziegler and Nichols [1]. It is based on the fact that for many processes under feedback control by a proportional controller, increasing the gain will eventually drive the loop to instability. On the way to instability, the process output will start oscillating, with decreasing damping. On the verge of instability, the oscillations will not be damped, and thus will have a constant amplitude in time; this is what Ziegler and Nichols call the *ultimate cycle*. This corresponds to a particular point of the frequency response of the system, known as the *critical point*. The corresponding controller gain K_u and the period of oscillation T_u are then used to compute the tuning constants according to the rules presented in Chapter 6. Many other tuning methods are available. A popular method is the Cohen-Coon, or process reaction curve method, based on features of the step response of the system. A variant of the Ziegler–Nichols method is the quarter-decay response method, where the tuning constants are adjusted so that the oscillations of the system decrease by a factor of four every period.

7.2.2 Model-Based Methods

Some other methods are based on a performance index, using the difference between the actual and the desired response, that is numerically minimized to yield optimal tuning constants. The performance indices used are the Integrated-Square-Error (ISE), the Integrated-Absolute-Error (IAE) and the Integrated-Time-Multiplied-Absolute-Error (ITAE). These methods require a parametric model of the process, generally in transfer function form. When a model of the process noise is also available, then tuning constants for the regulation problem can be obtained using these optimization-based techniques. Also, for specific models, a pole placement or minimum-variance control design will yield a controller from the PID family, or a Dahlin controller. For example, the minimum-variance controller for a first-order-plus-dead-time (FOPDT) process corrupted by first-order integrated-moving-average (IMA) noise is a Dahlin controller. A PID can be tuned from a pole-placement design using a second-order model. It is also possible to tune the PID controller in the frequency domain, from marginal stability considerations.

Example — Level Control

Consider the system given by:

$$\underbrace{y(t)}_{\text{noise}} = \frac{K}{1-B} \underbrace{u(t-1)}_{\text{input}} + \underbrace{w(t)}_{\text{noise}} \tag{7.1}$$

where B is the backward shift operator, i.e., $By(t) = y(t-1)$. If the noise is described by:

$$\underbrace{w(t)}_{\text{noise}} = \frac{1-cB}{1-B} \underbrace{e(t)}_{\text{white noise}} \tag{7.2}$$

then, the minimum-variance controller is:

$$u(t) = \frac{1-c}{K}(y_{sp} - y(t)) \tag{7.3}$$

This is a proportional controller with $K_c = (1-c)/K$.

If the noise is described by:

$$\underbrace{w(t)}_{\text{noise}} = \frac{1-cB}{(1-B)^2} \underbrace{e(t)}_{\text{white noise}} \tag{7.4}$$

then, the minimum-variance controller is:

$$u(t) = \frac{(2-c)-B}{K(1-B)}(y_{sp} - y(t)) \tag{7.5}$$

This is a PI regulator with $K_c = (2-c)/K$ and $T_i = (2-c)/(1-c)$. In the presence of dead time, a model-based method will not give a PID controller, but a Dahlin controller, a Smith predictor, or a minimum-variance controller.

As a prologue to adaptive control, it is important to realize that model-based tuning consists of two important steps:

1. Modelling of the process dynamics.
2. Model-based control design.

The first step is also known as the identification stage, and is now discussed in more details.

7.3 Recursive Identification

Very often, first-principles modelling is not possible, or not reliable enough. The alternative is then to perturb one of the process inputs, and based on the observed behavior, to fit a simplified linear model (e.g., a transfer function) that best describes that behavior. This is the field of process or system identification [2]. The method most used in industry, the step response method, is the simplest, but also the least reliable of all.

7.3.1 Identification Methods

7.3.1.1 Least-Squares Method

Within the control engineering community, the most popular method is the least-squares method. Let the dynamic system be described by

$$y(t) = \sum_{i=1}^{n} -a_i y(t-i) + \sum_{i=1}^{n} -q_i u(t-i) + w(t) \qquad (7.6)$$

where $u(t)$ and $y(t)$ are, respectively the input and ouput of the plant and $w(t)$ is the process noise. Defining

$$\begin{aligned} \theta^T &= [a_1 \cdots a_n q_1 \cdots q_n] \\ x^T &= [-y(t) \cdots - y(t-n) u(t-1) \cdots u(t-n)] \end{aligned} \qquad (7.7)$$

the system above can be written as

$$y(t) = x^T(t)\theta + w(t) \qquad (7.8)$$

With N observations, the data can be put in the following compact form:

$$Y = X\theta + W \qquad (7.9)$$

where

$$\begin{aligned} Y^T &= [y(1) \cdots y(N)] \\ W^T &= [w(1) \cdots w(N))] \\ X &= \begin{vmatrix} x^T(1) \\ \vdots \\ x^T(N) \end{vmatrix} \end{aligned} \qquad (7.10)$$

If, for each point, we define the modelling error as

$$\epsilon(t) = y(t) - x^T(t)\theta \tag{7.11}$$

then the least-squares performance index to be minimized is:

$$J = \sum_{1}^{N} \epsilon^2(t) \tag{7.12}$$

or using the matrix notation above

$$J = [Y - X\theta]^T [Y - X\theta] \tag{7.13}$$

Differentiating with respect to θ and equating to zero then yields $\hat{\theta}$, the least-squares estimate of θ as:

$$\hat{\theta} = \left[X^T X\right]^{-1} X^T Y \tag{7.14}$$

7.3.1.1.1 Properties of the least-squares estimate

The least-squares estimate is said to be consistent if it is unbiased, that is, if

$$E(\hat{\theta}) = \theta \tag{7.15}$$

For the least-squares estimate, this occurs only in two cases:

1. The noise sequence $w(t)$ is uncorrelated and zero-mean, or
2. $w(t)$ is independent of $u(t)$ and the model is a moving average, that is, no a term is estimated.

Thus, in general, despite its simplicity the least-squares method will not be used because it gives biased estimates in the presence of colored noise. Alternative methods such as the maximum-likelihood method must be used instead.

7.3.1.2 Maximum-Likelihood Method

The maximum-likelihood method considers the ARMAX model below where u is the input, y the output, e is zero-mean white noise with standard deviation σ:

$$A(B)y(t) = Q(B)u(t - k) + C(B)e(t) \tag{7.16}$$

where

$$A(B) = 1 + a_1 B + \cdots + a_n B^n$$
$$Q(B) = q_1 B + \cdots + q_n B^n \quad (7.17)$$
$$C(B) = 1 + c_1 B + \cdots + c_n B^n$$

The parameters of A, Q, C as well as σ, are unknown. Defining

$$\theta^T = [a_1 \cdots a_n b_1 \cdots b_n c_1 \cdots c_n]$$
$$x^T = [-y(t) \cdots - y(t-n) u(t-1) \quad (7.18)$$
$$\cdots u(t-n) e(t-1) \cdots e(t-n)]$$

the ARMAX model can be written as

$$y(t) = x^T(t)\theta + e(t) \quad (7.19)$$

Unfortunately, one cannot use the least-squares method on this model since the sequence $e(t)$ is unknown. In the case of known parameters, the past values of $e(t)$ can be reconstructed from the sequence:

$$\epsilon(t) = [A(B)y(t) - Q(B)u(t-k)]/C(B) \quad (7.20)$$

Defining the performance index to be minimized as:

$$V = \frac{1}{2}\sum_{t=1}^{N} \epsilon^2(t) \quad (7.21)$$

the maximum-likelihood method is then summarized by the following two steps.

1. Minimize V with respect to $\hat{\theta}$, using for instance a Newton–Raphson algorithm. Note that ϵ is linear in the parameters of A and B but not in those of C.
2. Estimate the noise variance as:

$$\hat{\sigma}^2 = \frac{2}{N}V(\hat{\theta}) \quad (7.22)$$

7.3.1.3 Properties of the maximum-likelihood estimate (MLE)

1. If the model order is sufficient, the MLE is consistent, that is, $\hat{\theta} \to \theta$ as $N \to \infty$.
2. The MLE is asymptotically normal with mean θ and standard deviation σ_θ.
3. The MLE is asymptotically efficient, that is, there is no other unbiased estimator giving a smaller σ_θ.

Because of those attractive properties, the maximum-likelihood method is the preferred identification technique, and is available in most software packages offering control system design and analysis capabilities.

7.3.2 Recursive Identification Methods

There are many situations when it is preferable to perform the identification on-line, such as in adaptive control. In this case, previous identification methods need to be implemented in a recursive fashion, that is, the parameter estimate at time t should be computed as a function of the estimate at time $t-1$ and of the incoming information at time t. The field of recursive identification has been the subject of intensive research in the last decade. For an in-depth look at this field, the reader is referred to the book by Ljung and Söderström [3] on the topic.

7.3.2.1 Recursive Least-Squares (RLS)

We have seen that, with t observations available, the least-squares estimate is:

$$\hat{\theta}(t) = \left[X^T(t)X(t)\right]^{-1} X^T(t)Y(t) \qquad (7.23)$$

with

$$Y^T(t) = [y(1) \cdots y(t)]$$
$$X(t) = \begin{bmatrix} x^T(1) \\ \vdots \\ x^T(t) \end{bmatrix} \qquad (7.24)$$

Assuming that one additional observation becomes available, the problem is then to find $\hat{\theta}(t+1)$ as a function of $\hat{\theta}(t)$ and $y(t+1)$ and $u(t+1)$. Defining $X(t+1)$ and $Y(t+1)$ as

$$X(t+1) = \begin{bmatrix} X(t) \\ x^T(t+1) \end{bmatrix} \qquad Y(t+1) = \begin{bmatrix} Y(t) \\ y(t+1) \end{bmatrix} \qquad (7.25)$$

and defining $P(t+1)$ and $P(t)$ as

$$P(t) = \left[X^T(t)X(t)\right]^{-1} \qquad P(t+1) = \left[X^T(t+1)X(t+1)\right]^{-1} \qquad (7.26)$$

after some manipulations, one can write

$$P(t+1) = \left[X^T(t)X(t) + x(t+1)x^T(t+1)\right]^{-1}$$
$$\hat{\theta}(t+1) = P(t+1)\left[X^T(t)Y(t) + x(t+1)y(t+1)\right] \quad (7.27)$$

In order to avoid the matrix inversion, one must use a classic result from matrix theory, known as the matrix-inversion lemma. The use of this lemma and some simple matrix manipulations then give

$$\epsilon(t+1) = y(t+1) - x^T(t+1)\hat{\theta}(t) \quad (7.28)$$

$$\hat{\theta}(t+1) = \hat{\theta}(t) + \frac{P(t)x(t+1)}{1 + x^T(t+1)P(t)x(t+1)}\epsilon(t+1) \quad (7.29)$$

$$P(t+1) = P(t) - \frac{P(t)x(t+1)x^T(t+1)P(t)}{1 + x^T(t+1)P(t)x(t+1)} \quad (7.30)$$

Note that the recursive least-squares algorithm is the exact mathematical equivalent of the batch least-squares, and thus has the same properties. The matrix P is proportional to the covariance matrix of the estimate, and is thus called the covariance matrix. The algorithm has to be initialized with $\hat{\theta}(0)$ and $P(0)$. Generally, $P(0)$ is initialized as αI where I is the identity matrix and α is a large positive number. The larger α, the less confidence is put in the initial estimate $\hat{\theta}(0)$.

7.3.2.2 Recursive Extended Least Squares, and Recursive Maximum-Likelihood

While it is possible to develop an exact recursive version of the least-squares algorithm, it is not possible for the maximum-likelihood method. The difficulty comes from the facts that $e(t)$ is not known, and that the likelihood is a nonlinear function of C.

The first technique can be seen as an extension to RLS. The ARMAX model can be rewritten in a compact form:

$$\begin{aligned} \theta^T &= [a_1 \cdots a_n, q_1 \cdots q_n, c_1 \cdots c_n] \\ x^T(t) &= [-y(t) \cdots - y(t-n), u(t-k-1) \cdots \\ & \quad u(t-k-n), e(t-1) \cdots e(t-n)] \\ y(t) &= x^T(t)\theta + e(t) \end{aligned} \quad (7.31)$$

If $e(t)$ were known, simple RLS could be used. But $e(t)$ is unknown, and so it has to be approximated. Because in $x(t)$ only past values of e appear, they can be back calculated from information available at time t. The approximation that has been shown best both from theory and simulation studies is the residual $\eta(t)$ defined as:

$$\eta(t) = y(t) - \hat{y}(t|t) = y(t) - x^T(t)\hat{\theta}(t) \quad (7.32)$$

Defining the θ vector and the x vector as in:

$$\begin{aligned}\theta^T &= [a_1 \cdots a_n, q_1 \cdots q_n, c_1 \cdots c_n] \\ x^T &= [-y(t) \cdots -y(t-n), u(t-k-1) \cdots \\ &\quad u(t-k-n), \eta(t-1) \cdots \eta(t-n)]\end{aligned} \quad (7.33)$$

then results in a scheme that is described by the same equations as the recursive least-squares above. The RELS estimate can be shown to converge to the true parameters under fairly weak conditions.

The other approach, the recursive maximum likelihood (RML) attempts to approximate the maximum likelihood by minimizing:

$$V(t) = \frac{1}{2}\sum_{i=1}^{t}\varepsilon^2(i) \quad (7.34)$$

where ε is the prediction error:

$$\varepsilon(t) = y(t) - \hat{y}(t|t-1) = y(t) - x^T(t)\hat{\theta}(t-1) \quad (7.35)$$

Because $V(t)$ is a nonlinear function in C, it is approximated by a Taylor series truncated after the second term. The resulting scheme is then:

$$\epsilon(t+1) = y(t+1) - x^T(t+1)\hat{\theta}(t) \quad (7.36)$$

$$\hat{\theta}(t+1) = \hat{\theta}(t) + \frac{P(t)x_f(t+1)}{1 + x_f^T(t+1)P(t)x_f(t+1)}\epsilon(t+1) \quad (7.37)$$

$$P(t+1) = P(t) - \frac{P(t)x_f(t+1)x_f^T(t+1)P(t)}{1 + x_f^T(t+1)P(t)x_f(t+1)} \quad (7.38)$$

where $x(t)$ is as in the RELS, and x_f is a filtered regresser obtained as:

$$x_f(t) = x(t) + \left(1 - \hat{C}(B)\right)x_f(t) \quad (7.39)$$

Thus, apart from that filtering, the RML is very similar to the RELS. Although slightly more complex, the RML is shown to converge under even more general conditions than the RELS.

7.3.3 Tracking Time-Varying Systems

The recursive estimators presented so far all suffer from the same pitfall: after some time the estimation gain will be near zero, and the parameter estimates will essentially not change anymore. This is because the underlying assumption is that the true parameters are time-invariant. However, in practice, and especially when applying adaptive control, one has to track time-varying parameters. The recursive least-squares algorithm is the exact mathematical equivalent to the batch one, and minimizes:

$$J(t) = \frac{1}{t} \sum_{i=1}^{t} \left[y(i) - x^T(i)\hat{\theta}(t) \right]^2 \tag{7.40}$$

In the above performance index, all points in $[1, t]$ have the same weight. If the plant is thought to be time-varying, then there should be a mechanism by which more recent data have more weight than old data that no longer represent the dynamics of the plant at time t. This mechanism is akin to forgetting, and can be achieved by exponential discounting of old data, through the use of a *forgetting factor* λ in the modified performance index:

$$J(t) = \frac{1}{t} \sum_{i=1}^{t} \lambda^{t-i} \left[y(i) - x^T(i)\hat{\theta}(t) \right]^2 \tag{7.41}$$

The recursive least-squares algorithm then becomes:

$$\epsilon(t+1) = y(t+1) - x^T(t+1)\hat{\theta}(t) \tag{7.42}$$

$$\hat{\theta}(t+1) = \hat{\theta}(t) + \frac{P(t)x(t+1)}{\lambda + x^T(t+1)P(t)x(t+1)} \epsilon(t+1) \tag{7.43}$$

$$P(t+1) = \left\{ P(t) - \frac{P(t)x(t+1)x^T(t+1)P(t)}{\lambda + x^T(t+1)P(t)x(t+1)} \right\} \frac{1}{\lambda} \tag{7.44}$$

In choosing λ, one has to trade-off between the tracking ability of the algorithm and the long-term quality of the estimates near steady-state. The smaller λ is, the faster the algorithm can track, but the more the estimates will vary, even if the true parameters are time-invariant. Also, a small λ may cause blowup of the covariance matrix P, since in the absence of excitation, the covariance matrix update equation essentially becomes:

$$P(t+1) = P(t)\frac{1}{\lambda} \tag{7.45}$$

in which case P grows exponentially, leading to wild fluctuations in the parameter estimates. One way around this problem is to vary the forgetting factor, according to the prediction error ϵ, as in:

$$\lambda(t) = 1 - k\varepsilon^2(t) \tag{7.46}$$

Thus, in case of low excitation, ϵ will be small, and λ will be close to 1. In case of large prediction error, λ will decrease. A number of alternatives and fixes have been proposed over the years. Recently, a scheme that incorporates many of those ideas has been proposed [4]. It is called the Exponential Forgetting and Resetting Algorithm, or EFRA:

$$\epsilon(t+1) = y(t+1) - x^T(t+1)\hat{\theta}(t) \qquad (7.47)$$

$$\hat{\theta}(t+1) = \hat{\theta}(t) + \alpha \frac{P(t)x(t+1)}{1 + x^T(t+1)P(t)x(t+1)}\epsilon(t+1) \qquad (7.48)$$

$$P(t+1) = \frac{1}{\lambda}P(t) - \alpha \frac{P(t)x(t+1)x^T(t+1)P(t)}{1 + x^T(t+1)P(t)x(t+1)}$$
$$+ \beta I - \gamma P^2(t) \qquad (7.49)$$

where I is the identity matrix, and α, β, γ, and λ are constants. An interesting property of the EFRA algorithm is that the covariance matrix can be proved to be bounded at all times, and on both sides as:

$$\sigma_{\min} I \le P(t) \le \sigma_{\max} I \qquad \forall\, t \qquad (7.50)$$

where in first approximation σ_{min} and σ_{max} are given by:

$$\sigma_{\min} = \frac{\beta}{\alpha - \eta} \qquad \sigma_{\max} = \frac{\eta}{\gamma} + \frac{\beta}{\eta} \qquad (7.51)$$
$$\text{with} \quad \eta = \frac{1-\lambda}{\lambda}.$$

Using the values recommended in [4], that is, $\alpha = 0.5, \beta = \gamma = 0.005$, and $\lambda = 0.95$, yields $\sigma_{min} = 0.01$ and $\sigma_{max} = 10$. The EFRA algorithm has proved very robust both in simulations and in industrial applications, and its use is therefore strongly recommended.

7.4   Adaptive Control

As we recall from the previous section, model-based tuning consists of two phases:

1. Model building, that is, *idendification*.
2. Controller design, using the *identified model*.

Adaptive control can be thought of as an automation of this two-stage procedure used by control engineers to develop a control scheme, that is, process identification and control design. The major difference is that the procedure is performed on-line, in real-time and without human supervision. The methods presented below consider the estimated parameters as the true process parameters, thus ignoring the uncertainty inherent in the parameter estimation procedure. When doing so, one is said to enforce the *certainty-equivalence* principle. For a comprehensive treatment of adaptive control, see the book by Åström and Wittemnark [5].

Definition: Self-Tuning:

Continuous updating of controller tuning constants. Used for truly time-varying plants.

Definition: Autotuning:

Periodic, usually on demand tuning. Once tuning constants are obtained, they are frozen and used until next tuning request. Used for time-invariant, or very slowly time-varying plants.

7.4.1 Indirect Adaptive Control

Indirect adaptive control is a straightforward mechanization of the model-based tuning methodology, as illustrated in Figure 7.2. The parameter estimator consists of one of the recursive identification schemes previously discussed. Using the certainty-equivalence principle, the parameter estimates are then used to design the controller as though they were the true plant parameters. Various combinations of identification and control design techniques are possible, and thus many different schemes can be proposed. For the indirect adaptive controller to behave as expected, it is important that the parameter estimates converge to their true value. This means that, in general, the use of simple RLS will not be sufficient. This also assumes sufficient prior knowledge

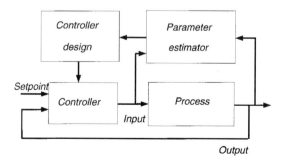

Figure 7.2 Indirect adaptive control scheme.

of the plant structure, that is, dead-time, number of poles and zeros, as well as an input signal which is sufficiently rich in order to excite all the modes to be identified. Another aspect of indirect adaptive control is that the controller design stage has to be implemented with great care so as to avoid the possibility of numerical problems, due for instance to common poles and zeros in the identified transfer function. This means that indirect adaptive control schemes are generally computation intensive.

Twenty years ago, this computational load made this approach unattractive for practical applications. This led to the development of the so-called direct adaptive controllers, discussed in the following section.

7.4.2 Direct Adaptive Control

Sometimes, it is possible to reparameterize the estimation problem in terms of the controller parameters, instead of the process parameters. The advantage offered by this approach is that the controller design stage is then unnecessary, and thus it reduces the computational requirements. Figure 7.3 depicts the principle of a direct adaptive controller. Because the parameters that are estimated are directly those of the controller, once the estimation is done the controller tuning is trivial. This makes those schemes very compact, and fast to execute.

This reparameterization also makes the analysis simpler for direct schemes than for indirect ones. The price to pay for all this is a decreased flexibility compared to indirect schemes. Indeed, once the controller structure is chosen, and the reparameterization of the model performed, any change in the control design technique means a complete redesign of the scheme.

7.4.3 Adaptive Predictive Control

Recently, adaptive predictive control techniques have become popular, particularly for applications in the process industries, where large and varying time-delays pose a

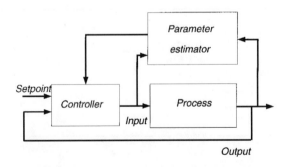

Figure 7.3 Direct adaptive control scheme.

major challenge to control engineers. A popular algorithm is the Generalized Predictive Controller recently proposed by Clarke et al. [6]. It is based on the minimization of the following quadratic performance index:

$$J = E\left\{\sum_{j=n_1}^{n_2}[y(t+j) - w(t+j)]^2 + \rho\sum_{j=1}^{n_u}[\nabla u(t+j-1)]^2\right\} \quad (7.52)$$

where

$w(t+j)$ is a sequence of future set points.
n_1 is the minimum prediction horizon.
n_2 is the maximum prediction horizon.
n_u is the control horizon.
ρ is the control weighting factor.

In order to perform the minimization of J, $y(t+n_1), \cdots, y(t+n_2)$ have to be predicted, given the current knowledge at t. Then, the minimization has to be performed over the independent variables $\nabla u(t), \cdots, \nabla u(t+n_u-1)$. Although at each control interval n_u control actions are computed, only the first one, $\nabla u(t)$, is implemented; this is called the receding-horizon approach.

Most often in GPC, the plant is modelled as a Controlled Auto-Regressive Integrated Moving Average (CARIMA) process described by:

$$A(B)y(t) = Q(B)u(t-k) + C(B)e(t)/\nabla \quad (7.53)$$

where A, B, and C are polynomials of degree n, $\nabla = 1 - q^{-1}$ is the difference operator, and $e(t)$ is a white noise sequence. The presence of the integrator $1/\nabla$ in the noise model reflects the nonstationary nature of the disturbance, and will result in integral action in the controller, a desirable feature in process control.

For the sake of simplicity, we now assume $C(B) = 1$. Now, consider the following equation, known as the diophantine equation, where F_j and G_j are uniquely defined polynomials of respective degrees $n-1$, and $j-1$.

$$1 = A\nabla F_j(B) + B^j G_j(B) \quad (7.54)$$

Multiplying Eq. (7.53) by $F_j(B)B^{-j}$, and substituting $A(B)\nabla F_j(B)$ from Eq. (7.54), after some simple manipulations one gets the j-step ahead prediction for $y(t+j)$ as:

$$\hat{y}(t+j) = G_j y(t) + Q\nabla F_j u(t+j-k) \quad (7.55)$$

In the r.h.s. of Eq. (7.55), terms can be regrouped in components that are known at time t, and the future Δu that have to be computed:

$$\hat{\mathbf{y}} = \mathbf{R}\tilde{\mathbf{u}} + \mathbf{f} \quad (7.56)$$

where:

$$\begin{aligned}\hat{\mathbf{y}} &= [y(t+n_1)\cdots y(t+n_2)]^T \\ \tilde{\mathbf{u}} &= [\nabla u(t)\cdots \nabla u(t+n_u-1)]^T \\ \mathbf{f} &= [f_{n_1}(t)\cdots f_{n^*}(t)]^T\end{aligned} \qquad (7.57)$$

The vector $\mathbf{f}$ contains the known components, while $\mathbf{R}$ is a $(n_2 - n_1 + 1) \times n_u$ matrix whose elements are the impulse response parameters r_i of the plant:

$$\mathbf{R} = \begin{bmatrix} r_{n_1-1} & 0 & \cdots & \cdots & 0 \\ r_{n_1} & r_{n_1-1} & 0 & \cdots & 0 \\ r_{n_1+1} & r_{n_1} & r_{n_1-1} & 0 & \vdots \\ \vdots & \vdots & \vdots & \ddots & \vdots \\ r_{n_1+n_u-2} & r_{n_1+n_u-3} & \cdots & r_{n_1} & r_{n_1-1} \\ \vdots & \vdots & & & \vdots \\ r_{n_2-1} & r_{n_2-2} & \cdots & \cdots & r_{n_2-n_u} \end{bmatrix} \qquad (7.58)$$

The sequence of present and future control actions that minimize J is then given by:

$$\tilde{\mathbf{u}} = \left[\mathbf{R}^T \mathbf{R} + \rho I\right]^{-1} \mathbf{R}^T (\mathbf{w} - \mathbf{f}) \qquad (7.59)$$

where $\mathbf{w} = [w(t+n_1)\cdots w(t+n_2)]^T$.

7.4.4 *Implementation Issues*

The class of adaptive controllers briefly introduced in the previous pages can be proven globally stable and convergent under some fairly restrictive and idealistic conditions. In particular, the process time delay must be known, and the model order must be at least that of the process. In reality, these two conditions are rarely, if ever, satisfied. Indeed, in practice, the model structure is always less complex than that of the actual process. We then say that there is unmodelled dynamics. The adaptive controller has to stay stable and performant even in the presence of unmodelled dynamics. In other words, it has to be robust. To achieve robustness, it is important to have a good description of the process over the bandwidth of interest. Signals outside that bandwidth must then be filtered out so that the estimator does not try fit the process in a bandwidth the model is not meant for. Thus, very often the regressor is filtered through a bandpass filter before the estimates are computed. The other important issue is the lack of proper excitation to the process. Indeed for the estimator to work properly, it is imperative that the process be sufficiently excited in the bandwidth of interest. In the case of lack of proper excitation, one may simply turn the estimator off by passing the prediction error through a dead zone, or one may decide to send an intentional external perturbation in order to excite the process. For more on implementation issues, see for instance [7].

7.4.5 Another Parameterization

One way to design a robust adaptive control requiring minimal a priori information and capable of handling time-delay plants (common in process control) is to abandon the usual transfer function models and instead develop an unstructured adaptive control scheme using an orthonormal series representation [8]. The set of Laguerre functions is particularly appealing because it is simple to represent, is similar to transient signals, and closely resembles Padé approximants. The continuous Laguerre functions are defined as:

$$L_{i(s)} = \sqrt{2p} \frac{(s-p)^{i-1}}{(s+p)^i} \quad , i = 1, \cdots, N \quad (7.60)$$

Alternatively, it is possible to define discrete Laguerre functions as:

$$L_k(B) := \frac{\sqrt{1-a^2}}{B^{-1}-a} \left(\frac{1-aB^{-1}}{B^{-1}-a} \right)^{k-1} \quad (7.61)$$

By discretizing each block of the continuous Laguerre functions, or directly from the discrete Laguerre functions, a discrete-time state-space representation is obtained:

$$\begin{aligned} l(t+1) &= Al(t) + bu(t) \\ y(t) &= c^T l(t) \end{aligned} \quad (7.62)$$

In this representation, A is a lower triangular $N \times N$ matrix, and b an $N \times 1$ vector. The vector c contains the Laguerre gains needed to represent the signal $y(t)$ and embodies all the knowledge about the process dynamics. It is also known as the Laguerre spectrum of the system. The Laguerre gains can be estimated via a simple recursive least-squares scheme, and can be shown to be unbiased even in the presence of colored noise and unmodelled dynamics. It is then possible to design an adaptive predictive control law based on the above state-space representation.

7.5 Autotuning

Most often, autotuning is used in reference to PID controllers. Over the last decade, many methods have been proposed to automatically tune PID controllers, some of which are now being used in commercial systems. Here, we shall briefly present some of the most important techniques. For more on PID autotuning, see the book by Åström and Hägglund [9].

7.5.1 The Relay Method

All methods discussed so far are based on models that attempt to represent the plant dynamics in the entire frequency range of interest, that is, up to the Nyquist frequency. However, a popular PID manual tuning method relies on the knowledge of only one point of the plant frequency response. It takes its roots in the Ziegler–Nichols ultimate cycle method. In this method, the proportional gain is increased until the closed-loop system sits at the verge of instability with the plant output in a limit cycle of constant period and amplitude relies on the determination of the critical point on the plant Nyquist chart, that is, the point that corresponds to a phase shift of -180 degrees. In the Ziegler–Nichols method, this is achieved by increasing the proportional gain. In Ziegler–Nichols automatic tuners, this limit cycle can be induced by introducing a nonlinearity in the loop. An advantage of such a method is that the loop is not taken to the verge of instability, and that the amplitude of the output oscillation can then be controlled.

The first documented PID autotuner based on self-induced limit cycle is discussed by Kitamori [10]. Kitamori adds, in parallel with the PID regulator, a saturation element that eventually results in the superimposition of a self-excited oscillation with limited amplitude on the process output. Then, based on the measurement of the limit cycle amplitude and period, tuning constants are generated using the Ziegler–Nichols tuning rules. This being an analog PID controller, everything, including the amplitude and period detection, as well as the tuning constant adjustment are realized with analog circuitry.

More recently, Åström and Hägglund [11] have proposed a similar way to tune discrete PID controllers. The idea is to put the plant under relay feedback, as in Figure 7.4. It is then very likely that the system will start to oscillate and reach a limit cycle. The study of such systems is generally done through harmonic analysis, via the Fourier transform. If the system in Figure 7.4 is self-oscillating, then the output will be a periodic signal. Assuming the plant is a high-order system with low-pass characteristics, then one can limit the analysis to the first harmonic of the oscillation, assuming that the higher-order harmonics win be severely damped by the plant.

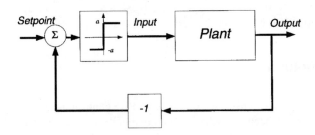

Figure 7.4 Plant under relay feedback.

Consider a pure relay, as in Figure 7.4. Let the error signal $e(t)$ feeding the relay be described by its first harmonic, i.e.:

$$e(t) = e_0 \sin \omega_0 t \tag{7.63}$$

Then, we want to express the output $u(t)$ of the relay by its first harmonic:

$$u(t) = u_1 \sin(\omega_0 t + \varphi_1) \tag{7.64}$$

This can be done by expanding $u(t)$ as a Fourier series:

$$u(t) = \bar{u} + \sum_{i=1}^{\infty} a_i \sin(i\omega_0 t) + b_i \cos(i\omega_0 t) \tag{7.65}$$

or

$$u(t) = \bar{u} + \sum_{i=1}^{\infty} u_i \sin(i\omega_0 t + \varphi_i) \tag{7.66}$$

where $u_i = \sqrt{a_i^2 + b_i^2}$, $\tan \varphi_i = \dfrac{b_i}{a_i}$

$$\bar{u} = \frac{1}{T} \int_0^T u(t)\, dt \tag{7.67}$$

$$a_i = \frac{2}{T} \int_0^T u(t) \sin(i\omega_0 t)\, dt \tag{7.68}$$

$$b_i = \frac{2}{T} \int_0^T u(t) \cos(i\omega_0 t)\, dt \tag{7.69}$$

where $T = 2\pi/\omega_0$.

Limiting the series expansion to the first term, and computing the above integrals yields:

$$\bar{u} = 0; \quad a_1 = \frac{4a}{\pi}; \quad b_1 = 0; \tag{7.70}$$

Thus,

$$u(t) = \frac{4a}{\pi} \sin \omega_0 t \tag{7.71}$$

Now, define the *describing function* as the transfer function between $e(t)$ and $u(t)$. A rapid inspection of Eqs. (7.63), (7.71) shows that, as far as the first harmonic is concerned, the relay can be described by the following equivalent transfer function:

$$N = \frac{4a}{\pi e_0} \tag{7.72}$$

Note that this describing function is a function of the signal's amplitude e_0 but not of its frequency ω_0. For the system of Figure 7.4 to be in a limit cycle, no energy loss must occur in the loop. In other words, the gains of the feedback and feedforward paths must be equal. If $G(i\omega)$ is the plant transfer function, the condition for a self-oscillating loop is expressed mathematically as:

$$N(e_0)G(i\omega_0) = -1 \tag{7.73}$$

This condition is illustrated graphically via the Nyquist plots of the $G(i\omega)$ and of $-1/N(e_0)$ on Figure 7.5. The intersection of the two plots defines the characteristics of the oscillation. Note that in this case, the intersection occurs at the critical point, i.e. the point at which the plant has a phase shift of -180 degrees. This is the same point found by the Ziegler–Nichols ultimate cycle method. Of course, for an oscillation to occur, the plant must have a phase shift of more than 180 degrees.

Based on the amplitude and period of the limit cycle, it is then possible to compute the tuning constants using various methods. The first that comes to mind is to use the Ziegler–Nichols tuning rules. In [11], other tuning rules are also derived, based for instance on gain margin specifications. When a relay with hysteresis is used, phase margin specifications can serve as the basis for tuning. By performing experiments

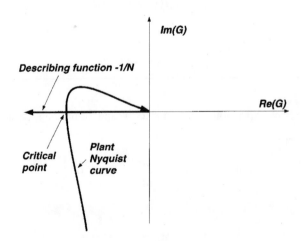

Figure 7.5 Nyquist plots for system under relay feedback.

with varying hysteresis, one can estimate more than one point on the plant Nyquist curve, and use more sophisticated tuning techniques [11].

7.5.2 Pattern Recognition

A popular empirical method for tuning PID controllers is based on the characteristics of the system transient response, either following a set-point change, or load disturbance. In [12], an automation of such empirical techniques is proposed. This technique continuously monitors the error signal as a function of time, and performs a waveform analysis on this signal whenever it exceeds a preset value. The salient features of the error signal are then extracted as shown on Figure 7.6. From Figure 7.6, the damping and overshoot are defined as follows:

$$\text{overshoot} = \frac{P_2}{P_1} \qquad \text{damping} = \frac{P_3 - P_2}{P_1 - P_2}$$

Based on those values, tuning constants can be evaluated, using for instance Ziegler–Nichols tuning rules. It is also possible to build a rule-based system, using rules derived from experience and from extensive simulation studies.

7.5.3 Model-Based Methods

Many commercial PID controllers with autotuning use a model-based method. An on-line identification technique is used to estimate a parametric model of the process. Two basic methodologies are then used to obtain the tuning constants of a PID controller. One may for instance design an adaptive controller based on pole placement. Of course, to obtain a PID regulator, one must choose a very specific model structure. Thus, very often second-order transfer function models without delay are estimated. The other methodology is to use an optimization-based technique, using for example

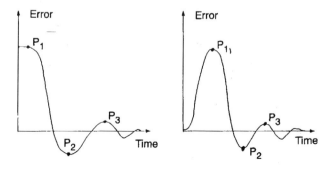

Figure 7.6 Features of the error signals (a) Set point change. (b) Load disturbance.

an ISE or ITAE criterion. This is particularly useful when a delay-free, second-order model cannot describe the process, but one still wishes to use a PID controller.

7.5.4 Commercial Products

As a result of the increased availability of low cost-microprocessors, and memory, most PID controllers now come with an autotuning feature. Control trade journals regularly review PID controllers, and the reader is encouraged to check recent journals to learn about current offerings. A recent review of temperature controllers is available in [13]. Many controllers use one of the model-based techniques previously described. One of the first self-tuning PID controllers to reach the market uses a heuristic pattern-recognition scheme to extract the features of that transient response. Those features are then used to obtain the controller parameters using tuning rules inspired from Ziegler–Nichols [14]. This controller will automatically retune itself every time the deviation from the expected behavior exceeds a prescribed level. The relay tuning method previously described has also led to a commercial product [9]. Contrary to the previous controller, this one provides on-demand rather than continuous tuning. This controller can also build a gain scheduling table on its own, a handy feature for nonlinear precesses.

7.6 Applications

7.6.1 Glass Furnace Bottom Temperature Control

The glass industry contains many processes where temperature control may have a significant impact on product quality, as well as on the efficiency and profitability of the operation. A successful application of adaptive control to temperature control of an end-port glass furnace is described in [15]. The example below uses the same model to illustrate some of the techniques discussed in the previous sections.

The raw material is fed at the side of the furnace. At one end, two gas burners provide the needed heat to melt the raw materials. The molten glass naturally flows to the working end. Experience has shown that to control two important qualities of the glass, that is, the fining (absence of gas bubbles), and the homogeneity, it is necessary to tightly control the bottom temperature. This is a difficult control problem, characterized by large time constants, and lack of good physical model. It thus seems an ideal application of the technioues described in this chapter. The general structure of the control scheme is as shown in Figure 7.7. The bottom temperature is controlled by manipulating the top temperature set point. In turn, the top temperature is controlled by manipulating the gas flow set point to the burners.

In [15], the following model is proposed for the furnace:

$$A(B)y(t) = P(B)u_1(t-1) + Q(B)u_2(t-1) + C(B)e(t) \qquad (7.74)$$

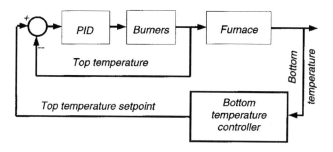

Figure 7.7 Bottom temperature cascade control scheme.

where

$$A(B) = 1 - 1.113B - 0.642B^2 + 0.757B^3$$
$$P(B) = 0.061 - 0.0032B - 0.057B^2$$
$$Q(B) = -0.063 + 0.0017B + 0.060B^2 \quad (7.75)$$
$$C(B) = 1 - 0.317B - 0.726B^2 + 0.101B^3$$

where $y(t)$ represents the bottom temperature, $u_1(t)$ represents the top temperature set point, and $u_2(t)$ represents the load to the furnace to be treated as a measured disturbance. This model corresponds to a sampling interval of 2 hr. Figure 7.9 shows the behavior of an adaptive generalized predictive controller on a glass furnace simulated by the equations above. The adaptive controller uses the EFRA estimator described earlier, with $\alpha = 0.99, \beta = 0.05, \lambda = 0.98$, and $\gamma = 0.005$. The parameter estimate and regressor vectors are respectively:

$$\begin{aligned}\theta^T &= [a_1 a_2 a_3 q_1 q_2 q_3 r_1 r_2 r_3 c_1 c_2 c_3] \\ x^T(t) &= [-y(t-1) \cdots -y(t-3) u_1(t-1) \cdots \\ & \quad u_1(t-3) u_2(t-1) \cdots u_2(t-3)]\end{aligned} \quad (7.76)$$

The initial P-matrix is chosen as $5I$, where I is the identity matrix. The initial parameter estimate vector $\hat{\theta}(0)^T$ is chosen as [0 0 0 0.1 0 0 -0.002 0 0].

The parameters of the GPC controller are $N_2 = 5$, $N_u = 1$, and $\rho = 0.1$. In addition to the feedback regulator, a simple static feedforward control action is computed from the measured load disturbance as:

$$u_f(t) = -\frac{\hat{Q}(1)}{\hat{P}(1)} u_2(t) \quad (7.77)$$

where $\hat{Q}$ and $\hat{P}$ are the estimates of those polynomials. The input to the plant is then computed as:

$$u_1(t) = u_r(t) + u_f(t) \quad (7.78)$$

where $u_r(t)$ is the feedback control action computed by the GPC algorithm. Figure 7.8 shows the result of a simulation, with initial conditions as outlined above. It can be seen that after the learning period, the control system responds very well to load disturbances.

7.6.2 Lime Kiln Cooler-Feeder Control

Figure 7.9 depicts a lime kiln cooler-feeder control system. The hot lime is discharged from the kiln into the cooler where it is primarily cooled by an air flow induced by the cooler fan. The goal here is to try to maintain an even discharge temperature distribution in the four feeders while maintaining the cooler level as constant as possible.

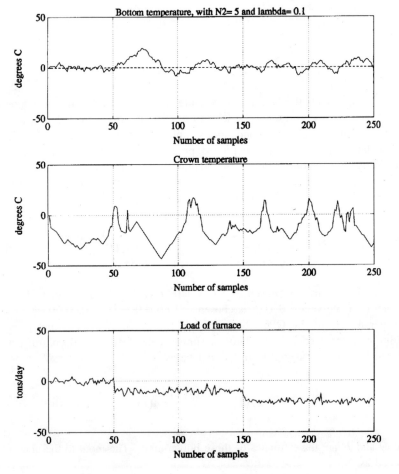

Figure 7.8 Generalized predictive control of simulated glass furnace temperature.

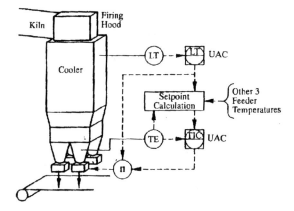

Figure 7.9 Lime kiln cooler feeder control system. (Courtesy of Universal Dynamics Ltd.)

To control the feeder temperatures, each feeder rate is manipulated using a vibrating trough. This is usually done manually by the operator. The benefits of improved temperature control are threefold. First, because the cooling air enters the kiln firing hood as secondary air, temperature variations will adversely affect the operation of the kiln, and the lime quality. Second, because calcination actually continues in the cooler, temperature variations will result in further lime quality variations. Finally, too hot a lime may damage the conveyor belt to the point of setting it on fire. The cooler level as well as the temperatures are controlled by the same feeder rates. There is also a strong interaction between the four feeders. The decoupling between the level and the four temperatures is achieved through a proprietary scheme. Of interest to us is each individual temperature controller denoted as UAC on Figure 7.9. Each of these controllers is an adaptive predictive controller based on a Laguerre function representation, as described in Section 7.4.5 [8]. The time delay in the system can vary from 45 to 90 min. Figure 7.10 shows some results obtained in a real production plant. The temperature set points for the four feeders are different due to different thermocouple placements. The improvement in temperature variability is quite obvious from Figure 7.10. Temperature deviations are reduced by a factor of nearly seven, compared to manual control. The resulting improvement of lime quality, that is, a more consistent slaking rate, has allowed that particular plant to significantly augment its production of premium grade.

7.7 Conclusions

This chapter has described some of the techniques used in recursive identification, autotuning, and adaptive control. Until recently, those techniques were reserved to academic, exploratory work. However, the field has now matured at the same time as computing power is becoming more readily available. Those techniques are thus

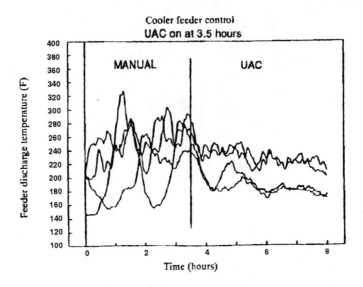

Figure 7.10 Lime kiln cooler feeder control system. (Courtesy of Universal Dynamics Ltd.)

playing an increasingly more important role in process control, including temperature control. Obviously, in a short chapter, it is impossible to do justice to such a broad topic. However, it is hoped that the material presented here has been sufficiently motivating for the reader to investigate it in more detail by reading some of the references listed in the bibliography.

References

1. Ziegler, J. and Nichols, N., Optimum settings for automatic controllers, *Trans. ASME* **64**, 759–768 (1942).
2. Ljung, L. *System Identification: Theory for the User*. Prentice-Hall (1987).
3. Ljung, L., and Söderström, T., *Theory and Practice of Recursive Identification*. MIT Press (1983).
4. Salgado, M.E., Goodwin, G.C., and Middleton, R., A modified least squares algorithm incorporating exponential resetting and forgetting. *Int. J. Control* **47**, 477–491 (1988).
5. Åström, K. and Wittenmark, B., *Adaptive Control*. Addison-Wesley (1989).
6. C.M. Clarke, D.W., and Tuffs, P., Generalized predictive control. Parts 1 and 2. *Automatica* **23**, 137–160, (1987).
7. Wittenmark, B., Adaptive control: implementation and application issues, in *Adaptive Control Strategies for Industrial Use* (S. Shah and G. Dumont, eds.). Springer-Verlag (1989).
8. Zervos, C., and Dumont, G., Deterministic adaptive control based on Laguerre series representation. *Int. J. Control* **48**, 2333–2359 (1988).
9. Åström, K., and Hägglund, T., *Automatic Tuning of PID Controllers*. Instrument Society of America, Research Triangle Park, NC (1988).

10. Kitamori, T., Test production of automatic adjusting process controller (in Japanese), in *7th SICE Symposium*, pp. 409–410 (1968).
11. Aström, K., and Hägglund, T., Automatic tuning of simple regulators with specifications on phase and amplitude margins. *Automatica* **20**, 645–651 (1984).
12. Bristol, E., Pattern recognition: An alternative to parameter identification in adaptive control. *Automatica* **13**, 197–202 (1977).
13. Laduzinski, A., New ideas combine with basics and apply to temperature control, *Control Engineering*, pp. 52–56, October 1989.
14. Kraus, T., and Myron, T., Self-tuning PID controller uses pattern recognition approach. *Control Engineering*, pp. 106–111, June 1984.
15. Wertz, V., and Demeuse, P., Application of Clarke-Gawthrop type controllers for the bottom temperature of a glass furnace. *Automatica*, **23**, 215–220 (1987).

CHAPTER 8

Methodologies for Temperature Control of Batch and Semi-Batch Reactors

Richard S. Wu and Eugene P. Dougherty

8.1 Introduction

Intense global competition has recently prompted a vigorous attempt to improve quality of manufactured products and processes to make them. Process control methodologies have been developed for steady-state continuous processes, which are commonly used for the large-scale production of commodity products. But specialty products are generally made by semi-batch or batch processes, which are inherently dynamic and thus never reach steady state. It is often not clear how the methodologies for continuous processes should be applied to manufacture specialty products, for which quality demands can be exceedingly high.

This chapter reviews four process control methodologies that we have found useful in solving industrial control problems: time series analysis, dynamic process modeling, feedforward–feedback control methods, and statistical process control. We show how these control methodologies can be used in batch and semi-batch processes, and demonstrate how these have been applied to achieve better batch process control and better specialty product quality. Our goal is to familiarize our readers with these methods so that they can apply them prudently to their own industrial control problems. The end result should be better-controlled, safer processes that produce high-quality specialty products.

8.2 Time Series Analysis

8.2.1 Model Identification

Design of a good process controller requires the engineer to be familiar with the process of interest. Knowledge of which variables must be under strict control,

---

Richard S. Wu and Eugene P. Dougherty, Rohm and Haas Company, P. O. Box 219, Bristol, PA 19007, USA

which variables are most suitable to manipulate, how the variables relate to each other, and how they respond to disturbances and changes in the process are all very important. In point of fact, most modern controller design methods require a quantitative process model, often referred to as the transfer function, which relates, in time and in magnitude, the variable(s) to be controlled to the variable(s) to be manipulated. Determination of a good process model, then, is key to controller design.

One way to determine the model is to carry out a thorough, in-depth theoretical analysis of the process based on fundamental physical and chemical principles. As explained in Section 8.3, this dynamic process modeling approach can be very demanding and difficult to implement, particularly for complex processes. In the present section, we consider simpler, more empirically based approaches to determine process transfer functions.

Even a good dynamic process model contains many parameters such as heat transfer or mass transfer coefficients, which tend to be site specific. Therefore these parameters must be determined empirically.

In what follows, we treat the case of a single-input, single-output (SISO) control algorithm for the sake of clarity. Of course, the techniques can be generalized to multiple inputs and outputs, resulting in matrix equations.

A common way to determine a process function is the process response curve method [1]. In this method, a process is operated until it is steady or quiescent, at which point the controller is set to the manual mode. Then, the process variable chosen to be the input or independent variable is intentionally raised or lowered by a single large step (see Figure 8.1). The variable is maintained at this new level until a new steady state is achieved. The output variable is then recorded, together with the time required to attain the new steady state.

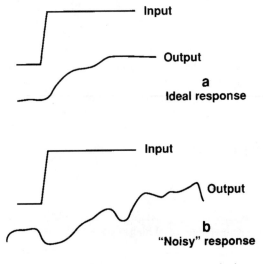

Figure 8.1 Process response curve method.

The above approach, however, has several serious drawbacks. First, a large step change may be required to obtain a significant response, especially if disturbances occur or noise levels are high. This large step change may unfortunately generate a large amount of poor-quality product. Second, a large step change may also result in the process responding in a nonlinear fashion, and thus may not give an accurate model of the real process that we wish to describe.

Third, process disturbances and noise levels may be so high that identifying the initial and final steady states may not be straightforward (see Figure 8.1b). Fourth, in real time, noise is not totally random, but tends to be "autocorrelated," that is, correlated with previously observed values, which themselves are noisy. This, of course, makes model identification even more difficult. Finally, the process may not be stable unless at least some control is exercised (i.e., it may be "open loop unstable"). A process that operates under "closed loop" control cannot be analyzed by the process response curve method.

Model identification using a pseudo-random binary sequence (PRBS) test and time series analysis can overcome all the drawbacks mentioned above. The PRBS method involves either addition or subtraction of a small amount from the normal controller output (hence, it is binary). Figure 8.2 is a schematic of a typical PRBS process experiment. Switching between addition or subtraction is done according to a schedule based loosely on the expected time constant of the process. Because the time constant is never precisely known, the actual switching is done using a random number generator, to determine if the process transfer function exhibits both high-frequency (short time constant) and low-frequency (long time constant) dynamic behavior.

In our view, the PRBS test represents the most practical method for identifying a process transfer function. First, the controller need not be set to manual, but can be set to either manual or to automatic, provided that the PRBS signal is added to the normal output from the controller. PRBS/time series methods enable one to identify an unstable process model under closed-loop control by relating the output response to the randomly varying input PRBS [2]. The PRBS method requires only small magnitude steps up and down to be taken, steps much smaller than that required for the large, single-step process response curve method (compare Figures 8.1 and 8.2). With small steps, the PRBS method is unlikely to perturb the process into a highly nonlinear, unstable regimen. Signal-to-noise ratios can be improved as needed

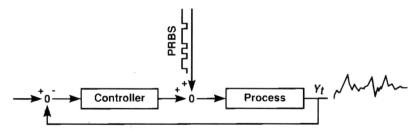

Figure 8.2 A PRBS experiment.

by simply increasing the time required for the PRBS experiment, not by increasing the step height.

To be sure, the maximum allowable magnitude of the PRBS should be small enough to ensure that the final product remains within specification limits. The average switching time t should be approximately $t/4 < \tau < t/2$, where τ denotes the process time constant. If the magnitude of the PRBS is small, then a long duration of the test time should be used.

One important advantage of the PRBS/time series approach is its ability to identify both the deterministic model together with the stochastic (i.e., noise) model for the process. Because, as noted earlier, noise is generally autocorrelated in time, identification of the noise structure is key to good controller design. Moreover, there is a well-developed statistical diagnostic checking method [3] to compare alternative models and to assess how well the fitted models match the data. This feature is particularly important for processes that are noisy or slowly drift around. Finally, there are good computer software packages available to implement the time series approach: SAS/ETS [4] and the McMaster University suite of programs [5] are two popular packages. Indeed, for further details on the overall time series analysis approach, we suggest that the reader consult the Advanced Process Control Course Notes, available from McMaster University [5].

8.2.2 Model Structure

The transfer function model can be expressed in the following equation:

$$Y_t = \frac{\omega_0 - \omega_1 B - \omega_2 B^2 - \ldots}{1 - \delta_1 B - \delta_2 B^2 - \ldots} X_{t-f} \qquad (8.1)$$
$$+ \frac{\theta_0 - \theta_1 - \theta_2 B^2 - \ldots}{1 - \phi_1 B - \phi_2 B^2 - \ldots} \frac{a_t}{(1-B)^d}$$

where B is the backward shift operator, f is the number of whole periods of delay, and $(\omega, \delta, \phi, \theta)$ are parameters estimated from fitting the data.

Equation (8.1) consists of two parts: the deterministic model and the stochastic (i.e., noise) model. Deterministic models are generally familiar to control engineers: familiar examples include first-order plus deadtime or second-order plus deadtime models. The stochastic model describes the noise, which results from disturbances on the process output that have not been accounted for in the deterministic model. The $(1-B)^d$ in the noise term means that the process can be nonstationary.

Nonstationary behavior characterizes most models in the process industries. Such processes will drift away from the steady-state value without closed-loop control. Unlike stationary processes, nonstationary processes require some sort of integral control.

To clarify these points, consider the example of a first-order plus deadtime model:

$$Y = \frac{g \exp(-T_d S)}{\tau S + 1} X \tag{8.2}$$

The time series or discrete model corresponding to Eq. (8.2) is given by:

$$Y_t = \frac{(\omega_0 - \omega_1 B)}{(1 - \delta B)} X_{t-f-1} + \frac{(\theta_0 - \theta_1 B)}{(1 - \phi_1 B)} \frac{a_t}{(1 - B)} \tag{8.3}$$

$$\delta = e^{T/\tau}; \quad \omega_0 = g(1 - \delta^{1-c}); \quad \omega_1 = g(\delta - \delta^{1-c})$$

where the time delay $T_d = (f + c)T$. T denotes the sampling period. f is the integer number of whole periods of delay, and c is the additional fractional period of delay.

8.2.3 Controller Design

Knowledge of the process model allows us to design a good process controller. We consider first the design of a constrained minimum variance controller (CMVC).

Clarke and Hastings-Jones (CHJ) [6] developed a technique to compute a family of CMVC algorithms from time series models of the form of Eq. (8.1). This equation applies to a single manipulated variable. The controller minimizes the following objective function:

$$O_\alpha = E\{(Y_{t+b+1} - Y_{sp})^2 + \alpha((1 - B)^d X_t)^2\} \tag{8.4}$$

where O_α is the objective function, E refers to the expectation value of the quantity in brackets, Y_{sp} is the set point, X_t is the manipulated variable, and α is the constraint parameter.

The CMVC is of the following general form:

$$(1 - B)^d X_t = \frac{a_0 + a_1 B + a_2 B^2 + a_3 B^3 + \ldots}{b_0 + b_1 B + b_2 B^2 + b_3 B^3 + \ldots} (Y_t - Y_{sp}) \tag{8.5}$$

A computer program developed at McMaster University calculates the CMVC [5] to minimize O_α for any α, the constraint parameter, which ranges from 0 to 1. As Eq. (8.4) shows, $\alpha = 0$ imposes no constraint on the manipulated variable, whereas $\alpha = 1$ restricts variations on the manipulated variable and thus penalizes the control variable more.

To ensure process safety, we prefer that changes to manipulated variables be done gradually, not drastically, because big changes made to the manipulated variable may lead the process into an unstable, nonlinear regime (see Section 8.2.1). Because the controller has been designed over a range of conditions for which linearity applies, the overall controller performance may suffer in such a nonlinear regime.

Thus safety and overall controller performance considerations lead us to design a controller that is robust. A robust controller permits some variation in the output (control) variable so as to minimize the variation in the input (manipulated) variable. As Figure 8.3 shows, this can be done by changing the constraint parameter α. By tuning this single parameter to the proper setting, safety and stability can be obtained with only a small price to be paid in controller performance.

There is still another reason to design robust, suitably constrained controllers. As mentioned previously, modern process controllers are designed based on a model consisting of the dynamic information about the process. Inevitably, there is some mismatch between the true process and the model. This may result from errors in model identification or from unanticipated changes in the plant process over time. Some examples include fouling, which reduces the heat transfer coefficient; or perhaps a reduction in the activity of a catalyst as it is used up over time. Despite model mismatch, the controller must still perform adequately (i.e., robustly). The constraint parameter can be used to make the process less sensitive to minor disturbances or model mismatch. It may be tuned to obtain either a rapid response ($\lambda \approx 0.01$) or a high degree of stability ($\lambda \approx 0.99$), either high performance or high robustness. The "see–saw" (Figure 8.4a) shows the robustness/performance dichotomy in a simple graphic way. The key to good process control is to achieve the balancing act of high controller performance and reasonable robustness to disturbances. Our experiences,

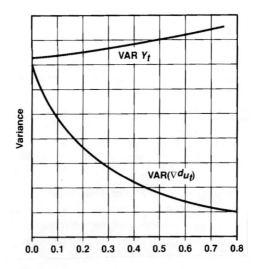

Figure 8.3 Typical sketch of the constraint parameter (λ) versus the variance of the control variable (Y_t) and the manipulated variable changes ($\nabla^d u_t$).

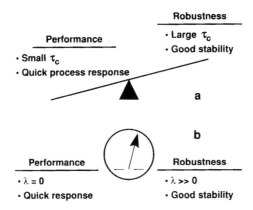

Figure 8.4 A "Balancing act": control performance versus robustness.

and Figure 8.3, indicate that intermediate values of λ, those in the 0.2–0.4 range, strike this compromise or balancing act best.

Many plants do not have systems in place to allow a controller to be used in the CMVC form of Eq. (8.5). Most plants do, however, have proportional, integral, derivative (PID) controllers, which are inexpensive and easy to implement and fine tune. At the present time, PID controllers are still the most commonly used controllers in the process industries.

One form of a PID controller is its so-called velocity form:

$$\nabla X_t = P \nabla e_t + I \frac{T_p}{60} e_t + D_k \frac{60}{T_p} (e_t - 2e_{t-1} + e_{t-2}) \tag{8.6}$$

where T_p is the controller poll time.

References 7 and 8 show how the CMVC [Eq. (8.5)] can be recast into the velocity form of the PID controller [Eq. (8.6)], using some simple approximations and algebraic rearrangements. We have shown that it is straightforward to design an appropriate CMVC using the CHJ method, recast it algebraically, and then implement it as a common PID controller [7].

Internal Model Control (IMC) [8] is another attractive approach to control, one that exhibits many similarities to the time series/CMVC methods previously described. The IMC approach addresses the performance/robustness dichotomy directly and quantitatively.

A block diagram of the IMC control structure is provided in Figure 8.5. The feedback signal is given by

$$\tilde{d} = (p - M)u + D \tag{8.7}$$

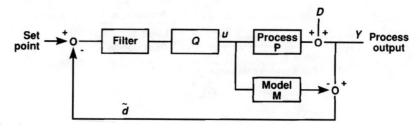

Figure 8.5 Internal model control (IMC).

If the model is perfect ($P = M$) with no disturbances ($D = 0$), then $\tilde{d} = 0$. This simple structure very directly expresses the notion of model–plant mismatch (uncertainty of the process).

As stated earlier, many plants would like to implement a standard PID controller. A method for implementing the IMC in standard PID form is described by Morari and Zafiriou [9]. Their approach is known as the IMC tuning rule for PID control. In this approach, a single adjustable parameter τ_c, is specified by the user. Once it has been specified and the model has been defined, a table of controller gains can be determined [9]. A large value of τ_c gives a more robust result, whereas a smaller value gives a quicker response to a disturbance. In this sense, this IMC tuning parameter is perfectly analogous to the constraint parameter of CMVC (see Figures 8.3 and 8.4). One conceptual advantage to the IMC approach is that τ_c has greater physical meaning than the constraint parameter of the CHJ method and thus may allow greater use of proper engineering judgment. The important point is that IMC methods can be used to yield good PID controller performance and yet still remain robust [9].

For the reasons given above, we prefer either IMC tuning or the CMVC approach over the more traditional Ziegler and Nichols [1,10] and Cohen and Coon [1,10] tuning methods. Although these latter methods can be very useful, the IMC and CMVC methods allow robustness to be tuned in using a single parameter.

8.3   Dynamic Process Modeling

8.3.1   The Philosophy of Computer Modeling and Simulation

For the past three decades there has been a trend toward more quantitative approaches to solving design and control problems in the process industries. The rapid development of computer technology has largely made this trend possible. At the present time, large, complex sets of algebraic, ordinary differential or even partial differential equations can be solved using relatively inexpensive desktop computers. This sort of quantitative analysis has made it possible to investigate alternative process designs, to control processes more precisely, and, perhaps most important, to provide a deeper understanding of the internal mechanisms of the processes studied [11].

Computer modeling and simulation allows scientists and engineers to answer "what if" questions: what if we bought new equipment, what if we changed our raw material addition schedule, what if we used a continuous rather than a batch process, what if we started to cool before the temperature set point was reached, and so on. Generally, process simulation examines such problems by depicting a scenario, manipulating the proper parameters, and evaluating the results [12], often before action is taken or specific experiments are planned.

As we shall see, computer modeling is a high-level task, requiring an educational background that is both demanding and diverse. It requires process knowledge, engineering know-how, knowledge of fundamental physical and chemical principles underlying the process, as well as some familiarity with computer technology and mathematical methods. Indeed, although the original "bottleneck" to this approach was that the equations could never be solved in one's lifetime, one may argue that the bottleneck to modeling nowadays is really the limit to one's educational background.

8.3.2 Building and Using Dynamic Process Models

There is a fairly well-defined approach to mathematical model building [11]. The approach is given in the flow chart provided in Figure 8.6.

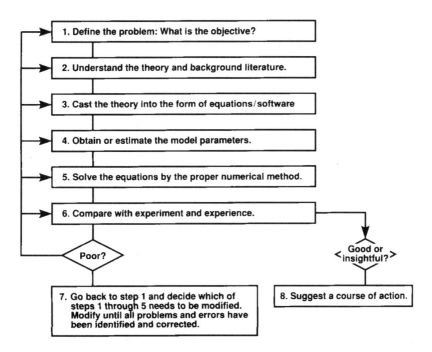

Figure 8.6 How to build a computer model.

The first step, defining the problem, is most crucial. This can usually be done only by people who have experience and background pertaining to the process to be studied, plus knowledge of the abilities and limitations of process modeling. Once the problem has been suitably defined and objectives set, then understanding the theory and literature pertaining to the problem is a time consuming, yet necessary part of the task to solve the problem. Often the real technical skill is exhibited at the third stage of the model-building process: formulating the theory as clear, unambiguously defined equations that can be solved by computer. The fourth step, parameter determination, demands a very resourceful individual. Computerized searching techniques and skilled librarians can be most helpful at this stage. Unfortunately, it may still be necessary to do experiments to estimate key parameters (or convince others to do so) in order for a model to be accurate enough to make predictions. This may slow down the process, unless the proper experimental facilities exist. The fifth step, traditionally the most difficult one, prohibited this method of quantitative analysis from being productive back as recently as the 1960s. But in the 1970s and 1980s, dramatic advances in computer technology have made it possible to solve very complex sets of equations efficiently and inexpensively. Despite this powerful technology, the computer model predictions often do not make sense immediately. Assumptions made in the model, and in the model-building process, have to be questioned, checked, and verified, preferably by well-designed experiments. It may be necessary to reformulate and rerun a computer program hundreds of times to ensure that it is genuinely capable of accurate predictions.

Finally, once a model has been built, run, and validated, it can be enormously helpful and useful. We have used modeling to guide experimentation, to design processes, to assess costs and potential profitability of new process alternatives, and, to be sure, to control temperature. At Rohm and Haas we have also even found this approach helpful in serving our customers: customers have asked our salespeople to have us run simulations of a copolymerization model for the monomer products we sell them. This technical service helps us retain satisfied customers and requires only minimal effort, if the dynamic models are in place.

There are a variety of different types of computer models one can envisage, usually characterized by the types of equations solved or the types of problems to be solved [12]. For example, there are linear programming models used in optimization and policy determination, spreadsheet/database models used in cost analyses, steady-state unit operation models used in plant design, probabilistic models used for safety analyses, and control loop real-time modeling (described in other chapters in this book).

The present focus is on dynamic process modeling, useful in treating batch and semi-batch processes. In a dynamic process model, activities are described as a function of time. The model calculates the states of the system as a function of time and (often) as a function of the parameters that can be changed in the process. As a dynamic model, it does NOT assume that steady-state conditions apply. Dynamic process modeling is most useful in understanding how nonlinear dependencies among variables and coupling among smaller subprocesses affect the process as a whole. In the following two subsections, we show examples of dynamic process models, one simple and one complex, with a focus on temperature control.

8.3.3   A Simple Dynamic Process Model for Temperature Control

In what follows we describe a relatively simple process for a semi-batch exothermic reactor controlled by a PID temperature controller. In this analysis we follow the flow chart given in Figure 8.6 to show how the model-building process really works.

Figure 8.7 shows a schematic of the reactor system we wish to examine. Our aim is to control the temperature of this semi-batch reactor and to maintain high productivity (using maximum cooling) at the same time. The problem is to design a simple (PID) feedback temperature controller to manipulate the feed rate of a key exothermic reactant in such a way that temperature remains under control (within limits). We use a relatively simple model consisting of simple mass and energy balances (including the kinetics), together with the equations for the PID controller. The unsteady-state heat balance around a jacketed reaction kettle is given by:

$$M\,C_p = \frac{dT_r}{dt} = F_f C_{pf}(T_f - T_r) + R_r \triangle (H_r) - U\,A(T_r - T_j) \qquad (8.8)$$

where
   M is the mass of the reactor in lbs
   F_f is the feed rate in lbs/hr
   C_p and C_{pf} are the reactor and feed heat capacities in BTU/(lbs-deg F)
   T_r and T_f are the reactor and feed temperatures in deg F

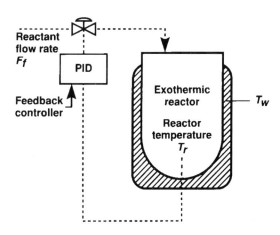

Figure 8.7   Schematic of semi-batch reactor system with PID temperature controller.

R_r is the reaction rate in lb/(hr-ft^3)
V is the reaction volume in ft^3
ΔH_r is the heat of reaction in BTU/lb
U is the overall heat transfer coefficient in BTU/(hr-ft^2-deg F)
A is the heat transfer area in ft^2
T_j is the average jacket (cooling water) temperature in deg F.

The reaction rate is given approximately by a first-order rate law. with an Arrhenius temperature dependence:

$$R_r = A \exp\{-E_a/(R(T_r + 459))\} C_r \qquad (8.9)$$

where
A is the preexponential factor in hr^{-1}
E_a is the activation energy in BTU/(lb-mole)
R is the universal gas constant in BTU/(lb-mole-deg R)
C_r is the concentration of the reactant in lb/ft^3.

The mass balances for the total reactor mass M and for a particular reactant r are given by

$$\frac{dM}{dt} = F_f \qquad (8.10a)$$

$$V\frac{dC_r}{dt} = \frac{F_f C_{r,\text{in}}}{d_r} - R_r V \qquad (8.10b)$$

where $C_{r,\text{in}}$ is the concentration of r in the inlet stream and d_r is the density of r (in lbs/ft^3). (Density changes are assumed to be negligible for this process.)

The energy balance around the cooling water jacket is given by

$$\frac{d}{dt}(M_j C_{pj} T_j) = F_j C_{pj}(T_{j,\text{in}} - T_j) - U A (T_j - T_r) \qquad (8.11)$$

where $V_j, C_{pj}, M_j, T_j, T_{j,\text{in}}$, and F_j are defined analogously to the definitions given for the variables in Eqs. (8.8) and (8.10). The PID equation provided in Eq. (8.7) applies, with F_f as the manipulated variable and T_r as the control variable.

Equations (8.8)–(8.11) and (8.6) constitute a system of ordinary differential and algebraic equations. The parameters in these equations were estimated either from pilot plant kinetic studies or from material properties available in the literature. These equations can be solved by standard methods, so long as reasonable initial values have been specified [13].

The SimuSolv computer program [14] was used to solve the actual equations. SimuSolv is well suited to dynamic process modeling. Besides making it easy to specify/program the model equations, SimuSolv permitted us to add noise to the output to simulate the effects of minor disturbances.

The results of one simulation are provided in Figure 8.8. As can be seen from Figure 8.8a, the concentration C_r increased to a maximum, before decreasing once the temperature and reaction rate became sufficiently high. The jacket temperature T_j dropped from its initial value of 80 deg C to about 65 deg C, remaining constant for most of the process. These simulation results are for a fixed cooling water flow rate.

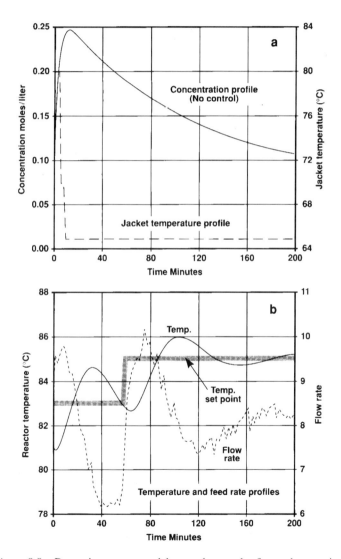

Figure 8.8 Dynamic process model control example: first-order reaction.

Figure 8.8b shows that the present PID temperature controller provides some measure of control, but it is far from perfect. The temperature profile lags the set point for practically the entire process. Also, temperature control requires fairly wide swings in the reactant flow rate F_f, which ranges from 6 to 10 lbs/min in the present simulation. Finally, the simulation predicts, not surprisingly, that the biggest control problems are to be expected at the beginning of the process: after 120 min, both the temperature and flow rate profiles have settled down to nearly constant values.

In summary, a fairly simple model can be quite powerful in determining sensitivities to related variables, assessing various control strategies, and estimating control parameters.

8.3.4 The SCOPE Model: A Sophisticated Dynamic Process Model

The SCOPE (Simulation and Control of Emulsion Polymerization) [15,16] model is a very sophisticated dynamic process model that treats batch and semi-batch emulsion copolymerizations in jacketed reactors. It consists of simultaneous differential and algebraic equations that compute material balances for each species of interest and energy balances for the emulsion reactor and jacket. Kinetic equations from the emulsion polymerization literature have been incorporated into the model. Diffusion-limited termination and propagation reactions are assumed to handle the gel effect. Classic copolymerization reactivity ratio theory is used to compute instantaneous and average copolymer compositions.

SCOPE also computes emulsion particle size and molecular weight. Particles are nucleated by micelles or precipitation and rapidly microcoagulate to form particles of a uniform diameter. The ratio of monomer to surfactant dictates how many particles are formed. A histogram approach couples nucleation and growth to compute the entire particle size distribution. Molecular weight distributions are computed using the method of moments.

The level of detail probed in the SCOPE model required several man-years to develop fully. These details have already been published [15,16], and will not be repeated here. In spite of this excruciating detail, there are still problems with the accuracy of the SCOPE model and key aspects of emulsion polymerization are missing. Thus, still more sophisticated models have been developed [17]; and we are improving and extending the SCOPE model as well [18]. Still, no matter how many improvements we make and no matter how much detail we include, there will always be some model–plant (i.e., SCOPE–emulsion process) mismatch.

Yet model–plant mismatch can be dealt with, as we have pointed out in Section 8.2. In addition, we have found SCOPE to be tremendously useful and insightful in our efforts for process control. Moreover, we have found SCOPE useful in synthesis design, process design, technical service applications, and even process control. Finally, it has been a useful training tool for new emulsion polymerization researchers.

To illustrate the utility of the SCOPE model, we include Figures 8.9 and 8.10, reprinted from ref. 16. These figures plot key model outputs versus time for three different process strategies employed in a styrene/Methyl methacrylate (MMA) semi-batch emulsion process. Three computer simulation runs were carried out to evaluate the three strategies: the base case run employed a PID temperature controller similar to that described in Section 8.3.3, with a temperature set point of 50 deg C; the "KPS × 2" run was similar, except that the initiator (potassium persulfate) concentration was doubled; the "SET PT. = 60" run was similar to the base case run as well, except that the set point was chosen to be 60 deg C instead of 50 deg C.

Figure 8.9a shows that the polymerization rate changes dramatically midway through the process as a result of the combined effect of the temperature and the strong gel effect typically exerted by MMA and styrene in free-radical polymerizations [15]. This increase occurs at an earlier time for the high initiator run. The particle size profile (Figure 8.9c) follows the polymerization rate profile, with some shrinkage occurring as the less dense monomer converts to the more compact copolymer. The

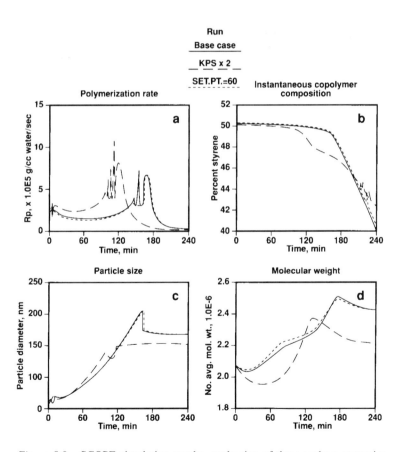

Figure 8.9 SCOPE simulation results, evaluation of three scaleup strategies.

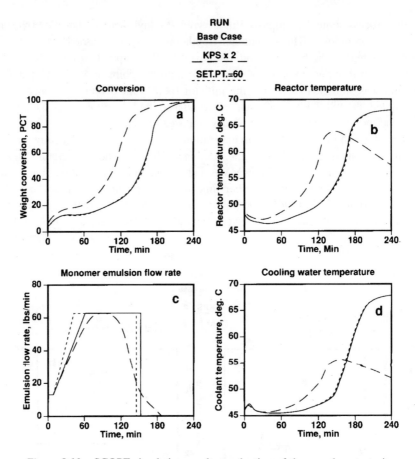

Figure 8.10 SCOPE simulation results, evaluation of three scalup strategies.

copolymer composition for this nearly ideal system is fairly well behaved (Figure 8.9b), but the instantaneous molecular weight profiles (Figure 8.9d) are intriguing. The high initiator run predicts the molecular weight to decrease, then increase, before leveling out at the end of the process. On the other hand, the molecular weight profiles for the two other runs look similar and predict higher molecular weights overall.

Figure 8.10a shows the conversion profile follows the polymerization rate profile, as expected. Figure 8.10b shows the temperature increases earlier for the high initiator run, but surprisingly, temperature control was better overall: the temperature range was only 48–64 deg for the high initiator run, whereas it ranged from 45 to 70 deg for the two other runs. Variation in the jacket temperature (Figure 8.10d) was also less. Such high temperatures could be attributed to the control algorithm, which set the monomer emulsion flow rate (Figure 8.10d) to its maximum value for much of the run while the temperature was below the desired set point. This high flow rate eventually caused the set point to be exceeded after the rate had increased and the exotherm had begun.

In summary, models such as SCOPE, which take a long time to develop, can be enormously useful in problems such as emulsion polymerization, where interrelationships among variables are very complex and difficult to predict without a good quantitative model.

8.4 Feedforward and Feedback Temperature Control

8.4.1 Why Feedforward

It is easier to make good decisions when the level of reliable and accurate information increases: greater information content leads to better decisions in fields as diverse as economics, politics, marketing, and, to be sure, process control.

Traditional feedback control is passive and reactive rather than proactive. That is, when a disturbance affects a process, a traditional feedback controller will not act until the controller actually senses the effect of that disturbance. For a chemical process exhibiting a long time constant, a feedback control action (more properly a **REACTION**) is taken typically too late. This delayed reaction means that it will take a long time to bring the process back to the desired process set point. To prevent this from happening, a feedback controller can be set with a very high gain. The drawback to a high gain controller, however, is that it may be too sensitive to minor disturbances. That is, the control algorithm sacrifices some stability in order to ensure that the controlled variable is maintained close to its set point.

On the other hand, if the principal variables affecting the process are known or can be accurately measured, then the control action can be computed (based on a model for the process). Such information can be directly used to control the process. This more proactive, information-rich, anticipatory feedforward control mode is clearly preferred over the more passive, reactive feedback control mode. This is especially true for batch or semi-batch processes, which, by their very nature, do not attain a steady state, but, instead, change dynamically with time, often in a way that can be modelled or predicted.

8.4.2 A Simple Form for the Feedforward Controller

Feedforward computations use a mathematical model to describe the steady state or the dynamic material or energy balances for an unsteady-state process. The mathematical equations in this model may be either linear or nonlinear. We have found simple models to be surprisingly effective in temperature control. As mentioned in Section 8.3, however, even sophisticated models are never perfect, so the feedforward computations (model predictions) are never perfectly accurate. There is inevitably some degree of model–plant mismatch; disturbances (such as raw material impurities) enter into the plant in ways that are virtually impossible to model. Model–plant mismatch, then, leads naturally to a process controller having both feedforward AND feedback (FF/FB) control elements. A good dynamic process model (see Section 8.3) should be sufficiently accurate to predict the effects and sensitivities of the major disturbances expected. With such a model, the feedback controller does not need to be carefully tuned, and may intentionally be detuned slightly. Detuning will dramatically improve the stability over a more precisely-tuned, high-gain, feedback-only controller.

The following example, based on a very simple steady state-energy balance for temperature control, demonstrates the usefulness of a FF/FB controller. Figure 8.7 and Figure 8.11, which provides more detail, depict a semi-batch process: cold reactants are gradually added into a tank reactor, but no product is removed until the reaction is completed. Semi-batch processes are commonly used to handle highly exothermic reactions: the sensible cooling of the cold reactant feed offsets the heat release due to the exothermicity. Moreover, semi-batch processes are convenient for manufacturing a variety of products in the same reactor. Semi-batch processes, however, are inherently nonlinear because the contents in the reactor increase constantly over time. Furthermore, as the feed rate changes, the temperature of the reactor can exhibit an inverse response: increasing the feed rate decreases the reactor temperature for a short time. Unfortunately, this temporary decrease in the reactor temperature is ordinarily followed by a dramatic increase in temperature once the exothermic chemical reaction rate increases sufficiently.

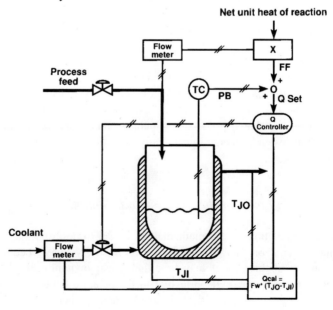

Figure 8.11   Feedforward/feedback control schematic for a semi-batch reactor.

One big problem with semi-batch reactions is that many products are made in the same reactor. Tuning a controller for each of these products is simply not practical. However, a simple FF/FB control strategy can be designed to work effectively to handle a wide spectrum of products.

The feedforward control terms include a simple energy balance consisting of the sensible cooling due to the cold reactant feed and the heat of reaction. The sensible cooling rate is given by:

$$Q_{\text{sens}} = F_f C_{p_{\text{in}}} (T_r - T_f) \tag{8.12}$$

The notation is similar to that of Eqs. (8.8)–(8.11). The heat release rate is the product of the reactant feed rate and its exothermicity:

$$H_1 = \Delta H_r F_f \tag{8.13}$$

Overall, then:

$$Q = H_1 - Q_{\text{sens}} \tag{8.14}$$

The feedback controller is a PID controller, although, as we shall see, a PD controller ($I = 0$) may provide greater flexibility:

$$FB = -\left(K_1 e + K_2 \int e \, dt - K_3 \frac{dT_r}{dt} \right) \tag{8.15}$$

where e is the difference between the reactant temperature and the set point:

$$e = T_{sp} - T_r \tag{8.16}$$

The controller output is the sum of both the feedforward and the feedback parts expressed in units of energy per unit time (BTU/min):

$$Q_{set} = FF + FB \tag{8.17}$$

The rate that the reactor temperature increases is linearly related to the rate of heat removal by the cooling water jacket according to:

$$M C_p \frac{dT_r}{dt} = F_f C_{pf} (T_f - T_r) + Q - Q_j \tag{8.18}$$

Thus

$$\frac{dT_r}{dt} \propto Q_j$$

Thus the FF/FB controller output is used in a cascade control arrangement: Q_{set} is set using Q_j, which, in turn, is determined by the jacket water flow rate and jacket temperature. This cascade controller maintains the reactor temperature (T_r) close to the desired set point exceptionally well.

8.4.3 Simulation Example

The following is an example to illustrate FF/FB control. In this simulation the true plant was modelled according to a first-order chemical reaction described in Section 8.3.3. The FF/FB control scheme was described in Section 8.4.2.

Simulation results are provided in Figures 8.12–8.15. A PD controller is used as the feedback controller: this controller provides the kind of rapid response required for a semi-batch reactor system exhibiting fast dynamics. With a PD controller, there is no integration action per se, but the FF part of the control algorithm ensures that there is no bias or offset relative to the set point (see Figure 8.12b). On the other hand, the feedback only controller (Figure 8.12a) exhibits the constant offset expected of a typical PD controller [1,10].

Figure 8.13b shows that the FF/FB controller, in contrast to the FB only controller (Figure 8.13a), performs very well despite the large step change of the reactant feed rate occurring at 30 min. The FF/FB controller significantly outperforms the FB controller, and yet is still very robust. To see just how robust, we simulated the effect of model–plant mismatch by deliberately underestimating or overestimating the process heat of reaction by 30% in the feedforward control algorithm. Nevertheless, as Figure 8.14 shows, the controller performance is still good. Here the model–plant mismatch can be overcome (compensated for) by the feedback component of the algorithm. In both cases, the feedforward component handles the steady-state heat load while the feedback component handles the dynamic transients.

Both the performance and robustness of the FF/FB are further illustrated in Figure 8.15, in which the chemical reactivity was assumed to be lost (perhaps due to an impurity or blunder) for a 20-min period starting at 60 min. Despite this shock to the system, the closed-loop performance was very good. As Figure 8.15 shows, even with a 50% loss in reactivity, the reactor temperatures remained close to the desired set point throughout this period, and excellent performance was reestablished by 105 min.

This rather simple example demonstrates that with a very simple energy balance model, a FF/FB controller makes significant strides in improving both the controller performance and robustness.

Perhaps the most important point concerning the applicability of FF/FB control strategy is that the FB controller usually does not have to be tuned again for each product run in a versatile, flexible semi-batch reactor. This is because the FB controller is used only to handle the mismatch between the feedforward model and the actual plant. On the other hand, the FF/FB controller can be slightly modified for as many products as is practical by entering a precalculated unit heat of reaction from the

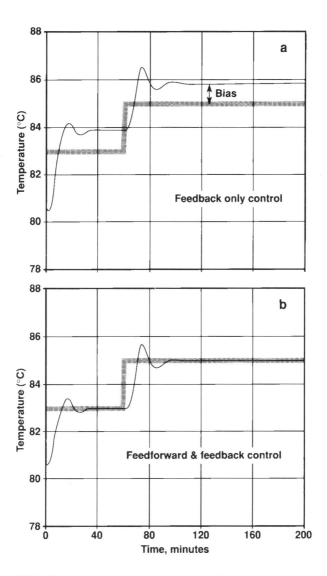

Figure 8.12 Plot of time verses temperature, with set-point change at 60 min.

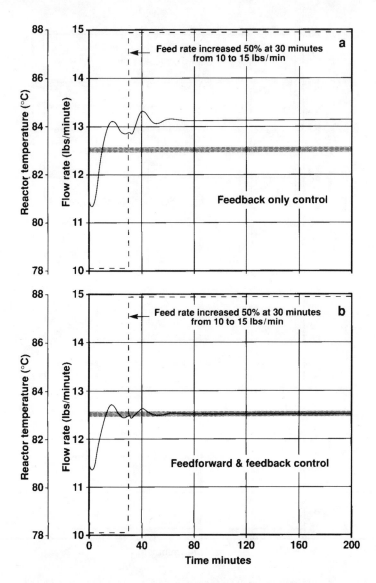

Figure 8.13 Plot of temperature and feed rate verses time.

8. Methodologies for Temperature Control   185

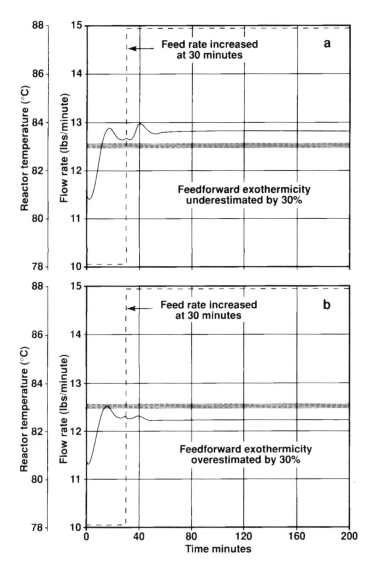

Figure 8.14 Demonstration for feedforward feedback controller (feed rate changed during simulation).

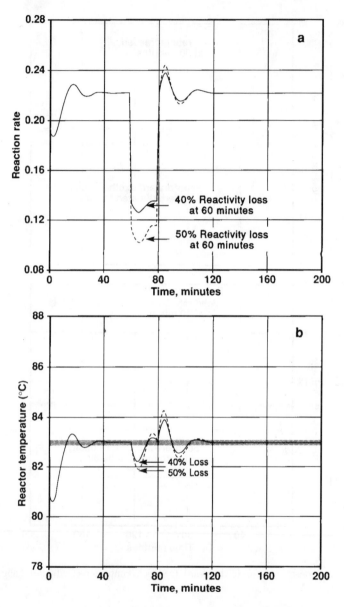

Figure 8.15 Demonstration of robustness for a feedforward and feedback control. While feed was held constant at 10 lbs/min, a loss of reactivity at 60 min was presumed, followed by resumption of normal rate at 80 min.

recipe into the process control computer before the semi-batch process is actually run. While the feed is being gradually added, the feedforward controller calculates the heat load by measuring the feed rates of the various reactants on line. Thus this simple FF/FB control algorithm is powerful; it can be used for many different products and product grades.

8.4.4 Generic Model Reference Control

In the process control literature, for highly nonlinear processes, we have found two recent developments based on the reference system synthesis [19,20] that are, in reality, remarkably similar to the FF/FB control concept we have outlined previously. An article entitled "Temperature Control of Exothermic Reactors Using Generic Model Control" [20] can be used to illustrate this similarity for a simple batch process.

The energy balance around a batch reactor is given by:

$$\frac{dT_r}{dt} = \frac{[Q - UA(T_r - T_j)]}{M C_p} \quad (8.19)$$

Here M is the weight of reactor contents, Q is the heat released by the reaction, and the other variables are defined as we have already described for Eqs. (8.8)–(8.11).

According to the Generic Model Control (GMC) [19,20], the manipulated variable, the jacket temperature T_j, is given by:

$$T_j = [T_r - Q/UA] + \frac{M C_p}{UA}\left[K_{11} e + K_{12} \int e\, dt\right] \quad (8.20)$$

By inspecting the steady-state energy balance around the reactor and solving this equation for T_j, we obtain the result:

$$\frac{dT_r}{dt} = 0 = \frac{[Q - UA(T_r - T_j)]}{M C_p} \quad (8.21a)$$

implies that

$$T_j = T_r - Q/UA \quad (8.21b)$$

We now consider Eq. (8.21b) as the feedforward model equation. If we add a feedback equation of the usual PID form, the FF/FB controller becomes:

$$T_j = [T_r - Q/UA] + [K_p e + K_I \int e\, dt] \quad (8.22)$$

(FF term) \qquad (FB term)

One can see at once the equivalence of the GMC approach and the FF/FB approach we have been developing in this chapter: Eqs. (8.20) and (8.22) are identical except that the GMC equation has a variable FB controller gain term including $M\,C_p/(UA)$. In both cases, however, the on-line estimation of Q, the rate of heat released by the chemical reaction, is required [21]. Readers can find a detailed description of on-line energy estimation methods in ref. 21.

8.5 Statistical Process Control and Engineering Process Control

8.5.1 Deming Philosophy of Continual Improvement

Recently, all over the world, Professor W. Edwards Deming's philosophy of on-going improvement of product quality has been universally embraced by both process and small parts manufacturing industries. Use of statistical process control (SPC), a basic tenet of the Deming philosophy, is now a generally accepted part of the manufacturing process. Judicious use of SPC charting techniques [the familiar Shewhart (e.g., $\bar{X}$BAR-R) charts and CuSUM (cumulative sum) charts] not only improves quality but also reduces rework, resulting in substantial productivity improvements and economic benefits [22].

In this section, we show how the same SPC techniques are related to engineering process control objectives. SPC techniques to achieve improved product quality are related to and consistent with engineering process control methods to adjust a process to run as closely as possible to a desired target [22].

8.5.2 Statistical Charting Techniques, Autocorrelation, and Process Control

A big problem with using standard statistical process control techniques is that data from process industries are often serially correlated. That is to say, the average drifts in time. This is particularly true in batch or semi-batch processes. We have already discussed the problem of autocorrelation in the section on time series analysis (Section 8.2.1). In essence, if the autocorrelation is statistically different from zero, then the control limits on a Shewhart chart have to be adjusted. This adjustment is needed to compute the process capability C_{pk} correctly and to apply the well-known Western Electric rules [23] (e.g., the rules that assignable causes must exist for each point that is 3 sigma units away from the centerline, or for 6 points consecutively above the centerline, and so on).

A CuSUM chart can be used to detect a shift in the mean data over time, something that a process control engineer would certainly want to know. The CuSUM chart signals process deviations from a target value, by plotting a running sum of the deviation values. When successive deviation values are small and normally distributed about zero, this plot is fairly horizontal [24]. However, if the deviations are large or biased either high or low, then a mean shift can result. The magnitude of this mean shift and the statistical significance of the shift can be ascertained using either a simple computational procedure or the so-called "V-mask" [22,24] graphical rule (see Figure 8.16).

If the deviations are high or biased, then the data may be autocorrelated in time. The autocorrelation coefficient, which can be easily calculated by most statistical computer packages, leads naturally to the exponentially weighted moving average (EWMA) model. We can see this by examining the EWMA forecast:

$$\hat{y}_{t+1} = z\, y_t + (1 - z)\, \hat{y}_t = \hat{y}_t + z\, e_t \tag{8.23}$$

where the hat (ˆ) indicates the forecast, z is the autocorrelation coefficient, and e_t is defined as the observed error at time t (difference between the forecast and the actual value). As you can see, the EWMA model is a specific model of the general class of time series models [Eq. (8.1)]. A slightly modified version of the EWMA model may also be defined as:

$$\hat{y}_{t+1} = \hat{y}_t + z_1\, e_t + z_2 \sum_{t=0} (e_t - e_{t-1}) \tag{8.24}$$

The forecast $\hat{y}_{t+1}$ is equal to the present predicted value plus three quantities: one proportional to e_t and the second a function of the sum of all the e_t values, and the third a function of the first difference of the e_t. The correspondence to Eq. (8.6), the PID feedback control equation, is quite clear. Indeed, the EWMA equation [Eq. (8.23)] or its slightly modified form [Eq. (8.24)] can be viewed as a dynamic control mechanism to keep a process mean on target whenever sequential data on

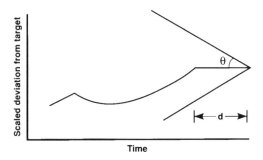

Figure 8.16 "V"-mask method for determining whether a mean "shift" has occurred in data taken as a function of time.

the manufacturing process are available [22]. If experiments can be done without any control, that is, in an "open-loop" fashion, the parameters in Eq. (8.27) can be estimated using historical data and standard regression techniques.

8.5.3   Closed-Loop Controller Performance Assessment

As mentioned in Section 8.2, safety and stability concerns require that industrial processes never be run under completely open-loop conditions; that is, some form of closed-loop control is imperative. It would be desirable to know whether or not the closed-loop controller being used is performing as well as it really should be. In other words, we would like to be able to assess the performance of a closed-loop controller quantitatively. Dr. Tom Harris [22,24] has established such a procedure. He notes that the best possible control in the mean square sense is realized when the minimum variance controller (MVC) is used. When the MVC is used, the autocorrelation function of the process output should, in theory, be zero beyond lag f (f is defined as the number of whole periods of delay plus 1). In practice, this is never realized due to modeling inadequacies and process disturbances (i.e., model–plant mismatch). However, the autocorrelation function can be easily calculated and graphically displayed. If the autocorrelation function of process output is statistically greater than zero beyond lag f, then the controller can be improved. This technique represents a simple and quantitative way to determine whether or not a controller is poorly designed and thus if it needs to be better tuned.

To illustrate this technique, we examine three sets of data shown in Figures 8.17 and 8.18. The data were obtained for the production of fine chemicals in a large, jacketed reactor using a semi-batch process (see also Figures 8.7 and 8.11). Reactor temperatures were controlled using the maximum productivity mode of Section 8.3.3. In this mode the jacket cooling has been fixed at a high value; a reactant feed rate is manipulated to maintain the reactor temperature. If the reactor temperature is too high, then the controller will call for a lower feed rate.

The original controller tuning constants were obtained using the procedure outlined in the section on time series analysis (Section 8.2). A slightly modified control strategy was then adopted to improve reactor productivity. New tuning constants for the controller were obtained using the dynamic process modeling technique described in Section 8.4. The new control strategy, together with the modified tuning constants, were then implemented in a very large reactor. Although the control results looked reasonably good, we were not sure if the PID controller we were using was a minimum variance controller (MVC). Figure 8.17a shows that control was pretty good: the reactor temperatures of all three batches was maintained to within a fraction of deg C. However, we wanted to know if the controller could be further tuned to achieve even better performance.

Autocorrelation coefficients of reactor temperature were plotted in Figure 8.17b. As you can see, the autocorrelation function of process output is, for this process,

8. Methodologies for Temperature Control 191

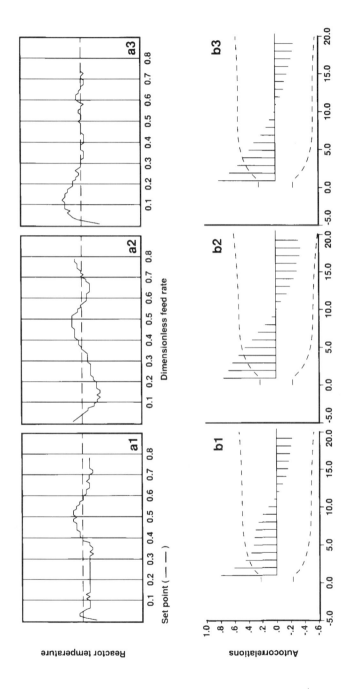

Figure 8.17 Autocorrelated plant temperature data. Dotted lines in b1, b2, and b3 indicate 95% confidence limits for reactor temperature autocorrelations.

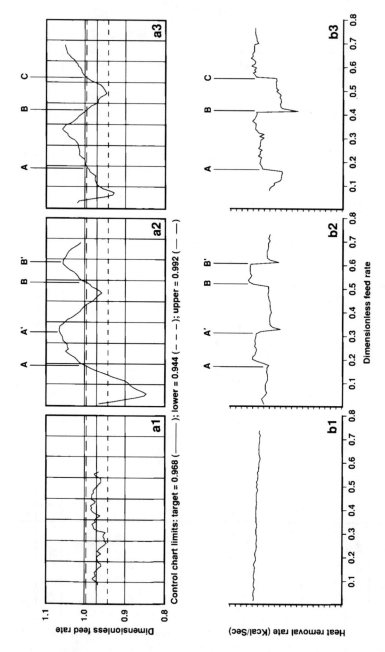

Figure 8.18 EWMA feed rate plots and heat removal rate plots.

statistically significantly less than zero beyond lag 3 (the number of whole periods of delay plus 1). Because our time series transfer function has a lag of 3, then, this controller cannot be tuned further to achieve better performance.

8.5.4   Special Cause Identification under Autocorrelation

When autocorrelation is present in data, the aforementioned SPC charting techniques can be used to determine if special causes are responsible. By plotting the error (technically, a single-point Shewhart chart), the exponentially weighted moving average (with a suitably chosen value of the autocorrelation parameter z), and the exponentially weighted moving variance, we can often determine if something special or unusual has happened to a process. (Professor Tom Harris [22,25] has written PC software to calculate autocorrelation coefficients and to produce these charts easily and conveniently.)

Consider Figure 8.19 as an example of how these charting techniques can be used to identify special causes in process data. Theses data, a series of pressure measurements, were taken for a proprietary process run in the laboratory that should have reached a steady state, but clearly had not done so. Early in the process, a high-frequency pattern in the pressure data persisted, as evidenced by the power spectrum, which plots intensity versus frequency for these data (see Figure 8.20). Later on, the process lined out to a steadier (yet not perfectly steady) value. Early in the process, both the mean and the variance were slightly higher than later in the process. After reviewing the data, these charts and the operator's notes, we noticed that the operator had made several adjustments to the process early in the run. In particular, the operator was continually monitoring and then slightly changing the pump speed to get exactly the feed rate called for by the operating procedure. The frequent adjustments made to the pump speed resulted in the high-frequency pattern in the pressure data noted in Figures 8.19a and 8.20. Once the operator had decided that the feed rate had been properly set, he stopped adjusting the pump. At this point, the high-frequency pattern in the pressure data disappeared and the overall variance was reduced. Unfortunately, the reason for the lower frequency pattern noted later in the run could never really be unequivocally ascertained.

8.5.5   Determination of Process Disturbances under Feedback Control

In the previous subsection, we treated the problem of identifying special causes in process data that may or may not be autocorrelated in time. In the present subsection, we treat the case of determining when process upsets or disturbances have occurred for a process operating under feedback control.

When a process is under feedback control, the process output is no longer the appropriate variable to be used for SPC plotting purposes [22]. The controlled variable

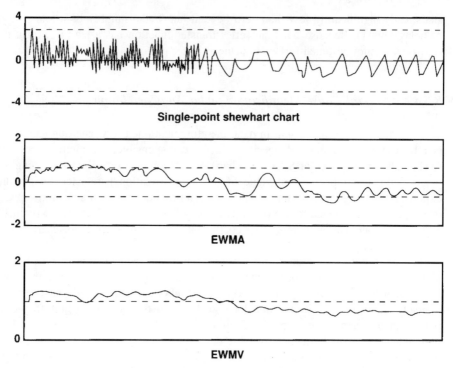

Figure 8.19 SPC charts for data taken as a function of time.

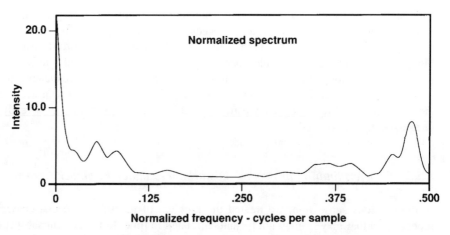

Figure 8.20 Spectral analysis of data shown in Figure 8.18. Note high- and low-frequency peaks.

8. Methodologies for Temperature Control   195

(the output) will be kept at or near the setpoint by the controller all the time; thus the SPC plot will not reveal any process upsets. In other words, the controller actually masks any disturbances (i.e., special causes). We cannot further improve the process if we cannot identify the time and magnitude of the disturbances. To identify the disturbances under feedback control, it is better to chart the manipulated variable. Furthermore, because the manipulated variable will be autocorrelated because of the action of the feedback controller, the exponentially weighted moving average (EWMA) plot of the manipulated variable should be used [22].

To illustrate this point, we return to the data we analyzed in section 8.5.3. In that section, we determined that control was good, and that the control algorithm was a minimum variance controller. However, there still may be "special causes" to contend with. Figure 8.18(a1) shows the EWMA plot for the feed rate for one of the batches, which, by our analysis of the energy balances, did not experience any external cooling disturbances [see Figure 8.18(b1)]. On the other hand, the EWMA plots for the feed rates of two other batches, shown in Figures 8.18(a2) and 8.18(a3), indicate external cooling disturbances at certain times. Moreover, the times that the EWMA charts indicated when the disturbances occurred agree well with the actual occurrences of disturbances as indicated by the energy balance plots [see Figures 8.18(b2) and 8.18(b3)].

Therefore, an EWMA plot of the manipulated variable can be a simple yet powerful diagnostic tool to find out when disturbances (or special causes) occur, even under closed-loop feedback control.

Acknowledgments

We would like to acknowledge the Rohm and Haas Company for permission to publish this work. We would like to thank Jeff Nathanson and John McGregor for many valuable comments. Finally, we would especially like to thank Dottie Saxton and Chris Campbell for their help in preparing this manuscript.

References

1. Coughanowr, D.R. and Koppel, L.B., *Process Systems Analysis and Control*. McGraw-Hill (1965), see esp. pp. Chap. 10, 241–242, 312–314. See also, Shinskey, F.G., *Process Control Systems*. McGraw-Hill, (1979).
2. Box, G.E.P. and MacGregor, J.F., *Technometrics* **16**, 391 (1974).
3. Box, G.E.P. and Jenkins, G.M., *Time Series Analysis: Forecasting and Control*. Holden-Day (1976).
4. *SAS/ETS Users' Guide*, SAS Institute, Cary, NC (1983).
5. MacGregor, J.F., Taylor, P.A., and Wright, J.D., *Advanced Process Control: An Intensive Short Course*, unpublished notes, McMaster University, Hamilton, Ontario, Canada, May 1984.
6. Clarke, D.W. and Hastings-Jones, R. *Proc. IEEE* **118**, 1503 (1971).

7. Dougherty, E.P., Westkaemper, P.H., and Wu, R.S., in *Computer Applications in Applied Polymer Science II* (Provder, T., ed.) *ACS Symp. Ser.* **404**, (1989).
8. Seagall, N.L. and Taylor, P.A., *I EC Process Des. Dev.* **25**, 495 (1986).
9. See, for example, Morari, M. and Zafiriou, E., *Robust Process Control*. Prentice-Hall (1989).
10. Smith, C.L., *Digital Computer Process Control*. Intext (1972).
11. Franks, R.G.E., *Mathematical Methods in Chemical Engineering*. John Wiley & Sons (1979).
12. Williams, P., Process simulation: a tool for on-line optimization. *Chem. Process.* July 1989, pp. 65–70.
13. Press, W.H., Flannery, B.P., Teukolsky, S.A., and Vetterling, W.T., *Numerical Recipes: The Art of Scientific Computing*, Cambridge University Press (1986), esp. Chap. 15.
14. Steiner, E.C., Blau, G.E., and Agin, G.L., *Introductory Guide to SimuSolv Modeling and Simulation Software*. Dow Chemical Company (1986).
15. Dougherty, E.P., *J. Appl. Polymer Sci.* **32**, 3051 (1986).
16. Dougherty, E.P., *J. Appl. Polymer Sci.* **32**, 3079 (1986).
17. Richards, J.R., Congalidis, J.P., and Gilbert, R.G., *J. Appl. Polymer Sci.* **37**, 2727 (1989).
18. Dougherty, E.P., in press (1994).
19. Bartusiak, R.D., Georgakis, C., and Reilly, M.J., *Chem. Eng. Sci.* **44**, 1837 (1989).
20. Cott, B.J., and Macchietto, S., *I E C Res.* **28**, 1177 (1989).
21. Wu, R.S., Dynamic thermal analyzer for monitoring batch processes. *Chem. Eng. Prog.* pp. 57–61. (1985).
22. MacGregor, J.F., Hunter, J.S., and Harris, T.J., *SPC Interfaces*, unpublished notes for a short course, Burlington, Ontario, Canada, May 1990.
23. *Statistical Quality Control Handbook*. AT&T (1956).
24. Doherty, J., Detecting problems with SPC. *Control*, November 1990, pp. 70–73.
25. Harris, T.J., *Can. J. Chem. Eng.* **67**, 856 (1989).

CHAPTER 9

Integrated Temperature Control Applications in a Computer Control Environment

Martin Dybeck

9.1 Introduction

It is very likely that temperature control was mankind's first practical use and application of process control. One needs to only consider the first time that man recognized the tremendous potential of the fermentation process when fruit juices or other starchy plant extracts were left to sit at a certain temperature range for several days. Somebody later recognized that through boiling and condensing, the early form of distillation control, there was even more "tang" in the resulting liquid. As vessels were needed to hold this wonderful new elixir, the art of pottery and baking clay at the right temperature became more refined. People also soon recognized that food remained palatable a little longer by applying heat to it for a certain time — the early concepts of sterilization.

Temperature control has come a long way since those early days with the advent or more accurate and reliable instrumentation for both measurement and control of temperature in the 1960s through the 1980s. More recently, the application of intelligent control, artificial intelligence (AI), diagnostics, and modeling have added another dimension to the control of temperature and other related variables.

9.2 Integrated Temperature Control through Distributed Process Computers

Digital control systems with real time continuous and batch control capabilities vastly increased the applications of automated temperature control in the industry.

Martin Dybeck, Life Sciences International, 1818 Market Street, Philadelphia, PA 19103, USA

One of the increasingly important objectives in chemical manufacturing is safety, improved diagnostics, and preventive maintenance. On-line fault diagnosis and predictive maintenance checks not only reduce costly downtime and production loss, but can also prevent many a hazardous condition. The following are some relatively straightforward but very effective examples of this type of on-line process check.

9.2.1   Temperature/Pressure Verification

In highly exothermic batch reactions such as vinyl chloride monomer polymerization to form polyvinyl chloride (PVC), it is absolutely critical that the temperature and pressure transmitters are always correctly calibrated. The kinetics of VC polymerization are such that above a certain temperature, an exponentially increasing amount of cooling is required to control the polymerization. The temperature control profile of certain PVC resin types run within 6–10% of this critical high temperature (10–15 deg F below the temperature where the cooling system has difficulty controlling the reaction). To allow for a potential 2–5 degree overshoot during heat-up, it is important that the temperature transmitters are accurately calibrated to within 1–2 degrees. A downward drift of more than 5 degrees could bring the reaction close to the temperature of "no return" if there are also simultaneous heat-up problems.

To allow the computer to provide continuous 24-hr calibration checks, a second, back-up temperature transmitter together with a pressure transmitter is installed. The two temperature readings are now continually compared to be within 4 degrees of each other. Simultaneously, a vapor pressure calculation uses the pressure reading together with Antoine's Equation to calculate a theoretical temperature from the vinyl chloride vapor pressure.

$$\log P_v = A - \frac{B}{T + C} \tag{9.1}$$

$$T = \frac{B}{A - \log P_v} - C \tag{9.2}$$

To provide maximum accuracy in this calculation, several sets of the constants A, B, and C were used for different ranges of pressure. Also the amount of converted resin in the vinyl makes a difference in the vapor pressure and must be taken into account. Thus the constants are a function of pressure and time. Usually three pressure ranges and three time periods into reaction provide sufficient accuracy, thus requiring nine different sets of A, B, and C to cover all conditions.

If the ΔT between the two temperature transmitters is greater than a fixed range, the reaction or heat-up is halted. This allows the operator to check the equivalent temperature from the vapor pressure. Depending on the plant policy, he then makes the decision of which temperature transmitter to use in the cascaded control scheme and continue the reaction, or possibly to abort the batch. Similarly, if the theoretical temperature deviates too much from the two actual temperature readings, a decision will be made to calibrate the pressure transmitter.

9.2.2   Predictive Maintenance on a Heat Exchanger

In the previous example, we assumed that the cooling system was working at or near capacity. In a highly exothermic reaction, a steady decrease in efficiency of a heat exchanger can eventually also have serious consequences. In less exothermic processes, it is more of an economic liability due to longer batch times. An example is the manufacture of ethoxylate-based surfactants. Ethylene oxide is gradually added to an alcohol/catalyst mixture in a batch reactor. The rate of ethoxylate addition is directly proportional to the rate of conversion, which is to a large extent affected by the rate of heat removal. A decrease in heat removal capacity means a slowdown in ethylene oxide feed, and thus a prolonged reaction. A 20–30% reduction in heat exchanger capacity often results in a 30–50% increase in batch times. The rate of heat exchanger fouling or plugging of tubes will be affected by the geography of the plant and the type of water used (i.e., such as river water) and the configuration of the heat exchanger itself.

An effective maintenance plan through both regular and computer-predicted cleaning schedules can keep the batches running at optimum and safe conditions.

If the reactor configuration includes the cooling water or the material to be cooled inlet and outlet temperature and a flow measurement, a straightforward heat transfer calculation $q = F\,c_p(\Delta T)$ can be used to track the change of heat removal capacity in BTU/hr from week to week for each reactor.

If insufficient transmitters, that is, measurements, are available to calculate the BTU removal, a suggested option might be to statistically track the position of the output of the controller that regulates the flow. At a fixed heat removal capacity, a fixed temperature set point, and a relatively constant cooling water temperature, a constant amount of cooling water should be required. As fouling or plugging decreases the heat exchanger performance, a proportionally larger amount of cooling water (or reduced amount of reactant) will be required to keep the temperature at set point. This relative change in the control valve position can be used as a warning to signal that the heat exchanger has dropped below an acceptable amount of heat removal capacity, and that it is time for a backflush or other maintenance.

9.3   Process Optimization: The "Hyperplane" Technique

In the field of optimization of continuous control, especially those involving reactor kinetics, a variety of methods such as linear programming exist that pose varying degrees of difficulty in development. One successful yet relatively easy to implement technique is called "hyperplane search" and uses multivariable statistical analysis as its basis [1]. As a stable, robust, and highly adaptive algorithm, the hyperplane technique always improves or holds a desired parameter (i.e., profitability, product quality, etc.) over time.

In any plant or process that is energy or material cost intensive such as petrochemical and steel manufacturing plants, there are many opportunities to optimize process conditions and save energy or raw material dollars. The hyperplane optimization method has its origin in statistical regression analysis and can be adapted to supplement gradient search methods for real-time optimization.

Complex kinetic processes present a challenge in that the interaction and relationship among all the independent controllable variables are not always clearly definable or even understood. In addition, different independent variables have varying and sometimes opposite effects on the key dependent variables. Thus, improving one quality variable drives another specification the wrong way or drives up the cost of production. In a perfect world, one could eventually find the optimum and leave the process at those settings. In the real world though, conditions and especially the noncontrollable, external independent variables change over time and the process does not stay at its optimum. It is this requirement of on-going real-time adjustment that is so critical if one is to keep a process near or at its optimum. Hyperplane search is a very effective yet simple method to address this very challenge.

The hyperplane technique generates a least-squares fit of an objective function as a linear function of chosen manipulated variables. The objective function (i.e., cost, product quality, or specification) can be dependent on any number of variables, but must be impacted by the chosen manipulated variables (i.e., temperature, feed rate, speed). The "curve fit" is based on recent sampled data so that only current plant performance impacts its progress. The system searches for the optimum by looking at each slope of the regressed objective function versus manipulated variable and incrementing that manipulated variable into the direction of improving profit or alternatively lower cost.

An example objective function (the "y" value) may be to minimize the pounds of steam per pounds of product. Next, a set of controllable independent variables ("x" values) must be chosen that have a direct impact on the objective function. It is recommended that no more than one or two x variables be selected to keep the calculation and the optimization simple and as direct as possible. Examples of x variables include: a temperature, a material flow or concentration, a motor amperage or speed, or any other recipe variable that is easy to manipulate and track via a control system. The objective function (steam cost) will now be set up as a function of the manipulated or controllable variables.

$$y = f(x_1, x_2, \ldots x_n) \tag{9.3}$$

(where preferably $n \leq 2$)

9. Integrated Temperature Control Applications

Next we linearize the model, forming an equation with y (steam cost) as a function of the manipulated variables

$$y = a_0 + a_1 x_1 + a_2 x_2 + \ldots a_n x_n \tag{9.4}$$

$a_0 =$ constant
$a_1 =$ slope of y in x_1 direction
$a_n =$ slope of y in x_n direction

For least-squares implementation, we calculate $(E_i)^2$ where $E = $ error of $y_1 - y_i$, and solve for a_0 and a_1 as a function x, y.

$$\sum (E_i)^2 = \sum (y_i^2 + a_0^2 + a_1^2 x_i^2 - 2a_0 y_i \tag{9.5}$$
$$- 2 a_1 x_i y_i + 2 a_0 a_1 x_i)$$

Therefore

$$\frac{\partial \sum E^2}{\partial a_0} = 2 \sum a_0 - 2 \sum y + \sum a_1 x = 0 \tag{9.6}$$

Thus

$$a_0 = \frac{\sum y - a_1 \sum x}{N} \tag{9.7}$$

where $N = $ total number of x, y data pairs

$$0 = \frac{\partial \sum E^2}{\partial a_1} = 2 \sum a_1 x^2 - 2 \sum xy + 2 \sum a_0 x \tag{9.8}$$

Therefore

$$a_1 = \frac{N \sum xy - \sum x \sum y}{N \sum x^2 - \sum x \sum x} \tag{9.9}$$

if $z_i = (x_i - x)$ or $x_i = (z_i + x)$
then

$$a_1 = \frac{\sum yx}{\sum z^2} \tag{9.10}$$

Through ongoing analysis and use of process data, the constant a_n will be continually updated. The sign of $a_n(+/-)$ determines in which direction the manipulated variable must be moved to minimize or maximize y (in this case minimize the steam

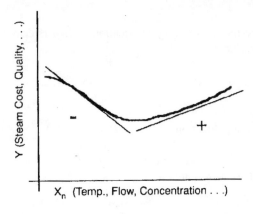

Figure 9.1

cost). If there is a local minimum such as shown in Figure 9.1, a positive sign on a_n indicates that the manipulated variable x_n must be decreased to lower the cost near the minimum or maximum.

When developing this equation on actual process data, the following procedure is recommended:

- Collect data when process dynamics have settled out and are relatively stable.
- Average data collected as a single value (hourly or batch averages).
- Keep the latest 10–12 x, y pairs, discarding the oldest when a new one is collected.
- Calculate sign of a_n and move x_n in the direction of optimum y value.
- Check constraints of variables.

The optimizer is thus continuously sampling data from the process, regressing, choosing the direction to improve the objective variable (in this case reducing steam cost), and moving towards the objective.

The hyperplane algorithm is a practical example of an adaptive searching optimizer that could have many potential applications in kinetic processes, especially in the presence of a computer control system. In areas where clear physical or model data are unavailable, an open-ended optimizer such as this can provide significant savings.

Reference

1. Bozenhardt, H., *Hyperplane: A Case History. Control Engineering Conference*, May 1986.

CHAPTER 10

Servo Temperature Control of a Batch Reactor

Thomas W. Campbell

10.1 Introduction

Temperature control of batch reactors is difficult for two reasons: batch reactors are integrators of energy and the process gain is a nonlinear function of volume, kettle temperature, utility temperature, and valve position.

An integrating process is one in which the heat losses to the atmosphere are insignificant. Uninsulated vessels containing as little as 20 gallons can be considered integrators of energy. The problem this poses is one of controller sufficiency. If an integrating process is exposed only to step-set-point disturbances, the minimally sufficient servo controller is a proportional (P) controller. The term "minimally sufficient controller" is used here to denote the simplest controller structure that is capable of rejecting a specific disturbance for a given process. However, if the process is exposed to step-load disturbances, the minimally sufficient servo regulator controller is a proportional–integral (PI) controller. The problem is that the structure of the minimally sufficient controller depends on the structure of the disturbance. For non-integrating processes this is not the case and makes controller design and tuning much easier.

The second problem cuts right to the core of control theory — the issue of linearity. The prime assumption of classical control theory is that the process is stationary and linear, that is, the process transfer function can be expressed as a rational polynomial in the Laplace or z-domain. This means the parameters that

---

Thomas W. Campbell, Eastman-Kodak, Kodak Park, Rochester, NY 14650, USA

constitute the transfer function — the delay, the gain, and the time constant(s) — will remain unchanged for all operating conditions. This also implies that the process does not change from batch to batch. Unfortunately this is a poor assumption for most batch reactors.

The process gain is a very strong function of operating temperature, utility temperature, volume, and valve position. The delay is similarly affected but to a lesser extent. The time constant is the only term that can be assumed to be relatively stationary.

For step-set-point disturbances, tuning equations are presented that depend only on the process transfer function. These equations guarantee a critically damped closed loop response which for our purposes is the optimal closed loop response. Optimality will be discussed and described mathematically but it should *not* be construed with linear quadratic gaussian (LQG) type optimality. It must be remembered that the optimality criterion used here arose not out of the calculus of variations but rather from demands of scientists concerned with product quality and efficient batch process operation. Mathematics has a name for what the scientists are demanding: a critically damped response.

Controller tuning of batch reactor temperature loops used to be a time consuming iterative procedure that would ordinarily take several days to complete. This is no longer the case. Process and disturbance transfer functions and the tuning equations are all that are needed to design a set-point controller and to tune it. The process transfer function can be determined by simple identification experiments.

It will also be shown that, after a process is linearized, the closed-loop performance is limited only by the process delay. This is not a startling revelation. What is significant is that the performance is quantifiable. Because intrinsic delay will be shown to be the sole determinant of closed-loop performance, it is no longer necessary to build a plant to know its performance. Many plant designs can be evaluated on paper before any investment capital is spent.

All results in this chapter apply to the application of non-delay-compensated proportional, integral, derivative (PID) control to first- or second-order processes with delay but with no zeros in the transfer function. The plant is assumed to be subjected only to step servo disturbances. The rationale for this is explained in the section on the optimality criterion. The time constant(s) of the process are assumed to be stable or semistable (not unstable). With these provisos, process invertibility will not be addressed but assumed.

The z-domain will be used exclusively to analyze the control problem. The z-domain has many advantages. The most important mathematical advantage is that delays require no special treatment. They become part of the transfer function polynomial and as such lend themselves to eigenvalue analysis. This single property is principally responsible for the serendipitous discovery of the controller equation for PID tuning and the plant performance metric.

The theory generated here is applicable to any first-order or second-order process, not just integrating processes. Naturally all of the limitations expressed above must also be met.

10.2 Plant Description

The plant of interest to us is a 50-gallon batch reactor. The batch reactor is jacketed but the jacket does not flood during heating or cooling. This is an important point in the design of a batch chemical reactor. A "falling film" reactor typically performs better than a flooded jacket reactor by a factor of five or more. Hence plant performance can be significantly enhanced by using a "falling film" or a dimpled jacket reactor.

Cooling is effected by cold water spraying onto the kettle liner. Water is distributed around the kettle through a ring in the upper part of the jacket. This ring is perforated with holes to direct the spray of water onto the outer kettle wall. The flow of water is controlled by a control valve.

Likewise, heating is effected by releasing steam into the jacket through the use of a steam ring in the base of the kettle. A diagram of the plant is shown in Figure 10.1.

Unfortunately, it is necessary to admit the existence of a modest reaction exotherm as reactants flow into the vessel and react. In addition, the reactants may be at temperatures where they too introduce a modest load disturbance. Experiments can determine whether a set-point control strategy can meet this specification.

It is unwise at this point to perform a process identification. Process identification contains an implicit assumption of process linearity and stationarity. The next section tests the strength of these assumptions.

10.3 The Linearity and Stationarity Assumptions

As discussed previously, a primary assumption of conventional control and identification theory is that the plant dynamics are stationary. This means that the parameters

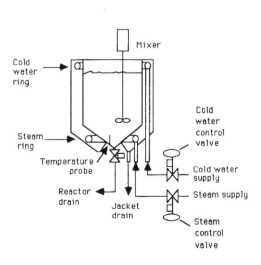

Figure 10.1 Process diagram.

that constitute the transfer function — the delay, the gain, and the time constant — are constant in value over the entire operating regime. This implies that the process does not change from batch to batch nor does the process change as a function of the operating conditions.

For batch reactors, it is generally a good assumption that the time constant does not change with respect to very much of anything. Integrators seem to stay integrators.

A change in the effective process delay is the most serious challenge to the stationarity assumption. The process delay is the most important process variable from the standpoint of stability. If the delay increases twofold, the volume within the stability envelope decreases by more than it would if the process gain were to change by a factor of two. The stability envelope is a surface generated by any combination of P, I, and D coefficients that delineate the boundary between an unstable closed-loop process and a stable closed-loop process.

Although the observed delay in a kettle does change, it does not appear to change significantly except on plant startup. On plant startup, the utility lines — steam and water — leading to the reactor are often at room temperature. When the control valves are first opened, the expected change in temperature very often does not happen until the lines are purged of the room temperature utilities.

The gain is also assumed to be constant. This is generally a very poor assumption. The process gain is affected by volume, temperature, viscosity, mixer speed, and thermal conductivity of the fluid. The next section shows that the valve characteristic, valve deadband, and valve crossover should be added to this ever-lengthening list.

10.3.1 Effect of Valve Characteristic on Plant Stationarity

The gain of an integrating process is measured by opening the steam valve (or cold water valve) a set amount and observing the steady-state heating (or cooling) rate. The gain, as used here, is the steady-state heating (cooling) rate divided by the valve position. The implication of a constant gain system is that the heating (cooling) rate must change proportionately to valve position. This is almost never true.

Figure 10.2 is a plot of the plant heating rate as a function of steam valve position. For the linearity assumption to be true, this curve should be linear with respect to valve position as demonstrated by "the ideal heating rate curve" in Figure 10.2. Instead this heating rate curve is very flat at initial openings and increases rapidly above 30%. The process gain is the slope of this curve. The process gain at 70% valve open is five times the process gain at 10% valve open. The implications of this gain curve are poor response near set point and relatively good response far from set point.Figure 10.3 is a plot of the valve coefficient, C_v, as a function of steam valve position. The valve used here is a half inch equal percentage Bauman valve. Indeed the process gain curve does appear to have the same characteristic shape as the C_v curve although not quite as pronounced. One might expect that installing a valve with a more linear characteristic would be warranted here. That is one solution. Another solution is to use software to compensate for this effect.

10. Servo Temperature Control of a Batch Reactor   207

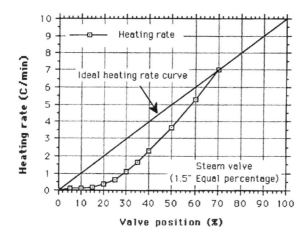

Figure 10.2 Heating rate dependence on steam valve position.

Figure 10.4 is a plot of the plant cooling rate as a function of cold water valve position. This cold water valve has high initial gain (cooling rate slope). Opening the valve more than 45% has only a marginal effect on the overall cooling rate. This valve has the same valve coefficient curve as the steam valve. Refer to Figure 10.3. This valve is an equal percentage valve. For example, when the valve is open 45% the orifice is open only 25%. One might conclude here that the valve needs to be reduced in size and we appear to need a more equal percentage characteristic to compensate for what appears to be an inverse equal percentage characteristic. Figure 10.4 underscores

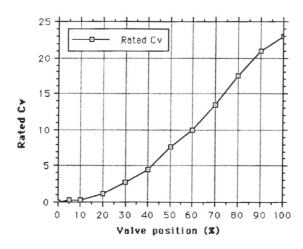

Figure 10.3 Valve coefficient curve for steam and CW valve.

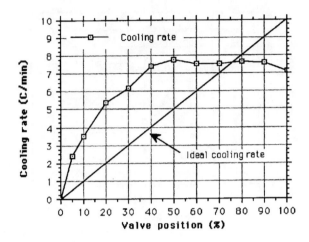

Figure 10.4 Cooling rate dependence on CW valve position.

that it is important to size valves based not on the availability of cold water but instead on the ability to transfer heat to the cooling medium from the vessel.

Comparing Figures 10.2 and 10.4 suggests that this process will suffer from extreme gain imbalance. At 5% open, the cooling rate is 2.4 deg C/min whereas the heating rate is 0.2 deg C/min. There exists a factor of 10 gain imbalance at this point of initial valve travel. When a process is operated at set point under a condition of no loads, the controller neither heats nor cools — both valves are closed. Because the process will spend most of its time near set point (i.e., at steady state), the linearity of the process gain as a function of valve position for the initial valve travel, say 0–10%, is most important.

10.3.2 *Effect of Gain Balance on Plant Stationarity*

Figure 10.5 combines the information in Figures 10.2 and 10.4 to display the gain curve of the process as a function of valve position.

If an identification experiment were conducted at this point, the results would be difficult to interpret. A single transfer function is not representative of either the heating process or the cooling process. Indeed, Figure 10.5 demonstrates the importance of identifying the heating process independently of the cooling process and at different valve positions — unless the valve gains are first linearized.

Figure 10.5 suggests a linearization strategy. The suggested range for the PID controller is from 2100% to + 100%, with the output from the PID controller split as follows: outputs above 0% are sent to the steam valve and outputs below 0% are sent to the cold water valve. Each of these outputs can be separately scaled in software to enable independent gain linearization.

10. Servo Temperature Control of a Batch Reactor 209

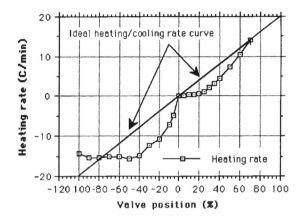

Figure 10.5 Overall heating rate curve dependence on valve position.

10.3.3 *Effect of Valve Deadband and Crossover on Plant Stationarity*

Figure 10.6 demonstrates the effect of valve deadband on the gain curve from Figure 10.5. Deadband introduces a discontinuity in the gain curve. This discontinuity reflects the inability of the controller to cause any effect until its output exceeds the deadband.

Without the use of integral action in the controller, valve deadband may introduce a persistent temperature offset from set point. Valve deadband can be eliminated without having to resort to integral action by introducing a positive bias in the output to the valve (in software) or by recalibrating the valve.

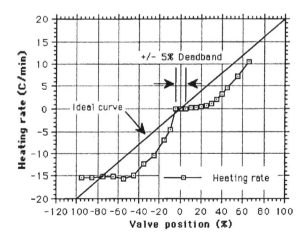

Figure 10.6 Effect of deadband on the heating rate curve.

10.3.4 Effect of Valve Crossover on Stationarity

Valve crossover occurs when the steam valve and the cold water valves are both open over part of their travel. Figure 10.7 depicts what valve crossover might do to the gain curve as a function of valve position at a particular temperature. Sometimes the use of valve crossover is intentional, but, in the case of an integrating process, it introduces uncertainty into the balance point of the process.

The balance point of the process is the output value of the controller during steady-state operation where the process is at set point. When there is no valve crossover and no deadband, the balance point is 0% output. In the presence of valve crossover, the balance point of the plant is a function of temperature. The effect of valve crossover is to introduce offsets of varying magnitude as a function of temperature.

10.3.5 Effect of Temperature on Plant Stationarity

Figures 10.8 and 10.9 show how the maximum heating and cooling rates vary as a function of temperature. The cooling rate appears to increase linearly with temperature. The heating rate decreases monotonically but not linearly with temperature. There is a factor of two difference between the magnitudes of the minimum and the maximum heating rates. There is a factor of three difference between the magnitudes of the minimum and the maximum cooling rates. Thus, the heating and cooling gains are not stationary as a function of temperature.

The magnitude of these gain changes taken individually is large enough to warrant concern about whether gain balance can be preserved. Unfortunately, these gain changes must be considered together because they move inversely with respect to each other. In the worst case, the ratio of the cooling gain to the heating gain can

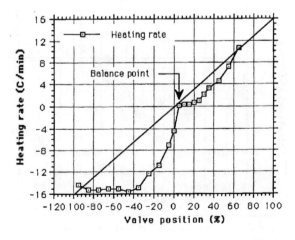

Figure 10.7 Effect of valve crossover on the heating rate curve.

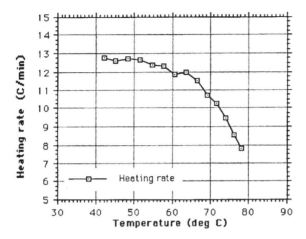

Figure 10.8 Heating rate dependence on reactor contents temperature.

change by up to factor of six. No controller can be expected to perform well under these conditions.

10.4 Plant Identification

The data in the preceding section demonstrate the large variability of the process gain as a function of valve position and operating temperature. Valve deadband and valve crossover are nonlinearities that commonly afflict control valves. The effect of temperature alone on the process gain is enough to cause great concern over process

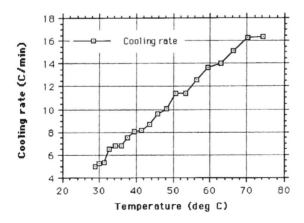

Figure 10.9 Cooling rate dependence on reactor contents temperature.

stationarity. The effect of valve position on the process gain introduces still another source of nonlinearity. These realities conspire to make the results of a single process identification meaningless.

The assumption of linearity in transfer function structure is supportable given that the valve deadband nonlinearity is removed. The assumption of parametric stationarity is not supportable unless the effects of temperature, valve position, valve crossover, and volume (which has not been discussed) are canceled by appropriate transformations.

The data in the preceding section most notably suggest that the cooling and heating processes may have such large differences in delay time and gain parameters that they need to be identified separately. If one does not perform the above recommended linearizations, then identification experiments as a function temperature, volume, and valve position for the heating and cooling processes taken separately (and the heating and cooling process taken together) may need to be conducted. Such an involved experiment would undermine the usefulness of identifying the process at all and would yield results less compelling than experiments specifically focused at revealing the underlying sources of nonlinearity or nonstationarity.

It is recommended that all sources of nonlinearities be removed or be minimized before any identification is conducted.

The plant transfer function is perhaps the single most important piece of information that one can determine. The transfer function is the mathematical description of how the plant converts inputs to outputs. Linear transfer function models are generally considered simply out of convenience. Recognition of this overt assumption is key, as experiments such as those discussed in the previous section can be designed and conducted to test how linear the process really is.

The transfer function tells us the equivalent linear dynamics of the plant: the time constants, frequencies of oscillations, delays, and steady-state values. Because plant stability is the single most important factor in the design of any control scheme, it is important to conduct identification experiments where the process has the greatest gain and greatest delay. The greatest process gain might occur when the vessel is operated under low-volume conditions. The greatest delay might occur when the vessel is operated with the greatest expected volume. A "pseudo" transfer function can be built that has these elements. The parameters of this pseudo transfer function may not actually resemble the actual parameters of the process under any single set of conditions. Instead the parameters represent a composite process that has the smallest stability envelope. The tuning parameters must reside within the stability envelope for the pseudo process to be stable. Because of the way the pseudo process is constructed, the actual process has a stability envelope that cannot be smaller than that of the pseudo process and hence the real plant is guaranteed to be stable.

Equation (10.1) is the pseudo transfer function for the batch reactor described in Section 10.2.

$$P(z) = \frac{0.0267}{z^{12}(z-1)} u(z) \tag{10.1}$$

Equation (10.1) states that the temperature, $P(z)$, rises at a rate of 0.0267 deg C/s for every percentage of positive valve travel, $u(z)$. Likewise, it cools at 0.0267 deg C/s for every percentage $u(z)$ is negative, that is, the cooling valve is open. There are 12 s of delay. This means that the effect of each controller action is not observable until 12 s after it occurs. The time constant of the process is infinite as indicated by the "$(z-1)$" term in the denominator of Eq. (10.1).

10.5 Control Objectives

This section outlines briefly the control objectives typically desired for temperature control of a batch reactor and then discusses issues pertinent to each objective.

Objective 1: Attain the temperature set point rapidly without overshooting when step-set-point changes occur.

Overshoots on step changes can be caused by zeros on or near the unit circle in the closed-loop error transfer function, $E(z)$, or by an underdamped closed-loop response. Avoidance of zeros on the unit circle and tuning the controller such that the process has a critically damped response to step-set-point changes will ensure that the process responds as rapidly as possible and without oscillation or overshoot of the set point.

Objective 2: Tolerate some offset from set point during a ramped set-point change.

The presence of one integrator in the process and control transfer functions taken together will yield a closed-loop response that will reject step disturbances and suffer only from a constant offset when subjected to ramp-set-point disturbances. This objective adds no new constraints.

Objective 3: Do not overshoot the set point after the set-point ends ramping.

If a critically damped closed-loop response is provided, this objective will also be met.

Objective 4: Tolerate less than 0.1 deg C offset when the set point is held constant.

If the process is truly linear and stationary and subjected to no load disturbance, this objective should be easily met.

Objective 5: Tolerate less than 0.25 deg C offset 1 min after the cessation of any impulsive load disturbance

A significant load disturbance is the addition of a large quantity of some reactant that may be at a different temperature than the bulk reactants or may generate or consume energy as a result of a reaction. Therefore significant load disturbances are allowed as long as they are brief. This objective specifies how quickly the reactor must recover from such a load.

10.6 Controller Optimality

Controller optimality is usually difficult to express in mathematical terms. From the previous section on controller objectives, a step-set-point disturbance is the primary disturbance unless the controller we devise cannot meet Objective 4. In addition, a critically damped response is the desired response to a step change in set point.

Root locus is used here to express and evaluate optimality. There are no sources of high-frequency disturbances. Hence the root locus of the plant is sufficiently rigorous to describe optimality and robustness. More importantly, it allows us to deal directly with the poles and zeros of the process and controller. These structural entities are what determine the closed-loop response of any control system.

The control problem is one of creating a controller that forces the process to have a critically damped response to a step change in set point. Because the objective of any controller is to eliminate error, the closed-loop error, $E(z)$, is used to evaluate optimality.

10.7 Theoretical Development

The PID controller is the optimal controller for any first- or second-order process that has no delay and no zeros such as the one described in Eq. (10.2).

$$P(z) = \frac{\omega_0}{(z - p_1)(z - p_2)} \qquad (10.2)$$

For such a process, the zeros of the PID controller can be chosen to exactly cancel the poles of the process. With proper tuning the resulting closed-loop performance can be made to be "dead beat." This means that the process described by Eq. (10.2) achieves its set point in two scans.

$P(z)$, the process transfer function, is composed of two poles at p_1 and p_2. The numerator contains only the constant term ω_0. The real world rarely presents us with such an ideal process. A better description of reality includes time delay as shown in Eq. (10.3).

$$P(z) = \frac{\omega_0}{z^d(z-p_1)(z-p_2)} \quad (10.3)$$

The d poles at the origin, from the z_d term, represent the d units of delay in the process. Again, the zeros of the PID controller can be chosen to exactly cancel the poles of the process. But usually there are not enough zeros in a PID controller to cancel all of the delay poles. Hence the closed-loop response can no longer be made "dead beat." The PID is not optimal only because it does not have delay compensation.

$C(z)$, the PID controller transfer function, is written in its simplest form in Eq. (10.4).

$$C(z) = K_p + K_i \frac{z}{(z-1)} + K_d \frac{(z-1)}{z} \quad (10.4)$$

K_p is the proportional gain, K_i is the integral gain, and K_d is the derivative gain. PID algorithms can be coded in a variety of ways and can have many additional features that Eq. (10.4) does not have. Such additional features include trapezoidal discretization, derivative on process instead of on error, and filtering of the derivative error to minimize the controller noise introduced by discrete sampling or electrical noise.

It is assumed that there is no electrical or discretization noise. Equation (10.4) can be expressed as a rational polynomial as shown in Eq. (10.5).

$$C(z) = \frac{(K_p + K_i + K_d)z^2 - (K_p + 2K_d)z + K_d}{z(z-1)} \quad (10.5)$$

Equation (10.5) can be expressed as a transfer function having two zeros in the numerator, two poles in the denominator, and a premultiplicative factor as shown in Eq. (10.6). Only the two zeros, a and b, and the premultiplicative factor, α, are adjustable. The act of tuning of the PID controller requires the appropriate assignment of values to a, b, and α.

$$C(z) = \alpha \frac{(z-a)(z-b)}{z(z-1)} \quad (10.6)$$

To translate Eq. (10.5) into Eq. (10.6) requires the use of Eqs. (10.7a)–(10.7d).

$$K_d = \alpha\, ab \quad (10.7a)$$
$$K_p = \alpha\, (a + b - 2ab) \quad (10.7b)$$
$$K_i = \alpha\, (1 - a - b + ab) \quad (10.7c)$$
$$\alpha = (K_p + K_i + K_d) \quad (10.7d)$$

When $a = p_1$ and $b = p_2$, the zeros of the controller exactly cancel the poles of the process. This leaves only one unknown in the controller described by Eq. (10.6) to be specified via tuning, α. For the purposes of this investigation, the zeros of the controller will always be assigned such that they cancel the poles of the process. This is the standard procedure in the design of pole placement set-point controllers for invertible processes.

The set-point disturbance affecting the process is mathematically described by Eq. (10.8).

$$S(z) = \frac{zs}{(z-1)} \qquad (10.8)$$

$S(z)$ is the z-domain representation of a step. The z domain transfer function of $S(z)$ is a simple integrator. Equation (10.8) simply states that the application of an impulse of unit height results in a step of height s. Small s is a scalar value that translates the unit pulse into a step having magnitude s.

The set-point control problem has the objective of forcing the process variable to follow a prescribed set point. For the chemical industry, set points usually follow steps or ramps. Because a constant offset from a ramp-set-point disturbance is generally always tolerated, it is sufficient to examine step-set-point disturbances exclusively. Loads on the system are assumed to be insignificant for the servo control problem.

Figure 10.10 is a block diagram of a set point control problem. Note the conspicuous absence of any load.

It goes without saying that the objective of the controller is to eliminate error. To accomplish this objective, the closed-loop error transfer function must have no poles on or outside the unit circle. In the z-domain, if the closed-loop poles are outside the unit circle, the closed-loop response is unstable. If the poles are on the unit circle, the response is neither stable nor unstable: the process wanders.

The closed loop response of the error of the process when subjected to a step-like set-point disturbance is expressed in Eq. (10.9) where $S(z)$, $P(z)$, and $C(z)$ represent the z-domain transfer functions as defined previously.

$$E(z) = \frac{S(z)}{(1 + P(z)C(z))} \qquad (10.9)$$

Equation (10.10) results when Eqs. (10.2), (10.6), and (10.8) are substituted into Eq. (10.9).

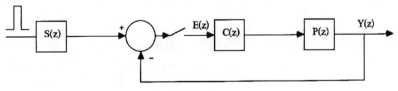

Figure 10.10 Servo control block diagram.

$$E(z) = \frac{\frac{zs}{(z-1)}}{\left(1 + \frac{\omega_0}{z^d(z-p_1)(z-p_2)} \frac{\alpha(z-a)(z-b)}{z(z-1)}\right)} \qquad (10.10)$$

Equation (10.11) is a more convenient representation of Eq. (10.10).

$$E(z) = \frac{zs}{(z-1)\left(1 + \frac{\omega_0}{z^d(z-p_1)(z-p_2)} \frac{\alpha(z-a)(z-b)}{z(z-1)}\right)} \qquad (10.11)$$

To reject the servo disturbance in Eq. (10.11), the servo disturbance pole [the $(z-1)$ premultiplicative term in the denominator of Eq. (10.11)] must be canceled by an integration pole in the $P(z)C(z)$ product. The integrator pole of the controller stands ready to accomplish this task given that $\alpha > 0$. But before we commit the controller to having an integrator we should recognize that if the process were to have an integrator pole, $p_1 = 1$ or $p_2 = 1$, then the process could accomplish this task also and a degree of freedom in the controller would be saved. If there is no controller action, $\alpha = 0$, Eq. (10.11) reduces to the transfer function of the servo disturbance, Eq. (10.8). Hence there must be some controller action if the disturbance is to be rejected.

Equation (10.12) is a condensed version of Eq. (10.11).

$$E(z) = \frac{z^{(d+2)}(z-p_1)(z-p_2)s}{\left(z^{(d+1)}(z-p_1)(z-p_2)(z-1) + \omega_0\alpha(z-a)(z-b)\right)} \qquad (10.12)$$

We know from Eq. (10.1) that the identified plant has only one integrating pole. The $(z-p_2)$ term can be taken from Eq. (10.12) to reflect the closed-loop error transfer function of a first-order process with delay as shown in Eq. (10.13).

$$E(z) = \frac{z^{(d+2)}(z-p_1)s}{\left(z^{(d+1)}(z-p_1)(z-1) + \omega_0\alpha(z-a)(z-b)\right)} \qquad (10.13)$$

If one of the controller zeros is set equal to the process integrator pole, Eq. (10.13) simplifies into Eq. (10.14).

$$E(z) = \frac{z^{(d+2)}s}{\left(z^{(d+1)}(z-1) + \omega_0\alpha(z-b)\right)} \qquad (10.14)$$

Equation (10.14) has two remaining degrees of freedom, α and b. If we set $b = 0$, Eq. (10.14) becomes Eq. (10.15).

$$E(z) = \frac{z^{(d+1)}s}{(z^d(z-1) + \omega_0\alpha)} \qquad (10.15)$$

Over an infinite time horizon the speed of response of Eq. (10.15) is controlled by the magnitude of the largest pole. When the largest pole is minimized, the plant rejects disturbances most quickly. When there is no controller action, the largest pole is in fact the disturbance pole, $(z - 1)$. The remaining poles, contributed by the delay term, lie at the origin.

Figure 10.11 demonstrates the functionality of the magnitude of the maximum pole on the proportional gain, K_p. As soon as some small quantity of controller action is effected, the disturbance pole moves inside the unit circle while the delay poles move out from the origin. As more controller action is applied to the system, one delay pole moves out to meet the disturbance pole that is moving inward. At this point the two poles will combine, form imaginary parts, and begin moving outward together. The point of intersection is where the magnitude of the largest pole is minimized. When proportional control is used, $\alpha = K_p$. The value of α that minimizes the value of the maximum pole is described by Eq. (10.16). From Eq. (10.16) or Figure 10.11, $P_{\max}$ equals 0.9231 when a proportional gain of 1.1026 is used.

$$\alpha_{\text{optimal}} = \frac{1}{\omega_0} \frac{d^d}{(d+1)^{(d+1)}} \tag{10.16}$$

Equation (10.16) demonstrates that the optimal gain of the controller is strictly a function of the inverse of the process gain, ω_0, and a complicated function of the process delay. Because the poles and the gain of the process are canceled by the controller, the speed of response of the closed-loop process is dependent solely on the process delay. In the world of reality, heat transfer and utility limitations also provide an upper bound on the closed-loop response in batch chemical reactors.

When Eq. (10.16) is used for tuning and substituted into Eq. (10.15) the magnitude

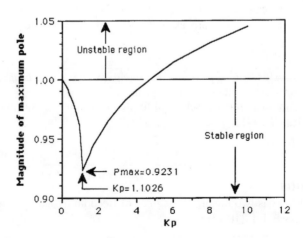

Figure 10.11 Dependence of maximum pole magnitude on controller tuning.

of the largest closed-loop pole can be determined through the use of Eq. (10.17). The magnitude of the largest pole tells us how fast we can expect the process to reject disturbances over an infinite time horizon.

Equation (10.17) is the relation that describes the magnitude, in the z-domain, of the largest pole of Eq. (10.15) when the tuning equations defined above are used.

$$\|p(\alpha_{\text{optimal}})\|_{\max} = \frac{d}{(d+1)} \tag{10.17}$$

Equation (10.17) is always less than unity when α_{optimal} is used. For the process described by Eq. (10.1) and tuned as above, $P_{\max} = 12/13 = 0.9231$. This equation proves that a PID controller can control a process having any amount of delay if it conforms to the above mentioned limitations.

Converting Eq. (10.17) into real-time units requires Eq. (10.18).

$$\tau = \frac{-\Delta t}{\ln(\|p(\alpha_{\text{optimal}})\|_{\max})} \tag{10.18}$$

Equation (10.18) states that the disturbance rejection time constant, τ, equals the negative of the sampling time, Δt, divided by the natural log of the magnitude of the maximum pole of the characteristic equation of Eq. (10.15).

The disturbance rejection time constant of the process described by Eq. (10.1) is 12.5 s or slightly greater than the process delay. Equation (10.19) is an excellent approximation of Eq. (10.18).

$$\tau = d\,\Delta t \tag{10.19}$$

Simply put: the optimal tuning of the system described in Eq. (10.15) will have a disturbance rejection time constant approximately equal to the (real-time) delay in the process. This result has important ramifications for the design of processes: the optimal performance of a process is limited by the delay in the process (given that all the other assumptions are satisfied, i.e., linearity, etc). This single result allows the process engineer to determine the performance of a process or control scheme a priori (i.e., before building the plant to measure control performance). It allows the process designer to focus on the one aspect of the job that is most critical to the performance of the process and is not easily changed during debug operations: the intrinsic process delay.

10.8 Results

Figure 10.12 is a simulation of the plant described by Eq. (10.15) using the tuning equations developed in the previous section. Thirteen seconds after the set point is changed, the process temperature begins to change. For a step change of 10 deg, it

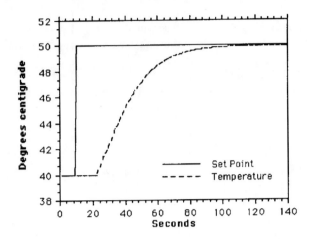

Figure 10.12 Closed-loop response to a step servo disturbance.

takes 90 s for the process to fall within 0.1 deg C of set point. Although this seems slow by typical servo motor control standards, it is enormously fast for a batch reactor temperature control response time. Most importantly, there are no oscillations on its approach to set point. Even though the temperature response appears over damped, it is not. If K_p is increased even minutely above its optimal value, the response would generate an oscillation the magnitude of which would be a function of how far above α_{optimal} K_p is increased.

The value of these results is to demonstrate how a PID controller can be constructed to reject a step servo control disturbance in such a way that a critically damped response results. Our customer objectives are such that the critically damped response is the optimal response.

It has been shown in Eqs. (10.17)–(10.18) that the closed-loop response is a function only of the process delay (given a process that is linear and stationary). More important, a crude estimate of the delay is all that is necessary to estimate the fastest disturbance rejection rate (time constant) for the closed-loop process given that a non-delay-compensated PID controller will be used. The power of this one fact is that process performance can be evaluated with only minor investment in time required for estimating the process delays. The process does not need to be built. Paper studies can screen various schemes so that only the best designed scheme will be the one actually constructed. Time and cost savings, thus, can be quite significant. Finally even process engineers poorly versed in process control can design high-performance processes by evaluating process delay times and by conducting the sort of analysis provided in this chapter.

CHAPTER 11

Modifications of a 500-Gallon Batch Reactor to Provide Better Data Acquisition and Control

R.J. Sadowski and C.G. Wysocki

11.1 Introduction

Back in the early 1970s, BP Research (then Standard Oil of Ohio) installed a 500-gallon reactor for polymer development work. In the mid 1970s, instrumentation was added to allow calorimetric measurements on the reactor. The process data was sent to a mainframe GE-4010 computer via underground cable from the separate pilot plant building.

After the project was completed, the computer interface with the reactor fell into disuse. Since then, the terminals were removed and the mainframe computer was altered several times and moved between locations. Eventually, the computer interface was lost.

After some time, new uses were found for this multipurpose reactor, and its piping was changed to meet the new demands. The piping, though, became quite complicated and difficult for operators to follow. In the mid 1980s, several major new projects warranted a major retrofit to update the reactor mechanically, simplify the piping and install new instrumentation and a data gathering system.

Meetings on the projects were held and potential users were surveyed for their needs. The following modifications to the 500-gallon reactor system were agreed on (see Figure 11.1):

- Addition of an agitator on the hold tank with the capability to handle viscosities up to 10,000 cps.

R.J. Sadowski and C.G. Wysocki, BP Research, Cleveland, OH 44128, USA

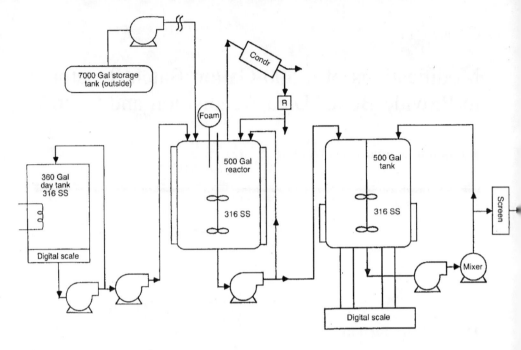

Figure 11.1   500-Gallon Reactor Pilot Plant.

- Addition of a temperature-controlled feed tank.
- Addition of pumps to the feed tank, reactor, and hold tanks to allow both pumping from one vessel to another and recirculation within the vessels
- New piping for both the process and utilities. The process and vacuum lines required stainless steel.
- Thermocouples on the coolant lines to the reactor, hold tank jacket, and condenser. Additional thermocouples were added on the reactor batch to indicate temperature uniformity.
- Flowmeters on the reactor, hold tank, and condenser coolant lines.
- New process controllers.
- A data gathering system with computational capability.
- Bulk storage for raw materials.
- Improved material handling
- Means to measure product weight.

11.2   Functional Requirements of the Control and Data Acquisition System

In addition to the modifications described in the introduction, several functional requirements were specified for the control system. These requirements were high priority ("musts"), moderately high priority ("very desirable"), or low priority ("nice to have"). The "musts" included the following:

- Provide temperature control of the 500-gallon batch reactor via a cascade control system.
- Provide controller tuning parameters [proportional, integral, derivative (PID)] that can be changed while a batch is in progress. We wanted the flexibility to allow the operators to change the parameters or to have the parameters revert automatically to predetermined settings.
- Provide a "foam control" to override the pressure control signal. This could simply be a limit on the pressure control.
- Control the direct injection of steam to the reactor jacket for high-temperature operation. Change the secondary control loop to control the pressure of steam in the jacket.
- Introduce tempered water to the 360-gallon "day tank" coils if the temperature exceeds either high or low limits.
- Monitor feed to the reactor via weight loss in the day tank.
- Alarm and advise the operator of out of spec conditions. Some conditions may require shutdown.
- Be easily reconfigured for different types of processes.
- Be expandable.
- Be user friendly. Operators with a high school education should be able to start up a batch without engineering assistance other than normal written instructions.

"Very Desirable" requirements included the following:

- Calculate heat release levels based on process data (jacket and condenser flows and temperatures).
- Provide the capability to change controller set points based on heat release or conversion rate. This could be an advisory function to the operators.
- Provide a printout of batch status on demand.

Finally, it would be "Nice to Have" a self-tuning capability. In some of the batch processes, the system gain changes dramatically during the course of the reaction. Ideally, the tuning parameters should be changed to accommodate the system gain changes.

11.3 The Control and Data Acquisition System

This section describes our experiences with the data acquisition and control system we selected. The vendor names are mentioned, because these met our particular functional requirements most satisfactorily. Naturally, our readers may have different requirements and choose different systems, but may encounter similar problems.

The control system we selected uses single loop digital controllers interfaced to a PC-based operator station. The hardware consists of Bailey Loop Command Controllers interfaced to an Indtech PC (an IBM AT clone). A software package called ONSPEC by Heuristics was chosen for data logging, alarming, trending, and both on-line and background calculations. Figure 11.2 is a schematic of the control hardware.

Table 11.1 lists the separate functions of the ONSPEC and the Bailey systems. The ONSPEC system is capable of direct digital control and has control block modules available. However, we decided to use the Bailey Loop Command controllers for several reasons:

1. We planned to do numerous on-line calculations that we thought might slow down or compromise the primary control functions.
2. The pilot plant already has several other installations using the Bailey Network 90 System. The operators were familiar with it but had little experience with direct digital control.
3. The Bailey controllers are microprocessor-based and have been configured to perform routine calculations themselves. The results are then sent to the PC for further processing.
4. If the computer failed, the Bailey controllers would maintain control.

In addition to the Bailey controllers, it was necessary to purchase a separate cabinet

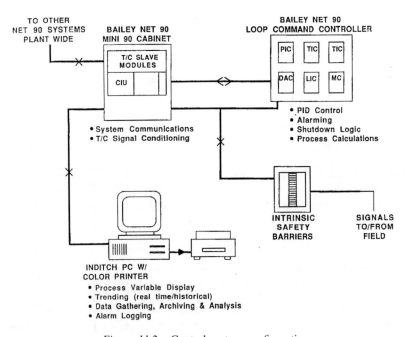

Figure 11.2 Control system configuration.

Table 11.1 Functions of the Bailey Controller and the On-Spec Program

Bailey Controller
Conventional control
Alarming
Shut down logic
Time delays
Totalization
Temperature difference calcs
Temperature averaging
On Spec
Monitoring of multiple points
Data logging
Alarm logging
Graphical trending of data
Graphical display of process
Process
Calculations
Action based on calculated values
Process simulation
Print process data and displays

to house the modules used to link the system into a plantwide communications network. Here the thermocouple signals are converted to digital for use by both the controllers and the computer. Because the reactor was in a hazardous area, we were required to install intrinsic safety barriers (ISBs) on all of the electronic signals going to the process. The 4–20 ma signals from the ISBs could be wired directly to the controllers.

We originally examined four different software systems. All four were satisfactory, but they all lacked the driver program for the Bailey controllers. The driver program is special software that allows the computer and the controllers to exchange information. It was difficult to find someone to write this driver for a reasonable price.

After reevaluation of our previous control system bids, we chose Heuristics' ON-SPEC software. It was one of the few that claimed it could interface with the Bailey controllers. As it turned out, Heuristics marketed a read only driver program for the Bailey system.

After considerable delay, Heuristics contracted with a software shop to complete writing the driver.

This experience taught us how important it is to find a software system that already has a driver written for your control system. Also, we would suggest to the readers that they see a complete system in operation before making a purchase. Moreover, they should know ahead of time exactly what data you want passed between the two systems. Just because a driver exists, it may not do everything you want it to do. Once you have determined a driver's limitations, find out who will meet your specifications, how long it will take to develop, and how much it will cost. Be prepared to wait several months before having the software written and debugged.

When the ONSPEC program first starts, the operator sees a menu of displays to choose from (Figure 11.3). Although some displays are already configured, most of them must be configured by the user with a special drawing program. The screens can show current data points and can be made interactive through user-programmed function keys (Figure 11.4). One can start pumps, do calculation routines, or change process set points. Process alarms appear one at a time at the bottom of the display. In addition, a full screen alarm summary can be called up (Figure 11.5).

11.4 Process Calculations and Graphics

We purchased a data trending package with the ONSPEC software called SUPER-TRENDS (Figure 11.6). This package gives high resolution trend plotting of process

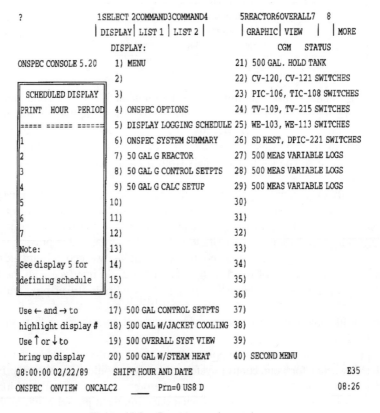

Figure 11.3 Operator station main menu.

11. Modifications of a 500-Gallon Batch Reactor   227

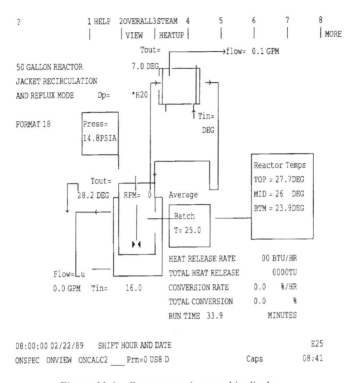

Figure 11.4   Operator station graphic display.

data. Both historical as well as current data can be viewed. Scales and data points can be changed while on-line to allow a more detailed examination of the data. The data can also be printed out in tabular form on demand.

Process calculations are done with an interactive spreadsheet program ONCALC2 (Figure 11.7). Each cell in the spreadsheet corresponds to a location in the main equivalence table. Data from the process can be accessed and transmitted back to the process while on-line.

11.5   On-Line Energy Release Calculations to Estimate Reactor Conversion

We have used the program to calculate heat release data from the process by measuring the heat pickup in the coolant. If we know the heat of reaction, we can calculate the reaction rate. These data can be further integrated to give cumulative conversion. One can even use this calculated value to change the set point on a process controller.

```
                    1 ALARM 2 ALARM 3 ALARM 4 CLEAR 5 PREV 6 PAGE 7 PAGE 8
                    |SUMMARY| SILENCE| ACKNWLG| HISTORY| DISPLAY|  UP   | DOWN  |MORE
                    Alarm history display          Most recent on bottom     1
13:54:28 02/17/89   ONSPEC START                                            E00
15:13:25 02/17/89   ONSPEC STOP
15:15:02 02/17/89   ONSPEC START
15:19:25 02/17/89   ONSPEC STOP
15:20:56 02/17/89   ONSPEC START
15:24:25 02/17/89   ONSPEC STOP
15:26:48 02/17/89   ONSPEC START
15:33:40 02/17/89   ONSPEC STOP
15:35:33 02/17/89   ONSPEC START
16:00:00 02/17/89   SHIFT HOUR AND DATE
00:00:00 02/18/89   SHIFT HOUR AND DATE
08:00:00 02/18/89   SHIFT HOUR AND DATE
16:00:00 02/18/89   SHIFT HOUR AND DATE
00:00:00 02/19/89   SHIFT HOUR AND DATE
08:00:00 02/19/89   SHIFT HOUR AND DATE
16:00:00 02/19/89   SHIFT HOUR AND DATE
00:00:00 02/20/89   SHIFT HOUR AND DATE
08:00:00 02/20/89   SHIFT HOUR AND DATE
16:00:00 02/20/89   SHIFT HOUR AND DATE
00:00:00 02/21/89   SHIFT HOUR AND DATE
08:00:00 02/21/89   SHIFT HOUR AND DATE
ONSPEC   ONVIEW  ONCALC2   ALTCON    Prn= US8 D           Caps         13:46
```

Figure 11.5 Alarm summary.

The next discussion gives the basis for the on-line heat release and conversion calculations. The conversion calculation is based on the laws of energy conservation where:

$$Q_i + Q_R = Q_o + Q_A \quad (11.1)$$
$$\text{Heat In} \quad \text{Generation} \quad \text{Heat Out} \quad \text{Accumulation}$$

The rate of heat generation Q_R is proportional to the weight of material (m) reacted:

$$Q_R = \frac{dm}{dt} \Delta H_r \quad (11.2)$$

Where ΔH_r is the heat of reaction per unit weight.

The heat accumulation results in an increase (dT) in batch temperatures (T_B). The rate of heat accumulation (Q_A) can be expressed by:

$$Q_A = W_B \, C_{PB} \, \frac{dT_B}{dt} \quad (11.3)$$

Where W_B is the total batch weight and C_{PB} is the specific heat of the batch contents.

11. Modifications of a 500-Gallon Batch Reactor   229

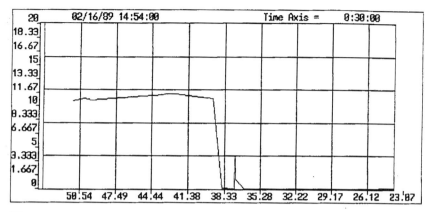

IN
FT166 CW
TO OVHD
10.6594
GPM
20
0

Figure 11.6   Trend chart window.

In a typical batch reaction, heat is either removed from the reactor or added to the reactor through the jacket. Additional heat is lost to the surroundings. Heat removal rate Q_o through the jacket is proportional to the temperature increase (ΔT_c) of the coolant flowing plus losses. This relationship can be expressed as follows:

$$Q_o = F_c \, \rho_c \, C_{pc} \, \Delta T_c + Q_L \tag{11.4}$$

Where:
F_c is the coolant flow rate.
ρ_c is the coolant density.
C_{pc} is the specific heat of coolant.
ΔT_c is the temperature difference between coolant inlet and outlet ($T_{ci} - T_{co}$).
Q_L is the heat loss to surroundings.
In the case of heat being added through the jacket ΔT_c will be positive and the Q_i term can be dropped.

Heat losses to the surroundings (Q_L) are proportional to the temperature difference ΔT_s between the transfer surface and the surroundings. This can be written:

$$Q_L = UA\Delta T \tag{11.5}$$

Where:
U is the overall heat transfer coefficient between the fluid losing heat and the surroundings.
A is the effective heat transfer area for loss to the surroundings.

```
    :   A    :   B    :  BDDNSPECDIntelligentDCalculatorDDDDDD01-21-88
 1     0.00          .
 2     0.00          . Filename         : 500CONV1.DNC
 3     0.00          . Sheet number     : 2
 4     0.00          . Last Sheet       : 3
 5     0.00          . Remaining memory : 23311
 6     0.00          . Scan Rate        : 5
 7     0.00          . Comments:
 8     0.00          . 1. Conv & heat release calcs
 9     0.00          . 2. See display 35 to setup and strt
10     0.00    0.00  . 3. 2/09/89 version CG Wysocki
11             0.00  . 4. General Calcs
12             0.00  .
13             0.00  . PgUp - Move to previous Sheet
14             0.00  . PgDn - Move to next Sheet
15                   .
16                   .
DDDDDDDDDDDDDDDDDDDDDDDDDDDDDDDDDDADDDDDDDDDDDDDDDDDDDDDDDDDDDDDDDDDDDDDDD

The logical expression below controls the execution of this sheet.
IF FLG10 ON AND SHEET(1) OFF

B 3 Text                    Type / for Commands      AutoCalc: OFF
```

Figure 11.7 Interactive spread sheet screen.

During isothermal operation, Q_L should be fairly constant and will be assumed so in this development. We determined the heat loss by holding the batch contents at a steady temperature without reaction and getting a calculated value by the monitor.

Substituting all these heat balance relationships into Eq. (11.1), we have:

$$\frac{dm}{dt} \Delta H_r = F_c \, \rho_c \, C_{pc} \Delta T_c + Q_L + W_B \, C_{PB} \frac{dT_B}{dt} \qquad (11.6)$$

To determine the rate of reaction, we can solve equation (6) for dm/dt giving:

$$\frac{dm}{dt} = \left(F_c \, \rho_c \, C_{pc} \Delta T_c + Q_L + W_B \, C_{PB} \frac{dT_B}{dt} \right) \bigg/ H_r \qquad (11.7)$$

Or expressed in terms of percent conversion rate (CONV1) based on total available reactant (m_T),

$$\mathrm{CONV1} = \frac{\dfrac{dm}{dt} \, 100}{m_T} \qquad (11.8)$$

Note that this relation gives conversion rate independent of any changes in fouling on the walls which can change the heat transfer coefficient.

The total weight of reactant (M) converted at any time (t) can be determined by rearranging and integrating Eq. (11.7) or:

$$M = \int_0^m dm = \frac{1}{\Delta H} \int_{t_0}^t \left(F_c\, \rho_c\, C_{pc}\, \Delta T_c + Q_L + W_B\, C_{PB}\, \frac{dT_b}{dt} \right) \quad (11.9)$$

Expressed in terms of total conversion (CONV):

$$\text{CONV} = \frac{M\, 100}{m_T} \quad (11.9)$$

One of the big advantages of this conversion monitor is to minimize the sampling requirements for reactions containing hazardous materials. Also, you get quick feedback that can be used for process control.

11.6   Choice of Instruments

When we started out we were not sure how accurately we could predict conversion. We did a differential error analysis to determine the cumulative effect of the errors in measurement of flows, temperature, heat capacity, etc. Also, the analysis showed the sensitivity of the final result to these individual errors. These results were used for writing the instrument purchasing specifications. The following explains the basis for the analysis.

If we have a quantity F which is related to several values ($X_1, X_2 \ldots$) as:

$$F = f(X_1, X_2 \ldots) \quad (11.10)$$

Small variations in each of the terms (X_i) in the function will then cause a variation in F related by:

$$dF = \left(\frac{\partial F}{\partial X_1} \right) dX_1 + \left(\frac{\partial F}{\partial X_2} \right) dX_2 \ldots \quad (11.11)$$

Each term on the right hand side of Eq. (11.12) represents the contribution of an error in X_i to the error in F or dF. The partial differential:

$$\frac{\partial F}{\partial X_1}$$

represents the sensitivity of the term.

For error in the reaction rate as calculated by heat release, we can partially differentiate Eq. (11.6) with respect to each of the variables. Putting the terms in the form of Eq. (11.12), we get:

$$dQ_R = \left(\frac{\partial Q_R}{\partial F_c}\right) dF_c + \left(\frac{\partial Q_R}{\partial F_c}\right) d\rho_c + \left(\frac{\partial Q_R}{\partial C_{Pc}}\right) dC_{Pc} + \left(\frac{\partial Q_R}{\partial \Delta T_c}\right) d\Delta T_c$$
$$+ \left(\frac{\partial Q_R}{\partial Q_L}\right) dQ_L + \left(\frac{\partial Q_R}{\partial W_B}\right) dW_B + \left(\frac{\partial Q_R}{\partial C_{PB}}\right) dC_{PB}$$
$$+ \left(\frac{\partial Q_R}{\partial T_B}\right) dT_B + \left(\frac{\partial Q_R}{\partial \Delta H}\right) (d\Delta H) \qquad (11.12)$$

If dx_i components are independently distributed and symmetrical with respect to positive and negative values, then we can write:

$$\overline{(dQ_R)^2} = \sum_{i=1}^{n} \left(\frac{\partial Q_R}{\partial X_i}\right)^2 \overline{(dx_i)^2} \qquad (11.13)$$

If we know the measurement errors associated with each of the x_i terms, they can be substituted for dx_i and the equations solved. This analysis showed that temperature and flow measurements make the largest contribution to the error in reaction time. Therefore, resistance temperature detectors or matched pairs of thermocouples are recommended to increase the accuracy of the calculation. We once tried turbine meters for flow measurement, but they broke down when we went to steam service on the jacket and rust got into the lines. In this latest revamp we used vortex flowmeters as a suitable compromise between accuracy and durability.

11.7 Project Planning and Costs

Figure 11.8 is the project schedule. We produced the project schedule on an Apple computer using the MacProject program, which proved very helpful in keeping the project on track. It forced us to have each of the craft groups tell us what they needed before they could begin or complete their job. It also pointed out additional manpower requirements that were not obvious beforehand. By supplying all the project participants with this schedule, they were able to better appreciate how important it is to keep on time. The MacProject program calculated the project critical path and generated a bar graph of all events in time sequence. A similar bar graph display showed a summary of time and expenses required by each craft. While the MacProject program was helpful, it was still not adequate by itself for project control.

A spreadsheet program was written in-house to track percent completion of various tasks and of the overall job. We compared scheduled hours versus actual hours used for each of the groups involved. A monthly summary was sent to each group manager with explanations for any variances.

Tables 11.2–11.6 show the project costs. Table 11.2 shows the overall project cost summary. The project used almost 5000 in-house manhours to complete (Table 11.3). These include both supervisory and capitalized time. Contract services totaled $34,000, close to the original bid. A breakdown is given in Table 11.4. The $128,000 equipment cost is broken down in Table 11.5. Instrumentation accounted for almost $44,000 of this cost and is further broken down in Table 11.6.

Table 11.2. Project Cost Summary

Manpower	
Capitalized and expense	4852 Manhours
Other	
Contracts (time and materials)	$34,000
Equipment	$128,500
Software and support	$8,200

Table 11.3 Manhours by Group

Process engineering	84
Electrical engineering	264
Instrument engineering	983
Mechanical engineering	180
Drafting	358
Instrument installation	241
In-house electrical	85
Mechanical installation	1153
Total	3348

Table 11.4. Contract Services (Time and Materials)

Revamps on vessels	$9,700
Electrical installation	16,900
Insulation	1,800
Hood and fan installation	5,600
Total	$34,000

Table 11.5. Equipment

Mixers and impellers	$24,100
Instrumentation	43,900
Piping	15,600
Mechanical	34,700
Computer, monitor, and printer	10,200
Total	$128,500
Software and support	$8,200

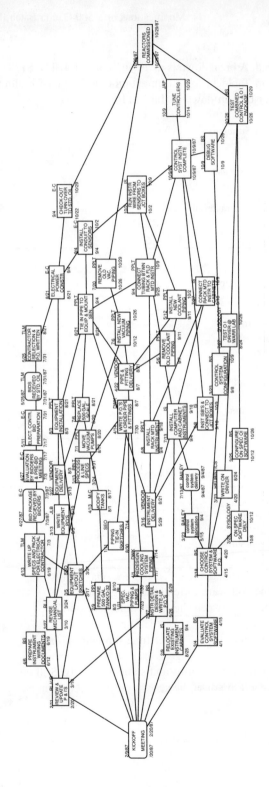

Figure 11.8 500 Gallon reactor schedule.

Table 11.6. Instrument Breakdown

Controllers (Bailey)	$23,700
Control valves	5,200
Intrinsic safety barriers	5,000
Digital scales	10,000
Total	$43,900

11.8 Summary of Our Results and Experiences

As we stated at the beginning, our 500-gallon multipurpose reactor and its supporting equipment has been modernized to provide:

- Improved materials handling
- Improved data collection
- The capability for advanced control
- On-line calculation capability
- Greater process flexibility

The project took about 10 months to complete, about 3 man-years worth of effort, and over $128,000 worth of equipment. The question is: has this been worth it? Our experience suggests that the answer is a qualified yes. When the system is working properly and used regularly it provides a much greater understanding of what is going on in the process and is a convenient way of storing and retrieving the data. Perhaps the most important benefit is the ability to use the on-line conversion calculations to regulate the feed rate of one or more components to a batch. In spite of the benefits, there were still some problems to overcome.

When we first started up we found that signals from the weight scales lost significant figures as the signals went through the Bailey controllers. We solved this problem by taking the digital weight signal direct to the PC via an RS-232 connection. This required some additional software to read the weight signal.

Temperature differences between the jacket inlet and outlet required smoothing of the data to obtain a readable rate. Also, it is necessary to delay the reading of the outlet temperature to account for the travel time through the jacket.

The first year of operation was plagued by a lot of system crashes. Some of the crashes were caused by lightning storms and static electricity. Still others were caused by the PC and system itself. Most of the system crashes were eliminated when the 286 chip was replaced with a 386 chip and 4 mb RAM. The hard disc was reconfigured so it operated only on Concurrent DOS rather than part on MSDOS. The system now runs about 2 months without a failure.

Index

Acrylontrile, 53
Adaptive control, 136, 147
   adaptive predictive control, 148, 158–159
   direct adaptive control, 148
   implementation of, 150
   indirect adaptive control, 147
   relation to hyperplane search, 198, 200
Adhesives, 95
Adiabatic behavior, 27–28, 45, 47, 49
Advection, 87–88
Agitation, 8
Analog-to-digital converters, 121
Antoine's Equation, 197
Apple computers, 230
   MacProject, 230
Arrhenius Dependence, 6, 42, 75, 172
Artificial intelligence 195–196
Åstrom and Hagglund, 151–152
Åstrom and Wittenmark, 147
Autocorrelation, 164, 186
   coefficients, 187, 190–192
   function, 187–188
Autoregressive moving average, 140, 149
Autotuning controllers, 147, 151–152
   relay method, 153

Bacterial contamination, 11
Bailey
   loop command controllers, 222–223, 233

   network 90, 222–223
Baker, 84
Balance
   macroscopic, 20
   microscopic, 20
Barkelew, 47
Becqueral, 102
Bias, 125, 207
Bilinearity, 131
Bioburden, 11
Bismaleimide (BMI) resins, 90–91, 95
Boilers, 124, 132
Brinkman Number, 30–31, 81, 87–88

Calcination, 158–159
Callendar-Van Dusen Equation, 108–109
Calorimetric measurements, 220
Carreau Power-Law Equation, 80
Cascade control, 113, 119, 121, 221, 128
Cell growth, 7
   rate constants describing, 11
Certainty-Equivalence Principle, 147
Characteristic times, 21, 22, 45, 101
Chips, computer
   286, 233
   386, 233
Clarke, 148, 165
Closed loop, 163, 187–189, 214, 218

Cohen-Coon Tuning Method, 138, 168
Commercial products, 155–156
Compensation
  delay, 213
  dynamic, 129, 131–132
  lead-lag, 131
  steady-state, 129
  for variable gain, 127
Computer modeling, 169
Conduction, 20, 23, 25, 29, 55, 88
Conservation equations, 79
  energy, 19, 81
  mass, 19, 81
  momentum, 19, 81
    convective term, 81
    viscous term, 81
Constraints, 200
Controller design, 147, 165, 171
Convection, 20, 29, 38, 40
Cooling, 203, 205
Cooney, 7
Copolymer composition, 174
Copper, 95
Costs, 200
  project, 232–233
Couette Distribution, 84
Crosslinking, 77, 79, 88
Cure cycle, 88, 95
Cure yemperature, 79
CuSUM charts, 185–187
  V-mask, 187

Dahlin Controllers, 137–138
Damkohler Number, 23, 61
Damping, 155
  critically damped, 202
  overdamped, 217
Darcy's Equation, 15
Data acquisition, 222–224
Davy, 106–107
Deadband, 126, 127, 207
Deadtime, 119, 123, 126–127
  mismatch, 124
Deadzone, 125, 126
Decoupling, 132–133
Delamination, 95
Delay, 121, 204, 218

and performance, 217, 218
and stability, 204
Deming, 185
Derivative action, 119, 125
Describing function, 154
Deterministic models, 165
Dhar, 91
Diafiltration, 12
Diagnostic tools, 192, 195–196
Differential Scanning Calorimetry (DSC), 91
Diffusion, molecular, 55
Diffusivity
  species, 80
  thermal, 24
Digital control, 120, 195–196
Dimensionless energy balance, 59–60
Dimensionless numbers, 22
Dimensionless temperature, 42
Diophantine Equation, 149
Displays, graphic, 224, 225
Distillation columns, 120
Distributed Parameter Phenomena, 40, 58
Disturbances, 168
  cancellation of, 133
  determination of, 192
  rejection of, 128, 215–216, 217
  sensitivity to, 177
  Servo, 202
  set point, 214
Disulfide bridges, 11
DNA, 7
Doolittle, 75
Drag velocity, 82
Dynamic Process Modeling, 169, 170–171, 190
Dynamic transients, 180

Economics, 197
Eigenvalues, 63
Electric heaters, 124
Emulsion particles
  molecular weight, 173, 174
  particle size, 173
Emulsion polymerization, 173
Encapsulation, 95
Endothermic reactions, 40
Endotoxins, 10

Engineering Process Control, 186
Enzymes, 7
Equations of change, 19
Error analysis, 229
Escherichia Coli (E. Coli), 7, 10
Ethylene oxide, 197
Exothermic reactions, 40, 55, 123, 128, 175–176
Explosions, 41
Exponential Forgetting and Resetting Algorithm (EFRA), 146, 157
Exponentially-Weighted Moving Average Model (EWMA), 187, 190, 192
Extensive properties, 99
Extruders, 82–83, 88

Fail-safe devices, 112
Feedback control, 97, 111, 117, 125
  determination of disturbances, 192
Feedforward control, 111, 129–131, 178
Feedforward-Feedback (FF-FB), 132, 157, 178–180
  controls relationship to GMC, 184–185
Fermentation, 5, 7–8, 195–196
Filtering, 119, 121, 124, 213
Filtration, 11
  microfiltration, 15
  ultrafiltration, 15
    membranes, 16
Finite difference methods, 83
Finite-element analysis, 74, 83–85, 87–88, 95
First-order plus deadtime
  minimum variance controller, 138
  model, 165
Flow meters, 220
  turbine, 230
  vortex, 230
Fluid mechanics, 82
Foam control, 221
Forgetting factor, 145
Fouling, 166, 229, 198
Fourier Number, 25
Fourier series, 153
Fourier transforms, 153
Fourier's Law, 24
Frank-Kamenetskii, 55

Freeman and Carroll, 91–94
Frequency, 190
Furnaces, 117
  for batch reactors, 201–202
  glass furnace bottom, 156
    temperature control gain, 112, 115, 118, 119, 122
  heating vs. cooling, 201–202
  imbalance, 205–207
  scheduling, 136, 156
  variable, 167, 204, 208

Galerkin Weighted Residual Method, 86
Gaussian elimination, 105
Gauss-Legendre Numerical Integration, 86
Gelation, 95, 97–98
Generalized predictive controller, 200, 210
Generic model control, 183–185
  equivalence to FF-FB, 185
Glass fibers, 91
Glass transition temperature (Tg), 75, 78

Half-life, 22
Harris, 187
Hastings-Jones, 165
Heat capacity, 116, 118
Heat (energy) balance equations
  steady state, 179, 183–184
  unsteady state, 172
Heat evolution (heat generation), 7, 42, 43, 45, 53, 61
Heat exchangers, 117, 120, 121, 124, 130
  inlet and outlet temperatures, 198
Heat of reaction, 53
Heat release, 221, 225–226
Heat removal, 221, 40, 42, 43, 45, 56–57
  temperature sensitivity of, 46
Heat transfer, 55
  capability, 7
  coefficients, 8, 221, 80, 172
Heuristics, 222–223
Hugo and Wirges, 68
Hydraulic radius, 24, 25
Hyperplane searching, 198–200
Hysterisis, 125

Identification, 147, 158, 202, 210
  least-squares method, 139

properties of, 140
maximum likelihood method, 140
  properties of, 141
  step response method, 139
Incompressibility, 87–88
Initiator decay, 37, 47
Instrumentation, 99
Instrument Society of America (ISA), 106–107
Integral action, 114, 165
Integrated Absolute Error (IAE), 115, 123, 138
Integrated Moving Average (IMA), 138
Integrated Square Error (ISE), 138, 155
Integrated Time-Absolute Error (ITAE), 138, 155
Integrators, 125, 202, 211
Intensive properties, 99
Interfacing, 222–223
Internal Model Control (IMC), 167–168
Internal Model Control (IMC) Tuning Rule, 168
International Practical Temperature Scale, 100
Interpolation functions, 85
Inverse response, 179
Isothermal behavior, 27–28, 30–31, 47–48
  quasi-isothermal, 47, 50

Jacket temperature, 183–184

Kaeble, 79
Kaotrope, 12
Kerimid 601, 90–91, 94–95
Kinetics
  first-order, 22
    adiabatic, 46
    irreversible, 68
  n-th order, 47, 90
  pseudo-first-order, 36, 37
  second-order, 22, 35
Kitamori, 153

Lags, 121–122, 187
  first-order dominant, 116, 123, 203, 212
  multiple, 123
  primary and secondary, 115–117, 118, 123

  second-order dominant, 124, 203, 212
Laguerre functions, 151–152, 158–159
Laminates, 95
Laplace Domain, 201–202
Law of Homogeneous Materials, 103
Lead, 119
Least squares, 139–140, 199
Leva, 14
Lime kiln cooler-feeder control, 158–159
Limit cycles, 153
Linearity assumption, 203, 205–206, 210
Linearization strategy, 207
Liquid chromatography, 13
  column performance, 15
Load
  disturbance, 155, 178, 203
  insignifance for servo control, 214
  for on-off controllers, 124
  response, 113–114, 129
  variable load, 118, 120
  zero-load, 118, 125
Loop interaction, 133

Mainframe computers, 220
Maintenance 146
Maleimide, 90
Manipulated variable(s), 192, 199
Master curves, 77
Material and energy balances, 178, 179
Maximum productivity mode, 187
McMaster University, 164, 165
Membrane separation, 15
Methyl methacrylate (MMA), 174
Microorganisms, 5, 9
Minimum variance controllers, 139, 187, 192
  Constrained Minimum Variance Controller (CMVC), 165–166
Mismatch
  deadtime, 124
  model-plant, 166, 168, 173, 178, 180
Model-based control, 117, 121, 123, 155
Model building, 169
Models, examples of
  control loop real time, 170
  linear programming, 170
  probabilistic, 170

spreadsheet, 170, 225–226
unit operations, 170
Molecular diffusion, 39
Molecular weight distribution, 36, 173, 174
Monod, 6
Morari and Zafiriou, 168
Motors, 125–126
Multivariable statistical analysis, 198

National Institute of Standards and Technology (NIST), 100, 109
Negative feedback, 112, 119, 122, 124, 126
Newtonian fluid, 87–88
Newton-Raphson Iteration, 87–88, 141
Newton's Law of Cooling, 25, 28
Nodes, 87–88
Noise, 123
   autocorrelated, 164
   discretization, 213
   electrical, 213
Nonlinearity, 124, 181–182
   removal, 133
Nonstationary processes, 165
Numerical methods, 83
Nusselt Number, 26, 32, 58
Nutrient consumption, 7
Nyquist frequency, 153
Nyquist plots, 154

Objectives, control, 211
Offset, 211, 212
On-line calculations, 225–228
   conversion, 225–228
   heat release, 225
On-off controllers, 124
ONSPEC, 222, 223, 225–226
   ONCALC2 Spreadsheet, 225
   SUPERTRENDS, 224–225
Open loop, 187
Optimality, 202, 212
   LQG, 202
   root locus, 212
Optimization, 6
   hyperplane, 198–200
Oscillations, 113, 114, 115, 125, 153
Overshoot, 113, 114, 120, 123, 155
Oxygen uptake, 7

Pade approximants, 152
Pappalardo, 91
Parametric sensitivity, 41, 48–49, 53
Pattern recognition, 155, 156
Peclet Number, 32, 81
Performance, 117, 136, 166, 199
   of closed-loop controllers, 187, 202
   criteria, 114
   of FF-FB controllers, 180
   indexes, 138
      quadratic, 148
   limitation by process delay, 217, 218
   of model-based controllers, 123
Personal computers
   IBM AT, 222–223
   Indtech, 222–223
PID taud controller, 122–123, 129
Poiseuille Distribution, 83–84
Pole placement, 138, 214
Poles, 213–214
Polyimides, 90–91
Polymer
   activation energies for viscous flow of, 75
   melts, 74
   processing, 74
   viscosity, 74
Polymerization, 34
   chain addition, 43, 47, 57
   condensation, 34
   degree of, 34
   ionic, 35
   rate of, 175–177
   reactors, 40, 120, 195–196, 197
Polymer reaction engineering, 19
Polyvinyl chloride (PVC), 196
Positive feedback, 122, 124
Pottery, 195–196
Power spectrum, 190
Pressure, 190, 197
Preventive maintenance, 195–198
Principle of Equal Reactivity, 35
Process capability, 186
Process reaction curve, 138
Propagation
   addition, 37, 50
   random, 34

step, 35
Proportional controllers (P), 139, 202, 216
Proportional-Integral-Derivative (PID), 111, 114, 117, 221, 173, 179
  autotuning, 153
  design of, 171
  interacting, 120, 129
  lack of delay compensation, 213
  noninteracting, 120
  relationship to EWMA model, 187
  relationship to MVC, 190
  tuning of, 136, 187, 202
  velocity form, 167, 173
Proportional plus derivative (PD), 119, 126, 180
Proportional plus integral (PI), 119, 139, 202
Proteins, 5
  biologically active oxidized form, 13
  denaturation of, 10
  refolding, 11, 12–13
  stability of, 10, 12
Pseudo-Random Binary Sequence (PRBS), 163–164
  switching time for, 164
Purification, 5
Purification processes, examples of, 12

Radiation, 99
Ramps, 214
Random Access Memory (RAM), 225–228
Ray, 68
Reactors
  batch, 37, 113, 181–182, 186, 197
    unmixed, 40
  Bench scale, 50
  Continuous Stirred Tank (CSTR), 39
  continuous tubular, 40
  plug flow, 38
  polymerization, 40
  semi-batch, 174, 178–179, 186
    jacketed, 183–184, 187
  stirred tank, 119
  temperature control of, 179
  tubular reactor, 38
Recursive identification, 139, 142
Recursive Least-Squares (RLS), 142–143
  extended version (RELS), 143–144

Recursive maximum likelihood, 144
Recycled material, 76–77
Reference junction, 103–104
Reference temperature, 59–60
Regression analysis, 198
Resistance Temperature Detectors (RTDs), 230
Resistance Temperature Devices (RTDs), 108, 109
Resistance thermometry, 106–108
Response curve method, 163
Response time, 101, 102
Reynolds Number, 14, 81
Rhone-Poulenc, 90
Robustness, 118, 123–124, 136, 166
Routh-Hurwitz Criteria, 63, 68
RS-232, 230

Safety and control, 115, 195
Sampling, 157, 213
SAS/ETS, 164
SCOPE model, 173
Seeback coefficient, 102
Self-tuning controllers, 147
Semenov, 42, 47, 55
Semi-batch processes, 174, 178–179
  nonlinearity of, 179
Sensible cooling, 179
Sensors, 99
  installation, 101
Servo control, 214
Servo disturbances, 202
Servo motor, 217
Set-point change, 221, 155
Set-point disturbances, 202, 214
Set-point response, 113, 123
Shear, 73–74
  shear rate, 80, 84
  shear thinning, 88
Shewhart charts, 185–186, 190
Sichina, 91
Siemens, 108
Simulation, 280
SimuSolv computer program, 173
Single Input Single Output (SISO) Control, 163
Smith predictor, 122

protection, 132
WLF Equation, 75, 79

Z-domain, 201–202, 214

Zeros, controller, 214, 215
Ziegler-Nichols Tuning Method, 137, 153, 154–155, 156
Zienkiewicz, 83–84

Software, drivers, 224
Somatotropins, 12
Spans, 121
Special causes, 190
Split-range control, 8, 207
Spores, bloom, 11
Spreadsheet programs, 225–226, 232
Stability, 42, 200
   analysis, 42, 58, 63, 68
   of PID controllers, 124
   problems with for feedback control, 177
Stanton Number, 32
Stationarity, 203–204, 207, 208
Stationary proceses, 165
Statistical Process Control (SPC), 185–186, 192
Steady state, 63, 115, 178, 280
   vs. dynamic properties, 112
   lack of for on-off control, 124
   multiplicity, 58
Steam injection system, 221
Sterilization, 9
Stochastic models, 165
Stokes flow, 81
Styrene, 53, 174
Surfactants, ethoxylated, 197

Temperature
   definition, 99
   steady state, 101
Temperature control system, 8
Tempered water system, 221
Theoretical considerations for control, 212
Thermal conductivity, 80
Thermal degradation, 77
Thermal ignition, 40, 42, 49
Thermal runaway, 40, 47, 57
   early approximation, 43, 47, 55
Thermistors, 108, 109
Thermocouples, 106, 222–223, 230, 220
   calibration, 106–107
   types of, 106–107
Thermoelectric effect, 102
Thermosets, 76, 88
Thermowells, 101
Time constants, 118

   closed-loop, 168
Time-proportioning controllers, 125–126
Time series analysis, 163, 190
Time-temperature superposition, 77
Time temperature transformation, 78
Time-varying systems, 145
Torsional braid analysis, 78
Transfer function, 162, 164, 190, 202, 207
   delay, 204, 211
   gain, 204
   model equation, 164
   pseudo-transfer function, 211
   time constant, 204
Transmitters
   pressure, 197
   temperature, 197
Transport phenomena, 19, 40, 79
   momentum transport, 32
Trapezoidal discretization, 213
Tuning, 137, 168, 187, 217
Turbulence, 39

Valves, 126
   ball, 127
   butterfly, 127
   characteristic, 204
   coefficient (Cv), 205–206
   crossover, 209
   deadband, 207
   equal-percentage, 126
      Bauman, 205–206
   friction, effects of, 127
   linear, 126
   motor-driven, 124, 125
   positioning, 127
   quick-opening, 126
   solenoid, 124
Vinyl chloride, 195–196
Viscoelasticity, 77
Viscosity, 40
   temperature dependence of, 29
Viscous Energy Dissipation (VED), 28, 32, 40, 80, 83, 87
Vitrification, 78

Warpage, 95
Western Electric rules, 186
Windup, 120, 129